# U.S. HISTORY AND GOVERNMENT

### (Revised)

## Andrew Peiser

*Assistant Principal for Social Studies*
*Sheepshead Bay High School, Brooklyn, N.Y.*

## Michael Serber

*Assistant Principal for Social Studies*
*Forest Hills High School, Forest Hills, N.Y.*

AMSCO

## AMSCO SCHOOL PUBLICATIONS, INC.
### 315 Hudson Street / New York, N.Y. 10013

*To our wives Barbara and Adele, and our children Rick, Jackie, Brett, Ellen, and Richard, for their patience, support, and understanding, and to our students.*

When ordering this book, please specify:
*either*  **R 547 P** (Paperback)
   *or*  **R 547 H** (Hardbound)

ISBN 0-87720-878-6 (Paperback)
ISBN 0-87720-882-4 (Hardbound)

Revised 1995

# PREFACE

# History from a New Angle

Every history of the United States looks at our nation's past through a different lens—a special angle of vision that authors bring to their subject. Before reading further, you should know the features that give this text, U.S. HISTORY AND GOVERNMENT, its unique character.

1. **Full Description of the U.S. System of Government**  As the book's title suggests, this text treats both the history *and* the government of the United States. The first chapter, Origins of the Constitution, describes the founding of the republic and the drafting of the U.S. Constitution and Bill of Rights. The second chapter, Government in the United States, connects past to present by describing the federal government and state and local governments as they exist today.

2. **Emphasis on the Twentieth Century**  The current century (1901 to 2000) is almost over. Our own generation and the generations of our parents and grandparents have lived through a time of turmoil and rapid change. We, the authors, take the view that understanding the trends and events of this century is critical if we Americans are to cope successfully with the forces of change propelling us into the future. Therefore, as many as 13 of the text's 19 chapters deal with events of the twentieth century.

   As the foundation for understanding our own century, early historical chapters (1, 3, 4, 5, 6, and 7) present a concise, comprehensive overview of the colonial period, the early national period, reform in the Age of Jackson, and industrialization in post-Civil War America.

3. **Inclusion of the Experiences of Women and Ethnic Minorities**  Traditional histories of the past tended to focus

primarily on the experiences and contributions of the dominant minority—white males of Anglo-Saxon ancestry. Unlike such histories, this text describes a multiethnic, pluralistic society whose strength derives from a variety of groups including Native Americans, African Americans, Asian Americans, Hispanic Americans, and European Americans. The experiences of American women are also recognized in this text as critically important to the nation's development.

4. **Primary Source Readings**   This text allows Americans of the past to speak for themselves. Included in every chapter are primary source readings of two kinds:

- **Documents:** excerpts from presidential addresses, Supreme Court cases, and other official papers of the U.S. government. Example: the Monroe Doctrine, the Emancipation Proclamation, a fireside chat by President Franklin Roosevelt, and *Brown v. Board of Education of Topeka.*

- **Observers of American Life:** passages from personal journals, magazine articles, and popular literature commenting on daily life and social and economic conditions. Examples: an African American's comments on racial discrimination in the 1870s, a soldier's letter from the trenches in France in 1918, and a journalist's interview with teacher-astronaut Christa McAuliffe in 1986.

5. **The United States in a Global Context**   Our nation did not develop in a vacuum. From its beginning, the United States influenced and was influenced by changes that were global in scope—the worldwide Industrial Revolution, for example. This text highlights the world setting—or global context—for national events and trends. See, for example, the Global Context maps on pages 44 and 82 and the description of the Industrial Revolution on page 160. Both the title and content of the concluding unit, Living in a Global Age, make clear that national policy cannot be separated from world developments.

6. **Logical, Easy-to-Study Organization**   History can be an untidy subject consisting as it does of thousands of facts that may seem overwhelming. The subject becomes manageable and meaningful only when care is taken to arrange facts in an orderly, easy-to-follow sequence. We think the clearest and most logical way to show relationships among historical topics is to present them in outline form:

| Outline Structure | Example (from Chapter 1) |
|---|---|
| I. First main topic | I. A Brief History of Two Ideas |
|    A. Subtopic |    A. Representative Government |
|    B. Subtopic |    B. Limited Government |
| II. Second main topic | II. The American Revolution |
|    A. Subtopic |    A. Causes of British-American Conflict |
|    B. Subtopic |    B. The Declaration of Independence |

As you scan this text, you will see that main ideas and supporting subtopics stand out boldly in the numbered and lettered headings.

7. **Concise Treatment of Topics**   The building blocks of a survey course in U.S. history are the smaller topics and episodes: the Whisky Rebellion of 1794, the Compromise of 1850, the sinking of the battleship *Maine* in 1898, and so on. Although entire books have been written on such episodes, this text treats them as concisely as possible. For example, we treat the sinking of the *Maine* in just one paragraph (rather than a full page).

8. **Glossary of Key Terms in Every Chapter**
   - What happened at the **Boston Tea Party?** (See the Glossary at the end of Chapter 1, page 19).
   - In 25 words or less, what is a system of **checks and balances?** (See the Glossary at the end of Chapter 2, page 64.)

   For reinforcing knowledge of vocabulary and key events, this text presents important terms in bold type and succinctly defines them in an end-of-chapter glossary.

9. **Cause-and-Effect Charts and Diagrams**   Consider any event in history, and you will find that it has both causes leading to it and effects arising from it. Each chapter of this text not only describes the cause-effect sequence for a major event but also *shows* the sequence visually in the form of a chart or diagram. See, for example, the cause-effect chart for the Mexican War and the Civil War (page 124) and the cause-effect diagram for the Great Depression (page 327).

10. **Other Graphic Study Aids**   Crucial to the study of history is an accurate sense of time. Since the flow of time from decade to decade is abstract, it helps if you can visualize that flow through some graphic device. That is the purpose of the illustrated time frames beginning each chapter. See, for example, the time frame for Chapter 3, page 73, and Chapter 4, page 104.

Another unique device is the occasional "word wheel," which looks like this:

Coming at the end of a chapter section, the word wheel's purpose is to link a main idea (the rim of the wheel) to supporting details (inner parts of the wheel). Questions beneath the wheel challenge you to explain how each detail supports the main idea of the reading.

11. **Multiple-Choice Questions for Review**   Every chapter ends with a series of multiple-choice questions. The first set of questions ("Reviewing the facts") reinforces knowledge of basic facts and key terms. The second set ("Reviewing the main ideas") carries the level of thinking to a higher level and focuses on the central themes and ideas of the chapter. The third set ("Developing critical thinking skills") focuses on a map, graph, table, or political cartoon.

12. **Relating Facts to "Enduring Issues"**   Separation of powers, the rights of women, and the rights of ethnic groups are three constitutional issues that give thematic unity and importance to a course in U.S. history. A total of 13 such enduring issues have been identified by the Political Science Association and the American Historical Association. Every end-of-chapter review includes a question that asks you to explain how certain historical events illustrate a given "enduring issue."

13. **Essay Questions on Two Levels**   An important skill is the writing of short essays that are well organized and well supported with factual information. At the end of every chapter of this text are essay questions of two kinds. Level 1 questions are more complex and challenging than Level 2 questions. Both levels help you to prepare for essay questions on standardized exams.

**14. Study Techniques to Prepare for a Final Exam** A special chapter in the Appendix, How to Study for a Final Exam in U.S. History and Government, presents a detailed, 14-day plan for reviewing a full-year course. It suggests proven test-taking strategies for successfully dealing with both short-answer questions and essay questions.

The nation to which we belong, the United States of America, derives its unique identity and character from more than 200 years of history. As teachers and writers of that history, we feel privileged to introduce our nation's remarkable history to you.

*Andrew Peiser*
*Michael Serber*

# ENDURING ISSUES

The 13 issues below are ones that Americans have debated ever since the Constitution was created in 1787. Undoubtedly, they will continue to enter into public debates for years to come. In "Test Yourself" (the questions at the end of every chapter), there is a section called "Enduring Issues." When answering questions in that section, you can review what each issue means by turning to this page.

1. *National power—limits and potential*
   How much power is the national government capable of exercising under the Constitution? To what extent should the government's powers be limited?

2. *Federalism—the balance between nation and state*
   What kinds of powers should the national government exercise compared to those powers entrusted to the individual states?

3. *The Judiciary—interpreter of the Constitution or shaper of policy?*
   Should the U.S. Supreme Court play a major role in making policy for the nation? Or should it restrict itself to ruling narrowly on cases of law?

4. *Civil liberties—the balance between the government and the individual*
   The government has the responsibility of keeping order as well as preserving individual rights. What is the proper balance between order on the one hand and liberty on the other?

5. *Rights of the accused and protection of the community*
   A person accused of a crime has certain rights to be treated fairly. The community also has a right to be protected from criminal acts. Under what circumstances do the rights of the community override an accused person's rights?

6. *Equality—its definition as a constitutional value*
   The Constitution guarantees "equal protection of the laws" for all citizens. What does this phrase mean in specific cases?

7. *The rights of women under the Constitution*
   In the course of U.S. history, to what extent have women won equal rights and equal protection relative to men?

8. *The rights of ethnic and racial groups under the Constitution*
   In the course of U.S. history, to what extent have ethnic and racial minorities won equal rights and equal protection relative to the majority?

9. *Presidential power in wartime and foreign affairs*
   How have the powers of the president increased in response to wars and other international crises? To what extent should the growth of presidential power in wartime be permitted?

10. *Separation of powers and the capacity to govern*
    In our political system, there is a separation of powers among the legislative, executive, and judicial branches of government. If the three branches are in conflict, it becomes difficult to make policy for the national welfare. Is there a danger of government's being paralyzed as a result of too much conflict among rival branches?

11. *Avenues of representation*
    To what extent are all citizens effectively represented in the legislative, judicial, and executive branches of government?

12. *Property rights and economic policy*
    In a free-enterprise system, the independent decisions of private businesses play a major role. To what extent should the government be permitted to regulate business and take an active role in the economy?

13. *Constitutional change and flexibility*
    Should the Constitution be amended? In what ways can the federal government adjust to changing times without calling for major changes in the Constitution?

# CONTENTS

Contents

# UNIT ONE

# Constitutional Foundations

*In 1976 the American people* celebrated the two hundredth anniversary of the signing of the Declaration of Independence. Eleven years later, in 1987, they celebrated the two hundredth anniversary of the drafting of another remarkable document, the U.S. Constitution. The first chapter in this unit describes the historic origins of these two documents, which still serve as the basis for our government today.

Let the following chart introduce you to other major topics in the unit:

| Chapter | Topics |
|---|---|
| 1. Origins of the Constitution | • How government can be limited to protect citizens' rights<br>• Why the American colonies revolted against British rule<br>• How the U.S. Constitution made up for weaknesses in an earlier plan of government |
| 2. Government in the United States | • The powers given by the Constitution to three branches of government<br>• How the Supreme Court has interpreted different provisions of the Bill of Rights<br>• The role of state and local governments in the federal system |
| 3. The Constitution Tested: The Early Republic | • How a two-party system developed<br>• The beginnings of sectional conflict between North and South<br>• Democratic reforms in the time of Andrew Jackson |
| 4. The Constitution Tested: Westward Expansion and Civil War | • How two Mexican territories, Texas and California, became part of the United States<br>• Why the South seceded from the Union after Lincoln was elected<br>• Why the North won the Civil War |

1

# Chapter *1*

# Origins of the Constitution

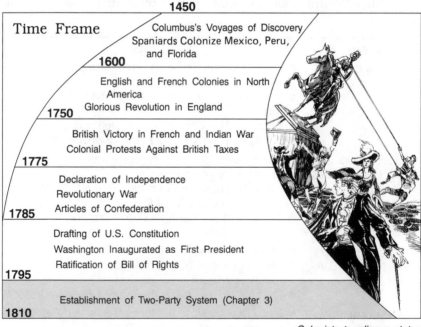

| Time Frame | |
|---|---|
| **1450** | Columbus's Voyages of Discovery |
| | Spaniards Colonize Mexico, Peru, and Florida |
| **1600** | |
| | English and French Colonies in North America |
| | Glorious Revolution in England |
| **1750** | |
| | British Victory in French and Indian War |
| | Colonial Protests Against British Taxes |
| **1775** | |
| | Declaration of Independence |
| | Revolutionary War |
| | Articles of Confederation |
| **1785** | |
| | Drafting of U.S. Constitution |
| | Washington Inaugurated as First President |
| | Ratification of Bill of Rights |
| **1795** | |
| | Establishment of Two-Party System (Chapter 3) |
| **1810** | |

*Colonists toppling a statue of George III*

## *Objectives*

- To trace the origins of the U.S. system of government.
- To define and illustrate two ideas: representative government and limited government.
- To explain the British-American conflict leading to revolution.
- To evaluate the importance of the Declaration of Independence.
- To compare and contrast the Articles of Confederation and the Constitution.

In the revolutionary year 1776, a young Virginian named Thomas Jefferson wrote: "We hold these truths to be self-evident: That all men are created equal...."

These words are included in a document that declared the independent existence of a new nation, the United States of America. The government of this nation was unique because it was founded on the ideal of equal rights for all citizens. In practice, large numbers of Americans—especially women and people of African descent—did not enjoy the rights granted to white males. But the ideal of equal rights was never abandoned, and eventually those who believed in it changed the U.S. government to make it conform more closely to Jefferson's phrase, "all men are created equal."

This chapter will explain the revolutionary ideas contained in the Declaration of Independence (1776), the U.S. Constitution (1787), and the U.S. Bill of Rights (1791). The chapter will also explain how and when these ideas originated.

*Note:* Terms printed in **bold type** are defined in a glossary at the end of this chapter.

# I. A Brief History of Two Ideas

A major purpose of studying U.S. history is to know and appreciate those fundamental ideas that have given our system of government its unique character. Two such ideas are:

- **Representative government.** Government's laws are legitimate only if they are approved by the people's elected representatives.
- **Limited government.** Government's powers should be strictly defined and limited by the provisions of a constitution and a bill of rights.

When both ideas are put into practice, a nation's system of government may be called a **democracy**.

## A. REPRESENTATIVE GOVERNMENT

Throughout world history, governments controlled by monarchs (kings, queens, and other hereditary rulers) have been far more common than governments that represent the people. The origins of representative government in the United States can be traced to three historic sources: ancient Rome, medieval England, and colonial America.

**The Roman Republic (500–27 B.C.)**   In ancient times, Romans of the upper, or patrician, class were represented in a lawmaking body called the senate. Romans of the lower, or plebeian, class were represented in assemblies, which had the power to elect certain high-ranking officials.

**The English Parliament**   Centuries later, beginning in 1295, kings of England would periodically call upon representatives of both the English nobility and the middle class to meet as a **Parliament** (or advisory group) to consider laws and taxes. Over time, the Parliament acquired more power relative to the king and became an established part of the English political system. A major step in this direction was the Glorious Revolution of 1688, when Parliament forced James II to give up the throne.

**Colonial Assemblies (1619–1776)**   The settlers in England's American colonies brought with them their country's tradition of representative government. In 1619 the settlers of Jamestown in Virginia founded the **House of Burgesses** as America's first representative assembly for making laws. The next year, 1620, English Pilgrims aboard the *Mayflower* agreed that the laws for their Plymouth Colony in Massachusetts would be subject to the colonists' approval and consent. The document presenting their agreement was later known as the **Mayflower Compact**.

During the next 150 years other English colonies were founded from New Hampshire in the north to Georgia in the south. The laws of each were made, in part, by a popularly elected assembly. Colonial governors appointed by England's king were often successfully opposed by the assemblies. By 1760 it was generally conceded that the assemblies controlled the vital **power of the purse**—the power either to approve or reject a proposal for a new tax.

**The Limited Nature of Colonial Democracy**   Despite the power of the elected assemblies, none of the English colonies was fully democratic. After all, only a minority of the people was permitted to vote for representatives. Prohibited from voting were all women, all slaves, and many white males who owned no property. Furthermore, in most of the colonies, the governor was appointed by England's king, not elected by the qualified voters. Even so, considering that all white male property owners could vote, the basis for a future democracy was well established during colonial times.

## B. LIMITED GOVERNMENT

The concept of a government limited by law had fundamentally the same origins (Rome, England) as the concept of representative government.

**Roman Law** In the courts of ancient Rome, judges were careful to follow regular procedures for judging a defendant's guilt or innocence. Thus, Roman officials could not act in any way they pleased, but had to stay within the bounds established by a written code of laws.

**English Common Law** The judges of medieval England recognized that the same legal principles should be applied equally and fairly to all citizens. Their decisions in thousands of court cases came to be known as the English **common law**.

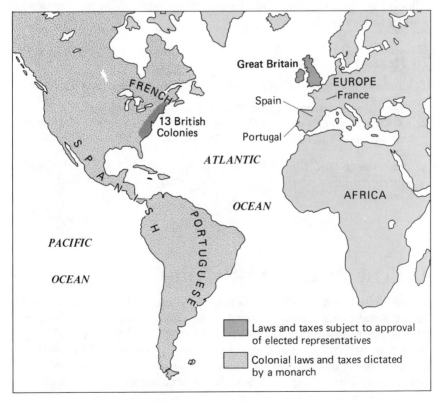

The global context: colonial America, 1750

**English Documents Guaranteeing Civil Rights**   In 1215 a group of rebellious nobles compelled England's tyrannical King John to agree to the terms of the **Magna Carta**. Among the rights guaranteed in this much celebrated document were (a) the right to be tried by a jury of average citizens and (b) the right of the Great Council (a group of nobles) to approve the monarch's proposed taxes.

In 1688 a revolt by the leaders of Parliament against King James II led to the drafting of the English Bill of Rights (1689). This document guaranteed a number of basic liberties including the right to a speedy jury trial and protection against excessive **bails** and fines. Most important, the consent of Parliament was required for collecting taxes, suspending laws, and maintaining an army.

**Locke's Theory of Natural Rights**   To justify the revolt of 1688, an English philosopher named John Locke wrote an influential book (*Two Treatises on Government*, 1689) in which he argued that people were born with certain rights to life, liberty, and property. The purpose of government, said Locke, was to protect people's "natural" rights. Locke's philosophy was one expression of the **Enlightenment,** a liberal age in European thought that challenged authoritarian beliefs and practices of the past.

## *In Review*

The following questions refer to section I: A Brief History of Two Ideas.

1. Identify and define the two ideas treated in this section.
2. Explain how each of the following contributed to the development of representative government: (a) ancient Rome and (b) medieval England.
3. Referring to the "Global Context" (map, page 5), contrast the British system of colonial rule in the 1700s with the Spanish and French systems.

# II. The American Revolution

The British empire grew much larger as a result of a war between Great Britain and France for control of North America—a war known as the **French and Indian War** (1754–1763). Although Great Britain won the war and gained Canada, its victory led almost immediately to growing conflict with its 13 American colonies. Eventually, the Americans' protests against British tax policies turned into full-scale revolution and war.

# A. CAUSES OF BRITISH-AMERICAN CONFLICT

**Change in British Policy** Before the French and Indian War, Great Britain had generally allowed the colonies to govern themselves without much interference. Its colonial policy was one of **salutary neglect** (*salutary* meaning "beneficial"). That policy came to an abrupt end when Britain won the war and acquired Canada from the French. With an expanded empire to govern, Great Britain decided to enforce its trade laws and station troops in the colonies as a permanent military force. Even worse, from the colonists' point of view, was the decision to collect new taxes to pay for the costs of the past war and the new empire.

**Resistance to British Taxes** When the British Parliament and king decided to tax the American colonies without the consent of their assemblies, many colonists believed that their rights were under attack. They protested vehemently against (1) a **stamp tax** (1765) on colonial newspapers and legal documents and (2) **import taxes** (1767) on shipments of British tea, glass, and other articles. Resistance to these taxes took the form of boycotts (refusal to buy British goods), riots (mob action against tax collectors), and dumping British tea into Boston Harbor (the **Boston Tea Party**).

**British Retaliation** Acts of British retaliation only angered the colonists further. Two events were especially alarming to Americans: (1) In the **Boston Massacre** (1770) a crowd of people was fired upon by British troops, and four British Americans and one African American, Crispus Attucks, were killed. (2) The **Intolerable Acts** (1773) closed Boston Harbor to shipping as punishment for the Boston Tea Party. In effect, Boston's economy was nearly shut down by British action.

**Battles of Lexington and Concord** The first shots of the American Revolution were exchanged in the Massachusetts towns of Lexington and Concord. On April 19, 1775, British troops marched into Lexington and fired upon a small band of armed Americans. Continuing to Concord, the British were driven back by large numbers of farmers firing at them from behind trees and stone walls.

**Thomas Paine's Arguments for Independence** Even after the bloody encounters at Lexington and Concord, most Americans thought of fighting the British only for the purpose of defending their rights. They rejected the idea of fighting for independence. But many changed their minds after reading *Common Sense*, a pamphlet by Thomas Paine. Referring to tyrants as "royal brutes," Paine boldly set forth arguments for American independence. He wrote that it made no

Outbreak of the Revolutionary War at Lexington

sense for a small island kingdom like Great Britain to rule over vastly larger American lands at such a great distance.

**Decision for Independence**  On two occasions, delegates from the different colonies met in Philadelphia to plan united action in defense of their rights. The First Continental Congress (1774) petitioned the British government to repeal its taxes and overturn other harsh measures. But the British made no concessions. The Second Continental Congress (1776) met after British and Americans had clashed at Lexington and Concord and then at Bunker Hill outside Boston. On July 4, 1776, Congress announced its decision to declare the independence of a new nation, the United States.

## B. THE DECLARATION OF INDEPENDENCE

Congress's reasons for declaring independence were eloquently stated by Thomas Jefferson, the main author of the Declaration of Independence. His arguments were both general and specific.

**General Arguments for Independence**  Drawing upon the theories of John Locke, the Declaration argues that "all men are created equal" in their right to the enjoyment of "life, liberty, and the pursuit of happiness." Furthermore, government "derives its power from the consent of the governed." In short, the first and most famous section of the Declaration argues that governments must be (1) representative of the people and (2) limited in power by a recognition of basic human rights. Furthermore, when any government violates people's natural rights, then the people have the additional right to "alter or to abolish" that government.

**Specific Arguments for Independence**  A second section of the Declaration lists specific grievances against the British king in order to demonstrate that the colonists' rights were repeatedly violated. The grievances included: (1) the dissolving of colonial assemblies, (2) the keeping of British troops in the colonies, and (3) "imposing taxes without our consent."

## DOCUMENTS: THE DECLARATION OF INDEPENDENCE

*This excerpt from the 1776 document that gave birth to the United States argues that, under certain circumstances, people have a right to rebel against an established government.*

*According to Jefferson, when do people have this right? Do you agree that the right exists?*

We hold these truths to be self-evident: That all men are created equal; that they are endowed by their Creator with certain unalienable rights; that among these are life, liberty, and the pursuit of happiness.

That to secure these rights, governments are instituted among men, deriving their just powers from the consent of the governed.

That whenever any form of government becomes destructive of these ends, it is the right of the people to alter or to abolish it, and to institute new government, laying its foundation on such principles

Thomas Jefferson

and organizing its powers in such form as to them shall seem most likely to effect their safety and happiness. Prudence, indeed, will dictate that governments long established should not be changed for light and transient causes; and, accordingly, all experience hath shown that mankind are more disposed to suffer, while evils are sufferable, than to right themselves by abolishing the forms to which they are accustomed. But when a long train of abuses and usurpations, pursuing invariably the same object, evinces a design to reduce them under absolute despotism, it is their right, it is their duty, to throw off such government, and to provide new guards for their future security.

## Actions and Reactions
### (events leading to revolution)

| British Action → | Colonial Reaction → | British Response |
| --- | --- | --- |
| 1. Attempt to collect stamp tax (1765) | Riots and protests; tax collectors "tarred and feathered" | Repeal of stamp tax (1766) |
| 2. Attempt to collect import taxes on paint, lead, tea (1767) | Boycotts, riots, increased anger | British troops sent to Massachusetts |
| 3. Arrival of British troops (1768) | More protests; citizens killed in Boston Massacre (1770) | Import taxes repealed, except for a reduced tax on tea |
| 4. Tea Act (1773) | Destruction of British tea in Boston Tea Party (1773) | Decision to punish Boston by harsh measures |
| 5. Intolerable Acts close Boston Harbor (1774) | Meeting of First Continental Congress in Philadelphia to protest British acts (1774) | Orders to arrest resistance leaders |
| 6. British march on Lexington and Concord to confiscate supply of gunpowder (1775) | Militia ("Minutemen") warned of British march by Paul Revere, and William Dawes | Shots exchanged; military conflict; British retreat to Boston |
| 7. British troops in Boston prepare for war | Meeting of Second Continental Congress; | British reinforcements sent to Boston |
| 8. British reject colonists' petition for recognition of their rights; King George III hires German (Hessian) troops | Thomas Paine publishes *Common Sense*; Congress adopts Declaration of Independence (1776) | After eight years of war, Britain signs peace treaty (1783) recognizing U.S. independence |

**Continuing Importance of the Declaration**   The revolutionary ideas in the Declaration of Independence have had a profound effect on world history. Inspired by its principles of equal rights and popular consent, peoples of many nations have used the Declaration to justify their own struggles for independence against oppressive governments.

## C. THE WAR FOR INDEPENDENCE

This chapter focuses on the origins of the U.S. government, not on military battles and campaigns. Nevertheless, since independence was won through war, you should know some of the highlights of the American war for independence (or Revolutionary War).

**Early Defeats**   The first year of war was a desperate one for the largely untrained, disorganized troops led by the American general, George Washington. Fighting a losing battle in defense of New York City (July 1776), Washington's army barely managed to escape disaster by retreating across the Hudson River to New Jersey. By the end of the first year, British troops, as well as hired troops from Hesse in Germany, occupied two of the colonies' most important cities, Boston and New York. The American capital, Philadelphia, fell to the British and Hessians the following year.

**Turning Points, Trenton and Saratoga**   Desperately needing a victory to keep American hopes alive, Washington launched a surprise attack on Trenton, New Jersey, on Christmas night, 1776. The Hessian defenders of Trenton were routed. A second turning point was a decisive American victory at Saratoga, New York, in 1777 against a British army commanded by General John Burgoyne. Americans showed enough strength in this battle to convince France to give them military and naval assistance.

**Victory at Yorktown**   The last years of the war were fought in the South. Aided by French naval support and reinforced by French troops, Washington's army forced Britain's commanding general, Lord Cornwallis, to surrender his army at Yorktown, Virginia (1781). Two years later, American and British diplomats signed a peace treaty in Paris ending the war. In the treaty, Great Britain recognized the existence of the United States as an independent nation. The western border of the new American nation was to be the Mississippi River.

### *In Review*

The following questions refer to section II: The American Revolution.

1. Identify three acts of the British Parliament that led to protest in the American colonies.
2. Compare John Locke's ideas with Thomas Jefferson's ideas in the Declaration of Independence.

3. Discuss the ways in which the Declaration of Independence expressed both the idea of representative government and the idea of limited government.

# III. Creating the Constitution

Both during and after the American Revolution, delegates from the 13 original colonies, which later became states, met as a Congress to make laws for the United States. This Congress of the Revolution met for six years (1775–1781) before a document called the **Articles of Confederation** set forth the U.S. government's official powers.

## A. THE ARTICLES OF CONFEDERATION (1781–1788)

The Articles of Confederation was the first constitution (written plan of government) for the United States. Government under the Articles soon proved unsatisfactory for reasons explained in this section.

**Confederate System**   A **confederation,** or confederate plan of government, gives to the central (national) government only a few powers relative to the greater powers exercised by state governments. In the colony of New York, long before the Revolution, the six nations of the Iroquois had formed a confederate system for cooperating for their mutual benefit. Their form of government was known as the Haudenosaunee political system. Colonial leaders knew about this system, and it may have influenced the confederate plan of government adopted in 1781 by those who wrote the Articles of Confederation.

**Organization of the National Government**   The U.S. government under the Articles consisted simply of a one-house lawmaking body, the **Congress** (or Continental Congress). There was neither a separate executive branch to enforce the laws nor a separate system of national courts to interpret the laws. Each state was represented equally in Congress by a delegation that could cast just one vote on each issue.

**Powers of the National Government**   Congress was given the power to declare war, make peace, and conduct foreign affairs. But it lacked the power to collect taxes directly and relied upon grants of money from the states to pay its expenses. To pass any law in Congress required a two-thirds majority.

**Strengths and Weaknesses**   Congress under the Articles had two major achievements: (1) bringing the Revolutionary War to a successful end and (2) establishing a workable plan (the *Northwest Ordinance,* 1787) for governing the western lands between the Appalachian

Mountains and the Mississippi River. On the other hand, Congress was handicapped by its dependence on the states for tax revenues. It could not regulate commerce between the states, and the paper currency it issued was nearly worthless. The Articles of Confederation could not be changed without the *unanimous* agreement of all 13 states.

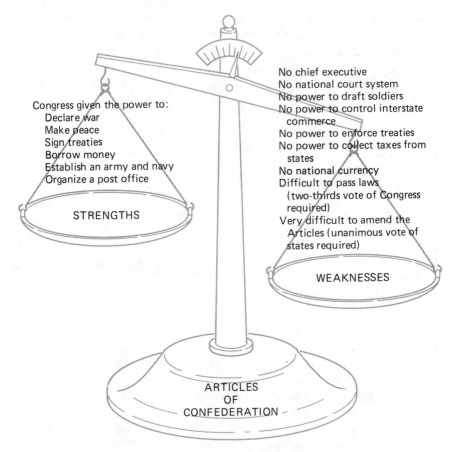

Congress given the power to:
Declare war
Make peace
Sign treaties
Borrow money
Establish an army and navy
Organize a post office

STRENGTHS

No chief executive
No national court system
No power to draft soldiers
No power to control interstate
  commerce
No power to enforce treaties
No power to collect taxes from
  states
No national currency
Difficult to pass laws
  (two-thirds vote of Congress
  required)
Very difficult to amend the
  Articles (unanimous vote of
  states required)

WEAKNESSES

ARTICLES
OF
CONFEDERATION

Strengths and weaknesses of the Articles of Confederation

## B. THE CONSTITUTIONAL CONVENTION

In the 1780s economic troubles and political unrest caused many Americans to doubt whether their young country could long survive under a weak central government. Particularly alarming was a violent protest by Massachusetts farmers (**Shays's Rebellion,** 1786) against the collection of a state tax. To increase Congress's powers to deal with various troubles, delegates from the different states met in a convention in Philadelphia in the summer of 1787. Soon the majority in the convention was persuaded by James Madison and other Virginia delegates to replace the existing plan of government (the Articles) with an entirely new constitution.

**Conflicts**   Delegates disagreed sharply on three issues:

1. *Representation.* The larger states like Virginia insisted that representation in the newly organized Congress should be proportional to the size of each state's population. Smaller states like New Jersey wanted representation to be the same for all states.

2. *Slavery.* Because slaves made up a large part of the South's population, Southern delegates proposed that slaves be counted

---

## OBSERVERS OF AMERICAN LIFE: Poem by a Young Woman

Born in Africa, Phillis Wheatley was kidnapped at the age of nine and brought to Massachusetts as a slave. Her master's wife taught her to write. In 1773, as a teenager, she published a volume of poetry— only the second book of poems to be published by a woman living in America. The following poem was addressed to a British noble, the Earl of Dartmouth.

No more *America* in mournful strain
Of wrongs, and grievance unredress'd complain,
No longer shall thou dread the iron chain,
Which wanton *Tyranny* with lawless hand
Has made, and which it meant t'enslave the land.
Should you, my lord, while you pursue my song,
Wonder from whence my love of *Freedom* sprung,
Whence flow these wishes for the common good,
By feeling hearts alone best understood,
I, young in life, by seeming cruel fate
Was snatch'd from *Afric's* fancy'd happy seat:
What pangs excruciating must molest,
What sorrows labour in my parent's breast?
Steel'd was the soul and by no misery mov'd
That from a father seiz'd his babe belov'd
Such, such my case. And can I then but pray
Others may never feel tyrannic sway?

in a state's population for representation purposes but not for tax purposes. Northern delegates proposed just the opposite—counting slaves for tax purposes but not for representation.

3. *Trade.* Southern delegates thought foreign commerce should *not* be taxed, because their region relied heavily on importing manufactured goods from Great Britain. A tax would make foreign goods more expensive. Northerners thought foreign commerce *should* be taxed, since their region was beginning to manufacture goods that competed with foreign imports. A tax on foreign goods might help local industries to grow.

**Compromises**   Each conflict at the convention was resolved through compromise.

1. The **Great Compromise** created a Congress of two houses: the House of Representatives where states would be represented proportional to their populations; the Senate where states would be represented equally.

2. A compromise on slavery provided that three fifths of a state's slave population would be counted for purposes of both taxation and representation.

3. A compromise on trade gave Congress the power to tax imports but not exports.

# C. HOW THE CONSTITUTION DIFFERED FROM THE ARTICLES OF CONFEDERATION

The Constitution created a central government for the nation that was considerably stronger than the original U.S. government under the Articles of Confederation. The new plan of government differed from the Articles in these respects:

**A Separate Executive Branch**   The president was to act as the leader of an **executive branch** for enforcing Congress's laws. (Under the Articles there was no executive branch and no president with executive responsibilities.)

**A Separate Judicial Branch**   To settle cases of law under the Constitution, a separate U.S. court system, or **judicial branch,** was established. (Under the Articles there was no national court system.)

**A Two-House Legislature**   The **legislative branch,** Congress, was to consist of two houses, a Senate and a House of Representatives. (Under the Articles Congress had only one house.)

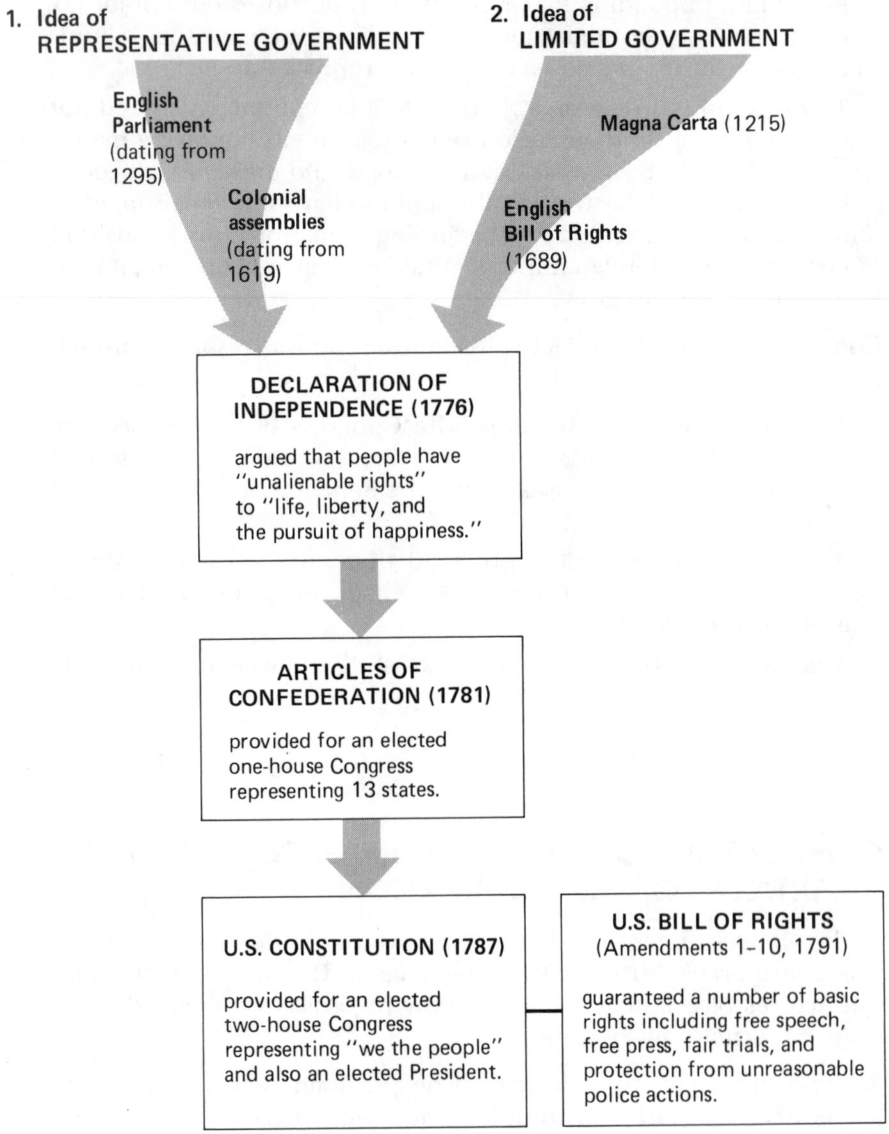

**1. Idea of
REPRESENTATIVE GOVERNMENT**

**2. Idea of
LIMITED GOVERNMENT**

**English
Parliament**
(dating from
1295)

**Magna Carta** (1215)

**Colonial
assemblies**
(dating from
1619)

**English
Bill of Rights**
(1689)

**DECLARATION OF
INDEPENDENCE (1776)**

argued that people have
"unalienable rights"
to "life, liberty, and
the pursuit of happiness."

**ARTICLES OF
CONFEDERATION (1781)**

provided for an elected
one-house Congress
representing 13 states.

**U.S. CONSTITUTION (1787)**

provided for an elected
two-house Congress
representing "we the people"
and also an elected President.

**U.S. BILL OF RIGHTS**
(Amendments 1–10, 1791)

guaranteed a number of basic
rights including free speech,
free press, fair trials, and
protection from unreasonable
police actions.

Sources of major ideas in the U.S. Constitution

**Greater Power for Congress** Congress was given the power to collect taxes on imports. (Under the Articles Congress had no tax-collecting powers.)

**Federal in Form (Not Confederate)** The powers of government were divided between a strong central government and strong state governments. Such an arrangement is known as a **federal system**. (Under a confederate form of government, the central government is generally weaker than the state governments.)

## D. DEBATE ON RATIFICATION

In September 1787, the delegates who framed, or created, the Constitution submitted it to the states for their approval. A great debate followed on whether or not the new plan of government should be substituted for the Articles of Confederation. Favoring the ratification of the Constitution was a group called the **Federalists**; opposing it were the **Antifederalists**.

**Federalist Arguments** A series of essays by three Federalists (James Madison, Alexander Hamilton, and John Jay) explained the need for a federal plan of government to replace the confederate plan (the Articles of 1781). Each essay presented reasons for thinking that the Constitution would strengthen the national government and protect liberty at the same time. When published as a book, the *Federalist Papers* became a classic work in defense of a representative government whose powers are evenly distributed among three branches.

**Antifederalist Arguments** Opponents of ratification included two leaders of the American Revolution, Patrick Henry and Samuel Adams. They feared that the central government under the Constitution might become too strong and crush people's liberties. As originally written, the Constitution lacked a **bill of rights.** Antifederalists pointed to this omission as proof that people's rights would not be respected.

**Federalist Victory** Each state called a special convention in which delegates voted for or against the proposed Constitution. Federalists won the first three states easily by large majorities. But vigorous opposition in Massachusetts and Virginia was overcome only after the Federalists promised to add a bill of rights as the new government's first order of business. Even so, the vote to **ratify,** or approve, the Constitution was far from unanimous. New York's convention, for example, voted to ratify by the slim majority of 30–27. Ratification by the required number of states (nine) was accomplished in June, 1788.

## E. THE FIRST CONGRESS AND THE FIRST PRESIDENT

After the Constitution was ratified, steps were taken in each state to elect senators and representatives to the First Congress (that is, the first Congress to meet under the new Constitution). In addition, a group of **electors** (special voters for president and vice president) were chosen by the 13 states. The electors agreed by unanimous vote that George Washington should be the first president. By April, 1789, both the first president and the first Congress had been sworn into office. Thus, the Constitution drafted in 1787 was put into effect less than two years later.

*Note:* The next two chapters will describe (1) the unusual procedures for electing a U.S. president and vice president and (2) the main accomplishments of George Washington as president.

## F. ADDING THE BILL OF RIGHTS

A bill of rights is a document setting forth the kinds of actions that government officials may *not* take. Its purpose is to prevent abuses of power and protect people's liberties. Soon after the Constitution was adopted, one of the first acts of the new Congress was to propose a series of amendments. When ratified by the states in 1791, the first ten amendments to the Constitution became known as the U.S. Bill of Rights.

Among the rights guaranteed in the Bill of Rights are the following:

- Freedom of religion
- Freedom of speech and the press
- Fair trial
- Freedom from unreasonable searches by the police
- Freedom from cruel and unusual punishments.

These rights and others will be described in detail in Chapter 2.

In the diagram on page 16, "Sources of Major Ideas in the U.S. Constitution," observe how the U.S. Bill of Rights continues a long history going back to 1215 and the Magna Carta—the history of people forcing government to recognize strict limits on its powers.

Observe, too, that the two-house Congress under the Constitution represented only a *part* of the American population—white men who owned property. In later chapters, you will see how this partially representative government became more fully democratic.

## *In Review*

The following questions refer to section III: Creating the U.S. Constitution.

1. Identify two issues at the Philadelphia Convention of 1787, and explain how they were resolved through compromise.
2. Define (a) confederation and (b) federal system.
3. Summarize the ways in which government under the Constitution was stronger than government under the Articles of Confederation.

## GLOSSARY OF KEY TERMS: CHAPTER 1

**Antifederalists** those Americans who opposed the ratification of the Constitution in 1787.

**Articles of Confederation** the first document to serve as a constitution for the United States (adopted 1781, replaced by the current Constitution 1788).

**bail** a sum of money paid to a court by a criminal defendant to ensure that the person, if released from jail, will appear for his or her trial.

**bill of rights** a document that spells out those rights of citizens that may not be violated by government officials. (The English Bill of Rights was adopted in 1689, the U.S. Bill of Rights in 1791.)

**Boston Massacre** an incident (1770) in which five citizens of Boston were killed by British troops.

**Boston Tea Party** an incident (1773) in which a shipment of British tea was destroyed by citizens of Boston as a protest against the British tax on tea.

**common law** a written record of judges' decisions from as far back as the Middle Ages that still guide the way a court defines legal rights and wrongs.

**confederation** a system of government in which state or local governments have more power than the national government.

**Congress** the lawmaking body of the United States consisting originally of only one house (under the Articles of Confederation), currently two houses (under the Constitution).

**Declaration of Independence** a document of 1776 announcing the decision of 13 British colonies to be an independent nation, the United States of America.

**democracy** a form of government that protects people's rights and gives final authority to the voters and their elected representatives.

**electors** a small group authorized by the Constitution to cast official ballots for president and vice president.

**Enlightenment** an era in European history (about 1690–1790) characterized by tolerance for religious differences and the use of reason to solve problems.

**executive branch**   that part of government that specializes in enforcing the laws.

**Federalists**   those Americans who supported the ratification of the Constitution in 1787; later, citizens and politicians belonging to the Federalist party.

**federal system**   a political system in which a central government for the nation and local governments for the states both exercise considerable power.

**French and Indian War**   a war between Great Britain and France (and their Indian allies) ending in 1763 in British control of much of the North American continent, including Canada.

**Great Compromise**   a plan at the Constitutional Convention (1787) for settling a dispute over representation of the different states. A two-house Congress was agreed upon: a Senate to satisfy the less populous states, a House of Representatives to satisfy the larger states.

**House of Burgesses**   lawmaking body in colonial Virginia; the first representative assembly in North America.

**import tax**   a tax collected on merchandise from abroad that is imported into a country.

**Intolerable Acts**   laws adopted by the British Parliament (1773) to punish those responsible for the Boston Tea Party; one provision closed the port of Boston to trade.

**judicial branch**   that part of government that specializes in interpreting how laws apply to specific cases; a court system.

**legislative branch**   that part of government that specializes in making laws.

**limited government**   government that must recognize strict limits on its power and must not infringe on the rights of citizens.

**Magna Carta**   a document signed by England's king in 1215 promising to respect certain rights.

**Mayflower Compact**   an agreement by Pilgrim settlers of Plymouth Colony, in which they pledged to participate in making laws for the colony.

**militia**   a force of volunteer soldiers trained to serve temporarily in an emergency.

**Northwest Ordinance**   a U.S. law of 1787 setting forth a system for governing western lands.

**parliament**   the lawmaking body in Great Britain, and also in other nations that have adopted the British system.

**power of the purse**   the power to authorize the collection of a tax and to determine who shall pay the tax.

**ratify**   to approve, usually by vote of a legislature.

**representative government**   government in which laws are made by officials elected by the people.

**salutary neglect**   British policy (before 1763) of overlooking colonial violations of Britain's trade laws and allowing the colonies to govern themselves.

**Shays's Rebellion**   a revolt of Massachusetts farmers in 1786 against the tax policies of the state government.

**stamp tax**   a widely resisted British tax of 1765 on the sale of paper articles (newspapers, legal documents).

# TEST YOURSELF

## A. Multiple Choice: Facts, Main Ideas, Skills

*On a separate sheet of paper, write the number of the word or expression that, of those given, best completes the statement or answers the question.*

### Reviewing the facts

1. At the constitutional convention of 1787, the issue of how to count slaves was settled by (1) Northerners yielding to Southerners (2) Southerners yielding to Northerners (3) blacks yielding to whites (4) a compromise involving concessions by both Northerners and Southerners

2. Which document argues that people have a right to revolt against an oppressive government? (1) the U.S. Bill of Rights (2) the Mayflower Compact (3) the Declaration of Independence (4) the U.S. Constitution

3. Antifederalists opposed the ratification of the Constitution because (1) it gave too much power to the states (2) it lacked a bill of rights (3) it failed to give Congress enough power (4) it was unfair to the smaller states

4. Which of the following does *not* describe government in the American colonies before 1763? (1) a policy of salutary neglect (2) representative assemblies (3) a heritage of limited government (4) laws prohibiting slavery

5. Both the Articles of Confederation and the U.S. Constitution provided for (1) a Congress with legislative powers (2) a president with executive powers (3) a Supreme Court with judicial powers (4) local governments with veto powers

6. Which pair of events occurred at about the same time? (1) signing of the Magna Carta and first meeting of the House of Burgesses (2) Boston Tea Party and passage of the Intolerable Acts (3) signing of the Declaration of Independence and the American victory at Yorktown (4) Boston Massacre and Shays's Rebellion

## Reviewing the main ideas

**7.** A major criticism directed against the Articles of Confederation was that power was given primarily to (1) military leaders (2) the national government (3) a president (4) state governments

**8.** The ideals of Roman law and the Mayflower Compact contributed most significantly to the growth of the principle of (1) the consent of the governed (2) religious freedom (3) separation of powers (4) racial equality

*Base your answers to questions 9 and 10 on the statements below and on your knowledge of social studies.*

*Speaker A:* "We should reject any plan of government that makes no mention of such basic rights as freedom of speech and freedom of religion."

*Speaker B:* "For every power granted to the executive branch there should be a comparable power granted to the legislative branch."

*Speaker C:* "Our nation should be viewed as a loose compact among the states. The chief concern of the central government should be the conduct of foreign affairs."

*Speaker D:* "The laws of the national government and the state governments must both be subject to the supreme law of the land: the Constitution."

**9.** Which two speakers would most likely have voted *against* the ratification of the U.S. Constitution in 1787? (1) A and B (2) B and C (3) A and C (4) C and D

**10.** The kind of government created by the Articles of Confederation is described by Speaker (1) A (2) B (3) C (4) D

**11.** Which development was a result of the other three? (1) the practice of representative government in England's colonies (2) provisions in the U.S. Constitution for a Senate and a House of Representatives (3) the founding of the House of Burgesses (4) the practice of electing members of England's Parliament

**12.** In the debate over ratification, which of these was an important factor in overcoming objections to the Constitution? (1) the political skill of compromise (2) tactics of force and intimidation (3) strict devotion to the ideal of equality (4) general distrust of state governments

## Developing critical thinking skills

*Base your answers to questions 13 and 14 on the table on page 23 and on your knowledge of U.S. history and government.*

**U.S. Population by Region, State, and Race, 1790**
(in thousands)

| Region and State | Total | Race White | African-American |
|---|---|---|---|
| New England | **828** | **812** | **16** |
| Connecticut | 238 | 233 | 5 |
| Massachusetts | 379 | 373 | 6 |
| New Hampshire | 142 | 141 | 1 |
| Rhode Island | 69 | 65 | 4 |
| Middle Atlantic | **1,317** | **1,254** | **63** |
| Delaware | 59 | 46 | 13 |
| New Jersey | 184 | 170 | 14 |
| New York | 340 | 314 | 26 |
| Pennsylvania | 434 | 424 | 10 |
| South | **1,738** | **1,104** | **634** |
| Georgia | 83 | 53 | 30 |
| Maryland | 320 | 209 | 111 |
| North Carolina | 394 | 288 | 106 |
| South Carolina | 249 | 140 | 109 |
| Virginia | 692 | 414 | 278 |

Source: *Historical Statistics of the United States*

13. The table would be most useful for a research report on (1) a comparison of the populations of North and South in 1790 (2) regional politics during the time of George Washington (3) slavery in the Middle Atlantic states in 1790 (4) representation in Congress in the 1790s
14. Which generalization is supported by evidence in the table? (1) African Americans were in a majority in the South. (2) Virginia in 1790 was the most populous of the 13 states. (3) The greatest number of white males lived in the New England states. (4) Slavery existed in all 13 states in 1790.

## B. Word Wheel

Explain how each labeled section of the wheel expressed the idea of representative govenment.

## C. Enduring Issues

*Select* two *of the enduring issues from column A. For each issue chosen, explain how the historical example in column B relates to the issues.*

| A. Enduring Issues | B. Historical Examples |
|---|---|
| 1. Federalism—the balance between nation and state | The decision to replace the Articles of Confederation with the Constitution |
| 2. Equality—its definition as a constitutional value | Political ideas in the Declaration of Independence |
| 3. Avenues of representation | The Great Compromise |
| 4. Constitutional change and flexibility | The addition of the Bill of Rights |

## D. Essays

### Level 1

The roots of American democracy may be traced to colonial times.

**1.** Identify *three* events in the British colonies (before 1776) that contributed to democratic institutions.

**2.** Choose *two* of the events named in question 1. Discuss the importance of *each* event chosen in preparing the way for democratic government.

### Level 2

The U.S. Constitution and the Bill of Rights set limits on the powers of government.

**A.** List *three* limits on the powers of the U.S. government.

**B.** Base your answer to part B on your answer to part A. Write an essay showing that the U.S. Constitution and the Bill of Rights limit the powers of government.

# Chapter 2

# Government in the United States

## *Objectives*

- To define and illustrate basic principles of the U.S. Constitution including federalism, separation of powers, and checks and balances.
- To identify and understand the importance of key clauses in the Constitution.
- To understand how the legislative, executive, and judicial branches of the U.S. government are organized.
- To know the main provisions of the U.S. Bill of Rights.
- To evaluate the importance of selected landmark cases of the U.S. Supreme Court.
- To know how the principle of separation of powers is carried out by state and local governments.

The form of government created by the framers of the Constitution in 1787 has endured for more than 200 years. No other written constitution in the world has been in force for so long. Let us examine the features of the Constitution that have made our government both stable and flexible enough to respond well to the changing needs of American society.

# I. Main Parts of the U.S. Constitution

The Constitution begins with its most famous paragraph, the **Preamble**. Then follows the main body of the document, which consists of seven major parts known as articles. Added to the document after it was written and ratified are ten **amendments**, known as the Bill of Rights, and 16 other amendments adopted at different times in U.S. history.

## A. THE PREAMBLE

Recall that the Constitution's creators—or framers—wanted to improve upon the Articles of Confederation of 1781, which had established a loose association of states. Therefore, to give authority to the people of the entire nation, the Preamble asserts that the new U.S. government was being established by "we the people" rather than by the individual states. The Preamble identifies the goals of the new government as follows:

We, the people of the United States, in order to form a more perfect union, establish justice, insure domestic tranquillity, provide for the common defense, promote the general welfare, and secure the blessings of liberty to ourselves and our posterity, do ordain and establish this Constitution for the United States of America.

## B. THE THREE BRANCHES

The Constitution gives the powers of government to three separate groups, or branches: the legislative branch, the executive branch, and the judicial branch.

**The Legislative Branch: Congress**   Article I describes the organization and powers of the lawmaking, or legislative, branch—the U.S. Congress. It says that Congress shall consist of two groups of lawmakers, each meeting in a separate chamber, or "house": the House of Representatives and the Senate. In addition to listing the powers of Congress for passing laws, Article I also describes (1) the method for electing members of each house, (2) the qualifications for election, (3) terms of office in the House and Senate, and (4) the procedures for making laws.

**The Executive Branch: President and Vice President**   Article II describes the law-enforcing, or executive, branch. It says that the chief executive (official in charge of the law-enforcing branch) shall be the president. It also mentions the vice president but says little about this official's responsibilities.

Article II describes (1) the president's powers, (2) the president's four-year term of office, (3) the method of electing the president and vice president, and (4) the method for removing the president by **impeachment** (an accusation of wrongdoing followed by a trial).

**The Judicial Branch: Supreme Court and Lower Courts**   Article III describes the judicial branch—the federal court system that interprets the laws of Congress as they apply to specific cases. The Constitution mentions both "inferior" courts (or lower courts) and a Supreme Court. It describes (1) the term of office for federal judges and (2) Congress's power to establish new courts. Concerning the **jurisdiction** (assigned area of responsibility) of the courts, it distinguishes between cases that go directly to the Supreme Court (the highest, most powerful court) and cases that may be heard first by lower federal courts.

## C. THE STATES, THE AMENDMENT PROCESS, AND THE SUPREME LAW

The main body of the original Constitution (the part written in 1787) concludes with four short articles on miscellaneous matters.

**Interstate Relations**  Article IV describes relations among the states and "their obligations toward one another." The article says that a person charged with breaking the laws of one state and fleeing to another may be **extradited** (or returned) to the original state. The article also describes (1) how U.S. territories may enter the Union as new states and (2) the responsibility of the federal government to protect states from invasion and "domestic violence" (rioting).

**The Amendment Process**  Article V describes methods for amending the Constitution. (See below, pages 55–56.)

**The Supremacy Clause**  According to the so-called supremacy clause in Article VI, "The Constitution, and the laws of the United States . . . shall be the supreme law of the land." (This clause was the basis for historic decisions of the Supreme Court by which it declared national laws to be supreme over state laws.) Another clause in Article VI says that a person's religion may never be a qualification for holding public office.

**Ratification**  The seventh and last article of the original Constitution is no longer in force. It describes the method by which the Constitution was to be submitted to the states in 1787 for ratification, or approval.

## D. THE BILL OF RIGHTS (AMENDMENTS 1 TO 10)

As explained in Chapter 1, the Bill of Rights refers to the first ten amendments to the Constitution. These amendments were proposed by Congress in 1789 and ratified as a group in 1791. Originally they protected citizens from the powers of the *federal* government only. Later the rights guaranteed by these amendments were applied to state governments as well. (See the section on the Fourteenth Amendment, page 52.)

## E. AMENDMENTS 11 TO 26

After the adoption of the Bill of Rights, the Constitution was changed by amendment only 16 times from 1795 (adoption of the Eleventh Amendment) to 1971 (adoption of the Twenty-sixth Amendment). Among the most important of these amendments are:

- *The Twelfth Amendment*: modifying the system for electing a president and vice president

- *The Thirteenth Amendment*: abolishing slavery
- *The Fourteenth Amendment*: guaranteeing equal rights of citizenship to all groups
- *The Fifteenth Amendment*: guaranteeing voting rights to citizens of all races
- *The Sixteenth Amendment*: providing for the collection of a federal income tax
- *The Seventeenth Amendment*: providing for the election of U.S. senators by direct popular vote (rather than by vote of the state legislatures)
- *The Nineteenth Amendment*: guaranteeing voting rights to women as well as men
- *The Twenty-sixth Amendment*: guaranteeing voting rights to young adults aged 18 or older.

For a summary of all of the later amendments (11 to 26), see the chart on pages 57–58.

# II. Principles of the U.S. Constitution

The framers of the Constitution created a government based on three principles: federalism, separation of powers, and checks and balances.

## A. FEDERALISM: THE POWERS OF CENTRAL AND STATE GOVERNMENTS

A **federal system** of government is one in which political power is divided, more or less evenly, between a central government for the nation and the individual state governments.

**Division of Powers**  The federal system of the Constitution replaced the confederate system established by the Articles of Confederation in 1781. Recall that the Articles of Confederation provided for a weak central government (a one-house Congress) and much stronger state governments. As a result the central government of the 1780s was unable to govern effectively. Framers of the Constitution attempted to remedy this situation by increasing the powers of the central government while reserving other powers for the states.

**Delegated Powers**  Powers given to the central government are those affecting the entire nation. Such powers—known as **delegated powers** or enumerated powers—are ones specifically named by the Constitution. They include collecting taxes, coining money, maintaining the armed forces, regulating trade, and making treaties.

**Reserved Powers**  Those powers reserved to the states by the Tenth Amendment include any and all powers that the Constitution neither delegates to the central government nor denies to the states. Although they are not named by the Constitution, **reserved powers** include the states' traditional authority over such matters as health and safety, marriage and divorce, the regulation of business, and the licensing of professions.

**Concurrent Powers**  **Concurrent powers** are those exercised by *both* the federal government and the state governments. Examples of these powers include building roads and highways, borrowing money, collecting taxes, and operating courts.

## B. SEPARATION OF POWERS: THREE BRANCHES

**Separation of powers** refers to a system for distributing legislative, executive, and judicial powers of government among three separate branches. The framers of the Constitution created such a system by giving to each of the three branches of the federal government its own special area of responsibility. The Congress as the legislative branch was to be responsible for making the nation's laws. The president as the chief executive was to be responsible for enforcing the laws. The federal courts as the judicial branch were to be responsible for interpreting the laws.

By creating three branches, each with a different area of responsibility, the framers hoped to prevent one official or group of officials from acquiring all or most of the powers of government.

## C. CHECKS AND BALANCES

The third great principle of the Constitution, **checks and balances**, concerns the system by which the three branches interact with each other.

**Definition and Purpose**  The framers gave each branch some powers to participate in the decisions of the other branches. This fact forces each branch to try to gain the approval of the other branches for its policies and decisions. If it fails to win such approval, its policies may be defeated. Such a system of partially shared responsibility is called checks and balances, because each branch has the ability to check, or block, the actions of the other branches. Powers are distributed in a balanced way so as to prevent any one branch from dominating the others.

**Example: The Lawmaking Process**  Take as an example of the checks and balances system the process for enacting a U.S. law.

Although Congress has primary responsibility for lawmaking, the president participates in the process by signing proposed laws passed by both houses of Congress. The president may also decide to **veto** (reject) an act of Congress. The president thereby checks Congress. Congress, however, has the power to countercheck. It may override the president's veto by passing the proposed law again with a two-thirds vote of approval in each house (rather than the simple majority required for original passage). If the override is accomplished, an act of Congress becomes law without the president's signature.

Suppose that a bill becomes law (either with or without the president's approval). Then the law may be challenged in the federal courts. The Supreme Court may be called upon to consider whether

## Checks and Balances

**The president acts . . .**

**Another branch checks . . .**

| The president acts . . . | Another branch checks . . . |
|---|---|
| 1. Makes a treaty with a foreign government. | The Senate rejects the treaty (fails to ratify it by a two-thirds vote). |
| 2. Commits certain "crimes and misdemeanors." | The House impeaches the president; then the Senate votes to remove the president from office. |
| 3. Vetoes an act of Congress. | Congress overrides the veto by a two-thirds vote of each house. |
| 4. Makes an appointment to a cabinet post. | The Senate rejects the president's nominee. |

**Congress acts . . .**

**Another branch checks . . .**

| Congress acts . . . | Another branch checks . . . |
|---|---|
| 1. Enacts a bill. | The president vetoes Congress's act. |
| 2. Enacts a bill that is signed by the president. | The Supreme Court declares Congress's act to be unconstitutional. |

**The Supreme Court acts . . .**

**Another branch checks . . .**

| The Supreme Court acts . . . | Another branch checks . . . |
|---|---|
| 1. Declares an act of Congress unconstitutional. | Congress proposes a constitutional amendment. |
| 2. Declares an action of the president unconstitutional. | The president appoints a new justice to the Supreme Court (if there is a vacancy). |

or not the law is allowed by the Constitution. If the Supreme Court decides that the law is *not* constitutional, then it is no longer considered a valid law. In this way the Supreme Court checks Congress (and checks the president as well, if he or she had signed the original bill).

**Other Examples**  In the statements below, each clause introduced by "*but*" represents a constitutional power given to one branch to enable it to check another branch's actions.

*The president may*:

- nominate federal judges, including the justices of the Supreme Court; *but* the Senate must confirm, or approve, such appointments by majority vote.

- nominate cabinet officials and the heads of executive agencies, *but* the Senate must approve such appointments by majority vote.

- sign treaties with other nations, *but* the Senate must approve such treaties by a two-thirds vote.

- propose laws, *but* Congress must agree to enact the proposed laws.

- carry out duties stated in the Constitution; *but* if the president acts improperly, he or she may be impeached (accused) by a majority vote of the House of Representatives and removed from office by a two-thirds vote of the Senate.

*Congress may*:

- attempt to influence the Supreme Court by voting to increase the number of justices; *but*, once selected, Supreme Court justices vote independently on all judicial questions.

- appropriate (set aside) funds for a government program, *but* the president might delay spending the money.

*The Supreme Court may*:

- declare an action of the president to be unconstitutional; *but* if the president defies the Court's ruling, only Congress can initiate impeachment proceedings.

- declare a law to be unconstitutional, *but* Congress may propose an amendment to the Constitution that would permit the law to stand if it is passed a second time.

## In Review

The following questions refer to section I: Main Parts of the Constitution and section II: Principles of the U.S. Constitution.

1. Define *federalism, separation of powers,* and *checks and balances.*
2. Explain how the first three articles of the Constitution carry out the principle of separation of powers.
3. Identify four constitutional amendments adopted after 1860 that made American government more democratic.

# III. The Congress

As the legislative branch of government, Congress has the major responsibility for making the nation's laws.

## A. BICAMERAL ORGANIZATION

Congress is **bicameral**, meaning that it is divided into two houses: a House of Representatives and a Senate. Each house must vote separately on all bills. The chart summarizes the differences between the two houses.

### The Two Houses of Congress

| | House of Representatives | Senate |
| --- | --- | --- |
| Number of members | 435; seats apportioned to each state according to the size of that state's population. | 100; each state represented by two senators. |
| Term of each member | Two years; may be re-elected to an unlimited number of terms; all members subject to election at the same time. | Six years; may be reelected to an unlimited number of terms; only about one third of Senate seats subject to election in the same year. |
| Member's qualifications | At least 25 years old; U.S. citizen for at least seven years; resident of the state from which he or she was elected. | At least 30 years old; U.S. citizen for at least nine years; resident of the state from which he or she was elected. |
| Member's constituency (the people represented by each member) | Citizens residing within a congressional district (part of the state). | All citizens of the state. |
| Presiding officer | Speaker of the House | Vice president of the United States |

**Apportionment of Seats in the House of Representatives**  A
chief difference between the House and the Senate is that the House
is affected by population change, while the Senate is not. Every ten
years, a **census** (count) is taken to determine the populations of the
50 states. In a process called reapportionment, a state that has gained
population relative to other states will gain seats in the House. At the
same time, a state that has lost population relative to other states
will lose seats. The total number of House seats, however, remains
the same (435) from one census year to the next. In the Senate each
state is allotted just two seats. Currently, since there are 50 states,
the total number of senators is 100.

**Special Powers and Rules of the Senate**  The Constitution gives
to the Senate certain lawmaking powers that it alone exercises. Only
the Senate gives its "advice and consent" to treaties made by the
executive branch. Only the Senate votes on whether or not to accept
the president's nominations for high-level federal officials.

Each house determines its own rules for conducting business. A
rule peculiar to the Senate allows for unlimited debate on the Senate
floor. Because of this rule, a small group of senators may attempt to
defeat a bill favored by the majority simply by **filibustering**. This is
the technique of speaking endlessly, thereby delaying a vote on the
bill and weakening the majority's determination to pass it.

**Elections to Congress**  Elections to Congress are held in every even-
numbered year—1992, 1994, and so on. All members of the House
are subject to election at the same time. In the Senate, where members
serve for six years, only one-third of the senators are elected at one
time. The second third are elected two years later and a final third
two years after that. Because terms are staggered in this way, the
Senate is more of an ongoing body than the House.

## B. POWERS

The powers delegated to Congress by Article I of the Constitution
include the power to collect taxes, borrow money, regulate trade,
coin money, declare war, raise and support armed forces, and establish
a post office.

**The Elastic Clause**  The last legislative power listed in Article I is
known as the **elastic clause** because it gives Congress the ability to
expand, or stretch, its specific powers to meet a variety of circumstances. According to this clause, Congress may make "all laws that
are necessary and proper" for carrying out its other powers. Because
of the elastic clause Congress can adapt to change by legislating on
matters that were unknown back in 1789 (for example, regulating TV

broadcasting). Powers derived from the elastic clause are known as **implied powers**.

**Limits on Power**   Besides granting certain powers to Congress, the Constitution also prohibits Congress from enacting certain kinds of laws. For example, Congress may *not* pass laws that allow it to (*a*) collect taxes on imports, (*b*) grant titles of nobility, (*c*) favor the ports of one state over those of another state, or (*d*) suspend the writ of **habeas corpus** except in an emergency. Such a writ is a document issued by a judge to protect citizens from being thrown in jail without a valid reason. The writ requires that the jailed person be brought promptly into court so that a judge can decide whether the person is being lawfully detained. (If not, the judge orders the prisoner's immediate release.)

# C. PROCEDURES FOR MAKING LAWS

Meeting in one body, Congress could not possibly deal with the thousands of bills (proposals for laws) that come before it each year. Therefore, it relies upon committees to screen out bills that are not worthy of attention.

**Committees and Subcommittees**   Committees of both the House and the Senate specialize in different areas of lawmaking. There are standing (permanent) committees, for example, on agriculture, foreign affairs, armed services, commerce, and labor. Before any bill is voted upon by either the House or the Senate, it is first considered by an appropriate committee (one that specializes in the subject of the bill). A committee often divides itself into smaller working groups, or subcommittees, that study bills in depth and report back to the full committee. Guided by a subcommittee's written report, the committee votes on whether to approve the original bill as is, defeat the bill as is, or approve an amended (changed) version of the bill.

**Floor Votes**   If a Senate bill is approved by committee, it then goes to the "floor" (or meeting place) of the full Senate for debate and vote. (If it is a House bill, it goes to the House floor.) The senators or representatives may debate the merits of the bill and propose amendments. To be passed, or enacted, the bill must receive the "yea" (yes) votes of a majority of those present. After passage of a bill by one house, the bill then goes to the other house for its consideration and vote.

**Conference Committee**   Often the House and the Senate pass bills that are very similar but not identical. For these bills to merge into one, the differences in them must be ironed out by a conference committee, consisting of members from both houses. If this committee agrees to a compromise, two identically worded bills go back to the full House and full Senate for a final vote.

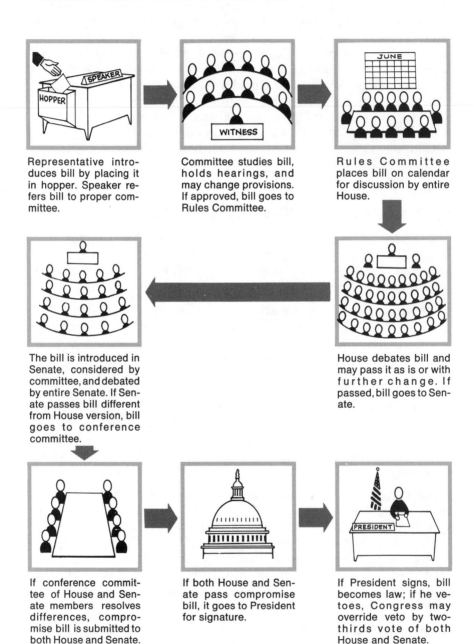

Representative introduces bill by placing it in hopper. Speaker refers bill to proper committee.

Committee studies bill, holds hearings, and may change provisions. If approved, bill goes to Rules Committee.

Rules Committee places bill on calendar for discussion by entire House.

The bill is introduced in Senate, considered by committee, and debated by entire Senate. If Senate passes bill different from House version, bill goes to conference committee.

House debates bill and may pass it as is or with further change. If passed, bill goes to Senate.

If conference committee of House and Senate members resolves differences, compromise bill is submitted to both House and Senate.

If both House and Senate pass compromise bill, it goes to President for signature.

If President signs, bill becomes law; if he vetoes, Congress may override veto by two-thirds vote of both House and Senate.

How a bill becomes a law

**Action by the President** If enacted by both houses, the bill—known at this stage as an act of Congress—goes to the president, who may either sign it or veto it.

- If it is signed, it becomes a law.
- If it is not signed, whether or not the act becomes a law depends on how long Congress continues in session.
  (1) If Congress is in session *longer than ten days* after passing an act, a president wishing to veto the act must promptly return it to Congress with an explanation for vetoing it. Congress then has an opportunity to override the veto by a two-thirds vote. (See page 31.)
  (2) If Congress is in session *fewer than ten days* after passing an act, the president can defeat the act simply by failing to sign it. This method of vetoing is known as the **pocket veto**.

# D. INFLUENCE OF PRESSURE GROUPS

How a member of Congress votes on a certain bill depends in part on whether the bill is favored or opposed by voters in the lawmaker's home district. Voters who wish to influence the lawmaking process may do so either as members of special interest groups or as individuals.

**Group Action** Many businesses, labor unions, and other organizations have a special interest in influencing the decisions of Congress because certain laws directly affect them. (For example, farmers have a special interest in agriculture bills; senior citizens have a special interest in Social Security bills.) To oppose or support bills that affect them, special interest groups organize letter-writing campaigns, place advertisements, and hire **lobbyists** (professional representatives) to visit members of Congress in their offices. Many special interest groups form **political action committees** (PACs) to contribute money to the campaigns of members of Congress.

**Individual Action** Also influencing government policy are those citizens who take the trouble to communicate their views to their elected representatives. They may either write letters to a representative or senator or visit a lawmaker's district office within the home state. Also, members of Congress may send out a mass mailing to **constituents** (the voters in their district) asking them to respond to questions on public issues. Of course the final expression of public opinion comes on Election Day when voters decide by majority vote whether those who currently represent them in government should be reelected.

# IV. The President

When the Constitution was written, the executive branch was meant to have the same amount of power as the other two branches. In recent years, however, many historians believe that the presidency has become more powerful than either Congress or the Supreme Court. In this section we will examine the growth of presidential power as well as the rules of the Constitution relating to the presidency.

## A. PRESIDENTIAL LEADERSHIP

The president has many roles to play as a chief executive, military leader, legislative leader, diplomatic leader, and ceremonial leader.

**Chief Executive**  The Constitution states that the president shall be "chief executive," or head of government. In this capacity, the president directs the work of cabinet heads and supervises agencies that make up the executive branch. The enforcement of all federal laws and programs is ultimately the responsibility of the president.

Among the dozens of government agencies that directly assist the nation's chief executive are:

- The Office of Management and Budget (OMB), which prepares a spending plan for the year for the U.S. government
- The Central Intelligence Agency (CIA), which gathers information on foreign matters affecting the national security
- The National Aeronautics and Space Administration (NASA), which directs U.S. exploration in space.

Those officials who head the major departments of the federal government form a cabinet of advisers to the president. George Washington was the first president to make use of a cabinet, which then consisted of four members. Today it is more than three times that number. Cabinet positions include the secretaries of agriculture, commerce, defense, education, energy, health and human services, housing and urban development, interior, justice, labor, state, transportation, treasury, and veterans affairs.

Today the executive branch employs about three million government workers (or civil servants) and spends more than one trillion dollars a year. The president's chief responsibilities include giving leadership to this immense organization and recommending a workable budget to Congress.

**Military Leader: Commander in Chief**  The president is the commander in chief of the armed forces. As a civilian, the president outranks every general and admiral. The most important military decisions must be approved by the president. For example, when U.S. troops were sent into Panama in 1990 to overthrow and capture the dictator Manuel Noriega, the action had the approval of President Bush.

**Legislative Leader**  In the role of legislative leader, the president either signs or vetoes acts of Congress. The president recommends new laws in an annual State of the Union address. For example, President Lyndon Johnson recommended to Congress an ambitious Civil Rights Act, which he persuaded Congress to pass and then signed into law in 1964. Another legislative power is the president's ability to call Congress into special session after it has adjourned for the year.

**Diplomatic Leader**  The Constitution gives to the president the power to (1) make treaties (with the approval of two thirds of the Senate), (2) receive ambassadors from other countries (and thereby recognize foreign governments), and (3) nominate U.S. ambassadors to other countries (with the approval of a majority of the Senate). For example, in 1803 President Thomas Jefferson arranged a treaty with France by which that country's huge Louisiana territory was added to the United States. Because of his diplomatic powers, the president is the chief maker of U.S. foreign policy.

**Ceremonial Leader: Chief of State**  In many nations, the **chief of state** (a ceremonial leader) is different from the chief executive (head of government). Great Britain, for example, has both a prime minister who acts as the political leader and a monarch who acts as the ceremonial chief of state. In the United States, the president serves in both roles. In the chief of state's role, the president speaks for the nation when traveling abroad and at home tries to inspire the American people to honor their traditions and live up to their ideals.

**Judicial Role**  Occasionally, the president participates in the judicial process by granting either a **pardon** (forgiveness for a federal crime) or a **reprieve** (delay of punishment). When a vacancy occurs on the Supreme Court, the president nominates a new justice, submitting the choice to the Senate for its confirmation, or approval.

## B. THE ELECTION PROCESS

Every four years, on the second Tuesday in November, millions of eligible voters aged 18 or older enter voting booths to elect a president and vice president. Of course the election process does not begin on the day of election but many months earlier. Let us review the main stages of the long campaign for the presidency.

**Nominating Candidates for President and Vice President** Those wishing to be president begin their campaign by seeking the nomination of either the Democratic party, the Republican party, or one of several minor parties. In the summer of a presidential election year, each political party holds a national convention at which delegates from the 50 states vote for the party's nominees for president and vice president.

How are convention delegates chosen? Most of the delegates to a party's convention are elected by the voters belonging to that party. Such preconvention elections are known as **primaries**. Each party holds its own primary.

The candidate who wins his or her party's primary election in a state receives most or all of that state's delegate votes at the national convention. In recent elections a single candidate in each party won enough primaries to be assured of winning nomination at the party's convention. After the convention votes for a presidential nominee, this person usually selects someone to be the party's candidate for vice president.

**The Fall Campaign** Following the conventions, the campaign moves to the next and final stage. Campaigning together as "running mates," the presidential and vice-presidential nominees of each party travel the nation seeking votes in the general election in November. They also devote much time to appearing on television—a medium that now plays a decisive role in the campaign process.

**The Electoral College** People who vote on Election Day may think that they are voting directly for a president and vice president. In fact, they are voting for a number of electors (either Republican electors or Democratic electors) who are authorized by the Constitution to cast ballots for president and vice president.

Electors are assigned to the 50 states according to the size of a state's delegation in Congress. Nevada, for example, had one representative and two senators in 1988, giving it three electors. California had 45 representatives and two senators, giving it 47 electors.

The candidate who wins a majority of "popular" votes (those cast by the people) wins *all* of that state's electoral votes. The winning group of electors in each state make up that state's electoral college. The electors cast ballots for president and vice president about one month after the popular election in November. Almost always the electors can be counted upon to cast their ballots for the candidates favored by a majority of the people.

**If There Is No Majority** If there are more than two major candidates in the race for president and no one wins a majority (more than 50 percent) of the electoral ballots, the Constitution provides that the election be decided by a special vote in the U.S. House of Representatives. In the House the delegation of each state is given just one vote. The candidate who wins a majority of the House vote is elected president.

## UNUSUAL ELECTIONS

**Election of 1800:** Tie vote broken by the House of Representatives. Electoral Vote: Jefferson, 73; Burr, 73.

Since no candidate had an electoral majority, the election was decided by the House of Representatives. The winner: Jefferson.

**Election of 1824:** Defeat of the most popular candidate

| Candidate | Popular Vote | Electoral Vote |
|---|---|---|
| Andrew Jackson | 153,544 | 99 |
| John Quincy Adams | 108,740 | 84 |
| William H. Crawford | 46,618 | 41 |
| Henry Clay | 47,136 | 37 |

Since no candidate had an electoral majority, the election was decided by the House of Representatives. The winner: John Quincy Adams.

**Election of 1876:** Defeat of the more popular candidate.

| Candidate | Popular Vote | Electoral Vote |
|---|---|---|
| Samuel J. Tilden | 4,284,020 | 184 |
| Rutherford B. Hayes | 4,036,572 | 185 |

This disputed election was resolved by a special commission in favor of Hayes.

**Election of 1888:** Defeat of the more popular candidate.

| Candidate | Popular Vote | Electoral Vote |
|---|---|---|
| Benjamin Harrison | 5,447,129 | 233 |
| Grover Cleveland | 5,537,857 | 168 |

The winner, Harrison, had less than a majority of the popular vote.

**Election of 1912:** Three-way race.

| Candidate | Popular Vote | Electoral Vote |
|---|---|---|
| Woodrow Wilson | 6,296,547 | 435 |
| Theodore Roosevelt | 4,118,571 | 88 |
| William H. Taft | 3,486,720 | 8 |

The winner, Wilson, had less than a majority of the popular vote.

**Arguments For and Against the System**   Our election system has long been a subject for debate. Some people argue that the system should be kept unchanged. Others advocate a variety of methods for either eliminating the electoral college or modifying it. (See chart, Debating the Electoral College.

## C. RULES OF SUCCESSION

Every nation must be concerned with developing orderly procedures for replacing its chief executive if that person should die or

---

## DEBATING THE ELECTORAL COLLEGE

Examine these arguments for and against the electoral college system. Then decide which position you support and why.

| Arguments For | Arguments Against |
|---|---|
| 1. The system is democratic since electors vote according to the majority will of each state. | 1. A far more democratic system would be one in which people vote directly for a president and vice president. There is no need for a second election involving only a small number of electors. |
| 2. The federalist system emphasizes the importance of the states. As the electoral college permits voting to be expressed state by state, the federalist principle is carried out. | 2. Although it rarely happens, electors *can* vote contrary to the wishes of the majority of voters. In a democracy, this is a dangerous possibility. |
| 3. The system is good for minority groups, since candidates must appeal to them in order to win election in a large urban state. | 3. If three or more candidates compete for the presidency, there is a good chance that the election will be decided— not by the people—but by the House of Representatives. |
| 4. The system is good for lightly populated states since it guarantees each of them at least three electoral votes. | 4. The system is *too* good for a lightly populated state like Nevada whose three electoral votes give it greater weight in the election total than its population justifies. |

fall seriously ill. In the United States the rules of **succession** are spelled out in an act of Congress and two amendments to the Constitution.

**Act of Presidential Succession**   An act of Congress of 1947 states that the vice president shall automatically become president if the president dies. It then lists those officials who would become president if *both* the president and vice president died at once. Next in line after the vice president would be the Speaker of the House, then the president pro tempore of the Senate, and then the department heads in the cabinet in the order in which the departments were created, beginning with the secretary of state.

**Twenty-second Amendment**   Adopted in 1951, the Twenty-second Amendment provides that no person may serve more than two elected terms as president. (*Historical note*: This amendment was adopted after Franklin D. Roosevelt had won election to the presidency four times, causing some people to worry about a president becoming too powerful.)

**Twenty-fifth Amendment**   This amendment, adopted in 1967, describes what would happen if the president is disabled by illness or injury. It allows for three possibilities: (1) The disabled president may prepare a written statement saying that he or she is unable to carry out presidential powers and duties. After this statement is received by leaders of both houses of Congress, the vice president will then serve temporarily as acting president. (2) The vice president, if supported by a majority of the cabinet, could submit a written declaration to the leaders of Congress stating that the president is unable to "discharge the powers and duties of his office." Then the vice president serves as acting president. (3) In a third circumstance the president may believe that he or she is capable of carrying out presidential duties, while the vice president and a majority of cabinet members think the president is incapable. Congress would then have the power to decide the issue. If the president's view is to be overruled, a two-thirds vote of Congress is required.

## D. REMOVING A PRESIDENT BY IMPEACHMENT

The Constitution says that a president who commits "crimes and misdemeanors" may be forced to leave office by a procedure known as **impeachment**. First, the House of Representatives decides by majority vote whether or not to impeach, or accuse, a president of acting either dishonestly or unlawfully. If the impeachment bill is passed, the Senate then meets as a trial court presided over by the chief justice of the Supreme Court. Two thirds of the senators must vote for conviction if an impeached president is to be removed.

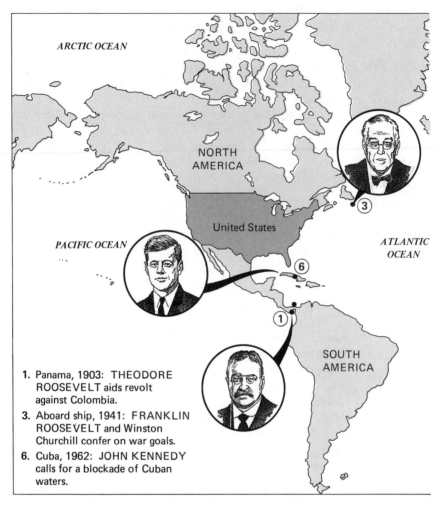

ARCTIC OCEAN

NORTH
AMERICA

United States

PACIFIC OCEAN

ATLANTIC
OCEAN

SOUTH
AMERICA

1. Panama, 1903: THEODORE
   ROOSEVELT aids revolt
   against Colombia.
3. Aboard ship, 1941: FRANKLIN
   ROOSEVELT and Winston
   Churchill confer on war goals.
6. Cuba, 1962: JOHN KENNEDY
   calls for a blockade of Cuban
   waters.

The global context:

Only one president, Andrew Johnson, was ever impeached by the House (but then acquitted by the Senate). Richard Nixon resigned office in 1974 *before* the House voted on a bill of impeachment.

## E. GROWTH OF PRESIDENTIAL POWER

The office of U.S. president is today considered the most powerful elected position in the world. However, it was not always so powerful. In 1789 the United States was a nation of only four million people. It had a new and untried government, an agricultural economy, and a tiny army and navy. Today it is a mighty industrial nation with one

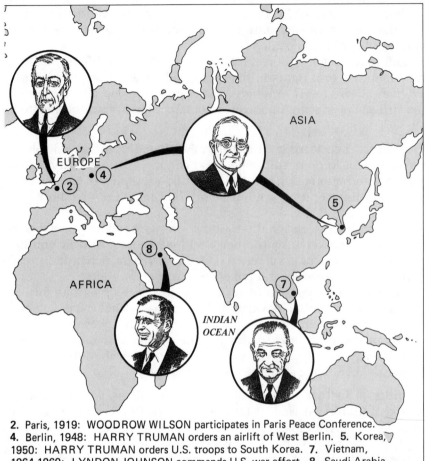

2. Paris, 1919: WOODROW WILSON participates in Paris Peace Conference.
4. Berlin, 1948: HARRY TRUMAN orders an airlift of West Berlin. 5. Korea,
1950: HARRY TRUMAN orders U.S. troops to South Korea. 7. Vietnam,
1964-1969: LYNDON JOHNSON commands U.S. war effort. 8. Saudi Arabia,
1990: GEORGE BUSH orders U.S. troops to fight war in the Persian Gulf.

presidential decisions in foreign affairs

of the largest armed forces in the world. As the power of the nation
has grown, so has the power of the presidency. The growth of
presidential power in both domestic affairs and foreign affairs can be
traced to the beginning years of the twentieth century.

**Presidents' Leadership in Domestic Affairs** In the early 1900s,
three successive presidents—Theodore Roosevelt, William H. Taft,
and Woodrow Wilson—responded vigorously to public demands for
honest and efficient government. Reforms championed by these
presidents (see Chapter 8) won the admiration of millions of citizens.

Vigorous leadership was provided by Franklin D. Roosevelt in the

1930s in meeting the economic crisis of the Great Depression and leading the nation to victory in World War II. In the twentieth century no other president did more than Roosevelt to increase the power and prestige of the presidency.

Adding further to the central role of modern presidents was the movement for civil rights in the 1950s and 1960s. Four presidents—Truman, Eisenhower, Kennedy, and Johnson—generally supported the struggle of African Americans to obtain relief from discriminatory laws.

**Presidents' Leadership in Foreign Affairs**   The increased role of the president in domestic affairs has been matched by an increased role in international affairs. (For dramatic examples of presidential actions in this century, see the map, The Global Context, on pages 44–45.)

As a leader of one of the world's strongest military powers, a president meets often with other world leaders at **summit conferences**. A successful conference usually results in expanded presidential power overseas and enhanced prestige at home.

The necessity for quick decision making in a crisis has further added to presidential power. In the fast-paced age of jet planes, nuclear weapons, and missile-delivery systems, the awesome responsibility of deciding how to respond to a perceived military attack must usually be entrusted to a single leader, rather than to the much slower deliberation of Congress's 535 members.

**Additional Factors**   Modern electronic technology allows presidents to speak to and be viewed by the entire nation. On television the president is seen almost daily (unlike the average member of Congress, who appears on national TV news infrequently, if at all).

Because the federal government has expanded to include agencies that affect all aspects of our lives, from health to Social Security to housing, the president's ability to influence our lives through presidential appointments and policies has also expanded.

## *In Review*

The following questions refer to section III: The Congress and section IV: The President.

### Word Wheel

Which section of the wheel on page 47 is described by each phrase?

**1.** Elected head of the executive branch

**2.** Power to ratify treaties

**3.** Members elected for two-year terms

4. Power to vote for or against nominees to cabinet posts
5. Presides over cabinet meetings
6. The smaller part of the legislative branch
7. Proposes a legislative program in an annual State of the Union message
8. Known for filibustering
9. May use the veto power to check Congress
10. Chiefly responsible for making U.S. foreign policy

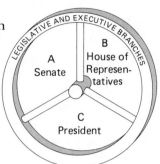

# V. The Supreme Court

In Article III the framers of the Constitution established a federal judiciary, or court system, as the third branch of government. Article III gives certain powers to a Supreme Court but leaves to Congress the responsibility of organizing the lower courts. Let us examine the organization of the federal courts, the jurisdiction of the Supreme Court, and some of the most significant Supreme Court decisions.

## A. ORGANIZATION OF THE FEDERAL COURTS

In 1789 Congress passed a Federal Judiciary Act, which organized the federal court system. It set up a **district court** (or lower court) in each state. Three circuit courts (or **appeals courts**) were created with power to review the decisions of the district courts. Since then, as the nation grew, so did the number of courts. In 1990 there were 94 district courts and 12 circuit courts, in addition to the one highest court—the U.S. Supreme Court.

**Trial Courts** Most trials for cases involving federal laws are held in district courts. Such courts have what is known as **original jurisdiction** for conducting trials.

**The Appeals Process** If a lawyer believes that a trial has been unfair, he or she may appeal the district court's decision to a circuit court. If unsuccessful there, the lawyer may further appeal to the Supreme Court as "the court of last resort." Cases begun in a state court may also be heard by the Supreme Court following a hearing by that state's appeals court. However, the Supreme Court is not required to hear all appeals. It may decide either to hear a case on appeal or not to hear it.

**Justices on the Supreme Court** Congress has the power to determine the number of justices who shall sit on the Supreme Court.

The first Supreme Court had six justices; today there are nine (one chief justice, eight associate justices). A decision in a case is made by majority vote. One of the justices in the majority is assigned the task of writing the constitutional reasons for the Court's decision.

**Life Tenure** According to the Constitution, Supreme Court justices and all other judges in the federal government "shall hold their offices during good behavior." Thus, there is no fixed limit on a judge's term of office. In effect a federal judge may be in office for life or until he or she voluntarily retires. An important result of this rule is that a federal judge feels no pressure to make decisions to win the favor of politicians or the popularity of voters.

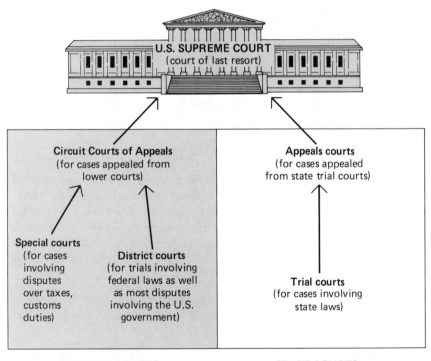

FEDERAL COURTS                                    STATE COURTS

Federal courts, state courts, and the appeals process

## B. JURISDICTION OF THE SUPREME COURT

The Supreme Court is the only court in the federal system that has two types of jurisdiction: original jurisdiction and appellate jurisdiction.

**Original Jurisdiction**  In a small number of cases, the Supreme Court is authorized by the Constitution to act as a trial court (a court with original jurisdiction). Such cases include those involving (1) ambassadors and (2) disputes between states.

**Appellate Jurisdiction**  The Supreme Court also has the authority to review cases appealed to it from lower courts. In these cases it has **appellate jurisdiction**. In each case it may decide either to uphold the decision of the lower court or to overturn that decision.

## C.  LANDMARK DECISIONS OF JOHN MARSHALL

John Marshall, the fourth chief justice of the United States, served from 1801 to 1835. He was remarkably successful in establishing the Supreme Court as an independent and influential force in the federal government. Three of his most important decisions are summarized here:

***Marbury v. Madison* (1803)**  Just before leaving office, President John Adams appointed William Marbury to be a judge in a federal court. The next President, Thomas Jefferson, ordered his secretary of state, James Madison, *not* to carry out the appointment. Marbury appealed to the Supreme Court, arguing that a 1789 law granted the Supreme Court the power to force Madison to give Marbury his appointment. But Chief Justice Marshall, writing the majority opinion of the highest court, argued that the 1789 law of Congress applying to Marbury's case was not authorized by the Constitution. Thus, the law was **unconstitutional**—null and void.

*Effect*: The Supreme Court's decision in this case established the principle of **judicial review**, which is a federal court's power to determine whether or not an act of Congress is allowed by the Constitution.

***McCulloch v. Maryland* (1819)**  At issue in this case was whether a state government (Maryland) could collect a tax from a bank that had been chartered by the U.S. government. Marshall argued that states could *not* tax a federal agency because, according to the Constitution, the federal government was meant to be supreme. Marshall stated that "the power to tax is the power to destroy." On another question Marshall argued that Congress's powers could be interpreted loosely to authorize the creation of a national bank.

*Effect*: This case established the idea that a state law could be nullified (declared void) if it was found to be in conflict with a federal law.

***Gibbons v. Ogden* (1824)**  At issue in this case was whether a state (New York) could grant to one and only one steamship company the

# DOCUMENTS: *McCULLOCH V. MARYLAND*

John Marshall

Could the state of Maryland tax a bank created by the U.S. Congress? Did Congress have the constitutional power to create such a bank? Here is John Marshall's answer to these questions in the landmark case of *McCulloch v. Maryland* (1819).

On a separate piece of paper, state in your own words the argument that Marshall makes.

We admit, as all must admit, that the powers of the government are limited, and that its limits are not to be transcended. But we think the sound construction of the constitution must allow to the national legislature that discretion, with respect to the means by which the powers it confers are to be carried into execution, which will enable that body to perform the high duties assigned to it, in the manner most beneficial to the people. Let the end be legitimate, let it be within the scope of the constitution, and all means which are appropriate, which are plainly adapted to that end, which are not prohibited, but consist with the letter and spirit of the constitution, are constitutional . . . .

right to operate on an interstate waterway (the Hudson River). In his decision Marshall stated that trade is commerce, that commerce between states was controlled by the U.S. Congress, and therefore that New York's law was invalid.

*Effect*: The ruling clarified the concept of interstate commerce and increased the authority of the federal government to regulate businesses that operate in more than one state.

**Impact of Marshall's Decisions** Taken as a whole the many cases decided by Chief Justice Marshall increased the power of the national government relative to that of the states. Also, by the repeated application of judicial review, Marshall greatly expanded the power and influence of the Supreme Court.

# VI. The Bill of Rights

Ever since the 1940s and 1950s, some of the most important decisions of the Supreme Court concerned the meaning of specific clauses of the Bill of Rights (amendments 1 to 10 of the Constitution). Every citizen should know the basic provisions of the Bill of Rights, since they are fundamental to defining Americans' two greatest political ideals: liberty and justice.

## A. MAIN PROVISIONS

In the summary that follows, notice that most provisions of the Bill of Rights define something that government officials are *not* permitted to do.

**Freedom of Religion**   Congress may not interfere with a person's right to worship according to his or her own conscience (First Amendment).

**Separation of Church and State**   Congress may not favor one religion over another by giving special support to any church, synagogue, or other religious institution (First Amendment).

**Freedom of Speech, Press, Assembly, and Petition**   Congress may make no law that interferes with a person's freedom to express ideas in speech and writing. Nor may officials of the U.S. government stop people from demonstrating (or assembling) in a peaceful manner. Nor may people be punished for petitioning the government for a change in policy (First Amendment).

**Right to "Keep and Bear Arms"**   Citizens may not be denied the right to carry weapons for use in a state **militia** (a group of volunteer soldiers trained for the common defense) (Second Amendment).

**Right Against Unfair Police Searches and Seizures**   Government officials must obtain a judge's permission—or **search warrant**— before they can conduct a search of a person's property. A warrant must describe "the place to be searched and the persons or things to be seized." It may be issued to a police officer only if a judge is convinced that there is "probable cause" of criminal evidence being found (Fourth Amendment).

**Rights of Persons Accused of Breaking U.S. Laws**   The following rights of an accused person are guaranteed in the Fifth Amendment and the Sixth Amendment.

- The accusation, or **indictment**, of a federal court must be made by a **grand jury**.
- No **double jeopardy**: A person acquitted by a jury cannot be tried again on the same charge.
- No person can be forced to give testimony or evidence that may be used against him or her at a trial.

- An accused person is guaranteed "a speedy and public trial."
- An accused person has the right to a trial by an impartial jury.
- An accused person has the right to be informed of the criminal charges against him or her.
- An accused person has the right to be represented by a lawyer and to have the government assist in producing witnesses on his or her behalf.

**Right to Due Process**   No person may be deprived of "life, liberty, or property without due process of law" (Fifth Amendment).

**Rights Concerning Bail and Punishment for Crime**   A person awaiting trial may not be charged an excessive amount for bail (a sum of money to obtain release from jail pending trial). A person convicted of a crime may not be punished for it in "cruel and unusual" ways (Eighth Amendment).

**Rights Reserved to the States**   Whatever powers are neither delegated to the federal government nor denied to the states belong to the governments of the different states and to the American people (Tenth Amendment).

## B. THE FOURTEENTH AMENDMENT

Adopted in 1791 the first ten amendments—or Bill of Rights—protected citizens from abuses of the *federal* government only, not from unfair state laws. This partial protection continued for more than 75 years until 1868. In that year the Fourteenth Amendment was added to the Constitution. Northern victors of the Civil War wanted the amendment to be a means of protecting the rights of freed slaves. Of course the amendment applied to all other Americans as well.

The Fourteenth Amendment provides that no *state* may deny its citizens either "due process of law" or "equal protection of the laws." Often, in the twentieth century, the Supreme Court has used the due process clause of the Fourteenth Amendment to expand the protections of the first ten amendments. Therefore, instead of applying only to federal laws, the Bill of Rights now applies to state laws as well.

# VII. Interpreting the Bill of Rights

In the twentieth century many of the most important decisions—or landmark decisions—of the Supreme Court involved various provisions of the Bill of Rights. Let us examine some of these landmark decisions and the basis for them.

# A. DECISIONS ON FIRST AMENDMENT RIGHTS

The rights protected by the First Amendment are fundamental to a free society. The amendment guarantees every citizen's right to freedom of religion, freedom of speech, freedom of the press, freedom of assembly, and freedom of petition.

**Separation of Church and State**   The First Amendment states that Congress may "make no law respecting an establishment of religion." In other words government may not do anything to favor or give preference to any religious practice or group. Thomas Jefferson said that "a wall of separation between church and state" should keep government from interfering in religious matters. In recent years many Supreme Court decisions have affirmed and clarified this idea.

- In the case of *Engel* v. *Vitale* (1962), the Supreme Court ruled that prayer in public schools was unconstitutional because it violated the principle of separation of church and state.

- In *School District of Abington Township [Pennsylvania]* v. *Schempp* (1963), the highest court ruled that Bible reading in public schools violated the First Amendment.

**Freedom of Speech and the Press**   Freedom of speech and the press means that nobody may be penalized for criticizing government officials and policies. However, under certain circumstances affecting the public safety, the right to express ideas freely may be limited.

- In *Schenck* v. *United States* (1919), Justice Oliver Wendell Holmes said that speech could be limited if it presented a "clear and present danger." As an example of such a danger, he said, "free speech would not protect a man in falsely shouting fire in a theatre and causing a panic."

- In *Tinker* v. *Des Moines School District* (1969), the Supreme Court decided that students could not be penalized for wearing black armbands to school to protest the Vietnam War. The Court argued that students do not "shed their Constitutional rights to freedom of speech or expression at the schoolhouse gate."

- In a controversial case of 1989, *Texas* v. *Johnson*, the Supreme Court decided that a person who had deliberately set fire to an American flag as an act of protest could not be punished by state officials, because flag burning could be considered a form of symbolic speech protected under the First Amendment.

**Freedom of Assembly**   The First Amendment guarantees the right of people to assemble peacefully and to petition the government "for a redress of grievances."

- For example, in *Collin* v. *Smith* (1978), the Supreme Court agreed with an appeals court ruling that said that the American Nazi party had a right to march in the city of Skokie, Illinois, even if this act of "peaceable assembly" offended other people in the community.

From the above cases, we see that the Supreme Court uses its power of judicial review to define what each clause of the First Amendment means in a specific situation.

## B. DECISIONS ON THE FOURTH, FIFTH, AND SIXTH AMENDMENTS

In the 1960s, under the leadership of Chief Justice Earl Warren, the Supreme Court decided a great number of cases that tested the meaning of the Fourth, Fifth, and Sixth Amendments.

**Search and Seizure** The Fourth Amendment protects citizens against police officers making "unreasonable" searches and seizures of personal property. Two decisions concerning search and seizure were especially important.

- In *Mapp* v. *Ohio* (1961), the Supreme Court ruled that evidence obtained without a valid search warrant may not be admitted into a state court.
- In *Katz* v. *United States* (1967), the Court ruled that wiretapping requires a search warrant. A person's privacy (not just property) is protected by the Fourth Amendment.

**Rights of Accused Persons** The rights guaranteed in the Fifth and Sixth Amendments concern the procedures that the courts and the police must use to ensure fair treatment of persons arrested for crimes. (See pages 51–52 for a list of these rights.)

- In *Gideon* v. *Wainwright* (1963), the Supreme Court under Earl Warren ruled that if an accused person is too poor to hire a lawyer, a state is obligated to provide one at public expense.
- In *Escobedo* v. *Illinois* (1964), the Court ruled that anyone taken to a police station for questioning has the right to be represented by a lawyer.
- In *Miranda* v. *Arizona* (1966), the Court ruled that at the time of arrest, a person must be told his or her rights to remain silent and to have an attorney present.

## C. DECISIONS CONCERNING "CRUEL AND UNUSUAL PUNISHMENTS"

Is it constitutional to execute a convicted criminal for violent crimes? Or are such executions forbidden by the Eighth Amendment's ban against "cruel and unusual" punishments? In two landmark cases of the 1970s, the Supreme Court ruled on this matter.

- In *Furman* v. *Georgia* (1972), the Court ruled that the death penalty is not constitutional *unless* the state has clear and consistent rules for applying the penalty uniformly to people of all races and social classes.

- In *Gregg* v. *Georgia* (1976), the Court ruled that the death penalty is constitutional if the nature of the crime is made the sole factor for imposing the sentence.

### *In Review*

The following questions refer to section V: The Supreme Court, section VI: The Bill of Rights, and section VII: Interpreting the Bill of Rights.

1. Define *original jurisdiction, appellate jurisdiction, judicial review, unconstitutional, separation of church and state,* and *due process of law.*
2. Explain how the Fourteenth Amendment extended the protections of the Bill of Rights.
3. Identify three rights of an accused person that are guaranteed by the U.S. Bill of Rights.

# VIII. The Constitution as a "Living Document"

Scholars have called the U.S. Constitution a "living document" because it is flexible enough to change with the times. Our constitutional system may be changed in two ways: (1) by formal amendment and (2) by informal adjustments and decision making.

## A. FORMAL PROCEDURES OF AMENDMENT

Article V of the Constitution describes the formal procedures for proposing and ratifying amendments. Although several procedures may be used, the most common of them involves two steps:

*Step One*: Congress proposes an amendment by a two-thirds vote of each house.

*Step Two*: The proposed amendment is considered by the legislatures of the states. If approved or ratified by at least three fourths of the states, the amendment is added to the Constitution.

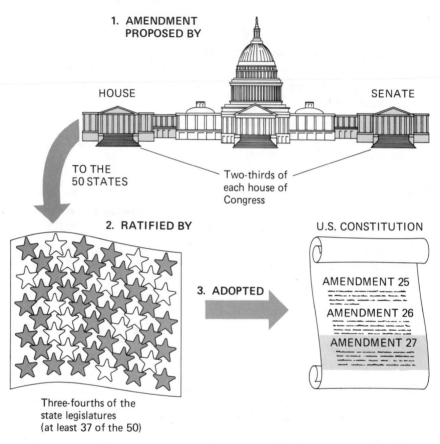

The most common method for amending the Constitution

## B. METHODS OF INFORMAL CHANGE

The Constitution is a flexible "living document" not only because it can be changed by formal amendment but also because it allows informal methods of change.

**Congress and the Elastic Clause**   Congress would be unable to cope with changing times if it were not for the so-called elastic clause (or "necessary and proper" clause) in Article I of the Constitution. Because of this clause, Congress is empowered to legislate on a vast number of subjects that were unknown when the Constitution was

## A Summary of Amendments 11 to 27

| Amendment | Year Adopted | Main Provisions |
| --- | --- | --- |
| Eleventh | 1798 | Citizens of other states or of foreign countries cannot sue a state in federal court without that state's consent. |
| Twelfth | 1804 | Electors from each state shall cast two separate ballots—one for president, one for vice president. |
| Thirteenth | 1865 | Slavery in the United States is abolished. |
| Fourteenth | 1868 | All persons born in the United States are U.S. citizens, who are entitled to due process of law and equal protection of the laws. |
| Fifteenth | 1870 | No government in the United States may prevent citizens from voting because of their race. |
| Sixteenth | 1913 | Congress has the power to collect taxes on incomes without dividing the taxes among the states according to their population. |
| Seventeenth | 1913 | The two U.S. senators from each state shall be elected by a direct vote of the people of the state. |
| Eighteenth (Also known as the Prohibition Amendment) | 1919 | The manufacture and sale of intoxicating beverages in the United States is prohibited. |
| Nineteenth | 1920 | No government in the United States may prevent citizens from voting because of their gender. |
| Twentieth (Also known as the "Lame Duck" Amendment) | 1933 | The terms of office of the president and vice president end at noon, January 20. The terms of office of members of Congress end at noon, January 3. |
| Twenty-first | 1933 | The Eighteenth Amendment is repealed. |
| Twenty-second | 1951 | No person can be elected more than twice to the office of president. |
| Twenty-third | 1961 | Residents of the District of Columbia may participate in the election for president and vice president by choosing three electors. |

## A Summary of Amendments 11 to 27 (*continued*)

| | | |
|---|---|---|
| Twenty-fourth | 1964 | No government in the United States may collect a poll tax from citizens as a requirement for voting. (A poll tax is a tax collected from voters before they are issued ballots.) |
| Twenty-fifth | 1967 | If the cabinet and the Congress determine that the president is disabled, the vice president will temporarily assume the duties of president. |
| Twenty-sixth | 1971 | No government in the United States may prevent persons 18 or older from voting on account of their age. |
| Twenty-seventh | 1992 | Congress cannot vote itself a pay increase until an election of representatives intervenes. |

written. For example, it can regulate airplane traffic, set speed limits on interstate highways, and provide for a minimum wage. Such regulations are permitted because they may be viewed as "necessary and proper" means of regulating interstate commerce. (Only interstate commerce—trade crossing state lines—is mentioned in the Constitution—not airplanes, interstate highways, and minimum wages.)

**The Supreme Court and Judicial Review**   Judicial review is the power of the Supreme Court to rule on the constitutionality of federal and state laws. Each case decided by the highest court involves a question of how the words of the Constitution apply to a unique set of circumstances. Of course the circumstances keep changing. In the 1880s and 1890s many cases involved the issue of regulating railroads and oil companies—institutions that were unknown to the Constitution's framers. In the future, issues involving computer technologies will probably make up a large number of Supreme Court cases. No matter what the issue, the Supreme Court uses its power of judicial review to adapt the Constitution to changing circumstances.

**The Presidency and the Unwritten Constitution**   The **unwritten constitution** refers to traditions that have become part of our political system. Note these examples: (1) Most elected offices are filled by two major political parties, the Republicans and the Democrats, even though there is no mention of political parties in the Constitution. (2) After the first president, George Washington, declined to serve more than two terms, later presidents made the same decision. The "'two-term tradition," as it was called, was finally broken in 1940, when Franklin Roosevelt ran successfully for a third term. He also won a fourth term in 1944. (Later, in 1947, supporters of the two-term tradition persuaded the nation to adopt the Twenty-second Amendment, which limited the president to two elected terms.) (3) The Constitution says nothing about the cabinet. But early in his presidency, George Washington made a habit of meeting with a cabinet of four advisers. Since then, presidents have asked Congress to add new cabinet positions to meet the needs of changing times.

# IX. The States in the Federal System

Citizens of the United States are also citizens of the states in which they reside. While the U.S. government takes responsibility for national problems and foreign affairs, states have authority for dealing with local issues such as education, public safety, and public health. The organization of state governments is similar to that of the national government. Each of the 50 states has its own constitution, which

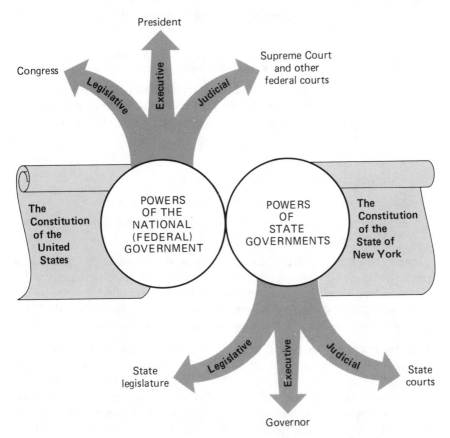

Separation of powers in the federalist system

provides for the separation of powers among a legislative branch, a judicial branch, and an executive branch headed by a governor.

## A. ADMISSION OF NEW STATES

Thirty-seven of the 50 states were admitted to the Union *after* the Constitution was written in 1787. The Constitution provides for changing a territory governed by Congress into a state that has its own government and constitution. First, a territory formally applies to Congress for statehood. The territory must submit a proposed state constitution that has been approved by the people of the territory. By majority vote Congress may either accept or reject a territory's application for statehood.

At times Congress may attach conditions to statehood. In 1896, for example, Utah was admitted as a state on the condition that it not allow polygamy (the practice of being married to two or more persons at the same time).

The last two territories to apply for admission, Hawaii and Alaska, won statehood in 1959.

## B. STATE LEGISLATIVE BRANCH

Like the U.S. government, each state government has a representative legislature whose members debate and vote upon proposed laws for the state. Representing the citizens who elect them, state lawmakers vote on issues like these:

- Should more state prisons be built?
- Should penalties for crimes be changed?
- Should more funds be set aside for mass transit?
- Should passing a state test be a requirement for graduating from high school?

**Bicameral Organization**   Like Congress almost all state legislatures have two houses, both of which must approve bills by majority vote. In New York State the larger of the two houses is called the Assembly and the smaller house the Senate. Nebraska is the only state that has a single legislative body; its members are called senators.

**The Politics of Redistricting**   Periodically, district lines for the houses of the state legislature are changed to reflect shifts in population. The state legislature has the power to vote on how the new district boundaries shall be drawn. Often, by a common practice called **gerrymandering**, politicians belonging to the majority party in the legislature draw district lines so as to favor their own political party. To restrict this practice, the U.S. Supreme Court has ruled in

*Baker* v. *Carr* (1962) that legislative district lines must reflect the principle of "one man, one vote." In other words, districts must be roughly equal in population to ensure that residents of the districts are equally represented. Despite this requirement district lines can still be twisted out of shape—or gerrymandered—to make it easier for the candidates of one political party to win election.

## C. STATE EXECUTIVE BRANCH

Every state's chief executive is the governor. Just as the president enforces the laws of Congress, the governor's primary role is to carry out, or enforce, the laws of the state. To assist in this complicated task, each state governor directs a number of executive departments and agencies, each responsible for a different function (for example, a highway department to maintain state roads, an education department to supervise state schools).

**The Governor's Influence on Legislation** The governor provides legislative as well as executive leadership. He or she proposes a legislative program (series of bills) and tries to persuade a majority of state lawmakers to vote for it. A governor, like the president, has the power to veto bills.

Every year governors recommend a state budget (taxing and spending plan) to the legislature. To persuade the legislature to approve the proposed budget, governors make full use of their executive authority, access to the media, and political influence as party leaders.

**A Governor's Other Duties** Another power of the governor is to nominate the heads of executive departments and agencies. In many states the governor also appoints state judges. Usually a governor's appointments require the approval of one of the two houses of the legislature.

Another of the governor's functions is to act as commander in chief of the state National Guard (a military force consisting of citizen volunteers). In times of emergency, natural disaster, or riot, the governor orders National Guard units into action. If necessary the governor may also request that the president call federal units into service.

A governor may grant **pardons** (forgiveness for a crime) or **reprieves** (postponement of a punishment) to persons convicted of state crimes.

## D. STATE JUDICIAL BRANCH

Each state has its own court system, consisting of both lower courts for trying cases and higher courts for hearing appeals.

**Function**  The three main functions of state courts are (1) to hear criminal cases involving violations of state laws, (2) to settle legal disputes between citizens, and (3) to resolve cases involving the interpretation of the state constitution.

**The Judicial Process**  Before any criminal case goes to trial, a group of citizens called a grand jury (large jury) decides whether there is enough evidence to **indict**, or accuse, a certain person of committing a crime. If so the indicted person stands trial in a state trial court, where a **petit jury** (smaller jury) decides the person's guilt or innocence. If found guilty the convicted person may appeal the case to a state appeals court. A second appeal may then be made to the highest state appeals court (often called the state supreme court). If the case involves a federal issue or an interpretation of the U.S. Constitution, a final appeal may be made to the U.S. Supreme Court.

In making their decisions, state courts must be guided not only by the rules of the state constitution, but also by the rights guaranteed by the U.S. Constitution.

## E.  INTERSTATE RELATIONS

Because each state is free to make laws and regulations of its own, there could be a problem of states competing with each other rather than working together for their mutual good. But two factors help to alleviate the problem: provisions of the U.S. Constitution and interstate agreements, or compacts.

**"Full Faith and Credit"**  Imagine, for a moment, these possibilities:

- Your automobile license is not recognized as valid when you drive out of state.
- Your high school diploma is considered legitimate only by your own state.

Fortunately, neither event could occur because Article IV of the Constitution requires that states give "full faith and credit" to each other's laws, licenses, and official documents. For example, the state of Florida must honor the licenses granted by New York State to New Yorkers traveling in Florida. However, the scope of the "full faith and credit clause" is limited. A state may require that its lawyers and teachers meet its own licensing standards and may refuse to acknowledge an out-of-state certificate in these professions as valid.

**Interstate Compacts**  States that share a common border often recognize that they have a mutual interest in solving a common problem. By signing interstate compacts, the governors of neighboring states establish regional agencies managed by officials from those states. An example is the Port Authority of New York and New Jersey, which operates interstate bridges and tunnels on either side of the Hudson River.

## F. LOCAL GOVERNMENTS

Within states there are smaller units of government for counties, villages, towns, and municipalities (cities). Each unit has its own governing bodies for carrying out duties within its jurisdiction. Most municipalities, for example, have their own police, fire, sanitation, and health departments.

**Officials** Local officials such as mayors, city managers, and county executives act in the role of chief executive, supervising the departments of the municipal or county government. Members of city councils and county boards of supervisors (or freeholders) have legislative powers for making local regulations called **ordinances**. In making their decisions, both legislative bodies and executive officials must be careful to conform to state laws.

**Finances** Funding for public schools and other local institutions comes mainly from **property taxes** collected on the value of residents' homes and local businesses. These tax revenues are supplemented by grants of money from both the state and federal governments.

# Summary: The Strengths of Our Constitutional System

How can we explain the remarkable fact that a constitution created more than 200 years ago is still the basis for one of the most successful and stable governments in the world? The reasons are many:

- The Constitution is a brief and flexible set of guidelines, allowing the government to adapt to change. Thus, each generation has been able to interpret the Constitution in terms of changing needs and conditions. At the same time, the traditional values and principles of the Constitution are still respected.
- The Preamble emphasizes that the Constitution is a document of the people, not of the states.
- The principles of separation of powers and checks and balances have helped to block the possibility of one of the three branches wielding absolute power.
- The Bill of Rights has served to protect individual liberties.
- Amendments to the Constitution have extended voting rights to all groups in the adult population.

## *In Review*

The following questions refer to section VIII: The Constitution as a "Living Document," and section IX: The States in the Federal System.

1. Illustrate the idea that the Constitution is a "living document."
2. Compare separation of powers in state government with separation of powers in the federal government.

## GLOSSARY OF KEY TERMS: CHAPTER 2

**administration**   the management of governmental affairs.

**agency**   an administrative division of government with specific functions.

**amendment**   an addition to or change in the U.S. Constitution; also, a change in a law or proposed law.

**appeal**   to make a request to a higher court for the rehearing or review of a case.

**appeals court**   a federal court that is intermediate in authority between the U.S. district courts and the Supreme Court and may review cases originally tried in the district courts.

**appellate jurisdiction**   the authority of a higher court to review a case originally tried in a lower court.

**appropriate**   to set aside public funds for a specific use, such as paying for schools.

**bail**   money or credit deposited with a court to allow an arrested person to be temporarily released from jail on the assurance that he or she will appear for trial at the proper time.

**bill**   a proposal for a law.

**checks and balances**   a system by which one branch of government may oppose and defeat the policies or decisions of other branches.

**committee**   a group of people chosen from a larger group (such as the full membership of a legislature) to consider, investigate, and report on an assigned topic or public issue.

**concurrent powers**   powers that are exercised jointly by both the U.S. government and state governments.

**constituents**   voters represented by a particular official.

**delegated powers**   powers granted to the U.S. government that the Constitution mentions directly and explicitly; also known as enumerated powers.

**district court**   a U.S. court that conducts trials for a specific area, or district.

**division of powers** dividing power between a central government and state governments.

**double jeopardy** the placing of an accused person on trial a second time for the same offense after that person had been found innocent in the first trial.

**due process of law** a constitutional guarantee that persons under legal investigation receive fair treatment from government officials.

**elastic clause** a clause in the U.S. Constitution giving to Congress the power to pass laws that are "necessary and proper" for carrying out Congress's other specific powers.

**electoral college** a group of politicians elected by the voters to perform the formal duty of electing the president and the vice president.

**"equal protection of the laws"** a clause in the Fourteenth Amendment guaranteeing the same legal rights and privileges for all citizens.

**federal government** the U.S. government; or the central government of any nation that has a federal system.

**gerrymandering** the practice of state legislatures drawing district lines in such a manner as to make it either easier or more difficult for the candidates of one political party to win election.

**grand jury** a group of citizens who decide whether there is enough evidence to indict (accuse) a certain person of a crime.

**habeas corpus** an order requiring that a detained (or jailed) person be brought before a court at a stated time and place to decide whether the person's detention is proper and lawful.

**impeach** to accuse an official of wrongdoing—an accusation that *may* lead to the person's being removed from office.

**implied powers** powers of the U.S. government that derive from the so-called "elastic clause" (see above).

**indictment** a formal written accusation charging one or more persons with a crime.

**judicial review** the Supreme Court's power to determine whether or not an act of Congress is allowed by the Constitution.

**judiciary** the part of government that administers the courts and interprets the laws in specific cases.

**jurisdiction** the legal power to hear and decide cases.

**legislature** the lawmaking branch of a government.

**lobbyist** a person, acting for a special interest group, who tries to influence legislators' votes on proposed laws.

**naturalize** to confer the rights of citizenship upon someone who had been born in a foreign country to foreign parents.

**nominate** to name or appoint to an office or position.

**ordinance** a regulation by a local government.

**original jurisdiction**   the authority of a court to be the first to hear a case and conduct a trial.

**pardon**   a chief executive's power to forgive a convicted person for a crime.

**petit jury**   a group of citizens who hear testimony at a trial and decide upon a verdict.

**poll tax**   a payment once required for voting in some states (now prohibited by the Twenty-fourth Amendment).

**preamble**   an introduction to a document, such as a constitution, stating the overall purpose of the document.

**primary election**   a preliminary election in which voters choose between the candidates competing for a political party's nomination.

**property tax**   a tax on the value of privately owned property such as houses and stores.

**ratification**   the approval of a proposed treaty or constitutional amendment.

**reprieve**   a chief executive's power to postpone a convicted person's punishment.

**reserved powers**   powers such as police protection and education that remain with the states after other powers were delegated to the national government by the Constitution.

**search warrant**   a legal document authorizing or directing a police officer to search a specified person or place for stolen articles or items to be used as evidence in court.

**self-incrimination**   to make oneself appear guilty of a crime by one's own statements or answers.

**separation of powers**   a system for distributing the legislative, executive, and judicial powers of government among three separate branches or departments.

**succession**   the process by which one official follows another into a given office.

**unconstitutional**   not in accordance with or permitted by the U.S. Constitution (or state constitution).

**unwritten constitution**   traditions in government that are consistently practiced even though they are not specifically written into the Constitution.

**veto**   the power of a chief executive (the president or state governor) to refuse to sign a bill passed by the legislature.

# TEST YOURSELF

## A. Multiple Choice: Facts, Main Ideas, Skills

*On a separate sheet of paper, write the number of the word or expression that, of those given, best completes the statement or answers the questions.*

### Reviewing the facts

1. The principle of federalism as established by the U.S. Constitution provides for the  (1) separation of powers of the three branches of government  (2) placement of ultimate sovereignty in the hands of the state governments  (3) division of power between the state governments and the national government  (4) creation of a republican form of government

2. A power shared by both the state governments and the federal government is the power to  (1) regulate interstate commerce  (2) issue money  (3) declare war  (4) collect taxes

3. The section of the U. S. Constitution that grants Congress the power to "make all laws which shall be necessary and proper for carrying into execution the foregoing powers ..." has come to be known as the  (1) great compromise  (2) supremacy clause  (3) due process provision  (4) elastic clause

4. The constitutional power to regulate commerce allows the federal government to exercise control over  (1) post offices and post roads  (2) interstate trade  (3) international relations  (4) the value of money

5. Which situation in the United States is an illustration of lobbying? (1) A defeated candidate for the Senate is appointed a member of the president's cabinet.  (2) A special interest group hires a person to present its views to certain members of Congress.  (3) Federal public works projects are awarded to a state.  (4) Two members of Congress agree to support each other's bills.

6. The main responsibility of Congress is to  (1) make laws for the people of the United States  (2) enforce the laws of state legislatures  (3) command the armed forces  (4) regulate state legislatures

7. Which is generally considered to be a major weakness of the electoral college system for selecting a U.S. president?  (1) Electoral votes are unevenly distributed among the states.  (2) A candidate can win the popular vote but lose the presidency.  (3) Too much time elapses between the general election and the counting of electoral votes.  (4) Candidates tend to ignore the states with a majority of young voters.

8. In the United States, the electoral college system influences presidential candidates to  (1) make personal appearances in every state  (2) campaign extensively in states with large populations  (3) state their platforms in very specific terms  (4) seek endorsements from state governors

**9.** Judicial review gives the U.S. Supreme Court the power to   (1) grant pardons to prisoners held in federal penitentiaries   (2) examine the qualifications of judges appointed to lower courts   (3) decide on the constitutionality of laws   (4) impeach the president

**10.** The framers of the Constitution gave voters the most direct participation in the selection of the   (1) House of Representatives   (2) Senate   (3) president   (4) Supreme Court

**11.** The significance of the Supreme Court case of *Marbury* v. *Madison* is that   (1) a federal law was declared unconstitutional   (2) the principle of states' rights was greatly strengthened   (3) the separate but equal principle was established   (4) the constitutionality of a national bank was upheld

**12.** The due process clause in the U.S. Constitution requires that   (1) all labor-management contracts must be reviewed by a commission of the federal government   (2) members of minority groups must be given preferential treatment in employment   (3) the selection of the president and vice president must follow an established set of steps   (4) a standard set of procedures must be followed before any action is taken to punish persons accused of breaking the law

**13.** The U. S. Supreme Court has ruled that accused persons who cannot afford a lawyer must   (1) be provided with a lawyer at government expense   (2) plead guilty to the offense   (3) act as their own defense   (4) not stand trial until someone can be found to pay a lawyer

**14.** In order to enforce rights for minorities, the Constitution added the Twenty-fourth Amendment, which outlawed   (1) segregation in schools   (2) the poll tax   (3) discrimination on the basis of race or color   (4) slavery

**15.** New states may be admitted to the Union as a result of   (1) an amendment to the Constitution   (2) a majority vote of the existing states   (3) a majority vote of Congress   (4) a presidential order

## Reviewing the main ideas

**16.** The idea that the U.S. Constitution establishes a central government of limited powers is best supported by the provision that   (1) Congress may make no law restricting freedom of speech   (2) Congress has the power to make all laws that are "necessary and proper"   (3) the president shall act as commander in chief of the armed forces   (4) the Supreme Court shall have both original and appellate jurisdiction

**17.** The fact that the U. S. Constitution provides for federalism and a system of checks and balances suggests that   (1) the original 13 states sought to dominate the national government   (2) its writers desired the national government to rule over the states   (3) its writers feared a concentration of political power   (4) the American people supported a military government

**18.** Why does the U.S. Constitution establish a system of checks and balances? (1) to provide a means of electing members of Congress (2) to keep one branch of government from becoming too powerful (3) to allow the Supreme Court to judge cases of law (4) to limit the term of office of the president

**19.** All of the following situations illustrate the constitutional principle of checks and balances *except*: (1) the Senate rejects a presidential appointment (2) the House of Representatives votes to impeach the president (3) the Supreme Court declares a law unconstitutional (4) the president acts as both chief of state and chief executive

**20.** Which constitutional provision indicates that the authors of the original Constitution did not completely trust the common voter to make decisions? (1) the electoral college (2) the veto power of the president (3) direct election of senators (4) election to the House of Representatives

**21.** In a presidential election, the electoral vote was distributed as follows:

Candidate ..................... A    B    C    D
Percentage of electoral vote ...... 38    38    16    8

Based on this information, which is a valid statement about the outcome of the election? (1) Candidate A was declared the winner immediately after the election. (2) Candidate A became president and Candidate B became vice president. (3) Another presidential election was held in order to determine a winner. (4) The president was chosen by a vote of the House of Representatives.

**22.** Which is the most important reason why the office of president became increasingly powerful after World War II? (1) greater involvement of the United States in world affairs (2) a trend toward industrialization in the United States (3) greater coverage of world affairs by the news media in the United States (4) increased restrictions on the rights of U.S. citizens to participate in government

**23.** Most of the authority of the U.S. Supreme Court is based on its power to (1) propose legislation to Congress (2) change the distribution of power as outlined in the Constitution (3) amend the Constitution (4) interpret the Constitution

**24.** The fact that the U. S. Constitution can be interpreted differently at different times allows the government to (1) take any action favored by the political party in power (2) meet the needs of a changing society (3) eliminate the system of checks and balances (4) determine the circumstances under which war may be declared

**25.** How did the Supreme Court under Chief Justice John Marshall influence U.S. history? (1) The Court stimulated the states' rights movement by supporting the idea that states could reject acts of Congress. (2) The Court's decisions in many cases helped to strengthen the federal government. (3) The Court weakened the judiciary by refusing to deal with controversial issues.    (4) The Court became heavily involved in foreign affairs.

**26.** The need for a warrant to conduct a lawful search is an indication that  (1) the crime rate is increasing in the United States  (2) the person about to be searched is really innocent  (3) individuals are protected against government power  (4) there is an excessive concern for the rights of criminals

**27.** In the United States, informing suspects of their legal rights during an arrest procedure is required as a result of  (1) customs adopted from English common law  (2) state laws  (3) decisions of the U. S. Supreme Court  (4) laws passed by Congress

*Speakers A, B, C, and D have been accused of violating a law but think that they were unfairly treated by the police and the courts. Base your answers to questions 28 through 32 on their statements and on your knowledge of Supreme Court cases involving the Bill of Rights.*

Speaker A: I was found guilty of a serious crime in a federal court. My conviction was based largely on the testimony of anonymous witnesses whose identities were concealed by the prosecution so as "to ensure their safety."

Speaker B: I was indicted in a state court for the crime of murder. At the conclusion of the trial, the jury could not reach a verdict. As a result I was retried for the same offense.

Speaker C: I was arrested on suspicion of arson and questioned by the police for several days. During that time I confessed in order to get some rest. The police never told me I had a right to call a lawyer, but I wouldn't have been able to pay for one anyway.

Speaker D: I was arrested for giving a talk on a street corner. The police said I was inciting to riot. A police judge convicted and fined me on the grounds that I was creating a "clear and present danger." I maintained that my freedom of speech was violated.

**28.** Which speaker is trying to plead double jeopardy?  (1) A   (2) B   (3) C   (4) D

**29.** The right of an accused person to cross-examine his or her accusers was violated in the case of Speaker  (1) A   (2) B   (3) C   (4) D

**30.** The constitutional right not to be forced to testify against oneself was violated in the case of Speaker  (1) A   (2) B   (3) C   (4) D

**31.** In cases like that of Speaker C, the U.S. Supreme Court has ruled that the accused  (1) has an obligation to answer police questions that are reasonable  (2) has a right to be advised by a lawyer whether or not to answer a police officer's questions  (3) should not have been arrested solely on suspicion of arson  (4) should have been furnished with a public defender after confessing

**32.** In cases like that of Speaker D, the U.S. Supreme Court has ruled that  (1) the accused cannot plead the First Amendment when charged with violating local laws   (2) the accused should have been tried in a federal court on the riot charge   (3) freedom of speech does not include the right to endanger public safety   (4) freedom of speech does not include the right to make speeches in public in support of a religious belief

## Developing critical thinking skills

*Base your answers to questions 33 to 35 on the cartoon below and on your knowledge of U.S. history and government.*

33. What point of view toward the rights of an accused person is expressed by the cartoon?   (1) In criminal proceedings, an accused person has many more rights than the victim.   (2) The police are inclined to ignore an accused person's rights.   (3) An accused person is likely to receive a fair trial.   (4) An accused person is not likely to receive a fair trial.

34. The section of the Constitution that defines an accused person's rights is   (1) the Preamble   (2) the first three articles   (3) the first ten amendments   (4) the supremacy clause

35. We can infer that the creator of the cartoon would most likely favor   (1) more training for the police   (2) more careful procedures for determining an accused person's guilt or innocence   (3) less concern about the rights of the accused   (4) less concern about the welfare of the victim

## B. Enduring Issues

*Select* two *of the enduring issues from column A. For each issue chosen, explain how the historical example in column B relates to the issue.*

---

| A. Enduring Issues | B. Historical Examples |
| --- | --- |
| 1. The Judiciary—interpreter of the Constitution or shaper of policy | Landmark decisions of the U.S. Supreme Court under John Marshall |
| 2. Rights of the accused and protection of the community | Landmark decisions of the U.S. Supreme Court under Earl Warren |
| 3. Presidential power in wartime and foreign affairs | President Bush's actions in Panama and the Middle East (see map, "The Global Context") |

---

## C. Essays

### Level 1

Throughout U.S. history certain enduring issues have been involved in cases brought before the Supreme Court. Paired below are three such issues and Supreme Court cases that dealt with them.

- Role of the judiciary—*Marbury* v. *Madison* (1803)
- Federalism, the balance between nation and state—*McCulloch* v. *Maryland* (1819)
- Rights of the accused—*Miranda* v. *Arizona* (1966)

Select *two* of the issues listed above. For *each* one chosen, briefly summarize the facts of the given Supreme Court case, state the Court's decision in the case, and explain how that decision provided an answer to the enduring issue.

### Level 2

The principle of checks and balances is a key part of our constitutional system.

**A.** 1. State *one* way that the president may check Congress.
  2. State *one* way that the Supreme Court may check Congress.
  3. State *two* ways that Congress may check the president.

**B.** Using examples from part A, explain how the principle of checks and balances helps to keep one branch of the U.S. government from dominating the other two branches.

# Chapter *3*

# The Constitution Tested: The Early Republic

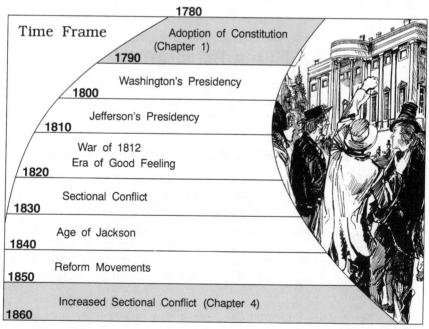

| Time Frame | |
|---|---|
| **1780** | |
| | Adoption of Constitution (Chapter 1) |
| **1790** | |
| | Washington's Presidency |
| **1800** | |
| | Jefferson's Presidency |
| **1810** | |
| | War of 1812 Era of Good Feeling |
| **1820** | |
| | Sectional Conflict |
| **1830** | |
| | Age of Jackson |
| **1840** | |
| | Reform Movements |
| **1850** | |
| | Increased Sectional Conflict (Chapter 4) |
| **1860** | |

*The inauguration of Andrew Jackson*

## *Objectives*

- To identify the most important policies of the early presidents and evaluate their effect on the U.S. political system.
- To define the conflict between sectionalism and nationalism.
- To analyze and compare the first political parties in the United States.
- To understand the social and economic origins of sectional conflict.
- To describe democratic reforms in the era of Andrew Jackson.

The U.S. political system consists of much more than the words of the Constitution. Continually shaping and reshaping that system from day to day are the actions of government leaders in all three branches.

The first presidents to lead the executive branch strongly affected not only their times but also the future development of the U.S. government. This chapter tells of the problems they confronted, the decisions they made, and the long-term effects of their decisions.

# I. Policies of Five Presidents

Would the federal system of government created by the Constitution work well or poorly? Because the system was new and untried in the 1790s, nobody could be certain of the answer.

## A. MAKING DOMESTIC POLICY: WASHINGTON AND ADAMS

The first president, George Washington, served two terms, after winning election in 1789 and again in 1793. More than any later president, Washington made decisions and adopted policies that profoundly influenced the nature of American government. In his first term Washington decided to (1) form a cabinet, (2) put down a rebellion, and (3) advocate bold measures for financing the costs of government.

**The First Cabinet (1789)** A cabinet consists of high-level officials who meet as a group to advise the chief executive. Cabinet meetings are not mentioned in the Constitution. But Washington's decision in 1789 to appoint a secretary of state (Thomas Jefferson), a secretary of the treasury (Alexander Hamilton), a secretary of war (Henry Knox), and an attorney general (Edmund Randolph) established the cabinet as a permanent institution of the executive branch.

**The Whisky Rebellion (1794)**  To raise revenue, Congress placed a federal **excise tax** on the distilling of whisky. (An excise tax is a tax on the sale of a product made within the country collecting the tax.) News of the whisky tax provoked an armed revolt among whisky-producing farmers in western Pennsylvania. Washington's decision to send troops to put down the rebellion demonstrated that the federal government had real power to act effectively in a crisis (unlike the confederate government of the 1780s that could do nothing about Shays's Rebellion).

Not everyone approved Washington's use of a large army to deal with the rebellion. Thomas Jefferson, the secretary of state, said the government's action was like using "a meat axe to kill a spider."

**Hamilton's Financial Plan**  Washington's secretary of the treasury, Alexander Hamilton, proposed a series of measures for strengthening the finances of the U.S. government. Hamilton's financial plan was eventually enacted by Congress after a bitter struggle. Included in the plan were (1) a means for funding (paying off) the past debts of the states and the national government, (2) the creation of a national bank for depositing both tax revenues and merchants' loans to the U.S. government, and (3) tariffs to protect new American industries from foreign competition.

**Forming of Political Parties: The Federalists**  Conflict over Hamilton's financial plan was one reason that two political parties emerged in the 1790s. Leading the two parties were rival members of Washington's cabinet—Alexander Hamilton and Thomas Jefferson. Hamilton's party, the Federalists, favored government policies that would serve the interests of Northern merchants and, to a lesser extent, of Southern planters. Merchants approved Hamilton's program for the following reasons.

- They thought it would help the national government to become strong and stable. (Stable government promotes a healthy economy.)
- They wanted a national bank to serve as a source of loans for new businesses.
- They hoped tariffs (taxes on foreign goods) would protect new, or "infant," industries in the United States from foreign competition.

On constitutional issues, Federalists argued for **loose construction**, the idea that government had many powers that were implied by the Constitution's "necessary and proper" clause.

## America's First Political Parties

| | Federalists | Democratic-Republicans |
|---|---|---|
| Leaders | Alexander Hamilton<br>John Adams<br>John Marshall | Thomas Jefferson<br>James Madison<br>James Monroe |
| Geographic strength | Strongest support among merchants of the Northeast | Strongest support among farmers of the South and West |
| Position on Hamilton's financial plan | Favored all parts of the plan (establishing central bank, funding the debt, protecting infant industries) | Opposed all parts of the plan |
| Position on constitutional issues | Favored *loose construction* of the Constitution to give the national government maximum power | Favored *strict construction* of the Constitution to limit the national government's power and safeguard the independent powers of the states |
| Position on foreign policy | Though partial to the British, supported Washington's Proclamation of Neutrality | Though partial to the French, supported Jefferson's attempts to maintain U.S. neutrality during the Napoleonic wars |

**Forming of Political Parties: The Democratic-Republicans** Opposing the Federalists was a second political party, the Democratic-Republicans. Led by Thomas Jefferson, this party favored government policies that would promote the interests of farmers and the common people. It opposed Hamilton's financial plan for the following reasons.

- Full payment of the national debt by buying back government bonds would benefit speculators (those who buy and sell bonds and other property in the hope of making huge profits). Many bondholders had obtained government bonds at a reduced rate and stood to make a fortune if the government bought them at full value.

- A national bank would provide loans for Northern merchants but would be less likely to lend money to Western and Southern farmers.

Unlike the Federalists, Jefferson and the Democratic-Republicans argued for **strict construction** of the Constitution, meaning that the federal government should do no more than what specific clauses of the Constitution allowed.

During the Federalist era a two-party system became an important and enduring part of American government.

**Alien and Sedition Acts (1798)**  Conflict between the two parties was particularly bitter during the presidency of Washington's successor, John Adams (1797 to 1801). A Federalist majority in Congress enacted two laws whose chief purpose was to intimidate the supporters of the Democratic-Republicans. The Alien Act authorized the president to deport aliens (foreigners residing in the United States) who were thought to be dangerous to the public safety. The Sedition Act authorized the government to fine and imprison newspaper editors who printed any "scandalous and malicious writing" about the government.

State legislatures in Virginia and Kentucky passed resolutions that protested these measures and claimed the right to **nullify** (disregard) them as unconstitutional. These resolutions expressed the views of Thomas Jefferson, who argued that the Alien and Sedition Acts violated citizens' basic rights.

**End of the Federalist Decade: The Election of 1800**  The first 13 years of U.S. government under the Constitution were dominated by three leaders: George Washington, Alexander Hamilton, and John Adams. That era ended in 1800 when Adams was defeated for reelection by two candidates of the Democratic-Republican party— Thomas Jefferson and Aaron Burr. Because Jefferson and Burr were tied with the same number of electoral votes, the election was decided by a vote of the House of Representatives. Jefferson finally emerged as the winner, but only after much confusion in Congress and suspense in the nation at large.

To avoid tie votes in the future, Congress proposed changing the electoral college system by means of the Twelfth Amendment (adopted by the states in 1804). The original Constitution had provided that each elector was to cast two ballots, both for president. Now, according to the Twelfth Amendment, each elector would cast one ballot for president and a second ballot for vice president. (The amendment worked well; since its adoption there have been no tie votes like that of 1800.)

# B. MAKING DOMESTIC POLICY: JEFFERSON

As a Democratic-Republican, President Jefferson was committed to the idea of states' rights and strict construction of the Constitution. And yet Jefferson's policies as president did not differ greatly from those of his Federalist predecessors. He discovered that in his role as U.S. president, his first duty was to strengthen the nation. To do this, he reluctantly changed his view of the Constitution. The issue that prompted a change of mind was this: Should the president agree to purchase from France the vast Western territory called Louisiana?

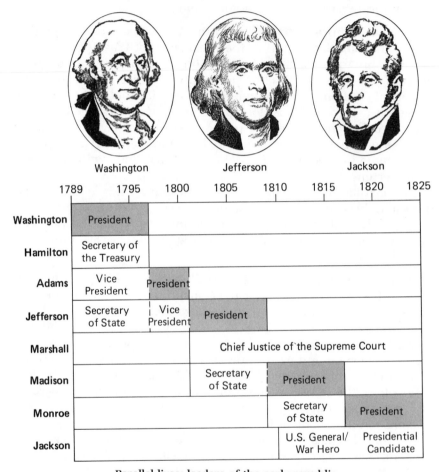

Parallel lives: leaders of the early republic

**Opportunity to Purchase Louisiana** By 1800 pioneer families had moved beyond the Appalachian Mountains into Kentucky, Tennessee, and Ohio. These lands were already part of the United States. On the Mississippi River, however, the city of New Orleans as well as the unexplored lands of Louisiana to the west were under French rule. In 1803 the French emperor Napoleon made the extraordinary offer to sell New Orleans and the Louisiana territory to the United States for a bargain price (about $15 million).

**Jefferson's Constitutional Dilemma**  In considering whether or not to buy New Orleans and the Louisiana territory, Jefferson faced a constitutional dilemma. No clause in the Constitution authorized the national government to expand the country's borders. As a strict constructionist, Jefferson could not justify making the purchase. But to turn down the offer of Louisiana would be to miss out on the greatest land sale in history.

**Decision for Loose Construction**  Jefferson's opponents in the Federalist party argued for a loose construction of the Constitution. According to this view the national government had many powers that were implied by the "necessary and proper" clause of the Constitution. Reluctantly, Jefferson adopted the loose construction view when, in 1803, he asked the Senate to ratify the treaty with France for the purchase of Louisiana.

**Effects of the Louisiana Purchase**  Purchase of the huge territory west of the Mississippi more than doubled the land area of the United States. With the full support of Congress and President Jefferson, an expedition set out from St. Louis in 1804 to explore the newly acquired lands. Reports brought back by the explorers Meriwether Lewis and William Clark prepared the way for later settlement of the American West.

The Louisiana Purchase—and the states later formed from it

## C. MAKING FOREIGN POLICY

Compared to other countries of the world, the United States in the 1790s was in a unique position. Unlike the kingdoms of Europe, the United States was a **republic** with a written constitution. (A republic is a form of government in which officials are elected by vote of the people.) Unlike the Spanish colonies to the south (including Florida and Mexico) and the British colony to the north (Canada), the United States before 1800 was the only sovereign nation in the Western Hemisphere. Through the early years of the American republic, the foreign policies of five presidents were shaped by the following goals:

- Defense of U.S. rights as a sovereign republic
- Westward expansion
- Support of the people of Latin America in their struggle for freedom from foreign rule
- **Neutrality** (giving support to neither side in a foreign war).

**Washington and the French Revolution**   In France a revolution overthrew the French monarchy in 1789 (the same year that the U.S. Constitution went into effect). Viewed as a threat to the monarchies of Europe, the revolutionary government of the French Republic fought for its survival against invading armies of Britain, Austria, and Spain.

In the United States public opinion was sharply divided on whether or not to give assistance to the French Republic. Through his two terms as president, George Washington followed a policy of neutrality. In his Farewell Address to the American people, Washington urged that the United States "steer clear of permanent alliances with any portion of the foreign world."

**John Adams and the XYZ Affair (1797)**   The next two presidents, John Adams and Thomas Jefferson, adopted Washington's policy of neutrality toward the conflict in Europe. During Adams's presidency the French navy seized American ships at sea. French diplomats (identified only as X, Y, and Z) demanded bribes for their assistance in stopping the French government's abuses of U.S. rights. Angered by the **XYZ Affair**, many Americans called for war. Their slogan was: "Millions for defense but not one cent for tribute." Adams avoided an open declaration of war against France. Even so, in 1798, French and American naval forces fought on the high seas. When Napoleon took control of the French government, he and Adams negotiated a settlement, although it did not resolve all differences.

**Jefferson and the Napoleonic Wars**   During Jefferson's presidency the military conqueror, Napoleon, crowned himself emperor of France, thereby ending the French experiment with republican government. To fight Napoleon at sea and cut off supplies to Napoleon's empire, British warships often stopped and searched U.S. merchant ships, removed cargo, and forced (or **impressed**) American sailors to serve in the British navy. The French also stopped American shipping and violated U.S. rights as a neutral nation.

To prevent further violation of U.S. rights, Jefferson persuaded Congress to place an **embargo** (a prohibition on trade) on the shipment of American goods to Europe. But New England merchants and shipbuilders protested bitterly because the embargo badly hurt their business. The embargo was lifted after a two-year trial (1807 to 1809).

**Madison and the War of 1812**  The fourth president, James Madison (1809 to 1817), also attempted to defend U.S. rights at sea without going to war. But another issue arose in the West that increased tensions between Great Britain and the United States. Reacting to the pressure of Americans settling on their lands, Indians in the region of the Great Lakes were persuaded by their leader, Tecumseh, to fight a war against the settlers. Westerners complained bitterly that the weapons used by Tecumseh's forces had been supplied by Britain. Furthermore, a faction of young Southerners and Westerners in Congress—the so-called "**war hawks**"—thought that a war with Britain might give the United States an opportunity to acquire British Canada.

Congress declared war against Great Britain in 1812. At first the War of 1812 went badly for the United States. An American invasion of Canada failed. Later, British forces captured Washington, D.C., and set fire to government buildings, including the Capitol and the White House. But these defeats were offset by a U.S. naval victory on Lake Erie (1813) and a military victory led by Andrew Jackson at New Orleans (1815). A treaty ending the war said not a word about U.S. neutral rights and awarded no compensation (neither territory nor money) to either side. (Also in 1815, peace was restored in Europe when Napoleon was finally defeated and exiled.)

After the War of 1812 (also called the "second war for independence"), Great Britain ended its much resented policy of stopping American ships and seizing their cargoes. The United States emerged from the war as a respected member of the community of nations.

**Monroe and Latin American Independence**  Inspired by the examples of the American Revolution and the French Revolution, rebel groups in South and Central America led successful revolts against the colonial rule of Spain, Portugal, and France. But President James Monroe (1817 to 1825) and his secretary of state John Quincy Adams feared that the monarchies of Europe might try to reconquer the newly established Latin American republics. As a warning to Spain and other European powers, Monroe wrote a message to Congress later known as the **Monroe Doctrine**. It stated:

- The Western Hemisphere (North America and South America) was closed to any further colonization by a European power.
- The United States would firmly oppose attempts by a European power to intervene in the Western Hemisphere.
- The United States would not involve itself politically in the affairs of Europe.

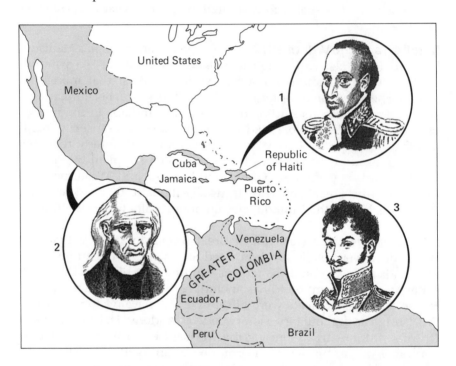

**1.** Toussaint L'Ouverture, leader of an uprising in Haiti in 1791. **2.** Miguel Hidálgo y Costilla, whose speech for independence in 1810 touched off Mexico's revolt against Spain. **3.** Simón Bolívar, leader of the struggle to liberate Venezuela, Colombia, Ecuador, and Peru (1811 to 1824).

The global context: liberators of Latin America

Monroe's policy had the full support of Great Britain and the new nations of Latin America. For more than one hundred years, the Monroe Doctrine was viewed by American leaders as the foundation for U.S. policy toward Europe and Latin America.

# DOCUMENTS: THE MONROE DOCTRINE

The statement below of U.S. foreign policy toward Europe and the Western Hemisphere was included in President Monroe's State of the Union message to Congress in 1823. On a separate piece of paper, describe the events in the Western Hemisphere that caused Monroe to make this statement. To what extent, if at all, do you think Monroe's policy should guide U.S. foreign policy in the 1990s?

In the wars of the European powers in matters relating to themselves we have never taken any part, nor does it comport with our policy so to do. It is only when our rights are invaded or seriously menaced that we resent injuries or make preparation for our defense. With the movements in this hemisphere we are of necessity more immediately connected. . . . We owe it, therefore, to candor and to the amicable [friendly] relations existing between the United States and those powers to declare that we should consider any attempt on their part to extend their system to any portion of this hemisphere as dangerous to our peace and safety. With the existing colonies or dependencies of any European power we have not interfered and shall not interfere. But with the Governments who have declared their independence and maintained it . . . we could not view any interposition for the purpose of oppressing them, or controlling in any other manner their destiny, by any European power in any other light than as a manifestation of an unfriendly disposition toward the United States. . . .

## *In Review*

The following questions refer to section I: The Policies of Five Presidents.

1. Compare Hamilton's view of the Constitution with Jefferson's view of it.

2. Discuss the long-term effect of each of the following presidential decisions: (a) Washington's decision in 1789 to meet with a cabinet of advisers; (b) Jefferson's decision in 1803 to purchase the Louisiana territory; (c) Madison's decision in 1812 to go to war; and (d) Monroe's decision in 1823 to declare U.S. policy toward Latin America.

# II. The Sections: North, South, and West

Political change is often driven by economic forces. We see this clearly in the young American nation where, in the early 1800s, three regions, or sections, developed different economies. The economic differences of the North, the South, and the West caused political strains and growing conflict.

## A. NEW INDUSTRIAL ECONOMY IN THE NORTH

In the early 1800s the building of new factories in the North began to change that region into a center of industrial growth. Why did the North industrialize more rapidly than other sections?

**Geographic Factors Aiding Industrial Growth**  Geography was an important factor. Many rivers in the North (1) provided water power for driving machinery and (2) served as natural highways for transporting goods. Connecting the rivers was a network of roads and canals. The completion of the Erie Canal in 1825 enabled goods to be shipped in one continuous voyage between New York City and ports on Lake Erie. Also, for trade with Europe, the North had a number of excellent ports. Thousands of immigrants arriving in the ports of Boston and New York provided cheap labor for the North's textile mills.

**Political Factors Aiding Industrial Growth**  Alexander Hamilton of New York used his political influence to encourage the North's industrial growth. Partly because of Hamilton's efforts Congress established a national bank whose activities benefited Northern merchants. Then, after the War of 1812, Congress passed a tariff act (1816) that taxed foreign imports and made it easier for new American textile mills to compete against British mills. In 1816, to replace Hamilton's first national bank, Congress chartered a second Bank of the United States, which provided loans to businesses and helped industry to grow.

**Technological Factors Aiding Industrial Growth**  Another factor in the growth of industry was technological progress. A system for using standard, interchangeable parts to manufacture rifles was invented by Eli Whitney. The invention of the steamboat by Robert Fulton and others increased the speed of water transportation. The building of railroads in the 1830s and 1840s greatly improved the speed and efficiency of transporting goods by land.

# B. COTTON-GROWING ECONOMY IN THE SOUTH

In colonial times the South's economy depended far more on farming than on commerce. This emphasis became even greater in the early 1800s when Southern planters grew rich by growing a single crop: cotton. Why did cotton suddenly emerge as the South's most important crop?

**Increased Cotton Production** To supply their booming textile mills, British manufacturers of the 1780s and 1790s needed ever greater quantities of cotton. Cotton was easily grown in the American South. But removing seeds from cotton had been a slow and laborious process until 1793, when Eli Whitney invented the cotton gin. This machine made it extremely profitable for Southerners to grow cotton for the textile mills springing up in both Great Britain and the American Northeast.

**Increased Use of Slave Labor** Greater demand for cotton had the unfortunate result of increasing the use of slaves to plant and pick cotton. Congress banned the importation of slaves in 1808. But the law was largely ignored in the South where cotton growers now considered slaves to be an economic necessity. Slaves continued to be bought and sold at auction.

Besides working in the cotton fields, slaves also provided the skilled labor (such as carpentry, blacksmithing, and barrel making) that enabled plantations to operate as nearly self-sufficient economic enterprises. In the plantation houses African-American women performed vital services as cooks, seamstresses, and caretakers of the white owners' children.

Because only Africans and their descendants were held as slaves, whites tended to view themselves as a superior race while treating slaves and free blacks alike as social inferiors. Racist attitudes hardened in the 1800s and became extremely difficult for later generations to overcome.

**Slave Revolts** Some slaves found their condition of lifelong bondage so intolerable that they revolted against it. They did so even while recognizing that there was little hope of success and that the penalty for revolt was death. Some uprisings, such as the one planned by Denmark Vesey in South Carolina in 1822, was discovered before being carried out. Other revolts, such as the one led by Nat Turner in Virginia in 1831, were soon halted and brutally punished, after some whites were killed.

**African-American Music** Freedom, though denied, was greatly desired. One outlet for expressing this desire was in the religious songs composed by African Americans—songs known as spirituals. Slaves who sang such spirituals as "Swing Low, Sweet Chariot" gave vent to deep yearnings for freedom that were not allowed to be spoken.

**Political Conflict over Slavery**    Before the invention of the cotton gin, some Southerners as well as Northerners wanted slavery to be abolished by law. But in the 1800s, as slave labor became more important, Southern whites were nearly unanimous in supporting slavery. They argued that slaves were a form of property and that the Constitution itself permitted slavery. In the North, however, one state after another prohibited its citizens from owning slaves. A small but dedicated group of mostly Northerners, called **abolitionists**, demanded that slavery be abolished everywhere. A more moderate group of antislavery Northerners wanted to stop slavery from spreading into the Western territories beyond the Mississippi.

Conflict over the slavery question caused North and South to view each other with increasing distrust.

## C. RAPID GROWTH OF THE WEST

The history of a third section, the West, is the story of constant movement, growth, and change. The **frontier** (an imaginary line dividing settled areas from the wilderness) was pushed ever westward to the Appalachian Mountains (by 1763); to the Mississippi River (by 1812); and finally across the Great Plains to the Pacific Ocean (by 1845). Settlers in the Western territories formed governments and soon won admission to the Union as new states.

**The Expanding Frontier**    The 1783 treaty with Britain ending the American Revolution established the Mississippi River as the Western boundary of the new American nation. During the next 20 years, pioneer families cleared the forests of Kentucky, Tennessee, and Ohio and made these territories into new states of the Union.

President Jefferson's purchase of the Louisiana Territory from France in 1803 extended U.S. boundaries far beyond the Mississippi all the way to the Rocky Mountains. Thus, a vast new frontier beckoned to trappers, explorers, and pioneering farmers. By the end of the 1840s farmhouses and mining shacks of American pioneers were found as far west as California and Oregon.

**"Manifest Destiny"**    In the 1800s many Americans came to believe that their country was destined to expand westward. They spoke of the *"manifest destiny"* of the United States to expand at least as far as the Pacific coast and to be the dominant nation in North America. Large parts of the West, however, were already settled by Mexicans.

From the Mexicans' point of view, the U.S. idea of "manifest destiny" posed a challenge and a threat.

**Government Policies Supporting Expansion**  Congress passed a number of laws to encourage the settlement of the West. Senator Henry Clay of Kentucky proposed an ambitious plan for linking the economic fortunes of East and West in a scheme he called the "American system." Adopting Clay's idea, Congress voted to finance the building of Western roads and canals. Also, for Easterners' benefit, Congress voted for a high tariff on European imports that would encourage Westerners to buy their supplies from Eastern manufacturers. Thus, by aiding both West and East, Clay hoped to tie the nation together as one economic unit.

## *In Review*

The following questions refer to the map below and to section II: The Sections: North, South, and West. Answer by referring to the letters on the map, A–E.

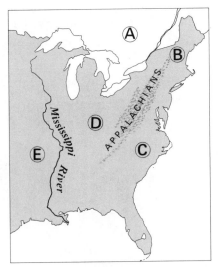

1. Into which section of the United States was slavery first introduced?

2. Which territory did "war hawks" in Congress hope to take from British control during the War of 1812?

3. Which region of the United States objected to the War of 1812, even though it suffered the most from British seizure of American ships?

4. Which section of the United States did both Henry Clay and Andrew Jackson represent?

5. Purchase of which territory in 1803 doubled the land area of the United States?

# III. Nationalism and Sectionalism

Through the early 1800s a serious dispute arose about the nature of the federal system under the Constitution. Nationalists interpreted the system one way, while sectionalists interpreted it a different way. The chart ("Comparing Nationalism and Sectionalism") explains their different points of view.

## Comparing Nationalism and Sectionalism

|  | Nationalism | Sectionalism |
|---|---|---|
| Definition | *Nationalism* is the belief that a person owes his or her political loyalty to the nation and its central government. | *Sectionalism* is a feeling of strong attachment and loyalty to a particular section or region. |
| Views of the Constitution | American nationalists of the 1800s believed the states were permanently bound together in an unbreakable union. | Sectionalists thought the states were joined loosely and voluntarily in a union that could be dissolved at any time. |

Voluntary
constitutional
ties

## A. NATIONALISM AND SECTIONALISM IN THE WAR OF 1812

In 1812, less than 30 years after the end of the American Revolution, the United States again went to war with Great Britain. For the most part, America's attitudes in the war (1812 to 1815) were strongly nationalistic. But during the war there was also one incident of extreme sectionalism. (For causes of the War of 1812, review section I.)

**Consequences of War**   A chief consequence of the war was the boost it gave to the spirit of nationalism. Examples of wartime patriotism were many. For his sensational victory at New Orleans in 1815, Andrew Jackson instantly became a national hero. A witness to one of the battles, Francis Scott Key, was inspired to express his national pride in a song, "The Star-Spangled Banner"—later adopted as the U.S. national anthem. People recognized that the treaty of peace of 1814 gave nothing to either side. But many Americans felt proud simply to have fought the mighty British Empire to a draw.

**Sectionalist Protest in New England**   However, not everyone was thrilled by the war news. In New England members of the Federalist party were so opposed to the war that they called a convention to protest it. Meeting in Hartford, Connecticut, from December 15, 1814 to January 5, 1815, convention delegates seriously considered pulling the New England states out of the Union. No action was taken, but the sectionalist outburst warned of worse troubles to come from a different region: the South.

## B. THE ERA OF GOOD FEELINGS

After the War of 1812 the United States was united as never before, as a tide of nationalist feeling swept through all sections, North, South, and West. The Federalist party was widely condemned for its antiwar convention in Hartford. Soon afterward this party ceased to be a major force in American politics.

The Democratic-Republican candidate for president, James Monroe, was practically unopposed in his two campaigns for president (1816 and 1820). The eight years of his presidency (1817 to 1825) have been called the **Era of Good Feelings**.

But two disputes in this era revealed that sectional resentments lay just beneath the surface of the nationalist calm. The first dispute concerned slavery.

**The Missouri Compromise**   Southern slave owners who moved to the Missouri Territory brought their slaves with them. In 1819 the people of Missouri applied for their territory to be admitted to the

Union as a new state—a state permitting slavery. There was much debate. Both Northerners and Southerners were well aware that Missouri's admission would end the fragile balance of power between slave states of the South and free, or nonslave, states of the North. Finally in 1820 Congress passed a compromise measure. According to this **Missouri Compromise**,

- Missouri would enter the Union as a slave state
- Maine would enter the Union as a free state
- All territory north of the 36°30′ line of latitude in the lands of the Louisiana Purchase would be closed to slavery.

This agreement did not apply to Western lands (such as California or New Mexico) that the United States did not yet own. Thus, the crisis over slavery in the West was not solved, only put off to a later time.

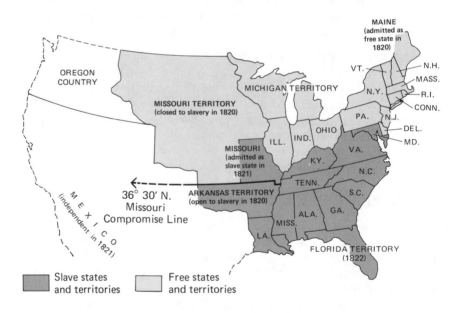

The Missouri Compromise

**The Election of 1824** A second dispute concerned party politics. By 1824 the Democratic-Republican party had split into several groups, each hoping to elect a different candidate to the presidency. Of the four candidates Andrew Jackson—hero of the War of 1812—had the most popular votes. But no candidate received the majority of electoral votes required to win election. As the Constitution provided in these circumstances, the House of Representatives decided the election. The House, after much political wrangling, voted in favor of the candidate from Massachusetts, John Quincy Adams. Jackson and his supporters were outraged, charging that the election had been stolen. They formed a new party, thus ending the brief Era of Good Feelings in which there had been only one national party.

# IV. The Age of Jackson

The two parties that emerged in the 1820s were the Democratic party of Andrew Jackson and the National Republican party of John Quincy Adams and Henry Clay—a party later known as the Whigs. In the presidential election of 1828, Jackson won both the popular vote and the electoral vote by an impressive margin. Jackson's dynamic leadership during his two-term presidency (1829 to 1837) stamped itself on his era: the **Age of Jackson**. The era is remembered for two things: (a) its sectional conflicts and (b) its democratic reforms.

## A. SECTIONAL CONFLICTS

The chief issue that heated sectional tempers during Jackson's presidency was an economic one: the tariff.

**The Tariff Issue**　When the United States went to war in 1812, Americans were stopped from importing factory goods from Great Britain (the wartime enemy). Without competition from abroad, new American factories sprang up in the North and made handsome profits. In peacetime Congress tried to continue the good times for "infant" (beginning) U.S. industries by raising tariff rates in 1816, 1818, 1824, and 1828. The effect of high tariffs on Northern industry was generally positive. Tariffs not only lessened foreign competition but also enabled Northern manufacturers to raise the prices of consumer goods. But the effect of high tariffs on the South was doubly negative. First, the tariffs made manufactured goods more expensive to buy. Second, the tariffs reduced the market for British cotton cloth. This meant that the South would sell less cotton to Britain, its chief customer. Many Southerners had already been hurt by earlier tariffs. The passage of even higher tariffs in 1828 seemed to them good cause for revolt. They said they could not stand for this "**Tariff of Abominations**" (hated tariff).

**The Nullification Issue**　The leader of Southern resistance to high tariffs was John C. Calhoun of South Carolina. While serving as vice president under Andrew Jackson, Calhoun wrote and published an important essay championing the right of states to defy national law.

Calhoun argued that every state had a right to ignore, or nullify, any act of Congress that in the state's judgment violated the Constitution. The right of **nullification** applied to the Tariff of 1828, said Calhoun, because it benefited one section of the country at the expense of another.

To President Jackson, Calhoun's nullification ideas seemed treasonable. Angrily opposing the vice president's words at a political dinner in 1830, the president made a short speech that warmed the hearts of nationalists. "Our Union," he said, "it must be preserved."

In 1832 Congress eliminated some parts of the Tariff of 1828, but this mostly benefited Northern manufacturers. Many Southerners were still dissatisfied. South Carolina called a special state convention, which declared the tariffs of 1828 and 1832 "null, void, and no law." In its Ordinance of Nullification, South Carolina threatened to withdraw from the Union if the federal government tried to enforce the collection of tariffs in Southern ports. In other words South Carolina talked of **seceding** (leaving the Union to become an independent republic).

**Henry Clay's Compromise**   President Jackson threatened to send troops into South Carolina to uphold the Union and enforce the tariff law. But then Senator Henry Clay saved the day by proposing a compromise. Clay persuaded Congress to pass a new tariff act in 1833, which provided for a gradual reduction of tariff rates. South Carolina then repealed its Ordinance of Nullification. For the moment violent conflict between the sections was avoided.

**The Bank Issue**   Another conflict in the Age of Jackson pitted merchants of the Northeast against farmers of the West. The dispute involved the second Bank of the United States, whose 1816 charter was up for renewal. Jackson suspected the bank of serving only the interests of wealthy Easterners. At the same time he thought the bank discriminated against ordinary people—especially Western farmers. He accused the bank of readily granting loans to merchants and manufacturers while denying loans to Western farmers. In 1832 Jackson vetoed an act of Congress that would have renewed the bank's charter. He boldly defended his controversial decision in his 1832 campaign for reelection. The Whig candidate for president, Henry Clay, supported the bank and thought Jackson had made a disastrous mistake to attack it. But President Jackson proved his popularity with the people, winning reelection by a huge majority.

## B. TREATMENT OF NATIVE AMERICANS

Andrew Jackson was a champion of democracy for people of his own social class. In other words he favored Western farmers and pioneers. But he had little sympathy for people who were nonwhite.

# CONTROVERSIAL ACTS OF A CONTROVERSIAL PRESIDENT

Andrew Jackson's actions as president were bold and controversial. If you had been a U.S. citizen in the 1830s, which actions would you have supported, and which would you have opposed?

| Action | Argument For | Argument Against |
|---|---|---|
| 1. Jackson threatens to send troops to South Carolina to prevent it from seceding. | No state should be allowed to leave the Union, thereby destroying it. | If states had been free to enter the Union, they should be equally free to withdraw from it. |
| 2. Jackson vetoes the rechartering of the second Bank of the United States. | The bank represented the interests of wealthy Easterners. Its policies discriminated against farmers, particularly Western farmers. | The bank was a stable institution that kept U.S. currency from expanding too rapidly and provided loans necessary for the growth of American industry. |
| 3. Jackson orders the removal of Cherokee Indians from Georgia. | The president has an obligation to promote the interests of U.S. citizens only. The Cherokees belonged to an alien nation. | The Cherokees were peaceful farmers who had accepted many aspects of U.S. culture. The seizure of their land was a violation of basic human rights. |

This explains, in part, his decision concerning Cherokees and other Native American tribes who lived east of the Mississippi River. He decided that they should be forced to abandon their villages and homes to move hundreds of miles to the west where whites had not yet settled. Jackson reasoned that the policy of Indian removal would put an end to conflict between whites and Native Americans.

**Indian Resettlement Act**  In 1830 Congress passed and Jackson signed the Indian Resettlement Act. Under the terms of the act, the U.S. government signed more than ninety removal treaties with various

Native American tribes. Some tribes left peacefully for the lands set aside for them in the "Indian Territory" west of the Mississippi River (later to become the state of Oklahoma). Other tribes fought before being forced to submit.

**Cherokee "Trail of Tears"**   The most tragic of the forced removals occurred in 1838, when some 15,000 Cherokees from Georgia (men, women, and children) trekked westward for 800 miles through cold and rain. On this **"Trail of Tears,"** many died from starvation. Earlier, in a Supreme Court case, Chief Justice John Marshall had ruled that the Cherokees had a right to remain on their land. But President Jackson ignored the Court's ruling.

## C. DEMOCRATIC REFORMS

Throughout U.S. history there have been periods when people campaign widely for reforms in society and government. The first period of such reforming effort occurred during the Age of Jackson. Reformers embraced a number of causes: votes for women, improved treatment of the mentally ill, free public education for children, abolition of slavery, and more democratic procedures for nominating candidates for office.

**Universal Suffrage for White Males**   In George Washington's time (the 1780s and 1790s), most state laws required that voters own a certain amount of property. Those lacking sufficient property were barred from voting. But in the new century, between 1800 to 1830, state after state acted to remove property requirements for voting. By the time Jackson was elected president in 1828, virtually all white males aged 21 or older were permitted to vote.

**New Democratic Campaigns for Election**   As voting rights were extended to the masses, candidates for office adopted new techniques for reaching great numbers of voters. Political parties conducted elaborate campaigns for their candidates, using banners, rallies, speeches, and debates. Parties also changed their methods for nominating candidates. Instead of **caucuses** (meetings among party leaders only), Jackson's Democratic party and Clay's Whig party held nominating conventions in which party delegates from different states voted to select party candidates.

**The Spoils System**   President Jackson adopted as his motto: "To the victor belongs the spoils." As the victor in the election of 1828, Jackson dismissed from federal employment some officials who were not Democrats and replaced them with his own Democratic supporters. The rewarding of political supporters with government jobs is known as the **spoils system**. Later presidents, whether Whig or Democrat, followed Jackson's example. Those who supported the spoils system considered it democratic at the time, because it meant that government jobs would go to ordinary people ("the common man"), not to a specially educated and privileged group.

## DOCUMENTS: DECLARATION OF SENTIMENTS

*More than a hundred women and men traveled to the home of Elizabeth Stanton in Seneca Falls, New York, in 1848. Here they drafted a declaration about women's rights that in style and form closely imitated the Declaration of Independence. Instead of accusing King George III of tyranny, this document accused men of many offenses against women.*

*On a separate piece of paper, tell to what extent American women today have won rights not granted them in 1848.*

The history of mankind is a history of repeated injuries and usurpations on the part of man toward woman, having in direct object the establishment of an absolute tyranny over her. To prove this, let facts be submitted to a candid world.

He has never permitted her to exercise her inalienable right to the elective franchise.

He has compelled her to submit to laws, in the formation of which she had no voice. . . .

Having deprived her of this first right of a citizen, the elective franchise, thereby leaving her without representation in the halls of legislation, he has oppressed her on all sides. . . .

He has taken from her all right in property, even to the wages she earns. . . .

He has monopolized all the profitable employments, and from those she is permitted to follow, she receives but a scanty remuneration. . . .

**Elizabeth Cady Stanton was 33 years old when she called the Seneca Falls convention. Joining Lucretia Mott and other reformers, she objected to being kept out of "male-only" political meetings. Until her death in 1902, she worked tirelessly for laws that would grant women the rights long denied them, including the right to vote. From 1869 to 1890, she led the National Woman Suffrage Association as its president.**

# CAUSES AND EFFECTS

## Reviewing Selected Events (1790 to 1850)

| Cause | Effect |
| --- | --- |
| The Whisky Rebellion suppressed by federal action (1794) | Increased power and prestige of the national government |
| Conflicting policies of Hamilton and Jefferson (1790s) | Development of a two-party system |
| Alien and Sedition Acts (1798) | Virginia and Kentucky Resolutions challenge national authority. |
| Tie vote in the election of 1800 | Twelfth Amendment changes the procedures for electing a president and vice president. |
| French emperor, Napoleon, needs to focus on costly war in Europe. | Louisiana Territory (1803) purchased from France, doubling U.S. territory |
| Great Britain violates U.S. rights on the Atlantic Ocean; "war hawks" favor expansion. | Outbreak of the War of 1812 |
| The Hartford Convention offends nationalist feelings. | End of Federalist party (about 1815) |
| Latin Americans revolt against Spanish rule. | Monroe Doctrine (1823) |
| Increased production of cotton in the South following invention of the cotton gin | Increased Southern dependence on slavery |
| Missouri applies for admission as a state. | Sectional conflict resolved temporarily by the Missouri Compromise (1820) |
| Congress votes high tariffs (1828). | Southerners claim the right to nullify federal laws. |
| Desire for Indian lands | Acute hardship of Indians as they are forced to leave their homelands ("Trail of Tears," 1838) |
| Growing population of new states in the West | American politics becomes more democratic, as a "man of the people," Andrew Jackson, comes to power (1828). |
| Meeting of reformers at Seneca Falls Convention, 1848 | Beginning of a long campaign for woman's suffrage and equal rights for women |

**Movement for Women's Rights** Even though they were barred from voting, women were extremely active in the reform movements of the 1830s and 1840s. One group of reformers declared at a convention at Seneca Falls, New York (1848), that "all men *and women* are created equal." Among the rights listed in their declaration were the following:

- The right of women to vote and hold office
- The right of married women to hold property in their own name
- The right of women jobholders to manage their own income
- The right of women to be the legal guardians of their own children.

**Movement for Controlling the Sale of Alcohol** In the 1840s women took the lead in an antidrinking campaign called the **temperance movement**. Women reformers were concerned about husbands and other male relatives who spent their wages on liquor rather than on useful goods for the family. Temperance advocates persuaded lawmakers in several states to prohibit the production and sale of alcoholic beverages.

**Movement for State Institutions for the Mentally Ill** An ex-schoolteacher, Dorothea Dix, discovered to her horror that the mentally ill were often chained, beaten, and abused. Dix worked tirelessly to call public attention to these horrors and to establish state institutions where the mentally ill could receive decent care. She persuaded several states to supervise the care given to patients in special "asylums" set aside for them.

**Movement for Public Schools** Until the Age of Jackson most children did not go to school. Education was primarily for privileged boys whose parents paid fees for them to attend private schools. Recognizing that democracy depended upon citizens who could read, write, and reason, reformers like Horace Mann and Henry Barnard advocated systems of public education paid for by the states. Massachusetts and New York led the way by establishing state systems of elementary schools where attendance was compulsory and free of charge for children aged eight to fourteen. By 1850 New York had extended its public education system to offer instruction from grades one to twelve.

## *In Review*

The following questions refer to section III: Nationalism and Sectionalism and section IV: The Age of Jackson: Sectional Conflict and Democratic Reform.

**1.** Define *sectionalism, nationalism, nullification, secession, temperance,* and *spoils system.*

**2. Word Wheel**

Do you agree or disagree with this statement? *Between 1800 and 1840 conflict between North and South became more and more serious.*

Support your position (agree or disagree) by commenting on *two* of the topics in the word wheel.

## GLOSSARY OF KEY TERMS: CHAPTER 3

**abolitionists**  reformers who wanted slavery to be declared illegal in all states.

**Age of Jackson**  a period known for democratic reform and corresponding roughly to the years of Andrew Jackson's presidency (1829 to 1837).

**Alien and Sedition Acts**  laws of Congress of 1798 passed by a Federalist majority to suppress criticisms by the opposing party.

**Bank of the United States**  a bank created by the U.S. government to deposit its tax revenues, issue paper money, and make loans to businesses and governments.

**caucus**  a meeting of a small group of party leaders to select the party's candidates for elective office.

**embargo**  a government order prohibiting the shipment of goods to other nations.

**Era of Good Feelings**  the time of Monroe's presidency (1817 to 1825) when the Democratic-Republican party was unchallenged by a major rival.

**excise tax**  a federal tax on the sale of goods made in the United States.

**frontier**  an imaginary line dividing settled areas from the wilderness.

**impressment**  the British practice of removing sailors from American ships and forcing them into service in the British navy.

**Indian removal**  Andrew Jackson's policy of requiring Indian tribes in the East to migrate to lands west of the Mississippi River.

**interchangeable parts**  the components of a machine or tool that are made exactly alike in order to speed up the assembly of the finished product.

**loose construction**   the belief that the U.S. Constitution may be interpreted broadly to allow maximum power to the national government.

**"manifest destiny"**   a popular belief of many Americans of the early 1800s that the United States was bound to expand westward to the Pacific coast.

**Missouri Compromise**   a temporary solution to sectional conflict over slavery in which the lands of the Louisiana Purchase were divided into a Southern section where slavery would be permitted and a Northern section where it would be excluded.

**nationalism**   a feeling of strong attachment and loyalty to the nation.

**neutrality**   the policy of not taking sides in a war between other nations.

**nominating conventions**   meetings of political parties to decide upon candidates for different offices.

**nullification**   the idea that a state has the right to ignore a federal law.

**republic**   a form of government in which officials are elected by vote of the people.

**secession**   a state's decision to separate itself from all previous ties and obligations to a federal union.

**sectionalism**   a feeling that political loyalty to one's own region should be supreme.

**Seneca Falls Convention**   a meeting of reformers in Seneca Falls, New York, in 1848 that launched the movement for women's rights.

**spoils system**   the practice of appointing people to government offices on the basis of their loyalty to a political party rather than their qualifications for holding office.

**strict construction**   the belief that the national government can exercise only those powers that are clearly and specifically stated by the U.S. Constitution.

**tariff**   a tax on imported goods.

**"Tariff of Abominations"**   the South's term for the high tariff rates enacted by Congress in 1828.

**temperance movement**   a reform movement advocating that the sale of alcoholic beverages be prohibited by law.

**"Trail of Tears"**   the extreme suffering of the Cherokees in 1838 as they were forced by federal law to leave their homelands in the Southeast for lands in the West.

**"war hawks"**   a group of U.S. Congressmen from the Western states who urged that the United States declare war against Britain in 1812.

**XYZ Affair**   a diplomatic incident (1797) in which French diplomats offended American public opinion by suggesting U.S. payment of a bribe.

# TEST YOURSELF

## A. Multiple Choice: Facts, Main Ideas, Skills

*On a separate sheet of paper, write the number of the word or expression that, of those given, best completes the statement or answers the question.*

### Reviewing the facts

1. As the first president, Washington adopted policies that guided later presidents. An example was his (1) support for states' rights (2) support for Western farmers who complained that they were over-taxed (3) selection of a cabinet to assist in making governmental decisions (4) insistence on serving several terms as president

2. Alexander Hamilton believed that a major role of the federal government was to (1) establish and control public schools (2) support and encourage business and industry (3) promote the superiority of the agrarian way of life (4) allow the states to make important national decisions

3. The main purpose of the Monroe Doctrine was to (1) exclude Portugal from Latin America (2) encourage France to protect the Western Hemisphere (3) create an alliance of Latin American nations (4) warn European nations not to interfere in the affairs of nations in the Americas

4. Which issue was involved in the Missouri Compromise? (1) high tariffs (2) an excise tax on whisky (3) slavery in the Western territories (4) improvements in road building and canals

5. Which belief was essential to the doctrine of nullification? (1) The states created the federal government and therefore could overturn federal laws. (2) The federal government had been created by federal interests. (3) Individuals could decide for themselves whether or not to obey a law. (4) The Southern states had made a mistake in joining the Union.

6. Which of the following is *not* an accurate statement about slavery? (1) Slavery was based primarily on race. (2) Between 1800 and 1850 the number of slaves declined. (3) Several Northern states abolished slavery. (4) Southern whites believed slaves were a form of property.

7. A believer in "manifest destiny" would most likely favor (1) further exploration and settlement of the West (2) increased tariffs on European goods (3) attempts to limit immigration into the United States (4) development of industry in the South

8. One reason that Westerners opposed the Bank of the United States was that they (1) feared inflation (2) believed the bank favored debtors (3) believed deposits were mismanaged (4) believed that Eastern business interests received most of the benefits

9. During the Age of Jackson, Native American tribes (1) moved to urban areas in large numbers (2) sought to form alliances with

other minority groups    (3) were forced to move westward    (4) chose to adopt the culture of white settlers

10. The spirit of American nationalism was greatly stimulated by    (1) the Alien and Sedition Acts    (2) the War of 1812    (3) the Hartford Convention    (4) the protective tariffs of the 1820s

11. "The people backed him, but the men of property—bankers, merchants, manufacturers—disliked him." This statement best applied to    (1) James Madison    (2) James Monroe    (3) John Quincy Adams    (4) Andrew Jackson

## Reviewing the main ideas

12. Which factor contributed to the rise of the first political parties in the United States?    (1) a dispute over Hamilton's financial plan    (2) a law to establish the cabinet    (3) an amendment to the U.S. Constitution    (4) the Embargo Act

13. Which is the best summary of early U.S. foreign policy?    (1) The United States tried to follow a policy of neutrality but eventually declared war against a European nation.    (2) The United States never followed its own policy of neutrality.    (3) The United States consistently followed a strong anti-European policy.    (4) U.S. policy lacked direction and goals.

14. Which of the following best illustrates the idea that the American political system changes informally over a period of time?    (1) the adoption of the Twelfth Amendment    (2) the emergence of a two-party system    (3) Congress's declaration of war in 1812    (4) the writing of the Monroe Doctrine

15. The foreign policies of Washington, Jefferson, and Monroe were similar in that they    (1) aided the French Republic    (2) favored England    (3) were hostile to England    (4) sought to avoid involvement in European affairs

16. Which of these most clearly illustrates the president's power as chief executive?    (1) Washington's appointment of a cabinet    (2) Monroe's policy toward Latin America    (3) Jefferson's leadership of the Democratic-Republican party    (4) Marshall's decision in *Marbury* v. *Madison*

*Base your answers to questions 17 to 19 on the discussion below and your knowledge of U.S. history and government.*

*Speaker A*: On all sides we see the threat of the national government becoming all-powerful and crushing the liberties of the states.

*Speaker B*: The time will come—and I rejoice to think of it—when the United States will stretch from sea to shining sea.

*Speaker C*: The tariff laws are an abomination to our section, and we must resist them with all our strength.

*Speaker D*: Because the Union is one and inseparable, we cannot permit the states to defy the laws of Congress.

**17.** Which speakers are most likely to stress the importance of states' rights?  (1) A and B  (2) A and C  (3) C and D  (4) B and C

**18.** Which speaker is most likely to be an advocate of westward expansion?  (1) A  (2) B  (3) C  (4) D

**19.** Andrew Jackson's policies as president were most like those of speaker  (1) A  (2) B  (3) C  (4) D

**20.** "An industrialized Northeast, a plantation South, and a small-farms West cannot peacefully exist in the same nation." The subject of this quotation is  (1) sectionalism  (2) protectionism  (3) nationalism  (4) federalism

## Developing critical thinking skills

*Base your answers to questions 21 and 22 on the map below and your knowledge of U.S. history and government.*

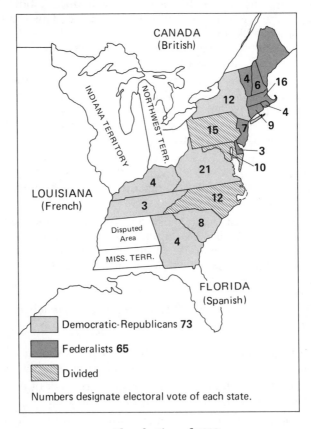

The election of 1800

**21.** Which of these conclusions is supported by evidence in the map?   (1) The Federalists were generally more popular than the Democratic-Republicans. (2) Slaves did not vote in the election of 1800. (3) The population of Massachusetts in 1800 was greater than that of New York. (4) Voter turnout in Virginia was greater than in any other state.

**22.** Which generalization about the election of 1800 is accurate?   (1) The Federalist party was strongest in the Northeast. (2) The Federalist party was strongest in the South. (3) Democratic-Republicans lost the election. (4) Democratic-Republicans had greater support in the North than in the South.

## B. Enduring Issues

*Select* two *of the enduring issues from column A. For each issue chosen, explain how the historical example in column B relates to the issue.*

| A. Enduring Issues | B. Historical Examples |
| --- | --- |
| 1. National power, limits and potential | Hamilton's view of how the U.S. Constitution should be interpreted |
| 2. Federalism, the balance between nation and state | South Carolina's Ordinance of Nullification |
| 3. The rights of women under the U.S. Constitution | Seneca Falls Convention |
| 4. The rights of ethnic and racial groups under the U.S. Constitution | The institution of slavery |

## C. Essays

### Level 1

Select *three* of the topics listed below and explain how *each* changed the American nation.

> Louisiana Purchase
> War of 1812
> Monroe Doctrine
> Missouri Compromise

### Level 2

President Washington believed that a policy of neutrality was very important for the United States.

**A.** Describe *one* action of President Washington and *one* action of President Jefferson that supported a policy of neutrality.

**B.** Base your answer to part B on your answer to part A. Explain how the United States tried to remain neutral during the early years of the nation (1790 to 1810).

# Chapter *4*

# The Constitution Tested: Westward Expansion and Civil War

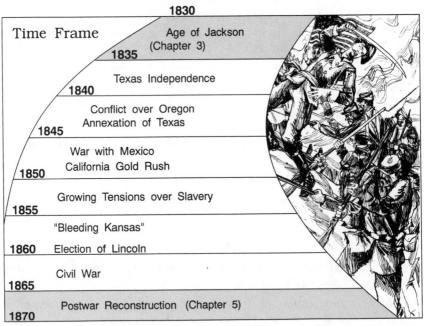

| Time Frame | 1830 | |
|---|---|---|
| | Age of Jackson (Chapter 3) | |
| 1835 | | |
| | Texas Independence | |
| 1840 | | |
| | Conflict over Oregon Annexation of Texas | |
| 1845 | | |
| | War with Mexico California Gold Rush | |
| 1850 | | |
| | Growing Tensions over Slavery | |
| 1855 | | |
| | "Bleeding Kansas" | |
| 1860 | Election of Lincoln | |
| | Civil War | |
| 1865 | | |
| | Postwar Reconstruction (Chapter 5) | |
| 1870 | | |

*Civil War battle, 1864*

## *Objectives*

- To explain how expansion in the West increased the sectional conflict between North and South.
- To examine how a dispute over Oregon was settled peacefully, while another dispute over Texas and the Southwest resulted in war.
- To identify the causes and consequences of the U.S. war with Mexico.
- To identify the causes and consequences of the Civil War.
- To compare the points of view of Northerners and Southerners on the slavery issue.

Recall from Chapter 3 that many Americans believed it was their nation's "manifest destiny" to expand to the West. This feeling was particularly strong in the 1840s. During that expansionist decade the United States went to war with Mexico to fulfill its ambitions of "manifest destiny." A decade of westward expansion was followed by a decade of sectional conflict leading finally to the Civil War between North and South in 1861. Expansion, sectional conflict, and the Civil War are the main subjects of this chapter.

# I. Westward Expansion

Four Western territories were added to the United States between 1845 and 1853:

- Texas (annexed by an act of Congress in 1845)
- Oregon (added by a treaty with Britain in 1846)
- California and much of the Southwest (ceded by Mexico in 1848)
- southern Arizona and New Mexico (purchased from Mexico in 1853).

Let us see how each addition came about.

## A. HOW THE UNITED STATES ACQUIRED TEXAS

The first new territory added to the United States in the 1840s was Texas. In colonial times Texas, California, and lands in between had been part of the Spanish Empire. When Mexicans revolted against Spanish rule in 1821, Texas and California became the northern part of the new nation of Mexico.

**Texan Independence**   In the 1820s Texas was inhabited by only a few thousand Mexicans. The open land attracted pioneer families from the United States. Most were from the South and many owned slaves. By the mid-1830s there were more American settlers in Texas than Mexicans. The Americans often defied Mexico's laws, including its law against the holding of slaves. When Mexico tried to stop further American immigration, the Americans already there revolted and declared Texas an independent nation (1836).

Determined to put down the revolt, Mexico's president, Antonio López de Santa Anna, led troops into Texas. His forces overwhelmed and killed the Texan defenders who were occupying the Alamo, a church mission turned into a fort. Soon afterward, however, during a battle on the San Jacinto River, the Texans captured Santa Anna, who was forced to grant their demand for independence.

**Issue of Texas Annexation**   For nine years, 1836 to 1845, Texas was a completely separate and independent nation: the "Lone Star Republic." Its leaders applied for admission to the Union as a state. But for years the proposed **annexation** (formal addition) of Texas failed to receive a favorable vote in Congress. The chief obstacle was slavery. Northerners opposed annexation of Texas because slavery was well established there. Solidly supporting Texas annexation were the slave states of the South. Finally, in 1845, the issue was settled in the South's favor when Congress passed a joint resolution admitting Texas to the Union as the 28th state.

## B. FIGHTING FOR TEXAS AND CALIFORNIA: WAR WITH MEXICO (1846 TO 1848)

After its loss of Texas, Mexico still held vast lands in the Southwest (what is today Arizona, New Mexico, Utah, Nevada, and California). Many Americans looked upon these lands as part of their country's "manifest destiny" to expand. But Mexico was angered by U.S. annexation of Texas and refused to discuss U.S. offers to purchase Mexican lands. Tensions grew and war threatened.

**Causes of War**   A Democratic president, James K. Polk, believed strongly in expansion. His desire to gain Western lands was largely responsible for the outbreak of a war with Mexico. The immediate cause of the war was a disputed boundary between Texas and Mexico. Was this boundary marked by the Nueces River, as Mexico claimed? Or was it farther south on the Rio Grande, as the United States claimed? When Mexican troops fired upon U.S. troops within the disputed territory, President Polk asked Congress for a declaration of war. As his reason Polk said that Mexico had "shed American blood on American soil."

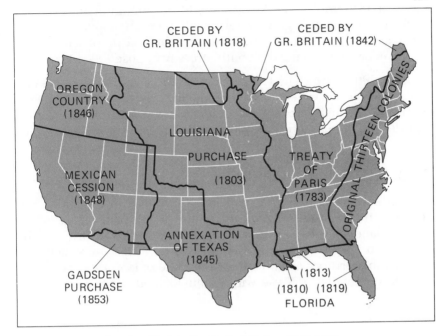

CEDED BY GR. BRITAIN (1818)

CEDED BY GR. BRITAIN (1842)

OREGON COUNTRY (1846)

LOUISIANA PURCHASE (1803)

TREATY OF PARIS (1783)

ORIGINAL THIRTEEN COLONIES

MEXICAN CESSION (1848)

ANNEXATION OF TEXAS (1845)

GADSDEN PURCHASE (1853)

(1813)
(1810)  (1819)
FLORIDA

Lands added to the United States, 1783–1853

**Invasion of Mexico**    Two U.S. armies struck south into Mexican territory. One army under Zachary Taylor occupied northern Mexico, while a second army under Winfield Scott forced Mexicans to surrender their capital, Mexico City, in 1848.

**Revolt in California**    A third American army under Stephen Kearny marched westward to California. There it joined a band of American settlers, who had earlier revolted against Mexican rule. Mexican defenders were quickly overcome, and California in 1848 became American territory.

**Peace Terms**    In the treaty ending the Mexican War (Treaty of Guadalupe Hidalgo, 1848), the United States paid the token sum of $15 million to Mexico for the huge territory extending from Texas's western border all the way to the California coast. In addition, the United States agreed to relieve Mexico of responsibility for paying $3.2 million in debts to U.S. citizens. The Rio Grande was established as the U.S.-Mexican border.

**Gold Rush in California**    Soon after the war, one of the American settlers of California discovered gold on his land. News of the discovery touched off massive excitement in the East and throughout the world. Fortune hunters poured into California in search of golden nuggets. "California or bust" was the slogan of thousands of people who joined the great 1849 **gold rush**. Most met with disappointment. Even so, California's population grew so rapidly that it soon qualified to apply to Congress for statehood. But because California proposed to be a nonslave, or "free," state, the South strongly opposed its admission.

**Gadsden Purchase**  The last section of land acquired from Mexico was won without violence. This land—the so-called Gadsden Purchase—was bought from Mexico in 1853 for $10 million. (James Gadsden was the American diplomat who arranged the deal.)

## C. DISPUTE OVER OREGON

President Polk and other expansionists were eager to possess not only the rock-and-desert country of the Southwest, but also the forested lands of the Northwest: the territory known as Oregon. The obstacle to U.S. possession of Oregon was Great Britain, which also claimed the territory as far as the 54°40′ line of latitude in northern Canada. (See map.) A U.S. war with Britain loomed as a real possibility.

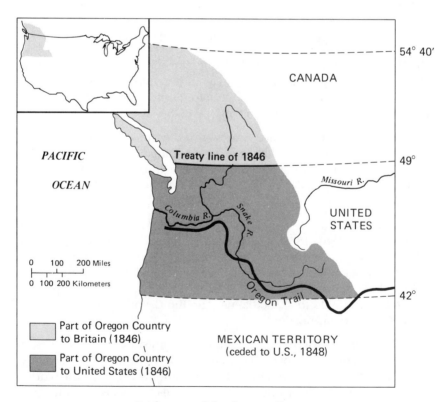

Settlement of the Oregon dispute

# OBSERVERS OF AMERICAN LIFE: IMMIGRANTS TO CALIFORNIA

This description of San Francisco after the gold rush was published in 1855 in Frank Soulé's *The Annals of San Francisco*. After remarking that German and French immigrants were most commonly seen on city streets, the author focuses on the thousands of people arriving yearly from China.

On a separate piece of paper, tell whether or not you think the author had racial biases. Support your answer with examples from the reading.

Upward of 20,000 Chinese are included in the general number of arrivals [in 1852] above given. Such people were becoming very numerous in San Francisco, from whence the recent immigrants from their country scattered themselves over the various mining regions of California. At one period of 1852 there were supposed to be about 27,000 Chinese in the state. A considerable number of people of "color"...also arrived. These were probably afraid to proceed to the mines to labor beside the domineering white races, and therefore they remained to...make much money and spend it in San Francisco, like almost everybody else. Mexicans from Sonora and other provinces of Mexico, and many Chileans, and a few Peruvians from South America, were likewise continually coming and going between San Francisco and the ports of their own countries. The Chinese immigrants had their mandarins [high-ranking scholars], their merchants, rich, educated, and respectable men, in San Francisco; but all the Mexicans and Chileans, like the people of Negro descent, were of the commonest description....

**Conflicting Claims**   Since the early 1800s, the United States and Great Britain had agreed to joint occupation of the vast Oregon territory. But in 1844 many Americans wanted control of the entire territory and would no longer accept joint occupation. They heartily approved the Democratic campaign slogan: "**Fifty-four forty or fight!**" which meant: make Great Britain give up all of Oregon to the 54°40' line.

Although both nations wanted control of Oregon, both also had strong reasons for avoiding war. Great Britain wanted to preserve its good trade relations with the United States. The United States, at war with Mexico in 1846, had no desire to see Great Britain come to Mexico's aid.

**Settlement**  Diplomats on both sides managed to work out a compromise. A British-American treaty of 1846 divided the Oregon territory into two roughly equal halves. The northern half went to Great Britain. The southern half (below the 49th parallel of latitude) went to the United States. Two long-term results of the treaty were (1) the border between Canada and the United States was extended to the Pacific and (2) relations between Great Britain and the United States were much improved.

### In Review

The following questions refer to section I: Westward Expansion.

1. Identify the causes of conflict between each of these: (a) Mexico and American settlers of Texas in 1836; (b) Great Britain and the United States in 1845; and (c) the United States and Mexico in 1846.
2. Explain why many Northerners opposed the annexation of Texas.

# II. Growing Sectional Conflict (1850 to 1861)

During his term of office (1845 to 1849), President Polk achieved his goal of expansion to the Pacific. However, expansion came at a price. As new territories were added, arguments over whether to allow slavery in the West became more and more heated. Various compromises were proposed, and two of them were tried. But as we shall see, despite these compromises, the South eventually seceded and Civil War began.

## A. COMPROMISES OVER SLAVERY

Recall that in 1820 (well before the war with Mexico), Congress had adopted the Missouri Compromise as a means of resolving the slavery question. According to this compromise, slavery would be allowed in Missouri but prohibited in all other territory north of 36°30' latitude. But after the war with Mexico and the addition of California, the Missouri Compromise was no longer acceptable either to Northerners or Southerners. Congress therefore worked out a second compromise—the **Compromise of 1850**. (To compare the slavery compromises of 1820 and 1850, see the chart on page 111.)

**The Issue of California**  Because of its rapid settlement during the gold rush, California was the first of the new territories to apply for admission as a state. The South was alarmed because California insisted on being admitted as a free (nonslave) state. This would upset the balance of free states and slave states established by the Missouri Compromise. It would increase the representation in Congress of the Northern, nonslave states and give the North an absolute majority in the Senate as well as the House. Southern cotton farmers feared that the Northerners in Congress might try to block them from taking their slaves into the Southwest territories won from Mexico. They threatened to defy any antislavery law that the North might attempt to pass.

**The Compromise**   To settle the dispute, Senator Henry Clay of Kentucky proposed another compromise:

- California would be admitted to the Union as a free state. In other parts of the Mexican Cession (Arizona, New Mexico, Utah, and Nevada), settlers would decide by majority vote whether or not to allow slavery. The issue, in other words, would be decided by "**popular sovereignty**."
- The practice of buying and selling slaves at public auction in Washington, D.C., would be abolished.
- Government officials in the North would assist in the capture of escaped slaves and return them to their masters in the South. This **Fugitive Slave Act** would be strictly enforced, with heavy fines for those who disobeyed. Although Congress voted for Clay's compromise, there was widespread resistance among Northern abolitionists to the Fugitive Slave Act.

### A Comparison of Two Compromises

|  | Missouri Compromise | Compromise of 1850 |
|---|---|---|
| Terms to satisfy the South | Admit Missouri as a slave state | Strictly enforce a new fugitive slave act |
| Terms to satisfy the North | Admit Maine as a free, nonslave state | Admit California as a free state; abolish the auctioning of slaves in the District of Columbia |
| Other terms | Divide the lands of the Louisiana Purchase at the 36°30′ line; prohibit slavery north of the line; allow it south of the line | In the Southwest territories, submit the slavery question to vote of the people ("popular sovereignty") |

## B. THE KANSAS-NEBRASKA ACT (1854)

Only four years after Congress agreed to the Compromise of 1850, another proposal was made about slavery in the Western territories. This time the proposal concerned territories on the Great Plains— the Kansas Territory and the Nebraska Territory.

**Changing the Law**   Both Kansas and Nebraska were located north of the 36°30' line. According to the Missouri Compromise of 1820, no slaves would be permitted north of the line. But in the 1850s Southerners objected to this restriction and hoped to do away with it by amending the law. Stephen Douglas, a U.S. senator from Illinois, encouraged Southern hopes. Douglas proposed that settlers in Kansas and Nebraska decide for themselves whether or not to allow slavery in their territories. Congress voted in favor of Douglas's proposal, and the **Kansas-Nebraska Act** became law. Its most important provisions were these:

- The terms of the Missouri Compromise no longer applied to Kansas and Nebraska.
- Instead, the people of these territories would exercise "popular sovereignty" by voting on whether or not to allow slavery.

**The Violent Outcome**   Voting is one way to settle an issue; fighting is another. In Kansas, after the passage of Senator Douglas's bill, fighting broke out between Southern, proslavery settlers and Northern, antislavery settlers. Armed clashes between Northerners and Southerners in "Bleeding Kansas" warned of the nationwide civil war that would soon follow.

## C. THE ABOLITIONIST MOVEMENT

Most people in the North were unconcerned about the existence of slavery in the South. Nevertheless, a small minority of Northern whites, as well as free blacks, spoke out strongly against slavery. Since they wanted to outlaw or abolish slavery in the South, they were known as abolitionists. The following were the best-known abolitionist leaders.

**Harriet Beecher Stowe**   Harriet Beecher Stowe, a white woman from Connecticut, was the author of one of the most influential novels ever written: *Uncle Tom's Cabin*. It tells the story of a kind-spirited and elderly slave, Uncle Tom, who is savagely beaten and killed by a vicious slave overseer, Simon Legree. The book's publication in 1852 caused a sensation in both the North and the South. Northerners were morally outraged by its depiction of the evils of slavery. Southerners were deeply offended by the book, complaining that it presented a false picture of Southern society. After the Civil War erupted, President Lincoln met with Harriet Beecher Stowe, remarking that she was "the little woman whose book made such a great war."

**Harriet Tubman**   As a young black woman, Harriet Tubman escaped slavery and then spent a lifetime leading others to freedom. She was one of the estimated 50,000 people who escaped slavery by journeying to the North over secret routes and stopovers. The network of abolitionists who helped slaves escape was known as the **Underground Railroad**. Tubman was a principal organizer of the secret "railroad." Because of her heroic efforts for her people, she has been called the "Moses" of the antislavery movement.

**Frederick Douglass**   After escaping slavery, Frederick Douglass dedicated himself to the cause of African-American freedom and equal rights. He spoke to large crowds about the injustice of slavery and argued forcefully for its abolition. He also published his arguments in a newspaper he founded—a newspaper written by African Americans.

**William Lloyd Garrison**   A white reformer, William Lloyd Garrison, helped to begin the abolitionist movement by publishing an antislavery newspaper, *The Liberator*, in 1831. His writings and speeches demanded an immediate end to slavery without compensating the slave owners for their loss. Because slavery was permitted by the U.S. Constitution, Garrison condemned that document as "a covenant with death and an agreement with Hell."

**John Brown**   Another white abolitionist, John Brown, believed in using violence to fight slavery. In Kansas in 1856, Brown and his sons murdered five supporters of slavery in retaliation for the deaths of antislavery settlers. Then at Harper's Ferry, Virginia, in 1859, Brown led an attack on a federal arsenal, probably with the hope of arming slaves for a revolt against their masters. But the plot failed, and Brown was captured and hanged. Northern abolitionists hailed Brown as a martyr, but Southerners viewed him as a crazed fanatic. Sensational newspaper accounts of the raid on Harper's Ferry added to the growing hostility between North and South.

## D. LANDMARK DECISION: THE DRED SCOTT CASE

The antislavery writings and speeches of the abolitionists increased sectional tensions. The Supreme Court's decision in the **Dred Scott case** of 1857 increased tensions even further.

**Facts of the Case**   Dred Scott had lived in Missouri as a slave before being taken by his owner to Illinois, a free state. Returning to the slave state of Missouri, he went to court to sue for his freedom. He argued that he had lived in free territory and therefore should be declared a free citizen. His case eventually was appealed to the U.S. Supreme Court.

**Supreme Court's Decision**   In 1857 the Supreme Court ruled that Scott's petition was *not* valid. The reason the Court gave was extremely controversial. Chief Justice Roger Taney, a Southerner, argued as follows:

- Even free African Americans could not sue in a federal court, since they were not citizens of the United States.
- Slaves brought into free territory remained slaves because they were a form of property. Owners could not be denied their property rights without due process of law.
- The Missouri Compromise, which had excluded slavery from free territory, was unconstitutional because it denied slave owners their property rights.

**Public Reaction**   Southern slave owners were glad that the Supreme Court's decision completely confirmed their views. But in the North, many people were shocked to think that all Western territories were now thrown open to slavery.

## E. RISE OF THE REPUBLICAN PARTY

The Democratic party was a national party with strength in all three sections: North, West, and South. It was a political force for keeping the nation united. The Democrats were challenged in the 1850s by a new party that was sectional, not national. The Republican party, founded in 1854, drew all of its support from the North and the West. In the South it was looked upon with suspicion and hostility as an antislavery, anti-Southern party.

**Republican Goals**   Various antislavery groups (Whigs, Northern Democrats, and abolitionists) came together in the 1850s to form the Republican party. As stated in the Republican platforms of 1856 and 1860, the new party stood for the following:

- Keeping slavery out of the Western territories (Note that the abolition of slavery in the South was a goal of only a minority of Republicans; it was not the official goal of the party.)
- Enacting a high protective tariff to encourage Northern industries
- Building a nationwide, or transcontinental, railroad stretching from the Atlantic coast all the way to the Pacific.

Stopping the spread of slavery was the Republicans' chief objective.

One Republican who spoke out forcefully on the issue was Abraham Lincoln.

**Lincoln-Douglas Debates**  Lincoln was a lawyer and state legislator from Illinois who in 1858 became the Republican candidate for a U.S. Senate seat. The person holding that seat and running for reelection was the famed Democratic leader in the Senate, Stephen Douglas. In various towns in Illinois, the tall Republican debated the much shorter Democrat ("the "Little Giant," as Douglas was called) on the slavery issue. Douglas defended his position on "popular sovereignty"; Lincoln attacked it. Said Lincoln in one debate: "The Republican party looks upon slavery as a moral, social, and political wrong. They insist that it should be treated as a wrong; and one of the methods of treating it as a wrong is to make sure that it should grow no longer." Although Lincoln lost to Douglas in the Senate race, his strong arguments in the debate won national attention.

**Election of 1860**  Angry feelings between Northerners and South-erners dominated politics in 1860 as Republicans and Democrats met in national conventions to choose their candidates for president. The Republicans nominated Lincoln. A majority of Democrats nominated Stephen Douglas, a moderate on the slavery issue. But Southern Democrats wanted a candidate of their own, who would be committed to the proslavery interests of their section. These Southerners nom-inated John Breckinridge as a third candidate. A fourth candidate, John Bell, was nominated by a new party: the Constitutional Union party. In this four-way race, Lincoln emerged as the winner. From the South's point of view, it was the worst possible outcome.

**Secession of the South**  Only one month after Lincoln's election, South Carolina announced its decision to secede from the Union. Other Southern states followed South Carolina's example. By March, 1861, Northern states and Southern states were acting as two separate nations. The Union had come apart.

## F. REASONS FOR SECESSION

Why did the South secede? Historians who have studied the coming of the Civil War point to several forces that built to a climax in 1860.

**1. Cultural and Economic Differences**  The plantation South dif-fered greatly from the industrial North. The way of life on a Southern plantation was based on a single family's ownership of land worked by a large number of slaves. The courtly manners of the owners of the plantation house represented the customs of an older age. In contrast, the more commercial North was rapidly developing new customs and values in keeping with a new industrial age.

The two regions' differing economies meant that they were often at odds on important political questions, such as the tariff.

**2. Regional Loyalties**  Nationalism was weaker in the South than in the North. Southerners felt a great attachment to their own region and jealously guarded states' rights. They were convinced that the states had every right to secede from the Union if the national government tried to interfere too much with local matters.

**3. Southerners' Mistaken Belief in Easy Victory**  Many Southerners believed that secession could be achieved peacefully and that the North would not go to war over it. Even if war came, Southerners were confident that the industrial world's need for their cotton would bring support from abroad for Southern independence. If the South won the backing of just one nation, Great Britain, it was felt that the Southern cause would surely triumph in peace or war. As one Southerner put it: "Should the South produce no cotton for three years England would topple headlong and carry the whole civilized world with her except the South. No, you dare not make war on cotton. No power on earth dares to make war upon it. Cotton is king."

**4. Lack of National Leadership**  It so happened that the presidents of the 1850s (Millard Fillmore, Franklin Pierce, and James Buchanan) were not strong leaders. In Congress, too, leadership was lacking when it was most needed. Hopes for holding the Union together suffered a setback when two nationalist senators, Henry Clay and Daniel Webster, both died early in the 1850s.

**5. Slavery as a Moral Issue**  The issue of slavery aroused strong feelings on both sides. Although most Southern whites owned no slaves, they supported slavery as part of the Southern way of life. In the 1850s more and more Northerners began to view slavery as a moral issue and also as an institution that could not live side by side with democracy. Lincoln expressed this view in a speech of 1858: "A house divided against itself cannot stand. I believe that this government cannot endure permanently half slave and half free. I do not expect the Union to be dissolved; I do not expect the house to fall; but I do expect it will cease to be divided. It will be all one thing or all the other."

**6. Combined Effect of Many Incidents**  In the 1850s one incident after another kept stirring up feelings of suspicion and hostility. After the publication of *Uncle Tom's Cabin* (1852) came John Brown's raids in Kansas (1856), the Dred Scott decision (1857), the hanging of John Brown at Harper's Ferry (1859), and the election of an antislavery Republican as president (1860).

## G. FIRING ON FORT SUMTER

The secession of South Carolina and other Southern states did not necessarily mean war. All depended on the response of the federal government and its new leader, President Lincoln. A month after Lincoln's inauguration, an incident occurred that was the immediate cause of civil war. Fort Sumter, an island fortress in the harbor of Charleston, South Carolina, was held by U.S. forces. South Carolina insisted that the fort be surrendered to the South. Lincoln refused. Southern guns bombarded the fort, and thus the war began.

### *In Review*

The following questions refer to the word wheel and section II:
Growing Sectional Conflict (1850 to 1861).

**Word Wheel**

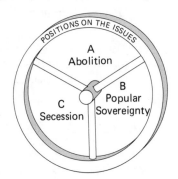

For each person identified in phrases 1 to 8, tell whether he or she was most likely to have favored: (*a*) abolition, (*b*) "popular sovereignty," or (*c*) secession.

1. An admirer of William Lloyd Garrison and Frederick Douglass in the 1840s
2. A voter for John Breckinridge in 1860
3. An African-American teenager living in Boston in the 1850s
4. A white citizen of South Carolina in 1861
5. A Virginian outraged by the news of John Brown's raid on the federal arsenal at Harper's Ferry
6. A slave owner in the Kansas territory in 1855
7. A critic of the Supreme Court's decision in the Dred Scott case
8. An admirer of Senator Stephen Douglas

# III. The Civil War

Eleven Southern states were loosely joined under their own national constitution and central government. They called their nation a **confederacy** (the Confederate States of America). For four years

(1861–1865), the Confederate army of the South fought for independence against a Northern army committed to preserving the Union and putting down the "rebellion."

## A. ADVANTAGES OF EACH SIDE

In general, the South had a better army for fighting a short war, but the North's vast economic resources gave it the advantage in a longer war.

### North and South in the Civil War

| Union Advantages | Confederate Advantages |
|---|---|
| 1. *Population*. The North's population (22 million in 1860) was more than twice that of the South (six million free citizens, three million slaves). | 1. *Strategic position*. In war it is generally easier to defend a position than it is to attack it. Instead of launching risky offensives, the Confederacy needed only to beat back Northern assaults. |
| 2. *Economic resources*. The Union's numerous factories and farms were capable of producing the massive amount of war goods and food supplies needed for victory. In contrast the South had little industry and its farms produced chiefly cotton, not food. In addition the North's railroad system was far superior to the South's. | 2. *Preparation for war*. Southerners had a stronger military tradition than Northerners. Most of them knew how to shoot and ride and needed less training than the raw recruits in the Union army. |
| 3. *Political leadership*. Though hardworking and dedicated, the Confederate president, Jefferson Davis, did not have the leadership ability of the Union president, Lincoln. | 3. *Military leadership*. On the whole Southern generals like Robert E. Lee and Thomas J. ("Stonewall") Jackson were much superior to Northern generals. |
| 4. *Foreign relations.* The United States was recognized throughout the world as a legitimate nation. The South's efforts to win the support and recognition of Great Britain and other nations ended in failure. | 4. *Morale*. Because Southern troops were fighting in defense of their homeland, their morale, or fighting spirit, was usually greater than that of Northern troops. |
| 5. *Naval superiority*. The South had very few ships of war compared to the North's strong navy. Thus, the North was able to blockade Southern ports and cut off vital supplies. | |

## B. TURNING POINTS IN THE WAR

In the first years of war, 1861 to 1862, the South won most of the important battles. But by the summer of 1863, it became clear that momentum had shifted to the Union. Three battles—one at sea, two on land—may be viewed as turning points.

**Battle of the Ironclads**   In the long run, using its navy to blockade Southern ports was the North's most effective weapon. The blockade badly weakened the Confederacy by cutting off European shipments of guns and other war supplies. In an attempt to break the blockade, the South attached iron plates to the sides of a captured Union ship, the *Merrimac* (renamed *Virginia*). The ironclad warship did heavy damage to the North's wooden sailing ships. But after a Union ironclad, the *Monitor*, fought the *Merrimac* (*Virginia*) to a draw in 1862, the South was unable to challenge the North's blockade. The battle of two ironclad ships was the first in history.

**Battle of Gettysburg**   With war supplies running low, the South's brilliant general, Robert E. Lee, decided to take the offensive in a bold, do-or-die invasion of the North. In the Pennsylvania farm town

Some of the 7,058 men killed at Gettysburg

of Gettysburg, three days of fighting (July 1 to 3, 1863), ended in a desperate charge across an open field by the South's General George Pickett. Both sides suffered thousands of deaths at Gettysburg. But the Union army was clearly the victor, as the surviving remnant of Lee's army marched wearily back to Virginia.

**Siege of Vicksburg**   Only one day later, July 4, 1863, Union troops under General Ulysses S. Grant forced the surrender of a strategic

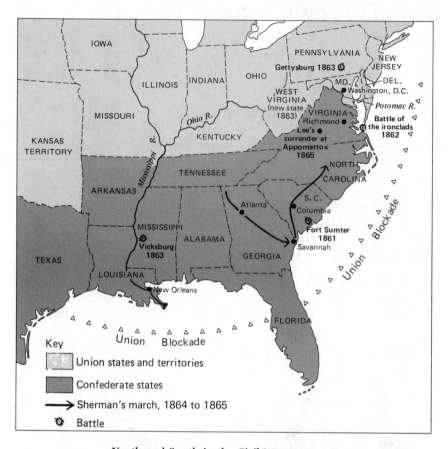

North and South in the Civil War, 1861–1865

fortress at Vicksburg on the Mississippi River. This victory gave the North complete control of the Mississippi River and thus split the South in two. Three Confederate states on the west side of the river (Texas, Arkansas, and western Louisiana) were separated from the rest of the Confederacy.

## C. THE FINAL CAMPAIGNS

After Gettysburg and Vicksburg, the Civil War continued to consume thousands of lives, as opposing armies under Grant and Lee fought each other in bloody combat in a densely wooded region in Virginia. At the same time, in 1864, an untold number of Southern farmhouses were put to the torch by Union troops marching through Georgia and South Carolina.

**Sherman's March to the Sea**  The Northern army was led by General William T. Sherman on a campaign of destruction eastward from

Tennessee to the Georgia coast and then northward to the Carolinas. For the first time in the war, civilian property was deliberately destroyed as an act of policy. "War is hell," said Sherman, and he made the South feel the full truth of his statement.

**Richmond and Appomattox**   As the capital of the Confederacy, Richmond in central Virginia was a target of Northern military campaigns throughout the war. For four years Confederate armies saved the capital from being taken. But finally, on April 2, 1865, Lee's battered army gave way and a Union army marched into Richmond. Seven days later, Lee surrendered his army to Grant at Appomattox Court House. The war was over.

## D. LINCOLN'S LEADERSHIP

Lincoln was reelected president in 1864. But only one month after beginning his second term (April, 1865), he was assassinated by an embittered actor and Southern sympathizer, John Wilkes Booth. Why do historians consider Lincoln to have been one of the nation's greatest presidents? The explanation lies in his firm beliefs and excellent judgment.

**His Firm Political Purpose**   Lincoln made it clear from the beginning that his one goal as president was to save the Union. All of his actions and decisions were directed at achieving this overriding purpose.

**His Political Shrewdness and Courage**   Lincoln was subject to much criticism from the press, the public, and even Republican politicians. As a politician himself, he had a keen sense of when to give in to political pressures and when to take the risk of making an unpopular decision. Patiently, he tried out different generals until one of them, Grant, emerged as the most capable.

**His Decision to Emancipate Slaves**   Although Lincoln personally opposed slavery, he waited through almost two years of war before taking action on the issue. In his **Emancipation Proclamation** (January 1, 1863) Lincoln declared that slaves in the Confederate states were now free men and women. Of course the Confederate states did not recognize Lincoln's authority, and thus his proclamation had little immediate effect on slavery. Nevertheless, it signaled a new direction for the nation and an understanding that slavery would probably be abolished everywhere if the North won the war.

**His Speeches**   Nobody expressed the democratic ideal more beautifully than Lincoln. His **Gettysburg Address**, a two-minute speech dedicating a military cemetery at Gettysburg, Pennsylvania, ranks among the most memorable and inspiring speeches in history. The speech ends in a series of simple yet stirring phrases: "...that we here highly resolve that these dead shall not have died in vain; that this nation, under God, shall have a new birth of freedom; and that government of the people, by the people, for the people, shall not perish from the earth."

# DOCUMENTS: THE EMANCIPATION PROCLAMATION

Lincoln's proclamation of January 1, 1863, extended only to those states that were then "in rebellion against the United States." Unaffected by it were five states still in the Union where slavery was legal: Missouri, Kentucky, Maryland, Delaware, and West Virginia.

On a separate piece of paper, tell whether or not you think Lincoln's proclamation should have applied to the "loyal" states as well as the "rebellious" ones.

And, by virtue of the power and for the purpose aforesaid, I do order and declare that all persons held as slaves within said designated states and parts of states are, and henceforward shall be, free; and that the executive government of the United States, including the military and naval authorities thereof, will recognize and maintain the freedom of said persons.

And I hereby enjoin upon the people so declared to be free to abstain from all violence, unless in necessary self-defense; and I recommend to them that, in all cases when allowed, they labor faithfully for reasonable wages.

And I further declare and make known that such persons of suitable condition will be received into the armed service of the United States to garrison forts, positions, stations, and other places, and to man vessels of all sorts in said service.

And upon this act, sincerely believed to be an act of justice, warranted by the Constitution upon military necessity, I invoke the considerate judgment of mankind and the gracious favor of Almighty God.

# E. THE CONTRIBUTIONS OF AFRICAN AMERICANS AND WOMEN

Although the Civil War was fought primarily by men in uniform—most of whom were white—African-American men as well as women of both races were unavoidably drawn into the conflict.

**Heroes of the Battlefield**  When the war began, neither the North nor the South allowed African Americans to enlist in its armed forces. Thousands of free blacks in the North attempted to enlist but were turned away. As the war progressed the U.S. government changed its policy to permit both emancipated Southern slaves and free Northern blacks to serve in racially segregated (separate) army units. At first they were assigned to tasks other than fighting—for example, cooking meals and building fortifications. But beginning in 1863 African-American troops (usually under the command of white officers) were trained to fight and then sent into battle. They served with distinction. By war's end over 180,000 African Americans had joined the Union armed forces and about 38,000 had lost their lives. Twenty-two were awarded the nation's highest military honor, the Medal of Honor (sometimes known as the Congressional Medal of Honor).

**Victims of Draft Riots**  Enlistment in the Union army was voluntary until 1863, when Congress passed a law that drafted (compelled) young men of a certain age into military service. In New York City, whites who did not want to serve rioted against the draft law. They took out their anger against African Americans, who competed with them for factory jobs. During four days of street violence, countless African Americans were beaten by the raging mob, and many were lynched.

**Women's Experience**  Before the war, women were accustomed to working long hours both on the farm and as wage-earning mill workers. During the war, as hundreds of thousands of men left home to wear a uniform, women had to work even longer hours to fill the labor gap. Employed in factories for wages as low as 25 cents a day, women provided much of the labor force needed to produce uniforms, weapons, and other war goods.

The need for nurses in the war opened up an important profession for women. Under the energetic leadership of Dorothea Dix and Clara Barton, women volunteers took to the battlefield to care for the wounded. After the war Clara Barton continued her pioneering efforts in the nursing field by organizing the American Red Cross in 1877.

## Two Wars: Causes and Consequences

Behind every war there are both underlying causes (forces that bring nations or groups into conflict) and immediate causes (specific events that touch off armed conflict). Also, all wars have important consequences for both winners and losers.

| | Causes | Consequences |
|---|---|---|
| War with Mexico | *Underlying causes:* Americans' territorial ambitions and belief in "manifest destiny" • Migration of Southern pioneers into Texas (Mexican territory)<br><br>*Immediate causes:* annexation of Texas by the United States • Dispute over Texan-Mexican border | 1. Long-term resentment of Mexico toward the United States<br>2. U.S. acquisition of California and territories of the Southwest<br>3. Increased sectional conflict on the slavery issue (whether to allow slaves in the newly acquired territories) |
| Civil War | *Underlying causes:* Economic differences between North and South and the resulting dispute over tariffs • Intense conflict over slavery as a moral issue (as well as a political and economic issue) • Differing views of the U.S. Constitution and the degree to which states may defy national laws • Constant renewal of the slavery controversy as a result of westward expansion<br><br>*Immediate causes:* Lincoln's election as president • Southern states' decision to secede • Southern forces' firing on Fort Sumter | 1. Economically the South was devastated; politically it was subject to domination by a Congress controlled by Northerners.<br>2. Slavery was abolished; all African Americans were free citizens of the United States.<br>3. Three important amendments were added to the U.S. Constitution (see Chapter 5).<br>4. The national Union was preserved.<br>5. The federal system was understood to be one in which national laws were supreme; secession of a state would never again be seriously considered. |

## *In Review*

The following questions refer to section III: The Civil War.

1. Explain why *each* of the following events is considered a turning point in the Civil War: (a) the Union victory at Gettysburg, (b) the Union victory at Vicksburg, and (c) the battle between two ironclads.

**2.** Discuss the importance of *each* of these to Northern victory in the Civil War: (*a*) Lincoln's leadership, (*b*) the Northern economy, and (*c*) the freeing of slaves by Union troops after the Emancipation Proclamation.

# GLOSSARY OF KEY TERMS: CHAPTER 4

**annexation**   the process by which one nation enters into union with another nation (as Texas was annexed to the United States in 1845).

**"Bleeding Kansas"**   the violent conflict between proslavery and antislavery settlers in the Kansas Territory after 1854.

**blockade**   in wartime, an attempt by a nation's navy to prevent supplies from reaching the ports of its enemy.

**Compromise of 1850**   a series of measures by which Congress attempted to resolve the intensified conflict over slavery following the war with Mexico.

**Confederacy**   the name for the republic of 11 seceded states in the South during the Civil War.

**Dred Scott case**   a controversial Supreme Court case of. 1857 that angered abolitionists by declaring that slaves were not citizens and could not claim their freedom even in Northern states.

**Emancipation Proclamation**   a document by President Lincoln declaring the slaves of the Confederate states to be free.

**"Fifty-four forty or fight!"**   a popular slogan of Western expansionists demanding that Great Britain yield to the United States all of the Oregon territory.

**Fugitive Slave Act**   part of the Compromise of 1850 requiring that nonslave states and territories return escaped slaves to their owners.

**Gettysburg Address**   a short speech by President Lincoln (1863) eloquently stating the ideals for which the North fought during the Civil War.

**gold rush**   a frenzied migration of people to an area reported to have large deposits of gold.

**Kansas-Nebraska Act**   a federal law of 1854 that opened the territories of Kansas and Nebraska to the possibility of slavery being established there by popular vote (or "popular sovereignty").

**Lincoln-Douglas debates**   a series of political debates in Illinois (1858) between two candidates for the U.S. Senate, Abraham Lincoln and Stephen Douglas; the debates established Lincoln's reputation as an antislavery Republican.

**"popular sovereignty"**   a method for resolving the issue of slavery in the Western territories by giving the people of a territory the power to vote for or against allowing slavery in the territory.

**Sherman's march to the sea**   a military campaign through Georgia led by the Union general William Sherman in which civilian property as well as railroads and military supplies were deliberately destroyed.

**slave trade**   the buying and selling of slaves at public auctions and the importing of slaves from Africa.

**Underground Railroad**   the escape routes used by Southern slaves in fleeing to freedom in the North and Canada.

# TEST YOURSELF

## A. Multiple Choice: Facts, Main Ideas, Skills

*On a separate sheet of paper, write the number of the word or expression that, of those given, best completes the statement or answers the question.*

### Reviewing the facts

1. The main obstacle to the annexation of Texas during the 1840s was   (1) the danger of war with Mexico   (2) the desire of the federal government to first settle the Oregon boundary dispute   (3) the threat of intervention by Great Britain   (4) the feeling of antislavery leaders that annexation was a plot to extend slave territory

2. The expression "Fifty-four forty or fight!" is associated with   (1) the Texan war for independence   (2) the U.S. war with Mexico   (3) the California gold rush   (4) the Oregon territory

3. A U.S. war with Great Britain over the control of Oregon was avoided as a result of   (1) intervention by France   (2) Britain's agreement to give up all claims to the territory   (3) President Polk's desire for peace at all costs   (4) a compromise settlement

4. Which of the following is the correct order of events?   (1) Kansas-Nebraska Act, Missouri Compromise, Compromise of 1850   (2) Missouri Compromise, Compromise of 1850, Kansas-Nebraska Act   (3) Compromise of 1850, Kansas-Nebraska Act, Missouri Compromise   (4) Missouri Compromise, Kansas-Nebraska Act, Compromise of 1850

5. The Dred Scott decision was significant because it   (1) supported the Compromise of 1850   (2) brought an end to slavery in the territories   (3) established that slavery was legal in any territory   (4) ruled that slaves could sue their owners in a federal court

6. Unlike the Missouri Compromise, the Kansas-Nebraska Act   (1) provided for the admission of Kansas as a slave state   (2) provided for the admission of both Kansas and Nebraska as nonslave states   (3) said nothing about slavery   (4) allowed settlers to determine whether their territories would be slave or free

7. According to the idea of "popular sovereignty," major political

questions should be decided by  (1) Congress  (2) the state legislatures  (3) the electoral college  (4) the voters

8. The Kansas-Nebraska Act had the effect of  (1) increasing cooperation between North and South  (2) increasing tension between slave states and free states  (3) putting an end to slavery in the Western territories  (4) giving the abolitionists their first political victory

9. The Republican party took the position that  (1) slavery must be ended throughout the nation  (2) slavery should not be allowed in the Western territories  (3) each territory should decide for itself whether to allow slavery  (4) slavery was less important than other issues

10. Lincoln's election as president in 1860 demonstrated that he  (1) had the support of both the North and the South  (2) had the support of a majority of Americans  (3) was basically a sectional candidate  (4) was considered a compromise candidate

11. Compared to the South, the North in the Civil War had the advantage of  (1) a larger industrial base  (2) more experienced military leaders  (3) better trained soldiers  (4) fighting for a superior cause

12. The Battle of Gettysburg was significant because it  (1) led to an immediate end to the war  (2) opened an invasion route to the North  (3) inflicted a major loss on General Lee's army  (4) cut off supplies to states west of the Mississippi River

## Reviewing the main ideas

13. Policies based on the idea of "manifest destiny" led to all of the following except  (1) war with Mexico  (2) the annexation of Texas  (3) increased sectional conflict over slavery  (4) the decline of the Democratic party

14. An underlying cause of the Civil War was  (1) the North's unwillingness to compromise on the tariff issue  (2) the Supreme Court's unwillingness to make decisions about slavery  (3) the sectional tensions created by the issue of slavery  (4) the Democratic party's commitment to the cause of abolitionism

15. Which statement best describes the condition of African Americans in the South before the Civil War?  (1) They gained some civil rights by appealing to their masters.  (2) They were considered citizens but were denied basic constitutional rights.  (3) Some were granted freedom as a result of Supreme Court decisions.  (4) They were treated as the property of those who purchased them.

16. The primary goal of Lincoln's presidency was to  (1) uphold the national honor  (2) preserve the Union  (3) free all slaves  (4) strengthen the Republican party

17. During the period between 1820 and 1860, the two issues that dominated U.S. politics were  (1) national security and relations with Great Britain  (2) westward expansion and slavery  (3) big

business and economic growth   (4) the environment and states' rights

**18.** The basic constitutional issue resolved by the Civil War was the   (1) definition of presidential power   (2) process by which a territory becomes a state   (3) supremacy of the federal government over the states   (4) civil liberties of prisoners of war

## Developing critical thinking skills

*Base your answers to questions 19 and 20 on the graph below and on your knowledge of U.S. history and government.*

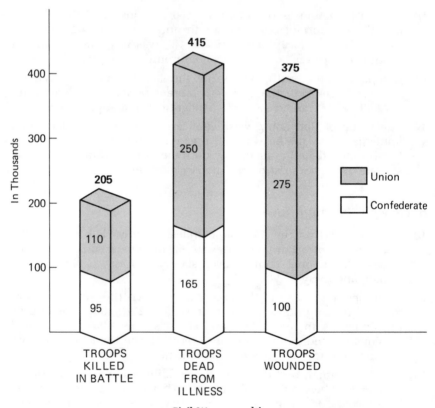

Civil War casualties

**19.** Which generalization about the Civil War is best supported by the evidence in the graph?   (1) In all categories Union casualties were greater than Confederate casualties.   (2) In all categories Confederate casualties were greater than Union casualties.   (3) Union soldiers were more likely to be killed in battle than to be wounded.   (4) Compared to Union soldiers, Confederate soldiers were more likely to be wounded but less likely to die from illness.

**20.** It can be inferred from the graph that, in a typical Civil War battle, the total wounded on *both* sides was likely to be   (1) less than the number killed   (2) about equal to the number killed   (3) greater than the number killed   (4) about equal to the number killed added to the number dead from illness

## B.  Enduring Issues

*Select two of the enduring issues from column A. For each issue chosen, tell how the historical example in column B relates to the issue.*

| A.  Enduring Issues | B.  Historical Examples |
| --- | --- |
| 1. Federalism, the balance between nation and state | Southern states' decision to secede from the Union |
| 2. The judiciary, interpreter of the U.S. Constitution or shaper of policy | The Dred Scott case |
| 3. Rights of ethnic and racial groups under the U.S. Constitution | The Fugitive Slave Act |
| 4. Presidential leadership in wartime | Lincoln's presidency |

## C.  Essays

### Level 1

*Select two of the events or movements given below. For each one selected, discuss one way in which that event or movement tended to promote either nationalism or sectionalism in the United States.*

- "Manifest destiny"
- The annexation of Texas
- Abolitionism
- The rise of the Republican party

### Level 2

Until 1861 compromise helped the United States to avoid civil war.

**A.**  1. Identify *two* compromises that helped the nation avoid civil war before 1861.

2. Identify *two* of the events of the 1850s that led to a civil war.

**B.**  Base your answer to part B on your answer to part A. Explain how compromise failed to prevent a civil war.

# UNIT TWO

# Industrialization (1865 to 1900)

*Northern victory in the Civil War* was a triumph not only of Union armies but also of the North's industrial economy. The chapters in this unit describe a period when industrial growth, especially in the North, moved at a dizzying pace. Between 1865 and 1900 the South was transformed, the West was settled, and the East was swept up in a tide of industrial and urban change. By the end of the century, the United States—once a small and struggling republic—was one of the leading nations of the world.

| Chapter | Topics |
| --- | --- |
| 5. The Reconstructed Nation | • How the rights of African Americans were guaranteed after the Civil War |
| | • How Southern whites reacted to the occupation of Northern troops |
| | • The origins of racial segregation in the South |
| 6. The Rise of Business, Labor, and Agriculture | • The effects of the Industrial Revolution on businesses, workers, and farmers |
| | • Why labor unions grew in importance after the Civil War |
| | • Why farmers of the South and West joined a new political party in the 1890s |
| 7. Adjusting to Industrialism: The Western Frontier and Eastern Cities | • How the Great Plains were settled by farmers and cattle ranchers |
| | • The effect of Western settlement on Native Americans |
| | • The opportunities and problems of urban life before 1900 |
| | • The changing pattern of immigration from colonial times to the early twentieth century |

*Chapter* **5**

# The Reconstructed Nation

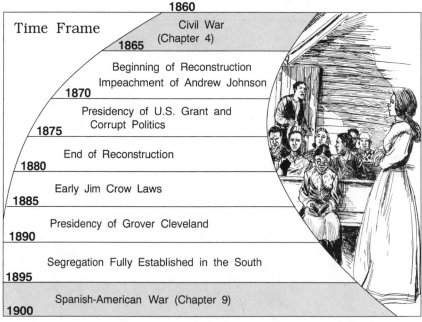

| Time Frame | | |
|---|---|---|
| **1860** | | |
| | Civil War (Chapter 4) | |
| **1865** | | |
| | Beginning of Reconstruction Impeachment of Andrew Johnson | |
| **1870** | | |
| | Presidency of U.S. Grant and Corrupt Politics | |
| **1875** | | |
| | End of Reconstruction | |
| **1880** | | |
| | Early Jim Crow Laws | |
| **1885** | | |
| | Presidency of Grover Cleveland | |
| **1890** | | |
| | Segregation Fully Established in the South | |
| **1895** | | |
| | Spanish-American War (Chapter 9) | |
| **1900** | | |

*Class for freed slaves*

## *Objectives*

- To understand the changing nature of American society—and especially Southern society—from 1865 to 1895.
- To evaluate different plans for bringing the Southern states back into the Union after the Civil War.
- To describe the factors that prevented full freedom for African Americans after their emancipation from slavery.
- To compare the points of view of Northerners and Southerners during the era of Reconstruction.
- To describe the long-term social, political, and economic consequences of the Civil War and Reconstruction.

General Lee's surrender to General Grant at Appomattox Court House in 1865 brought the Civil War to an end. The South lay in ruins. The Confederacy was no more. The triumphant Northerners who controlled the U.S. government now faced the problem of "reconstructing," or reshaping, the governments of the defeated Southern states so that they might rejoin the Union. For 12 years after the war (1865 to 1877), Northern troops occupied parts of the South. These postwar years are known as the era of **Reconstruction**.

# I. Three Plans of Reconstruction

Except for Antietam and Gettysburg, every battle of the Civil War had been fought in the South. After four years of armies marching over the land, the South's economy was in a pitiful state. The wartime destruction of property was vast and incalculable. In addition Southern planters and farmers faced the loss of their labor force, as Union armies carried out Lincoln's Emancipation Proclamation and set free three and a half million slaves.

In the North, there were two major questions for the Republican government in Washington to decide: (1) On what terms should Southern states be readmitted to the Union, and (2) how were the rights of former slaves to be protected? Different plans for answering these questions were proposed and heatedly debated.

## A. LINCOLN'S PLAN

President Lincoln favored lenient treatment of the South. He wanted the seceded states to rejoin the Union, not as conquered territories, but as states equal in status to those of the North. Lincoln proposed two conditions for a seceded state's being admitted back into the Union: (1) Ten percent of the state's voters would be required to take an oath of allegiance to the United States, and (2) the new state government would be required to guarantee the abolition of slavery. Lincoln's hopes for putting this plan into effect were abruptly ended in April, 1865, by an assassin's bullet.

## B. ANDREW JOHNSON'S PLAN

After Lincoln's murder, Vice President Andrew Johnson became the new president. Johnson was deeply distrusted by many Northern Republicans because he had been a Democrat from Tennessee, one of the Southern slaveholding states.

The new president proposed a plan of reconstruction similar to Lincoln's. He proposed three conditions for readmitting a seceded state to the Union: (1) Ten percent of the state's voters would be required to take an oath of loyalty to the U.S. Constitution; (2) the state must ratify the Thirteenth Amendment abolishing slavery; and (3) it must deny the right to vote to a few Confederate leaders, while granting that right to all other Southern white men.

## C. RADICAL REPUBLICANS' PLAN

Many Republicans in Congress supported an entirely different Reconstruction plan from that of Lincoln and Johnson. They thought the South should be punished for its role in the war and that the seceding states should be treated as conquered territories. The plan favored by abolitionists like Senator Charles Sumner of Massachusetts and Congressman Thaddeus Stevens of Pennsylvania was harsh toward Southern whites but helpful to Southern blacks. The Republicans in Congress who supported such a plan were known as **Radical Republicans**.

The Radical Republicans wanted to prevent Confederate leaders of the past from ever holding political office again. They also wanted to ensure that Southern blacks would be guaranteed the same political and legal rights as whites. Their plan of Reconstruction proposed the following:

- No state would be allowed to deprive anyone born on American soil of the rights of citizenship. No state could deprive a person of the right to vote because of that person's race or former status as a slave. (These guarantees were written into the Fourteenth and Fifteenth Amendments to the U.S. Constitution.)

- No military leader or political officeholder of the defeated Confederacy would be permitted to hold state or federal office in the postwar period. (This provision was included in the Fourteenth Amendment.)

- The South would be occupied by federal troops and governed by army generals. The troops would be withdrawn from a state after it had adopted a new state constitution acceptable to Congress.

## D. THREE AMENDMENTS PROTECTING THE CIVIL RIGHTS OF AFRICAN AMERICANS

During Andrew Johnson's presidency (1865 to 1869) the Radical Republicans dominated Congress. So great was their power that they were able to enact their Reconstruction plan despite the president's opposition and repeated vetoes. By far the most important measures passed by the Radical Republicans were three amendments to the U.S. Constitution guaranteeing the rights of freed slaves.

**The Thirteenth Amendment (1865)**   Going well beyond Lincoln's Emancipation Proclamation, this amendment declared slavery to be illegal in every state of the Union. Through this amendment the Northern abolitionists fully achieved their objective.

**The Fourteenth Amendment (1868)**   This amendment defined the rights of American citizenship as follows: "All persons born or naturalized in the United States, and subject to the jurisdiction thereof, are citizens of the United States and of the state wherein they reside." In addition, the amendment prohibited a state from interfering with the "privileges and immunities" of citizens of the United States. Thus, all African Americans (including freed slaves) were to be U.S. citizens with rights equal to those of other citizens.

As discussed in Chapter 2, the Fourteenth Amendment prohibited states from depriving a person of life, liberty, or property without *due process of law* (see Glossary, Chapter 2). Neither could a state deny a citizen the *equal protection of the laws.* The significance of this was that the rights protected by the Constitution now applied to state governments as well as the federal government.

**The Fifteenth Amendment (1870)**   This amendment said that voting rights could not be denied to a person because of that person's "race, color, or previous condition of servitude." In effect, the amendment guaranteed voting rights to African Americans.

## E. "BLACK CODES" IN THE SOUTH

The first year after the Civil War, 1865, was a time of terrible confusion. Southerners held state conventions in order to organize new postwar governments for their respective states. President Johnson accepted the conventions as legitimate if they complied with the terms of his Reconstruction plan. From South Carolina to Texas, each convention drew up a list of measures for limiting the movements and restricting the rights of former slaves. These measures, known as the "**Black Codes**," prohibited blacks from doing the following:

- Carrying firearms
- Starting businesses
- Appearing on the streets after sunset
- Renting or leasing farmland
- Traveling without a permit.

Southern whites argued that the codes were necessary to keep order. But to other Americans it seemed all too obvious that the codes were meant to deprive freed blacks of civil rights.

## F. RADICAL REPUBLICAN LAWS FOR GOVERNING THE SOUTH

Radical Republicans condemned the "Black Codes" and argued that the state conventions in the South were not legitimate. To accomplish their two goals (protecting Southern blacks and punishing Southern whites), the Radical Republican leaders pushed through Congress a series of Reconstruction laws.

**The Freedmen's Bureau (1865)**   This new agency of the U.S. government was given the ambitious task of aiding more than three million former slaves ("freedmen") in adjusting to freedom. It operated schools in the South for blacks, recognizing that as slaves, they had been deliberately deprived of the skills of literacy. The bureau also provided emergency aid in the form of clothing, food, and medical supplies.

**Civil Rights Act (1866)**   To combat the "Black Codes," this law gave the federal government the authority to protect the civil rights of blacks.

**Military Reconstruction (1867)**   Congress divided the South into five military districts. Each district was occupied by federal troops and commanded by a military governor (instead of an elected civilian governor).

**Conditions for Readmitting a Seceded State to the Union (1867)**
The state conventions of 1865 were deemed illegitimate. A state wanting to be readmitted to the Union had to draw up a state constitution that accepted the terms of the Fourteenth Amendment. One part of this amendment disqualified former Confederate leaders from holding office.

**Force Acts (1870 to 1871)**   These laws authorized federal troops to break up terrorist organizations such as the **Ku Klux Klan** formed by Southern whites to intimidate black voters.

## G. IMPEACHMENT AND TRIAL OF ANDREW JOHNSON

Andrew Johnson was not a popular president. He antagonized the Radical Republican leaders in Congress by repeatedly using his veto power to try to block their Reconstruction plan. The lawmakers managed to override each veto by the required two-thirds vote.

**Impeachment**   In 1867 Congress passed, over the president's veto, an act that would have changed the constitutional system of *checks and balances* (see Glossary, Chapter 2) in Congress's favor. This Tenure of Office Act prohibited the president from firing a cabinet officer without the Senate's approval. After the act was passed, Johnson defiantly announced the firing of his secretary of war, Edwin Stanton. In 1868 the House of Representatives responded by voting to impeach the president.

**Trial**   At Johnson's trial on impeachment charges, the Senate fell just one vote short of the two-thirds majority required to remove an official from office. Thus, barely saved from removal, Johnson continued as president until the end of his term.

### In Review

The following questions refer to section I: Three Plans of Reconstruction.

1. Compare President Johnson's plan of Reconstruction with that of the Radical Republicans.
2. Define each term: *Reconstruction,* *"black codes,"* and *impeachment.*
3. Explain how the conflict between Congress and President Johnson in 1868 illustrates the principle of checks and balances.

# II. Reconstruction Governments in the South

The state governments organized in the South after 1867 were extremely controversial. The reason for the controversy was that Southern whites and Southern blacks looked at Reconstruction from entirely different points of view. For whites, already embittered by Confederate defeat, Northern control of their state governments was an insult. For blacks, on the other hand, Reconstruction was an all-too-brief period of potential freedom and equal opportunity (enforced by federal law).

Let us look at Reconstruction from the differing points of view of three groups: Northern politicians, Southern blacks, and Southern whites.

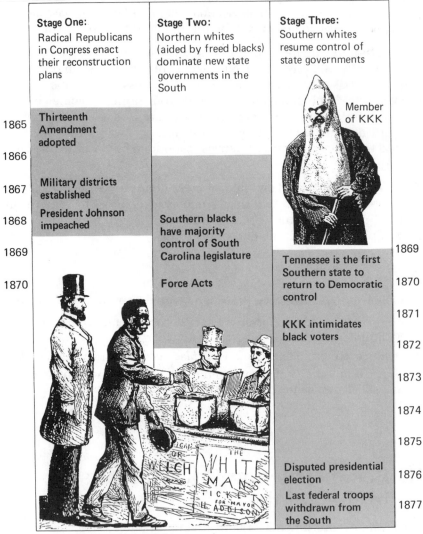

| Stage One: Radical Republicans in Congress enact their reconstruction plans | Stage Two: Northern whites (aided by freed blacks) dominate new state governments in the South | Stage Three: Southern whites resume control of state governments |
| --- | --- | --- |
| | | Member of KKK |
| 1865 Thirteenth Amendment adopted | | |
| 1866 | | |
| 1867 Military districts established | | |
| 1868 President Johnson impeached | Southern blacks have majority control of South Carolina legislature | |
| 1869 | | 1869 Tennessee is the first Southern state to |
| 1870 | Force Acts | return to Democratic control 1870 |
| | | 1871 KKK intimidates black voters 1872 |
| | | 1873 |
| | | 1874 |
| | | 1875 |
| | | Disputed presidential election 1876 |
| | | Last federal troops withdrawn from the South 1877 |

Cartoon of a freedman voting

Three stages of Reconstruction

## A. THE POINT OF VIEW OF NORTHERN POLITICIANS

In the postwar years thousands of Northerners moved to the South, seeing opportunities there for both economic gain and political power. Shielded by federal troops, the Northerners campaigned for election to seats in the new legislatures created by the South's new state constitutions. They ran as Republicans and counted upon Southern blacks to vote Republican on Election Day.

**Republican Victories**   In 1868 elections were held in seven Southern states. Aided by the nearly unanimous support of freed blacks, Northern Republicans won four of the seven governorships, ten (out of 14) seats in the U.S. Senate, and 20 (out of 35) seats in the U.S. House of Representatives.

**Extravagant Use of Public Funds**   A chief task of the newly organized legislatures was to help rebuild all that had been destroyed during the war. For this purpose large sums of money were voted by the Republican legislators. However, some of the money intended for rebuilding was taken by the legislators for their personal profit.

## B. THE POINT OF VIEW OF SOUTHERN BLACKS

For Southern blacks, making the transition from slavery to freedom was an enormous challenge. At first they had high hopes that the U.S. government would protect their rights and help them to take their place in Southern society as landowning farmers.

**Economic Hopes**   In the early years of Reconstruction, it was widely rumored that every black family in the South would be given a chance at economic independence by receiving from the government **forty acres and a mule**. Blacks' hopes were encouraged by Congressman Thaddeus Stevens and other Radical Republicans, who favored the idea of distributing land to freed slaves.

**Political Hopes**   The adoption of the Fifteenth Amendment gave African Americans solid grounds for believing that the U.S. government would do all in its power to protect their civil rights as voters.

**Economic and Political Reality**   The reality was a bitter disappointment. Congress never acted on the idea of providing forty acres and a mule. Also, the Fifteenth Amendment's guarantee of voting rights proved to be misleading. At first Northern troops tried to protect the right of blacks to vote. But, as we shall see, many Southern whites were determined to stop blacks from voting.

**Participation in Reconstruction Governments**   In the early years of Reconstruction (about 1868 to 1872), blacks had the full support of Northern Republicans and U.S. troops. In this period many African Americans won election to seats in Southern legislatures. In one house of South Carolina's legislature, they were in the majority. Black citizens may have been better represented in the lawmaking process during Reconstruction than at any time before or since.

**African Americans in Congress**   During Reconstruction 14 African Americans from the South served in the U.S. Congress. Among them were Senator Hiram Revels of Mississippi, Congressman Robert Smalls of South Carolina, and Congressman Jeremiah Haralson of Alabama. Half of the black lawmakers were former slaves; half had attended college. As a group they championed a number of causes including protection of civil rights and federal aid to education.

## C. THE POINT OF VIEW OF SOUTHERN WHITES

The chief interests of Southern whites during Reconstruction were to (1) revive their war-torn economy and (2) regain control of their state governments. They viewed the Reconstruction governments as hateful and scorned the Northern whites and Southern blacks who took part in them.

**The Hated "Carpetbaggers" and "Scalawags"**   Northerners who came south were accused of profiting from the region's economic distress and political weakness. They were scornfully nicknamed "**carpetbaggers**" (fortune hunters who carry all their belongings in a single travel bag). Even worse in the eyes of Confederate loyalists were those Southern whites who cooperated with the Northerners. These "**scalawags**," as they were called, were thought to have only one motive: to share in the Northerners' corrupt, money-making schemes.

**Terrorist Raids**   Many whites were so hostile to Reconstruction that they decided to use violent means to attack it. In every Southern state, groups of whites formed secret societies such as the Knights of the White Camelia and the Ku Klux Klan (KKK). The chief victims of the nightly raids were Southern blacks, who were beaten and sometimes killed. "Scalawag" whites were also intimidated.

# III. Corruption in the Grant Era

Southern whites accused "carpetbaggers," "scalawags," and blacks in the state legislatures of being corrupt. (**Corruption** is any attempt by public officials to participate in illegal activities.) But the Reconstruction governments in the South were no more corrupt than state and local governments in the North. Everywhere, at all levels of government, the post-Civil War years may well have been the most corrupt period in U.S. history.

A man tragically associated with the swindles of his time was a war hero who, in 1868, was elected president—Ulysses S. Grant.

## A. ELECTION POLITICS: "WAVING THE BLOODY SHIRT"

In campaigning for Grant for president in 1868, Republicans stirred up the hatreds and resentments of wartime. They reminded voters of the South's "rebellion" and urged them to vote for Grant because of his large role in saving the Union. The campaign technique, common at the time, of denouncing the wartime enemy was known as **"waving the bloody shirt."**

In 1868 and again in 1872 the technique was effective. In both election years Grant defeated his Democratic opponent. One reason for his success were the votes that he received from African Americans in the North and the South, who were almost unanimously Republican.

## B. SCANDALS IN NATIONAL POLITICS

On the battlefield Ulysses S. Grant had been a good honest soldier. He remained personally honest throughout his eight years in the White House. But he was politically inexperienced and deceived by those he appointed to cabinet posts and other federal offices. As a result his administration was tainted by several scandals.

**The Crédit Mobilier Scandal** Shocking headlines told of a railroad construction company (Crédit Mobilier) selling its stock at bargain prices to the vice president and several members of Congress in return for political favors.

**Other Scandals** Other high-level officials including Treasury Department agents and Grant's secretary of war were involved in various schemes to enrich themselves at public expense.

## C. SCANDALS IN LOCAL POLITICS

The most notorious scoundrel in the post-Civil War period was the Democratic "boss" of New York City, William M. Tweed. Rigging elections to city offices for his tightly organized band of followers (the so-called Tweed Ring), "Boss" Tweed used his political power to steal public money. His favorite trick was to pay extravagant sums to city contractors and demand half the money back in "under the table" payments.

Newspaper articles exposed the corruption at city hall. Even more influential were the political cartoons of Thomas Nast showing Tweed as a vulture (see page 142). New York's honest and capable governor, Samuel Tilden, ordered the prosecution of the Tweed Ring, and the "boss" himself went to prison in 1872.

## OBSERVERS OF AMERICAN LIFE: CARTOONS OF THOMAS NAST

In one cartoon by Thomas Nast, the tiger represents Tammany Hall, a club of Democratic politicians under "Boss" Tweed's control. Mangled in the arena is a figure labeled THE REPUBLIC. In the gallery we see the bearded and big-bellied Tweed presiding over the slaughter. The cartoon's caption reads: "The Tammany Tiger Loose—'What are you going to do about it?'" What New York's voters did about it in the November election of 1871 was to vote the ring officials out of office.

In a second cartoon, "Let Us Prey," how is Tweed characterized? What was his prey?

## *In Review*

The following questions refer to section II: Reconstruction Governments in the South and section III: Corruption in the Grant Era.

1. Define *"carpetbagger."* Then describe how "carpetbaggers" were viewed by (a) Southern whites and (b) Southern blacks.

2. **Word Wheel**

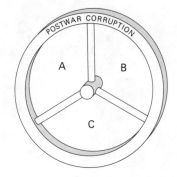

How would you illustrate the idea that politics after the Civil War was generally characterized by corruption? In one paragraph on the topic, include three facts (A, B, and C) that illustrate it.

# IV. End of Reconstruction

Northern and Republican control of state governments in the South began to weaken in 1869. In that year Tennessee became the first Southern state after the war to elect a government dominated by Democrats. One by one, other Southern states also elected Democratic majorities. By 1877 there were no more Reconstruction governments.

## A. REASONS FOR THE CHANGE

Why did Northern Republicans allow Southern Democrats to regain political control of the South?

**Change in Public Opinion**  As time passed, many Northern whites grew tired of the Reconstruction issue. They became less concerned about protecting the rights of African Americans and more interested in private pursuits. By 1875 the Civil War lay 10 years in the past. Many people wanted to put the war behind them by withdrawing troops from the South.

**Amnesty Act**  As public opinion shifted, the Radical Republicans lost their grip on Congress. Toward the end of Grant's first term, a

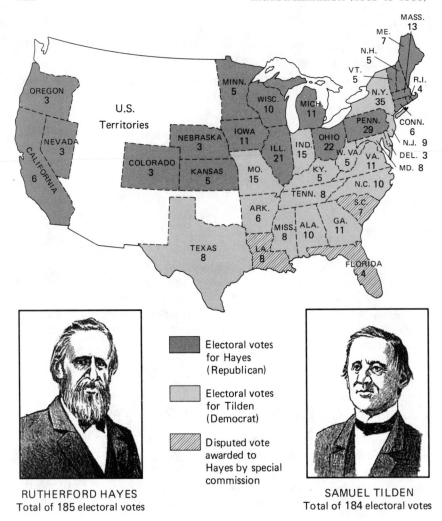

RUTHERFORD HAYES
Total of 185 electoral votes

Electoral votes
for Hayes
(Republican)

Electoral votes
for Tilden
(Democrat)

Disputed vote
awarded to
Hayes by special
commission

SAMUEL TILDEN
Total of 184 electoral votes

**The election of 1876**

more moderate Congress enacted the Amnesty Act (1872), which restored voting rights to about 160,000 former Confederates.

**Increase in Terrorist Pressure**   Secret societies like the Ku Klux Klan increased in number and strength. Despite the Force Acts federal troops had little success capturing and bringing to justice those responsible for the KKK's beatings and lynchings. Though some blacks took up arms in defense of their homes and families, they were eventually forced to submit to white pressure. In time, it became clear that the federal government either could not or would not enforce its own civil rights laws. Rather than jeopardize their lives, many Southern blacks stopped going to the polls to vote.

## B. ELECTION OF 1876

Finally Republicans ended Reconstruction in order to win an extremely close presidential election.

**Disputed Election Results in Three States**  In the election year 1876 federal troops occupied just three Southern states: South Carolina, Florida, and Louisiana. In all other states of the South, the troops had left and the Democrats had returned to power. In these Southern states without troops, the Democratic candidate for president, Samuel Tilden of New York, won every electoral vote. Only in the three states with federal troops was the Republican candidate, Rutherford Hayes, able to claim a victory. But Tilden also claimed victory in these states, pointing to a set of Democratic voting returns that contradicted the Republican returns. A special commission was called to investigate whether the election had been won by Hayes or Tilden. Since Republicans on the commission outnumbered Democrats, the decision went for Hayes—declared the winner by just *one* electoral vote. So angry were the Southern Democrats at this point that some talked of taking up arms and fighting another civil war if necessary.

**Compromise of 1877**  The political crisis was solved by compromise. Meeting in secret, Republican leaders and Democratic leaders agreed that Hayes (Republican) would be the next president. In exchange, Hayes would immediately order the last federal troops to leave the South. By withdrawing these troops Republicans were in effect abandoning Southern blacks to rule by the white majority. Northern commitment to Reconstruction was over.

# V. The South After Reconstruction

The South that emerged from the Civil War and Reconstruction was profoundly different from the antebellum (prewar) South. In all areas of Southern life, institutions arose that endured for generations.

## A. POLITICAL CHANGES

After Reconstruction ended, the Republican party almost ceased to exist in several Southern states.

**The Solid South**  Southern whites generally blamed the Republican party for the hardships they suffered from war and Reconstruction. After Reconstruction they made sure that the Democratic party in their region would be strong enough to win every state and local election. In a short time the South became virtually a one-party region. It was the "**Solid South**" (solid for the Democratic party).

From 1880 to 1924 Democratic candidates for president won *all* the electoral votes of the Southern states.

**National Supremacy** Because of their defeat in the war, Southerners reluctantly conceded that the national government and the U.S. Constitution were supreme. Never again would a Southern state threaten to secede from the Union. (Even so, Southern states continued to champion the idea of states' rights.)

**Disenfranchisement of African Americans** To **disenfranchise** is to take voting rights away from a person or group. Confederate officers had been briefly disenfranchised by the Fourteenth Amendment. After Reconstruction the South disenfranchised black citizens in order to ensure the control of the Democratic party. Each Southern state passed a number of laws that made it either difficult or impossible for African Americans to vote. (See the following chart.)

### Methods Used to Disenfranchise

| Method | Voting Law | How the Law Discriminated Against African Americans |
| --- | --- | --- |
| 1. Literacy test | Voters must take a test demonstrating an ability to read and write. | Slaves had not been taught the skills of literacy. State examiners could deliberately pass whites and fail blacks. |
| 2. Poll tax | Citizens must pay a tax to the state before being allowed to vote. | Most blacks were poorer than most whites and could not afford to pay the tax. |
| 3. "Grandfather clause" | A person whose grandfather had voted before 1867 could vote without having to pass a literacy test. | Only whites had grandfathers who voted before 1867. |

## B. ECONOMIC CHANGES

What was to replace the great cotton plantations and the slavery system of the prewar period? Who was to plant and harvest the crops? Who was to own and manage the land? During and after Reconstruction, the economic system that developed in the South gave whites ownership of most of the land, while blacks worked the land as tenants and sharecroppers.

## OBSERVERS OF AMERICAN LIFE: TESTIMONY OF A CONGRESSMAN

Born a slave in 1847, John R. Lynch of Mississippi enrolled in a school as soon as federal troops freed his family. He won election to the reconstructed legislature of Mississippi and went to Washington in 1872 as a member of the U.S. House of Representatives. This account of his experience with racial prejudice was printed in the *Congressional Record.*

John R. Lynch

... Think of it for a moment; here am I, a member of your honorable body, representing one of the largest and wealthiest districts in the State of Mississippi, and possibly in the South; a district composed of persons of different races, religions, and nationalities; and yet, when I leave my home to come to the capital of the nation, to take part in the deliberations of the House and to participate with you in making laws for the government of this great Republic, ... I am treated, not as an American citizen, but as a brute. Forced to occupy a filthy smoking-car both night and day, with drunkards, gamblers, and criminals; and for what? Not that I am unable or unwilling to pay my way; not that I am obnoxious in my personal appearance or disrespectful in my conduct; but simply because I happen to be of a darker complexion. If this treatment was confined to persons of our own sex we could possibly afford to endure it. But such is not the case. Our wives and our daughters, our sisters and our mothers are subjected to the same insults and to the same uncivilized treatment.... The only moments of my life when I am necessarily compelled to question my loyalty to my Government or my devotion to the flag of my country is when I read of outrages having been committed upon innocent colored people and ... when I leave my home to go travelling.

**Farm Owners** After the destruction of wartime, only a few plantation owners could afford to keep their huge properties intact. Other planters divided their estates into small sections, which they sold as farms. Most of the land went to white buyers, although a small number of blacks also managed to become landowning farmers.

**Tenant Farmers**  Instead of selling the land, plantation owners often rented sections of it to tenants. In order to live and work on the land, **tenant farmers** provided their own seed, mules, and provisions.

**Sharecroppers**  The poorest Southerners (whites as well as blacks) lacked the money either to pay rents or to buy mules for plowing. In return for farming a piece of land, they paid a certain share of the crop to the landlord. **Sharecroppers**, as they were called, were often unable to pay their debts for many reasons—worn-out land, low prices for their cotton, and relatively high prices for farm supplies. Thus many African Americans were still economically in bondage (even though, legally, they were free from slavery).

## C. SOCIAL CHANGES

Both in the North and the South, many whites tended to regard blacks as their social inferiors. In some cities in both regions, they expressed their racial prejudice by forbidding blacks to mix with whites in public places (railroad cars, streetcars, restaurants, and hotels). Laws that segregated, or separated, the races in this way were known as **Jim Crow laws**.

**The Civil Rights Act of 1875**  During Reconstruction, Congress passed a civil rights act that prohibited owners of railroads, restaurants, and other public places from discriminating against African-American customers. For a few years the law was generally obeyed.

**The Spread of Jim Crow Laws**  Beginning in 1881, however, one Southern state after another adopted Jim Crow laws, which required the **segregation** (or racial separation) of public facilities. By the 1890s segregation was the rule everywhere in the South. African Americans were strictly prohibited from entering public places that had been reserved "for whites only."

## D. SUPREME COURT CASES ON SEGREGATION

Black citizens went to court to challenge the constitutionality of the Jim Crow laws. They argued that such laws violated the Fourteenth Amendment's clause guaranteeing equal protection of the laws. But the Supreme Court ruled otherwise.

**Civil Rights Cases (1883)**  In a series of cases, the Supreme Court concluded that Jim Crow practices in the South were allowed by the Constitution. It said that individual property owners had the right to keep out customers if they wished. The Fourteenth Amendment, said

**Causes and Effects**
Reconstruction and Post-Reconstruction in the South

| Cause | Effect |
|---|---|
| Lincoln is assassinated (1865) | Johnson, a less able president, takes office |
| "Black Codes" adopted by Southern conventions (1865) | Radical Republicans reject Johnson's plan of Reconstruction |
| Adoption of the Thirteenth Amendment (1865) | End of slavery in the United States |
| Conflict between Radical Republicans in Congress and the president | Impeachment of President Johnson (1868) |
| Presence of federal troops in the South | Southern blacks able to vote and hold office |
| Republican ambition to win the disputed election of 1876 | Withdrawal of last federal troops in the South |
| Southern whites regain full political control of their states | Many Southern blacks prevented from voting; racial segregation established through Jim Crow laws |
| Supreme Court's decision in *Plessy v. Ferguson* (1896) | Continuation for many decades of racial segregation in the South |

the Court, applied only to the actions of government officials, not to those of private citizens.

***Plessy v. Ferguson* (1896)** A black citizen of Louisiana, Homer Plessy, sued a railroad company for preventing him from entering a railroad car set aside for whites. Once again, in a landmark decision, the Supreme Court ruled in favor of the property owner and against the African-American petitioner. Because the railroad provided **"separate but equal"** facilities for blacks, the Court decided that the equal protection clause of the Constitution had not been violated. One justice, John Harlan, disagreed. In a dissenting opinion Justice Harlan argued that segregation threatened personal liberty and equality of rights. But for many years the majority on the Court used the standard of "separate but equal" to justify racial segregation.

## E. RESPONSE TO SEGREGATION

For a time African Americans were forced to obey the Jim Crow laws as an unpleasant reality of Southern life. Between 1890 and 1910 two leaders arose who took opposite positions on segregation.

**Booker T. Washington's Arguments**   One of those freed from slavery in 1865 was a nine-year old boy named Booker T. Washington. As a young man, in 1881, Washington founded the Tuskegee Institute in Alabama, a school dedicated to giving industrial and vocational training to African Americans. Washington took the position that blacks should not seek to be accepted into white society. A more realistic and important goal, he said, was to win economic opportunity by filling skilled, high-paying jobs. In a famous speech delivered in Atlanta in 1895, Washington said, "In all things that are purely social we can be separate as the fingers, yet one as the hand in all things essential to mutual progress."

**W. E. B. Du Bois's Arguments**   A younger man than Washington, W. E. B. Du Bois grew up in Massachusetts, where he excelled as a scholar, earning a Ph. D. degree from Harvard University. In a book published in 1903, *The Souls of Black Folk*, Du Bois challenged Washington's views on segregation. He agreed that vocational education for blacks was one important avenue of economic opportunity. On the other hand, he strongly disagreed with the idea that economic gains were any more important than civil rights. He urged African Americans to insist on their rights and to oppose the Jim Crow laws with all their strength.

## *In Review*

The following questions refer to section IV: The End of Reconstruction and section V: The South After Reconstruction.

1. Explain the significance of (a) the election of 1876, (b) the literacy test, and (c) *Plessy v. Ferguson*.
2. Summarize the factors that resulted in the end of Reconstruction.
3. Compare Southern society in 1890 with that of 1860.

## GLOSSARY OF KEY TERMS: CHAPTER 5

**"Black Codes"**   measures adopted by Southern whites in 1865 to restrict the freedom of blacks.

**"carpetbagger"**   Southern whites' name for a Northerner who came to the South during Reconstruction to exploit the region for personal gain.

**corruption**   any attempt by public officials to participate in illegal money-making schemes.

**Crédit Mobilier affair** a political scandal of the Grant era in which U.S. congressmen were bribed not to investigate the illegal practices of a railroad construction company.

**disenfranchisement** taking away the right to vote from those who already have it.

**forty acres and a mule** a plan proposed (but not adopted) by which the U.S. government would give forty acres of farm land and a mule to every freed slave.

**Freedmen's Bureau** a government agency during Reconstruction that provided schools, medical aid, and other services for people freed from slavery.

**"grandfather clause"** a law favoring white voters in the South by exempting them from taking a literacy test.

**Jim Crow laws** state and local laws that discriminated against African Americans by denying them access to "white-only" railroad cars, streetcars, restaurants, and other public facilities.

**Ku Klux Klan** one of the secret societies formed by Southern whites to intimidate and terrorize black voters.

**literacy test** a state voting requirement that a voter demonstrate an ability to read and write.

***Plessy v. Ferguson*** a Supreme Court case (1896) that approved the practice of segregating public facilities providing only that they be "separate but equal."

**poll tax** a state tax collected from voters at each election (such a tax is now prohibited by the Twenty-fourth Amendment).

**Radical Republicans** a group of Republicans in Congress who favored a plan of Reconstruction that was harsh to Southern whites but helpful to Southern blacks.

**Reconstruction** the postwar period from 1865 to 1877 when Southern states were occupied by federal troops and controlled by Northern politicians.

**"scalawag"** name commonly given to any Southern white who cooperated with the Republican plan of Reconstruction.

**segregation** the practice of separating people on the basis of race.

**separate but equal** the idea endorsed by the Supreme Court in the *Plessy* case that public facilities set aside for blacks could be separate provided that they were also equal to the facilities for white use.

**sharecropper** a farmer who owes a landlord a portion, or share, of each year's crop to pay for the use of the land.

**"Solid South"** the political allegiance of the white majority in the South to the Democratic party.

**"waving the bloody shirt"** the campaign technique of appealing to voters' hatred of the wartime enemy.

# TEST YOURSELF

## A. Multiple Choice: Facts, Main Ideas, Skills

*On a separate sheet of paper, write the number of the word or expression that, of those given, best completes the statement or answers the question.*

### Reviewing the facts

1. In his Second Inaugural Address (1865), Lincoln spoke of "malice toward none" and "charity for all," thereby indicating his desire to (1) punish the South severely (2) treat the South like conquered territory (3) provide for a quick readmission of Southern states into the Union (4) guarantee equal rights for former slaves

2. Which statement accurately compares Andrew Johnson's Reconstruction plan with that of the Radical Republicans? (1) Both plans aimed to punish Southern whites severely. (2) Johnson's plan was more lenient than that of the Radical Republicans. (3) Radical Republicans wanted to provide aid to Southern whites, while Johnson wanted to provide aid to Southern blacks. (4) Both plans welcomed the secessionist states back into the Union with few conditions.

3. The Fourteenth Amendment is important because, in addition to awarding citizenship to former slaves, it (1) guarantees women the right to vote (2) abolishes the poll tax (3) guarantees equal protection of the laws (4) provides protection against illegal searches and seizures of property

4. Reconstruction ended when Democrats agreed to the election of Rutherford Hayes, and Republicans promised to (1) withdraw federal troops from the South (2) give each freedman forty acres and a mule (3) do away with the electoral college (4) repeal the Fifteenth Amendment

5. Reconstruction emphasized each of the following *except*: (1) protecting the voting rights of former slaves (2) protecting the right of former slaves to run for and serve in elective office (3) providing land for former slaves in order that they might better earn a living (4) disenfranchising former leaders of the Confederacy.

6. During Reconstruction, African-American voters in the South generally (1) voted for Republican candidates (2) voted for Democratic candidates (3) showed no preference for either Republicans or Democrats (4) refused to participate in elections

7. Corruption in government is most often associated with the administration of (1) Abraham Lincoln (2) Andrew Johnson (3) Ulysses Grant (4) Rutherford Hayes

8. The purpose of Jim Crow laws was to (1) give full civil rights to African Americans (2) keep African Americans in a separate and inferior position (3) give economic incentives for business growth (4) provide equal opportunities for all citizens

9. In *Plessy* v. *Ferguson* the Supreme Court argued that (1) states could pass laws separating people on the basis of race as long as equal facilities were provided (2) segregation on the basis of race was unconstitutional (3) the Fourteenth Amendment outlawed practices that emphasized racial distinctions (4) separate but equal laws would create separate but unequal facilities

## Reviewing the main ideas

10. A major feature of Reconstruction was that (1) new federal laws and constitutional amendments attempted to ensure equal rights and opportunities for African Americans (2) the South rapidly developed into the nation's major industrial center (3) a spirit of cooperation existed between the president and Congress (4) new state governments in the South concentrated on ending corruption

11. Which was a significant characteristic of U.S. politics in the years immediately following the Civil War? (1) abolition of the spoils system (2) greater presidential concern for foreign affairs than for domestic affairs (3) disappearance of third-party movements (4) domination of national politics by the Republican party

12. Which was a major result of the Civil War? (1) Disputes between the North and the South were ended. (2) Whites accepted blacks as social equals. (3) Slavery was ended through the passage of an amendment to the Constitution. (4) The South returned to the way it was before the war.

13. Which statement provides the best evidence that the United States has become more democratic since the Civil War? (1) The United States has become one of the world's greatest powers. (2) The United States today has one of the highest standards of living in the world. (3) Laws have been passed to provide assistance to the poor. (4) Constitutional amendments have been adopted to guarantee the rights of all citizens.

*Assume that the following discussion took place just after the Civil War. Base your answers to questions 14 through 16 on this discussion.*

*Speaker A:* "The Emancipation Proclamation has already declared slaves to be free. We don't need constitutional amendments to guarantee rights already won by the war."

*Speaker B:* "The proposed amendments will not ensure the rights of blacks in the South. After whites regain control of their state governments, they will find ways to ignore the amendments and deprive blacks of their rights."

*Speaker C:* "As a member of the Republican party, I want to see these amendments adopted to ensure the voting strength of our party in the South."

*Speaker D:* "These amendments must be passed in order to guarantee equal rights for all Americans."

**14.** Two of the constitutional amendments under discussion are the (1) First and Fourth (2) Fifth and Tenth (3) Thirteenth and Fifteenth (4) Twenty-first and Twenty-third

**15.** Speaker C assumed that the Republican party could count on the votes of (1) former slaves (2) Western farmers (3) urban factory workers (4) former Confederate soldiers

**16.** Which speaker describes most clearly the political situation that actually occurred in the 1880s and 1890s? (1) A (2) B (3) C (4) D

**17.** The basic constitutional issue resolved by the Civil War was the (1) expansion of the president's war powers (2) extension of the right to vote to all adults (3) supremacy of federal authority over the states (4) civil liberties of citizens during wartime

**18.** Which provided the legal basis for racial segregation in the late nineteenth century? (1) Supreme Court decisions that excluded African Americans from voting (2) adoption of laws by the U.S. Congress (3) passage of Jim Crow laws by Southern legislatures (4) laws in Northern states that prevented African Americans from working in factories

**19.** The major purpose of state laws that established literacy tests, the poll tax, and the "grandfather clause" was to (1) increase educational opportunities for former slaves (2) create separate school systems for blacks and whites (3) deny voting rights to former slaves and their descendants (4) discourage blacks from voting

## Developing critical thinking skills

*Base your answers to questions 20 through 22 on the table below and on your knowledge of U.S. history and government.*

### Cotton and Tobacco Production in the South

|  | Cotton (millions of pounds) | Tobacco (millions of pounds) |
|---|---|---|
| Output during 1859 | 2,373 | 204 |
| Average yearly output, 1866 to 1870 | 1,213 | 89 |
| Average yearly output, 1876 to 1880 | 2,375 | 133 |

**20.** Which years in the table correspond with years of Reconstruction? (1) 1859 (2) 1866 to 1870 (3) 1876 to 1880 (4) none of the above

**21.** Just before the Civil War, cotton production was   (1) much greater than in the postwar years to 1870   (2) much less than in the postwar years to 1870   (3) about the same as in the postwar years to 1880   (4) less than the average output of tobacco in the 1870s

**22.** Which statement is *not* correct for the years given?   (1) In every year cotton production exceeded tobacco production.   (2) The production of both cotton and tobacco was greater in 1880 than in 1859.   (3) After Reconstruction the production of both cotton and tobacco increased significantly.   (4) Cotton production in 1880 was above the prewar level in 1859.

## B. Enduring Issues

*Select* one *enduring issue from column A and* one *example of that issue from column B. Write* two *paragraphs explaining how the selected example illustrates the selected issue.*

| A. Enduring Issues | B. Historic Examples |
|---|---|
| 1. National power, limits and potential | Conflict between President Johnson and Congress |
| 2. Federalism, the balance between nation and state | Adoption of the Thirteenth, Fourteenth, and Fifteenth Amendments |
| 3. Civil liberties, the balance between government and the individual | Supreme Court's decision in *Plessy v. Ferguson* |
| 4. Rights of ethnic and racial groups under the U.S. Constitution | Northern control of Southern legislatures during Reconstruction |
| 5. Equality, its definition as a constitutional value | Resistance of Southern whites to federal laws and amendments |

## C. Essays

*Level 1*

Throughout U.S. history, the federal government has pursued diverse goals. Listed below are some of its goals:

- To guarantee liberty and freedom to all citizens
- To protect the rights of minorities
- To meet the changing needs of society
- To encourage greater participation in the political process.

Select *two* of the goals listed. For *each* goal chosen, discuss a specific action that demonstrates how the U.S. government sought to achieve that goal during the era of Reconstruction.

*Level 2*

African Americans were greatly affected by events from 1865 to 1900.

**A.** 1. List *two* actions, policies, or laws that helped African Americans during this period.

   2. List *two* actions, policies, or laws that hurt African Americans during this period.

**B.** Base your answer to part B on your answer to part A. Evaluate whether African Americans were more helped or more harmed by events from 1865 to 1900.

*Chapter* **6**

# The Rise of American Business, Labor, and Agriculture

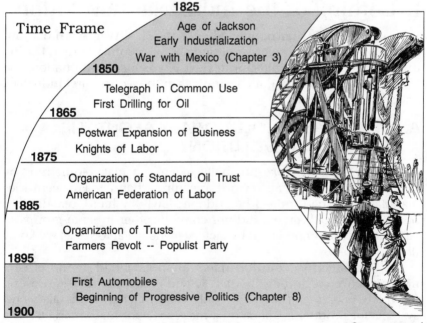

| Time Frame | |
|---|---|
| **1825** | |
| | Age of Jackson |
| | Early Industrialization |
| | War with Mexico (Chapter 3) |
| **1850** | |
| | Telegraph in Common Use |
| | First Drilling for Oil |
| **1865** | |
| | Postwar Expansion of Business |
| | Knights of Labor |
| **1875** | |
| | Organization of Standard Oil Trust |
| | American Federation of Labor |
| **1885** | |
| | Organization of Trusts |
| | Farmers Revolt -- Populist Party |
| **1895** | |
| | First Automobiles |
| | Beginning of Progressive Politics (Chapter 8) |
| **1900** | |

*Steam-powered
Corliss Engine, 1876*

## *Objectives*

- To understand how industrialization in the United States was part of a worldwide economic revolution.
- To know the ways in which American business changed from 1865 to 1900.
- To understand the response of the federal government to industrialization and business growth.
- To recognize the struggle of labor and labor organizations to achieve improved working conditions.
- To explain the causes of farmers' discontent and evaluate their political program.

In the last chapter we saw the dramatic changes in Southern society brought about by the Civil War. In this chapter we shall see the even more sweeping and lasting changes in the American economy brought about by the Industrial Revolution. What was this revolution, and how did the United States jump to a position of economic leadership in the world in the three dynamic decades following the Civil War?

# I. Coming of the Industrial Revolution

To understand what happened after the Civil War, we must first go back in time to the colonial period about a century earlier. During the 1700s, before the United States existed as a separate nation, the Industrial Revolution had its beginnings in the world's first industrial nation, Great Britain.

## A. WHAT WAS REVOLUTIONARY ABOUT THE INDUSTRIAL REVOLUTION?

The word *manufacture* originally meant "to make something by hand" (*manu-* is a Latin word meaning "hand"). For centuries manufacturing had indeed been done slowly by hand, usually in a home workshop. Workers did *not* come together in large groups to labor at machinery provided by factory owners. Factories as we know them did not exist.

The **Industrial Revolution** refers to an extended period of economic change (beginning about 1750 and continuing to the present) in which people invented not only new machines but also new systems for producing goods on a mass scale for mass markets. As a result of this revolution, manufacturing is now carried out in large factories, not in home workshops. The change in methods for producing goods revolutionized all aspects of life, including how we think about the world.

# B. GLOBAL CONTEXT: FROM GREAT BRITAIN TO THE UNITED STATES TO JAPAN

In the first hundred years of the Industrial Revolution, new methods of production were invented by the British and adopted by others, including the Americans and the Japanese.

**Beginnings in Great Britain**  The making of cotton cloth, or textiles, was the first industry to be revolutionized by machinery and methods of mass production. Several British inventors created machines for producing cotton thread. In 1785 a power loom was invented for rapidly weaving thread into cloth. The power for the mechanized loom was supplied by another invention—the steam engine (invented by James Watt in 1765).

Because each yard of machine-made cloth could be made at less cost than a yard of handmade cloth, it could be sold cheaply not only in Great Britain but throughout the world. Enterprising business persons could hope to make huge profits. But first they had to invest large sums of money for purchasing textile machines, building factories to house the machines, and paying workers to operate the machines.

**Rapid Development in the United States**  Americans were quick to adopt the revolutionary methods of the British industrialists. Recall from Chapter 3 that merchants of the Northeast were eager to compete with the British and sell inexpensive American textiles both at home and abroad. Recall too that Washington's secretary of the treasury, Alexander Hamilton, devised government programs that encouraged the development of American industries. His ideas for a U.S. bank and high tariffs were generally supported in the industrializing North, but they were opposed in the agrarian (farming) South.

**U.S. Advantages in the Race to Industrialize**  More than any nation on earth, the United States was richly endowed with the three resources needed for rapid industrial growth. Economists call these three types of resources: land (raw materials), labor (human energy and skill), and **capital** (tools, machinery, and money for investment). The diagram on page 160 identifies the specific factors that gave the United States an economic advantage in all three areas.

**The Critical Importance of Capital**  A **capitalist system** is one in which capital goods—tools, machinery, and factories—are privately owned and managed by competing businesses. Consider these advantages of the U.S. economy, in terms of capital alone:

- *A strong tradition of business enterprise.*  Even in colonial times merchants of Boston, New York, and Philadelphia had long been accustomed to risking capital in hopes of making a profit. The

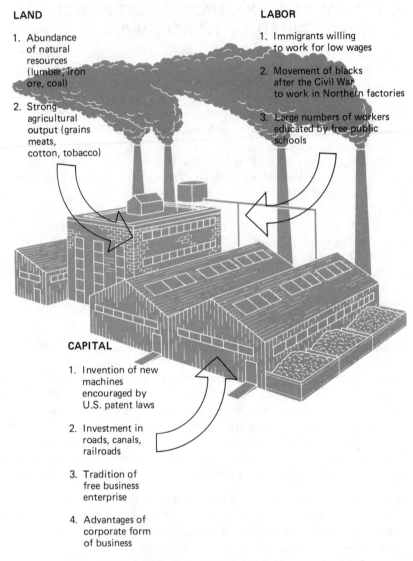

**LAND**

1. Abundance of natural resources (lumber, iron ore, coal)

2. Strong agricultural output (grains meats, cotton, tobacco)

**LABOR**

1. Immigrants willing to work for low wages

2. Movement of blacks after the Civil War to work in Northern factories

3. Large numbers of workers educated by free public schools

**CAPITAL**

1. Invention of new machines encouraged by U.S. patent laws

2. Investment in roads, canals, railroads

3. Tradition of free business enterprise

4. Advantages of corporate form of business

The basis of U.S. industrial expansion: land, labor, and capital

profits they earned from their business successes enabled U.S. banks to finance costly new ventures for the new industrial age.

- *Patent laws to encourage invention.* The U.S. Constitution gives to Congress the power to "promote the progress of science and useful arts" by issuing **patents** to inventors. A patent is a government document giving to the creator of an original object the exclusive right to make and sell that object for profit. Thousands of Americans recognized that a good idea for a useful gadget or machine could make their fortune. Of course not all of the would-be inventors succeeded. But those that did not only enriched themselves but also contributed to the Industrial Revolution.

- *Corporate form of business organization.* Another encouragement to business owners were state laws that enabled them to form **corporations**. A corporation is a business chartered, or formed, under state law. To raise capital, a corporation may sell shares of ownership—or stock—to the public. Anyone buying stock in a corporation was subject to lose no more than the sum originally invested in the stock. If the corporation could not pay its debts and went bankrupt, its stockholders (owners) were not personally liable, or responsible, for paying its debts. In other words, they could keep their houses and other personal property instead of losing everything to pay business debts. (Owners of other forms of businesses—proprietorships and partnerships—did in fact risk all that they owned.)

- *Investment in transportation.* Another advantage of the corporate form of business was the amount of investment money that corporations could raise for ambitious industrial projects such as building a railroad or digging a canal. Railroad companies and canal companies sold their stock to the public to capitalize, or finance, the building of these costly enterprises. People who bought stock in a railroad had faith in its money-making potential. They recognized that railroads and the rapid hauling of freight over long distances were the key to the industrial future.

## C. JAPAN'S DECISION TO INDUSTRIALIZE

By the time of the Civil War, the Industrial Revolution was more than 100 years old in Great Britain, about 70 years old in the United States, but had not yet begun in any country of Asia. In 1867 (two years after the Civil War) the situation in Asia changed almost overnight. The Japanese officials who came to power in that year decided that their country could compete with the British and the Americans only by mastering the new industrial methods. In a short time Japanese factories were producing impressive quantities of textiles, steel, machinery, and ships. The Industrial Revolution was now global in scope.

# II. Growth of American Industry After the Civil War

Northern industry made great strides in the 1850s, the decade just before the Civil War. By 1860 the nation's cities were linked by more than 30,000 miles of railroad track (three times the mileage of 1850). Every year the production of pig iron (crudely cast iron) set new records. Invention of the telegraph by Samuel F. B. Morse in 1844 speeded business communications.

The Civil War accelerated industrial production in the North but had a devastating effect on factories in the South. After the war Northern manufacturing firms broke all records for output, invention, and business growth. Some historians argue that the postwar business boom would have happened even if there had been no war. Others argue that the war acted as a major stimulant for business investment. But nobody questions that a postwar boom did in fact occur and that it changed the nation.

## A. RAILROADS ACROSS THE CONTINENT

A great achievement of Northern industry after the Civil War was the building of a transcontinental railroad across the vast Western plains to the Pacific coast. Though undertaken by two private railroad companies, the project had a lot of help from the federal government.

**Land Grants** The route of the proposed railroad passed over almost totally unsettled territory. To encourage railroad companies to risk their money on the colossal venture, the Republican majority in Congress voted to grant huge sections of land to the railroads all along the route. As shown on the map, sections of land were arranged

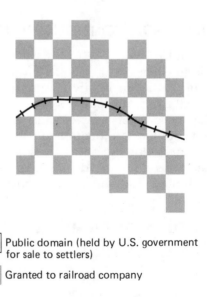

☐ Public domain (held by U.S. government for sale to settlers)

▨ Granted to railroad company

Checkerboard pattern of land grants to Western railroads

in a checkerboard pattern, half the land squares going to the railroad companies, half to be kept by the government for sale to would-be settlers.

**The Race to Lay Track**   Starting from Sacramento, California, crews hired by the Central Pacific Railroad cut tunnels through the Sierra Nevada, a great Western mountain range. Heading in the opposite direction from Omaha, Nebraska, crews of the Union Pacific Railroad fought off Indian attacks on the Great Plains and then blasted tunnels through mountain passes in the towering Rockies. After three years of work, the rival crews came together in 1869 in Promontory, Utah, where they hammered the last spike—a spike of solid gold.

**The Immigrant Contribution**   The grueling labor of building the first transcontinental railroad was undertaken by two groups of immigrants. The Central Pacific crew consisted of 10,000 men from China who were specially recruited for the task by agents of the railroad company. Many lost their lives in the dangerous work of building bridges and dynamiting tunnels. Another 10,000 men from Ireland, working for the Union Pacific, performed the feat of laying as much as four miles of track a day.

**Other Railroads**   After the completion of the first transcontinental railroad, other Western railroads followed in rapid succession. Between 1865 and 1900 railroad tracks in the United States went from 35,000 miles to 260,000 miles—an incredible eightfold increase in just 35 years. By the end of the century, the United States was tied together by many more miles of railroad track than existed in all of Europe (including Russia).

## B. NEW INDUSTRIES: STEEL

Another industry that boomed in the post-Civil War years was the manufacture of steel. Before the war the chief metal of the Industrial Revolution had been iron. It was known for a long time that steel was stronger and more durable than iron. But the process for making it was slow and costly. All this changed in 1856 when a British industrialist, Henry Bessemer, invented a process for blowing cold air through molten iron, thereby producing steel that had no impurities. The **Bessemer process** for making steel was adopted by an American industrialist, Andrew Carnegie, in 1867. Soon the United States led the world in steel production, with an output in 1901 of 13.5 million tons.

## C. NEW INDUSTRIES: OIL

Before the Civil War small lamps that burned either whale oil or vegetable oil were the chief means of lighting homes. In the 1850s it was discovered that kerosene made from petroleum was a relatively clean fuel for home lighting. But where was petroleum to be found in quantity? The answer came in 1859 when Edwin Drake dug a deep well in Titusville, Pennsylvania, and underground oil gushed to the surface. The digging of oil wells and the processing of oil to yield kerosene became a big business in the United States, particularly when a Cleveland businessman, John D. Rockefeller, entered the field (see page 166).

## D. NEW INDUSTRIES: CONSUMER GOODS

Recognizing that goods could be shipped by rail all over the country, inventors and business leaders began to create products that could be sold nationwide (rather than selling mainly to local customers, as in the past).

**Edison's Invention Factory**   One creative genius who changed American life with his ideas was the "Wizard of Menlo Park," Thomas Edison. Menlo Park in New Jersey was the site of Edison's most famous invention: a lightbulb whose bamboo filament glowed brightly when an electric current passed through it. Edison hired a team of scientists and engineers to assist him in his search for new products. Even more important than his hundreds of individual inventions (including the phonograph and the motion picture camera) was Edison's system for bringing talented people together to work jointly on a research project. His invention factory of the 1870s and 1880s is the direct forerunner of modern industrial laboratories.

**Department Stores for Urban Consumers**   Until the 1860s small specialty stores in the cities catered to the rich. Middle-class consumers felt out of place in such shops. But they delighted in wandering from department to department of a large New York City store erected by A. T. Stewart in 1862. This department store, as it was called, was widely imitated in other major cities. For the first time, shopping for consumer goods became a popular pastime for large numbers of urban Americans.

**Mail-Order Catalogs for Rural Consumers**   Most potential buyers of consumer goods lived on farms far from any city store. To reach these millions of rural Americans, a clever Chicago businessman, Montgomery Ward, mailed catalogs picturing his merchandise and invited people to mail back their orders for advertised items. The first catalogs were mailed in 1871 and drew orders from far and wide. Two other Chicagoans, Richard Sears and Alvah Roebuck, also built a hugely successful business in the 1890s mailing out catalogs even more enticing than Ward's and filling orders for everything from mousetraps to pianos.

### Changes in Business and Industry

|  | Age of Jackson (1825 to 1845) | Mid-Century (1845 to 1865) | After the Civil War (1865 to 1900) |
|---|---|---|---|
| Organization of business and advances in manufacturing | Growth of textile mills<br><br>Increased number of corporations | Isaac Singer's plant for making sewing machines, 1853<br><br>Bessemer process for making steel, 1856 | Standard Oil Trust organized, 1882<br><br>Trend toward bigger, consolidated business firms |
| Inventions in transportation and communication | Peter Cooper's first locomotive, 1830<br><br>Samuel F. B. Morse's telegraph, 1844 | Laying of transatlantic cable, New York to London, 1859 to 1865<br><br>First oil pipeline, 1865 | Cable streetcar in use in San Francisco, 1873<br><br>Alexander Graham Bell's telephone, 1876<br><br>Thomas Edison's phonograph, 1878 |
| Inventions in agriculture | John Deere's steel plow, 1837<br><br>Cyrus McCormick's reaper, 1831 | Introduction of grain elevators, 1850s<br><br>Mowing, threshing, and haying machines, 1850s | Giant combine harvester and thresher, 1880s<br><br>Corn-shucking machine, 1890s |

## E. ELECTRICITY AND THE REVOLUTION IN COMMUNICATIONS

In the new industrial age, using electricity to send messages greatly speeded up communications between businesses. Already connecting American cities before the Civil War were thousands of miles of telegraph wires. After the war the invention of the telephone (1874 to 1876) by a Scottish immigrant, Alexander Graham Bell, gave people the remarkable ability to talk with each other over long distances. By 1900 about 1.3 million telephones were in use in American homes and businesses.

# F. "CAPTAINS OF INDUSTRY" OR "ROBBER BARONS"?

Business growth after the Civil War owed much to the leadership of men who rose to the top of their industries. Among them were Cornelius Vanderbilt (railroads), Andrew Carnegie (steel), and John D. Rockefeller (oil). Admirers called them "**captains of industry**." Critics called them "**robber barons**."

**Andrew Carnegie**   Born in Scotland, Andrew Carnegie was one of thousands of immigrants who came to the United States in the 1840s with much hope but no money. As a teenager he worked in a cotton mill 12 hours a day, six days a week, for only 20 cents a day. His good fortune and unusual ability won him a job working directly for the president of the Pennsylvania Railroad. In a short time he was a millionnaire having invested wisely in railroad sleeping cars, iron mills, and finally steel.

As the hard-driving owner of his own steel company in the 1870s, Carnegie paid his workers low wages, drove hard bargains with railroad companies on their prices for shipping steel, and did all in his power to bankrupt competitors. In 1901 Carnegie sold his huge steel company to a group of bankers led by J. P. Morgan for nearly 500 million dollars. From a humble beginning as a 20-cents-a-day laborer, Carnegie had risen to become one of the world's richest and most successful men.

**John D. Rockefeller**   A native of Cleveland, Ohio, John D. Rockefeller invested his savings in an oil-refining company in 1865. Oil refining was then a fiercely competitive industry, and the chances of business failure seemed much greater than the chances of success. To ensure the survival of his own company, Rockefeller aimed to take control of the entire industry and drive all competitors out of business. He nearly succeeded. In 1870 when Rockefeller organized the Standard Oil Company, there were 200 competitors. Ten years later, only a few competitors were still in business, and Standard Oil accounted for 90 percent of the oil refined in the United States.

Rockefeller crushed his competitors by using the following tactics:

- He persuaded railroads to give **rebates** to Standard Oil—that is, to return to his company a portion of the railroad's shipping charges. This enabled him to charge the lowest prices for oil until his competitors were forced out of business.

- Whenever a competitor was struggling, Rockefeller moved in with an offer to buy out the firm.

- Instead of paying railroads' freight charges, Rockefeller increased his competitive advantage by shipping oil more cheaply over pipelines built and owned by Standard Oil.

**Critics and Defenders of the Business Leaders**   Carnegie and Rockefeller—as well as other business leaders of their age—did not concern themselves with fairness. Workers received low wages, and strikes were not tolerated. Competitors were put out of business by whatever means a big business chose to employ, including secret agreements with railroads and temporary reductions in prices. These practices lend support to the charge that industrial leaders of the late 1800s were "robber barons."

On the other hand, business leaders like Carnegie and Rockefeller made the industries that they dominated bigger and more productive than any that existed before. To do so, they risked tremendous amounts of money with no guarantee of success. The impressive result of their efforts lends support to those who would call them "captains of industry."

**Theories About the Capitalist System**   Many scholars and writers of the late 1800s supported the business practices of men like Carnegie and Rockefeller. They believed that the remarkable growth of the American economy proved that the capitalist system of free enterprise was working exactly as it should.

- *The theory of laissez-faire.*   According to a Scottish philosopher, Adam Smith, the surest road to economic progress was to allow businesses to compete freely and without legal restriction. Any government attempt to regulate business would only reduce the economic benefits to be gained from competition. Therefore, said Smith, the best government policy was **laissez-faire**—leave businesses alone without laws to restrict or regulate them. Although Adam Smith lived at the time of the American Revolution, his theory had wide influence a century later.

- *The theory of social Darwinism.*   A British biologist, Charles Darwin, advanced the theory that lower forms of life evolved into higher and higher forms as a result of an ongoing struggle for survival. Those who survived the struggle were the "fittest" of the species. A British philosopher, Herbert Spencer, applied Darwin's theory to the competitive world of business. In a theory known as **social Darwinism**, Spencer argued that those businesses that were strongest, fittest, and most efficient would survive. Weaker businesses deserved to fail and die out. Spencer wrote: "The American economy is controlled for the benefit of all by a natural aristocracy, and the leaders of this aristocracy were brought to the top by a competitive struggle that weeded out the weak, incompetent, and unfit and selected the wise and able."

- *The books of Horatio Alger.*   In the post-Civil War era Horatio Alger wrote immensely popular books for children and young adults. His stories all told of poor boys who, by hard work and lucky breaks, rose from rags to riches. The amazing career of Andrew Carnegie made many Americans think that Horatio Alger's success stories actually happened in real life.

### In Review

The following questions refer to section I: Coming of the Industrial Revolution and section II: Growth of American Industry After the Civil War.

1. Define *Industrial Revolution, capital, corporation, "captains of industry," laissez-faire,* and *social Darwinism.*
2. Identify five advantages of the United States in its ability to industrialize.
3. Discuss whether or not Andrew Carnegie deserved to be called a "robber baron."
4. Explain why the building of a transcontinental railroad was important to the industrial growth of the United States.

# III. Big Business and Government Policy

There was one central flaw in the argument for laissez-faire. If Rockefeller and Carnegie had their way, the final result of completely free competition would be no competition at all. Rockefeller's overriding goal, after all, was to eliminate his competitors. If he succeeded, his Standard Oil Company would be the one and only seller of kerosene. It would then be a **monopoly** (the situation in which one producer totally controls an industry). One consequence of monopoly control is the monopolist's ability to charge high prices for its products.

## A. THE TREND TOWARD CONSOLIDATION

In the 1870s and 1880s the trend toward monopoly control was all too clear. In every industry it seemed that businesses were becoming less and less competitive, more and more **consolidated** (joined together). First, let us see how big business firms became bigger. Then we shall see how government responded to the trend.

**Pooling Agreements** Railroad companies at first tried to suppress competition by a method called **pooling**. Railroad lines that once cut their fares in order to attract more business secretly agreed to charge exactly the same high fares. The railroads would also divide the total market for their transportation services, Railroad A serving one territory and Railroad B a different territory. Pooling did not work well, however, because participating companies found it too easy to cheat on their agreement.

**Trusts**   Rockefeller devised an ingenious method for bringing under his control many former competitors. The stock certificates of competing firms were traded for "trust certificates" in a new super-corporation called a **trust**. After competitors were at the brink of ruin, Rockefeller persuaded them to join his Standard Oil Trust, formed in 1882. If they refused, he threatened to drive them out of business. Other leading business firms in other industries were quick to follow Standard Oil's example. Soon, in addition to the oil trust, there was the steel trust, the tobacco trust, the sugar-refining trust, and many more.

**Holding Companies**   In the 1890s business leaders discovered a third method for consolidating. They formed corporations whose one function was to hold the stocks of several firms in the same industry. **Holding companies**, as they were called, held a majority of stocks in each company and thus had the power to dictate a common policy for all.

## B. THE BEGINNING OF FEDERAL REGULATION OF BUSINESS

To some extent state governments regulated businesses that operated within their borders. But until 1887 the federal government generally followed a policy of laissez-faire. Its laws encouraged business growth through tariffs, land grants, and patents. But it did very little to regulate business practices. In the 1880s, however, the voting public became more and more alarmed about companies like Standard Oil using "unfair" methods for eliminating competition. Responding to public pressures, Congress enacted two laws that marked the beginning of business regulation by the U.S. government.

**The Interstate Commerce Act (1887)**   To regulate certain practices of railroad companies, Congress created a commission (an official group with rule-making power). The Interstate Commerce Commission (ICC) was to enforce the following regulations:

- Railroad rates had to be "reasonable and just."
- Pools were illegal.
- Returning rebates to favored customers was illegal.
- Railroads could not charge more for a short haul than for a long haul.

At first the commission's powers were limited, but they were expanded by later amendments to the law.

**Sherman Antitrust Act (1890)**  This act provided that "every contract, combination in the form of a trust or otherwise, or conspiracy, in restraint of trade or commerce . . . is hereby declared to be illegal." The law, however, was poorly and vaguely written. Terms such as *trust, conspiracy,* and *restraint of trade* were not defined. As a result no trusts were successfully prosecuted in the 1890s. Even the sugar trust, which controlled 95 percent of the sugar industry, escaped the law's provisions. Weak as it was, the **Sherman Antitrust Act** established the principle that government should act to break up trusts and other forms of monopoly.

# IV. Organization of Labor

The growth of industry and big business created problems for industrial workers. Overworked and poorly paid, they found that they could do nothing as individuals to persuade corporate giants to treat them better. Therefore, in response to the organization of large corporations, workers organized large labor unions.

This section describes (a) the origins of the labor movement in the early 1800s and (b) the growth of labor unions in the late 1800s.

## A. HOW THE INDUSTRIAL REVOLUTION CHANGED WORKING CONDITIONS

As you know, the Industrial Revolution in the United States was well under way before the Civil War. As early as the 1820s it was clear that the life of a machine operator in a New England textile mill was far different from the life of a skilled craft worker in an old-fashioned home workshop. The chart below summarizes the differences.

**Working Conditions Before and After the Industrial Revolution**

| Before | After |
|---|---|
| Workers owned their own tools. | All tools and machines were owned by the employer. |
| Young workers had a good chance of someday becoming masters of their own workshops. | Young workers had little chance of raising enough capital to own their own factories. |
| Most workers were highly skilled in a craft such as carpentry, shoemaking, and barrel making. | Most factory workers were employed doing routine, unskilled work. |
| The employer and master of the shop worked side by side with other workers. | In a large factory, workers never saw the business owners or even the top managers. |

**Mill Workers**  Most of the wage earners in New England's textile mills were women and children under the age of 12. The mill owners required them to work 12 to 14 hours a day, six days a week. Wages were so low and working conditions so bad that a mill worker's life was compared to that of a slave. Critics of the factory system— especially Southerners—said that factory workers were nothing but "wage slaves." In general, however, working conditions in U.S. factories were considerably better than the terrible conditions inflicted on English laborers. Some American mill owners took an interest in the welfare of their workers, providing housing and meals. The cost of these benefits was deducted from the workers' pay.

**Early Unions**  Reacting to changing times and the harsh policies of many employers, workers in the same craft organized unions for collective (group) action. But these early unions were small, and employers generally resisted their demands to raise wages and shorten hours.

## B. WORKING CONDITIONS AFTER THE CIVIL WAR (1865 TO 1900)

After 1865, as business firms grew larger, the plight of factory workers tended to become even worse.

**Problems of Industrial Workers**  To minimize their labor costs, most manufacturers believed in keeping wages as low as possible. They saw nothing wrong with demanding from their workers a 60- to 70-hour workweek. Factories were often cold in winter, hot in summer. Ventilation was poor. Machines had few safeguards to prevent accidents. If an accident injured or killed a worker, it was considered the worker's fault, not the employer's. Wages in steel mills, slaughterhouses, and oil refineries were barely enough to put food on the table.

**Reasons for Worker Insecurity**  How were workers to combat these conditions? If they joined a union or participated in a strike, employers would almost certainly turn them out of their jobs. The daily grind was bad enough, but fear of unemployment was a nightmare.

Employers had no trouble finding replacements for striking workers. Every year thousands of immigrants eager for work arrived from Europe. Also competing for jobs were (1) women and children, (2) farm youths leaving the land for the cities, and (3) African Americans leaving the South in hopes of a better life in the North.

There were other sources of worker insecurity. First, jobs could be eliminated as employers substituted the tireless work of machines for the more costly labor of human beings. Second, business booms would come to a crashing halt in sudden depressions and panics. At such times hundreds of thousands of jobless people faced the awful prospect of many months of no wages and no income. Government aid in the form of unemployment insurance did not then exist.

## C. THE KNIGHTS OF LABOR

In spite of workers' fears, two national unions managed to recruit many thousands of members. The first union to become a major economic force was the **Knights of Labor**, organized in 1869.

**Membership Open to All**   Unlike earlier unions the Knights of Labor invited craft and industrial workers of all kinds to join it. Nobody was excluded. Skilled and unskilled workers were equally welcome. So were African-American workers and white workers, women and men, foreign-born and native-born.

**Goals and Methods**   Under the leadership of its president, Terence Powderly, the Knights of Labor avoided strikes for many years. Until 1885 it tried to settle labor disputes through **arbitration** (the judging of a dispute by an impartial person). It established **cooperatives**, in which workers owned and operated their own businesses. Most important to the Knights of Labor was the goal of winning employers' consent to an eight-hour workday.

**Sudden Rise and Equally Sudden Fall**   Abandoning its antistrike policy, the Knights of Labor surprised the nation by winning a major strike against a railroad company in 1885. Following the strike, membership in the union shot up to 700,000. But its triumph was short-lived. In 1886, in the Haymarket section of Chicago, someone threw a bomb into a crowd, killing several police officers and civilians. The Knights of Labor was wrongly blamed for the incident because one of the bomb throwers belonged to the union. After the Haymarket Riot, workers left the Knights of Labor in droves. By the 1890s membership had dwindled to an insignificant number.

**Reasons for Decline**   As a union the Knights of Labor had weaknesses that were as much responsible for its downfall as the Haymarket disaster. (1) Prejudices were difficult to overcome. Many skilled workers did not like being associated with unskilled workers. Many whites did not like being on equal terms with blacks. (2) The Knights of Labor probably gave too much attention to political goals (a graduated income tax, for example) and too little attention to bread-and-butter economic issues (higher wages and better working conditions.)

## D. THE AMERICAN FEDERATION OF LABOR

A second national union, the **American Federation of Labor (A.F. of L.)**, lasted much longer than the Knights of Labor. In fact, in altered form, it survives to this day as the largest union in the United States.

**Membership Limited to Skilled Workers**   The founder of the A.F. of L., Samuel Gompers, was a British immigrant who came to New York City as a teenager. As the leader of a union of cigar makers, he had the idea of bringing other crafts unions together in a single organization. The federation, or loose association, of unions that he organized in 1886 permitted the member unions (a union of cigar makers, a union of carpenters, and so on) to continue their separate existence. The A.F. of L. leadership would set overall policy for achieving the objectives held in common by the various crafts unions.

**Goals and Methods**   Under Gompers' leadership, the A.F. of L. focused strictly on bread-and-butter goals: higher wages, shorter hours, better working conditions. Once asked what he wanted for members of his union, Gompers replied simply "more." If Gompers thought a strike was a practical means of attaining an A.F. of L. objective, he approved it. If it was judged not practical, the strike was off and other tactics were tried.

**Gradual Growth**   Membership in the A.F. of L. grew steadily. By 1900, there were half a million workers belonging to crafts unions in the A.F. of L.

## E. DISCRIMINATION AGAINST WOMEN
## AND MINORITIES

Unions in the A.F. of L. tended to discriminate against black workers, excluding them from membership simply because of their race. The few unions that admitted African Americans forced them to meet in segregated units. The unfortunate result of this policy was that the excluded blacks were often used by employers to fill the jobs of striking union members. Their reputation as "strikebreakers" only increased the racial prejudice of the A.F. of L. membership.

Women were also discriminated against in the male-dominated A.F. of L. Yet women were commonly exploited by their employers even more than men. Conditions of work were notoriously bad in "sweatshops" where women sat at sewing machines for long hours stitching clothing at breakneck speed.

One of many young women who became active in the labor movement was Mary Kenney O'Sullivan. This energetic Irish American persuaded thousands of garment workers of New York City and Troy, New York, to join local unions. Then in 1903 she founded a national organization for women similar in purpose to the A.F. of L. Attracting members from both the middle class and working class, the National Women's Trade Union League concentrated on trying to improve wages and working conditions in those industries where women were employed in large numbers.

## OBSERVERS OF AMERICAN LIFE: A GARMENT WORKER IN BROOKLYN

A magazine, *The Independent*, printed this account of a young woman's daily routine working at a garment factory in Brooklyn, New York, around the year 1900.

On a separate piece of paper, tell whether or not you think factory conditions today are better than those described here. Support your answer with examples from your reading.

Two years ago I came to this place, Brownsville, where so many of my people are, and where I have friends. I got work in a factory making underskirts—all sorts of cheap underskirts, like cotton and calico for the summer and woolen for the winter, but never the silk, satin, or velvet underskirts. I earned $4.50 a week and lived on $2 a week, the same as before . . . .

At seven o'clock we all sit down to our machines and the boss brings to each one the pile of work that he or she is to finish during the day, what they call in English their "stint." This pile is put down beside the machine and as soon as a skirt is done it is laid on the other side of the machine . . . .

The machines go like mad all day, because the faster you work the more money you get. Sometimes in my haste I get my finger caught and the needle goes right through it. It goes so quick though, that it does not hurt much. I bind the finger up with a piece of cotton and go on working. We all have accidents like that. Where the needle goes through the nail it makes a sore finger, or where it splinters a bone it does much harm. Sometimes a finger has to come off. Generally, though, one can be cured by a salve.

All the time we are working the boss walks about examining the finished garments and making us do them over again if they are not just right. So we have to be careful as well as swift . . . .

## F. RADICALS IN THE LABOR MOVEMENT

The A.F. of L. took a conservative approach to issues dividing business and labor. Business leaders were not viewed as "the enemy," but only as reasonable adversaries who could be talked into making sensible business deals with unions. In contrast to this conservative approach were the radical ideas of two groups: the anarchists and the socialists.

**Anarchists** Those responsible for the Haymarket bombing in Chicago in 1886 were anarchists. They believed that the capitalist system and the political system that supported it could not be reformed and that violent means should be used to end them.

**Socialists** This group of radicals also opposed capitalism but advocated peaceful means for abolishing it. They organized a political party—the Socialist party—and hoped to elect enough Socialist candidates to give workers control of the government. If they succeeded, Socialists intended to give the government ownership and control of the nation's factories and railroads.

## G. VIOLENT CLASHES BETWEEN BUSINESS AND LABOR

Workers' strikes were extremely common in the post-Civil War era. Many ended in violence, as strikers clashed with police and state troops. These strikes involved labor disputes with some of the nation's biggest corporations.

**Great Railway Strike (1877)** The cause of this railroad strike was the announcement by the Baltimore and Ohio Railroad of a cut in workers' pay. The strike spread like wildfire from Baltimore to Pittsburgh to several cities in the Midwest. Open warfare broke out between the striking workers and soldiers in the Pennsylvania state militia. Finally President Rutherford Hayes sent in federal troops and the strike was broken.

**Homestead Strike (1892)** The Homestead Steel Plant in Pennsylvania was owned by Andrew Carnegie's steel company. Carnegie's business associate, Henry Frick, responded to a strike against the plant by calling in strikebreakers from the Pinkerton National Detective Agency. Fierce fighting broke out between the Pinkertons and the strikers, and many on both sides were killed. In the end, the strike was broken and the steel workers' union was crushed.

**Pullman Strike (1894)** George Pullman was the inventor and manufacturer of the Pullman sleeping car for comfortable railroad travel. In 1894 he announced a 25-percent reduction in wages. In protest the workers at Pullman went on strike. Led by Eugene V. Debs (later to become a Socialist), other railroad workers throughout the country refused to handle trains that included Pullman cars. President Grover Cleveland sent federal troops to end the strike. He

Strike at the Homestead Steel plant, 1892

justified his action on the grounds that U.S. mails were delayed by
the strikers' action. Debs was jailed, and his railway union was broken.

**Public Policy and Public Opinion**   Most Americans generally
supported the government's use of troops to break strikes. They
viewed strike leaders as revolutionaries who challenged the traditional
values of society. But a growing minority sympathized with the unions
and pointed to the unhappy plight of the workers—their low wages,
long hours, and unhealthy working conditions.

Government consistently sided with business against unions in the 1800s. But as you shall see, it would change its policies to support *both* business *and* labor in the next century.

## *In Review*

The following questions refer to section III: Big Business and Government Policy and section IV: Organization of Labor.

1. Explain why some Americans were alarmed by the growth of businesses like the Standard Oil Trust.
2. Describe two attempts by the U.S. government to regulate business.
3. Explain how the growth of labor unions was a response to the growth of business.
4. Compare the Knights of Labor to the American Federation of Labor.

# V. Agrarian Protest: Farmers Against the Railroads

For farmers the post-Civil War era was both the best of times and the worst of times. Because of advances in science and technology, American farmers were more productive than ever before. At the same time the prices that farmers received for each pound of cotton and each bushel of wheat were discouragingly low. In short, farmers succeeded as never before—and also failed as never before.

The situation was bewildering, but in this section we will try to understand it.

## A. THE AVAILABILITY OF CHEAP LAND

When the Republican party came to power in 1861, one of its primary goals was to support agricultural progress by practically giving away public lands in the West. For this purpose Congress gave land grants to Western railroads (see page 162). The lawmakers assumed, correctly, that the railroads would sell land to farmers at almost giveaway prices. Congress also enacted two laws for disposing of public lands.

**The Homestead Act (1862)**  By the terms of this law, any citizen or immigrant intending to become a citizen could acquire 160 acres of federal land simply by cultivating it for five years. Labor, not money, was the price of a homestead.

**The Morrill Act (1862)**  This act provided that huge tracts of federal land would go to the states. The one condition was that the states build colleges on the land for teaching "agricultural and mechanical arts." Such colleges, known as **land-grant colleges**, were extremely influential in teaching farmers how to increase their crop yields with new technology.

## B. FARMERS' DEPENDENCE ON RAILROADS, MERCHANTS, AND BANKS

While land was cheap, everything else about a farmer's business was expensive: farm machinery, tools, buildings, seed, horses, and mules. Another major expense was paying railroads to haul a farmer's crop to city markets and to store the crop temporarily in grain elevators. In other words a farm family started out with good land and dependable labor (their own) but lacked capital (the money with which to buy farm equipment and supplies).

Capital was provided to farmers in the form of merchants' credit and bankers' loans. Of course, every farmer hoped to repay the creditor or bank by selling a good-sized crop for a good price. But every year there was also the possibility of little rain, poor crops, and bad prices. If this happened several years in a row, a farmer's debts could grow to the point that a bank would lose patience and **foreclose**, or take possession, of the farm.

Naturally farmers resented being always at the mercy of railroads, merchants, and banks. They particularly resented it when they succeeded in growing a large crop only to receive prices for the crop far below the prices of the year before. This condition—good crop, poor price—happened year after year in the 1870s, 1880s, and 1890s. As prices sank, farm debts soared.

Twice farmers turned to politics to solve their problems. Midwestern farmers battled the railroads in the Granger movement of the 1870s. Then farmers of the South and West campaigned against Northeastern bankers in the Populist movement of the 1890s.

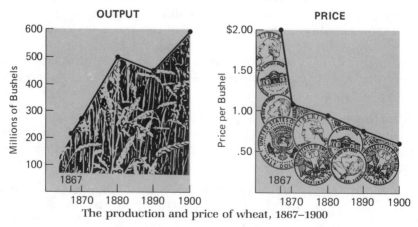

The production and price of wheat, 1867–1900

## C. THE GRANGER MOVEMENT

The Patrons of Husbandry, otherwise known as the **Grange**, was founded in 1867 as a society for bringing farm families together for social purposes. Soon, however, Grange meetings focused on troubling economic issues: how to cope with falling grain prices and rising railroad rates.

**Grangers' Grievances**  Farmers complained about the common railroad practice of charging low rates for a long haul (for example, Chicago to New York) and a much higher rate for a short haul (for example, Springfield, Illinois, to Chicago). Railroads competed with each other for business on the long route. They commonly made up for their losses by overcharging farmers for the less competitive shorter hauls.

Farmers also complained about another high charge for the storage of their wheat and corn in grain elevators. Farmers could choose to sell their grain directly to the elevator company, which then would sell it to the public. But the price farmers were offered by an elevator company was usually very low. How could farmers break free from the crushing rates charged by others?

**Farmers' Cooperatives**  One solution was for farmers themselves to build and operate their own grain elevators. The new elevators were financed with money contributed by Grange members to businesses known as **cooperatives.** A cooperative is an enterprise owned and operated by those using its services. Besides operating the grain elevators at reasonable rates, Grange cooperatives lowered prices for needed supplies by buying from merchants in great quantities.

**Granger Laws**  To fight high railroad rates, the Grangers took political action. They persuaded several state legislatures in the 1870s to pass laws regulating both the freight rates of railroad companies and the storage rates of elevator companies.

**Supreme Court Decisions For and Against Regulation**  Companies facing regulation under the so-called "Granger laws" challenged the laws in court. In the landmark case of *Munn* v. *Illinois* (1877), the Supreme Court decided that a state *could* set maximum rates for the storage of grain. But in a later case of 1886, the Supreme Court reversed itself. It declared that railroad rates set by state laws interfered with Congress's exclusive power to regulate interstate commerce. The next year, Congress enacted the Interstate Commerce Act (page 169). The regulatory commission created by the act (the Interstate Commerce Commission) continues to this day as the Grangers' most enduring contribution to American government.

## D. THE FOUNDING OF THE POPULIST PARTY

Farm prices rose briefly in the early 1880s, and Grange membership declined. But later in the decade prices again dropped lower and lower. At one point farmers burned their own corn for fuel rather than sell it at the prevailing low price. Embittered farmers in all parts of the country joined a movement that eventually became a new political party—the People's party, also known as the **Populist party**.

**Origins of the Movement**   The first organized response to falling farm prices was the formation of three farmer associations called "alliances." They were (1) the Northern Alliance with two million farmers from the Middle West and Northwest, (2) the Southern Alliance with three million white farmers of the South, and (3) the Colored Farmers National Alliance with about one million African-American farmers. In the South, an effort was made to include farmers of both races in a single alliance. But white alliance leaders feared that the presence of African Americans might deter many white farmers of the South from joining the movement.

**Birth of the Populist Party**   In 1890 leaders of the Northern Alliance organized independent parties to champion farmer interests. The next year, members of both the Northern and Southern alliances met in Cincinnati where they founded the Populist party.

**The Populist Platform of 1892**   Populist delegates assembled in Omaha, Nebraska, in 1892 for their party's first national convention. Included in their new party's **platform** (a statement of political ideas) were reform ideas that caused a sensation when reported in the nation's newspapers. For the time Populists' ideas sounded radical. They wanted:

- A **graduated income tax**—a tax on the incomes of rich people (the higher the person's income, the higher the tax rate)
- Establishment of savings banks in U.S. post offices
- Government ownership and operation of the railroads
- Government ownership and operation of telephone and telegraph companies
- Election of U.S. senators by direct vote of the people rather than by state legislatures
- An eight-hour workday for all factory workers
- State laws granting the **initiative** (voters' power to initiate ideas for new laws) and the **referendum** (voters' power to mark their ballots for or against proposed laws).

## DOCUMENTS: PLATFORM OF THE POPULIST PARTY

In their platform of 1892, the Populists accused both the major parties of neglecting the interests of the common people. On a separate piece of paper, tell whether or not you would have voted for the candidates of this new party if you had been a voter in 1892. Support your answers by referring to the arguments below as well as the specific reforms proposed by the Populists, page 180.

We have witnessed for more than a quarter of a century the struggles of the two great political parties for power and plunder, while grievous wrongs have been inflicted upon the suffering people. We charge that the controlling influences dominating both these parties have permitted the existing dreadful conditions to develop without serious effort to prevent or restrain them. Neither do they now promise us any substantial reform. They have agreed together to ignore, in the coming campaign, every issue but one. They propose to drown the outcries of a plundered people with the uproar of a sham battle over the tariff, so that capitalists, corporations, national banks, rings, trusts, watered stock, the demonetization of silver and the oppressions of the usurers [moneylenders] may all be lost sight of. They propose to sacrifice our homes, lives, and children on the altar of mammon [god of riches and greed]; to destroy the multitude in order to secure corruption funds from the millionaires.

Assembled on the anniversary of the birthday of the nation ... we seek to restore the government of the Republic to the hands of the "plain people," with which class it originated.

## E. THE POPULISTS' IDEA FOR INFLATED MONEY

American democracy benefited the most from the Populists' ideas listed above. But the Populists were *most* excited about a financial reform that, at the time, seemed to offer a surefire solution to their economic troubles. Between 1873 and 1890, no silver coins had been minted and circulated by the U.S. government. Only gold coins were minted, and because gold was a more valuable precious metal than silver, these coins were often kept and not spent. Money, therefore, was terribly scarce. Farmers saw a direct connection between the scarcity of money and the low prices they received for cotton and corn. The Populists offered a solution: raise farm prices by making the government coin more money—*silver* money.

In other words, the Populists wanted the U.S. government to bring about **inflation** (a regular increase in prices). The way to do it, they said, was to coin 16 silver dollars for every one gold dollar. Naturally, the farmers' fondness for silver coins was fully shared by silver miners, who became enthusiastic Populists in 1892.

## F. EARLY POPULIST TRIUMPHS, 1892

The coinage of silver and other reforms promised by the Populists in 1892 drew a lot of votes. The Populist candidate for president, James Weaver, won over a million votes (almost 9 percent of the total) as well as 22 electoral votes. Other Populists were elected to seats in the U.S. Congress and seats in state legislatures of the South and West. For a brand-new party it was an impressive showing.

## G. SILVER AGAINST GOLD IN THE ELECTION OF 1896

The president elected in 1892 was Grover Cleveland, a Democrat. In his four years in office, he became known for his support of gold as the only metal for U.S. coins. Most Democrats of the North and East agreed with Cleveland that gold represented "sound money" and that business confidence would suffer a terrible blow if silver coins were issued. The "gold-bug" Democrats, as they were called, were opposed by Democrats of the South and West, who favored the "free and unlimited coinage of silver."

**The Democrats' Nomination of Bryan** At the Democratic convention of 1896, the so-called "silver Democrats" were thrilled by the rousing speech of a young U.S. congressman from Nebraska, William Jennings Bryan. His speech (known as the "cross of gold" speech) declared that farmers would prevail over the bankers of the cities. Bryan brought the convention to its feet with his last sentence: "You shall not press down upon the brow of labor this crown of thorns, you shall not crucify mankind upon a cross of gold." In the vote for a presidential candidate, the conservative, "gold-bug" Democrats were defeated by the supporters of the "silver-tongued" candidate, William Jennings Bryan.

**The Populists' Nomination of Bryan** At the Populists convention of 1896, a majority favored the idea of nominating the Democrats' choice, Bryan. After all, they reasoned, who could match Bryan's ability to rally the nation behind the Populists' favorite cause, silver money? To satisfy those who opposed Bryan's nomination, the Populists chose a vice-presidential candidate different from the one picked by the Democrats.

**The Republican Victory** Even with the support of both the Democrats and the Populists, Bryan lost the election. He was defeated by the Republican candidate, William McKinley, who supported the use of gold and opposed the use of silver as currency. Although Bryan carried the South and much of the West, he failed to win the crucial electoral votes of the East. Many Eastern workers feared inflation and were persuaded by McKinley's campaign that silver money would cause high prices, which in turn would bring a depression and the loss of jobs.

## H. THE POPULISTS' CONTRIBUTION

The defeat of Bryan and improved farm prices after 1896 caused a rapid decline of the Populist party. After 1900 there were no more Populists elected to Congress.

Nevertheless many of the reforms in the Populist platform of 1892 were eventually adopted by the two major parties. In fact two Populist ideas became the basis for constitutional amendments:

| Populist Idea | Amendment |
| --- | --- |
| Graduated income tax | Sixteenth Amendment (adopted 1913) |
| Direct election of U.S. senators by popular vote | Seventeenth Amendment (adopted 1913) |

We see then that third parties, even if they fail to elect many candidates, can have a major influence on national policy.

### *In Review*

The following questions refer to section V: Agrarian Protest: Farmers Against the Railroads and to the word wheel.

**Word Wheel**

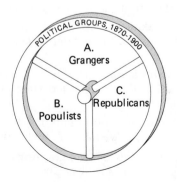

On a piece of paper, identify the group or groups in the wheel described by each phrase.

1. Joined a new political party.
2. Hoped that the free and unlimited coinage of silver might solve farmers' financial problems.
3. Gained passage of state laws regulating railroad rates.
4. Wanted Bryan to win the election of 1896.
5. Won the election of 1896.
6. Favored a number of reforms including public ownership of the railroads and a tax on the incomes of the rich.
7. Established a number of farm cooperatives.

## GLOSSARY OF KEY TERMS: CHAPTER 6

**American Federation of Labor (A.F. of L.)**   a national association of crafts unions founded in 1881.

**arbitration**   the judging of a dispute by an impartial person.

**Bessemer process**   an improved method for making steel, invented by Henry Bessemer in 1856.

**capital**   the buildings, tools, and machinery for producing goods and services; also, the money with which to purchase such buildings, tools, and machinery.

**capitalism**   the economic system in which the means of production are owned privately by many businesses competing for profits.

**"captains of industry"**   business leaders of the late 1800s.

**consolidation**   the process of combining separate business firms into a single large firm.

**cooperative**   a business owned and operated by those who purchase its products and services.

**corporation**   a form of business organization chartered by the state government and owned by shareholders who invest in the firm.

**"cross of gold" speech**   the speech by Williams Jennings Bryan that won him the nomination of the Democratic party in 1896.

**foreclosure**   a bank's taking possession of a piece of property (such as a farm or house) because of the resident's failure to repay the bank's loan.

**Grangers**   farmers who belonged to the Patrons of Husbandry, or the Grange, an organization that persuaded state legislatures to regulate railroad rates in the 1870s.

**holding company**   a corporation that, for the sake of eliminating competition, holds a majority share of stocks in several companies.

**Homestead Act**   a federal law of 1862 granting a section of land to any settler who worked the land for five years.

**industrialization**   the replacement of hand tools by power-driven machines and of home workshops by factories.

**Industrial Revolution**   the transformation of the world's economy that resulted from using machines to produce goods rapidly and cheaply for mass markets.

**inflation**   a general rise in prices over a period of time.

**initiative**   a procedure for making a state legislature consider a proposal for a law favored by a majority of voters.

**Interstate Commerce Act**   a federal law of 1887 outlawing unfair practices and establishing the first federal regulatory commission.

**Knights of Labor**   one of the first successful industrial unions organized in 1869 and open to all workers.

**laissez-faire**   the theory that business competition should not be regulated by the laws of government.

**land-grant college**   a college or university founded as a result of a federal grant of public land to a state government.

**limited liability**   a characteristic of a corporation by which shareholders risk the loss only of their original investment, not their personal property.

**monopoly**   the situation in which one producer has complete control of an industry.

**patent**   a government document that grants to one inventor the exclusive right to manufacture and sell his or her invention for a certain number of years.

**platform**   a political party's statement of its policies on election issues.

**pooling**   the attempt of two or more business firms to limit competition by charging the same prices and sharing the same market.

**Populist party**   a third party of the 1890s that represented the interests of farmers and campaigned for reforms in the American political and economic system.

**rebates**   the return to a buyer of part of the amount paid; a practice once common among railroads competing for the business of major corporations.

**referendum**   a direct vote of the people on whether or not to pass a certain state law.

**"robber barons"**   unscrupulous business leaders (term commonly used by critics of the industrialists of the late 1800s).

**Sherman Antitrust Act**   a federal law of 1890 declaring trusts to be illegal.

**social Darwinism**   the theory that society advances to higher levels as a result of free competition among businesses and the triumph of stronger firms over weaker ones.

**trust**   a business organization in which several competing firms are combined into one by the exchange of stock for trust certificates.

# TEST YOURSELF

## A. Multiple Choice: Facts, Main Ideas, Skills

*On a separate sheet of paper, write the number of the word or expression that, of those given, best completes the statement or answers the question.*

### Reviewing the facts

1. The growth of railroads was aided in part by (1) government assistance in the form of land and money (2) few geographic obstacles (3) support from Indian tribes in the West (4) the abolition of slavery

2. During the last half of the nineteenth century, the laissez-faire policy of the U.S. government was supported by (1) labor unions (2) big business (3) farmers (4) Populists

3. Which of the following products of the late 1800s would not have been widely available in the early 1800s? (1) flour and meat (2) books and shoes (3) kerosene and steel (4) lumber and cotton

4. The Sherman Antitrust Act of 1890 was intended to control (1) the consolidation of big business (2) the growth of labor unions (3) the power of farm organizations (4) the practices of railroad companies

5. During the late 1800s farmers supported free and unlimited coinage of silver mainly because they believed that it would lead to (1) the establishment of government farm price supports (2) the lowering of rates charged by railroads (3) lower prices for consumer goods (4) higher prices for farm products

6. Which statement best describes many of the reforms proposed by the Populist party? (1) They were just campaign promises. (2) They disappeared from public interest. (3) They were undesirable in a democratic country. (4) They were won through the efforts of other political parties at a later time.

7. The Populist movement of the 1890s can best be described as a (1) political coalition of farming interests directed against banking and railroad interests (2) trade union movement located in major Eastern cities (3) reform movement seeking to eliminate urban poverty and slums (4) political interest group desiring a war with Spain to protect U.S. interests in Cuba

### Reviewing the main ideas

8. Which is a true statement about economic growth of the North during and after the Civil War? (1) Small farmers used the sharecropping technique to attract farm workers. (2) The pace of industrial change was greater than before the Civil War. (3) Construction of railroads gradually declined. (4) Industrialization was confined to the Northeastern part of the nation.

9. Industrialization in the United States caused (1) a decrease in immigration (2) an increase in the power of big business (3) a decrease in the power of the United States (4) an increase in forest lands

10. Which was a major obstacle to union success from 1860 to 1900? (1) prohibition of labor organizations by the U.S. Constitution (2) general government support of business (3) excellent working conditions in U.S. factories (4) status of factory workers as equal partners with management

11. Which was a major problem faced by U.S. farmers in the 1890s? (1) lagging technology (2) lack of tariff protection (3) debts incurred for the use of capital (4) inflationary currency

12. A major aim of both the Granger movement and Populist movement was (1) the establishment of a gold standard for currency (2) mandatory government policies to end inflation (3) passage of laws for the public control of railroads (4) unlimited immigration of Asians

13. Minor parties have sometimes had a major impact on U.S. politics. This statement is best supported by (1) the Democratic politics of Grover Cleveland (2) the experience of the Grangers (3) the influence of the Populist platform (4) the Republican victory in 1896.

14. Which was most characteristic of the early factory system in the United States? (1) Factories provided workers with a voice in management and employment conditions. (2) Women and children were not allowed to work in factories. (3) Unsafe working conditions were common. (4) Most workers could look forward to being promoted to management jobs.

15. Which would a laissez-faire economist most likely favor? (1) government support of basic industries (2) high protective tariffs on imports (3) no government regulation of business (4) unemployment insurance and workers' compensation programs

16. Events from 1865 to 1900 show that (1) big business, farmers, and workers benefited equally from industrial changes (2) the federal government took the lead in protecting farmers and workers from the power of big business (3) the U.S. Supreme Court consistently ruled in favor of labor unions (4) the growth of big business led to the growth of both farm organizations and labor unions

17. A study of major railroad strikes of the late 1800s shows that the federal government (1) refused to interfere (2) demanded that owners negotiate fairly with union leaders (3) took action against the owners (4) sent in troops that ended the strikes

18. The Populist party was formed mainly to express (1) the desire of workers to form labor unions (2) the opposition of employers to further immigration (3) the desire of businesses to increase overseas investments (4) the discontent of farmers with their economic problems

**19.** Labor unions and big business would have disagreed most over   (1) policies for encouraging farm production   (2) high tariffs on European imports   (3) building the transcontinental railroad   (4) the use of troops to end strikes

**20.** One advantage of a corporation over other forms of business organizations is that a corporation can   (1) raise large amounts of capital   (2) operate without legal restraint   (3) operate without being taxed   (4) avoid labor troubles

**21.** One effect of a monopoly is to   (1) eliminate business competition   (2) keep prices low   (3) give consumers a greater choice of goods and services   (4) increase the influence of labor unions

## Developing critical thinking skills

*Base your answers to questions 22 and 23 on the cartoon below and on your knowledge of history and government.*

**22.** The threat depicted in the cartoon is   (1) the building of a transcontinental railroad   (2) the reforms proposed by the Grange   (3) the growing size and power of railroad companies   (4) a nationwide strike by crafts unions

**23.** The farmers in the cartoon probably would favor   (1) the formation of trusts   (2) the jailing of all anarchists and socialists   (3) a strict policy of laissez-faire   (4) state laws regulating unfair business methods

## B. Essays

*Level 1*

In the nineteenth century, the growth of industry had a major impact on two aspects of U.S. society, agriculture and labor.

1. For *each* of the two aspects of society listed, show in what ways the growth of industry had an impact.

2. Select *two* of the following movements for reform and explain how *each* tried to solve a problem related to the growth of industry.

Granger movement
Populist movement
Labor movement

*Level 2*

Since 1865 farmers and workers in the United States have faced many problems.

A. Identify *one* problem faced by U.S. farmers since 1865 and *one* problem faced by factory workers.

B. Base your answer to part B on your answer to part A. Write an essay discussing problems that farmers and factory workers faced after the Civil War.

# Chapter 7

# Adjusting to Industrialism: The Western Frontier and Eastern Cities

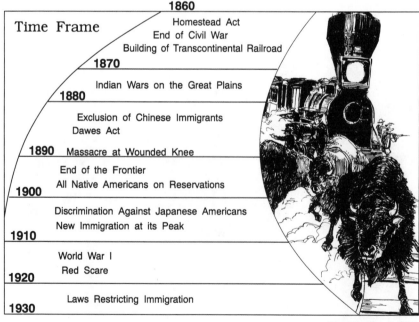

| Time Frame | |
|---|---|
| **1860** | Homestead Act |
| | End of Civil War |
| | Building of Transcontinental Railroad |
| **1870** | |
| | Indian Wars on the Great Plains |
| **1880** | |
| | Exclusion of Chinese Immigrants |
| | Dawes Act |
| **1890** | Massacre at Wounded Knee |
| | End of the Frontier |
| | All Native Americans on Reservations |
| **1900** | |
| | Discrimination Against Japanese Americans |
| | New Immigration at its Peak |
| **1910** | |
| | World War I |
| | Red Scare |
| **1920** | |
| | Laws Restricting Immigration |
| **1930** | |

*Slaughtering buffalo on the Great Plains*

## Objectives

- To understand the impact of Western settlement on Native Americans and U.S. society.
- To understand the impact of industrialization and urbanization on American life.
- To appreciate the immigrant contribution to American life and the development of a pluralistic society.
- To examine episodes of prejudice and discrimination from the point of view of ethnic minorities.
- To trace the changing role of women in response to industrialism.

Three great themes of American history come together in this chapter: (1) the settlement of the Western frontier, (2) the impact of industrialism on American society, and (3) the immigration to the United States of people from many countries and cultures. Like streams feeding into a common river, the three themes are part of a single story. It is a story of people on the move: people moving to the West, people moving to the cities, people moving from various lands to the United States. In the process the American nation was transformed.

# I. The Last Frontier

The frontier is an imaginary line that separates settled areas from the wilderness. As trappers, miners, and farmers moved west, the frontier moved with them.

## A. THE FRONTIER BEFORE 1850

Use the map on page 192 to review the main stages of the steady westward movement that, year after year, changed the location of the frontier.

- *First colonial century (1607 to 1700):* After almost one hundred years of settlement, the first frontier extended only about 300 to 400 miles inland from the Atlantic coast.
- *Founding of the nation (1776 to 1790):* Settlement advanced rapidly in this period. During the American Revolution Daniel Boone opened a trail through the Appalachian Mountains into Kentucky. But for the most part the Appalachians still defined the Western frontier when George Washington became president in 1789.

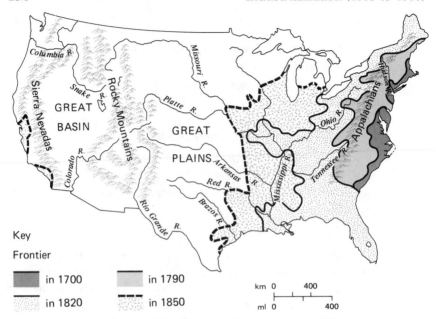

**Advance of the Western frontier, 1700–1850**

- *Early republic (1790 to 1820):* Flatboats and rafts on the Ohio River helped pioneering farm families move beyond the Appalachians to the wooded region that included Kentucky, Tennessee, Ohio, and Illinois. During the presidency of James Monroe (1817 to 1825), one section of the frontier lay just west of the Mississippi River.

- *Expansion to the Pacific (1830 to 1850):* The next Western lands to be settled were Texas, California, and Oregon. After the California gold rush of 1849, a small section of the Pacific coast was settled, but the huge area between the Far West (Oregon and California) and the region just west of the Mississippi River was still unsettled.

How did this "last frontier" of the American West (the lands between the settlements) finally yield to miners' pickaxes, cowboys' cattle, and farmers' plows?

**The Great American Desert**   Before 1850 the vast stretch of land between Missouri and California was popularly known as the Great American Desert because it seemed dry, barren, and impossible to farm. The region consisted of two main parts: (1) the flat grasslands of the Great Plains, stretching about 400 miles from the banks of the Missouri River to the steep slopes of the Rocky Mountains, and (2) the high plateau known as the Great Basin, stretching about 700 miles between two mountain ranges (the Rockies and the Sierra Nevada).

**Indians of the Plains**  Of course Indians had an entirely different view of the Great Plains. For them the plains were filled with plants and animals that richly supported their way of life. Millions of shaggy buffalo provided almost all that the Plains Indians needed: meat for food, pelts for clothing, skins for shelter, bones for tools, and dried manure for fuel. The buffalo-hunting tribes (including the Blackfeet, Cheyenne, Comanche, and Sioux) viewed the plains with religious awe and respect. To them the land and the life it supported were sacred. Unlike white settlers from the East, the Indians could not conceive of dividing the land into privately owned plots and using it for personal gain. In their view the land and its wealth belonged to all.

## B.  SETTLEMENT OF THE GREAT PLAINS

Starting about 1850, Easterners began to view the so-called Great American Desert in a new light. The settling of this region occurred in three stages. First came people hoping to strike rich deposits of gold and silver in the Western mountains. Then came people who hoped to make their fortune raising and selling cattle. Finally came the homesteaders (farm families) who hoped for enough rain to raise wheat and corn for a profit.

**The Mining Frontier**  Gold! The news of a gold strike in the Rocky Mountains touched off a rush westward in 1859 similar to the rush to California ten years earlier. More than 100,000 people were inspired to cross the Great Plains in wagons and search for gold near Pike's Peak in Colorado. In later years thousands of others were lured into the Western mountains by news of silver in Nevada, copper in Montana, and gold in the Black Hills of Dakota. In hundreds of remote places, mining towns sprang up almost overnight.

**The Cattle Frontier**  In Texas in the 1860s and 1870s the most promising way to make a living on the frontier was to hire a crew of cowboys for driving cattle to market. Millions of acres of the grassy plains were regarded by cattle owners as open grazing land. In other words cattle herds were privately owned, but the **open range** was used by all. The cowboys who tended the herds had to be as tough as the long-horned steers in their charge. They included European Americans, Mexican Americans, Native Americans, and African Americans. A former slave, Nat Love (known by the nickname "Deadwood Dick"), earned the admiration of other cowboys for his remarkable skills and feats of endurance on horseback.

**The Farming Frontier**  The passage of the Homestead Act in 1862 invited Eastern farmers to try their luck settling on the Great Plains. Those who did so were often referred to as **homesteaders.** Anyone who wished could acquire 160 acres of Western land simply by settling on it. Although intended for homesteaders, much of the land made available under the act was grabbed by speculators (those who buy something, not for use, but only for later sale to others at a higher price).

**The Role of the Railroads**  Railroad companies were even more eager than the U.S. government to encourage farmers to go west. After all, a railroad's chief business was hauling freight from one place to another. If there were no settlers on the empty plains, there would be no business for a Western railroad. To recruit settlers, railroad companies sent agents to Europe as well as to U.S. cities. Railroads' land grants from the U.S. government were offered for sale to would-be settlers at bargain prices. (Review Chapter 6.)

Railroads were also crucial to the cattle drives from Texas that altered life on the plains. The end of the cowboys' long journey was the railroad depot in Abilene, Kansas. Here the cattle were herded into railroad cars for shipment to the slaughter pens in Chicago and from there (as meat) to the restaurants and butcher shops of the East. In the 1860s a long-horned steer bought in Texas for $3 could bring between $30 and $40 when sold to a Chicago meat packer. Without the railroads as the connecting link, the cattleman's profit-making enterprise would have been impossible.

**The Role of New Technology**  Farming the hard sod of the plains posed a double problem. For one thing, rainfall was slight. For another, there were no trees from which to make the rail fences commonly used in the East to enclose sheep and other farm animals. Two inventions went a long way toward solving both problems: (1) Windmills on a homesteader's land provided the power for pumping up underground water, and (2) barbed wire (invented in 1874) enabled farmers to fence their lands without using much wood. In addition, improved steel plows enabled farmers to cut deep into the hard ground.

## C. ADJUSTING TO LIFE ON THE FRONTIER

The pioneering families of the 1860s and 1870s included immigrants from Europe, farm families from the East, and some African Americans recently freed from slavery. The first homesteaders to settle the Great Plains, coped daily with a daunting number of hazards and hardships.

**Sod Houses and Dugouts**  Because of the absence of trees, homesteaders built their first homes out of bricks made from the prairie sod. If the ground was hilly, they might simply dig a room out of the hillside for shelter. Doors and windows were covered with blankets and hides. If it rained, water seeped through the sod roof and formed puddles on the dirt floor of the typical one-room cabin. If it did not rain for months at a time, crops would wither, and dust would cover everything the family owned.

Farmers on the Great Plains were separated by great distances. Occasional neighborly get-togethers provided the only social life. After several seasons of disappointing harvests, dust storms, hot summers, cold winters, and uncomfortable living, many farm families gave up and moved back east.

**The Role of Women**   For women especially, life on the frontier was difficult and lonely. Daily they performed a never-ending round of chores. They worked the land, fed the chickens, churned the butter, cooked the food, sewed the linens, made the clothing, and tended the children. The number of children to be tended was often ten or more. Little time was taken for giving birth. It was common for a woman to do a full morning of work, give birth in the afternoon, and return to her chores the next morning.

Women were a civilizing force on the frontier. When they arrived in the rough-and-tumble mining camps and cow towns originally dominated by men, they managed to build more settled and peaceful communities. They made sure their towns had libraries, schools, even theaters. They acted as teachers, missionaries, librarians, and occasionally as doctors and dentists.

It was in the Western territory of Wyoming that women first achieved the right to vote in 1869. By 1910 women in most Western states voted in large numbers, while most women in the East were still denied voting rights. One reason for the West's leadership was men's realization that Western women had made many sacrifices and had played a crucial role in settling the last frontier.

# D. VIOLENT CONFLICT IN THE "WILD WEST"

The 25-year period after the Civil War (1865 to 1890) is the period most often dramatized in Western movies and TV shows. Gunfights did occur in the mining towns and cow towns of the newly settled West, but the fights did not erupt every minute, as in the movies. Let us try to separate the reality of Western life from the myth.

**Ranchers Against Farmers**   One cause of violent conflict was the barbed wire that farmers used to fence in their homesteads. The fencing angered cattle owners, who had always treated the grasslands as open range. Cowboys used wire cutters to open a path through the farmers' fences and let their cattle through. Gun battles, or "barbed-wire wars," broke out between farmers and cattle ranchers. In the 1880s the ranchers conceded defeat by fencing in their own grazing lands. After that the days of the open range were over.

**Vigilantes Against Outlaws**   Mining camps and cattle towns attracted many young men who were in a hurry to make their fortunes. Many found that it was easier to steal another miner's gold or rustle (steal) another rancher's cattle than to obtain them by honest work. To defend themselves and their property, most Westerners carried guns. Sometimes they used them to settle personal quarrels in shoot-outs (later made famous in Western movies).

In a remote town honest citizens could not always rely on government officials to capture cattle thieves and bank robbers. Therefore they carried out the law in their own way as vigilantes (a self-appointed police force). A suspected outlaw might be hanged without a full trial—or any trial at all. These crude procedures for dealing with crime on the frontier were known as **vigilante justice.**

**Soldiers Against Native Americans**   For more than 200 years (1607 to 1850) the frontier had been the scene of frequent fighting between Indian peoples (the original settlers of North America) and pioneer families (newcomers to the land). As the frontier moved west to the Mississippi River and beyond, the setting for the Indian-U.S. wars also shifted westward. The last chapter in the long conflict was fought on the last frontier—the Great Plains.

Recall from Chapter 3 the policy of Indian removal adopted by President Andrew Jackson in the 1830s. Indian peoples of the East, including the Cherokees, were forced to leave their lands for territory set aside for their use—the territory known then as the Great American Desert. U.S. treaties guaranteed the Indians' right to this land for "as long as the rivers shall run and the grass shall grow." But in the 1850s as settlers started building mining towns and cattle towns in this region, the way of life of Indian peoples was again threatened.

The Sioux, who hunted buffalo on the plains of Wyoming, were the first of many Plains Indians to attack U.S. military posts in the region. The high point of their war was a battle on the Little Bighorn River in Montana in 1876. Led by their chief, Crazy Horse, the Sioux killed 210 U.S. soldiers including Lieutenant Colonel George Custer. But in 1890 the U.S. Army took a terrible revenge, killing about 300 Sioux on Wounded Knee Creek in South Dakota. The fighting was less a battle than a massacre of people, including women and children, who were cut down as they fled from the scene. This event ended the resistance of the Sioux. Reluctantly they moved to a **reservation** in South Dakota. (A reservation is an area with fixed boundaries for Indian use.)

Other Indian peoples also fought against the loss of their hunting grounds to white settlers. But for them too, it was a losing battle. In Oregon in 1877 a tribe of about 500 Nez Percé tried to escape the fate of being forced onto a reservation by journeying over mountain trails

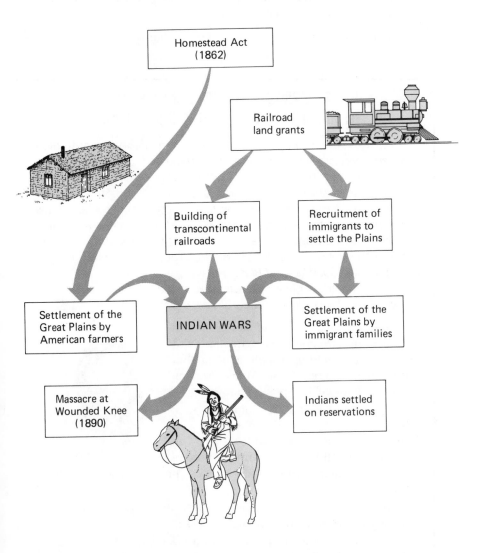

Chain of causes and effects: the last frontier

to Canada. But U.S. troops caught up with them, forcing the Nez Percé to surrender. It was a sad moment for their heroic leader, Chief Joseph, who said:

My people ask me for food, and I have none to give. It is cold, and we have no blankets, no wood. My people are starving. Where is my little daughter? I do not know. Perhaps even now she is freezing to death. Hear me, my chiefs. My heart is sick and sad. I have fought. But from where the sun now stands, I will fight no more, forever!

The Apaches of Arizona were the last Indian people to fight U.S.

## OBSERVERS OF AMERICAN LIFE: THE TESTIMONY OF STANDING BEAR

Standing Bear was the chief of the Poncas, a Native American tribe that had been ordered to leave its homeland in the Dakotas for the Indian Territory to the south. The Poncas had great difficulty adapting to the change. Many died, including Standing Bear's son. Standing Bear violated army rules when he left the reservation to bury his son in his former homeland to the north. He was placed under arrest. At his trial in 1879, he made a speech that was recorded by a witness and white friend of the Poncas, Thomas H. Tibbles. The excerpt below is from Tibbles's book, *Buckskin and Blanket Days*.

How does Standing Bear characterize the treatment his people have received from the U.S. government?

Standing Bear rose. Half facing the audience, he stretched his right hand out before him, holding it still so long that the audience grew tense. At last, looking up at the judge, he spoke quietly.

"That hand is not the color of yours, but if I pierce it, I shall feel pain. If you pierce your hand, you also feel pain. The blood that will flow from mine will be of

Standing Bear

the same color as yours. I am a man. The same God made us both."

Half facing the audience again, he let his gaze drift far out through a window. His tone grew tense.

"I seem to stand on the bank of a river. My wife and little

troops. After they submitted in 1900, Indian peoples lived peaceably—but unhappily—on reservations.

**Why Native Americans Lost Their Wars**    Although Indians challenged white settlers and U.S. troops, they never won a war against them. Why did they lose? They lost for three reasons. First, they fought as separate tribes rather than as a single, united nation. Second most tribes were small, often numbering fewer than a thousand people. Third, though they were equipped with rifles as well as bows and arrows, Native Americans lacked their foe's advanced weapons, such as the cannon and machine gun.

girl are beside me. In front the river is wide and impassable, and behind are perpendicular cliffs. No man of my race ever stood there before. There is no tradition to guide me."

Then he described how a flood started to rise around them and how, looking despairingly at the great cliffs, he saw a steep, stony way leading upward.... Finally he saw a rift in the rocks and felt the prairie breeze strike his cheek.

"I turn to my wife and child with a shout that we are saved. We will return to the Swift Running Water that pours down between the green islands. There are the graves of my fathers. There again we will pitch our tepee and build our fires.

"But a man bars the passage. He is a thousand times more powerful than I. Behind him I see soldiers as numerous as the leaves of the trees. They will obey that man's orders. I, too, must obey his orders. If he says that I cannot pass, I cannot. The long struggle will have been in vain. My wife and child and I must return and sink beneath the flood. We are weak and faint and sick. I cannot fight."

He paused with bowed head. Then, gazing up into Judge Dundy's face with an indescribable look of pathos and suffering, he said in a low, intense tone:

"You are that man."

No one who merely reads the speech can possibly imagine its effect on those people who knew of the Poncas' sufferings when they heard it spoken by the sad old chief in his brilliant robes.

*The U.S. judge ruled in favor of Standing Bear. He said the Poncas and their chief could return to their homeland in the Dakotas.*

# E. U.S. POLICY TOWARD NATIVE AMERICANS

Indian peoples of the plains lost not only their lands but also the buffalo herds upon which their way of life depended. The herds made an easy target for travelers who made a sport of killing buffalo from train windows. Hunting parties slaughtered buffalo for their furry hides, sold in the East as buffalo robes. By 1890 the great herds of buffalo, once numbering in the millions, had dwindled to less than a thousand.

**Hardships on the Reservations** The lands assigned by the U.S. government to different tribes of Native Americans were not their native lands. Reservation lands were often barren and poorly suited to supporting life. Unable to hunt for their food as in the past, Native Americans were reduced to lives of poverty and hopelessness. Agents of the U.S. government who ran the reservations were often corrupt, pocketing the funds intended for Indians' welfare.

**The Dawes Act** In the 1880s many U.S. citizens began to recognize that Native Americans were not being treated fairly. A reformer named Helen Hunt Jackson published *A Century of Dishonor* (1881), a book that described the many times that Native Americans had been deceived and cheated when the U.S. government violated its treaties with them.

Reform-minded lawmakers in Congress hoped to improve conditions on the reservations by encouraging Indians to adopt the lifestyle of American farmers. In 1887 Congress passed the **Dawes Act,** which offered 160-acre plots on the reservations to the heads of Indian households. It was assumed that Indian farmers would become self-supporting and **"Americanized"** (practicing the ways of the dominant white culture). An official appointed to enforce the Dawes Act said, "We will make of them American citizens and render future conflicts between them and the government impossible." But people with a hunting culture did not become model farmers overnight. Rather than taking homesteads for themselves, many rented or sold them to white settlers for cash.

**Changed Policy in the 1920s and 1930s** Early in the twentieth century two laws changed the status of Native Americans. By an act of Congress of 1924, all Indians born in the United States were granted full U.S. citizenship. By another law of 1934, the **Indian Reorganization Act,** the former policy of dividing reservation lands into individual plots was abandoned. The new policy permitted Indian peoples to own land in common as tribal property rather than as separate farms.

## F. IMPACT OF THE FRONTIER ON AMERICAN LIFE

The U.S. Bureau of the Census reported in 1890 that the frontier had ceased to exist. Taking note of this fact, a historian named Frederick Jackson Turner wrote about the passing of the frontier in an essay that received much public attention. He argued that the frontier had served the American nation as both a democratizing force and an outlet, or **safety valve,** for people seeking new economic opportunities.

Turner observed that life on the frontier tended to be more democratic than life in settled areas. People on the frontier judged each other, not according to social rank, but according to their abilities and strength of character. There was a sense on the frontier that everyone had an equal chance to succeed.

Furthermore, according to Turner, the Western frontier provided people living in crowded Eastern cities with a safety valve—a means of starting life over by moving to unsettled lands. While the frontier lasted, cheap land was always available to those seeking new opportunities.

Other scholars have pointed out weaknesses in Turner's thesis. They argue that American democracy owed far more to British influences in colonial times than to the frontier. Disputing the safety-valve theory, they point out that the trip West was costly and the poor could hardly afford to pay for a covered wagon and supplies.

Whether it was or was not a democratizing force, the frontier helped shape the American character. The passing of the frontier marked the end of a unique period in American history.

### *In Review*

The following questions refer to section I: The Last Frontier.

1. Identify (a) the Homestead Act, (b) the Dawes Act, (c) the Battle of Wounded Knee, and (d) Frederick Jackson Turner.
2. Describe the effect on Native Americans of (a) the removal policy of the 1830s and (b) the reservation policy of the 1880s and 1890s.
3. Explain how farmers overcame the problems of lack of water and lack of trees on the Great Plains.
4. "The frontier was a largely positive force in the life of the American nation." Evaluate this statement, explaining whether you agree or disagree with it.

# II. The Growth of Cities

While thousands of people moved west to settle the last frontier, millions of others moved to the cities of the East and Middle West.

The newcomers to the cities included both native-born Americans from rural areas and foreign-born immigrants from Europe and Asia.

## A. ATTRACTIONS OF CITY LIFE

People came to cities for both economic reasons (jobs) and cultural reasons (schools, museums, theaters, and sports).

**Jobs**  In the industrial age cities grew larger mainly because of the factories that were built in them. For shipping goods, industrialists would locate their factories near transportation centers such as railroad terminals and steamship ports. Workers would then move in to take advantage of the factory jobs. Near the factories, owners of real estate saw opportunities to rent housing to the workers and open shops catering to their needs. Thus as cities grew in population, the variety of services available to the public also grew.

**Public Services**  To cope with the increasing numbers of people, major cities like New York, Philadelphia, and Chicago adopted new systems for transporting people to and from work. After 1875 electric streetcars, subways, and elevated railways began to replace the horse-drawn streetcars of an earlier day. Impressive suspension bridges like the Brooklyn Bridge (completed in 1883) and tunnels improved the traffic flow between neighboring cities. The first skyscraper was built in Chicago in 1884; it was ten stories high and was widely imitated in other cities. The invention of electric elevators made it possible for people to shop on different floors of big-city department stores.

**Education**  City schools were larger and better equipped than the one-room schoolhouses of rural America. They offered a more varied and complete course of study. Also all the cultural resources of the city—the libraries, the museums, the concert halls—greatly enriched the education of city children.

**Cultural Attractions**  Many people were drawn from the farm to the city by the cultural excitement associated with urban life. In a city like New York, the rich and the middle class could dine in a restaurant or attend a new play at the theater whenever they wished. People of all classes could enjoy going to the city's baseball park or racetrack.

## B. PROBLEMS OF CITY LIFE

City life also had its problems. Among them were overcrowding, violent crime, and bad sanitation.

**Overcrowding**  Before unions became strong, factory workers received low wages—only a few cents an hour. For their housing they

Key
· 5,000 to 100,000 inhabitants
• 100,000 inhabitants and over

Urban America at the turn of the century, 1900

could afford to pay only very low rents. Landlords therefore built multifamily buildings called **tenements.** Designed to hold as many families as possible, each tenement was five or six stories high. It was built so close to neighboring tenements that a fire could spread through an entire neighborhood in minutes. Overcrowded tenements were a breeding ground for rats, roaches, and disease. Many residents died of tuberculosis and other diseases.

Jacob Riis, a New York City reporter, described one such tenement: "Here is a door. Listen! That short hacking cough, that tiny helpless wail—what do they mean? . . . Oh! a sadly familiar story. . . . The child is dying with measles. With half a chance it might have lived; but it had none. That dark bedroom killed it."

**Crime**   Urban poverty encouraged urban crime. As cities grew in size, so did the number of violent crimes—murders, burglaries, robberies. In tenement neighborhoods youths organized rival gangs that sometimes fought each other with weapons.

**Sanitation**   Disposing of garbage was another problem. Cities commonly dumped sewage into the same rivers and lakes that provided drinking water. As a result there were frequent outbreaks of typhoid fever, a disease transmitted by polluted water. Lacking bathtubs and running water, tenement dwellers had trouble keeping clean. Factory smokestacks polluted the air. Before the automobile was invented, droppings from thousands of carriage-pulling horses added to the city's foul odor.

## C. IMPACT OF URBANIZATION ON FAMILIES

Families in the crowded cities of the late 1800s had to adapt to changing conditions of the industrial-urban age. Also, city neighborhoods arose that showed a sharp division between three social classes: the working class, the middle class, and the wealthy class.

**Working-Class Families**  On a farm, members of the family worked together and saw each other from morning to night. But factory workers in the cities were seldom home. The daily routine among members of a worker's family was to split up during the day. For men working in factories and mines, the home became merely an evening refuge from the day's labor. One man's wages were seldom enough to pay the rent, so women and children of the household also had to seek employment. Since women and children were paid lower wages than men, they sometimes found it easier to hold a job in a time of economic depression. This tended to lower the self-esteem of unemployed men and to increase family tensions.

The jobs available to working-class women in the post-Civil War years were limited to low-paying work in factories and laundries and domestic work as cleaners and cooks in middle-class homes. New technologies of the 1880s and 1890s opened up thousands of jobs for women as typists and telephone operators.

**Middle-Class Families**  As cities grew, so did the numbers of Americans who belonged to society's middle class. (This class consists of people who have sufficient income to live in modest comfort.) In the period after the Civil War, the emerging middle class included shopkeepers, well-educated professionals (doctors, lawyers, teachers, and others), and salaried office workers who wore white collars and business suits to work. Office workers were known as "white-collar" workers to distinguish them from "blue-collar" factory workers.

The values of people in the middle class tended to be conservative— honoring the nation, upholding polite manners, and regularly attending religious services in a church or synagogue. Married women of the middle class were generally discouraged from working at a job. Instead of earning income, they were expected to devote themselves to the care of a family and also to engage in civic and charitable activities in the community. Many single women of the middle class pursued careers as teachers—the one profession in which women greatly outnumbered men.

**Conspicuous Consumption of the Wealthy Class**  The smallest class in society—the wealthy—were also the most visible. Those who made great fortunes from owning successful businesses (men like Andrew Carnegie and John D. Rockefeller) displayed their wealth so that all would notice and admire it. In New York City they built enormous mansions, hired hundreds of household servants, entertained friends on yachts and private railroad cars, bred racehorses, and paid huge sums for masterpieces of European art. The buying habits of the rich were called **conspicuous consumption** by an economist and keen observer of the time, Thorstein Veblen. He said that costly objects were bought by the wealthy, not because they were useful, but because they showed off the owner's success. The humorist Mark Twain called the late nineteenth century the **Gilded Age** because of the showy objects collected by millionaires. (To "gild" is to cover objects with a thin layer of gold.)

Although the rich spent lavishly on their private amusements, they also donated millions for public causes. Rockefeller, Carnegie, and others devoted the later years of their lives to enriching American culture by financing libraries, museums, universities, and medical research.

## OBSERVERS OF AMERICAN LIFE: GROWING UP IN NEW YORK CITY (about 1850)

Gene Schermerhorn was a man of 44 in 1886 when he began writing to a cousin about his memories of childhood growing up in New York City. In the excerpt below he compares the city of the 1850s with the city of the 1880s.

What aspects of daily life changed between the years of the writer's childhood and those of his adulthood? Would you think such changes were typical of most U.S. cities?

It seems hard to believe that Twenty-third Street—which is the first street in the city of which I remember anything, could have changed so much in so short a time. The rural scenes, the open spaces, have vanished; and the small and quiet residences, many of them built entirely of wood, have given place to huge piles of brick and stone, and to iron and plate-glass fronts of the stores which now line the street.

I was six years old when we moved to New York from Williamsburgh in 1848. We went to live in a house in this street just west of Sixth Avenue. . . .

This will give you an idea of the house; right next door was a small farm or truck-garden extending nearly to Seventh Avenue. Across the way were the stables of the 6th Ave Omnibus line; the stages starting here and going down Sixth Avenue, 8th Street and Broadway to the Battery. They afterwards started from Forty-sixth Street. I shall have more to tell about these Stage Lines for at this time there were no horse cars. Twenty-third Street and in fact all the streets in the neighborhood were unpaved. Here was my playground and a good one it was. There certainly was plenty of room, plenty of dirt (clean dirt) and plenty of boys; what more could be desired!

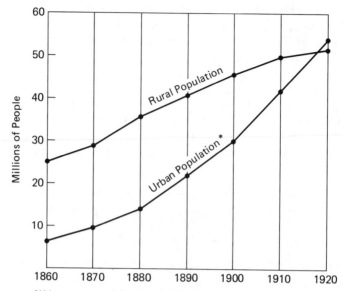

*Urban areas were defined by the U.S. Census Bureau as places with at least 2,500 inhabitants.

U.S. urban and rural population, 1860–1920

## D. ETHNIC NEIGHBORHOODS

As different groups of people moved into a city (some from Italy, some from China, some from rural America, and so on), they gathered in neighborhoods of their own nationality and ethnicity. (An ethnic group is one that shares a common cultural background.) At first the residents of **ethnic neighborhoods** lived in working-class tenements because job opportunities for non-English-speaking immigrants were mainly in the city's factories.

## E. POPULAR CULTURE

City people had opportunities for recreation and amusement different from the fishing, hunting, and picnicking that farm families enjoyed. In addition to the stage shows that had long been popular, city people in the late 1800s started cheering the "home team" in professional baseball games.

**Sports and Recreation** An amateur baseball game (one of the first on record) was played in Hoboken, New Jersey, in 1846. But the sport did not fully come into its own until after the Civil War. Cincinnati was the first city to have a professional team—the Red Stockings (now the Cincinnati Reds), formed in 1869. Football began entertaining crowds of spectators on college campuses in the 1870s. To give city youths some team exercise in the winter months, a teacher in

Springfield, Massachusetts, invented basketball in 1892. In each sport, people became fans of one team or another.

**Dime Novels and Penny Newspapers**   Another form of cheap entertainment were the one-penny and two-penny newspapers that circulated daily in every city. New York publishers like William Randolph Hearst and Joseph Pulitzer appealed to the urban masses by featuring articles on team sports and sensational crimes. Other publishers found that books sold well if they were on exciting subjects (like the outlaws of the West) and priced at only ten cents.

## F. HEALTH AND EDUCATION

The age of urban growth coincided with an age of scientific discovery. City doctors were challenged to find cures for diphtheria and other contagious diseases that, in urban crowds, turned into epidemics. City hospitals were built to meet the needs of a growing population. As a result of improved health care, the average life expectancy in the United States in 1900 was 47.3 years, compared to only 35.5 years a century earlier.

In the same period schools increased in number and improved in quality. More teachers received professional training. Cities raised money for new elementary schools and high schools. Between 1865 and 1900 enrollments at the elementary school level more than doubled. The number of high schools in the country went from only about 400 in 1860 to more than 6,000 in 1900. The general public approved the building of new schools, recognizing that an educated citizenry benefited everyone.

In response to the needs of a new industrial age, educators defined their goals differently. Formerly, they had concentrated on teaching basic literacy: reading, writing, and arithmetic. But after 1900 "progressive" educators believed that it was equally important to offer occupational training courses and to prepare students for citizenship.

## G. MUSIC, ART, AND LITERATURE

A growing urban population made it possible for talented Americans to make a living as professional artists, musicians, and writers. As the author of *The Adventures of Tom Sawyer* (1876) and *The Adventures of Huckleberry Finn* (1884), Samuel Clemens became a celebrity in the Gilded Age under the pen name Mark Twain. Early in the twentieth century Willa Cather achieved fame for *My Antonia* (1918), a novel of Western life. Henry James's *Washington Square* (1880) and Edith Wharton's *The Age of Innocence* (1920) depicted the social manners of upper-class New Yorkers.

Going to the opera became a popular pastime in the cities. In New York City the ornately decorated Metropolitan Opera House opened its doors in 1883. An original, distinctly American music of the period was composed by an African American and former slave, Scott Joplin. His music for the piano, including "Maple Leaf Rag" (1899), was known as ragtime, a lively and rhythmic music that influenced the development of jazz. In our times Joplin's music was used as the background for a popular 1973 movie, "The Sting."

### *In Review*

The following questions refer to section II: The Growth of Cities.

1. Compare the impact of industrialism on a working-class family with its impact on a middle-class family.
2. Identify four ways that the growth of cities after the Civil War affected American cultural life.

# III. Changing Patterns of Immigration

The United States has been called "a nation of immigrants" because all its citizens have ancestors who had once immigrated from another land. Even Native Americans are the descendants of an Asiatic people who probably migrated from Siberia to North America between 20,000 to 40,000 years ago. After Columbus's voyages of discovery in the 1490s, ships from Spain and Portugal brought the first immigrants from Europe. After that, immigration from Europe to North and South America continued for centuries—and continues to this day.

In the 50-year period after the Civil War (1865 to 1915), more immigrants arrived than ever before. They played a vital role in the settling of both the Western frontier and the Eastern cities.

## A. IMMIGRATION BEFORE THE CIVIL WAR

Before describing immigration after the Civil War, let us briefly identify the immigrant groups that first settled the British colonies and the United States *before* 1860.

**British Immigrants in Colonial Times**  A majority of those who immigrated to the British colonies from 1607 to 1776 came from the British Isles: England, Scotland, Wales, and Northern Ireland. Some immigrated for religious reasons. Puritans, for example, were persecuted for wanting to reform the Church of England. Other immigrants were unemployed city dwellers and debtors who hoped to find economic opportunities in the American colonies.

**Non-British Immigrants in Colonial Times**  A large number of immigrants to the British colonies did *not* speak English when they arrived. The Europeans among them came chiefly from France, Germany, Holland, and Sweden. (See graph on the next page.) Their

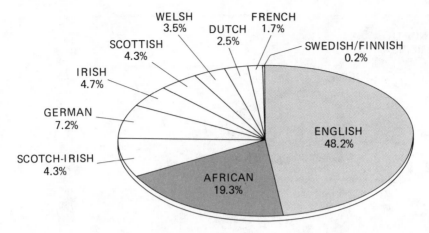

WELSH
3.5%

SCOTTISH
4.3%

DUTCH
2.5%

FRENCH 1.7%

SWEDISH/FINNISH
0.2%

IRISH
4.7%

GERMAN
7.2%

ENGLISH
48.2%

SCOTCH-IRISH
4.3%

AFRICAN
19.3%

Ethnic groups in the U.S. population, 1790

reasons for immigrating were similar to those of the English and Scottish. They wanted to escape from religious intolerance and seek opportunities to own land on the frontier.

**Forced Immigration of Africans**  A large number of people were shipped to the British colonies against their will. Born on the west coast of Africa, they were captured in wars between African kingdoms, sold to European slave traders, and forced to endure a frightening voyage across unknown waters to an unknown destination. African slaves were commonly used in Spanish America as early as the 1500s. In the British colonies the first slaves arrived in Jamestown, Virginia, in 1619. Through the 1600s and 1700s the slave trade continued to grow. By the time of the American Revolution, slaves in the original 13 states numbered between 750,000 and 850,000 and formed about 20 percent of the population. Thus, in George Washington's time, one American in five was of African ancestry.

A clause of the U.S. Constitution enabled Congress to prohibit the importation of slaves after 1808. Even so, the slave trade continued illegally. About a million Africans suffered the fate of being shipped to the South as slaves between 1808 and 1860.

**Early Republic: Immigration of British, Germans, and Irish**  The immigrant ships that arrived in U.S. ports after 1800 brought three main groups: the British, the Germans, and the Irish.

Thousands of British decided to leave their homeland mainly for economic reasons related to the Industrial Revolution. They had come to London and other cities looking for employment, but there weren't enough jobs for all the people seeking them. Desperately poor, they hoped to do better in the fast-growing American republic.

After a revolution in 1848—a revolution that failed—Germans

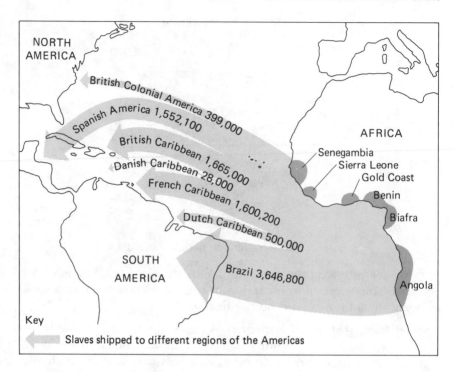

NORTH
AMERICA

British Colonial America 399,000

Spanish America 1,552,100

British Caribbean 1,665,000

Danish Caribbean 28,000

French Caribbean 1,600,200

Dutch Caribbean 500,000

SOUTH
AMERICA

Brazil 3,646,800

AFRICA

Senegambia
Sierra Leone
Gold Coast
Benin
Biafra
Angola

Key

Slaves shipped to different regions of the Americas

The global context: slave trade in the 1700s

immigrated to the United States in large numbers. Among them were many Jews. The Germans came for both political reasons (unhappiness over the defeat of their revolution) and economic reasons (seeking opportunities for farming and employment). As a group they added their voices to the antislavery movement, supported the growth of public education, and established successful farms in the Midwest.

The largest immigrant group before the Civil War were the Irish. In 1846 a plant disease known as blight killed the potato crop upon which the Irish relied for food. Thousands starved to death. For thousands of others, immigrating to the United States seemed the only way to survive the effects of the potato famine. The wave of Irish immigration was the first large-scale entry of Roman Catholics into U.S. society. Many Irish immigrants took positions of leadership in the Democratic party in large Eastern cities.

**Absorption of Latin Americans**   Before the U.S. war with Mexico in 1846, almost all Spanish-speaking Americans lived *outside* the United States in Latin American countries to the west and south. Mexican territory extended as far as Texas and California, whose populations consisted of both Indian tribes and citizens of Mexico.

When Mexico was defeated in war in 1848, the Mexicans of Texas and California automatically became citizens of the United States. Mexican Americans in California were soon joined by other Spanish-speaking people when news of California gold attracted thousands of Latin American immigrants.

In the U.S. territory of New Mexico in the 1850s, Spanish and English were both used as official languages of the territorial government. Government documents were printed in both Spanish and English. Thus, at least in the Southwest, there was a tradition of **bilingualism** (the practice of giving official recognition to two languages).

## B. THE DOMINANT AMERICAN CULTURE

The U.S. population has always represented a blend of two groups: (a) foreign-born people from many lands and (b) native-born Americans whose colonial ancestors had been immigrants but who long ago had lost touch with their family's immigrant past. Because the second group (the native-born) formed a majority, they tended to dominate U.S. society and to determine the prime cultural values of the nation. Although these values differed from one region to another, the following traits described American society in general in the nineteenth century (1800s).

**Individualism**   This was the belief that each person was completely responsible for his or her own actions. If a person attained economic success, it was assumed that the chief reason was his or her strength of character. Similarly, if a person failed, it was thought to be because of some fault or weakness of character.

**Puritanism**   During colonial times, especially in New England, the majority culture was strongly influenced by the teachings of a Protestant religion known as Puritanism. Protestant ministers in the North preached a stern Christian morality and taught that the inner soul of every person was essentially sinful or wicked. They believed that only a fortunate few were "predestined" (selected before birth) to be "saved" or accepted into God's kingdom. As part of their moral code, Puritans stressed the importance of working hard and carefully managing one's money and property.

**Rough Social Equality**   Native-born people of European descent tended to view each other as social equals, especially on the Western frontier. They stressed the importance of being neighborly and helpful to others.

**Belief in White Superiority**   Throughout the 1800s many white Americans in the North as well as the South believed that their race

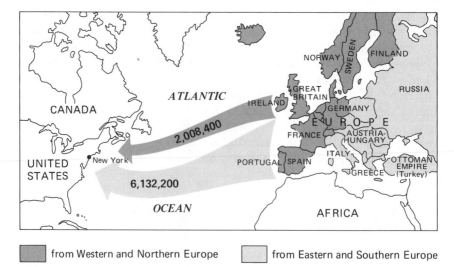

from Western and Northern Europe      from Eastern and Southern Europe

Peak years of European immigration, 1901 to 1910

was superior to other groups (Africans, Asians, Latin Americans, and Native Americans). They believed that the United States had a mission to bring the benefits of Western civilization to other regions and people. Americans of British descent viewed their culture as superior to the culture of other nationalities. Also many Protestants regarded their faith as superior to other religions.

These cultural values of the native-born European Americans influenced their attitudes toward foreign-born newcomers to the United States.

## C. THE "NEW IMMIGRATION"

During the 1860s and the decades following, the nature of the foreign-born population began to change. Immigrants from Italy, Austria-Hungary, Greece, Russia, and other countries of eastern and southern Europe arrived in increasingly large numbers. They were called "**new immigrants**" because their cultures were different from those of the earlier groups from western Europe.

**The Assimilation Issue**  **Assimilation** is the slow process by which a minority culture learns the customs of the dominant culture. Americans who spoke English and worshipped in Protestant churches considered themselves to be the guardians of the dominant U.S. culture. Even though they were descended from immigrants, they distrusted the "new immigrants" who arrived in the United States in the post-Civil War era. They were afraid that these immigrants would not assimilate easily into the English-speaking culture of the majority. Beginning in the 1870s the issue of whether or not to admit foreign-born people from all lands became a major issue in U.S. politics.

**Cultural Differences of the "New Immigrants"**    Immigrants of an earlier time had been much alike. Except for German immigrants they spoke the same language, English. Except for Irish immigrants and German Jews they were mainly Protestants. Even the Germans and Irish seemed to adjust easily to the dominant, English-speaking culture of the United States.

But few of the "new immigrants" (those arriving after 1880) were English-speaking and very few attended Protestant churches. The Italians were mainly Roman Catholics. The Greeks were Eastern Orthodox Christians. The Poles and Russians were largely Jewish. Besides their unfamiliar languages and religions, the new arrivals wore clothing and cooked foods that seemed strange to many native-born Americans. Could the newcomers learn to become Americans? Could they assimilate successfully? Newspaper editorials of the 1870s and 1880s raised fears and doubts about the newcomers.

The native-born became even more concerned after 1890 when the number of people arriving from southern and eastern Europe began to exceed the numbers from other regions. Between 1900 and 1910 total immigration averaged close to a million people a year (compared to less than 300,000 a year in the 1860s). Of the total arriving in 1910, there were about 700,000 people from the countries of southern and eastern Europe and only about 300,000 from all other countries.

# D. REASONS FOR IMMIGRATION

From one country to the next, the reasons for immigration varied. In general, however, every person's or family's decision to immigrate was based on two conclusions—one negative and the other positive.

- Negative conclusion: Conditions in the home country were bad and could not be tolerated.

- Positive conclusion: Conditions in the United States were likely to be much better than those at home.

Let us identify the specific conditions that caused different groups of Europeans to board ships for America.

**Population Pressures**    In the Industrial Age Europe was becoming overcrowded. A European population of 140 million in 1750 grew to 260 million in 1850 and 400 million in 1914. Farmlands were scarce compared to the abundance of lands on the Western frontier of the United States. Also, recognizing that the United States was industrializing at a rapid rate, many Europeans thought U.S. factory jobs might be easier to find and pay better wages than those near home. As one historian wrote, "The new machines [in the United States] provided jobs for the millions, so the millions appeared."

**Recruitment Campaigns** Railroad companies with Western lands to sell and steamship companies seeking passengers sent agents to Europe to promote the idea of immigration. Recruiters gave the impression that, after a few years of work, anybody could expect to become rich in the United States. Steamship lines offered tickets for the ocean voyage to New York City for as little as $25 a person.

**Economic Conditions** In southern Italy after 1880—and also in the Scandinavian countries of Sweden and Norway—it became more and more difficult for poor farmers to earn a living. From one generation to the next, the farms in Italy and Scandinavia were divided and subdivided to provide the sons of a family with land. Most farms had become too small to raise a profitable crop. Many Italians, Swedes, and Norwegians were landless and desperately poor.

**Political Oppression** Harsh laws could be as bad as economic troubles. As a religious and ethnic minority, Jews in Russia and Poland lived in fear of **pogroms**—sudden attacks on their communities in which Jews would be beaten and killed and their homes set on fire. In many countries of eastern Europe, people resented laws requiring boys of 15 and 16 to serve in a monarch's army.

### European Immigrants: When and Why They Came

| Nationality | Period of Greatest Immigration | Reasons for Immigrating |
| --- | --- | --- |
| Irish | 1840s and 1850s | Failure of potato crop and resulting famine |
| German | 1840s to 1880s | Economic depression; oppression following failed revolution |
| Scandinavian (Danes, Swedes, Norwegians, and Finns) | 1870s to 1900s | Poverty; shortage of farmland |
| Italian | 1880s to 1920s | Poverty; shortage of farmland |
| Jews from eastern Europe (including Poland and Russia) | 1880s to 1920s | Political oppression; religious persecution; poverty |

## E. ADJUSTING TO AMERICAN LIFE

The experience of leaving one's country and traveling to an unknown place is usually a difficult and painful one. Certainly it was difficult for Italians, Scandinavians, Greeks, and eastern Europeans whose

# OBSERVERS OF AMERICAN LIFE: THE LOWER EAST SIDE IN 1898

*After arriving from Russia in 1882, Abraham Cahan adjusted quickly to American life. He published a novel about the experience of Russian Jews in the 1890s and wrote an article about his New York City neighborhood, the Lower East Side. The following passage comes from Cahan's article in the* Atlantic Monthly, *1898.*

*In the author's view what characteristics of Russian-Jewish immigrants enabled them to preserve their own culture and also adapt successfully to American ways?*

Sixteen years have elapsed [since Cahan's arrival in New York City]. The Jewish population has grown from a quarter of a million to about one million. Scarcely a large American town but has some Russo-Jewish names in its directory, with an educated Russian-speaking minority forming a colony within a Yiddish-speaking colony,* while cities like New York, Chicago, Philadelphia, and Boston have each a ghetto [Jewish neighborhood] rivaling in extent of population the largest Jewish cities in Russia, Austria, and Rumania. The number of Jewish residents in Manhattan borough is estimated at 250,000, making it the largest center of Hebrew population in the world. . . .

The grammar schools of the Jewish quarter are overcrowded with children of immigrants, who, for progress and deportment, are raised with the very best in the city. At least 500 of 1,677 students at the New York City College, where tuition and books are free, are Jewish boys from the East Side. . . .

The 5,000,000 Jews living under the czar [in Russia] had not a single Yiddish daily paper even when the government allowed such publications, while their fellow countrymen and coreligionists who have taken up their abode in America publish six dailies (five in New York and one in Chicago), not to mention the countless Yiddish weeklies and monthlies, and the pamphlets and books which today make New York the largest Yiddish book market in the world.

* Yiddish is a language spoken by many European Jews.

way of life in the "old country" was far different from the way of life in their adopted country, the United States.

**Efforts to Assimilate**   Living in ethnic neighborhoods in U.S. cities, immigrants tried to preserve the customs and language that they had known in Europe. At the same time they tried hard to learn to speak

Lower East Side in New York City, 1900

English. Usually, immigrant children learned English and taught and adopted American ways far more readily than their parents. Schools taught only in English and sometimes changed an immigrant student's name to make it easier for native-born Americans to pronounce. At times immigrants or their children changed their own names in order to blend in more easily with the majority culture.

**Prejudice Against Foreign-born Workers**  Native-born American workers resented having to compete for jobs with people from a foreign country. Labor unions generally opposed immigration and refused to admit foreign-born members. Many employers shared the unions' antiforeign prejudice. Most immigrants therefore were forced to accept only the lowest paying jobs in factories, mines, and lumber camps.

**Living Conditions**  People living in the overcrowded tenements of the cities were mostly foreign-born. Tenement apartments were known as "railroad flats" because they were arranged in a straight line, one after the other. Families often had to share an already crowded apartment with relatives and friends recently arrived from Europe. Many apartments had no bathroom. A single toilet might be available for an entire floor. The grim living conditions of the typical immigrant family in New York City were fully described by Jacob Riis in his 1890 book, *How the Other Half Lives*—a book that shocked many middle-class readers.

## F. IMMIGRANTS FROM ASIA

In addition to European immigrants, who settled mainly in the East, there were large numbers of Chinese and Japanese immigrants who settled on the West Coast. By 1910 more than 300,000 Chinese immigrants and more than 150,000 Japanese immigrants had crossed the Pacific Ocean to work in the United States. Most were young men who had left their families at home and hoped to return to Asia after having saved a large sum of money.

## G. CONTRIBUTIONS TO THE AMERICAN ECONOMY

The Western frontier and Eastern cities alike depended upon the labor of immigrants. They provided the labor for the building of the first transcontinental railroad. They turned the prairies and forests of the Middle West into prosperous farms. They helped to make New York City the center for a booming garment industry. They opened small retail stores that would later grow into large department stores such as Macy's and Gimbels. They provided the necessary labor for the steel mills of Pittsburgh, Pennsylvania, and Birmingham, Alabama. They became the technicians, inventors, and scientists who helped to turn the dream of a mighty industrial empire into a reality.

## H. NATIVIST REACTION TO THE NEW IMMIGRANTS

A **nativist** is someone who believes that the foreign-born pose a threat to the majority culture and should be stopped from entering the country. At different times in the nineteenth century, nativists made organized attempts to exclude certain immigrant groups— especially Irish Catholics, east European Jews, Italians, Chinese, and Japanese.

**Know-Nothings** The first target of nativist anger were the Irish Catholics who immigrated in record numbers in the 1850s. American-born Protestants organized a secret society called the **Know-Nothings,** which, as a political party, tried to elect candidates who would promise to restrict, or limit, immigration. (Members of the society were called "know-nothings" because, when asked about the society's activities, they would answer, "I know nothing.")

**Fear of the "Yellow Peril"** In the 1870s there was talk of Asian people coming to the United States by the millions and overwhelming the American culture. In Western states and territories, anti-Chinese riots broke out to protest the so-called "**Yellow Peril.**" Two laws were passed in response to the nativist fears and prejudice.

- The **Chinese Exclusion Act** (1882) declared that no more Chinese would be permitted to immigrate to the United States.

- In the schools of San Francisco, Japanese children were required to attend segregated classes. Japan's government was deeply offended by this practice. President Theodore Roosevelt persuaded California's local governments to end their offensive school policies. In return Japan agreed to stop the further immigration of Japanese workers into the United States. This diplomatic understanding of 1907 and 1908 was known as the **Gentlemen's Agreement.**

**Causes of Nativist Feeling.**    How can we explain the nativist dislike for Asians, Eastern Europeans, and other immigrants?

- An *economic reason* was competition for jobs. Many native-born Americans feared that immigrants would deprive them of their jobs by working for very low wages. (In fact employers were the ones chiefly responsible for discriminating against native-born workers and taking advantage of immigrants' desperate need for work of any kind at any wage.)

- A *cultural reason* was the tendency of people belonging to a dominant culture to protect that culture against outside or "foreign" influences.

- A *psychological reason* was the nativist's desire to feel superior to others. This desire often takes a racist and nationalist form— the feeling that one's own race or nationality is superior to all others. Nativists expressed racist ideas by asserting that the newcomers from Eastern and Southern Europe were racially inferior and would produce a class of criminals and paupers.

- A *political reason* was a common fear among native-born Americans that many new immigrants might be connected with radical and revolutionary causes.

Nativist reaction was countered by those Americans who recognized the essential contributions of the immigrants. A New York writer named Emma Lazarus expressed this positive point of view in a poem that began: "Give me your tired, your poor, your huddled masses yearning to breathe free, the wretched refuse of your teeming shore. Send these, the homeless, the tempest-tossed, to me." Lazarus's poem is inscribed at the base of the Statue of Liberty, whose lamp started welcoming immigrant ships to New York Harbor in 1886.

**Red Scare**    A Communist revolution in Russia in 1917 fueled nativist fears about the loyalties of the huge foreign-born population. Nativists thought that there might be an attempt by foreign-born radicals to overthrow the U.S. government. Their fears turned to action in the **Red Scare** of 1919 and 1920. President Wilson's attorney general, A. Mitchell Palmer, organized a series of raids—the so-called **Palmer raids**—to arrest and deport immigrants suspected of disloyalty. Federal agents were told to enter homes, businesses, and the offices of political groups and search for damaging evidence. Often they did so without search warrants. Before the raids ended, nearly 600 people were forced to leave the United States as unwanted "Reds" (radical thinkers).

# I. LAWS RESTRICTING IMMIGRATION

The antiforeign attitudes of many native-born Americans were reflected in a series of immigration laws passed by Congress between 1882 and 1924. The first of these laws excluded Chinese immigrants and banned the immigration of people with "undesirable qualities" (paupers, prostitutes, and others). Later laws, adopted after World War I, were designed to discriminate against large classes of people—especially the new immigrants from southern and eastern Europe.

| Date | Immigration Law |
|------|-----------------|
| 1882 | Chinese Exclusion Act: Chinese were prohibited from immigrating. |
| 1882 | Paupers, convicts, and mentally defective persons were prohibited from immigrating. |
| 1891 | Prostitutes, polygamists, and diseased persons were prohibited from immigrating. |
| 1917 | Literacy test: Those unable to pass a reading test in their native language (or any other language) were prohibited from immigrating. |
| 1921 | First quota law: Yearly immigration from any country was limited to just 3 percent of the number arriving from that country in 1910. |
| 1924 | New quota law: (a) Yearly immigration from any country was limited to just 2 percent of the number arriving from that country in 1890. (b) No more than 150,000 immigrants were to be admitted yearly from a single country. (c) No Asian immigrants would be admitted. |

One purpose of the **quota laws** of the 1920s was to reduce to a bare minimum the number of immigrants arriving from Italy, the Soviet Union (formerly Russia), and other countries of southern and eastern Europe. A second purpose was to halt all immigration from Asia. The laws did in fact drastically reduce immigration to the United States. Earlier, during the peak period of immigration (1901 to 1910), more than eight million immigrants (mostly from Italy, Austria-Hungary, and Russia) had arrived. Because of the **restrictive immigration laws**, fewer than 350,000 immigrants arrived in the 1930s.

# J. THE ASSIMILATION ISSUE: THREE POINTS OF VIEW

To what extent should immigrants be expected to adopt the customs and the language of the American majority? To what extent should

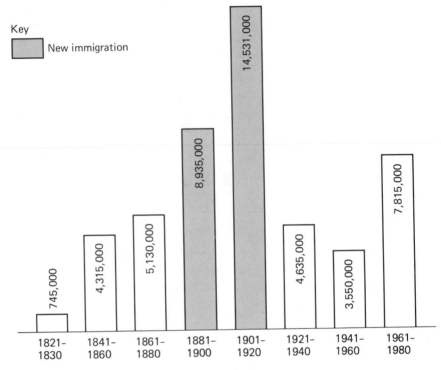

Key

■ New immigration

14,531,000

8,935,000

7,815,000

5,130,000

4,635,000

4,315,000

3,550,000

745,000

| 1821–<br>1830 | 1841–<br>1860 | 1861–<br>1880 | 1881–<br>1900 | 1901–<br>1920 | 1921–<br>1940 | 1941–<br>1960 | 1961–<br>1980 |

Immigration to the United States, 1821 to 1980

they preserve and cherish the culture of their birth? In a "nation of immigrants" such as ours, the question is a vital and continuing one. During the peak years of immigration (1901 to 1910), Americans debated three opposing points of view on the issue.

**Total Assimilation, or Americanization** According to this viewpoint immigrants should learn to speak English and become Americanized by adopting all aspects of American culture as quickly as possible. They should make an effort to rid themselves of customs derived from a foreign (non-American) culture.

**"Melting Pot" Theory** According to this idea immigrants from various nations would gradually and naturally blend into a single nation—the American nation. The culture of this "**melting pot**" nation would combine the best elements of the many cultures and nationalities of the foreign-born. Although based on these foreign cultures, the new American culture would be different from them— and also superior to them, since it combined their best features. The theory was democratic in that it respected elements from all cultures.

It was also nationalistic, since it regarded American culture as superior to others. Believers in the "melting pot" theory thought that English should be the common language for everyone—native-born and foreign-born alike.

**Cultural Pluralism**    According to **cultural pluralists** an English-speaking culture is not superior to any other culture. Instead, all cultures and languages of the foreign-born population should be respected as valuable. Each ethnic group should practice its own customs while also adjusting to the ways of the larger society. Today many cultural pluralists favor the idea of bilingualism—using Russian, Korean, or Spanish to teach science, math, and other subjects to foreign-born children rather than requiring them to cope in English. Their new language would be learned in periods set aside for English and also outside the classroom in the cafeteria and gym.

## In Review

The following questions refer to section III: Changing Patterns of Immigration and to the word wheel.

**Word Wheel**

Identify the group *or* groups described by each phrase.

**1.** Most likely to have approved the Palmer raids
**2.** Included among the "new immigrants"
**3.** Most likely to have opposed the immigration laws of the 1920s
**4.** Least likely to be cultural pluralists
**5.** Descended from immigrants
**6.** Settled in ethnic neighborhoods in Eastern cities
**7.** Similar in their social and political beliefs to the Know-Nothings

# GLOSSARY OF KEY TERMS: CHAPTER 7

**"Americanization"**   the view that immigrants to the United States should adopt all aspects of the majority culture.

**assimilation**   the process by which Native Americans and immigrants learned the ways of the majority culture.

**bilingualism**   the practice of giving official recognition to two languages.

**Chinese Exclusion Act**   a federal law of 1882 excluding Chinese people from immigrating to the United States.

**conspicuous consumption**   the practice of buying costly goods and services in order to impress other people.

**cultural pluralism**   the view that immigrant groups should retain their original cultures even while learning American ways.

**Dawes Act**   a federal law of 1887 that divided the tribal lands of Native Americans into individual plots.

**ethnic neighborhoods**   sections of a city populated by different nationalities.

**Gentlemen's Agreement**   an informal agreement (1907 to 1908) between President Theodore Roosevelt and the Japanese government that stopped further Japanese immigration to the United States.

**Gilded Age**   the period from 1865 to 1900 when industrial leaders amassed great fortunes and dazzled the public with their wealth.

**homesteaders**   settlers who moved to the West as farmers and sheep-herders and acquired land under the Homestead Act of 1862.

**Indian Reorganization Act**   a federal law of 1934 permitting Native Americans to hold lands in common rather than requiring ownership of individual plots.

**Know-Nothings**   a secret society and minor political party of the 1850s that opposed the immigration of Roman Catholics to the United States.

**literacy test**   the requirement of an immigration law of 1917 that immigrants be able to read at least one language.

**"melting pot"**   a theory that immigrant groups would eventually lose their original identity by blending into the mainstream culture.

**nativists**   native-born citizens who believe that the foreign-born pose a threat to the majority culture and should be stopped from entering the country.

**"new immigration"**   the large numbers of immigrants from eastern and southern Europe who came to the United States between 1880 and 1920.

**open range**   huge unfenced territory in the West used by ranchers to graze their cattle.

**Palmer raids**   government raids organized by Attorney General Palmer in 1919 and 1920 for the purpose of arresting and deporting immigrants believed to be Communists.

**pogroms**   outbreaks of violence against Jews in Russia and Poland, in which Jews were beaten and killed and their villages destroyed.

**quota laws**   immigration laws of the 1920s that severely limited the number of immigrants from eastern and southern Europe.

**Red Scare**   the period after World War I—1919 and 1920—when many Americans feared that communists were plotting to take over the U.S. government.

**reservation**   land set aside for the use of a Native American tribe or tribes.

**restrictive immigration laws**   federal laws for the purpose of limiting the total number of immigrants and especially the number of immigrants from eastern and southern Europe.

**safety valve**   the idea that the Western frontier provided dissatisfied Easterners with an opportunity to improve their lives by moving west.

**tenements**   multifamily houses in city neighborhoods that were occupied by working-class families.

**vigilante justice**   the practice of lynching (hanging) or otherwise punishing a suspected criminal without a formal trial.

**"Yellow Peril"**   the view that Asian immigrants in the late 1800s threatened U.S. society because of their cultural differences from the white majority.

# TEST YOURSELF

## A. Multiple Choice: Facts, Main Ideas, Skills

*On a separate sheet of paper, write the number of the word or expression that, of those given, best completes the statement or answers the question.*

### Reviewing the facts

1. The 1890 census indicated that an end had come to the  (1) "new immigration" from Europe  (2) era of railroad building  (3) policy of "manifest destiny"  (4) existence of a frontier

2. Which was most responsible for the rapid economic growth of cities during the nineteenth century?  (1) presence of theaters and libraries  (2) growth of industry  (3) rise of urban mass transportation  (4) the development of mass communication

3. During the 1800s most immigrants to the United States came because  (1) unskilled factory jobs were available  (2) the U.S. government lowered tariff rates  (3) they wanted to escape communism  (4) they were seeking political power

4. U.S. immigration restrictions of the 1920s severely reduced the number of immigrants from  (1) Great Britain and Scandinavia  (2)

eastern Europe and Asia   (3) Africa and Latin America   (4) Canada and Australia

5. The passage of the immigration acts of 1921 and 1924 indicated that the United States wished to   (1) restrict the flow of immigrants   (2) continue the immigration policies followed during most of the nineteenth century   (3) encourage cultural diversity   (4) play a larger role in international affairs

6. According to Frederick Jackson Turner, one effect of the frontier on U.S. society was to   (1) encourage the growth of democracy   (2) decrease economic opportunity   (3) limit the rights of women   (4) increase Americans' concern for the environment

7. How did the "new immigrants" who came to the United States between 1880 and 1920 differ from earlier immigrants?   (1) They were considered physically and mentally superior to earlier immigrants.   (2) They arrived before the closing of the frontier in the West.   (3) The countries they came from differed from those of the earlier immigrants.   (4) They came chiefly from northern and western Europe.

8. From the Red Scare of 1919 and 1920 it became clear that   (1) large numbers of Soviet agents had infiltrated the federal government   (2) communism tended to gain influence in times of economic prosperity   (3) loyalty oaths helped to prevent espionage   (4) people's fears of disloyalty could lead to the erosion of civil liberties

9. The Chinese Exclusion Act, the Gentlemen's Agreement, and the immigration laws of the 1920s were reactions to earlier U.S. policies of   (1) requiring proof of literacy   (2) permitting unlimited immigration   (3) restricting immigration to the middle and upper classes   (4) encouraging the immigration of scientists and intellectuals

10. Those believing in the idea of the "melting pot" predicted that   (1) each immigrant group would always maintain its separate identity   (2) all immigrant groups would eventually adopt an English culture   (3) a unique American culture would emerge from the blending of Old World cultures   (4) some immigrant groups would retain their culture while others would gradually blend into the mainstream culture

## Reviewing the main ideas

11. Between 1865 and 1890 what effect did westward expansion have on U.S. society?   (1) increased interest in Latin American politics   (2) increased economic opportunities   (3) decreased concern about industrialization   (4) increased respect for immigrants

12. What was a major reason that farmers did not settle the Great Plains before 1860?   (1) They had enough good land in the East.   (2) They had no way to stop cattle ranchers from using the Great Plains for grazing.   (3) They did not know how to cope with the absence of water and trees.   (4) Farm families were too small to provide enough labor to plant and harvest crops on the plains.

**13.** "If a nation expects to be ignorant and free, in a state of civilization, it expects what never was and never will be." Which idea is most strongly supported by this statement?  (1) compulsory education  (2) universal suffrage  (3) strong central government  (4) government's power to tax

**14.** What effect did U.S. population growth have on American Indians in the nineteenth century?  (1) It caused Indians to move to urban areas in large numbers.  (2) It forced Indians to move westward.  (3) It led most Indians to adopt the culture of the settlers.  (4) Most Indians formed alliances with other minority groups.

**15.** The growth of industry after the Civil War resulted in  (1) the decline of suburbs  (2) the growth of cities  (3) an increase in the number of farmers  (4) a decline in immigration

**16.** In the late 1800s overcrowding, crime, and poor sanitation characterized  (1) frontier life  (2) life in a farming community  (3) life in urban areas  (4) Indian life on the Great Plains

**17.** In the late 1800s the middle-class U.S. family was characterized by  (1) an increase in patriarchal control  (2) the expectation that women would stay home to care for children  (3) strengthening of the extended family  (4) encouragement of large families

**18.** Which is a long-range effect of industrialization on the status of women in the United States?  (1) decline of legal rights for women  (2) decline in the importance of formal education for women  (3) increase in employment opportunities for women  (4) increase in the percentage of women in domestic occupations

**19.** Which statement about immigration to the United States is accurate?  (1) Most immigration to the United States was completed by 1900.  (2) Immigrants from northern and western Europe have had the most problems in being assimilated into U.S. society?  (3) Immigration has been a result of circumstances abroad as well as in the United States.  (4) Immigrants have had little effect on American culture.

**20.** "U.S. society may be described as a stew in which each ingredient adds to the stew's flavor but still retains its own distinct identity." This statement best describes the concept of  (1) ethnocentrism  (2) cultural pluralism  (3) nativism  (4) social control

**21.** Which is the main way that ethnic groups have helped to shape the U.S. national identity?  (1) Most of the newer groups adopted all the ways of the earlier immigrants.  (2) Ethnic groups made large financial contributions to the arts.  (3) Each group attempted to become the dominant one in American society.  (4) Each group contributed its own cultural characteristics to the general culture of the nation.

**22.** Which statement describes the experience of most immigrants to the United States from 1800 to the present?  (1) They were resented by many native-born Americans.  (2) They settled in rural areas where cheap land was available.  (3) They were rapidly assimilated into the mainstream culture.  (4) They joined radical political parties to bring about economic reform.

*Developing critical thinking skills*

*Questions 23 and 24 refer to the line graph on page 206. Base your answers on that graph.*

**23.** We may conclude from the graph that the rural population of the United States exceeded the urban population until the year  (1) 1890  (2) 1900   (3) 1910   (4) 1920

**24.** We may infer from the graph that most U.S. citizens in 1880 lived (1) in small cities   (2) in large cities   (3) on farms   (4) in places with fewer than 2,500 inhabitants

## B. Enduring Issues

*Select two of the enduring issues from column A. For each issue chosen, explain how the historical example in column B relates to the issue.*

| A. Enduring Issues | B. Historical Examples |
|---|---|
| 1. Civil liberties—the balance between government and the individual | Deporting immigrants in the Red Scare of 1919 and 1920 |
| 2. The rights of ethnic and racial groups under the Constitution | The treatment of Native Americans in the 1870s and 1880s |
| 3. Equality—its definition as a constitutional value | Discrimination against Chinese and Japanese immigrants between 1880 and 1910 |

## C. Essays

### Level 1

U.S. immigration policy between 1789 and 1930 may be divided into two major periods:

Open immigration, 1789 to 1914 (except for Asians)
Restricted immigration, 1921 to 1930.

For *each* period given above, describe U.S. immigration policy. In a concluding paragraph, discuss reasons for the change in policy.

### Level 2

The growth of cities created new problems as well as opportunities.

**A.** List *three* problems of city life in the late 1800s. Then list *two* opportunities that caused people to move to cities.

**B.** Base your answer to part B on your answer to part A. Write an essay describing *either* the problems *or* the opportunities of city life in the late 1800s.

# UNIT THREE

# Progressivism and Imperialism (1890 to 1917)

*In the previous unit* you read about the social problems caused by industrialization. But by and large, neither state governments nor the federal government did much about these problems. Only toward the beginning of a new century—the twentieth century—did government take action. The first chapter in this unit describes what a group of reformers did to make government both more democratic and more actively involved in the nation's economic life.

A second chapter describes the effect of industrial growth on U.S. foreign policy. The effect was enormous because, after a brief war with Spain, the United States became one of the world's great powers.

| Chapter | Topics |
|---|---|
| 8. The Politics of Reform | • How industrial change led to movements for political reform |
| | • How two strong presidents—Theodore Roosevelt and Woodrow Wilson—provided national leadership for reform |
| 9. America Reaching Out | • Why the United States fought a war with Spain in 1898 |
| | • How the United States acquired an overseas empire that included Puerto Rico, Hawaii, and the Philippines |
| | • How Theodore Roosevelt used a "big stick" (the U.S. Navy) to achieve foreign policy goals |

# Chapter *8*

# The Politics of Reform

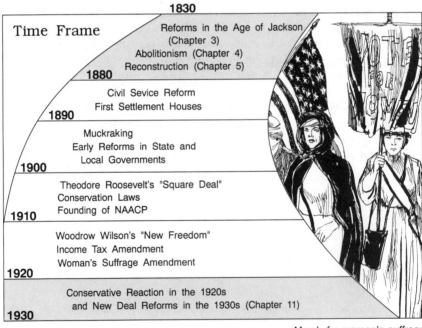

**Time Frame**

**1830**
Reforms in the Age of Jackson (Chapter 3)
Abolitionism (Chapter 4)
Reconstruction (Chapter 5)

**1880**
Civil Sevice Reform
First Settlement Houses

**1890**
Muckraking
Early Reforms in State and Local Governments

**1900**
Theodore Roosevelt's "Square Deal"
Conservation Laws
Founding of NAACP

**1910**
Woodrow Wilson's "New Freedom"
Income Tax Amendment
Woman's Suffrage Amendment

**1920**
Conservative Reaction in the 1920s and New Deal Reforms in the 1930s (Chapter 11)

**1930**

*March for woman's suffrage*

## *Objectives*

- To recognize that there have been several periods of reform in U.S. history including the Progressive Era.
- To identify and evaluate the reforms achieved by the Progressive movement.
- To be aware of the origins of movements to protect consumers, workers, the environment, and the rights of women and minorities.
- To describe the efforts of women and African Americans to bring about democratic reforms.
- To compare the reform politics of three presidents: Theodore Roosevelt, William Howard Taft, and Woodrow Wilson.

A democratic society is one in which everyone enjoys equal civil (or political) rights and equal economic opportunities. Defined in these terms, democracy is an ideal that has never been completely achieved in any country. But the United States is much closer to the democratic ideal because of the efforts of reformers of the past.

One of the most remarkable periods of reform began shortly before 1900 and reached a climax in the presidential election of 1912. The reformers called themselves "progressives" and gave a name to the era that they dominated—the **Progressive Era.**

# I. The Reform Tradition: A Review

Early reform movements paved the way for the progressive reforms at the turn of the twentieth century. Briefly, let us review these earlier movements.

## A. FROM REVOLUTION TO CIVIL WAR

Two wars fought on American soil—the American Revolution and the Civil War—were both caused, in part, by organized protests against acts of tyranny and injustice.

**American Revolution**  Between 1765 and 1775 groups of American colonists protested loud and often against the various attempts by the British government to tax them without the consent of their colonial assemblies. Most colonists had no desire to break away from British rule but only to defend their rights against unfair taxes and other abuses. Nevertheless, Americans' protests and demands for fair treatment eventually led to armed revolt.

**Reform in the Age of Jackson**  As originally written in 1787, the U.S. Constitution said nothing about voting rights. To make the U.S.

political system more democratic, a major movement for reform began in the 1820s, gathered force in the 1830s, and reached a peak in the late 1840s. It was associated with the democratic politics of President Andrew Jackson. Consider the many reforms of this period:

- Voting rights were extended by state laws to all white males above a certain age. (Property qualifications of the past were eliminated.)

- The spoils system (see Glossary, Chapter 3) made it possible for a greater number of people—not just the privileged few—to hold government offices.

- Candidates for office were chosen by national conventions open to many party members. (Formerly, candidates had been chosen at small meetings, or caucuses, of party leaders.)

- President Jackson's opposition to the second Bank of the United States was viewed by many thousands of voters as a courageous attack against the power of the wealthy and privileged class. (See page 92.)

- Helping the disadvantaged was another focus for reform in the 1840s. Dorothea Dix brought pressure on state governments to provide asylums for those suffering from mental illness.

- Recognizing that a democratic society depended on education for all citizens (not just a privileged class), Horace Mann and Henry Barnard led the reform movement that resulted in children of every social class attending tax-supported public schools.

**The Abolitionist Movement and Civil War**   Probably the most controversial reform movement of the pre-Civil War era was the movement to abolish slavery. Recall from Chapter 4 the work of abolitionist leaders—William Lloyd Garrison, Harriet Beecher Stowe, Frederick Douglass, and Harriet Tubman. The uncompromising demands of these reformers for an immediate end to slavery continued through the 1840s and 1850s. After slavery and other issues finally resulted in Civil War, the abolitionists influenced President Lincoln to issue the Emancipation Proclamation in 1863.

## B. REFORMS AFTER THE CIVIL WAR (1865 TO 1900)

After the Civil War, reformers concentrated on extending voting rights to all adult citizens and cleaning up the political corruption that marked the Gilded Age.

**Citizenship and Voting Rights for African Americans**   During Reconstruction (1865 to 1877), the Thirteenth Amendment abolished slavery, the Fourteenth Amendment guaranteed U.S. citizenship to former slaves, and the Fifteenth Amendment stated that the right to vote could not be denied "on account of race, color, or previous condition of servitude." (Review Chapter 5.)

**Movement for Woman's Suffrage** For almost one hundred years after the United States declared its independence in 1776, only men were permitted to vote. The first women to vote in a U.S. election lived on the Western frontier as residents of the territory of Wyoming. They cast their ballots in 1869, about 20 years after the movement for woman's suffrage (voting rights) had officially begun at the Seneca Falls Convention in New York in 1848. (See Chapter 3.) Participants in the movement, men and women alike, were known as **suffragists.** Their leaders included Susan B. Anthony, Elizabeth Cady Stanton, and Lucy Stone. Some suffragists concentrated on trying to persuade each state legislature to grant equal voting rights to women. Most of their triumphs came in the new states of the West—Utah, Wyoming, Colorado, and Idaho.

The approach favored by Susan B. Anthony was to win support for an amendment to the U.S. Constitution that would guarantee voting rights for women in *all* the states. This amendment was first introduced in Congress in 1878, but the male lawmakers rejected it. The suffragists persisted by reintroducing the amendment in every session of Congress for the next 40 years. Finally, in 1919 it was passed by Congress and in 1920 ratified by the states as the Nineteenth Amendment. It stated: "The right of citizens of the United States to vote shall not be denied or abridged by the United States or by any state on account of sex." Suddenly, the number of people eligible to vote in U.S. elections nearly doubled.

**Temperance Movement** Fighting alcohol abuse was another movement that attracted the energies of many women. Reformers in the **temperance movement,** as it was called, wanted to abolish the sale of alcoholic drinks in public places called saloons. They argued that excessive consumption of alcohol increased the poverty of working-class families. The most famous of the temperance crusaders were Frances Willard and Carrie Nation. Wielding a hatchet, Carrie Nation would march into the saloons of Kansas in the 1890s and destroy shelves of bottled liquor.

The temperance movement achieved its goal with the adoption in 1919 of the Eighteenth Amendment. Until its repeal in 1933, this amendment prohibited the manufacture and sale of alcoholic beverages in the United States.

**Civil Service Reform** Before the 1880s appointments to all federal offices were made on the basis of an applicant's politics, not on the basis of his or her fitness for holding office.

In 1881 President James Garfield was shot and killed by a man who had expected to be given a federal job after campaigning for Garfield. Failure to get the job led him to murder the president. Political reformers blamed the tragic event on the spoils system. They demanded a method for selecting government workers that was free of politics. Reformers proposed that postmasters and other officials be selected by means of an examination rather than by presidential appointment. Shortly after the assassination Congress passed the Pendleton Act (1883), which created a **civil service system** (an organization of government workers). Each job in the civil service would be filled by a person scoring highest on a civil service examination. As time passed, Congress added amendments to the Pendleton Act that brought more and more government jobs into the civil service.

**Reforms Proposed by the Populists**  Sweeping changes in the political system were proposed by the Populists in their party platform of 1892. Recall their demands for government ownership of the railroads, a graduated income tax, and more power to the voters to influence lawmaking. (Review Chapter 6.)

# II. Pressures for Reform in the Industrial Age

As the American nation became more industrial and urban, serious problems arose that cried out for attention. The progressive movement that began in the 1890s was an attempt to bring under control the problems created by industrial growth and change.

## A. INDUSTRIAL PROBLEMS AND PROGRESSIVE SOLUTIONS

The following chart lists the chief problems of the industrial age and the Progressives' attempts to deal with them.

| Industrial Problem | Progressive Solution |
|---|---|
| 1. *Monopolistic control of big business.* Recall the trusts and holding companies formed by John D. Rockefeller and other "captains of industry" to eliminate smaller businesses and establish total dominance of an industry. (Review Chapter 6.) | *Enforcement of antitrust laws.* The Sherman Antitrust Act of 1890 made it illegal for businesses to form trusts and other conspiracies "in restraint of trade." Progressive reformers wanted this act to be vigorously enforced by the U.S. Justice Department. However, reformers disagreed with one another on whether to view all or only some big businesses as harmful to the public interest. |

| Industrial Problem | Progressive Solution |
|---|---|
| 2. *Poor living conditions in urban slums.* Recall the conditions of overcrowded and unsanitary housing described by Jacob Riis. (Review Chapter 7.) | *Building codes; settlement houses.* Reformers urged city governments to adopt and enforce strict codes for regulating the construction of factories and tenement houses. The reformers also encouraged the voluntary efforts of middle-class women like Jane Addams who established settlement houses among the urban poor in an attempt to help and educate them. |
| 3. *Conflict between businesses and labor unions.* As described in Chapter 6, industrial workers were poorly paid, overworked, and underprotected from unhealthy and unsafe factory conditions. There were frequent strikes for better pay, shorter hours, and greater safety. | *State labor laws.* Reformers were alarmed by the number of strikes that disrupted the economy. Hoping for "industrial peace," they urged state legislatures to pass laws that would protect workers from unsafe conditions and force employers and insurance companies to compensate workers for injuries on the job. |
| 4. *Power of corrupt city bosses and their political machines.* In every major U.S. city, political bosses like William Tweed of New York City held a firm grip on political parties. (Chapter 5). Loyal party workers who took orders from the boss were rewarded with government offices. They used their offices to make dishonest deals with local businesses. Hundreds of party workers acted like a well-oiled **political machine** at election time, rounding up voters to elect candidates handpicked by the boss. | *Campaigns to elect honest, progressive candidates.* Newspapers played a major role in exposing the political tricks and corrupt practices of city bosses. The newspapers would endorse a list of reform candidates who opposed the rule of the boss and his machine. Progressives also hoped to break the power of corrupt politicians by increasing the power of voters. Their methods for accomplishing this (the primary, initiative, referendum, and recall) are explained on pages 238–239. |

## B. RISE OF THE MIDDLE CLASS AND THE MASS MEDIA

Progressive candidates for office depended upon the backing of (1) middle-class voters and (2) publishers of popular magazines and city newspapers. Since the Civil War, both groups had grown more important in U.S. society as a result of industrial change and the growth of cities.

**The Middle Class**   One of the chief characteristics of members of the middle class was their practice of reading popular books, magazines, and newspapers. They also took their civic duties seriously— the men by voting regularly and the women by participating in clubs and charities and sometimes joining reform movements. Most were native-born citizens who took pride in their country's traditions and growing strength.

**Newspapers and Magazines**   Inventions in the publishing business kept pace with inventions in other industries. By the 1870s city newspapers rolled off immense machine-driven presses (a far cry from the hand presses that Benjamin Franklin had used a hundred years earlier). The goal of every newspaper publisher was to increase daily readership and advertising pages. Two of the most successful publishers owned rival newspapers in New York City. Joseph Pulitzer owned the New York *World*, and William Randolph Hearst owned the New York *Journal*. Both reached an enormous public by selling newspapers for only a penny and running feature stories that appealed to people's appetite for scandal and sensation. The methods used by Pulitzer and Hearst were known as "**yellow journalism**." (The name derives from a popular cartoon, the "Yellow kid," featured daily in the *New York World*.)

Monthly magazines also circulated widely among middle-class Americans. Magazines like the *Ladies Home Journal* and *McClure's* carried lengthy articles about corruption in city government and shocking conditions in factories and slums. The writers of these articles played up dirty politics, or "muck"—all that seemed dishonest, immoral, and ugly. Theodore Roosevelt therefore referred to these writers as **muckrakers.**

**Muckraking Books and Articles**   Journalists were critically important to the Progressive movement. Their books and magazine articles gave millions of Americans an interest in righting the wrongs of their society. The following were the most influential muckrakers.

- Lincoln Steffens: His magazine articles and book, *The Shame of the Cities* (1904), revealed how thoroughly corrupt were the city politicians of his time.
- Ida Tarbell: Her thorough investigation of the monopolistic methods of John D. Rockefeller was published as a series of magazine articles and then as a book, *History of the Standard Oil Company* (1904).
- Henry Demarest Lloyd: In a best-selling book about big business, *Wealth Against Commonwealth* (1894), Lloyd wrote: "A small number of men are obtaining the power to forbid anyone else

to provide the people with fire in nearly every form known to modern life. They control the electricity and the gas, the kerosene and the candles. You cannot free yourself. You are under their control."

- Upton Sinclair: His novel *The Jungle* (1906) exposed the dreadful conditions in the meat-packing plants in Chicago. The public outcry following publication of this book led directly to a U.S. law providing for federal inspection of meat (the Meat Inspection Act, 1906). A related law, the Pure Food and Drug Act (1906), regulated the manufacture of foods.

Long after the era of Progressive reform ended, the muckrakers continued to influence later generations of journalists who, in our time, are known as investigative reporters.

## OBSERVERS OF AMERICAN LIFE: CONDITIONS IN A SAUSAGE FACTORY

Quoted below is one of the most nauseating paragraphs in American literature. It is a description of a sausage factory in Upton Sinclair's muckraking novel, *The Jungle*.

If you had been in Congress in 1906, would you have voted for a meat inspection law on the basis of this paragraph alone?

There was never the least attention paid to what was cut up for sausage; there would come all the way back from Europe old sausage that had been rejected, and that was moldy and white—it would be dosed with borax and glycerine, and dumped into the hoppers, and made over again for home consumption. There would be meat that had tumbled out on the floor, in the dirt and sawdust, where the workers had tramped and spit uncounted billions of consumption germs. There would be meat stored in great piles in rooms; and the water from leaky roofs would drip over it, and thousands of rats would race about on it. It was too dark in these storage places to see well, but a man could run his hand over these piles of meat and sweep off handfuls of the dried dung of rats. These rats were nuisances, and the packers would put poisoned bread out for them; they would die, and then rats, bread, and meat would go into the hoppers together. This is no fairy story and no joke; the meat would be shoveled into carts, and the man who did the shoveling would not trouble to lift out a rat even when he saw one—there were things that went into the sausage in comparison with which a poisoned rat was a tidbit.

The conservative view          The progressive view

## C. TWO VIEWS OF GOVERNMENT AND BUSINESS

Should government regulate business, or should it leave business alone? This question was at the heart of the debate between citizens who favored progressive reforms and other citizens who opposed them.

**The Conservative View**    People who took a conservative, anti-progressive view thought that businesses should be free to compete as they saw fit. In their view businesses should *not* be regulated by government commissions and agencies. In other words conservatives believed that the policy of laissez-faire (hands off business) should continue into the twentieth century.

**The Progressive View**    People who sided with progressive politicians thought the time had come to abandon laissez-faire. They wanted laws that would (1) stop businesses from competing in unfair ways and (2) provide some protection for consumers and the general public from the unpleasant effects of industrialism. In their view government should act toward businesses as a good police officer—making them obey rules that would ensure safety and fair treatment for all.

### *In Review*

The following questions refer to section I: The Reform Tradition: A Review and section II: Pressures for Reform in the Industrial Age.

1. Define *spoils system, civil service, suffragist, muckraker,* and *progressivism.*
2. Explain how progressive ideas for reform were a response to the growth of cities and industry.
3. Compare the conservative view of business competition with the progressive view.

# III. Reforms for Children, Workers, and Voters

In the early days of progressivism (from about 1890 to 1900), reformers focused on enacting progressive laws at the local and state levels. They did not seek progressive laws at the federal level until a progressive president, Theodore Roosevelt, came to power in 1901. In state and local politics progressives sought reforms that would help the poor, regulate factory conditions, and expand democracy in the voting booth. Although their efforts began in the 1890s, they had their greatest successes between 1900 and 1916.

## A. MOVEMENT FOR SOCIAL JUSTICE

Some progressives were most concerned about the welfare of people living in urban slums. They were at the forefront of what was called the **social justice movement.** Included in their ranks were Jacob Riis, newspaper reporter and author of *How the Other Half Lives* and Jane Addams, founder of Hull House, a settlement house in Chicago.

**Settlement Houses**  A **settlement house** was a building located in a poor immigrant neighborhood where women and children could go for help in adjusting to American life. Both Jane Addams's Hull House in Chicago and Lillian Wald's Henry Street Settlement in New York City provided activities for poor children to keep them from the dangers of unsupervised play on city streets. Their immigrant parents were offered free classes in English as well as classes in the arts, literature, and music. Jane Addams, Lillian Wald, and other social workers became experts on the problems of urban poverty. They used their knowledge to persuade state legislatures to enact laws for children's protection, especially laws to abolish **child labor.**

**Child Labor Laws**  In 1900 about 1.7 million children between the ages of 10 and 15 worked for pennies an hour on farms and in mines and factories (especially cotton mills and canning plants). Many child wage earners were as young as six and seven. Progressives in every state in the country campaigned vigorously to stop employers from exploiting children. By 1914 child labor laws had been enacted by nearly all the states, although some of the laws were weak and easily evaded.

## B. MOVEMENT TO REGULATE BUSINESS AND LABOR

Reformers were also concerned about the effects of long hours of work on the health of women. Florence Kelley, who worked with

Jane Addams at Hull House, was mainly responsible for an Illinois law prohibiting employment of women for more than eight hours a day. Women reformers in Massachusetts persuaded the legislature to enact a minimum wage law in 1912.

The courts, however, posed an obstacle. Business firms and their lawyers argued in court that state regulatory laws were unconstitutional because they infringed upon a property owner's rights. Lawyers cited the due process clause of the Fourteenth Amendment ("... nor shall any state deprive any person of life, liberty, or property, without due process of law"). Two landmark cases of the Supreme Court examined the issue. One case was won by the conservatives, a second case by the progressives.

**Case of *Lochner* v. *New York* (1905)**  A New York law prohibited bakers in the state from working more than a 60-hour week or a 10-hour day. The Supreme Court decided that the New York law violated a business owner's right under the Fourteenth Amendment not to be deprived of the use of property without "due process of law." The Court therefore ruled the state law to be unconstitutional.

**Case of *Muller* v. *Oregon* (1908)**  An Oregon law provided that women could not work more than ten hours a day in Oregon's factories and laundries. Defending the law before the Supreme Court, a brilliant lawyer named Louis Brandeis used scientific studies of women workers to demonstrate that women's health could be injured by overly long hours of physical labor. His arguments persuaded the Court to permit Oregon's law to stand. Brandeis later became the first American of the Jewish faith to serve on the U.S. Supreme Court.

## C. REFORMS IN THE ELECTION PROCESS

To overthrow the city bosses and their political machines, progressives proposed that voters be given greater power. Several states gave more power to the people in the following ways.

- The **initiative:** By signing a petition, a small percentage of voters could force the state legislature to consider a proposed law.
- The **referendum:** A proposed law could be submitted directly to the people to be voted upon in an election.
- The **recall:** In a special election, people could vote on whether or not to remove an elected official from office before the end of his or her term.
- The **Australian ballot,** or secret ballot: Instead of openly choosing a ballot issued by a political party, voters would enter a curtained booth and vote in secret using an official ballot printed by the state government.

- The **direct primary:** Instead of state conventions nominating candidates for office, the voters would nominate them by direct popular vote in a primary election (an early election before the general election in November).

A great leader in the fight for these reforms and others was the governor of Wisconsin, Robert ("Battling Bob") La Follette. In Wisconsin, as elsewhere, the railroads, bosses, and business interests were hard to beat, but La Follette managed to rally voters to his cause and overcome opposition in the legislature. The initiative, referendum, recall, and direct primary were among many reforms that gave Wisconsin a nationwide reputation as a "laboratory for democracy."

### *In Review*

The following questions refer to section III: Reforms for Children, Workers, and Voters.

1. Define *social justice, settlement house, initiative, referendum,* and *recall.*
2. Explain how Robert La Follette's reforms in Wisconsin resulted in greater democracy for the people of the state.

# IV. The Policies of Three Progressive Presidents

Between 1901 and 1921 three presidents led the movement for reform in national politics. They were Theodore Roosevelt (1901 to 1909), William Howard Taft (1909 to 1913), and Woodrow Wilson (1913 to 1921).

## A. THEODORE ROOSEVELT'S "SQUARE DEAL"

At 42 years of age, Theodore Roosevelt, affectionately called "Teddy" or T. R. by his many admirers, became the youngest president in U.S. history. He had been a progressive governor of New York in the 1890s, a hero of the Spanish-American War in 1898, and a successful candidate for vice president in the election of 1900. The Republican president in 1901, William McKinley, was known for his conservative policies during a previous term (1897 to 1901). An assassin shot and killed McKinley shortly after his second term began, and Theodore Roosevelt thus became president.

Almost immediately, the young president showed a bold style of leadership that excited the imagination of the voting public. He promised a **"square deal"** to all groups in the American population: labor as well as business, the poor as well as the rich. Said Roosevelt:

"While I am president I want the laboring man to feel he has the same right of access to me as the capitalist has. Our doors swing open as easily to the wage workers as to the heads of the big corporation."

As a champion of reform, Roosevelt acted on many fronts—busting trusts, pushing for new regulatory laws, settling labor disputes, and conserving the American wilderness.

**Roosevelt, the "Trust Buster"** Roosevelt was the first president to make a serious effort to enforce the Sherman Antitrust Act of 1890. People were amazed when he announced his decision to prosecute the Northern Securities Company, a powerful holding company that controlled several Western railroads. In 1904 the Supreme Court concluded that the president's move to break up Northern Securities was proper and constitutional. After this victory Roosevelt broke up other business combinations including the Standard Oil Company.

Although Roosevelt was popularly known as a **"trust buster"** (a breaker of monopolistic businesses), he was not an enemy of big business. He always distinguished between "good trusts" (those that acted responsibly) and "bad trusts" (those that ignored the public interest). Only the latter were targets for his trust busting.

**Settling the Coal Strike** Roosevelt demonstrated what he meant by a "square deal" for business and labor by settling a strike of Pennsylvania coal miners in 1902. Recall that earlier presidents had used troops to support big business and break strikes. Roosevelt showed an unusual respect for the cause of labor by inviting to the White House the leaders of *both* the coal miners' union and the mining company. The strike was settled when the company agreed to a shorter workday and a 10-percent increase in miners' wages.

**Regulating Railroads and Meat Packers** Roosevelt was also the first president to persuade Congress to enact a number of reform laws concerning interstate businesses.

- The Meat Inspection Act (1906) gave U.S. officials the power to check the quality and healthfulness of meats shipped in interstate commerce.
- The Pure Food and Drug Act (1906) banned the manufacture and sale of impure foods, drugs, and liquors and required commercially bottled and packaged medicines to be truthfully and fully labeled.
- The Elkins Act (1903) strengthened the Interstate Commerce Commission (created in 1887) by providing for the punishment of railroads that granted rebates (special reductions in price) to favored customers.

- The Hepburn Act (1906) gave the Interstate Commerce Commission the power to fix the rates that railroads charged for their services. It also strictly limited the free passes that railroads gave out to politicians and business owners.

**Conserving Forests and Rivers**    Perhaps the most important of Roosevelt's reforms were his efforts to protect the nation's natural resources. Having hiked and camped in the West, Roosevelt appreciated the beauty of wilderness areas and did not want to see them exploited recklessly by mining and lumbering companies. He stated that "the forest and water problems are perhaps the most vital internal problems of the United States." From the beginning to the end of his presidency, Roosevelt tried to win public support for **conservation**—the wise management and careful use of the natural environment. Inspired by his leadership, Congress passed two major conservation laws.

- The Newlands Reclamation Act (1902) provided that money from the sale of desert lands in the West be used to finance irrigation projects.
- The Inland Waterways Act (1907) provided for the appointment of a commission to study the use of the nation's major rivers.

In addition, President Roosevelt used a previously existing law to establish 149 national forests totaling more than 190 million acres. All such forests were publicly owned and strictly controlled by officials in the U.S. Forest Service.

## B. CONTROVERSY UNDER PRESIDENT TAFT

Roosevelt chose a trusted member of his cabinet, William Howard Taft, to be the Republican nominee for president in 1908. Roosevelt hoped that Taft would continue his progressive policies. Taft won the election easily. Although he believed in progressive ideas, Taft lacked Roosevelt's energetic style of leadership. Progressive Republicans in Congress—and even Roosevelt himself—soon grew impatient with him.

**A Second "Trust Buster"**    In one respect, Taft proved even more aggressive than his predecessor. He ordered the Justice Department to prosecute 90 businesses for violating the antitrust law (compared to 44 such cases prosecuted under Roosevelt).

**Losing the Progressives' Support**    On two issues—tariff reform and conservation—Taft failed to give the leadership that reformers expected from him. They were disappointed with the results of a struggle to lower tariff rates. Instead of lowering prices on imports, as progressives had wanted, the new Payne-Aldrich Tariff (1909) raised prices on many products. Taft signed the tariff act into law over the protests of progressive members of Congress.

Progressives were even more upset when Taft fired a leading conservationist, Gifford Pinchot, as the head of the Forest Service. As a friend of Pinchot, Roosevelt was especially angered by Taft's action. It seemed to many progressives that Taft was secretly going along with selfish business interests rather than fighting the good fight for conservation and low tariffs. Unhappy reformers in the Republican party invited Roosevelt to seek the Republican nomination for another term as president. The popular ex-president accepted.

## C. THE ELECTION OF 1912

The election of 1912 was one of the most unusual and exciting elections in U.S. history. It involved three major candidates for president (Roosevelt, Taft, and Woodrow Wilson) and a fourth candidate of a minor party (Eugene V. Debs).

**Taft, the Republican** Conservatives in the Republican party rallied around the president. They nominated Taft rather than Roosevelt.

**Roosevelt, the Progressive (Bull Moose)** Angered by their defeat in the Republican national convention, progressive supporters of Theodore Roosevelt decided to form a new political party. The Progressive party, as they called it, was also known as the "**Bull Moose**" **party** after its candidate, Roosevelt, described himself as "strong as a bull moose."

**Wilson, the Democrat** Though born in Virginia, Woodrow Wilson had moved to New Jersey as a college professor and won national attention as a progressive governor of that state. He was a newcomer in Democratic national politics in 1912 but managed to win the nomination of his party after a long and bitter struggle on the convention floor.

**Debs, the Socialist** Since 1900 the Socialist party had steadily gained in strength and numbers. It championed the interests of industrial workers and put forth the radical idea that all major industries should be owned and operated by the U.S. government. Its presidential candidate, Eugene Debs, campaigned with great energy and zeal.

**Election Results** Wilson won with 435 electoral votes. Neither Taft nor Roosevelt had much chance of pulling off a victory, since they divided the Republican vote between them. Roosevelt won 88 electoral votes, far better than Taft's 8 electoral votes. Debs received not a single electoral vote, even though he polled nearly one million popular votes. Since all the candidates claimed to be reformers—even Taft— it seemed that the entire nation was now eager for reform.

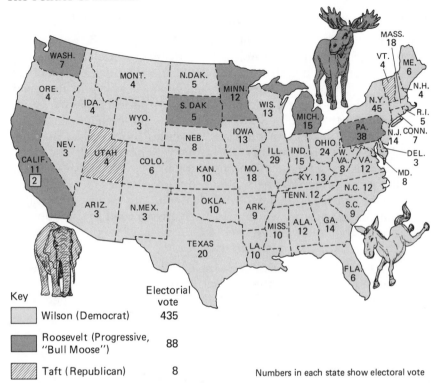

Key

Electorial vote

Wilson (Democrat)  435

Roosevelt (Progressive, "Bull Moose")  88

Taft (Republican)  8

Numbers in each state show electoral vote

The election of 1912

# D. WOODROW WILSON'S NEW FREEDOM

Wilson was only the second Democrat to be president since the Civil War. (Grover Cleveland had been the first.) In his inaugural address of 1913, he announced a sweeping program of economic reform, which he called the **New Freedom.** He proposed reforms of three kinds: a lower tariff, more effective regulation of big business, and a reformed system of banking.

**Fight for a Lower Tariff**  Addressing a special session of Congress, the new president said: "The tariff duties must be altered." When Congress balked, Wilson appealed to the American people to put pressure on their representatives. They did, and the Underwood Tariff became law (1913). One effect of the lower tariffs was to lower the prices of many consumer goods. Another effect was to remove the special protection that big business had enjoyed for more than 20 years (since the enactment of the very high McKinley Tariff of 1890).

**Regulation of Big Business**  The president also insisted upon a stronger antitrust law and a federal commission to ensure fair business practices. Again he struggled with Congress, and again he prevailed.

- The Clayton Antitrust Act (1914) This act greatly strengthened the Sherman Antitrust Act of 1890. Instead of the vague clauses of the original act, the new act listed specific business practices that would now be illegal. It said businesses could not grow bigger by organizing holding companies. (Review Glossary, Chapter 6.) Further, the new law said that the same people could not sit on the boards of directors of several companies. In other words, **interlocking directorships** were now illegal. Also illegal were secret agreements among companies to "fix" prices (charge the same prices for the same products).

   One clause of the Clayton Act pleased union leaders. It provided that labor unions, which had been prosecuted as monopolies under the Sherman Act, could no longer be prosecuted on charges of breaking the antitrust laws.

- The Federal Trade Commission Act (1914) The federal agency created by this act—the Federal Trade Commission (FTC)—was given power to: (1) investigate business practices suspected of being unfair and (2) issue orders demanding that companies "cease and desist" from acting in illegal ways, as defined by the antitrust laws.

**A New Banking System: The Federal Reserve**  Before Wilson became president, coins were the only form of U.S. currency. There were no dollar bills. Nor was there any federal system for expanding or contracting the supply of currency (money) when businesses' need for currency expanded or contracted. Wilson recognized that the growing industrial nation required an organized banking system.

In the past private banks would often have too little money in reserve (kept in their vaults). If hundreds of customers demanded the withdrawal of their money at the same time, a bank with a low reserve of currency might collapse (go bankrupt). Many banks failing at once would cause the whole U.S. economy to sink into a depression.

The progressive solution to this problem, supported by Wilson, was to create a system of central banks called the **Federal Reserve system.** Private banks would hold their cash reserves in 12 regional banks. General policy for these banks would be made by a small group of U.S. officials—the Federal Reserve Board. The regional banks could make loans to private banks around the country at interest rates set by the governing board. The loans would consist of a paper currency printed by the U.S. government as Federal Reserve notes (dollar bills). This is the currency that Americans have used ever since the Federal Reserve Act was passed by Congress in 1913.

The Federal Reserve system made it possible for the supply of

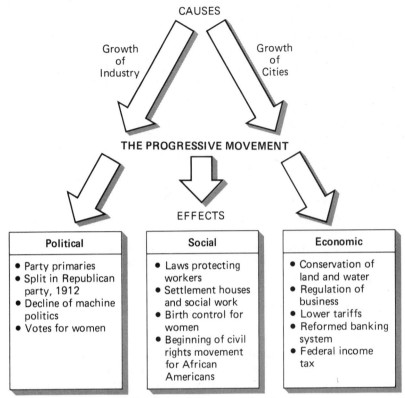

CAUSES

Growth of Industry

Growth of Cities

THE PROGRESSIVE MOVEMENT

EFFECTS

| Political | Social | Economic |
|---|---|---|
| • Party primaries<br>• Split in Republican party, 1912<br>• Decline of machine politics<br>• Votes for women | • Laws protecting workers<br>• Settlement houses and social work<br>• Birth control for women<br>• Beginning of civil rights movement for African Americans | • Conservation of land and water<br>• Regulation of business<br>• Lower tariffs<br>• Reformed banking system<br>• Federal income tax |

Causes and effects: the progressive movement

currency to increase or decrease according to the changing needs of business. Also, the interest rates charged by the Federal Reserve (regional) banks indirectly affected the interest rates of all banks and thus gave the U.S. government the power to influence the entire national economy.

**Child Labor** Late in his first term as president, 1916, Wilson decided to support a reform long urged by Jane Addams and other leaders of the social justice movement. He persuaded Congress to pass a law that prohibited the shipment across state lines of any products made by child laborers. However, this law was declared unconstitutional in a Supreme Court decision of 1918.

## E. TWO PROGRESSIVE AMENDMENTS

Reviving Populist ideas from the 1890s, Progressives also succeeded in changing the U.S. Constitution. Their two amendments for democratic reform both went into effect in the same year, 1913.

**Income Tax** The Sixteenth Amendment gave Congress the power to collect a tax on incomes and removed an earlier requirement that such a tax be apportioned according to a state's population. The tax was considered democratic because at first it was collected only from people with extremely high incomes. It was also a **graduated income tax,** or progressive income tax—a tax whose rate goes higher and higher as a person's reported income goes higher.

**Direct Election of Senators** The Seventeenth Amendment required that the senators from every state be elected by the voters of the state (not by state legislatures, as in the past).

# V. Women and Minorities in the Progressive Era

Movements for progressive reform affected all groups in the population—women and men, whites and nonwhites, the foreign-born and the native-born.

## A. WOMEN IN THE PROGRESSIVE MOVEMENT

Women such as Jane Addams and Florence Kelley were in the forefront of the movement for social justice. Several women were among the most active and effective labor leaders of the era; these included Mary Harris Jones, Mary Kenney O'Sullivan, and Rose Schneiderman. Women reformers also fought hard for causes that were of special concern to other women.

**Birth Control** Working as a nurse among immigrant families in New York City, Margaret Sanger observed many women of the working class risking their lives and suffering increased poverty because of frequent pregnancies and births. She believed that women should be given information on ways to prevent pregnancy, if they wished. In 1914 she started publishing a magazine on birth control and opened the first birth-control clinic in Brooklyn. Her clinic and her book *What Every Girl Should Know* (1916) launched a movement for informed parenthood that gained strength in later decades.

**Woman's Suffrage** The movement for woman's suffrage that began in 1848 continued into the Progressive Era. The older leadership (Susan B. Anthony and Elizabeth Cady Stanton) was replaced by a new generation of suffragists led by Alice Paul and Carrie Chapman Catt. Some men in the Progressive movement supported the women's crusade for voting rights. But many men, though reform-minded on other issues, thought women should not become involved in politics. The suffragists kept up the pressure on state legislatures, asking how the United States could be a democracy if women could not vote. They finally persuaded President Wilson to support the idea of an amendment guaranteeing woman's suffrage.

The Nineteenth Amendment (adopted in 1920) was nicknamed the Susan B. Anthony Amendment in honor of the great leader who had first championed it.

## B. FOREIGN-BORN MINORITIES

The experience of immigrants during the Progressive Era was both positive and negative. It was positive in the sense that immigration from Europe was still wide open in the years before World War I (1901 to 1914). But it was not open to the Chinese (excluded since 1882); nor was it open to the Japanese after Theodore Roosevelt's Gentlemen's Agreement with Japan in 1907.

Jewish immigrants from eastern Europe were often the target of native-born Americans' religious and cultural prejudices. To combat the unfair statements that were made about them, Jewish Americans organized the Anti-Defamation League in 1913.

Many Russian and Italian immigrants had never attended school because their homelands did not provide free public education. Lawmakers in Congress, including some progressives, favored a literacy test as a device for limiting immigration. Such a test would disqualify those immigrants who could not read in any language. Presidents Cleveland, Taft, and Wilson had each vetoed a literacy test bill, but a fourth bill passed into law in 1917 after Congress overrode President Wilson's veto.

## C. AFRICAN-AMERICANS' FIGHT AGAINST DISCRIMINATION

Recall from Chapter 5 the Jim Crow laws that established racial segregation in the South in the 1880s and 1890s. During the Progressive Era, African-American leaders challenged these laws and tried to win the support of white reformers.

**The Niagara Movement of W. E. B. Du Bois**  The chief leader of the movement for African-American rights was a Harvard-educated scholar, W. E. B. Du Bois. In 1905 he launched the movement at a meeting of reformers in Niagara Falls, Canada. (They met there because hotels on the New York side of the border refused to give them rooms.) The **Niagara Movement,** as it was called, focused on publicizing and protesting acts of injustice against African Americans. In 1909 members of the movement joined with white reformers in organizing the National Association for the Advancement of Colored People (NAACP).

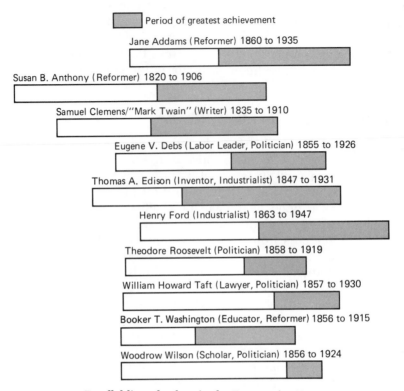

Parallel lives: leaders in the Progressive Era

Dedicated to defending the civil rights of African Americans, the NAACP stood ready to defend those accused of crimes merely because of their race. It also published a magazine, *The Crisis*, edited by Du Bois.

**The Antilynching Campaign of Ida B. Wells**   One of the NAACP's founders was an African-American reporter from Tennessee, Ida B. Wells. She was appalled by the number of African Americans who were lynched, or hanged, by mobs of whites. There were more than 1,100 deaths of this brutal nature between 1900 and 1914. Wells wrote a "muckraking" book about the lynching evil and dedicated her career to the cause of racial justice.

**Booker T. Washington at the White House**   The best known leader of African Americans in the Progressive Era was Booker T. Washington. (For Washington's background and point of view toward segregation, review Chapter 5.) Many white business leaders and politicians conferred with Washington about the education and training of African Americans for skilled industrial jobs. Washington was frequently called to the White House to advise Theodore Roosevelt.

After one such meeting in 1908, Washington ate lunch with the president. News of this event touched off a storm of criticism in the South.

**Segregation Policies of Woodrow Wilson** Though progressive in other ways, Wilson did not appear to be concerned about the civil rights of African Americans. He ordered the washrooms in federal buildings in the nation's capital to be strictly segregated. In each building African Americans were limited to using only one washroom. When a group of African Americans came to the White House to protest Wilson's policies, the president angrily dismissed them.

**Victories in the Supreme Court** Aside from the white reformers in the NAACP, most whites failed to consider the issue of civil rights for blacks. Even so, during the Progressive Era, NAACP lawyers managed to win a number of civil rights cases in the Supreme Court. Between 1915 and 1917 the Court declared the following to be unconstitutional:

- The "grandfather clause" (see Glossary, Chapter 5)
- A segregated housing law
- The practice of denying African Americans the right to serve on juries
- The practice of denying African Americans the right to run for office in party primaries

## In Review

The following questions refer to section IV: The Policies of Three Progressive Presidents and section V: Women and Minorities in the Progressive Era.

**Word Wheel**

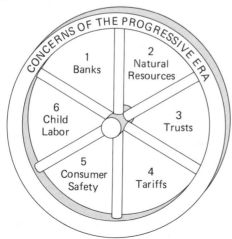

For each topic on the wheel, describe a specific reform of the Progressive Era that is associated with it. Write your answers to the six items on a separate piece of paper.

## GLOSSARY OF KEY TERMS: CHAPTER 8

**Australian ballot**   an election method requiring that voters cast ballots within the privacy of a curtained booth.

**"Bull Moose" party**   the nickname for the Progressive party, a third party organized by progressive Republicans in 1912 to support the candidacy of Theodore Roosevelt for president.

**child labor**   the employment in factories and on farms of children under the age of 14.

**civil service system**   an organization of government employees who are selected by strictly nonpolitical procedures—usually by means of a competitive examination.

**conservation**   a policy of carefully managing and protecting natural resources.

**direct primary**   a method by which voters belonging to a political party may elect the party's nominees.

**Federal Reserve system**   a system established in 1913 by which the U.S. government regulates the interest rates of private banks and influences the nation's supply of money.

**graduated income tax**   a type of tax in which high-income people are taxed at a higher rate than low-income people; also called *progressive income tax.*

**initiative**   the process by which a group of citizens may compel a state legislature to vote on a bill that the group favors.

**interlocking directorships**   a method for limiting business competition by placing the same persons on the executive boards of several companies.

**muckrakers**   writers who investigated alarming conditions in factories, city slums, politics, and other areas of American life.

**New Freedom**   Woodrow Wilson's program of progressive reforms, including a lower tariff, a new antitrust law, and a system for regulating banks and currency.

**Niagara Movement**   a movement founded by W. E. B. Du Bois to promote the civil rights of African Americans.

**political machine**   a tightly organized group of local politicians who loyally supported a party boss and made sure the voters in their neighborhoods turned out to support their party's candidates on Election Day.

**Progressive Era**   the period from about 1900 to 1917 when citizens and politicians worked for reforms in many areas of American life.

**recall**   an election in which voters decide whether or not to remove an official before the end of his or her term.

**referendum**   an election in which people vote on proposed laws.

**settlement house**   a building in a poor city neighborhood where residents received free services such as instruction in English and day care for immigrant children.

**social justice movement**   the various efforts by reformers to improve living and working conditions for the urban poor.

**"square deal"**   Theodore Roosevelt's program of reform; also, his view that both labor and business (as well as other groups in the population) should be fairly treated by government.

**suffragists**   women and men who campaigned for the right of women to vote.

**temperance movement**   a movement to abolish the manufacture and sale of alcoholic beverages.

**"trust buster"**   the nickname given to Theodore Roosevelt for his efforts to enforce the Sherman Antitrust Act of 1890.

**"yellow journalism"**   a newspaper's practice of featuring scandals, crimes, and other shocking events for the purpose of attracting more readers.

# TEST YOURSELF

## A. Multiple Choice: Facts, Main Ideas, Skills

*On a separate sheet of paper, write the number of the word or expression that, of those given, best completes the statement or answers the question.*

### Reviewing the facts

1. What problem did Elizabeth Cady Stanton and Susan B. Anthony hope to correct?  (1) scarcity of free public schools  (2) few legal and political rights for women  (3) inadequate medical care  (4) unfair treatment of ethnic minorities

2. Civil service reform in the 1880s was a reaction to  (1) the principle of separation of powers  (2) abuses in the electoral college system  (3) the spoils system  (4) the gold standard

3. Which might correctly be called a muckraker?  (1) a cartoonist with strong conservative biases  (2) a reporter during the Age of Jackson  (3) a conservationist in the time of Theodore Roosevelt  (4) a writer who investigates corruption in politics

4. Which helped to bring about a federal meat inspection law during the Progressive Era?  (1) a decline in farm exports  (2) economic demands of cattle ranchers  (3) a book by a muckraker  (4) a popular interest in trust busting

5. Jane Addams, Lillian Wald, and Jacob Riis were leaders of the movement for (1) antitrust laws (2) banking reform (3) social justice (4) temperance

6. The main purpose of the initiative, referendum, and recall was to (1) reduce federal control over local government (2) enlarge citizens' control over state and local governments (3) stimulate economic growth (4) restore the balance between state and federal power

7. The main purpose of party primaries was to (1) enable voters to select party candidates (2) increase the power of political bosses (3) reduce the number of candidates for president (4) establish a stronger link between state governments and the federal government.

8. Which statement expresses President Theodore Roosevelt's policy toward monopolies? (1) Government should not regulate big business. (2) Government should encourage businesses to combine. (3) Only trusts that fail to consider the public good should be prosecuted. (4) The antitrust laws are not capable of being fairly enforced.

9. Which statement is best supported by the election of Woodrow Wilson in 1912? (1) A new third party can affect the result of the election. (2) Democrats are more likely to be elected in times of war. (3) War heroes tend to be successful presidential candidates. (4) A declining economy usually results in the defeat of the party in power.

10. President Wilson's "New Freedom" included all of the following reforms *except* (1) a child labor law (2) a strengthened antitrust law (3) the abolition of Jim Crow laws (4) the reduction of tariff rates

11. A chief function of the Federal Reserve system was to (1) make loans to farmers (2) regulate international trade (3) balance the federal budget (4) regulate the amount of money in circulation

12. Which of these was *not* a goal of any progressive president? (1) consumer protection (2) civil rights for African Americans (3) tariff reform (4) conservation of natural resources

## Reviewing the main ideas

13. Reform movements in U.S. history have usually sought to (1) change American foreign relations (2) overthrow the capitalist system (3) improve social and economic conditions (4) increase the power of a privileged minority

14. The progressive movement is best described as an attempt to (1) promote political and economic democracy (2) preserve the traditional ways of an agrarian society (3) place major industries under government ownership and control (4) increase the supply of immigrant labor

15. Most progressives wanted the federal government to (1) follow a laissez-faire policy (2) reduce discrimination against members of minority groups (3) increase the power of big business (4) regulate business for the public good

16. Which statement describes both the "square deal" and the "New Freedom"? (1) They were the legislative programs of reforming presidents. (2) They stressed the importance of conservation. (3) They were chiefly supported by Republicans. (4) They included only political and legal reforms, not economic reforms.

17. "The ills of democracy must be cured by more democracy." The author of this statement would probably support all of the following *except* (1) woman's suffrage (2) the initiative and referendum (3) popular election of senators (4) higher tariff rates

## Developing critical thinking skills

*Base your answers to questions 18 through 20 on the cartoon below and your knowledge of U.S. history and government.*

18. Which of the following most accurately describes the subject of the cartoon? (1) the progressive ideas of Theodore Roosevelt (2) Theodore Roosevelt's approach to the problem of big business (3) the origins of the antitrust laws (4) Theodore Roosevelt as an outdoorsman and conservationist

19. The "Bad Trusts" bear represents those businesses that Theodore Roosevelt would have wanted to (1) break up (2) leave alone (3) regulate (4) assist

**20.** During what period was this cartoon probably created? (1) 1890 to 1900 (2) 1900 to 1910 (3) 1910 to 1915 (4) 1915 to 1920

## B. Enduring Issues

*Select two of the enduring issues from column A. For each issue chosen, explain how the historical example in column B relates to the issue.*

| A. Enduring Issues | B. Historical Examples |
|---|---|
| 1. The rights of women under the Constitution | The adoption of the Nineteenth Amendment |
| 2. The rights of ethnic and racial groups under the Constitution | The founding of the NAACP |
| 3. Property rights and economic policy | Trust busting under Theodore Roosevelt and William H. Taft |
| 4. Constitutional change and flexibility | The Supreme Court's decision in *Muller* v. *Oregon* |

## C. Essays

### Level 1

At different times in U.S. history, reform groups have arisen to deal with various economic, social, and political problems. There were:

- reforms in the Age of Jackson
- reforms in the 1880s involving the spoils system
- reforms in the Progressive Era.

**1.** Select *one* of the reform periods listed. For that period, describe one problem that concerned reformers.

**2.** Describe the reformers' proposed solution to the problem identified in question 1.

**3.** Discuss the extent to which the reform succeeded in solving the problem.

### Level 2

Between 1900 and 1920 people in the progressive movement tried to solve many problems of society.

**A.** List *two* specific problems that concerned reformers in this period.

**B.** Base your answer to part B on your answer to part A. Write an essay explaining how reformers in the Progressive Era tried to solve these problems.

# Chapter *9*

# America Reaching Out

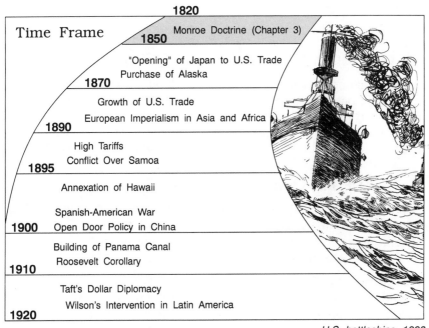

| Time Frame | |
|---|---|
| **1820** | |
| | Monroe Doctrine (Chapter 3) |
| **1850** | |
| | "Opening" of Japan to U.S. Trade |
| | Purchase of Alaska |
| **1870** | |
| | Growth of U.S. Trade |
| | European Imperialism in Asia and Africa |
| **1890** | |
| | High Tariffs |
| | Conflict Over Samoa |
| **1895** | |
| | Annexation of Hawaii |
| | Spanish-American War |
| | Open Door Policy in China |
| **1900** | |
| | Building of Panama Canal |
| | Roosevelt Corollary |
| **1910** | |
| | Taft's Dollar Diplomacy |
| | Wilson's Intervention in Latin America |
| **1920** | |

*U.S. battleships, 1898*

*Objectives*

- To explain the economic causes for U.S. expansion in the Pacific.
- To evaluate arguments for protectionism and free trade.
- To evaluate arguments for and against intervention in the affairs of Latin American nations.
- To analyze reasons for increased U.S. involvement in Asia and Latin America from 1890 to 1920.


The nineteenth century was near its end in 1898. Now more than 120 years old, the United States had established a worldwide reputation as a major industrial nation. But it was not yet fully recognized as a military power. This chapter tells about a war in 1898 that changed the U.S. role in the world. The change, however, did not come about overnight. It was based, as you shall see, on economic changes that had built up slowly over the course of the nineteenth century.

# I. Impact of Trade on Foreign Policy

Every nation's economic prosperity depends partly on its trade with other nations. Recognizing this fact, makers of U.S. foreign policy have always been concerned about both protecting and promoting U.S. trade. This section explains how trade in the early 1800s prepared the way for an expanded U.S. role in world affairs in the 1890s.

## A. TRADE BEFORE THE CIVIL WAR

Before the Civil War the main concern of foreign-policy makers was achieving the nation's "manifest destiny" to expand westward. Even then, however, trade also played a significant role in the policy decisions of U.S. presidents.

**Acquiring the Port of New Orleans**   When Jefferson became president in 1801, the city of New Orleans on the Mississippi River belonged to Spain and shortly afterward to France. Spain had often made it difficult for Americans to transport goods down the lower Mississippi River and through New Orleans into the Gulf of Mexico. For this reason, many Westerners wanted to take New Orleans by military force. War was avoided when France acquired the Spanish lands and decided to sell them. Jefferson accepted the French offer to buy both New Orleans and the Louisiana Territory to the west.

(Review Chapter 3.) By acquiring New Orleans, the United States achieved full control of its major trade route to the Gulf of Mexico and the West Indies.

**U.S. Goods for Export**  During the early 1800s the South's economy depended more and more on its exports of cotton and tobacco to Great Britain and other European nations. Manufacturers in the Northeast shipped increasing amounts of their products to South America and, to a lesser extent, to Japan and China. Shipments of wheat and corn from the Middle West fed growing numbers of British workers. In 1861 foreign trade reached record levels as more than two million tons of goods left U.S. ports.

**The China Trade**  Through the 1800s trade with Europe was much greater than trade with Asia. Although Chinese teas, porcelains, and silks were in great demand in the United States, the Asian trade grew slowly. American merchants had difficulty exporting U.S. goods to the Chinese Empire because the Chinese viewed their own civilization as superior to any other. High officials at the emperor's court had little interest in the cheap factory-made goods that Westerners brought with them to sell.

**The "Opening" of Japan**  For many years, Japan was even less interested than China in trading with Europeans and Americans. It became more open to trade after 1853, the year that Commodore Matthew Perry arrived in Japan with an American fleet. Perry wanted not only to open trade with Japan but also to gain assurances that Japan would assist shipwrecked U.S. sailors. He brought gifts demonstrating the benefits of industrial technology and, in a show of force, fired off the fleet's guns. Japanese officials were sufficiently impressed to sign a trade treaty with the United States. Soon afterward new leadership in Japan adopted a policy of learning Western technologies and making Japan into a modern industrial nation.

# B. INDUSTRIALISM AND IMPERIALISM IN EUROPE

Trade was vital not only to the United States but also to the nations of Europe. In fact, as time passed and Europe became more industrialized, trade became ever more important. After all, industrialism meant an increasing amount of factory-made goods and an increasing need to find buyers or markets for those goods. At the same time each nation needed more raw materials (cotton, coal, tin, oil, and so on) to keep turning out more clothing, machines, and other industrial products.

Where were new markets and new sources of raw materials to be found for Europe's growing factories? Every major European nation gave the same answer: colonies abroad. There were diamond mines to be discovered in Africa, sugar plantations to be started in Latin America, and millions of potential buyers for British cloth to be found in Asia. But Great Britain, Germany, and France saw no advantage in sharing overseas markets and raw materials. Each nation wanted exclusive control of a particular region—a control often attained by military force. A colony was something that the controlling European power could dominate for its own economic needs.

Spurred on by the rush to industrialize, the European powers entered a fiercely competitive race to build colonial empires. The policy of seeking colonies was known as **imperialism.** For several decades, beginning about 1840, the European countries competed to seize control of colonies in Asia, Africa, and South America. By 1900 Great Britain was clearly the leader in the competition, having won control of colonies that circled the globe. As the saying went, "The sun never sets on the British Empire." France, Germany, Italy, and even Belgium had many colonies of their own.

## C. U.S. EXPANSION IN THE PACIFIC

The United States was also industrializing at a fast pace in these last decades of the nineteenth century. It was natural to ask: Should the United States too become an imperialist power by acquiring colonies overseas?

In a sense, the United States had already acquired an empire in the West. In the early 1800s, "manifest destiny" had meant expanding U.S. territory to the Pacific Coast. The United States had achieved this goal by fighting a war with Mexico (1846 to 1848) and acquiring California. Now in the late 1800s some Americans hoped to expand U.S territory even farther west to islands of the Pacific.

In a 30-year period after the Civil War, the United States did acquire new territories far from its original borders. All these possessions— Alaska, Hawaii, and Samoa—were either on the Pacific coast or in the middle of the Pacific Ocean.

**The Acquisition of Alaska** The seal-hunting Eskimos and Aleuts had made the coast of Alaska their home for many centuries. A few Russians first settled on Alaska's coast in 1784 and began treating the coast and the vast, unexplored interior as a Russian colony. Russia continued to claim Alaska as its territory until 1867. In that year the U.S. Secretary of State William Seward signed a treaty with Russia agreeing to purchase Alaska for $7,200,000. The Senate ratified the treaty, even though many senators believed the distant lands to the far north to be worthless. Critics of the Alaska purchase called it "Seward's folly." In later years the discovery of Alaskan oil and gold proved that Seward's belief in his purchase was fully justified. (In 1959 Alaska was admitted to the Union as the 49th and largest state.)

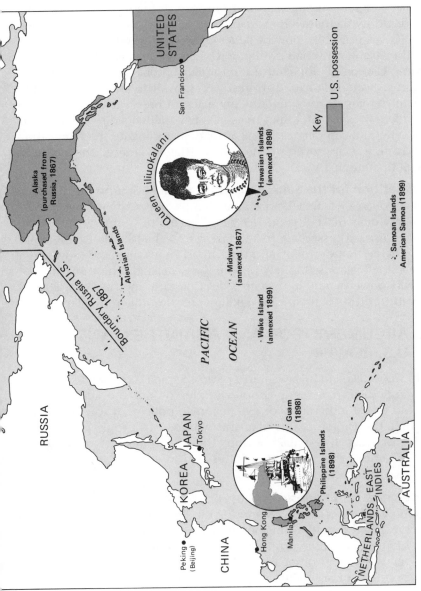

The global context: U.S. territories in the Pacific, 1900

UNITED STATES

San Francisco

Key

U.S. possession

Alaska
(purchased from
Russia, 1867)

Queen Liliuokalani

Hawaiian Islands
(annexed 1898)

Aleutian Islands

Boundary Russia U.S.
1867

Samoan Islands
American Samoa (1899)

Midway
(annexed 1867)

PACIFIC

OCEAN

Wake Island
(annexed 1899)

RUSSIA

Tokyo

JAPAN

Guam
(1898)

KOREA

Philippine Islands
(1898)

Peking
(Beijing)

Hong Kong

CHINA

Manila

NETHERLANDS EAST
INDIES

AUSTRALIA

**The Acquisition of Hawaii**   The acquisition of the Hawaiian islands in the Pacific Ocean is a good example of U.S. imperialism—and also of one president's opposition to imperialism. In the late 1800s a group of American sugar growers in Hawaii made several attempts to overthrow the native Hawaiian ruler. Finally in 1893, with the help of U.S. marines, a revolt by the sugar growers succeeded in overthrowing the strong Hawaiian monarch, Queen Liliuokalani. But President Grover Cleveland opposed an imperialist policy and rejected the sugar growers' plan for turning over Hawaii to the United States. Hawaii remained independent for a few more years. But the next president, William McKinley, was strongly influenced by imperialists in the Republican party. In 1898 a treaty providing for the annexation of Hawaii was approved by the Senate. (Hawaii entered the Union as the 50th state in 1959.)

**Competition for the Samoa Islands**   Far to the southwest of Hawaii lies a group of Pacific Islands called Samoa. A few Americans thought Samoa would make a good U.S. naval base. But Germany and Great Britain also expressed interest in taking over the islands. At one point it appeared that Germany and the United States might go to war over these small islands that few people knew existed. The threat of war passed, however, and in the late 1890s Germany and the United States agreed to divide Samoa, each taking control of different islands.

## D. ARGUMENTS FOR AND AGAINST EXPANDING U.S. POWER

In the 1890s when Hawaii and part of Samoa were acquired, there was much disagreement about whether or not the United States should adopt imperialist (or expansionist) policies. It was obvious to all that the United States, like the nations of Europe, was rapidly industrializing. It was also obvious that U.S. trade was growing. But did this mean that the United States had to enter the race to obtain overseas colonies?

**Arguments for Expansion**   Many U.S. businesses favored expanding U.S. power for *economic reasons.* Until about 1890 the settlement of the West had provided businesses with new markets for their farm machinery and other products. It also opened up rich sources of copper, silver, and other needed materials. But after the passing of the frontier, some business leaders looked for new economic frontiers—new markets, new investment opportunities—in the vast, non-industrialized world beyond U.S. borders.

Some Americans wanted to acquire overseas territories for *strategic reasons.* Alfred Thayer Mahan, a U.S. naval captain, published a book in the 1890s pointing out the importance of sea power to a nation like Great Britain. He argued that U.S. security also depended on having a strong navy. Since ships of the industrial age were now powered by coal-burning steam engines (not wind), the U.S. navy needed to establish bases in the Atlantic and Pacific Oceans where ships could pick up coal at strategically located islands. Furthermore, Mahan argued, increased U.S. trade with Asia and Latin America would depend upon a larger navy to protect that trade against European rivals.

Some people also proposed *cultural reasons* for expansion. For example, Protestant missionaries believed it was their moral duty to spread the message of Christianity to all parts of the world. One influential minister and author, Josiah Strong, argued that less developed regions of the world would benefit from being governed by the "advanced" civilizations of the West. He believed that the benefits of Christianity and U.S. civilization were practically one and the same.

**Arguments Against Expansion**  On the other hand some Americans were opposed to expansion for both moral and practical reasons. They thought the United States should follow President Washington's advice and focus on trade without political involvement. In their view democracy would suffer if the United States took over foreign places and thereby denied native peoples their political rights and independence.

Some feared that foreign involvement would lead to foreign wars. Even some businesses questioned the need for territorial gains, arguing that wars would harm rather than help overseas trade.

# E. THE TARIFF CONTROVERSY

The importance of trade throughout U.S. history is further shown by an issue that never went away: the tariff issue. Citizens and politicians have argued about the issue in the 1790s, the 1890s, and now again in the 1990s. Whenever the issue arises, the arguments for and against a high tariff are much the same.

**Arguments for Protectionism (High Tariffs)**  **Protectionism** is a policy of placing high tariffs on imported goods for the purpose of preventing such goods from competing against U.S. goods in U.S. markets. Tariff laws require U.S. merchants to pay a tax (or tariff) on the purchase of foreign-made goods. This tax is then passed along to American consumers in the form of higher prices for the imported items. In the 1790s Alexander Hamilton favored high tariffs to give "infant industries" in the United States an opportunity to compete against the more mature industries of Great Britain. In the 1890s U.S. industries were far from "infant." But manufacturers still sought tariff protection simply because it gave them an advantage in holding U.S. markets against foreign competitors. Another argument for protectionism is that jobs may be lost if American industries lose business to more cheaply priced goods from abroad. Republicans successfully used this argument in their 1896 campaign to elect William McKinley as president. McKinley's name was associated with a high tariff he had sponsored in 1890 when he was in the U.S. House of Representatives.

**Arguments for Free Trade (No Tariffs)** **Free trade** is a policy of placing no taxes, or tariffs, on imported goods. Those favoring such

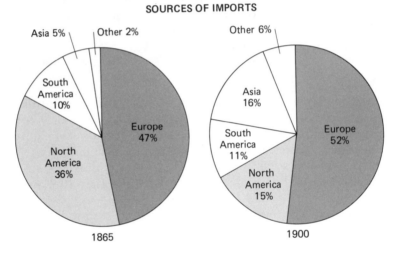

SOURCES OF IMPORTS

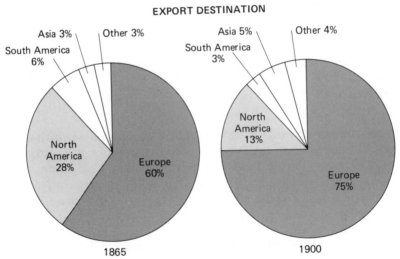

EXPORT DESTINATION

U.S. imports and exports, 1865 and 1900

a policy point out that consumers are best served when the prices they pay are as low as possible. A tariff on foreign goods can only make consumer prices go higher. If a tariff is so high that it keeps foreign goods from being sold at all, then consumers lose out altogether on an opportunity to buy the things they would ordinarily prefer to buy.

**A Hundred Years of Tariffs**   This chart summarizes the tariff in U.S. history from the days of Alexander Hamilton (1790s) to the days of William McKinley (1890s).

| Year | Tariff |
| --- | --- |
| 1789 | Enactment of Hamilton's tariff to protect U.S. infant industries |
| 1816 to 1818 | Tariffs to protect industries after the War of 1812 |
| 1828 | "Tariff of Abominations" favored by Northern industries but condemned by the South |
| 1833 | A lower, compromise tariff to prevent the Southern states from rebelling against the 1828 tariff. |
| 1865 to 1890 | High tariffs, including the McKinley Tariff of 1890 |
| 1898 | A high tariff on Hawaiian sugar resulting in increased public interest in annexing Hawaii |

## *In Review*

The following questions refer to section I: The Impact of Trade on Foreign Policy.

1. Define *imperialism, annexation, free trade, protectionism,* and *tariff.*
2. Compare the acquisition of Alaska with the acquisition of Hawaii. Comment on which of these events you think better illustrates the idea of imperialist expansion.
3. Explain how the growth of U.S. industrialism and trade in the 1800s affected U.S. foreign policy.

# II. The Spanish-American War

In 1895 a revolt against Spanish rule broke out in Cuba. Three years later the United States came to the support of the Cuban people by declaring war against Spain. More than any other event, this war represented a turning point in U.S. foreign policy. The swift and decisive U.S. victory in that war demonstrated that the United States was truly a major military power as well as a leading economic power. How did this brief but important war come about?

## A. IMMEDIATE CAUSES OF U.S. INVOLVEMENT

The American people's sympathy for the Cuban rebels played a large role in bringing about the U.S. war with Spain. Americans' sympathies were fanned almost daily by sensational headlines in the newspapers.

**"Yellow Journalism"**  Recall from Chapter 8 that newspapers of the 1890s attracted readers by playing up scandalous and sensational news. News stories that used big headlines, dramatic pictures, and emotional writing were known as "yellow journalism." Especially influential were the New York City newspapers owned by William Randolph Hearst and Joseph Pulitzer. Both publishers squeezed all the sensation they could out of the violent conflict in Cuba. Their reporters wrote of the terrible suffering of the Cuban people and the brutal acts of Valeriano Weyler, a Spanish general nicknamed "Butcher" Weyler. Reports of Spanish atrocities were often badly exaggerated.

**The De Lôme Letter**  Early in 1898 Hearst's New York *Journal* caused another sensation by printing a stolen letter that seemed to insult the U.S. president, William McKinley. The author of the letter was the Spanish minister to the United States, Dupuy de Lôme. Reading the letter, many Americans were outraged by the minister's description of the president as "weak and a bidder for the admiration of the crowd."

**Sinking of the *Maine***  Only a few days later came even more shocking news. The U.S.S. *Maine*, an American battleship anchored in the harbor of Havana, Cuba, had mysteriously exploded and sunk, killing about 250 of the ship's crew. It was not known then—or even today—what caused the explosion. But the newspapers made it seem as if Spain had deliberately blown up the U.S. ship. After this incident editorials in the "yellow press" urged that the U.S. government go to war to help liberate Cuba from Spanish rule.

## B. OTHER REASONS FOR U.S. INVOLVEMENT

Besides the public emotions stirred by sensational news stories, there were other reasons for war. A *strategic reason* was that military and naval planners thought Cuba might provide an ideal naval base for U.S. ships. They also argued that an island only 90 miles from Florida should not belong to a European power. An *economic reason* was that Americans had invested 50 million dollars in Cuba's sugar and tobacco plantations. One way to protect that investment was to drive out an unfriendly Spanish government and substitute a more friendly Cuban government.

## C. THE DECISION FOR WAR

Not everyone favored the idea of a war with Spain. Some business leaders feared that such a war might lead to the destruction of American-owned properties. There was also a good diplomatic reason for avoiding war. After the sinking of the *Maine*, Spain agreed to virtually all of the U.S. demands concerning Cuba. Spain pledged, for example, that it would eventually grant Cuba its independence.

Even so, President McKinley decided that most Americans expected him to take the country to war. In April, 1898, he asked Congress for a declaration of war against Spain. Congress readily complied.

# DOCUMENT: McKINLEY'S WAR MESSAGE TO CONGRESS, 1898

In April, 1898, President William McKinley wrote a lengthy message to Congress explaining why he believed the United States should declare war against Spain. The following is an excerpt from the president's message.

Of the four reasons for war given by McKinley, which do you regard as (1) the most important and (2) the least important? Why?

The grounds for such intervention may be briefly summarized as follows:

First, in the cause of humanity and to put an end to the barbarities, bloodshed, starvation, and horrible miseries now existing there, and which the parties to the conflict are either unable or unwilling to stop or mitigate. It is no answer to say this is all in another country, belonging to another nation, and is therefore none of our business. It is specially our duty, for it is right at our door.

Second, we owe it to our citizens in Cuba to afford them that protection and indemnity for life and property which no government there can or will afford, and to that end to terminate the conditions that deprive them of legal protection.

Third, the right to intervene may be justified by the very serious injury to the commerce, trade, and business of our people, and by the wanton destruction of property and devastation of the island.

Fourth, and which is of the utmost importance, the present condition of affairs in Cuba is a constant menace to our peace, and entails upon this government an enormous expense.

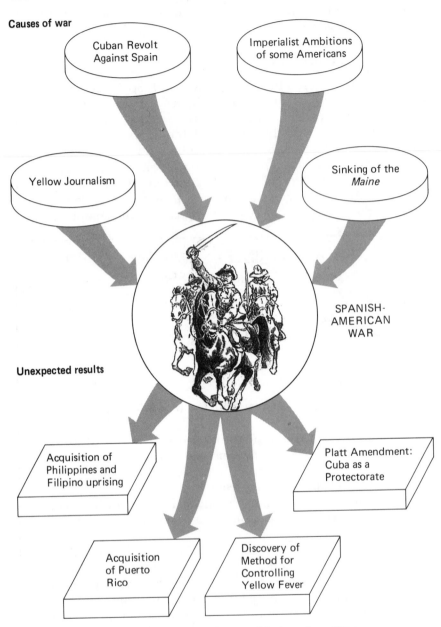

**Causes of war**

Cuban Revolt Against Spain

Imperialist Ambitions of some Americans

Yellow Journalism

Sinking of the *Maine*

SPANISH-AMERICAN WAR

**Unexpected results**

Acquisition of Philippines and Filipino uprising

Platt Amendment: Cuba as a Protectorate

Acquisition of Puerto Rico

Discovery of Method for Controlling Yellow Fever

Causes and effects: the Spanish-American War

## D. THE "SPLENDID LITTLE WAR"

The **Spanish-American War** lasted only about four months, and Americans won every major battle. From the U.S. point of view, it seemed a "splendid little war," as one American called it. It was fought on two fronts: the islands of Cuba and Puerto Rico in the Caribbean and the islands of the Philippines in the Pacific.

**Cuba and Puerto Rico**  In Cuba a troop of volunteers known as the Rough Riders won instant fame and glory by following their leader Theodore Roosevelt in a bold and successful charge up San Juan Hill. African Americans in the regular U.S. Army participated in the charge and spearheaded another attack in the Battle of El Caney. The battles of San Juan Hill and El Caney led to the Spanish surrender of the Cuban port of Santiago. At the same time the neighboring island of Puerto Rico—a Spanish colony since 1508—fell to the invading Americans.

**The Philippines**  In the Pacific the U.S. Navy distinguished itself in a devastating attack against the Spanish fleet in Manila Bay, near the Philippines' capital of Manila. Commodore George Dewey's overwhelming victory in this naval battle made him an American hero. But the attack, so far from Cuba, took most Americans by surprise. Many, including President McKinley, had to search to find the Philippines on a map. Only by reading the newspapers did Americans learn that the Philippines had been a Spanish possession since the 1500s. The Filipinos—like the Cubans—had been fighting for their independence from Spain when U.S. troops arrived. The Filipinos celebrated the American victory at Manila Bay, fully expecting independence to be the result. Instead, they were bitterly disappointed by the terms of the U.S.–Spanish treaty of peace.

## E. RESULTS OF THE WAR

These were the terms of the treaty, signed in December, 1898:

- Spain gave two islands to the United States: Puerto Rico in the Caribbean and Guam in the Pacific. (See map, page 271.)
- Spain granted Cuba its independence.
- Spain sold the Philippines to the United States for the bargain price of only $20 million.

Concerning the Philippines, American public opinion was sharply divided between those who wanted to govern them as U.S. territory and those who wanted the Asian islands to be independent.

**The Anti-Imperialist Argument**  Those arguing against U.S. control of the Philippines were known as **anti-imperialists.** Their leader was the Democratic candidate for president in 1900, William Jennings Bryan. Anti-imperialists warned that the United States would be abandoning its own commitment to democracy and the ideals of the Declaration of Independence if it ruled territory on the other side of the Pacific. Furthermore, they were afraid that the possession of Asian islands would inevitably involve the United States in Asian politics and wars.

**The Imperialist Argument**  Those favoring an imperialist policy, including Theodore Roosevelt, thought the United States had a duty to involve itself actively in world affairs. They argued that the acquisition of Pacific islands like Hawaii, Guam, and the Philippines was necessary for building the reputation of the United States as one of the world's great powers. Also, the argument went, the Philippines were bound to fall under the influence of one Western power or another. If that was so, then they were better off under U.S. rule than under a nondemocratic power like Germany or Russia.

**Suppressing the Filipino Revolution**  The Philippine people could not accept the idea of being traded from one colonial power to another. In 1899 the rebel troops that had fought against Spain turned their weapons against U.S. forces. To put down the uprising, President McKinley sent 70,000 additional troops to the Philippines. After nearly three years of vicious fighting in Philippine jungles, U.S. forces finally prevailed as the last rebel band surrendered in 1902.

**Cuba and the Platt Amendment**  What was to be done about the Spanish-speaking islanders in the Caribbean: the Cubans and the Puerto Ricans? Should they be treated any differently than the Filipinos? Although Spain had already granted Cuban independence, the U.S. position was unclear. President McKinley and Congress finally decided that Cuba should be permitted its independence—but with certain conditions attached. In 1901 these conditions were included in an amendment to an army bill. The **Platt Amendment,** as it was called, provided that:

- Cuba would sell or lease a piece of land to the United States for use as a naval and coaling station.

- Cuba would not permit a foreign power, other than the United States, from acquiring Cuban territory.

- Cuba would allow the United States to intervene in the country whenever it was necessary to protect American citizens residing in Cuba.

Cubans strongly protested these terms. But by a treaty of 1903, they finally accepted the Platt Amendment when the United States insisted upon it as the condition for removing U.S. troops. In effect, by agreeing to the Platt Amendment, Cuba became a U.S. **protectorate** (a nation whose foreign policy is partly controlled by a foreign power).

**The Status of Puerto Rico**   For economic reasons the people of Puerto Rico thought it would be to their advantage to be included in the U.S. empire. By the terms of a U.S. law (the Foraker Act, 1900), Puerto Ricans were allowed to elect representatives to their own legislature, but their governor was appointed by the U.S. president.

## In Review

The following questions refer to section II: the Spanish-American War.

1. Identify *the De Lôme Letter, the Platt Amendment, anti-imperialists,* and *protectorates.*
2. Explain both the long-range and short-range causes of the Spanish-American War.
3. Evaluate (a) the decision to go to war with Spain and (b) the decision to take possession of the Philippines.

# III. U.S. Policy Toward Latin America

Even as early as the 1820s, the United States was the strongest nation of the Western Hemisphere. Because of the relative strength of U.S. military forces, presidents tended to view countries to the south as needing U.S. protection from internal disorder as well as European control. But this point of view was often bitterly resented by Latin Americans, especially when U.S. troops were sent into their countries to "protect" them.

## A. CONTINUING IMPORTANCE OF THE MONROE DOCTRINE

Recall that the Monroe Doctrine of 1823 had warned Great Britain, France, Spain, and other European nations *not* to interfere in the internal politics of Latin American nations. (Review Chapter 3.) Implied in this warning was the idea that the United States would protect the countries of Latin America from outside interference. Also implied was the assumed right of the United States to send troops into any threatened country to the south.

The Platt Amendment that made Cuba a U.S. protectorate was an example of this policy—a policy that started almost 80 years earlier with James Monroe. In the first 20 years of the twentieth century, this policy would be applied again and again by the three presidents of the Progressive Era—Theodore Roosevelt, William H. Taft, and Woodrow Wilson.

## B. THEODORE ROOSEVELT AND THE PANAMA CANAL

A foreign policy of **intervention** is one in which military and naval power is used to achieve political goals. A prime example of such a policy is the story of the building of the Panama Canal.

**Early Attempts to Build a Canal**    As early as the 1850s, there had been ambitious plans to dig a canal through a narrow, 30-mile wide strip of land in Central America—the land known as Panama. Such a canal would cut in half the time required to sail from New York to San Francisco. It would greatly help the trade of all nations of the world and also eliminate the dangerous voyage over stormy seas at the tip of South America. In the 1880s a French business firm began work on a canal, but jungle diseases and inadequate funds put a stop to the venture. Another route for a canal was also considered— a route that led through Nicaragua (north of Panama).

**Roosevelt's Quarrel with Colombia**    In 1901 when Theodore Roosevelt became president, Panama belonged to the South American republic of Colombia. Roosevelt was extremely eager to begin digging a canal either through Panama or Nicaragua. He preferred the Panama route and offered to pay Colombia ten million dollars for the right to lease the land through which the canal would pass. But Colombia refused the president's offer. Roosevelt was furious. Since Colombia would not cooperate, he decided to support an uprising in Panama against Colombian rule.

**"Revolution" in Panama**    In 1903 the uprising took place as planned. It lasted only a few hours. U.S. naval forces were on hand in Panama to prevent Colombian troops from stopping the so-called "revolution." President Roosevelt wasted no time in recognizing the government of the new Republic of Panama. Of course this government quickly agreed to U.S. terms for leasing a canal zone through the country. Work on the canal began soon afterward.

**Evaluating Roosevelt's Intervention**    Did the president act correctly? He himself was proud of moving so boldly in Panama. Roosevelt later boasted: "I took Panama." But Colombians were outraged. They called U.S. actions a form of imperialist robbery. Years later President

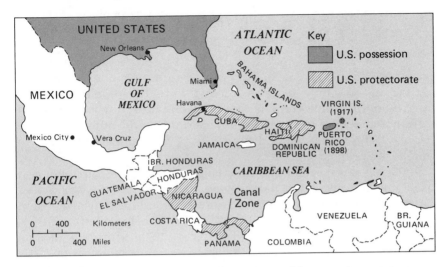

U.S. possessions and protectorates in the Caribbean, 1900 to 1917

Wilson persuaded Congress to award Colombia 25 million dollars as compensation for its loss of Panama.

**Building the Canal**   The building of the Panama Canal was one of the engineering marvels of the twentieth century. A wide strip of dense tropical vegetation had to be cleared from a canal zone 10 miles wide. A huge dam had to be built to control the canal's water level. Entire towns had to be erected to house all the workers. Overseeing these awesome projects was a brilliant army engineer, Colonel George W. Goethals.

The worst obstacles to the enterprise were two kinds of tropical mosquito that carried two killing diseases—malaria and yellow fever. During the Spanish-American War, Dr. William C. Gorgas had learned to eliminate the breeding places of the deadly mosquitoes whose bites had been responsible for the deaths of thousands of American soldiers in Cuba. Gorgas came to Panama to apply his knowledge to controlling the jungle mosquitoes. He succeeded well enough to save the lives of most canal workers.

Even so, thousands did die of malaria and yellow fever. Since most of the workers on the canal project were African Americans, most of those who died (4,500 out of a total of 5,500) were also African Americans.

After seven years of human toil, the "big ditch" was completed in 1914. Although no longer president in that year, Theodore Roosevelt lived to see ocean-going ships move through the canal that was begun under his administration.

## C. THE ROOSEVELT COROLLARY TO THE MONROE DOCTRINE

Roosevelt used the Monroe Doctrine to justify his interventionist policy in Latin America. He even added to the famous doctrine by issuing a "corollary" (logical extension) to it. The problem that led him to do this involved the failure of several Latin American nations to pay their debts to Great Britain, Germany, and other European nations. (The debts resulted from having used borrowed funds to purchase European imports.)

Roosevelt recognized that Europeans might become impatient and use force to collect the debts owed to them. He was afraid that Europeans wanting to colonize Latin America might use the debt problem as an excuse for taking political control of indebted countries. To avoid this possibility, he said the United States might intervene in a Latin American country if its debts were far overdue. The **Roosevelt Corollary** to the Monroe Doctrine read: "Chronic wrong-doing ... may in America, as elsewhere, ultimately require intervention.... In the Western Hemisphere the adherence of the United States to the Monroe Doctrine may force the United States, however reluctantly, in flagrant cases of such wrongdoing ... , to the exercise of an international police power."

Applying his corollary in 1904, the president sent U.S. troops to occupy the capital of the Dominican Republic, an island country in the Caribbean. The troops remained long enough to make sure that the Dominican Republic paid its debts.

## D. DOLLAR DIPLOMACY UNDER TAFT

The next president, William Howard Taft, continued Roosevelt's policy of intervention by sending U.S. marines into Nicaragua in 1912. His reasons for doing so were slightly different from Roosevelt's. Taft believed that the United States should protect the many American businesses that invested in Latin America. He also believed that the United States had the right to force a Latin American country to repay loans owed to U.S. banks. These reasons for intervening were given the name **"dollar diplomacy."** In the case of Nicaragua, Taft ordered in the marines when a civil war in that country threatened to prevent the repayment of a large U.S. bank loan.

## E. MORE MARINES IN HAITI AND THE DOMINICAN REPUBLIC

When Woodrow Wilson became president in 1913, he said that he did not believe in "dollar diplomacy." But he did believe in keeping order, especially in troubled areas close to the United States. In 1915 he sent marines to Haiti when a civil war erupted there. Two years later similar disorders in the Dominican Republic caused him to send more marines to that country. U.S. military forces remained in the Dominican Republic until 1925 and in Haiti until 1934.

Latin Americans throughout the region deeply resented the U.S. policy of intervention.

## F. "WATCHFUL WAITING" AND INTERVENTION IN MEXICO

Wilson's most serious problem in Latin America was the result of a 1910 revolution in Mexico. After the revolution began, opposing armies of Mexicans fought for control of their country's government. Since Wilson was committed to the ideal of democracy, he wanted to support a Mexican government that respected civil rights and permitted free elections. But he was often disappointed by the various governments that briefly came to power in Mexico.

**"Watchful Waiting"** Wilson especially disliked the ruthless methods of a Mexican dictator named Victoriano Huerta. Rather than recognize Huerta's government as fully legitimate, Wilson followed a policy of **"watchful waiting."** In other words he pledged to wait and see whether forces opposed to Huerta would soon overthrow him.

**Landing of Troops at Vera Cruz** In 1914 the jailing of several U.S. sailors in Mexico provided Wilson with a reason for taking action against Huerta. On the president's orders, U.S. troops occupied the Mexican port of Vera Cruz. The Mexican people were so offended by this U.S. action that even Huerta's political enemies rallied to his support. Wilson withdrew the troops after the "ABC Powers" of South America (Argentina, Brazil, and Chile) urged Huerta to resign from office. Huerta finally did so. But the new Mexican government of Venustiano Carranza was immediately challenged by rebel forces under Pancho Villa.

**Villa's Raids** In 1916 Villa tried to make himself a popular hero of the Mexican people by raiding a U.S. town in New Mexico and killing 19 Americans. Wilson retaliated for Villa's raids by sending a punitive expedition into northern Mexico. He avoided going to war, however. Early in 1917 he ordered the removal of U.S. troops and formally recognized the Carranza government as legitimate. Mexicans' bitter memories of U.S. intervention in their country had a negative effect on U.S.-Mexican relations for many years.

# IV. U.S. Policy Toward Asia

Two wars of the 1890s had serious consequences for the United States—and all other major powers of the world. One was the Spanish-

American War of 1898. Another was a war between Japan and China fought only a few years earlier, 1894 to 1895. The Japanese army and navy crushed the much weaker forces of the Chinese. It was clear that China was unable to defend itself against the imperialist ambitions of stronger rivals. It was also clear that Japan had become a major power in East Asia because of its successful efforts to industrialize.

After the United States acquired the Philippines, it too was involved in Asian politics. It too had to be concerned with the weakness of China relative to the strength of Japan.

## A. OPEN DOOR POLICY IN CHINA

After Japan defeated China, its armies occupied Korea and the Chinese island of Taiwan. Japan also won overall economic control of Manchuria in northern China. Manchuria became known as Japan's **"sphere of influence,"** which meant that Japan enjoyed special privileges in the region and more or less controlled its trade and industrial growth. Russia disputed Japan's control of Manchuria until 1904 when Russia's defeat in war forced it to give up its claim.

**The Competition for "Spheres of Influence"**   Following Japan's example, the European powers of France, Germany, Russia, and Great Britain forced the Chinese government to grant other "spheres of influence." It appeared as if all of China might be divided into such spheres. The U.S. government feared that Americans' long-standing trade with China might be cut off completely.

**John Hay's "Open Door" Notes**   John Hay was the secretary of state for two presidents, William McKinley and Theodore Roosevelt. To oppose the "spheres of influence" in China and keep the door open for U.S. businesses, Hay composed two diplomatic notes, one in 1899, the other in 1900. The first note called upon the European powers and Japan to agree to an **Open Door policy** in China. Such a policy would mean that all nations would have "equal trading rights" in China and that none would have to pay higher port fees or taxes than any other nation. The second note suggested that all powers in East Asia respect the **territorial integrity** of China. In other words no nation would compel China to give up the control of any of its own territory.

The various replies to Hay's notes were intentionally vague and evasive. But the U.S. government stood firmly committed to an Open Door policy in China. It would remain committed to that policy through the 1930s and early 1940s when Japanese troops occupied much of China. As we shall see, U.S. involvement in World War II was partly a response to Japan's violation of the Open Door.

**Key**

Japanese Possessions

Spheres of Influence

Russian    Japanese    German

British    French

The global context: spheres of influence in China about 1900

**The Boxer Rebellion**  The people of China resented the imperialist policies of the Western powers. Many joined a terrorist organization known as the Society of Righteous and Harmonious Fists—also known as the Boxers. Secretly they plotted to drive the "foreign devils" out of China. In 1900 the Boxers carried out their plot by attacking and killing Westerners residing in China. In the terrorist uprising, many Christian missionaries, including some Americans, lost their lives.

To rescue those trapped in the Chinese capital of Peking, the United States, Japan, and the European powers put together an unusual international army. This force crushed the **Boxer Rebellion** and threatened to impose harsh terms on the Chinese government. But the United States stood by its commitment to respect the territorial integrity of China and insisted that the other powers do likewise.

The Western powers forced China to pay them an **indemnity** (a sum of money to cover damages and deaths). But the U.S. Congress voted to return the U.S. portion of the indemnity to China. This gesture of friendship greatly impressed China's government. It used the returned money to pay for scholarships for Chinese students to attend U.S. colleges and universities.

## B. STRAINED RELATIONS WITH JAPAN

The growing power of Japan in the early twentieth century both impressed and worried U.S. policymakers. The president who did the most to shape U.S.-Japanese relations in these years was Theodore Roosevelt.

**Settlement of the Russo-Japanese War**  In 1904 Japan increased its reputation as a rising power by soundly defeating Russia in the **Russo-Japanese War.** Japan's government asked President Theodore Roosevelt to bring the war to an end by arranging a diplomatic conference on U.S. soil. The president was happy to act as mediator (someone not involved in a conflict who tries to arrange a settlement). The peace conference arranged by Roosevelt took place in 1905 at Portsmouth, New Hampshire. It succeeded in ending the war. For his role as peacemaker, Roosevelt was honored with the Nobel Peace Prize in 1906.

Japan was not happy with the terms of the compromise worked out at Portsmouth. True enough, Russia had conceded full control of Manchuria and Korea to Japan. But the Japanese had also wanted a sum of money as an indemnity, and this was denied.

**The Great White Fleet**  Roosevelt sometimes quoted a West African proverb: "Speak softly and carry a big stick." He believed, in other words, in what the newspapers called "big stick" diplomacy. Roosevelt was especially fond of using the U.S. Navy as his "big stick" for impressing other nations. To impress Japan with U.S. power, he ordered a fleet of battleships to sail around the world. Arriving in Tokyo Harbor, the handsome ships, painted white, were much admired by the Japanese who were also building a strong navy.

**Discrimination Issue**  Recall that Japan was offended by the practice in San Francisco schools of discriminating against the children of Japanese immigrants. Roosevelt managed to calm Japan by persuading California to end its segregation policies. For its part Japan agreed to restrict the immigration of Japanese workers to the United States.

**The 21 Demands**  During Roosevelt's presidency Japan agreed to respect the U.S. Open Door policy in China. But in 1915 Japan made a series of demands that challenged that policy. If China had consented to the so-called 21 Demands, it would have fallen under Japanese domination. But the U.S. and British governments both sent messages of protest to Japan. For the time being, this diplomatic action succeeded in preserving the independence of China.

## *In Review*

The following questions refer to section III: U.S. Policy Toward Latin America and section IV: U.S. Policy Toward Asia.

1. Identify *the Roosevelt Corollary, "watchful waiting," "sphere of influence," Open Door policy, Boxer Rebellion,* and *Russo-Japanese War.*
2. Describe Latin Americans' reaction to U.S. intervention in Mexico, Nicaragua, and Haiti.
3. Explain why the United States adopted an Open Door policy in Asia.

## GLOSSARY OF KEY TERMS: CHAPTER 9

**anti-imperialists**   those Americans who were opposed to the creation of an overseas empire.

**Boxer Rebellion**   an uprising in China directed against foreign influences and resulting in the deaths of many American and European missionaries.

**"dollar diplomacy"**   the policy of President William Howard Taft of promoting and safeguarding American business investments and bank loans in Latin America—if necessary, by using U.S. troops.

**free trade**   a policy of placing no taxes, or tariffs, on imported goods.

**imperialism**   a nation's policy of acquiring territory outside its borders.

**indemnity**   a payment for war damages made by a defeated nation to the victor.

**intervention**   the use of military force to support a political goal.

**Open Door policy**   the U.S. policy of supporting China's political independence and insisting on equal trading rights in China.

**Platt Amendment**   a U.S. law of 1901 that limited Cuba's power to conduct its own foreign relations.

**protectionism**   a policy of placing high tariffs on imported goods for the purpose of preventing such goods from competing against U.S. goods in U.S. markets.

**protectorate**   a country that is partly under the control of a stronger country.

**Roosevelt Corollary**   Theodore Roosevelt's interpretation of the Monroe Doctrine, asserting a U.S. right to send troops to an indebted Latin American nation and take over its finances.

**Russo-Japanese War**   a war between Russia and Japan in 1904 that increased Japan's power in East Asia.

**Spanish-American War**   a war between Spain and the United States in 1898 that extended the U.S. empire in both the Pacific Ocean and the Caribbean Sea.

**"sphere of influence"**   a region or zone in a weak country (such as China in 1900) that is largely under the control of a stronger, imperialist country.

**territorial integrity**   a country's freedom from another country's military or political control.

**"watchful waiting"**   Woodrow Wilson's policy in 1914 of refusing to give full recognition to the government of a Mexican dictator.

# TEST YOURSELF

## A. Multiple Choice: Facts, Main Ideas, Skills

*On a separate sheet of paper, write the number of the word or expression that, of those given, best completes the statement or answers the question.*

### Reviewing the facts

1. Which factor had the greatest influence on the U.S. government's decision to declare war against Spain in 1898? (1) campus demonstrations  (2) pressure from large corporations  (3) power of the press  (4) arguments of Cuban lobbyists in Congress

2. Which was a result of the peace treaty ending the Spanish-American War? (1) The United States acquired the Philippines. (2) Puerto Rico became an independent nation. (3) A civil war broke out in Mexico. (4) The United States announced an Open Door policy.

3. Theodore Roosevelt's interventionist policy is best illustrated by his (1) role in ending the Russo-Japanese War  (2) use of the U.S. Navy to support a revolt in Panama  (3) Open Door policy in China  (4) negotiations with Japan concerning Japanese immigrants

4. The Roosevelt Corollary to the Monroe Doctrine assumed the right of the United States to  (1) intervene in the internal affairs of a Latin American country  (2) collect the debts of a European country  (3) grant financial aid to less developed countries  (4) disregard any or all parts of the Monroe Doctrine

5. "Dollar diplomacy" indicated a U.S. desire to  (1) institute the dollar as an international currency  (2) give foreign aid to less developed countries  (3) protect the property of U.S. businesses located in foreign countries  (4) favor the nations of western Europe

6. A primary aim of the U.S. Open Door policy was to  (1) encourage the Chinese to emigrate to other nations  (2) prevent European powers from dividing up China  (3) develop China's industrial capacity  (4) introduce democratic government into China

**7.** Which president and foreign policy are *incorrectly* paired? (1) William McKinley—independence for the Philippines (2) Theodore Roosevelt—"big stick" diplomacy (3) William Howard Taft—"dollar diplomacy" (4) Woodrow Wilson—"watchful waiting"

## Reviewing the main ideas

**8.** Which statement best describes U.S. foreign policy *before* 1890? (1) It was chiefly concerned with the spread of democracy in the Western world. (2) It promoted global peace through international alliances. (3) It was committed to keeping European powers from interfering in the Western Hemisphere. (4) It attempted to bring about industrial growth in many regions of the world.

**9.** "In our infancy we bordered upon the Atlantic only; our youth carried our boundary to the Gulf of Mexico; today, maturity sees us upon the Pacific. Whether they will it or not, Americans must now begin to look outward." This statement from the late nineteenth century best reflects a U.S. foreign policy of (1) imperialism (2) isolationism (3) collective security (4) peaceful coexistance

*Speakers A, B, C, D, and E are discussing the Philippines. Base your answers to questions 10 through 12 on their statements and on your knowledge of U.S. history and government.*

*Speaker A:* "These poor, uncivilized, unchristianized people need our assistance if they are to be uplifted from their ignorance to a point at least approaching our level of civilization and accomplishment. The Philippines must be ours."

*Speaker B:* "These islands would certainly make excellent coaling stations for our great naval fleet which is growing each year as Congress approves additional funds for the construction of new ships."

*Speaker C:* "The shipping interests really find the Philippines to be excellent trading centers. Furthermore, they can be used to develop our commerce with China and Japan. We can use the islands as stopover and storage points for our merchant fleets."

*Speaker D:* "We have no alternative but to accept the Philippines as our own. God would not forgive us if we rejected his obvious faith and trust in our nation. Democracy must be carried to the four corners of the globe."

*Speaker E:* "Were our economic rivals to obtain the Philippines, it would be a commercial disaster for our nation. We entered the race late, but we must not fall behind now."

**10.** Each statement made by the speakers could be used to justify (1) imperialism (2) containment (3) coexistence (4) anti-imperialism

**11.** Which speaker presents a strategic reason for taking over the Philippines? (1) B (2) C (3) D (4) E

**12.** Speaker A's views are most similar to those of Speaker (1) B (2) C (3) D (4) E

**13.** Which statement reflects a foreign policy view held by both President James Monroe and President Theodore Roosevelt? (1) Revolutionary movements in western Europe must be opposed. (2) Close economic ties with Japan must be maintained. (3) Noninvolvement in world affairs is the wisest course for the United States. (4) U.S. influence in Latin America must be accepted.

**14.** Which was a characteristic of U.S. foreign policy from 1900 to 1915? (1) failure to acquire foreign possessions (2) involvement in European wars (3) frequent military interventions in Latin America (4) negotiation of treaties on the conservation of natural resources

**15.** The Platt Amendment and dollar diplomacy are examples of U.S. interest in (1) Europe and the Atlantic (2) Asia and the Pacific (3) South America and the Caribbean (4) the Middle East and Africa

## Developing critical thinking skills

*Base your answers to questions 16 through 18 on the map on page 275 and on your knowledge of U.S. history and government.*

**16.** Observe that there are no striped lines on the map of China representing the United States. From this we may conclude that (1) the United States became interested in China only after 1900 (2) the United States had no "spheres of influence" in China (3) China had not yet granted "spheres of influence" to any power (4) the Open Door policy was not taken seriously by the nations of Europe

**17.** The location of the Philippines may be described as (1) south of Japan, west of French Indochina (2) north of Japan, east of China (3) south of Japan, east of French Indochina (4) north of Japan, west of China

**18.** We may infer from the map that the territory *most* affected by the treaty ending the Russo-Japanese War was (1) the Philippines (2) Tibet (3) Taiwan (or Formosa) (4) Manchuria

## B. Enduring Issues

*Select* two *of the enduring issues from column A. For* each *issue chosen, explain how the historical example in column B relates to the issue.*

| A. Enduring Issues | B. Historical Examples |
| --- | --- |
| 1. National power—limits and potential | The U.S. decision to take possession of the Philippines |
| 2. Presidential power in wartime and foreign affairs | President Wilson's decision to send troops to Mexico |
| 3. Separation of powers and the capacity to govern | President McKinley's request for a declaration of war from Congress in 1898 |
| 4. Property rights and economic policy | President Taft's "dollar diplomacy" |

## C. Essays

*Level 1*

Developments in Latin America and Asia, such as those listed below, have had a significant impact on U.S. foreign policy.

*Latin America:* Cuban revolt against Spain
Independence of Panama
Revolution in Mexico

*Asia:* Division of China into "spheres of influence"
Emergence of Japan as a major power

Select two of the developments listed, and for each one selected, (1) discuss one way that the development affected U.S. foreign policy, and (2) identify and discuss one outcome of the policy pursued by the United States.

*Level 2*

**A.** U.S. presidents have often been challenged to make important decisions in foreign policy. Consider the actions taken by the following presidents:

| *President* | *Action* |
|---|---|
| William McKinley | ● Asked Congress to declare war against Spain |
| | ● Supported an Open Door policy toward China |
| Theodore Roosevelt | ● Arranged a treaty for the building of the Panama Canal |
| | ● Mediated treaty ending Russo-Japanese War |

Choose *one* action by each president. For *each* action chosen, state why the action was taken.

**B.** Base your answer to part B on your answer to part A. Write an essay discussing a foreign policy action of *either* President McKinley *or* President Roosevelt. Describe the action taken and explain the reason for it.

# UNIT FOUR

## At Home and Abroad (1914 to 1939)

*"Great War"* ... *Roaring Twenties* ... *Crash of 1929* ... *Great Depression.* These four phrases sum up the wrenching changes in American life treated in this unit. First came a war in Europe that eventually became a world war involving the United States and other non-European nations. Then came a decade of general prosperity (the 1920s), followed by a decade of hard times (the 1930s). To cope with the hard times, President Franklin Roosevelt offered a "new deal" to the American people. The U.S. government today still enforces many of the laws enacted during this era of great stress and change.

| Chapters | Topics |
|---|---|
| 10. World War I and Postwar Isolationism | • Why the nations of Europe suddenly went to war in 1914<br>• Why, despite a desire to stay out of the war, the United States was drawn into it<br>• How Americans turned their back on world affairs in the postwar years |
| 11. From Prosperity to Depression: The Twenties and Thirties | • How the automobile, the movies, and the radio affected American life<br>• Causes of the Great Depression<br>• Programs of economic relief, recovery, and reform under Franklin D. Roosevelt |

*Chapter* **10**

# World War I and Postwar Isolationism

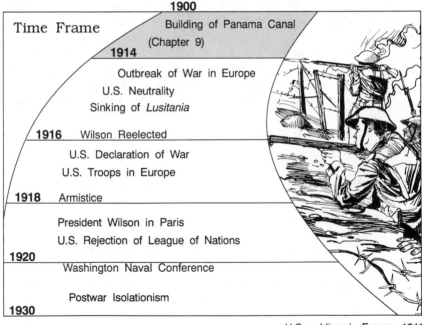

| Time Frame | 1900 | |
|---|---|---|
| | Building of Panama Canal (Chapter 9) | |
| **1914** | | |
| | Outbreak of War in Europe | |
| | U.S. Neutrality | |
| | Sinking of *Lusitania* | |
| **1916** | Wilson Reelected | |
| | U.S. Declaration of War | |
| | U.S. Troops in Europe | |
| **1918** | Armistice | |
| | President Wilson in Paris | |
| | U.S. Rejection of League of Nations | |
| **1920** | | |
| | Washington Naval Conference | |
| | Postwar Isolationism | |
| **1930** | | |

*U.S. soldiers in France, 1918*

### *Objectives*

- To identify the causes of World War I.
- To describe and explain the change in U.S. foreign policy from neutrality to involvement.
- To understand the impact of wartime on the civil liberties of Americans.
- To appraise U.S. contributions to peace and arms control after World War I.
- To evaluate whether or not the United States made the right choices during and after the war.

Before the outbreak of World War I, U.S. troops had fought overseas in Latin America (Cuba and Mexico) and in Asia (the Philippines), but they had never fought in Europe. How and why did the United States become involved in 1917 in a terribly destructive European war? What were the consequences of U.S. involvement?

In this chapter you will analyze choices in U.S. foreign policy both during and after World War I. You will also determine whether, in your judgment, the choices made were the right ones.

# I. Causes of "the Great War" in Europe

"The Great War," as it was called at the time, began in August, 1914, and ended in November, 1918. The United States participated in the war on the side of Great Britain and France only in the last 20 months beginning in April, 1917. Before analyzing how the United States became involved, you should understand how the war came about in Europe.

## A. LONG-RANGE CAUSES OF WORLD WAR I

All wars have both long-range causes and short-range causes. The chief long-range causes of World War I were the forces of nationalism, militarism, and imperialism. In addition, a system of **alliances** made it likely that a war between any two nations of Europe would result automatically in a much larger war involving the many allies of those two nations. These causes of war are defined and illustrated in the chart on page 286.

See also the accompanying map (page 287), and note especially the location of Serbia and its chief enemy, Austria-Hungary. It was the hostility between these countries that eventually brought all of Europe to the point of war.

## Causes of War, 1870 to 1914

| Causes | Examples |
| --- | --- |
| 1. **Nationalism:** a strong feeling of loyalty to an existing nation; also, the strong desire of people ruled by a foreign power to form their own independent nation. | a. French resentment over their loss to Germany in a war (1870 to 1871); French desire to regain the two territories (Alsace and Lorraine) lost in that war.<br>b. The desire of Poles, Serbs, Croats, Czechs, and other eastern European peoples to free themselves from rule by Austria-Hungary. |
| 2. **Militarism:** a nation's stress on building up its armed forces with the goal of having military and naval power greater than any of its rivals. | a. Germany's attempt to build a powerful navy capable of challenging Great Britain's navy.<br>b. Competition among the major powers of Europe to increase the size of their armies and equip them with superior weapons. |
| 3. **Imperialism:** the policy of acquiring colonies in the less industrialized continents of the world—Africa, Asia, and South America. | a. Germany's attempt to acquire African colonies was viewed by Britain and France as a challenge to their own colonies in Africa.<br>b. Russia's ambitions to acquire Turkish territory on the Mediterranean in order to have a warm water port. |
| 4. **Alliances:** the joining of nations by treaty into defensive systems; members of an alliance pledge to fight together against a common enemy if any member is attacked. | a. One alliance, known as the Triple Alliance, consisted at first of Germany, Austria-Hungary, and Italy. (In 1914 Turkey replaced Italy as the third ally.)<br>b. Another alliance, known as the Triple Entente, consisted of France, Russia, and Great Britain. |

In the 20 years before 1914, tensions between rival powers had been steadily building in Europe. Great Britain worried not only about Germany's ambitions for colonies and a strong navy but also about Germany's growing industrial economy. Austria-Hungary worried more and more about the rebellious attitude of Serbs and other Slavic peoples in its empire. The aging Austrian monarch worried too about support for Serbia by the world's largest Slavic nation, Russia. Russia in turn worried about Germany's support for its ally, Austria-Hungary.

## B. SHORT-RANGE CAUSES OF WORLD WAR I

The spark that ignited World War I was an assassination on the streets of Sarajevo—a city now in Yugoslavia, but then in Austria-Hungary. The victims of the shooting were the heir to the throne of Austria-Hungary, the Archduke Francis Ferdinand, and the archduke's wife. The assassin was a citizen of neighboring Serbia and a member of a band of Serbian terrorists. The terrorists hoped to bring about the collapse of Austria-Hungary so that Serbs within the empire could join independent Serbia.

Austria-Hungary blamed the nation of Serbia for the terrorist attack that killed the archduke. It presented Serbia with an **ultimatum** (a list of final demands). Serbia agreed to most of the demands. Even so, Austria-Hungary declared war on Serbia, and its heavy guns began bombarding Belgrade, the Serbian capital, on July 29, 1914.

The allies of the Austrians and the Serbs quickly called their armies

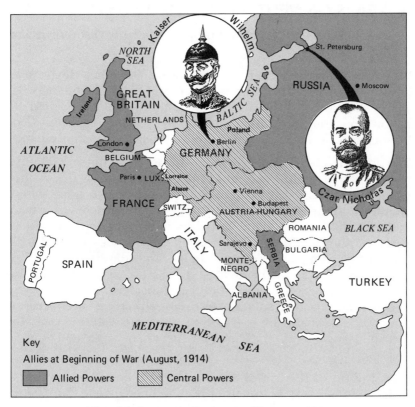

The global context: European alliances, 1914

into a state of readiness for war. A huge Russian army prepared to defend Serbia. Recognizing that Germany would defend Austria-Hungary against Russia, France and Great Britain prepared for war in defense of themselves and their Russian ally. On August 4, German armies marched into Belgium as the best invasion route for attacking France. By the end of the first week of August, all the major powers of Europe were at war.

# II. The U.S. Dilemma: Neutrality or Involvement?

Of course the United States in 1914 was not allied with any of the European nations. Since fighting against Great Britain in the War of 1812, it had remained strictly neutral and uninvolved in Europe's conflicts. Both President Woodrow Wilson and the American people hoped to keep the United States neutral from beginning to end of "the Great War."

## A. YEARS OF NEUTRALITY, 1914 TO 1916

As soon as war broke out in Europe, President Wilson proclaimed U.S. neutrality.

**Why Neutrality?**   In 1914 most Americans, including the president, believed that the war in Europe did not involve U.S. interests. They viewed the Atlantic Ocean as a great barrier that separated their nation from the problems of Europe. Also, many respected George Washington's advice not to become involved in "permanent alliances."

**Wartime Problems and Pressures**   However, as the war continued from month to month, it became clear that maintaining U.S. neutrality would not be easy. The United States continued to trade with the countries of Europe in wartime. It was one of its rights as a neutral nation. But Germany's hope for victory in the war depended in large part on cutting off supplies from reaching its enemies. It could achieve this goal by using a weapon new to warfare—the submarine.

Germany had by far the greatest number of submarines and used them with deadly effect against British ships. Beginning in early 1915 Germany also used its submarines to sink *any* ships—even passenger liners and merchant ships—if they crossed into waters close to Great Britain. Many of the ships carried American cargo and American passengers.

**The Sinking of the *Lusitania***   Disaster was bound to happen, and it did. In May, 1915, a British passenger liner named the ***Lusitania*** steamed into the "war zone" near Ireland where it was torpedoed and sunk by a German submarine. More than 1,000 people lost their lives, including 128 Americans. News of the tragedy shocked the American people into recognizing that their nation might be drawn into the war after all. It did not happen right away, however. Several strongly worded messages of protest from President Wilson persuaded Germany to abandon its policy of sinking unarmed ships without warning. Germany's promise was known as the **Sussex pledge** (named for another torpedoed ship).

**"He Kept Us Out of War"** A key issue of the 1916 campaign for president was whether or not the United States should build a stronger army and navy—just in case something might happen. The Democratic slogan for the reelection of Woodrow Wilson was: "He kept us out of war." The slogan helped Wilson to win, although he did so by only 23 electoral votes.

# B. LONG-RANGE CAUSES OF U.S. INVOLVEMENT

Despite Wilson's campaign slogan, he and many other Americans understood that neutrality might soon give way to military involvement. They realized that several powerful forces were pushing in the direction of involvement. These forces included the following:

**Sympathy for Great Britain and France** As citizens of an English-speaking nation, most Americans felt strong ties to Great Britain. They also sympathized with the French, remembering that France had assisted George Washington's struggling army and helped win U.S. independence. Also, Americans recognized that both France and Great Britain had democratic governments. Their enemies, on the other hand, were both ruled by monarchs—Germany by a kaiser, Austria-Hungary by an emperor.

**Economic Ties** The British navy effectively blockaded German ports. Therefore, most of U.S. trade during the war was with the British and the French. In fact, the United States sold millions of dollars of war materials to these two nations.

**Fear of German Power** Policymakers in the U.S. government feared German victory in the war for two reasons. First, the German economy before the war showed great strength, and its products competed strongly with U.S. goods in international markets. Second and more important, U.S. military leaders worried about threats to U.S. security if Germany won both the war and control of the Atlantic Ocean. German control of the Atlantic might hurt U.S. trade and would surely increase German ability to intervene in Latin America.

**British and French Propaganda** When the war began, German armies invaded the neutral country of Belgium in order to strike next

French propaganda depicting the Germans as murderers of Belgian civilians

at France. Americans viewed this invasion as cruel and unfair—the action of a bully. Skillful propagandists in Great Britain and France made the most of Germany's reputation as a military aggressor. They invented stories of German cruelty that were widely printed in U.S. newspapers. Pictures of the German kaiser, Wilhelm, made him appear especially villainous.

**Desperate Conditions in Europe**  As the war dragged on and on, people in all the belligerent (warring) nations suffered greatly. The death tolls on both the Eastern Front (Russia) and the Western Front (France) were staggering. By the end of 1916, millions had died from artillery fire, poison gas, tank attacks, and machine-gun bullets—and all in vain. There were no significant gains by either side. Civilians suffered almost as much as the soldiers, especially in Germany, where shipments of food supplies were cut off by the British blockade. The German people were hungry, nearly starved. Conditions in Russia were even worse. Here the only hope for relief from desperate poverty and suffering lay in revolution. The first revolution in Russia occurred in March, 1917.

Less than a month later, the United States declared war on Germany and Austria-Hungary. What persuaded President Wilson to change his policy from neutrality to war?

## C. SHORT-RANGE CAUSES OF U.S. INVOLVEMENT

Three events, including Russia's March revolution, brought about the change.

**Unrestricted Submarine Warfare**   In January, 1917, Germany decided that the time had come for desperate measures. It announced that its submarines would once again sink without warning all ships entering British waters. The military and political leaders who made this decision recognized that they were risking the entry of the United States into the war on the British side. But they hoped submarine damage to British shipping would end the war before U.S. troops could be trained for combat.

**The Zimmermann Telegram**   Early in 1917 the British had managed to intercept and decode a telegram sent by the German foreign secretary Arthur Zimmermann to a German diplomat in Mexico. The telegram instructed the German diplomat to tell Mexico that Germany might help it win back territories in Texas, Arizona, and New Mexico (territories lost in the 1840s). It would do so if Germany and Mexico both decided to declare war against the United States. The British sent the **Zimmermann telegram** to the U.S. government. Its publication in American newspapers caused a sensation.

**March Revolution in Russia**   In March, 1917, came news of the overthrow of the Russian czar, Nicholas II. Americans were excited by the news because they expected the new government in Russia to be democratic. President Wilson was especially pleased. As a leading champion of democracy, Wilson was willing to fight for democracies in Europe like France and Great Britain. Now that their ally, Russia, was more democratic, Wilson could lead the United States to war on the side of democracies.

## D. DECISION FOR WAR

On April 2, 1917, the president went to Congress to deliver one of the most eloquent and memorable speeches in U.S. history. He called Germany's submarine policy "warfare against mankind." He said: "It is a fearful thing to lead this great peaceful people into war, into the most terrible and disastrous of all wars." However, "the world must be made safe for democracy." Members of Congress stood up and cheered. Four days later, they voted almost unanimously for a U.S. declaration of war against Germany. (One of the few who voted against war was Jeannette Rankin, the first woman to serve in the House of Representatives.)

# E. AN ASSESSMENT: COULD U.S. INVOLVEMENT IN WORLD WAR I HAVE BEEN AVOIDED?

In the above history (sections A to D), we see the events and conditions leading to a decision for war. Many critics of U.S. policy in the "neutral years" argue that the United States was never truly neutral. If U.S. policy had been different, in their view, then involvement in the war could have been avoided. These are three of the critics' arguments.

**1. U.S. Economic Policy Was Never Neutral** An economic cause for involvement was the degree to which U.S. trade favored the Allies— Great Britain and France. British and French purchases of U.S. war supplies had been made on credit. (A much smaller amount of credit had been allowed the Germans for their purchases.) By 1916 Great Britain and France owed huge amounts of money, which would be paid back after the war—*if* they won. In a sense U.S. businesses and banks could not afford to see their best customers lose.

**2. German Submarine Policy May Have Been Justified** A nation at war must do all that it can to win. Germany's only advantage at sea was its superior force of submarines. In every other respect its navy was inferior to Great Britain's navy. The United States never asked the British to restrict the use of their battleships. If it had been truly neutral, it would have accepted Germans' use of their submarines.

**3. Americans Were Fairly Warned** Germany had issued warnings about the dangers of traveling into a "war zone." If the United States had wanted to avoid being drawn into war, it could have prohibited the travel of U.S. citizens aboard British ships.

## *In Review*

The following questions refer to section I: Causes of "the Great War" in Europe and section II: The U.S. Dilemma: Neutrality or Involvement?

**1.** Tell why each was a cause of the outbreak of war in 1914: (a) nationalism, (b) alliances, and (c) the assassination of Archduke Francis Ferdinand at Sarajevo in June, 1914.

**2.** Describe the U.S. response to Germany's submarine policy from 1915 to 1917.

**3.** Identify the two causes of U.S. involvement in World War I that *you* think were most important. Explain each choice.

**4.** Evaluate the arguments of those who thought the United States could have avoided going to war. Do you agree or disagree with them? Why?

# III. The United States at War, 1917 to 1918

Never before had the United States fought in a European war on European soil. To help win the war, Wilson and his advisers recognized that all the resources of the nation—farms, factories, businesses, labor unions, men, women, even children—had to participate in a determined national effort. Daily sacrifices would have to be made by everybody.

## A. MOBILIZING FOR WAR

For an entire year the main U.S. contribution to the Allied forces in France was to keep them supplied with food, guns, ships, airplanes, and other goods. This economic contribution was vital.

**Organizing the Factories** Called to the nation's capital to coordinate the war effort were a number of American business leaders. Chief among them was Bernard Baruch, who was asked by Wilson to head a new war agency—the War Industries Board. Baruch sent telegrams and mailed instructions to thousands of corporation presidents, explaining how they could change both their products and their methods for wartime needs. Partly because of Baruch's genius and energy, U.S. factories turned out vast quantities of war materials. Especially impressive was the spectacular growth of the U.S. chemical industry, which produced gun powder and explosives for the war.

**Organizing the Food Supply** Another brilliant and dedicated manager, Herbert Hoover, accepted Wilson's call to head up the Food Administration. Hoover went to work sending out pamphlets by the millions on how every American could contribute to U.S. victory by eating less food. He explained that the British were nearly out of food and they needed every ounce of bread and beef that could be saved in American homes. Americans soon grew accustomed to one "meatless" day and one "wheatless" day every week. The conservation effort made a huge difference in the amount of food shipped overseas in 1917 and 1918. When Hoover insisted that food would win the war, he exaggerated only slightly.

**New Jobs for Women and Minorities** War changed the nature of the American work force. As young men entered the armed forces, young women took their places in shipyards and factories. African Americans also filled factory jobs vacated by departing troops. The migration of African Americans to Northern cities, which had begun before the war, was significantly increased by the new job opportunities of wartime.

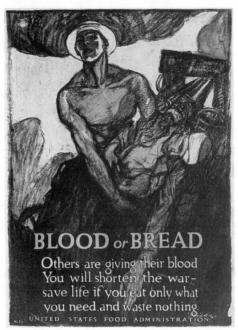

**BLOOD** *or* **BREAD**

Others are giving their blood
You will shorten the war—
save life if you eat only what
you need and waste nothing
UNITED STATES FOOD ADMINISTRATION

Poster for the Food Administration

On the farms of the Southwest, workers were needed to plant and harvest the crops. Between 1917 and 1920, about 100,000 Mexicans came to settle permanently in Texas, New Mexico, Arizona, and California.

## B. DISSENTERS IN WARTIME

Although most Americans supported the war, a few made speeches against it and refused to cooperate with the government's policies. The opponents of war were **dissenters**—people who actively opposed the majority view. In times of peace, the First Amendment of the Constitution protected a dissenter's rights to speak out boldly on any issue. But in wartime when the national security was at stake, might the Constitution be interpreted differently? During World War I this question arose in response to two laws: the Espionage Act and the Sedition Act.

**Espionage and Sedition Acts**   Congress passed the Espionage Act in 1917 and then the much harsher Sedition Act in 1918. These laws imposed heavy fines and prison sentences for the following antiwar actions: (1) spying and aiding the wartime enemy, (2) interfering with the recruitment of soldiers, (3) speaking against the government's campaign to sell bonds to finance the war, (4) urging resistance to U.S. laws, and (5) using "disloyal, profane, scurrilous, or abusive language" about the American form of government, flag, or military uniform. In addition the U.S. Post Office was given the right to remove from the mails any antiwar materials.

**Opponents of the War**    Dissenters opposed the war for different reasons. Some believed that the military draft threatened democracy because it might cause Americans to glorify military life. Others, including many socialists and anarchists, thought the war was little more than a capitalist scheme for making money. Still others, known as pacifists, opposed fighting in any war because they regarded war as a form of legalized murder.

Whatever the reason, each opponent of the war had to decide whether to heed the wartime laws of the country or to defy them by speaking out. About 1,500 who spoke out against the war were arrested under the Espionage and Sedition Acts. Eugene Debs, who had been the Socialist party's candidate for president, was sentenced to ten years in prison for making an antiwar speech. Emma Goldman, an anarchist, received a two-year prison term for her antiwar activities. After serving her sentence, she was deported to the Soviet Union.

**Case of *Schenck* v. *United States***    Another dissenter who went to jail was the general secretary of the Socialist party, Charles Schenck. Schenck had mailed about 15,000 leaflets urging men who had been drafted into military service to oppose the law. After being tried and convicted under the Espionage Act, Schenck appealed to the U.S. Supreme Court. He argued that his First Amendment rights to freedom of speech and the press had been violated.

In the case of ***Schenck* v. *United States*** (1919), the Supreme Court ruled against Schenck and upheld the constitutionality of the Espionage Act. Justice Oliver Wendell Holmes, writing the decision of a unanimous court, noted that the right to free speech was not absolute. In ordinary times, wrote Holmes, the mailing of Schenck's leaflets would have been protected under the First Amendment. However, Holmes went on, every act of speech must be judged according to the circumstances in which it was committed. For example, "the most stringent protection of free speech would not protect a man in falsely shouting fire in a theatre and causing a panic." Furthermore, speech that may be harmless in a time of peace may injure the public safety in a time of war.

The question to be asked, according to Holmes, was whether or not an act of speech posed a **"clear and present danger"** to the public. If it did, then Congress had the power to restrain such speech. The "clear and present danger" test, first stated in the *Schenck* case, was often applied in later Supreme Court cases involving the issue of free speech.

## C. FIGHTING THE WAR

An army can be recruited by (a) calling for volunteers and (b) compelling service by a procedure known as the **draft.** Woodrow Wilson believed that the latter method was both more efficient and more democratic (since members of every social class and ethnic group would be required to serve).

**The Draft**   At Wilson's request Congress passed the Selective Service Act in May, 1917. All male citizens of a certain age—21 to 30—were required to register for military service. Their names were then picked at random from fishbowls and other receptacles. Those called to service, if they passed a medical examination, were in the army—and in the war. By war's end a total of 2.8 million young men were drafted out of the 24 million who registered.

**The Weapons of World War I**   U.S. troops were trained in the use of new weapons that were the inventions of an industrial age. On land the two most deadly weapons were (1) the machine gun used to defend a trench against enemy attackers and (2) poison gas that was carried by wind currents into an enemy's trenches. Mustard gas attacked the skin causing huge blisters, horrible pain, and death. Armored tanks were also used for the first time in World War I. At sea Germany nearly crippled the British merchant fleet with another new weapon, the submarine. In the air, for the first time in the history of warfare, airplanes spied on enemy positions and fought each other in aerial "dogfights." (Bombing, however, was not a major factor until the next world war in the 1940s.)

**Pershing's Troops "Over There"**   In a popular song of World War I, George M. Cohan's "Over There," soldiers in U.S. training camps sang enthusiastically of "going over . . . we're going over . . . and we won't come back 'til it's over over there." In 1917 only a few thousand were ready to be sent to the trenches in France (the place "over there" where troops were meant to go). But in the summer of 1918 they arrived in France by the hundreds of thousands. Unlike the war-weary troops of Europe, the Americans jumped into the trenches fresh and ready for action. Commanding them was the American general, John J. Pershing.

**The Communist Revolution in Russia**   Meanwhile in November, 1917, a second revolution in Russia had overthrown the democratic government that had come to power in March. This time, the revolutionaries were Bolsheviks—or communists. They gave their country a new name, the Soviet Union, and promptly ended Russian suffering in the war by making peace with Germany. With Russia (the Soviet Union) out of the war, Germany and Austria-Hungary could

# OBSERVERS OF AMERICAN LIFE: A SOLDIER'S LETTER FROM THE WESTERN FRONT

U.S. soldiers in France wrote home about the sights and sounds of life (and death) in the trenches. This letter tells of one young soldier's experience preparing for his first battle. Why do you think almost every attack in World War I was preceded by an artillery barrage?

This was war; I was finally in it. I can not say that I was not excited; but I don't think I was afraid; only sort of apprehensive. Thank God! It was night, and I overlooked a great many horrors ...

"Please step high and over here. Thanks."

"What's matter? Wounded?"

"No. My pal is dying."

A little farther on a fellow lying on his back and looking straight up—and many such. Something seemed to grip me; I wanted to run, but those fellows ahead of me were cool enough; they were not afraid. Then we reached the "jumping-over" trench. Our battalion was scheduled to start at 6:30 A.M.

We were to have a barrage. Now I knew all about a barrage, but had never seen one in action. Everything was quiet after 3 A.M.; not a shell was fired. Fritz [the German enemy] was sending up lots of star shells, but that's his way. Six-fifteen, 6:25, 6:30. My God! All hell turned loose; my heart lost several beats and then caught up and overdid itself. Someone shouted, "Let's at them!"

Oh, it was a dandy barrage, and we walked over behind it without much opposition and took our objective. I threw my grenades at a couple of Huns in a bay and when they exploded (both Huns and grenades) I slid into a trench.

concentrate all their remaining strength on the Western Front. Could U.S. troops arrive in time to stop the German attack?

**The Last Big Push**  An all-out German offensive in March, 1918, almost succeeded in reaching its target, Paris. But the drive was finally halted and beaten back. Most U.S. troops arrived in time for a massive counterattack that eventually won the war. The first great thrust from September 12 to 16 was along a section of the front-line trenches called the St. Mihiel Salient. This was followed by another assault (beginning September 26), which drove the exhausted and demoralized Germans through a forest in northwestern France called the Argonne. By early November the retreating Germans had been pushed back almost to the border of their own country.

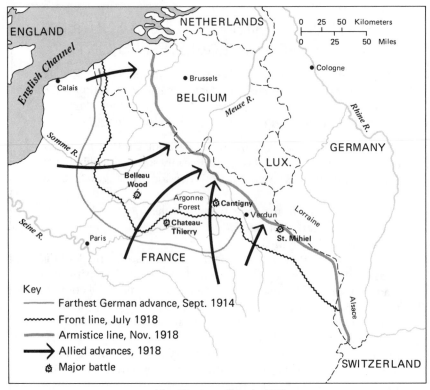

The Western Front, 1918

**Armistice!** Then the war ended. Curiously, the end came on the eleventh hour of the eleventh day of the eleventh month—November, 11, 1918. Germany signed an **armistice** (an agreement to stop fighting) and conceded defeat. The world war was over. In the United States crowds went wild with excitement and joy.

## In Review

The following questions refer to section III: The United States at War, 1917 to 1918.

1. Identify *dissenters*, Schenck *v.* United States, "*clear and present danger*," *the draft*, and *armistice*.

2. Describe the effects of U.S. participation in World War I on each of the following: (a) women and minorities (b) industry, and (c) the interpretation of the U.S. Constitution.

3. Describe the contributions of both the U.S. military and the U.S. economy in bringing World War I to a victorious conclusion.

# IV. The Peace Treaty: Ideals and Realities

Woodrow Wilson was an idealist. He wanted the war to result, not just in victory, but in a lasting peace settlement that was fair to all nations.

## A. THE FOURTEEN POINTS

In January, 1918, Wilson listed his goals for a peace settlement. This statement of goals became known as the **Fourteen Points.** The key points were:

- An end to the practice of making secret treaties
- Recognition of every nation's right to freedom of the seas in peace and war (especially, a neutral nation's rights to use the seas for trade and travel)
- Reduction of weapons
- Changing the borders of European countries according to the principle of **self-determination** (the many peoples of Austria-Hungary, for example, being allowed to decide to form nations of their own)
- Establishment of a new international organization, the **League of Nations**, to keep the peace by fairly resolving disputes between nations
- Placing European colonies in Africa, Asia, and Latin America under the control of the League of Nations.

Wilson explained the purpose underlying all points of his peace plan: "An evident principle runs through the whole program I have outlined. It is the principle of justice to all peoples and nationalities, and their right to live on equal terms of liberty and safety with one another...."

## B. WILSON IN PARIS

The Fourteen Points were so important to Wilson that he did something no earlier president had ever done. He traveled to a foreign country—France—to meet with other leaders and negotiate the terms of a treaty of peace. The losers of the war, Germany and Austria-Hungary, did not participate in the victors' discussions, which took place in the palace at Versailles, near Paris. At first Wilson had great influence because the people of Europe greeted him as a hero and even as a saint. But as the conference continued through the early months of 1919, the hard realities of European politics overwhelmed Wilson's idealistic plan for peace.

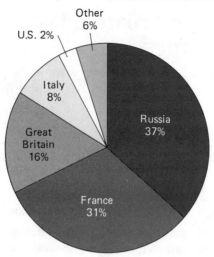

NOTE: Casualties (dead and wounded) for all allied powers were about
18 *million*! U.S. dead—112,432; U.S. wounded—230,074.

Allied casualties in World War I

**The Allies Seek Revenge**  Unlike Wilson, the leaders of France,
Great Britain, and Italy wanted a peace treaty that would punish
their wartime enemies. (Italy had entered the war on the side of the
Allies in 1915.) The victorious European powers had suffered huge
losses of life and property. They wanted to make sure that Germany
would never rise again as a major military power. They also wanted
a treaty that would force Germany to pay for war damages.

**The Treaty of Versailles**  The treaty that finally emerged from the
conference, the **Treaty of Versailles,** contained these provisions:

- Alsace-Lorraine (German territory since 1871) would again be
  part of France.

- Poland, whose independence had been lost for more than a
  hundred years, would again be an independent nation. It would
  receive from Germany a piece of territory, the so-called Polish
  Corridor, which would connect Poland to the Baltic Sea.

- Germany would lose all of its colonies, including three large
  colonies in Africa (Cameroon, German West Africa, and German
  East Africa).

- Germany's Saar Basin, a major coal-producing region in western
  Germany, would be controlled by France for 15 years.

- Germany would be required to pay a huge amount of money in
  **reparations** (payments for war damages).

- Germany would be made to disband its armed forces and agree never to have a future army of more than 100,000 men.

- Germany would be forbidden to manufacture and import war materials.

- Germany would accept full responsibility for causing the world war. (This provision was known as the **"war guilt" clause.**)

- A peacekeeping organization, the League of Nations, would be created to reduce the chance of future wars.

New nations of Eastern Europe, 1919

A separate treaty with Austria declared the old Austro-Hungarian Empire to be dissolved. It reduced Austrian territory to less than a third of its former size and recognized the existence of four new republics: Yugoslavia, Czechoslovakia, Austria, and Hungary.

**An Analysis of the Treaty**  The Treaty of Versailles was very harsh on Germany (although less harsh than France and Great Britain had originally wanted). Wilson succeeded in softening the treaty slightly and seeing a few of his Fourteen Points carried out in modified form. He recognized that the treaty was more vengeful than fair and might cause Germany to rebel against its terms. Even so, he was happy about one diplomatic victory. He had succeeded in persuading others at the conference to include the League of Nations as part of the treaty. All signers of the treaty would be committed to joining the League. Wilson hoped the League would eventually correct the treaty's faults.

## C. THE SENATE'S REJECTION OF THE LEAGUE OF NATIONS

Unfortunately for President Wilson, politics in the United States proved every bit as difficult as politics in Europe. Members of his own Democratic party generally supported the treaty that Wilson brought home with him from Paris. But Republicans in Congress were much less enthusiastic. Some were firmly opposed. To win approval of the Versailles treaty, Wilson had to win the votes of both Republican and Democratic senators.

**Isolationists and Reservationists** The Constitution provides that two thirds of the Senate must ratify all treaties. Wilson could count on a majority of senators supporting the treaty, but a two-thirds vote was uncertain. Republicans opposing the treaty included two groups: (a) **isolationists** who rejected the treaty outright because it would involve too many commitments abroad; (b) reservationists who would accept the treaty only if certain clauses were added to it—clauses called **reservations.** The leading reservationist in the Senate was Henry Cabot Lodge of Massachusetts, a bitter enemy of the president.

The chief issue in the struggle over the Versailles treaty was a clause providing that each member of the League of Nations would "respect and preserve as against external aggression the territorial integrity and existing political independence of all members of the League." In the opinion of the treaty's opponents, this clause meant that the United States might be drawn into a war that its own Congress did not approve.

**The President's Breakdown** Wilson took his case to the public. Traveling by train from town to town, he gave dozens of speeches in defense of the League and the treaty. But after a speech in Colorado, the president fell seriously ill. After arriving back at the White House he had a stroke that paralyzed one side of his body. For several months his poor health weakened his ability to provide leadership.

**Votes in the Senate**    In 1920 the Senate voted on whether to ratify the Treaty of Versailles. A majority voted in favor of the treaty with Senator Lodge's reservations. A two-thirds vote would have been possible if Wilson had supported these reservations. Instead, he instructed Democratic senators to vote no. A vote for the treaty without reservations also failed to win two-thirds approval.

**End of the Debate**    Had Wilson been willing to compromise, the treaty (with reservations) probably would have passed. Instead, the United States, which had proposed the League of Nations, was the only major power to vote against it. A separate U.S. peace treaty with Germany was signed by a Republican president, Warren Harding, in 1921. Since it contained nothing about the League of Nations, it passed the Senate easily.

# V. Postwar Isolationism

Warren Harding's election to the presidency in 1920 marked the beginning of a new decade—and the beginning of a new era in U.S. foreign policy. Wilson's internationalist policies were abandoned. In the 1920s and well into the 1930s, the prevailing mood in the United States was one of isolationism. In other words, most Americans thought the United States would be better off avoiding any further involvement in European troubles. Many regretted the decision to go to war because it surely had not made the world "safe for democracy," as Wilson had promised. In fact, it seemed possible—even likely— that a second world war might follow the first. But if such a war occurred, isolationists were determined to keep the United States out of it.

## A. EXAMPLES OF THE ISOLATIONIST TREND IN THE 1920s

U.S. foreign policy in the 1920s expressed the isolationist mood of the country.

**Avoiding International Commitments**    After the Senate rejected the Treaty of Versailles in 1920, the question was often asked: Should the United States join the League of Nations? This organization for settling disputes met in Geneva, Switzerland through the 1920s and 1930s. The United States never did join, although it sent observers to League meetings. The U.S. observers could discuss issues but could not vote.

Even without joining the League itself, the United States might have joined one of its special branches: the Permanent Court of International Justice, or World Court. The purpose of this court was to permit nations to settle their disputes peacefully by arguing their cases before a board of judges. Once again, isolationists in the U.S. Senate defeated every proposal for joining the World Court.

From these examples we see that the United States in the 1920s generally avoided making international commitments.

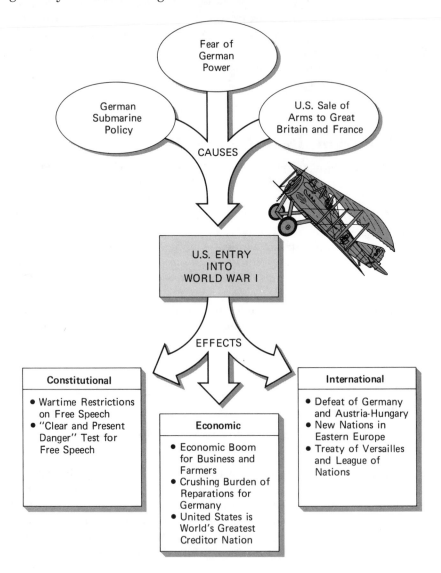

Causes and effects: U.S. entry in World War I

**Collecting War Debts**  On the other hand, U.S. policymakers believed that other nations should be committed to paying their debts to the United States. Because of its loans to Great Britain and France during the war, the United States in the 1920s was the world's greatest creditor nation (nation to whom debts were owed). During Harding's presidency Europeans owed more than $10 billion to the United States for their wartime purchases. The French government argued that such debts should be canceled since the French had lost many more lives in the war than the Americans and had fought much longer. But U.S. presidents of the 1920s insisted that the Allies pay back at least a sizable portion of the war debts.

**The Reparations Issue**  How much money should Germany be forced to pay the Allies in reparations? The Allies' answer: a crushing amount ($33 billion). The sum might have been more reasonable had the United States agreed to participate in the Allies' meetings on the issue. But in these isolationist times the United States once again preferred to stay out.

# B. EXAMPLES OF INVOLVEMENT IN THE 1920s

Isolationism, though strong, did not completely dominate U.S. policy in the postwar years. Following are three examples of the United States taking an interest in world affairs.

**Intervention in the Soviet Union**  In 1918 U.S. troops landed in the Soviet Union to aid Russian forces known as the "Whites" in their attempt to overthrow the new Communist government, the "Reds." The effort failed, and U.S. troops were withdrawn.

In 1921 policymakers adopted a more humanitarian approach. Recognizing that the Russian people were starving after years of war, the United States sent them millions of tons of food. Organizing the relief effort was the great wartime food manager, Herbert Hoover.

**Washington Conference**  President Harding and his secretary of state, Charles Evans Hughes, invited to Washington, D.C., representatives from all the major powers of the world. The subject of their talks was battleships and other ships of war. The question was how to limit the costly and potentially dangerous competition among the world's great naval powers. The five nations with the largest navies agreed to limit ship construction according to a certain ratio: United States (5), Great Britain (5), Japan (3), France (1.67), and Italy (1.67).

The **Washington Conference** helped the United States and Great Britain to keep down their governments' expenses on shipbuilding. But Japan was disappointed with its middle position. It wanted full **parity** (equality) with its Western rivals. In the 1930s the military leaders of Japan ignored the limits imposed by the Washington

Conference and built a navy strong enough to challenge both U.S. and British naval forces.

**Kellogg-Briand Pact**   Another example of U.S. involvement in the postwar world was its signing of a treaty with France in 1928. The **Kellogg-Briand Pact** invited all nations of the world to declare a common policy of never fighting an aggressive war. Eventually, 63 nations signed the pact, which was said to "renounce war as an instrument of national policy." Unfortunately for the cause of world peace, however, the pact was only a written statement. There was no real commitment to stopping an aggressor (war maker). If some nation chose to wage war, nothing in the treaty required the United States to act. In the isolationist 1920s, that was the way most Americans wanted it.

## In Review

The following questions refer to section IV: The Peace Treaty: Ideals and Realities and section V: Postwar Isolationism.

**1.** Identify *the Fourteen Points, self-determination, the League of Nations, the Treaty of Versailles, the Washington Conference,* and *the Kellogg-Briand Pact.*

**2.** Give two reasons for the rejection of the Treaty of Versailles by the U.S. Senate.

**3.** Define isolationism and give examples of this policy in the 1920s.

## GLOSSARY OF KEY TERMS: CHAPTER 10

**alliances**   groups of two or more nations that agree to come to each other's aid in the event of war.

**armistice**   an agreement by both sides in a war to stop fighting.

**"clear and present danger"**   the principle suggested by Justice Oliver Wendell Holmes (in *Schenck* v. *United States,* 1919) for determining whether or not an act of speech can be lawfully restrained or punished by government authorities.

**dissenters**   people who take a strong position on an issue in opposition to the majority position.

**draft**   a system for compelling a selected number of eligible persons to serve in the armed forces.

**Fourteen Points**   a statement by President Woodrow Wilson identifying the principles that he hoped would guide the peace negotiations after World War I.

**isolationists** those Americans who rejected the idea of the United States becoming involved in international organizations such as the League of Nations.

**Kellogg-Briand Pact** a treaty of 1928 in which 63 nations, including the United States, agreed never to go to war for aggressive purposes.

**League of Nations** an international organization of the 1920s and 1930s whose purpose was to resolve disputes between nations and, in extreme cases, to propose action to halt aggression.

*Lusitania* a British passenger ship sunk by a German submarine in 1915; the incident was a major cause of a shift in U.S. foreign policy away from neutrality toward involvement.

**militarism** a nation's policy of increasing the size of its armed forces in order to gain military and naval superiority over potential enemies.

**parity** the condition of being equal in rank or power.

**reparations** postwar payments made by a defeated nation to a victorious nation to compensate for war damages.

**reservations** statements placing limits on an agreement and identifying situations where the agreement does not apply.

*Schenck v. United States* a Supreme Court case of 1919 in which an antiwar protest was considered to represent a "clear and present danger" to the public welfare.

**self-determination** the right of the people of a common culture or nationality to form an independent nation.

*Sussex* **pledge** Germany's declaration in 1916, after the sinking of a passenger ship (the *Sussex*), that its submarines would not attack passenger ships or merchant ships without giving fair warning.

**Treaty of Versailles** the treaty of peace of 1919 arranged by leaders of the victor nations of World War I.

**ultimatum** one nation's written declaration threatening war unless another nation complies with all the demands in the document.

**"war-guilt" clause** a provision in the Treaty of Versailles placing the blame for World War I on Germany.

**Washington Conference** a conference of major powers in Washington, D.C. (1921 to 1922), resulting in an agreement to set limits on the size of each nation's navy.

**Zimmermann telegram** a message from Germany to Mexico (1917) proposing an alliance between them and suggesting Germany's willingness to help Mexico acquire U.S. territory in the Southwest.

# TEST YOURSELF

## A. Multiple Choice: Facts, Main Ideas, Skills

*On a separate sheet of paper, write the number of the word or expression that, of those given, best completes the statement or answers the question.*

### Reviewing the facts

1. Just before World War I, the major powers of Europe placed their hopes for national defense on (1) a system of alliances (2) an international court (3) the principle of self-determination (4) open agreements openly arrived at

2. At the outbreak of World War I in 1914, most Americans believed that their country should (1) aid the Allies (2) stay out of the war (3) immediately declare war against Germany (4) follow a policy of "watchful waiting"

3. The Zimmermann telegram and the *Sussex* pledge were diplomatic messages from (1) Great Britain (2) France (3) Germany (4) Austria-Hungary

4. Which was the main purpose of the formation of the League of Nations after World War I? (1) to promote international trade (2) to punish Germany for its role in the war (3) to bring about world peace (4) to oppose the spread of communism

5. Which statement best explains the relationship between Wilson's Fourteen Points and the Treaty of Versailles? (1) Wilson achieved total success in having the Fourteen Points serve as the basis for the treaty. (2) None of the Fourteen Points was incorporated into the treaty. (3) The treaty's only guarantee from the Fourteen Points concerned "freedom of the seas." (4) Wilson sacrificed many of his Fourteen Points in order to win the Allies' consent to a League of Nations.

6. Those opposed to U.S. membership in the League of Nations argued that (1) the League's headquarters would be located outside the United States (2) membership would be too expensive (3) the United States should avoid further involvement in the politics of Europe (4) the United States should attempt to change the League of Nations into a military organization

7. In terms of international trade and finance, the United States emerged from World War I (1) as a leading creditor nation (2) burdened with a huge trade deficit (3) owing a large war debt to Great Britain (4) determined to reduce its trade with Europe

8. The Washington Conference and the Kellogg-Briand Pact could best be used to support the conclusion that the United States (1) followed a strict isolationist policy in the 1920s (2) had some involvement in European affairs in the 1920s (3) was preparing for war in the 1920s (4) was establishing a new system of alliances in the 1920s

## Reviewing the main ideas

**9.** Before U.S. entry into World War I, U.S. foreign policy changed from isolationism to involvement mainly because  (1) the United States was obligated to honor commitments to the Allies  (2) U.S. interests were threatened by Germany's military power and use of submarines  (3) President Wilson believed in a policy of expansionism  (4) U.S. manufacturers lobbied for increased sale of weapons to all the warring powers

**10.** Which best explains the U.S. decision to enter World War I in 1917?  (1) the U.S. need for British products  (2) Wilson's ambition to be a war leader  (3) the widespread public belief that isolationism was wrong  (4) Germany's use of submarines

**11.** "Why, by interweaving our destiny with that of any part of Europe, entangle our peace and prosperity in the toils of European ambition, rivalship, interest, humor or caprice?" Which U.S. action best reflects the point of view expressed in this quotation?  (1) passage of legislation restricting immigration  (2) rejection of the Treaty of Versailles  (3) enactment of lower tariffs  (4) signing of the Kellogg-Briand Pact

**12.** After World War I most Americans wanted the United States to follow a foreign policy of  (1) remaining involved in overseas affairs  (2) supporting the League of Nations  (3) isolationism in world affairs  (4) using U.S. forces to maintain peace in Europe

## Developing critical thinking skills

*Base your answers to questions 13 and 14 on the cartoon below and on your knowledge of U.S. history and government.*

Interrupting the ceremony

13. The main purpose of the cartoon is to express opposition to which presidential action? (1) Woodrow Wilson's support of the Treaty of Versailles (2) Warren Harding's calling of the Washington Conference (3) Woodrow Wilson's response to the sinking of the *Lusitania* (4) Theodore Roosevelt's actions in Panama

14. According to the cartoon the United States should follow a policy of (1) collective security (2) noninvolvement (3) interventionism (4) imperialism

## B. Enduring Issues

*Select two of the enduring issues from column A. For each issue chosen, explain how the historical example in column B relates to the issue.*

| A. Enduring Issues | B. Historical Examples |
| --- | --- |
| 1. National power—limits and potential | U.S. military and economic contribution during World War I |
| 2. Presidential power in wartime and foreign affairs | Woodrow Wilson's role in the peace conference of 1919 |
| 3. Separation of powers and the capacity to govern | The U.S. Senate's rejection of the Treaty of Versailles |
| 4. Property rights and economic policy | U.S. insistence in the 1920s that Great Britain and France pay their war debts |

## C. Essays

*Level 1*

Major goals of U.S. foreign policy include the following:

- To foster foreign trade and U.S. economic interests
- To provide for the military security of the United States
- To promote the spread of democratic ideals in the world

Select *one* of the goals listed above. Then:

1. Describe an action of the U.S. government to support the goal (a) between 1900 and 1920 and (b) between 1921 and 1930.

2. Evaluate whether the action taken in *either* 1(a) *or* 1(b) achieved the goal.

*Level 2*

The foreign policies of U.S. presidents have both causes and consequences.

**A.** Listed below are foreign policy actions of two presidents during and after World War I.

| *President* | *Action* |
|---|---|
| Woodrow Wilson | Protested the sinking of the *Lusitania* and the *Sussex* |
| Woodrow Wilson | Proposed the Fourteen Points |
| Warren Harding | Called for the Washington Conference |

Choose *one* of the actions given above. State *one* reason for the action and *one* result of the action.

**B.** Base your answer to part B on your answer to part A. Write an essay discussing the foreign policy action you chose, including the reason for it and the result.

# Chapter 11

# From Prosperity to Depression: The Twenties and Thirties

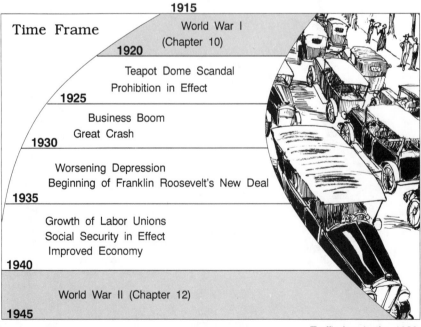

| Time Frame | |
|---|---|
| **1915** | |
| **1920** | World War I (Chapter 10) |
| **1925** | Teapot Dome Scandal<br>Prohibition in Effect |
| **1930** | Business Boom<br>Great Crash |
| **1935** | Worsening Depression<br>Beginning of Franklin Roosevelt's New Deal |
| **1940** | Growth of Labor Unions<br>Social Security in Effect<br>Improved Economy |
| **1945** | World War II (Chapter 12) |

*Traffic jam in the 1920s*

## *Objectives*

- To describe social changes in the postwar decade of the 1920s.
- To examine the causes and effects of the Great Depression on people and institutions.
- To compare the conservative politics of a decade of prosperity (the 1920s) to the reform politics of a decade of depression (the 1930s).
- To understand the interdependence of the world's financial and economic systems.
- To evaluate the impact of Franklin Roosevelt's policies on the U.S. economy, society, and politics.
- To examine both positive and negative changes in the life of women, African Americans, Native Americans, and other minorities.

From 1900 to 1917, the United States had moved under the banner of Progressive reform. In the 1920s, however, most Americans ceased to care about reform laws, and the U.S. government again adopted the old, nineteenth-century policy of laissez-faire. The government's return to "normalcy" (as President Harding called it) failed to recognize the realities of modern life. Society and the economy changed rapidly in the 1920s, even if government did not.

Economic boom in the 1920s was followed by economic bust in the 1930s. The disaster known as the Great Depression awakened political leaders to the need for more reform laws. Under the leadership of President Franklin D. Roosevelt, the U.S. government became more actively involved in the economy than ever before.

This chapter describes the strong contrast between two decades—the decade of prosperity (1920s) and the decade of depression (1930s).

# I. Conservative Politics of the Twenties

Politics often runs in cycles—a period of conservatism following a period of reform. For example, policies of the U.S. government changed dramatically from progressivism before World War I to conservatism after the war. Unlike the reform-minded presidents of the Progressive Era (Roosevelt, Taft, and Wilson), the three presidents of the 1920s (Harding, Coolidge, and Hoover) were conservative Republicans.

## A. PRESIDENCY OF WARREN G. HARDING

In the election of 1920 the Republican candidate, Warren G. Harding, defeated his Democratic opponent, James Cox, by a huge margin.

**Return to "Normalcy"**  In his campaign Harding promised that he would lead the American nation back to **"normalcy."** In other words he suggested a return to the quieter time before the world war and before the progressive politics of Woodrow Wilson. Once in office Harding showed his conservatism by doing very little to regulate business. He followed a laissez-faire policy like that of conservative presidents of the 1880s and 1890s.

**Teapot Dome Scandal**  Harding's presidency was marked by one of the worst scandals in U.S. history—known as the **Teapot Dome scandal.** Teapot Dome was the name of federally owned lands in Wyoming that contained huge reserves of oil. Secretary of the Interior Albert Fall leased the oil-rich public lands to several oil companies. In return for his cooperation, Fall received from the companies secret and illegal payments (bribes) totaling about $325,000.

Harding knew nothing about the corrupt dealings of Fall and other high-ranking officials, but he bore the responsibility for having appointed untrustworthy politicians to office. Before the scandals were fully investigated by Congress, Harding died suddenly in 1923.

## B. PRESIDENCY OF CALVIN COOLIDGE

The vice president, Calvin Coolidge, became president when Harding died and was then elected to office in his own right in 1924.

**"Silent Cal"**  Coolidge was a man of few words. His speeches were short; often, in social situations, he said nothing at all. Reporters referred to him as "Silent Cal."

**Conservative Policies**  Coolidge once said: "The business of America is business." The statement expressed Coolidge's policy of supporting big business rather than regulating it. He favored high tariffs to protect American businesses and less government spending to permit lower taxes. He relied upon the economic advice of Secretary of the Treasury Andrew Mellon—a banker and business leader.

## C. PRESIDENCY OF HERBERT HOOVER

When Coolidge decided not to run for reelection, the Republicans nominated Herbert Hoover as their candidate in 1928.

**Election of 1928**  Hoover's Democratic opponent was the first Roman Catholic candidate to be nominated for president by a major party. He was New York's popular governor, Alfred E. Smith. In a strongly Republican decade a Democrat like Smith had little chance of winning. Hurting Smith's chances even more was the prejudice of many voters against both Roman Catholics and New Yorkers. Hoover won the election by a landslide (a very large majority of the vote).

**Half a Year of Prosperity**   Time and again, throughout his career, Hoover had demonstrated unusual abilities as a leader. He had succeeded brilliantly as an engineer, a business leader, an administrator of war relief following World War I, and a cabinet member under Harding and Coolidge. Much was expected of the new president when he took the oath of office in March, 1929. Through his first six months in office, business prosperity continued, and President Hoover capably managed the government's executive branch. But in late October, 1929, the price of stocks on the New York Stock Exchange took a sudden and shocking plunge. The good times for President Hoover and millions of other Americans came to an end in the Great Depression that followed. What Hoover did—and failed to do—in this economic crisis will be described later in the chapter.

## D. LIMITED ROLE OF GOVERNMENT

All three presidents of the 1920s expressed faith in the workings of the American system of free enterprise. They believed that the growth of big business supported by a government policy of low taxes and high tariffs would create a more prosperous nation for all Americans. But as we shall see, this faith in business and conservative politics did not survive the Great Depression.

# II. Social Change in the Roaring Twenties

While prosperity lasted, most Americans cared less about politics than about the exciting amusements that were then coming into fashion. Young people in the cities and suburbs had automobiles, phonographs, radios, movies, major league sports, new dance steps, and a fast-paced music called jazz. Their fun, which lasted for about a decade, gave a name to their times: the Roaring Twenties.

## A. MASS CONSUMPTION OF NEW PRODUCTS

The telephone and phonograph had been invented in the 1870s. The first movies, the first automobiles with gasoline engines, and the first device for transmitting radio messages all appeared in the 1890s. The first successful flight of a heavier-than-air craft (airplane) occurred during the Progressive Era, in 1903. At first, however, these inventions were merely curiosities. Ownership of telephones and automobiles was limited to the rich. Only in the postwar decade, the 1920s, did the many marvels of the modern age become available to millions of American consumers.

**Henry Ford's Assembly Line**  An auto maker in Detroit, Michigan, had the idea of mass-producing his Model T cars so that they could be sold cheaply to people with average incomes. The method used by Henry Ford in manufacturing the Model T was as important as the car itself. Instead of having workers move about to pick up various automobile parts, Ford had them stand in one spot as the car being assembled moved past them on a moving conveyor belt. Without moving from his or her place in the assembly line, each worker repeated the same operation over and over. The assembly-line method saved time, cut production costs, and enabled Model T's to be sold in 1916 for a price of only $400. Ford's methods were copied in other industries. By 1920 U.S. factories everywhere had switched to the assembly-line method for mass-producing goods.

Advertisement in a 1920s magazine

**The Impact of the Automobile on American Life**    The automobile did for the twentieth century what the railroad had done for the nineteenth century. It boosted the American economy and transformed American society. Economically, the millions of automobiles sold in the 1920s stimulated the growth of other industries. The rubber industry expanded to produce tires. The oil and gasoline industry provided fuel. The steel industry produced millions of tons of metal for auto bodies. Roadside hotels and restaurants were built all over the country to take advantage of the motorists' fondness for travel and tourism.

During the 1920s millions of city dwellers moved to new housing in the suburbs. There they came to rely upon the family car for transportation as well as recreation. A new suburban way of life developed around the possession and use of an automobile.

Of course the automobile brought problems as well as benefits: drunken driving, fatal highway accidents, parking problems on city streets—and later, polluted air. But in the 1920s most Americans were delighted with the automobile and the way of life it made possible.

**Subways and Trolleys in the Growing Cities**    Public transportation in the cities also improved during the early years of the twentieth century. Shoppers and workers could now move about the city on subways, buses, and electrified trolley cars. Cities continued to grow rapidly. The 1920s was the first decade in U.S. history in which residents of urban areas outnumbered residents of rural areas.

**Crossing the Atlantic in an Airplane**    There was tremendous excitement in the 1920s about daring, record-setting journeys by airplane pilots. The feat that caused the greatest excitement was the crossing of the Atlantic Ocean from New York to Paris by Charles Lindbergh in 1927. Lindbergh became every American's hero. Returning by ship to the United States, he was welcomed by millions in a huge parade in New York City.

**Radio, Phonographs, and Movies**    By 1920 popular forms of entertainment had undergone a revolution. In addition to entertaining features in newspapers and magazines, there were now movies to see and phonograph records and radio shows to hear. Phonograph records preserved the voices of opera singers like Enrico Caruso and popular singers like Al Jolson. The practice of broadcasting shows on the radio—shows paid for by advertisers—began in the 1920s. For the first time people heard election results and major news stories at the moment that they happened.

In the 1920s the movie industry, which had begun in the East, found a new home on the West Coast. From studios in Hollywood, California, came hundreds of comedies, Westerns, and romances starring Charlie Chaplin, Mary Pickford, Rudolph Valentino, and others. The brief era of silent movies came to an end in 1927 when Al Jolson starred in *The Jazz Singer*, the first "talking movie."

**Effect of the Mass Media on Popular Culture**   The new forms of popular entertainment created a common culture for all Americans. Whether they lived in cities or on farms, people from East to West and North to South saw the same movies, listened to the same phonograph records, and adored the same celebrities. Everybody in the Roaring Twenties talked of aviators like Charles Lindbergh, movie stars like Rudolph Valentino, and sports heroes like baseball's Babe Ruth and football's Red Grange.

Advertising in the mass media also become part of the popular culture. People from coast to coast saw the same magazine ads for cigarettes, soft drinks, and cars. The repetition of these ads gave Americans everywhere the sense of belonging to a common national culture.

# B. EMANCIPATION OF WOMEN

The adoption of the Nineteenth Amendment in 1920 enabled women in every state to vote for president and other officials. But many women wanted more than the right to vote. Margaret Sanger continued her movement for birth control. Other women founded a political party whose main purpose was to work for an equal rights amendment. Those women did not involve themselves in politics began to challenge old assumptions about their role in society.

**The Flapper Look**   Many young women in high school and college experimented with a new style of dress. They raised hemlines above the knee and danced to the swinging beat of popular music. These young **flappers,** as they were called, shocked the older generation by wearing one-piece bathing suits and smoking cigarettes in public.

**Office Workers**   Refrigerators, washing machines, vacuum cleaners, and other household appliances became commonplace in the 1920s. These time-saving devices reduced the household chores that were traditionally assigned to women. They made it possible for women of the middle class to enter the work force in record numbers. But many jobs available to women were limited to support services— working for a man as a secretary or typist.

**Moral Questions**   Many older Americans, both men and women, worried about the new flapper fashions. They feared that greater freedom and full-time employment for women would lead to a breakdown of the traditional family. Traditional values seemed to be in serious danger.

## C. PROHIBITION AND ORGANIZED CRIME

Many citizens were also alarmed by the unexpected result of the Eighteenth Amendment, or Prohibition Amendment. This amendment, adopted in 1919, was the chief goal of Carrie Nation and other reformers in the temperance movement (review Chapter 8). It prohibited the manufacture and sale of wines, beers, liquors, and other alcoholic beverages in the United States.

**Defiance of the Law**    The new amendment failed to achieve its objective and caused millions of otherwise law-abiding citizens to obtain drinks illegally. The liquor was either manufactured illegally in the United States or smuggled across the border from Canada and other foreign sources. **Bootleggers** (those who made a business of supplying illegal beverages) made huge profits. In large cities like New York and Chicago, bootleggers organized criminal gangs that often managed to evade the law by corrupting the police. Thus, **Prohibition** was largely responsible for a huge increase in organized crime.

**Repeal**    Federal officials continued their losing battle to enforce Prohibition until 1933. In that year the Eighteenth Amendment was repealed (erased) by another amendment (the Twenty-first).

## D. CLASH OF CULTURES: THE SCOPES TRIAL

It was clear that an urban culture was fast emerging in the 1920s. Residents of rural areas felt that their more traditional culture was threatened by the new ways. The clash between the two cultures expressed itself in a spectacular and much publicized trial in Tennessee in 1925. The defendant was a biology teacher named John Scopes. He had purposely defied a Tennessee law against the teaching of Charles Darwin's theory of evolution in the public schools. The law had been passed because Darwin's ideas offended those Protestant groups who interpreted the Bible strictly.

A famous lawyer named Clarence Darrow defended Scopes. The prosecutor was a politician from an earlier era—William Jennings Bryan, the Democratic populist candidate for president in 1896 and former U.S. secretary of state. At one point in the trial, Darrow called Bryan as a witness and challenged Bryan's literal interpretation of the Bible. Reading about the trial in their newspapers, city people sided with Scopes and Darrow. Rural, church-going Americans sided with the prosecution. Although Scopes was convicted, he was fined only $100. A higher court in Tennessee later reversed the trial court's verdict.

Is it right or wrong to suppress the teaching of scientific ideas that conflict with traditional interpretations of the Bible? This issue was at the heart of the **Scopes trial** and continues to stir controversy in our own times.

# E. NATIVIST PREJUDICE AGAINST IMMIGRANTS

Life in the 1920s was generally good for people of the middle class who were largely native-born, white Americans. It was not so good for ethnic minorities and the foreign-born. Especially in rural communities there was distrust of big cities where large numbers of Italian and Jewish immigrants had settled. Although most immigrants were hardworking and law-abiding, many people accused the foreign-born of being responsible for city slums and crime.

**Strict Limits on Immigration**  Recall from Chapter 7 that immigration from eastern and southern Europe was severely restricted by **quota laws** enacted by Congress in 1921 and 1924. Another immigration law of 1929 limited total immigration to just 150,000 per year. Each country was assigned a small percentage of the total—a percentage (or quota) based upon the number of people from that country who lived in the United States in 1920. In addition the 1929 law prohibited any immigration from Asian countries.

**Growth of the KKK**  Recall that the Ku Klux Klan (KKK), was a secret society of Southern whites who had terrorized newly freed slaves after the Civil War. In the 1920s the Klan made a comeback. Millions of people in small towns of the South and the Middle West joined the society and wore the KKK's white hoods in town parades. The revived Klan tried to intimidate many groups—African Americans, Roman Catholics, Jews, and immigrants. In the early years of the decade, its growing membership made it an important force in the politics of many states. Oregon and Indiana, for example, both had governors who owed their election to the Klan's support.

**The Case of Sacco and Vanzetti**  Liberals blamed the antiforeign prejudices of many Americans for the deaths of two Italian immigrants. Nicola Sacco and Bartolomeo Vanzetti had been convicted in a Massachusetts court in 1921 of armed robbery and murder. As liberals pointed out, the evidence in the **Sacco-Vanzetti case** was weak, and the judge appeared to be biased against them. For years after the trial, there were worldwide protests and appeals for clemency. In 1927, however, both men were executed.

# F. AFRICAN AMERICANS IN NORTHERN CITIES

The 1920s was a time of significant change for African Americans, particularly for those who moved to Northern cities.

**Migration to the North**  Between 1910 and 1930 the number of African Americans in the North went from one million to 2.5 million.

Families of Southern blacks moved to Northern cities for two main reasons. First, they wanted to escape the segregation, or Jim Crow, laws of the South. Their resentment of these laws increased after World War I. African-American soldiers returning from Europe in 1919 had difficulty going back to being treated as second-class citizens. If they boldly defied whites' prejudice against them, they risked being jailed or even lynched (killed by a mob, usually by hanging). A second reason for moving to the North was the hope of a steady job for good pay.

**Race Riots in the North**  Many whites in the North felt threatened by the arrival of blacks in large numbers. In Chicago in 1919 riots broke out between blacks and whites on a segregated beach. A total of 38 people of both races died in the fighting. Race riots broke out in other Northern cities as well.

In Northern communities African Americans found segregation to exist not only on beaches but also in housing, schools, and clubs. The goal of racial fairness was far from being realized in any section of the country.

**Marcus Garvey**  While the NAACP worked for integration, a Jamaican immigrant named Marcus Garvey worked for the exact opposite. Coming to the United States in 1916, Garvey was deeply offended by the second-class status of African Americans. He decided that African Americans needed to take pride in their African heritage. In Jamaica he had organized the Universal Negro Improvement Association (UNIA), which sponsored a "Back to Africa" movement. In the United States the UNIA attracted about 500,000 members. Garvey urged African Americans *not* to seek acceptance by the white majority. Instead, he believed that they should build their own institutions and leave the United States for Africa, their ancestors' homeland.

Garvey's ambitions came to a sudden end. In 1925 he was tried and convicted of using the mails to defraud investors. In 1927 the U.S. government deported him to Jamaica.

**The Harlem Renaissance**  Many of the African Americans who moved to New York City between 1900 and 1930 settled in a neighborhood called Harlem. Here in the 1920s a number of talented African Americans rose to fame as writers, performers, and musicians. Their remarkable creativity during this period was called the **Harlem Renaissance.** Best known of the Harlem poets were James Weldon Johnson, Langston Hughes, and Countee Cullen. Among the celebrated actors living in Harlem were Paul Robeson, star of a number of Eugene O'Neill's plays as well as *Showboat.* Josephine Baker sang and danced her way to fame in night clubs in Philadelphia, New York, and Paris. Eubie Blake and W. C. Handy composed songs that are still heard today.

**Jazz**  African American musicians were the principal creators of the most popular music of the 1920s—jazz. They first played the music in New Orleans around 1900. By the 1920s jazz had traveled north to Chicago and New York City. Its vibrant, fast-moving beat expressed the spirit of the times. Among the greatest of the jazz musicians was the trumpet player and singer Louis Armstrong. He toured the world, playing for presidents and prime ministers, kings and queens.

**Discrimination in the Entertainment Industry**  Talent and ability did not lead to acceptance. Movies rarely used African Americans in other than stereotyped roles (servants, maids). Chorus lines were generally all-white. Even in Harlem, at the famous Cotton Club, African Americans would entertain, but were rarely seen as customers.

## In Review

The following questions refer to section I: Conservative Politics of the Twenties and section II: Social Change in the Roaring Twenties.

1. Discuss the significance of the following: *the Teapot Dome scandal, the Eighteenth Amendment, the Sacco-Vanzetti case,* and *the Harlem Renaissance.*

2. Identify the effects of the automobile on (a) the American economy and (b) American society.

3. Compare the politics of the 1920s to the politics of the period from 1900 to 1917.

# III. Economic Flip-Flop: From Boom to Bust

World War I had brought boom times to the U.S. economy. During the war American farms had fed much of Europe, and farm prices had risen to impressive levels. American industries had mobilized for war and produced vast quantities of military equipment.

But the war also produced an imbalance in the world economy—an imbalance that eventually led to a worldwide depression. We have seen that the peace treaty of 1919 forced Germany to pay the Allies a crushing sum of money in reparations. At the same time the victorious Allies (Great Britain, France, and others) owed vast sums to the United States for their wartime consumption of American-made foods and military supplies. The United States in the 1920s was the one nation to whom many other nations owed a huge debt. This fact produced the economic imbalance that was one cause of the economic collapse of 1929—the shocking event known to history as the **Great Crash.**

This section will describe the business boom of the 1920s and explain the forces that turned that boom into a decade-long depression.

## A. BOOM YEARS (1922 TO 1929)

The postwar U.S. economy underwent one bad year in 1921 before entering into a period of expansion and boom. The following events characterized the boom years.

**The Consolidation of Big Business**   During the presidencies of Harding, Coolidge, and Hoover, there was no more trust busting (breaking up of big business firms). Instead, big businesses flourished and grew bigger and more powerful every year. By 1929 the 200 largest U.S. corporations controlled 49 percent of all corporate wealth in the country.

**Dramatic Increase in Productivity**   As a worker spends less time accomplishing the same amount of work, we say that his or her **productivity** rises. New machinery and the use of assembly-line methods resulted in impressive gains in productivity during the 1920s.

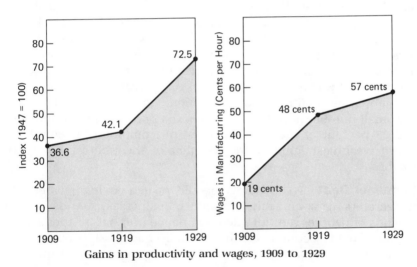

Gains in productivity and wages, 1909 to 1929

Although workers' wages also increased, they were far below the increases in productivity. An average factory worker earned $1,350 a year in 1929, compared to $1,100 a year in 1919.

**The Leading Role of the Automobile**   Gains in automobile production through the 1920s led to gains in many other industries (such as rubber, steel, oil, and highway construction). In only ten years the number of cars manufactured by U.S. companies increased more than threefold—from 1.5 million in 1919 to 4.7 million in 1929. By the end of the decade of prosperity, Americans owned more than 25 million cars.

**Bull Market on Wall Street**   Business was so good that average Americans with average income began buying the stocks of major corporations. As they invested larger sums in the stock market on New York City's Wall Street, the prices of most stocks went up and up. Month after month in 1928 people watched stock prices climb to record highs. It was a great **bull market** (the condition on a stock exchange when public confidence in stocks causes stock prices to rise).

## B. PROBLEMS IN THE U.S. ECONOMY

Many people thought that the boom would continue forever. They were mistaken. Looking back on the state of the U.S. economy during the 1920s, historians identify many underlying weaknesses that, sooner or later, were bound to cause trouble.

**Uneven Distribution of Wealth**   A nation's economic strength depends upon the ability of millions of citizens to buy the things that factories and farms produce. If wages are low relative to all that's offered for sale, much will go unsold and businesses will fail. In fact wages in the 1920s lagged far behind increases in production, as we have seen. Therefore, workers' purchasing power (ability to buy goods and services) was too weak to sustain many years of prosperity.

Much of the wealth in the U.S. economy in 1929 was in the hands of a small number of people. The richest 5 percent of the population had 25 percent of the total income. The combined income of the 36,000 wealthiest families equaled that of the poorest 12 million families.

**Consumer Debt**   To encourage people to keep buying new toasters, refrigerators, cars, and other products, businesses extended credit. Millions of people went into debt to finance purchases. After a while so much debt accumulated that a family had to stop buying new products just to make the monthly debt payments on all that they owed.

**Depressed Conditions on the Farm**   An important part of the U.S. economy was not at all prosperous in the 1920s. After 1921 farmers suffered from falling prices caused by European farms recovering from the war. Also better farm machinery produced surpluses of wheat and corn, which lowered their prices. Burdened with heavy debts, many farmers were too poor to purchase the great quantities of consumer goods that U.S. businesses were selling.

**Buying Stocks with Borrowed Money**  Another problem was the risky practice, common in the 1920s, of taking out a loan to purchase stocks. It was a common practice then to pay a small percent of a stock's purchase price with one's own money and finance the rest with a bank loan. Such a practice was called buying stocks "**on margin.**"

Take as an example a man who invested his entire savings of $1,000 to buy $10,000 worth of stock. This investor would be buying on 10-percent margin, that is, borrowing $9,000, or 90 percent of the price of the stock. Now suppose that the stock's market price went down by 10 percent or more. The bank that made the loan would have probably asked for more money from the investor. But the investor had no more money. The bank would then have sold the investor's stock for whatever the stock was worth. The investor would thereby have lost all of his savings. If the stock had fallen very far, the bank would have lost part of its loan of $9,000. Now multiply this one example by millions of investors and thousands of banks and you will get an idea of the potential dangers to the U.S. economy of investors going into debt in the 1920s to buy stocks "on margin."

## C. PROBLEMS IN THE INTERNATIONAL ECONOMY

Added to the debts of the American farmers, laborers, and buyers of stocks were the international debts left over from a costly world war. U.S. banks and businesses wanted all European nations to be

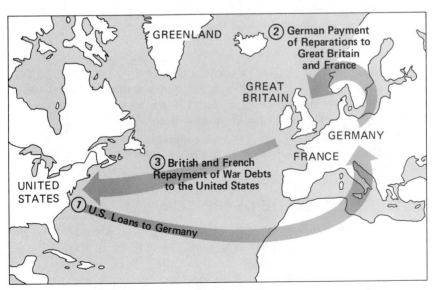

The global context: how U.S. loans financed international
prosperity, 1924 to 1929

able to buy American-made products. So they offered generous loans to Europeans to enable them to pay their war debts to U.S. companies. Such an arrangement could sustain prosperity only so long as U.S. banks were strong enough to keep making foreign loans. But if banks made too many loans to too many people, U.S. dollars might no longer be available to prop up the European economy.

The map on page 325 shows how U.S. loans to Germany helped to finance Germany's reparation payments to the Allies. This money in turn was used to finance the payments of the Allies' war debts to the United States. The process went round and round in a cycle to everyone's benefit.

Suddenly, however, the cycle of debt payments both in the United States and Europe came to a stop when stock market prices on Wall Street collapsed.

## D. THE STOCK MARKET CRASH

The bull market on Wall Street reached its highest point in September 1929. After that the prices of stocks started to go down—sometimes slowly, sometimes in frightening leaps. Bankers tried to save the market from losing any more ground. But on October 29, thousands of people panicked and ordered their brokers on Wall Street to sell at any price. On that "Black Tuesday" a record 16.5 million shares of stock were traded, almost all of them at prices far below what people originally paid for them. After that prices continued to sink lower and lower. By the end of December, the combined prices of Wall Street stocks had lost one third of their peak value in September.

The Great Crash on Wall Street had three consequences, all bad. First, the billions of dollars in savings that people had used to buy stocks were largely wiped out. Second, many individuals and businesses that owned stock on margin could not pay their debts and went bankrupt. Third, and perhaps most serious of all, people lost confidence in the economy. For years after the crash, they preferred to save what they could rather than to risk investing in new business ventures.

## E. THE WORLDWIDE DEPRESSION

In times of panic, people sometimes will do things that only make matters worse. That is what happened during the year that followed the Great Crash. It was understood that the U.S. economy was part of an international economy. The lifeblood of that larger economy was trade between nations. Tariffs that interfered with that trade could do damage to all nations, including the United States.

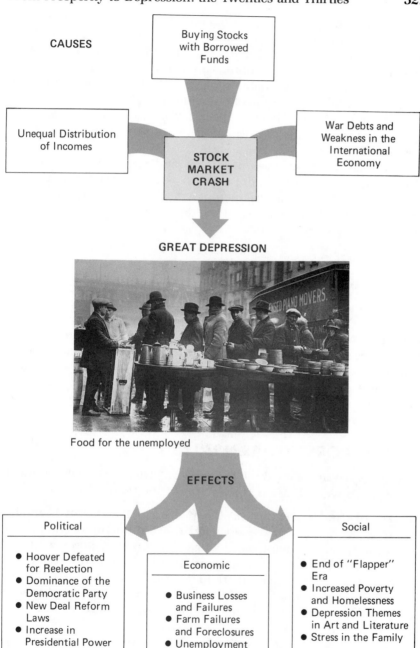

CAUSES

Buying Stocks
with Borrowed
Funds

Unequal Distribution
of Incomes

STOCK
MARKET
CRASH

War Debts and
Weakness in the
International
Economy

GREAT DEPRESSION

Food for the unemployed

EFFECTS

**Political**

- Hoover Defeated
  for Reelection
- Dominance of the
  Democratic Party
- New Deal Reform
  Laws
- Increase in
  Presidential Power

**Economic**

- Business Losses
  and Failures
- Farm Failures
  and Foreclosures
- Unemployment
- Loss of Personal
  Savings
- Lower Prices

**Social**

- End of "Flapper"
  Era
- Increased Poverty
  and Homelessness
- Depression Themes
  in Art and Literature
- Stress in the Family

Causes and effects: the Great Depression

And yet many politicians in Congress hoped to protect American industries from foreign competition by raising tariff rates. In 1930 they enacted a new tariff law—the **Hawley-Smoot Tariff**—that increased import taxes on more than a thousand items. The result was disastrous. European nations followed the U.S. example by raising their own tariffs. The volume of trade between the United States and Europe dropped to half of its peak level. (Even today those who oppose the idea of a protective tariff point to the negative effects of the tariff of 1930.)

After 1930 the economies of Europe and the United States sank deeper and deeper into a **depression** (a severe economic decline marked by business failures, unemployment, and low prices). Higher tariffs were not the only cause of the depression, but they surely did not help.

# IV. The Great Depression

By the middle of 1930 the signs of a worsening depression were everywhere. Farmers were deeper in debt than ever. Consumers were cutting back on the purchase of cars, radios, and other items. Businesses were laying off workers. Europeans and Canadians were buying fewer U.S. goods. Every month, from October 1929 to March 1933, the economic news seemed worse than the month before. These were hard months indeed—especially hard because Americans did not know when, if ever, the depression would end.

## A. THE WORST YEARS (1930 to 1932)

The worst years of the Great Depression, 1930 to 1932, corresponded to the years when Herbert Hoover was in the White House.

**Impact of the Depression on Daily Life**  In 1932 about 12 million workers—25 percent of the labor force—were unemployed. (In contrast, the unemployment rate in 1990 was under 6 percent.) Those fortunate enough to keep their jobs worked for much lower wages than in the 1920s. Prices paid to farmers were desperately low. Factories produced only half of the 1929 output. By 1932 about five thousand banks had closed their doors, forever cutting off customers from their savings.

Jobless persons who could not pay even the lowest rents were forced into the streets. For food they had no choice but to line up for free meals served by private charities and churches. The homeless slept in tents and shacks. They also found shelter in railroad boxcars and traveled about on freight trains. Jobless men and women sold apples on street corners in every large city.

**The "Bonus Army"**   One of the saddest events of the Great Depression occurred in the summer of 1932. About 17,000 veterans of World War I marched from their homes all the way to Washington, D.C., to convince the president and Congress to pay immediately the bonuses due to them at a later time. The **"Bonus Army,"** as they were called, set up makeshift shacks on the grounds of the Capitol. President

## OBSERVERS OF AMERICAN LIFE: ON THE ROAD WITH THE "BONUS ARMY," 1932

A writer on the staff of the New Republic offered a ride to two war veterans who had joined the "Bonus Army" on its march to Washington in 1932. The writer's account of what they told him is quoted below.

Why were the men so angry at the U.S. government? How do you think the government should have treated the marchers when they finally arrived in Washington?

Mile after mile we passed the ragged line as we too drove northward to the camp at Ideal Park. We were carrying two of the veterans, chosen from a group of three hundred by a quick informal vote of their comrades. One was a man gassed in the Argonne . . .; he breathed with an effort, as if each breath would be his last. [The Argonne was the region of France where American troops had fought heroically in the final push that ended World War I.] The other was a man with family troubles; he had lost his wife and six children during the retreat from Camp Marks and hoped to find them in Johnstown. He talked about his service in France, his three medals, which he refused to wear, his wounds, his five years in a government hospital. "If they gave me a job," he said, "I wouldn't care about the bonus. . . . Now I don't ever want to see a flag again. Give me a gun and I'll go back to Washington."—"That's right, buddy," said a woman looking up from her two babies, who lay on a dirty quilt in the sun. A cloud of flies hovered above them. Another man was reading the editorial page of a Johnstown paper. He shouted, "Let them come here and mow us down with machine guns. We won't move this time."—"That's right, buddy," said the woman again. A haggard face—eyes bloodshot, skin pasty white under a three days' beard—suddenly appeared at the window of the car. "Hoover must die," said the face ominously. "You know what this means?" a man shouted from the other side. "This means revolution."

Hoover ordered them to leave. When they refused, federal troops moved in with tanks and tear gas and broke up the encampment.

**Hoover's Policies** Hoover tried hard to revive the economy. These were his methods:

- Cutting taxes to enable consumers to buy more products
- Greatly increasing the amount of government money spent on public projects—the building of dams, highways, harbors, and so forth
- Persuading Congress to establish the Reconstruction Finance Corporation. This government enterprise provided federal funds to struggling banks, railroads, and insurance companies to keep them from going bankrupt.
- Persuading Congress to establish the Federal Farm Board. To help farmers through hard times, this agency had the power to purchase farm goods in order to keep prices from falling.
- Declaring a **debt moratorium** (temporary halt on the payment of war debts). Recognizing that the depression was worldwide, Hoover told European nations in 1931 that they could temporarily stop making payments on their debts.

**Evaluating Hoover's Policies** Despite the president's efforts, economic conditions did not improve. Many Americans accused Hoover of doing nothing to give direct relief to the poor and unemployed. His policies gave them the impression that he cared more about aiding businesses than aiding the common people. But Hoover disagreed with the idea of giving aid directly to the poor. He believed instead in what he called "rugged individualism." In his view government was less important to economic recovery than the decisions of private businesses and individuals. His belief in limited government action was in keeping with the beliefs of earlier presidents.

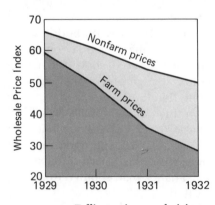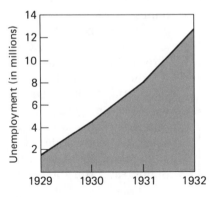

Falling prices and rising unemployment, 1929 to 1932

**A Vote for New Leadership**  But in 1932 most Americans were impatient with policies that did not seem to be working. They expressed their impatience by voting overwhelmingly for a change in leadership. In the election of 1932, Hoover as the Republican candidate lost by a huge margin to his Democratic challenger, Franklin D. Roosevelt.

## B. FRANKLIN D. ROOSEVELT'S NEW DEAL

The new president was part of the same wealthy New York family as Theodore Roosevelt, a distant cousin. But unlike Theodore (a Progressive Republican), the second Roosevelt in the White House was a Democrat.

**Political Career**  In 1920 Franklin Roosevelt had been the Democrats' unsuccessful candidate for vice president. Soon afterward he contracted polio, an often crippling disease, and his legs became paralyzed. For the rest of his life he worked in a wheelchair and wore heavy braces to support himself when he stood. But Roosevelt's personal charm and courage were unaffected by the handicap. He continued his career in politics, winning election as New York's governor in 1928 and 1930 and then as the U.S. president in 1932.

**Political Philosophy**  Roosevelt believed that government should do whatever it could to help people to overcome economic hardship. His approach differed from that of Hoover, who believed in a trickle-down theory for rescuing the economy. Recall that Hoover's programs like the Reconstruction Finance Corporation helped businesses. If businesses succeeded, then Hoover believed everyone would benefit indirectly from business profits trickling down to wage earners. Roosevelt, on the other hand, was more inclined to help people directly by giving them government jobs. The federal paychecks, in Roosevelt's view, would give people hope and also put money in the economy to make possible the buying of more goods and services.

Above all, Roosevelt believed in trying out many ideas for solving the economic crisis. In his 1932 campaign he had promised a "new deal" for the American people. Through his first term and part of his second term as president (1933 to 1938), the government programs that he favored were known as the **New Deal.**

**The "Hundred Days"**  By words and deeds the new president demonstrated an eagerness to fight the depression with all his strength. Listening to the radio, millions of Americans were reassured by the president's messages explaining his New Deal programs. He called his radio talks "fireside chats." People were amazed by all the laws that the president urged Congress to pass. In his first three months in office—almost exactly one hundred days—more important laws were enacted than in the entire decade of the 1920s. Recognizing that the times called for bold measures, the Democratic majority in Congress gave the president almost all that he asked. Among the laws passed in the **"Hundred Days"** were laws . . .

- to close banks temporarily
- to insure bank deposits
- to pay farmers to reduce their production (so as to boost farm prices)
- to encourage businesses in every industry to establish "fair" prices in order to stop and reverse the depression trend of sinking prices
- to provide for a minimum wage and a 40-hour workweek.

These and other laws created new government programs and agencies for dealing with the economic crisis. They gave people the impression that at last the U.S. government was acting vigorously for the public welfare.

## C. RELIEF, RECOVERY, AND REFORM

Roosevelt and his many advisers (a group called the "Brain Trust") had three main goals—**relief, recovery, and reform.** First, they wanted to provide relief to the poor and unemployed. Second, they wanted to bring about the recovery of business. Third, they wanted to reform the economic system and thus prevent the mistakes that had caused the depression. The following chart identifies New Deal agencies that were created for achieving each goal.

### New Deal Agencies and Their Purposes

| Agency (Year Established) | Purpose |
|---|---|
| Federal Emergency Relief Administration (FERA) (1933) | *Relief for the unemployed:* Gave federal money to the states, which used the money to help people in need. |
| Works Progress Administration (WPA) (1935) | *Relief for the unemployed:* Put unemployed workers on the federal payroll and organized special projects for them to do (raking leaves, painting murals, repairing schools, etc.). |
| Civilian Conservation Corps (CCC) (1933) | *Relief for the unemployed:* Provided young people with jobs in conservation (flood control, soil conservation, forest replanting, etc.). |

| Agency (Year Established) | Purpose |
|---|---|
| Agricultural Adjustment Administration (AAA) (1933) | *Recovery of agriculture:* Paid farmers to destroy a portion of their crops and livestock as a means of limiting production and raising farm prices. |
| National Recovery Administration (NRA) (1933) | *Recovery of business:* Encouraged business firms in every industry to agree upon prices and to draw up codes of fair practices. |
| Public Works Administration (PWA) (1933) | *Recovery and relief:* Used federal money to put people to work building bridges, dams, highways, and other public projects. |
| Federal Housing Administration (FHA) (1934) | *Recovery of housing industry:* Insured loans for the construction of new housing. |
| National Labor Relations Board (NLRB) (1935) | *Reform for labor unions:* Enforced the right of all workers to organize unions. |
| Social Security Board (SSB) (1935) | *Reform for the disabled, the unemployed, and the elderly:* Provided insurance benefits for those receiving no income because of old age, a physical handicap, or sudden loss of a job. |
| Securities and Exchange Commission (SEC) (1934) | *Reform of the stock market:* Regulated the stock market and required sellers of stocks to supply truthful information to the public. |
| Federal Deposit Insurance Corporation (FDIC) (1933) | *Reform of banking:* Provided government backing and insurance for bank deposits so that depositors would not risk loss of their money. |

Two other New Deal reforms should be noted. By an act of 1933, Congress increased the powers of the Federal Reserve Board to regulate bank loans. Another act—the Fair Labor Standards Act of 1938—set minimum wages and maximum hours for some workers. At first the minimum wage established by this law was 25 cents an hour.

# D. GOVERNMENT IN THE TENNESSEE VALLEY (TVA)

One of the most ambitious New Deal programs was an attempt to rescue an entire region from conditions of extreme poverty. The Southern lands watered by the Tennessee River were often flooded.

The farmers living near the river had no electric power and were desperately poor. In 1933 Congress created an agency to deal with these problems. The **Tennessee Valley Authority (TVA)** was given the power and the money to accomplish all of the following:

- Build dams to control floods
- Build power plants and provide electricity for the region
- Charge fair prices for the use of TVA-generated electricity
- Build reservoirs to hold needed water.

In a few years the TVA experiment was a proven success. Throughout the region that it served, people received relief in the form of TVA jobs. Recovery was evident in the farms that now had electric power. Reform was achieved through flood control and conservation.

## E. ROOSEVELT AND THE SUPREME COURT

During his first term as president, Roosevelt had a fairly easy time persuading a Democratic Congress to pass New Deal laws. But he had a much harder time with the conservative justices of the Supreme Court, most of whom had been appointed by Republican presidents.

**Two Acts Declared Unconstitutional**  Two programs that Roosevelt hoped would bring recovery were both declared unconstitutional by the nation's highest court. In one case (1935) a company in the chicken-raising industry complained about the law that had created the **National Recovery Administration (NRA).** The company's lawyer argued that the industry codes established under this law wrongly gave legislative power to the executive branch of government. The Supreme Court agreed that the NRA codes were too much like laws. Therefore, the National Industrial Recovery Act of 1933 was declared unconstitutional.

In a second case (1936) the Supreme Court considered whether a special tax could be collected to pay for the enforcement of the **Agricultural Adjustment Act** of 1933. It ruled against both the tax and the law.

**Attempt to "Pack" the Court**  Angered by the Supreme Court's decisions, Roosevelt proposed a scheme for increasing the number of justices from nine to 15. This would have enabled him to appoint justices who shared his liberal point of view. But the president was denounced by conservative critics for attempting to **"pack" the Court.** In 1937 Roosevelt's plan was defeated in Congress.

## F. POLITICS OF THE 1930s

Franklin Roosevelt was a controversial president. While most Americans admired him as a great leader, there were critics who attacked the president for doing too little about the economy and other critics who said he attempted too much.

**Changing the Democratic Party**   Roosevelt changed the nature of his party. Before the 1930s the Republicans had usually been in the majority in national politics. The Democratic party had long relied upon the solid support of Southerners whose views were generally conservative. But Roosevelt's New Deal appealed to great numbers of people in the Northern cities. It appealed to industrial workers, immigrants, African Americans, ethnic Americans, and people with liberal views. It also appealed strongly to farmers in all regions who were helped by New Deal programs. In the 1930s members of these different groups formed a majority. Their votes could be counted upon to elect Democratic majorities in Congress as well as a Democratic president, Franklin Roosevelt.

Campaign buttons from four elections: 1932, 1936, 1940, and 1944

**Breaking the Two-Term Tradition**   In 1936 Roosevelt was reelected president by a landslide. In 1940 he was elected to a third term and in 1944 to a fourth term. No president before him had ever served more than two terms. When Roosevelt ran for a third term, Republican critics accused him of breaking a **two-term tradition** that had been respected since the time of George Washington. After Roosevelt's death Congress proposed a constitutional amendment to prevent any future president from serving more than two full terms. The Twenty-second Amendment establishing this two-term limit was adopted in 1951.

**Extremist Attacks from Left and Right**   Because people were desperate in the 1930s, many wanted more radical changes than the reforms of the New Deal. At one extreme were Communists and Socialists who wanted the government to take over all major industries. (Socialists believed that radical change could be achieved peacefully through elections, while Communists looked forward to a violent revolt of the working class.) At the other extreme were racist and nationalist groups who thought the government should be run by a military dictator. Probably the most serious challenge to Roosevelt's leadership came from Louisiana, where a popular politician named Huey Long made the most of voters' discontents. As Louisiana's governor, Long promised to force the rich to "share the wealth" with the common people. But Long's ambitions for national power were cut short in 1935 when an assassin killed him.

**Conservative Critics of the New Deal**  Roosevelt was strongly criticized by business leaders as well as by conservative politicians in both the Democratic and Republican parties. They accused New Deal programs like the TVA of undermining the free-enterprise system. They thought such programs were hostile to business. "Creeping socialism," they said, was being substituted for the "rugged individualism" that had made the United States great.

**Liberal Defenders of the New Deal**  Liberals defended the New Deal by arguing that Roosevelt saved both democracy and the free-enterprise system. In their view extremist groups (Communists, Socialists, Fascists, and Populists like Huey Long) might have torn the nation apart if Roosevelt had failed to enact programs of economic relief. Liberals also argued that the reforms of the New Deal (the **Social Security system,** the regulation of the banking system, the minimum wage law, and others) simply extended the reforms of the Progressive Era. Their purpose was to avoid some of the bad effects of capitalism (such as bank failures, economic insecurity, and the possibility of depression) while preserving the good effects (such as freedom of choice, inventiveness, and economic growth).

## G. DID THE NEW DEAL BRING ABOUT RECOVERY?

Roosevelt's supporters argue that the New Deal succeeded, while critics argue just the opposite.

**Success of the New Deal**  During Roosevelt's first term the economy did show signs of recovery on all fronts. Compared to the low point of the Great Depression (1933), employment in 1936 was up, industrial production was up, farm prices were up, and business failures were down. By 1937 all of these indicators were very close to the prosperous levels of 1929 before the crash. New Dealers claimed credit for the improvement. (But Hoover and other conservative critics argued that the change would have come about anyway with or without all the government programs.)

**Failure of the New Deal**  The economy never fully recovered in the 1930s. Unemployment, while improving slightly, was far too great to say that prosperity had returned. During Roosevelt's second term, in 1937 and 1938, the economy took a sharp downward turn. Some viewed these years as a second depression. By 1939 the unemployed numbered 9.5 million (compared to 13 million in 1933). The next year, 1940, business again was booming, but the biggest reason for this was the coming of World War II, not New Deal programs.

Why did war result in the return of prosperity? It was mainly because the United States began supplying many millions of dollars of war goods to Great Britain. Confident of profitable sales to both the British and U.S. governments, businesses once again made sizable investments in new plants and machinery.

## In Review

The following questions refer to section III: Economic Flip-Flop: From Boom to Bust and section IV: The Great Depression.

### Word Wheels

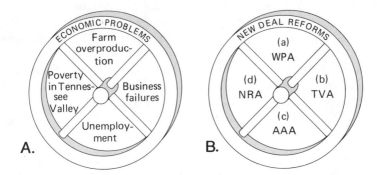

A.

B.

1. Explain why farm overproduction was considered to be a problem for farmers.
2. Identify each of the reforms in word wheel B.
3. On a separate piece of paper, match each economic problem in word wheel A to the New Deal reform in word wheel B that was supposed to correct the problem.

# V. Social Change in the Thirties

The Great Depression touched all aspects of American life. In this section, we shall explore its influence on popular culture, the arts, women, and minorities.

## A. THE GOLDEN AGE OF HOLLYWOOD

People did not stop going to the movies in the Great Depression. In fact, while other industries fell on hard times, the movie industry was never more glamorous or prosperous than in the 1930s. One reason for this was that, for only a few cents, people could briefly forget their troubles watching the great stars of Hollywood (for example: Shirley Temple, Clark Gable, James Stewart, and Judy

Garland) fall in love in a make-believe world. Most movies of the time such as *The Wizard of Oz* (1939) served people's needs for fantasy, adventure, romance, and fun. There were also great movies on serious social themes—movies that have become classics.

## B. REALISM IN ART AND LITERATURE

Gifted American artists and writers were inspired by the Great Depression to depict the lives of ordinary people struggling with hardship. Among the realist painters of the period were Thomas Hart Benton, Edward Hopper, and Ben Shahn.

The novelist William Faulkner and the playwright Lillian Hellman portrayed psychological and social tensions in Southern society. But the writer who most directly and vividly depicted the human misery of the Great Depression was John Steinbeck. In his novel *The Grapes of Wrath* (1939), Steinbeck created an unforgettable picture of Oklahoma sharecroppers ("Okies") being driven off their land and trying desperately to find work as peach pickers in California. It is a story of human beings swept away by cruel and impersonal economic forces.

## C. STATUS OF WOMEN

The freedom and fun that young women had as flappers of the 1920s did not last into the 1930s. The hemlines on skirts and dresses dropped to the ankle again, symbolizing the change to more serious and traditional values. In the Great Depression there were fewer job and career opportunities for women. Instead of pursuing a career, many women concentrated on the needs of their families.

On the other hand individual women of the 1930s achieved fame and high position in various fields. Amelia Earhart, for example, was to the 1930s what Charles Lindbergh had been to the 1920s. She became world-famous after flying a plane across the Atlantic—the first woman to accomplish this feat. Eleanor Roosevelt, wife of the president, went even farther than Franklin in championing liberal causes. She traveled around the nation visiting those hard-hit by the depression. She spoke out boldly and often on public issues. Soon she came to symbolize the "new woman" who was actively involved in national and world affairs.

Another public-spirited woman of the 1930s was Secretary of Labor Frances Perkins. As the first woman cabinet member, she had a distinguished record of service spanning 12 years. She administered many of the relief programs of the New Deal and helped bring about the abolition of child labor.

Amelia Earhart    Frances Perkins    Eleanor Roosevelt    Mary Bethune

# D. STATUS OF AFRICAN AMERICANS

Perhaps even more than whites, blacks suffered the full impact of the depression. The last to be hired, they were usually the first to be fired. There was one glimmer of hope, however. For the first time since the presidency of Abraham Lincoln, African Americans had the support of the president.

**Help from the White House** "Among American citizens there should be no forgotten men and no forgotten races." So said President Roosevelt, expressing his awareness that blacks had long been neglected by the U.S. government. Backing the president's words were New Deal programs that gave African Americans what they most needed—jobs. Many thousands of jobs were made available by the WPA and CCC.

Roosevelt also brought to the White House a "Black Cabinet," consisting of distinguished African-American leaders. Among them were Robert Weaver, an expert on urban housing problems, and Mary McLeod Bethune, an expert in education.

Perhaps most significant of all was the response of Eleanor Roosevelt to an incident of racial discrimination. In 1939 the great African-American opera singer Marian Anderson had been denied the right to perform at an important concert in Washington, D.C. When Eleanor Roosevelt learned of this, she invited Anderson to sing at the Lincoln Memorial.

The Roosevelts thus won a reputation for supporting the cause of racial justice. As a result, many thousands of African-American voters left the Republican party and became loyal Democrats.

**Continued Discrimination** Despite gestures of sympathy and support by the Roosevelts, African Americans continued to suffer from racism and discrimination. Even New Deal agencies discriminated against them. Under the industrial codes of the NRA (National Recovery Administration), white workers were allowed higher wage rates than black workers. Whites who sought employment from TVA were far more likely to be put on the payroll than African-American applicants.

By the 1930s, however, African Americans had learned how to resist and overcome some of the racist obstacles in their path. In Harlem a youthful leader named Adam Clayton Powell, Jr., organized a neighborhood boycott of stores that hired white workers only. Powell's followers carried signs that read: "Don't Buy Where You Can't Work." The campaign largely succeeded in ending the store owners' discriminatory practices. Powell was later elected to Congress where he represented the people of Harlem for 26 years (1944 to 1970).

# E. STATUS OF NATIVE AMERICANS

Native Americans had lived in poverty ever since the 1870s and 1880s when they had been forced to live on reservations. From their point of view, the economic depression had lasted 50 years *before* the stock market crash. The Great Depression was nothing new, except that whites now shared in the hard times.

The status of Native Americans did change, however, in 1934 when Congress passed the Indian Reorganization Act. (Review Chapter 7.) Instead of individuals owning plots of land on the reservations, the U.S. government now stressed tribal ownership and tribal authority. At the same time teachers in the reservation schools began to stress methods of scientific farming.

These changes were for the better. Even so, most Indians were still desperately poor. During the Great Depression there were fewer job opportunities outside the reservations and not enough income-earning opportunities on the reservations.

# F. CONTINUED PREJUDICE AGAINST IMMIGRANTS

Immigrants fared no better in the depression decade than they had in the 1920s. Native-born Americans' opposition to immigration extended even to the victims of Nazi persecution in Germany. Enforcing its quota laws, the U.S. government refused to allow the *St. Louis*, a ship filled with Jews fleeing Germany, to dock in Florida. The ship and its passengers had to return to Nazi Germany.

# G. THE GROWTH OF LABOR UNIONS

Factory workers suffered during the depression from wage cuts, frequent layoffs, and the daily *fear* of being unemployed. In the long run, however, workers benefited from the New Deal reforms that greatly strengthened their unions.

**The Wagner Act**   Named for its sponsor, Senator Robert Wagner of New York, the **Wagner Act** of 1935 launched a new era for American labor unions. It guaranteed to all workers the right to join the union of their choice and thus to "bargain collectively" with their employer on such issues as wages, hours, and factory conditions. To enforce the act, a National Labor Relations Board (NLRB) was empowered to compel employers to deal with whatever union the majority of workers chose to join. Firing anyone for joining a union was made illegal.

**Doubling of Union Membership**   Immediately after the Wagner Act became law, union membership shot upward. In just five years, 1935 to 1940, more than five million workers joined unions, doubling the total union membership and greatly increasing unions' bargaining power.

**Founding of the C.I.O.**   As unions grew more powerful, they started to compete among themselves. In 1935 the most powerful single union within the A.F. of L. was the United Mine Workers. Its aggressive leader, John L. Lewis, became impatient with the A.F. of L.'s policy of favoring unions of skilled crafts workers over the less skilled workers employed in automobile plants, steel mills, coal mines, and other industries. Lewis favored the organization of **industrial unions,** to which all workers in an industry—the unskilled and the skilled, African Americans and whites—could belong. Toward this end, he organized the **Congress of Industrial Organizations (C.I.O.),** which included his own miners' union, an auto workers' union, and others. In 1938 Lewis broke with the A.F. of L. completely, and the C.I.O. became a separate and rival organization.

**Sit-Down Strikes**   Industrial unions in the C.I.O. carried out strikes in the 1930s that shut down production for many months and resulted in major gains for labor. They devised the tactic of the **sit-down strike,** in which striking workers would simply occupy a factory and refuse to leave until their demands were met. The most dramatic and successful of such strikes shut down the automobile factories of General Motors in the winter of 1936 and 1937. The company finally yielded to almost all of the demands of the automobile workers' union.

## In Review

The following questions refer to section V: Social Change in the Thirties.

1. Identify *John Steinbeck, Frances Perkins, Marian Anderson, Adam Clayton Powell,* and *John L. Lewis.*
2. Summarize the effects of the Great Depression and the New Deal on the following (a) women, (b) African Americans, (c) Native Americans, and (d) labor unions.

## GLOSSARY OF KEY TERMS: CHAPTER 11

**Agricultural Adjustment Act**   a New Deal law of 1933 that encouraged farmers to reduce their production in order to raise farm prices; the law was declared unconstitutional in 1936.

**"Bonus Army"**   veterans of World War I who marched on Washington, D.C., in 1932 to persuade the government to make early payment of a veterans' bonus.

**bootleggers**   those who made a business in the 1920s of illegally selling liquors, wines, and beers.

**bull market**   a steady upward trend in the prices of corporate stocks.

**Congress of Industrial Organizations (C.I.O.)**   an association of industrial unions organized in the 1930s.

**debt moratorium**   the decision by President Hoover in 1931 to permit European nations not to pay their war debts while the Great Depression lasted.

**depression**   a severe economic decline marked by business failures, unemployment, and low prices.

**flappers**   young women of the 1920s who adopted an original style of dress and challenged traditional values.

**Great Crash**   the sudden and extreme decline in the price of stocks during the last week of October, 1929.

**Harlem Renaissance**   the national recognition in the 1920s of talented African-American artists, writers, and musicians who lived in the Harlem neighborhood of New York City.

**Hawley-Smoot Tariff**   a tariff law of 1930 that raised tariff rates on foreign imports and damaged the international economy.

**"Hundred Days"**   the first three months of Franklin Roosevelt's presidency during which Congress enacted many laws for fighting the Great Depression.

**industrial unions**   labor unions whose membership is open to all workers in an industry—unskilled workers as well as skilled workers.

**margin**   the practice of buying stocks for only a percentage of the market price and borrowing the rest.

**National Recovery Administration (NRA)**   a New Deal agency created in 1933 (declared unconstitutional in 1935) that established a set of rules, or codes, for doing business in different industries.

**New Deal**   the government programs begun under President Franklin Roosevelt to fight the Great Depression and achieve reform.

**"normalcy"**   Warren Harding's term for the state of affairs existing before World War I and the Progressive Era.

**"pack" the Court**   the phrase used by Franklin Roosevelt's critics to characterize his attempt to increase the number of justices on the Supreme Court.

**productivity**   the amount of economic goods or services that workers can produce in a given time.

**Prohibition**   the period in U.S. history (1920 to 1933) when the Eighteenth Amendment prohibited the manufacture and sale of alcoholic beverages.

**quota laws**   immigration laws of the 1920s that placed upper limits, or quotas, on the number of immigrants from a given country who would yearly be admitted to the United States.

**relief, recovery, and reform**   the three goals of Franklin Roosevelt's New Deal.

**"rugged individualism"**   Herbert Hoover's philosophy of stressing the importance of decisions made by private businesses for bringing about recovery.

**Sacco-Vanzetti case**   the controversial trial and execution of two Italian immigrants in the 1920s.

**Scopes trial**   a trial of 1925 involving a Tennessee law against the teaching of Charles Darwin's theory of evolution in the public schools.

**sit-down strike**   a labor union's method of occupying a factory for a long time in order to win concessions from management.

**Social Security system**   the system enacted in 1935 by which workers would be insured against the loss of income from retirement, injury, or unemployment; also, a system for providing welfare payments to disabled persons and children of the poor.

**Teapot Dome scandal**   a political scandal of the 1920s involving a cabinet member in Warren Harding's administration.

**Tennessee Valley Authority (TVA)**   a federal agency created in 1933 to provide electric power and flood control for people living in the valley of the Tennessee River.

**two-term tradition**   the custom of all presidents before Franklin Roosevelt of retiring from office after serving a maximum of two terms.

**Wagner Act**   a federal law of 1935 that guaranteed workers' right to join unions of their choice.

# TEST YOURSELF

## A. Multiple Choice: Facts, Main Ideas, Skills

*On a separate sheet of paper, write the number of the word or expression that, of those given, best completes the statement or answers the question.*

### Reviewing the facts

1. President Calvin Coolidge once said, "The business of America is business." This slogan is most closely related to (1) a laissez-faire

attitude toward the economy  (2) government ownership of heavy industry  (3) the elimination of protective tariffs  (4) legislation benefiting organized labor

**2.** A major weakness in the prosperity of the 1920s was that it was  (1) confined to the industrial states of the Northeast  (2) accompanied by runaway inflation  (3) based on large federal expenditures  (4) unevenly distributed through the population

**3.** Which contributed to the worldwide depression of the 1930s?  (1) loss of colonial markets due to colonial independence movements  (2) inability of the industrial nations to produce enough consumer goods  (3) decline in world trade caused by the imposition of high tariffs  (4) failure of Germany to pay reparations to the United States

**4.** An important cause of the Great Depression was that by the end of the 1920s  (1) the government controlled almost every aspect of the economy  (2) tariffs were so low that foreign products had forced many U.S. companies out of business  (3) investors were too cautious and put their money into government bonds  (4) factories and farms were able to produce far more goods than buyers could afford to purchase

**5.** The farm policy of the New Deal was designed to  (1) decrease federal involvement in agriculture  (2) reduce prices of farm products to aid factory workers  (3) enlarge farms by approving corporate mergers  (4) increase prices of farm products by reducing farm output

**6.** One purpose of the Social Security Act was to provide  (1) on-the-job training for unemployed workers  (2) aid to farmers  (3) income for retired workers  (4) funds to fight crime

**7.** The creation of the Tennessee Valley Authority is an example of  (1) federal intervention to meet regional needs  (2) experimentation with nuclear technology  (3) government's attempts to earn maximum profits in business  (4) a return to laissez-faire economics

**8.** During Franklin Roosevelt's first two terms, the strongest opposition to New Deal policies came from  (1) big business  (2) labor union members  (3) the poor  (4) African Americans

**9.** During the 1930s Congress defeated President Roosevelt's attempt to  (1) regulate stock market listings  (2) boost farm prices  (3) enlarge the membership of the Supreme Court  (4) establish a system of old-age insurance

**10.** Which statement best describes the labor movement during the 1930s?  (1) It grew rapidly once the right to organize was protected by law.  (2) Only organizations of skilled craft unions survived the Great Depression.  (3) Unions almost disappeared as a result of the Great Depression.  (4) Unions joined together to promote a socialist solution to the Great Depression.

*Reviewing the main ideas*

**11.** Which decade is best described by the phrases "return to normalcy" and "false prosperity ending in economic collapse"? (1) the 1890s (2) the 1920s (3) the 1930s (4) the 1940s

**12.** Which of these was most responsible for giving the 1920s the name Roaring Twenties? (1) technological improvements (2) social change (3) political reform (4) territorial expansion

**13.** Both Prohibition and the Scopes trial are evidence that during the 1920s (1) the reform spirit of the Progressive movement was as strong as ever (2) relations between blacks and whites began to improve (3) there was a conflict between old and new American ideals (4) the country was more receptive to socialist ideals

**14.** "The nation became urbanized, a process to which the automobile especially, as well as the radio, the moving picture, and the newspaper, contributed." Which is the first period in U.S. history to which this statement might have been applied? (1) 1890 to 1900 (2) 1901 to 1910 (3) 1920 to 1928 (4) 1933 to 1939

**15.** Which statement best summarizes President Franklin Roosevelt's approach to the Great Depression? (1) Provide government aid to many sectors of the economy at once. (2) Balance the federal budget. (3) Cut government spending to reflect lowered revenues. (4) Let the Federal Reserve system handle the recovery through monetary policies.

*The discussion below refers to the 1930s and the New Deal. Base your answers to questions 16 and 17 on this discussion and on your knowledge of U.S. history and government.*

*Speaker A:* "Our nation's economy has been ruined by costly government programs that destroy freedom of enterprise and individual initiative."

*Speaker B:* "I strongly disagree. Our economy will be helped by public works projects, unemployment insurance systems, and old-age retirement insurance. The New Deal is a peaceful and much needed revolution."

*Speaker C:* "We have had no revolution. We are simply witnessing the evolution of an idea that began in the days of Populism and Progressivism."

*Speaker D:* "We need not concern ourselves with whether these changes are revolutionary or evolutionary. The important thing is to conserve our resources and to do so through the democratic process."

**16.** The idea referred to by Speaker C is (1) a regulatory role for the government (2) the free and unlimited coinage of silver (3) civil rights for minorities (4) an income tax amendment

**17.** Which laws or events illustrate the positions taken by Speakers B and D? (1) National Industrial Recovery Act and the defeat of court packing (2) Eighteenth Amendment and Sacco-Vanzetti case (3) Social Security Act and Tennessee Valley Authority (4) Scopes trial and quota laws

**18.** A major result of Franklin Roosevelt's New Deal policy was that it (1) weakened the power of the chief executive (2) strengthened the policy of laissez-faire (3) increased the federal government's regulation of business (4) expanded the importance of states' rights

**19.** What was one lasting effect of the Great Depression on the United States? (1) Many programs from the 1930s still exist. (2) Big businesses never regained their former power. (3) Women attained equal economic rights. (4) Ever since the 1930s, the Republican party has dominated the presidency and Congress.

## Developing critical thinking skills

*Base your answers to questions 20 and 21 on the cartoon below and on your knowledge of U.S. history and government.*

"The Spirit of '37"

**20.** What point of view is expressed by the cartoon? (1) The New Deal was a military as well as a political force. (2) Congress accepted most of President Franklin Roosevelt's plans for dealing with the Great Depression. (3) President Roosevelt strictly followed the concept of checks and balances. (4) The judicial branch of the 1930s was controlled by the executive branch.

**21.** President Franklin Roosevelt's unhappiness with the situation described in the cartoon led him to (1) attempt to increase the number of U.S. Supreme Court justices (2) abandon many of his New Deal reforms (3) refuse to accept his party's nomination for a third term (4) turn over the responsibility for economic recovery to the states

## B. Enduring Issues

*Select* two *of the enduring issues from column A. For each issue chosen, explain how the historical example in column B relates to the issue.*

| A. Enduring Issues | B. Historical Examples |
|---|---|
| 1. Property rights and economic policy | The laissez-faire policy of the government in the 1920s encouraged business consolidations. |
| 2. National power—limits and potential | The Tennessee Valley Authority promoted the development of an entire region. |
| 3. The judiciary—interpreter of the Constitution or shaper of policy | The Supreme Court declared unconstitutional two New Deal laws created in 1933. |
| 4. Rights of the accused | Prejudice may have affected the verdict in the case of Sacco and Vanzetti. |
| 5. Separation of powers and the capacity to govern | Roosevelt attempted to "pack" the Supreme Court. |

## C. Essays

*Level 1*

Listed below are three goals of the New Deal. Select *one* goal to analyze.

Relief of human suffering
Recovery of the economy
Reform of business, labor, and society

**1.** Describe an action of the federal government in the 1930s to achieve the goal.

**2.** Discuss the extent to which the action was either successful or unsuccessful.

*Level 2*

At different times in its history, the United States has experienced serious economic problems. One such time was the 1930s.

**A.** List *two* specific economic problems that the United States faced at this time.

**B.** Base your answer to part B on your answer to part A. Write an essay explaining how the New Deal tried to deal with these problems.

# UNIT FIVE

# Foreign Policy in an Age of Global Crisis

*During the 30 years* described in this unit (1933 to 1963), U.S. foreign policy was turned upside down. At first the American people wanted to avoid foreign problems and foreign wars. But they discovered that a major power like the United States could not stay out of World War II. After fighting to victory in this war, Americans found that their nation had huge responsibilities for maintaining the peace and opposing the spread of communism. Three presidents (Harry Truman, Dwight Eisenhower, and John Kennedy) agreed that the United States was involved everywhere in the world in a fierce competition with the Soviet Union—a competition called the cold war.

| Chapter | Topics |
|---------|--------|
| 12. Peace in Peril: World War II | ● How acts of aggression by Germany and Japan threatened world peace |
| | ● The causes and consequences of U.S. involvement in World War II |
| 13. Peace with Problems: Beginnings of the Cold War | ● How nations of Asia and Eastern Europe came under Communist influence and control after World War II |
| | ● The policies adopted by U.S. presidents to oppose communism |
| | ● Chief trouble spots in the cold war: Berlin, Korea, China, and Cuba |

# Chapter *12*

# Peace in Peril: World War II

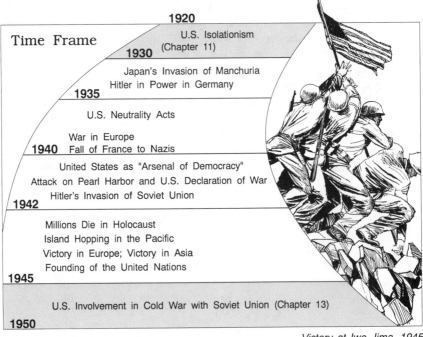

| Time Frame | **1920** | |
|---|---|---|
| | U.S. Isolationism (Chapter 11) | |
| | **1930** | |
| | Japan's Invasion of Manchuria | |
| | Hitler in Power in Germany | |
| | **1935** | |
| | U.S. Neutrality Acts | |
| | War in Europe | |
| | **1940** Fall of France to Nazis | |
| | United States as "Arsenal of Democracy" | |
| | Attack on Pearl Harbor and U.S. Declaration of War | |
| | Hitler's Invasion of Soviet Union | |
| | **1942** | |
| | Millions Die in Holocaust | |
| | Island Hopping in the Pacific | |
| | Victory in Europe; Victory in Asia | |
| | Founding of the United Nations | |
| | **1945** | |
| | U.S. Involvement in Cold War with Soviet Union (Chapter 13) | |
| | **1950** | |

*Victory at Iwo Jima, 1945*

*Objectives*

- To review the origins of U.S. isolationism and assess its impact on U.S. foreign policy in the 1930s.
- To recognize how military aggression posed increasing threats to U.S. security before 1941.
- To examine the impact of World War II on various groups.
- To summarize the military history of U.S. participation in World War II.
- To compare U.S. involvement in the United Nations after World War II with U.S. rejection of the League of Nations after World War I.

Through the 1930s the American people were absorbed by issues close to home: how to cope with the Great Depression and what to think of the New Deal. At the same time they were aware of events taking place in Europe and Asia that could lead to another war similar to the "Great War" of 1914 to 1918. In fact, war did erupt when Japan invaded China in 1937 and Germany invaded Poland in 1939. The German invasion of Poland touched off a second world war even more destructive than the first. Once again, the United States entered the war only after one of the warring nations, Japan, forced it to do so.

This chapter will examine why the United States hesitated to become involved in World War II and why, after becoming involved, it did not return to the isolationist policy of the past.

# I. The Isolationist Tradition in U.S. Foreign Policy

Recall from Chapter 10 that the United States did not expect to get involved in the "Great War" when it broke out in 1914. Until that time the traditional U.S. policy toward Europe had been one of isolationism (or noninvolvement) and neutrality (not taking sides in a foreign war).

Let us review briefly the origins and development of this policy from George Washington's presidency to Woodrow Wilson's decision for war.

## A. NEUTRALITY UNDER WASHINGTON

Washington was the first president to adopt a policy of neutrality toward warring European nations.

**Proclamation of Neutrality (1793)**  Shortly after a revolution toppled the French monarchy, France was attacked by its neighbors, who wanted to restore the monarchy to France. Many Americans wanted their country to aid the French in return for the support France had given to the American Revolution. Instead, President Washington issued a Proclamation of Neutrality in 1793. He stated that the United States would "pursue a conduct friendly and impartial toward the belligerent [warring] powers." In other words, the United States would be strictly neutral.

**Washington's Farewell Address (1796)**  Toward the end of his presidency, Washington reaffirmed his commitment to neutrality. His Farewell Address to the American people urged the United States to "steer clear of permanent alliances with any portion of the foreign world."

# B. ISOLATIONISM AND THE MONROE DOCTRINE

The fifth president, James Monroe, gave new meaning to a policy of noninvolvement in European affairs. His Monroe Doctrine warned European powers not to interfere with and not to attempt to colonize the newly independent countries of Latin America. (Review Chapter 3.) If Europeans did not interfere in the politics of the Western Hemisphere, Monroe pledged that the United States would not interfere in European politics.

For more than 100 years, makers of U.S. foreign policy gave both the Monroe Doctrine and Washington's Farewell Address as prime reasons for staying out of European alliances and wars. They also argued that the Atlantic and Pacific Oceans formed a natural protection against attack. Those who favored a policy of noninvolvement in world affairs were known as isolationists.

# C. EARLY OPPONENTS OF ISOLATIONISM

Industrialization and rapid economic growth dramatically changed the U.S. position in the world. As a result, by 1900, some Americans began to challenge the isolationist policies of the past.

**Imperialists**  A major result of the Spanish-American War (1898) was that the United States suddenly had overseas territories to govern—the Philippines in the Pacific and Puerto Rico in the Caribbean. The U.S. empire in the Pacific also included Hawaii, Samoa, and Guam. Those who approved the planting of the U.S. flag on overseas islands were known as imperialists. Chief among them was President Theodore Roosevelt.

**Internationalists**  In the first two decades of a new century (1900 to 1920), an influential group of newspaper editors and policymakers began to argue that U.S. involvement in world affairs was inevitable. Therefore, they said, the isolationist policies of the past should be abandoned as unrealistic. These critics of isolationism were known as **internationalists,** because they wanted the United States to take an active role in international affairs.

## D. WORLD WAR I AND THE POSTWAR REACTION

The outbreak of World War I plunged U.S. policymakers into a crisis. In just six years, 1914 to 1920, U.S. policy went from isolationism (avoidance of war) to internationalism (Wilson in Paris leading a peace conference) and back to isolationism (U.S. rejection of the League of Nations).

**From Neutrality to War**   In 1914 when war in Europe began, recall that Woodrow Wilson's first move was to proclaim U.S. neutrality. Only after German submarines attacked American shipping did he reluctantly ask Congress for a declaration of war. Wilson became a full-fledged internationalist after the war when he dedicated all his energies to winning public approval of the League of Nations.

**From War to Isolationism**   But after the U.S. Senate voted against the League and the Treaty of Versailles in 1920, most Americans grew tired of international politics. They even became disillusioned with the results of the war. In the 1920s public opinion generally favored a return to the traditional U.S. policy of isolationism. Presidents during the 1920s (Harding, Coolidge, and Hoover) were content to follow the isolationist mood of the country.

# II. Acts of Aggression in the 1930s

The 1930s was a time of depression at home and aggression abroad. Though Germany and Japan posed threats to world peace, Americans were determined to remain neutral and uninvolved. By 1941, however, the hope for U.S. neutrality collapsed with the Japanese attack on a U.S. naval base at Pearl Harbor in Hawaii. Young Americans once again put on uniforms and crowded into army transport ships to fight overseas. What caused this second turnabout from isolationism to involvement?

## A. THE RISE OF DICTATORSHIPS

Threats to the peace of Europe and the world came from three sources at once: the rise of a Fascist dictatorship in Italy, the rise of a Nazi dictatorship in Germany, and the rise of a military dictatorship in Japan.

**Fascists in Italy**   The type of government called **fascism** is one that glorifies war, preaches an extreme form of nationalism, and follows the commands of an all-powerful dictator. In Italy a party of Fascists led by Benito Mussolini seized power in 1922. Anyone who criticized Mussolini's regime risked severe punishment. Mussolini adopted a policy of military expansion. He ordered his army to bring glory to the Fascist cause by winning conquests in Africa. The African kingdom of Ethiopia, long an independent nation, made a valiant effort at resistance but fell to the Italian invader in 1936.

**Nazis in Germany**   After its defeat in World War I, Germany was faced with economic ruin, runaway inflation, and severe unemployment. As the Germans well knew, their country's economic plight stemmed largely from the penalties imposed upon it by the Treaty of Versailles. This treaty forced Germany to pay a crushing sum of money in reparations and also to surrender to France the coal mines of the Saar Valley. The treaty not only crippled Germany's economy but also wounded its national pride by forcing it to accept complete responsibility for causing World War I.

Hitler (left) and Nazi troops in Berlin

Many embittered Germans found an outlet for their hatred in the emotional speeches of Adolf Hitler, who led a Fascist-style party called the **Nazi party.** Hitler turned the rage and frustration of the German masses against a minority group, the Jews. In 1933 Hitler became chancellor (or prime minister) of Germany's government and then seized absolute power as the Nazi leader and dictator.

**German Aggression**   Hitler violated the terms of the Treaty of Versailles by ordering German troops into a neutral, demilitarized territory, the Rhineland (1936). Two years later, Hitler sent German troops into Austria and then announced his intention of seizing a territory in Czechoslovakia known as the Sudetenland.

**Militarists in Japan**   In Asia there were similar acts of **aggression** throughout the 1930s. The chief victim was China. The aggressor was Japan. A group of Japanese military leaders had come to dominate their country's government. Their nationalist beliefs and strong-arm methods resembled those of the Fascists of Europe. They wanted Japan to be the supreme power in East Asia. In line with this goal, Japanese troops marched into Manchuria in 1931 and then invaded China's heartland in 1937.

**Civil War in Spain (1936 to 1939)**   Also troubling to the democracies of the world was a vicious civil war in Spain. Beginning in 1936 Fascist forces attempted to overthrow Spain's republican government. Defenders of the government received military aid from the Soviet Union, while the Fascists received aid from Hitler's Germany and Mussolini's Italy. In 1939 Spain fell to fascism.

# B. THE BRITISH AND FRENCH RESPONSE

While Italy, Germany, and Japan followed a policy of military aggression, Great Britain and France followed a policy of appeasement.

**Appeasement at Munich**   **Appeasement** is the policy of yielding to the demands of a rival power in order to avoid armed conflict. British and French leaders applied this policy at the Munich Conference in 1938 by giving in to Hitler's demand to annex the Sudetenland. The Sudetenland was a region in northern Czechoslovakia where there was a large German-speaking population. In appeasing Hitler, the British and French hoped they could trust his assurance that he wanted only the Sudetenland and nothing more.

**Failure of Appeasement**   But only a few months after Munich, German troops occupied all of Czechoslovakia and then threatened Poland. By 1939 it was all too clear that appeasement had failed to

The global context: Nazi aggression in Europe, 1936 to 1939

stop Hitler and that the only way to stop him in the future would be through the use of armed force.

## C. THE U.S. RESPONSE

The American people were alarmed by news of the breakdown of peace in both Europe and Asia. Through the 1930s the majority wanted their country to remain neutral in order to avoid involvement in another world war.

**Neutrality Acts (1935 to 1937)**   Members of Congress were well aware of isolationist feelings in the country. Between 1935 and 1937 Congress enacted several laws whose purpose was to assure U.S. neutrality in the event of war. These **Neutrality Acts** provided for the following:

- No sale or shipment of arms to **belligerent nations** (nations involved in war)
- No loans or credits to belligerent nations
- No traveling by U.S. citizens on the ships of belligerent nations
- Nonmilitary goods purchased by belligerent nations to be paid for in cash and transported in their own ships.

This last provision was known as the **cash-and-carry principle.**

**Franklin Roosevelt's "Quarantine" Speech (1937)**  By 1937 President Roosevelt was growing more and more concerned about the aggressive acts of Japan, Germany, and Italy, and the Fascist threat in Spain. He was of course fully aware of the alarming series of events from 1931 to 1937:

- 1931: Japan invades Manchuria.
- 1935: Italy invades Ethiopia.
- 1936: Germany occupies the Rhineland.
- 1937: Japan invades China.

Responding to the Japanese invasion, Roosevelt gave a speech, known as the "**Quarantine**" **Speech**, in which he proposed that democratic nations join together to "quarantine" aggressor nations. The purpose of such a policy, he explained, would be "to protect the health of the [international] community against the spread of disease."

Isolationists were quick to criticize Roosevelt's "Quarantine" Speech. They warned that the president's proposed policy might lead to American involvement in war. Public opinion polls showed that most Americans agreed with the isolationists, not with the president. The largely negative reaction to Roosevelt's speech restrained the president from giving active assistance to the democracies of Europe. (In making foreign policy, even the strongest presidents hesitate to oppose the forces of public opinion.)

## In Review

The following questions refer to section I: The Isolationist Tradition in U.S. Foreign Policy and section II: Acts of Aggression in the 1930s.

1. Identify and define *isolationism, Washington's Farewell Address, fascism, appeasement,* and *Neutrality Acts.*
2. For each nation, give one example of an aggressive act committed in the 1930s by (a) Germany, (b) Italy, and (c) Japan.
3. "In 1937 the American nation strongly supported a policy of isolationism." Give two facts that could be used to support this statement.

# III. The Outbreak of World War II

Germany invaded Poland in September, 1939. This time, instead of continuing to appease Hitler, Great Britain and France both declared war against Germany.

## A. WAR IN EUROPE: EARLY GERMAN VICTORIES

During the first two years of World War II (1939 to 1941), the democracies (Great Britain, France, and their allies) suffered a series of crushing defeats. Slamming across the Polish border, wave after wave of German tanks and planes forced Poland to surrender within only 30 days. So rapid and overwhelming was the German method of attack that it was called **blitzkrieg,** which in German means lightning war. Next, German armies swept over Denmark and Norway. France managed only a brief resistance before it too fell to the Nazi invader in June, 1940.

Just before the war, in 1939, the Soviet leader Joseph Stalin had signed a **nonaggression pact** with Hitler. The two dictators had pledged that, if war broke out, their countries would not attack each other. Thus, when war did break out, the Soviet Union was neither a friend nor a foe of Germany.

With France beaten and the Soviet Union pledged to remain uninvolved, Great Britain in 1940 was the only nation with a chance of stopping Germany and its ally Italy from conquering all of Europe. Hitler planned to invade England in mid-September, 1940. To weaken his enemy beforehand, he ordered thousands of German planes to bomb London and other British cities. Nightly, the wailing of British air raid sirens warned civilians of German attacks. Fortunately, the British air force shot down enough German planes to cause Hitler to call off the invasion. Even so, Great Britain struggled alone for months as the last foe of Nazism to resist conquest.

## B. WAR IN ASIA: EARLY JAPANESE VICTORIES

As the Germans gobbled up huge pieces of Europe, the Japanese also made rapid gains in Asia. By 1941 much of northern China was under Japanese occupation. Naval and air assaults by Japan quickly brought the islands of Indonesia under its control. After France fell to Germany, the French colony of Indochina (present-day Vietnam, Laos, and Cambodia) fell to Japan. Early in 1942 the British colony of Singapore also fell to the invader.

## C. END OF U.S. NEUTRALITY

The outbreak of war and the success of the German and Japanese drives caused a sharp turnaround in U.S. public opinion. There was now much greater willingness to assist a democratic Great Britain in its battle against the dictators. Most Americans understood that German and Japanese victories in Europe and Asia would threaten U.S. security.

**Change in the Neutrality Laws (1939)**  In order to assist Great Britain after the German invasion of Poland, President Roosevelt moved quickly to change the earlier Neutrality Acts. According to the original law, only nonmilitary goods could be shipped to belligerent nations on a cash-and-carry basis. Military goods (weapons and ammunition) could not be sold to belligerent nations at all. Wanting to aid the democracies of Europe, Roosevelt persuaded Congress to pass a new Neutrality Act in 1939. It provided that U.S.-made war supplies could be sold to belligerents if they were paid for in cash and carried on the purchaser's own ships.

**Destroyer-Bases Agreement (1940)**  To help the British defend themselves against crippling submarine attacks, President Roosevelt agreed to transfer to Britain 50 U.S. destroyers (ships for use against submarines). In exchange the United States was given eight British naval and air bases extending from Newfoundland in Canada to a British colony in South America (British Guiana).

**Lend-Lease Act (1941)**  Under the pressure of daily German attacks, the British needed more war supplies than could be obtained by the cash-and-carry program. Recognizing this fact, Roosevelt persuaded Congress to authorize the lending, or leasing, of war supplies to Great Britain. He argued that the United States should act as the **"arsenal of democracy."** The passage of the **Lend-Lease Act** meant that the former policy of neutrality was now abandoned. Although the United States was not yet at war, it was committing much of its economic resources to help Great Britain fight off the German assault.

**Atlantic Charter (1941)**  On a battleship anchored off the coast of Newfoundland (Canada), President Roosevelt met with the British prime minister, Winston Churchill. Together they formulated a statement of common war aims known as the **Atlantic Charter.** These aims included:

- recognition of the right of all nations to self-determination (the right of a people to choose their own government)
- U.S.-British understanding that neither power would seek to gain territory from the war
- the disarmament (removal of weapons) of aggressor nations
- a "permanent system of general security" in the future.

## U.S. Response to European and Asian Wars, 1793 to 1941

| World Event | U.S. Response | Date |
|---|---|---|
| British-French war following French Revolution | Proclamation of Neutrality Washington's Farewell Address | 1793 1796 |
| Latin American republics win independence from Spain | Monroe Doctrine | 1823 |
| Cuban revolt against Spanish rule | Spanish-American War | 1898 |
| Beginning of World War I | Proclamation of U.S. neutrality | 1914 |
| German violations of U.S. neutral rights | U.S. declaration of war against Germany | 1917 |
| End of World War I | Rejection of the Treaty of Versailles by U.S. Senate | 1919 to 1920 |
| Rise of Fascist governments in Europe | Neutrality Acts | 1935 to 1937 |
| Spanish Civil War | No involvement or aid to either side in the conflict | 1936 to 1939 |
| Japanese invasion of China | Franklin Roosevelt's "Quarantine" Speech | 1937 |
| Beginning of World War II | Neutrality Acts amended to permit cash-and-carry purchase of war goods Destroyer-Bases Agreement Lend-Lease Act Atlantic Charter | 1939 1940 1941 1941 |
| Japan's continued aggression in Asia | U.S. embargo on oil and steel to Japan Freezing of Japanese assets | 1940 to 1941 1941 |
| Japan's surprise attack on U.S. naval base at Pearl Harbor | U.S. declaration of war against Japan | 1941 |

# D. JAPANESE ATTACK ON PEARL HARBOR

In 1941 the United States was committed to British defense. But it did not officially enter the war until a Japanese attack on a U.S. naval base in Hawaii gave it no choice.

**Causes of the Attack**  The attack came as a result of a fundamental conflict between the goals of Japan and the United States. Throughout the 1930s the makers of U.S. foreign policy had been alarmed by Japan's acts of aggression in China. They viewed such acts as violations of the U.S. Open Door policy. To limit Japan's capacity for making war, the United States in 1940 placed an embargo (stoppage of trade) on a list of U.S. exports that Japan needed to maintain its war machine. Under the embargo Japan could no longer purchase U.S. oil, aviation gasoline, scrap iron, and steel. Next, President Roosevelt froze all

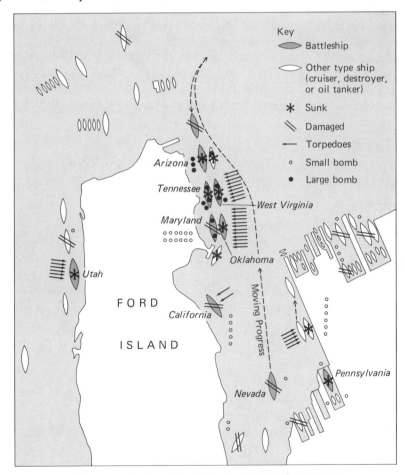

Japanese attack on Pearl Harbor, December 7, 1941

Japanese assets in U.S. banks. In other words Japan could no longer use these bank deposits for purchasing U.S. goods.

In 1941 Japanese military leaders believed that the United States might soon enter the war to oppose Japan's planned invasion of Indonesia. Therefore, the fateful decision was made to launch a surprise attack on the U.S. fleet in the Pacific. If the attack succeeded in destroying the fleet, Japan's generals hoped that the U.S. Navy might take a long time recovering from the blow—too long to stop Japan from winning all its war aims.

**Consequences of the Attack**  Early on a Sunday morning, December 7, 1941, hundreds of Japanese planes strafed and bombed a fleet of ships docked at the U.S. naval base at Pearl Harbor, Hawaii. In addition to eight battleships and 11 other ships that were either sunk or disabled, about 150 U.S. planes were destroyed and 2,335 soldiers and sailors were killed.

The next day, President Roosevelt asked Congress for a declaration of war against Japan. December 7, he said, was "a date which will live in infamy." Congress voted overwhelmingly for war. Then Japan's allies in Europe—Germany and Italy—declared war on the United States. Now that U.S. territory had been attacked, the American people put aside their isolationist feelings of the past and rallied to the war effort.

## In Review

The following questions refer to section III: The Outbreak of World War II and also to preceding chapters (9 and 10) on U.S. foreign policy.

**Word Wheels**

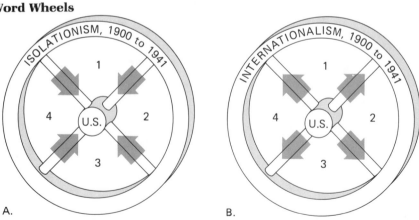

A.                                                              B.

1. For each word wheel, list four decisions by U.S. presidents that illustrate the policy shown.
2. Describe the causes that led the United States to change its policy from isolationism in 1939 to involvement in 1940 and 1941.

# DOCUMENTS: A FIRESIDE CHAT BY
# PRESIDENT ROOSEVELT, 1941

*Two days after the Pearl Harbor attack, President Roosevelt spoke to the American people over the radio. The following are excerpts from his "fireside chat" of December 9, 1941.*

*What lesson did Roosevelt think the American people had learned about the nation's security? What does his statement suggest about U.S. foreign policy in the future?*

On the road ahead there lies hard work—grueling work—day and night, every hour and every minute. I was about to add that ahead there lies sacrifice for all of us. But it is not correct to use that word. The United States does not consider it a sacrifice to do all one can, to give one's best to our nation when the nation is fighting for its existence and its future life.

In these past few years—and, most violently, in the past few days—we have learned a terrible lesson. It is our obligation to our dead—it is our sacred obligation to their children and our children—that we must never forget what we have learned.

And what we all have learned is this: There is no such thing as security for any nation—or any individual—in a world ruled by the principles of gangsterism. There is no such thing as impregnable defense against powerful aggressors who sneak up in the dark and strike without warning. We have learned that our ocean-girt hemisphere is not immune from severe attack—that we cannot measure our safety in terms of miles on any map.

# IV. The United States in World War II

On June 22, 1941, several months before Pearl Harbor, Hitler broke his nonaggression pact with Stalin by launching a massive assault against the Soviet Union. Thus, as 1942 began, Hitler faced three formidable foes: the United States, the Soviet Union, and Great Britain. His days of easy victory were over.

## A. ALLIED VICTORY IN EUROPE

It took the Allies more than three years (1942 to 1945) to win back the territories conquered by German and Italian armies in the first two years of war. The single most important turning point was Hitler's decision to invade the Soviet Union—a decision that proved to be a fatal blunder.

**Turning the Tide: Stalingrad, North Africa, and Sicily**  After initial successes the German invaders in the Soviet Union suffered a crushing defeat at the Battle of Stalingrad (1942 to 1943). Meanwhile, in the North African desert, a British force under General Bernard Montgomery defeated the Germans in a tank battle at El Alamein. Soon after, in 1943, combined assaults by British and American armies forced the surrender of the German army in North Africa. From their African bases, the Allies invaded the Mediterranean island of Sicily and then began a long and bloody campaign to liberate Italy.

**D-Day and the Final Drive to Victory**  On June 6, 1944 (code name: **D-Day**) allied forces left England in a massive drive to liberate France. The invading force included 11,000 planes, 600 warships and 176,000

U.S. troops landing on Normandy beaches, June 6, 1944 (D-Day)

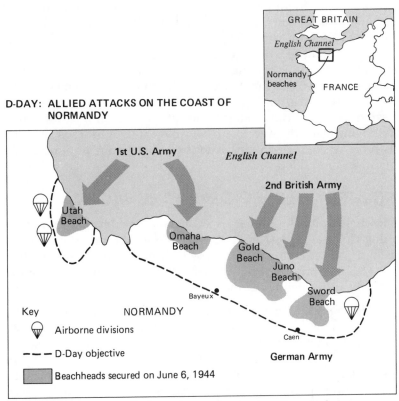

D-DAY: ALLIED ATTACKS ON THE COAST OF
NORMANDY

GREAT BRITAIN

*English Channel*

Normandy
beaches    FRANCE

1st U.S. Army        *English Channel*

2nd British Army

Utah
Beach

Omaha
Beach

Gold
Beach

Juno
Beach

Sword
Beach

Bayeux

Key                NORMANDY

Airborne divisions

— — — D-Day objective

Caen

German Army

Beachheads secured on June 6, 1944

D-Day: Allied attacks on the coast of Normandy

men. It was the largest amphibious (sea-to-land) assault in history. Crossing the English Channel, the assault force achieved its objective of securing beachheads on the coast of Normandy (northern France). From there Allied forces under General Dwight Eisenhower, the Supreme Allied Commander in Western Europe, fought for control of Normandy and then all of France. They liberated Paris in August and pushed eastward into Germany.

From the other direction Soviet troops also moved rapidly toward Berlin. In April, 1945, American and Soviet troops met for the first time on German territory near the Elbe River. Seeing that the end was near, Hitler committed suicide. Germany surrendered uncondi-tionally on May 7, 1945, ending the war in Europe.

**The Holocaust** As U.S. troops moved across Germany, they came upon concentration camps whose inmates were in a pitiful condition. They were mainly European Jews who had barely survived a policy of **genocide** (the extermination of an entire people) begun by Hitler in 1941. The survivors told horrifying stories of the Nazi practice of capturing Jews in all occupied countries of Europe and systematically either murdering them or working them to death in concentration camps. About six million Jews were killed in the **Holocaust** (systematic destruction of Jews by the Nazis).

Thousands of those who died in the Holocaust might have survived if the United States had changed its immigration policy. After Hitler had come to power in the 1930s and had begun to persecute the Jewish minority, many refugees from Nazi Germany hoped to gain admission to the United States. About 175,000 immigrants from German-controlled territory were accepted. But hundreds of thousands more were denied entry even though the immigrant quota for Germany was not filled.

## B. STRATEGY AND VICTORY IN THE PACIFIC

Following its attack on Pearl Harbor, Japan achieved a number of stunning victories and extended its power across much of Asia and the islands of the South Pacific. To win back territories lost in 1941 and 1942, including the Philippines, the U.S. armed forces had to fight a long and grueling campaign.

**"Island Hopping"**   In the Pacific, U.S. naval and military leaders developed a strategy known as **"island hopping."** In order to get within striking distance of Japan, American forces would concentrate on winning only the most strategically located islands, while leaving others under Japanese control. The fighting for each targeted island was fierce and bloody. Soldiers and marines rushed headlong toward enemy-held beaches under heavy fire, often without knowing the exact position of the enemy.

**Victories at Sea**   In the crucial contest between two strong navies, American ships and planes defeated Japanese forces in several major battles. A turning point in the war at sea was the U.S. victory at the Battle of Midway (1942), which probably saved Hawaii from enemy occupation.

**Atomic Bombs and Japanese Surrender**   In April, 1945, President Roosevelt died. His successor, Harry S Truman, had to decide what to do with a newly developed, immensely destructive weapon: the atomic bomb. At the time Truman and his military advisers were planning to invade the Japanese homeland in order to achieve final victory. They believed that such an invasion would result in the loss of hundreds of thousands of American soldiers.

If the president decided to use the new bomb, American lives might be saved. On the other hand, thousands of Japanese civilians would be condemned to death. Truman decided to use the bomb. He reasoned that the bomb's destructiveness might force Japan to surrender, and the planned U.S. invasion could then be canceled. On

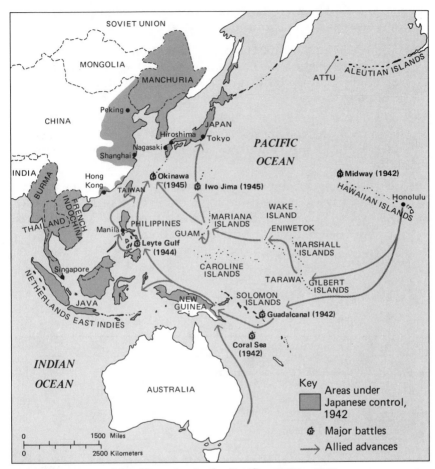

Island hopping in the Pacific, 1942 to 1945

August 6, 1945, a single U.S. plane dropped an atomic bomb on the city of Hiroshima. Three days later a second atomic bomb was dropped on the city of Nagasaki. The two explosions instantly killed more than 100,000 Japanese civilians. Many thousands of others died later from the effects of nuclear radiation.

As Truman hoped, the atomic bombs convinced Japan to surrender. General Douglas MacArthur presided over the ceremony of formal surrender aboard the U.S. battleship *Missouri* on September 2, 1945. Thus ended the most destructive war in history. (The total death toll for all nations: 17 million military deaths and probably more than twice that number in civilian deaths. The U.S. death toll: about 400,000.)

**Moral Question** Was the United States morally justified in dropping atomic bombs on Japan? Even to this day, the question continues to be raised and debated. These facts and possibilities should be considered when making your judgment:

- Although more than 100,000 people died from the atomic explosions, there might have been many times that number of dead (including Japanese civilians and soldiers) from the planned U.S. invasion of Japan.

- Instead of dropping atomic bombs on civilian targets, the United States could have demonstrated the new weapon's destructive power by dropping a bomb over the ocean close to the Japanese shore.

- After dropping a bomb on Hiroshima, the United States waited less than a week before dropping a bomb on Nagasaki. It could have waited longer to give Japan's government a chance to surrender before dropping the second bomb.

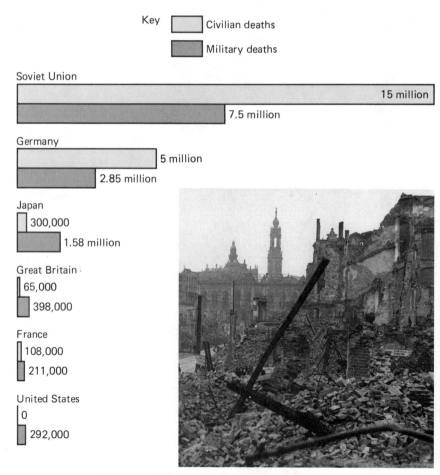

Key   □ Civilian deaths

■ Military deaths

Soviet Union

15 million

7.5 million

Germany

5 million

2.85 million

Japan

300,000

1.58 million

Great Britain

65,000

398,000

France

108,000

211,000

United States

0

292,000

**Military and civilian deaths in World War II**

# C. WARTIME CONFERENCES, 1943 TO 1945

During the last years of war, the leaders of the United States, Great Britain, and the Soviet Union arranged three meetings to discuss both military strategy and plans for dealing with the postwar world.

**Meetings at Teheran, Yalta, and Potsdam**   Franklin Roosevelt, Winston Churchill, and Joseph Stalin met at a "big three" conference at Teheran (Iran) in 1943. They met again at Yalta (Soviet Union) in 1945. After the death of Roosevelt (and soon afterward, the surrender of Germany), President Harry Truman represented the United States at a conference at Potsdam (Germany) in July, 1945.

At these different conferences, the "big three" agreed to a number of principles for treating a defeated Germany and a defeated Japan:

- Germany would be disarmed.
- Germany would be divided into four zones of occupation (British, American, French, and Soviet).
- "War criminals" in both Japan and Germany would be put on trial.
- Japan would be occupied chiefly by U.S. troops.
- Polish territory would be granted to the Soviet Union.

**Controversy over Yalta**   The agreement concerning Poland was made at Yalta. Critics of the agreement at the **Yalta Conference** accused Franklin Roosevelt of conceding too much to the Soviet Union and practically inviting the Soviets to occupy Poland and dominate Eastern Europe. Defenders of Roosevelt argued that the Soviet Union also made an important concession at Yalta. The Soviets agreed that, after the defeat of Germany, they would begin to wage war against Japan. Furthermore, Soviet troops were in Eastern Europe when the Yalta Conference took place. Roosevelt did not "give away" Eastern Europe to the Soviets; in effect, the region was already theirs.

# D. THE HOME FRONT

U.S. victory in World War II depended almost as much upon the work of civilians as upon the fighting of the armed forces. During nearly four years of U.S. participation in the war, all Americans had to adjust to the unusual demands of wartime.

**Impact of the War on Industry**   Allied hopes for victory depended largely on the speed with which U.S. factories could turn out war goods. Government officials encouraged companies in every industry to stop producing consumer goods and start producing bombs, bullets, and other military supplies. As the chief supplier of war materials, the United States acted as "the arsenal of democracy." The colossal buildup of U.S. arms production is revealed in the following pictogram.

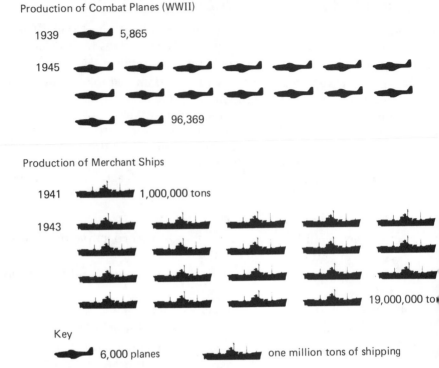

Production of Combat Planes (WWII)

1939 — 5,865

1945

96,369

Production of Merchant Ships

1941 — 1,000,000 tons

1943

19,000,000 tons

Key

6,000 planes      one million tons of shipping

"Arsenal of democracy": U.S. war production

**Impact of the Draft on Men**  Even before the United States entered the war, Congress enacted a selective service law, or draft, in September, 1940. Every man between the ages of 21 and 35 was required to register for possible induction into the armed forces. By 1945 a total of 12.5 million men and women were in uniform—approximately one out of three of the eligible group.

**Impact of the War on Women**  As young men were called into service, trained, and shipped overseas, women took up the slack in the work force. During wartime a great variety of jobs were open to women—jobs that had previously been reserved for men. The number of women in the U.S. labor force went from about 15 million in 1941 to about 19 million in 1945. A popular song of World War II, "Rosie the Riveter," celebrated the new status of women as key producers of ships, aircraft, and other war supplies.

American women also made contributions in the military by enlisting in support units (but not in combat units).

**Impact of the War on African Americans**  More than one million African Americans served in the U.S. armed forces during World War II. About half of them served overseas. Once again, their hopes for equal treatment were disappointed when they were placed in segregated units. On the home front, black civilians found employment in relatively high-paying jobs in defense plants in the North. The availability of such jobs greatly increased the migration of African Americans from Southern farms to Northern cities.

**Discrimination against Japanese Americans**   After Japan's attack on Pearl Harbor, many Americans treated citizens of Japanese descent with great suspicion and hostility. Thousands of Japanese Americans served loyally in the U.S. armed forces. Even so, their families suffered throughout the war from prejudice and discrimination. President Roosevelt yielded to the general prejudice by authorizing the removal of all Japanese Americans from their homes in California and other Western states. In 1942 the U.S. army seized 110,000 Japanese Americans and transported them to barracks within barbed-wire compounds called "relocation centers." Most were released before the war's end, but those suspected of disloyalty (about 18,000) were kept in a relocation center in California until Japan surrendered.

According to one historian, Arthur Link, the treatment of Japanese Americans in World War II was "the greatest single violation of civil rights in American history." But the Supreme Court did not see it that way. In a case decided in 1944, ***Korematsu v. United States,*** the Court determined that the removal of Japanese Americans was justified as a matter of military necessity. In recent years, however, many Japanese Americans who suffered loss and humiliation during World War II have received official apologies from the U.S. government as well as small sums of money to partly compensate for damages.

# V. Adjusting to Peace

Having fought in two horribly destructive world wars, the United States and its allies wanted to ensure that the future peace would be built on a firm foundation. Many people also wanted enemy leaders to be punished for the criminal slaughter of human life.

## A. WAR CRIME TRIALS IN GERMANY AND JAPAN

For nearly an entire year (from November 1945 to October 1946), a series of extremely unusual trials took place in Nuremberg, Germany. The defendants were former military and political leaders of the defeated Nazi government. They were accused of **"war crimes,"** especially the mass murders of Jews in Nazi concentration camps. Judges at the **Nuremberg trials** represented the victorious nations of World War II, including the United States. Of 24 defendants, 19 were convicted, and ten of these were executed. In addition, other military trials in Germany led to lesser punishments for some 500,000 former Nazis. Some Nazis who escaped capture were later found and brought to trial. For example, Adolph Eichmann was executed in Israel, and Klaus Barbie was imprisoned for life in France. The Nuremberg Tribunal established the precedent that national leaders could be held responsible for "crimes against humanity."

War crime trials were also held in Japan. More than 700 Japanese officers were executed for "war crimes," including the notorious leader of wartime Japan, Hideki Tojo.

## B. DEMOBILIZATION

In the United States, as soon as the war ended, the American public eagerly awaited the return of U.S. troops. **Demobilization** (cutting back the armed forces in peacetime) proceeded rapidly. In just two years, 1945 to 1947, as many as 11 million GI's (the World War II nickname for American soldiers) were released from service. To help the GI's adjust to civilian life, Congress had already enacted in 1944 a measure known as the **GI Bill of Rights.** Under this law, veterans were entitled to receive (1) free hospital care if they were sick or wounded, (2) grants and loans to pay for college, and (3) federally guaranteed loans for buying homes and investing in businesses.

## C. THE UNITED NATIONS AND THE END OF U.S. ISOLATIONISM

Hoping to build a more peaceful future, the United States and its allies sent representatives to a conference in San Francisco in April, 1945. Their purpose was to replace the League of Nations with a new peacekeeping organization. The **United Nations (UN),** as it was called, would be similar in purpose to the League (see chart). It would consist of representatives from different nations who would meet to settle disputes and stop acts of aggression like those that had led to World War II.

**The UN General Assembly and Security Council**  According to the UN Charter (the constitution of the United Nations), all member nations were entitled to vote in the UN General Assembly on almost any international issue. A smaller body, the UN Security Council, could call upon member nations to take military action in a crisis. But such a decision had to be approved by all five permanent members on the Security Council. The permanent members were the Soviet Union, Great Britain, France, China, and the United States. Six nonpermanent members of the Security Council—a number later increased to ten—would serve for two-year terms.

**Other UN Agencies**  Special UN agencies were established for various purposes. An Economic and Social Council would attempt to reduce hunger and improve health care in the poorer countries of the world. A Trusteeship Council would make decisions concerning the colonies given up by Germany and Japan. An International Court of Justice would decide legal questions referred to it by disputing nations.

**U.S. Membership in the United Nations**   In 1945, by a vote of 82 to 2, the U.S. Senate voted its approval of U.S. membership in the United Nations. In doing so, the United States signaled to the world that it would not again return to a policy of isolationism as in the past. As the world's most powerful nation—and also, briefly, the only nation with atomic weapons—the United States was now prepared to play a leading role in world affairs.

## In Review

The following questions refer to section IV: The United States in World War II and section V: Adjusting to Peace.

**1.** Identify and define *D-Day, the Holocaust, "island hopping," Yalta Conference*, Korematsu *v.* United States, *Nuremberg trials*, and *the United Nations*.

**2.** Discuss how U.S. entry into the war in 1941 contributed to Allied victory in both Europe and the Pacific.

**3.** Explain the significance of the Senate vote approving U.S. membership in the United Nations.

**Word Wheel**

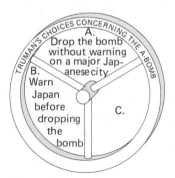

**4.** Identify a third alternative (C) for using (or not using) the atomic bomb in 1945. Give both an advantage or disadvantage for choosing alternative C.

## GLOSSARY OF KEY TERMS: CHAPTER 12

**aggression**   an unprovoked attack or warlike act by one nation against another.

**appeasement** the policy of giving in to the demands of a hostile or aggressive power in an attempt to avoid armed conflict.

**"arsenal of democracy"** Franklin Roosevelt's phrase for the U.S. role in World War II as a supplier of war materials to Great Britain.

**Atlantic Charter** a statement of common goals by Winston Churchill and Franklin Roosevelt following a meeting of the two leaders aboard a ship on the Atlantic Ocean in 1941.

**belligerent nations** nations at war.

**blitzkrieg** sudden, large-scale offensive warfare intended to win a quick victory.

**cash-and-carry principle** a U.S. policy in the 1930s of requiring a belligerent nation to pay for U.S. goods in cash and transport them in that nation's own ships.

**D-Day** U.S. code name for June 6, 1944, the day that Allied forces launched an invasion of the northern coast of France.

**demobilization** the disbanding of troops, usually after a war.

**fascism** a belief in a form of government characterized by a one-party dictatorship, militarism, and extreme nationalism.

**genocide** an attempt to kill all members of a certain nationality or ethnic group.

**GI Bill of Rights** a law of Congress (1944) granting a number of special benefits to veterans of World War II.

**Holocaust** the systematic killing of about six million Jews by the Nazi government of Germany.

**"island hopping"** a U.S. military strategy in World War II of attacking a selected number of islands in the Pacific in order to reach within striking distance of Japan.

**internationalists** those who believe in a U.S. policy of involvement in world politics.

***Korematsu* v. *United States*** a U.S. Supreme Court case of 1944 that upheld the authority of the U.S. government to confine Japanese Americans in relocation camps as a matter of national security in wartime.

**Lend-Lease Act** a law of Congress of 1941 authorizing the shipping of U.S. war supplies to Great Britain on credit.

**Nazi party** a German political party that its leader, Adolf Hitler, used to dominate Germany from 1933 to 1945.

**Neutrality Acts** a series of laws enacted by Congress in the 1930s to prevent the United States from becoming involved in a second world war.

**nonaggression pact** an agreement between two nations not to attack each other.

**Nuremberg trials** the postwar trial in Nuremberg, Germany, of Nazi leaders accused of "war crimes."

**"Quarantine" Speech**   a speech by President Franklin Roosevelt in 1937 in which he suggested that democratic governments act together to apply pressure on nations that commit acts of aggression.

**United Nations**   an international organization created in 1945 to settle conflicts between nations and to stop acts of aggression.

**"war crimes"**   acts of violence and brutality in wartime that violate international law and common standards of justice.

**Yalta Conference**   a meeting of the leaders of three Allied powers (the United States, the Soviet Union, and Great Britain), held in 1945 in Yalta, a city in the Soviet Union, in which the Soviet Union agreed to wage war against Japan, and the United States agreed to permit Soviet occupation of Polish territory.


# TEST YOURSELF

## A. Multiple Choice: Facts, Main Ideas, Skills

*On a separate sheet of paper, write the number of the word or expression that, of those given, best completes the statement or answers the question.*

### Reviewing the facts

1. The Neutrality Acts of 1935 to 1937 were designed to  (1) increase U.S. military preparedness for war  (2) prevent the United States from being drawn into wars  (3) make the United States the strongest naval power in the world  (4) encourage Great Britain to stand up to Nazi aggression

2. The policy most closely associated with the Munich Conference was (1) American isolationism  (2) Japanese imperialism  (3) British appeasement  (4) Italian fascism

3. The Neutrality Act of 1939 and the Lend-Lease Act of 1941 marked a change in policy from  (1) imperialism to isolationism  (2) isolationism to imperialism  (3) neutrality to involvement  (4) involvement to neutrality

4. Which policy decision was the *opposite* of the other?  (1) passage of the Neutrality Acts of 1935 to 1937—U.S. decision to join the United Nations  (2) embargo of the sale and shipment of U.S. oil to Japan—declaration of war against Japan  (3) British response to Germany's invasion of Poland—U.S. response to Japanese attack on Pearl Harbor  (4) Destroyer-Bases Agreement—Lend-Lease Act

5. Which cause is paired with the correct result?  (1) World War I ends—United Nations is formed  (2) Neutrality Acts are passed—Hitler comes to power in Germany  (3) U.S. embargo on the sale and shipment of oil and steel to Japan—Japan's attack on Pearl Harbor  (4) German troops occupy the Sudetenland—World War II ends

6. Truman's chief reason for dropping two atomic bombs on Japanese cities was to (1) test a new weapon under wartime conditions (2) bring World War II to a rapid end (3) retaliate for the bombing of Pearl Harbor (4) punish Japan for "war crimes"

7. World War II began in 1939 when Germany invaded (1) France (2) Great Britain (3) the Soviet Union (4) Poland

8. The policy of removing Japanese Americans from their homes during World War II was closely related to the problem of (1) a labor shortage during the war (2) racial prejudice (3) effects of the Great Depression (4) imperialism in Latin America

9. Franklin Roosevelt spoke of the United States as the "arsenal of democracy" when urging Congress to pass (1) the Neutrality Acts of 1935 to 1937 (2) the Neutrality Act of 1939 (3) the Selective Service Act of 1940 (4) the Lend-Lease Act of 1941

10. An immediate result of President Roosevelt's "Quarantine" Speech of 1937 was (1) isolationist criticism of the speech (2) the rapid decline of isolationist feeling in the United States (3) increased military aid to the democracies of Europe (4) Japan's decision to stop its invasion of China

## Reviewing the main ideas

11. Which of the following policies would be most consistent with President Washington's advice to "steer clear of permanent alliances with any portion of the foreign world"? (1) supporting a particular group or organization during a conflict with another nation (2) issuing a proclamation of U.S. neutrality in response to a foreign war (3) signing a mutual defense pact (4) providing weapons to emerging nations in Africa

12. U.S. foreign policy in the 1920s and 1930s was characterized by (1) appeasement of aggressor nations (2) imperialist pressures for overseas expansion (3) reliance upon the League of Nations (4) isolationism in world affairs

13. U.S. foreign policy between 1941 and 1945 could best be described as (1) isolationist (2) imperialistic (3) neutral (4) closely allied with European democracies

14. Which statement best describes the international situation in the mid-1930s? (1) Chinese aggression posed a threat to world peace. (2) Great Britain and France gave in to the demands of aggressor nations. (3) The League of Nations resolved a number of European conflicts. (4) The United States threatened to go to war with Japan.

15. Which was chiefly responsible for a U.S. policy of neutrality in the 1930s? (1) general economic prosperity of the period (2) disillusionment with World War I and its results (3) sympathy with Adolf Hitler's goals for Germany (4) President Franklin Roosevelt's lack of concern about foreign affairs

16. A nation that tries to avoid taking sides in a war is said to follow a

policy of (1) internationalism (2) imperialism (3) militarism (4) neutrality

17. Just before each of the two world wars, the politics of Europe was characterized by (1) increased concern for conflicts in Asia (2) defiance of the Monroe Doctrine (3) fear of German military power (4) acts of aggression by Great Britain and France

18. Between 1939 and 1941, U.S. foreign policy can best be described as (1) moving toward isolationism (2) moving from isolationism to involvement (3) moving toward imperialism in Latin America (4) moving away from imperialism in Asia

19. Which was a long-range cause of both World War I and World War II? (1) the weakness of Poland (2) Italy's demand for control of Eastern Europe (3) the assassination of a crown prince (4) German ambitions for greater military power

## Developing critical thinking skills

Base your answers to questions 20 and 21 on the cartoon below and on your knowledge of U.S. history and government.

The other road

**20.** The umbrella in this cartoon is a symbol of  (1) an act of war  (2) an unsuccessful policy  (3) resistance to Nazi Germany  (4) international cooperation

**21.** Which of the following statements is most clearly implied by the cartoon?  (1) World War II could have been prevented by further appeasement.  (2) Peaceful nations have usually been exploited.  (3) Appeasement has not prevented war.  (4) Human beings make progress despite war.

## B. Enduring Issues

Select two of the enduring issues from column A. For each issue chosen, explain how the historical example in column B relates to the issue.

| A. Enduring Issues | B. Historical Examples |
|---|---|
| 1. National power—limits and potential | Decision to drop atomic bombs on Japan |
| 2. Presidential power in wartime and in foreign affairs | The "big three" conferences at Teheran, Yalta, and Potsdam |
| 3. The rights of ethnic and racial groups under the Constitution | Treatment of Japanese Americans during World War II |

## C. Essays

### Level 1

U.S. presidents and Congress make foreign policy in response to specific circumstances. Examine this list of foreign policy actions:

> The Neutrality Acts of 1935 to 1937
> Roosevelt's "Quarantine" Speech of 1937
> Lend-Lease Act of 1941
> President Truman's decision to use the atomic bomb (1945)

**1.** Select three of the actions above. For each action chosen, describe the circumstances that led to it.

**2.** For one of the actions chosen in part 1, discuss whether or not you agree with it and explain.

### Level 2

Acts by other nations caused the United States to enter World War II.

**A.** List two actions by other nations that helped to bring about U.S. entry into World War II.

**B.** Base your answer to part B on your answer to part A. Write an essay explaining how actions by other nations caused the United States to enter World War II.

*Chapter* **13**

# Peace with Problems: The Beginnings of the Cold War, 1945 to 1963

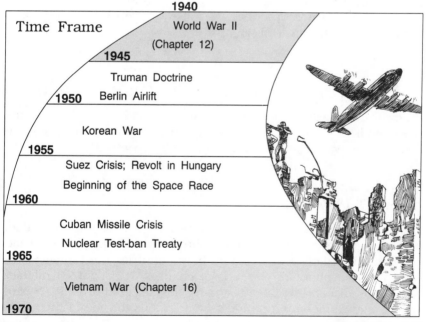

Time Frame

1940

World War II
(Chapter 12)

1945

Truman Doctrine

1950    Berlin Airlift

Korean War

1955

Suez Crisis; Revolt in Hungary

Beginning of the Space Race

1960

Cuban Missile Crisis

Nuclear Test-ban Treaty

1965

Vietnam War (Chapter 16)

1970

*Berlin Airlift, 1948*

*Objectives*

- To describe the global commitments of U.S. foreign policy after World War II.
- To explain the origins of the cold war rivalry between the United States and the Soviet Union.
- To compare U.S. policy toward Asia with U.S. policy toward Europe in the postwar period.
- To describe cold war conflicts in Eastern Europe, Berlin, Korea, Cuba, and other troubled areas of the 1940s and 1950s.

Out of the ashes of World War II arose a new and different world. One after another, new nations in Asia and Africa gained their independence from European control. With much of Europe in ruins, the world soon became dominated by two great powers, the United States and the Soviet Union. During the war these two nations had fought as allies against a common enemy, Germany. In the postwar period, however, cooperation between the superpowers would be replaced by distrust and hostility.

How did this change from wartime allies to postwar enemies come about? How did the conflict between the world's most powerful nations affect not only each other but also every other nation of the world? This chapter describes the postwar world and the rivalry between its most powerful nations.

# I. An Overview of the Postwar World

Recall that Germany surrendered in May, 1945, while Japan surrendered in September. Try to view the world of the late 1940s—the first five postwar years—as people at the time viewed it.

## A. THE DEFEATED NATIONS: GERMANY AND JAPAN

Although most U.S. troops went home shortly after the war ended, several army divisions remained abroad to occupy the defeated countries, Germany and Japan. In both countries the United States tried to bring about three kinds of changes. It sought (1) military change by disbanding and disarming the defeated armies, (2) economic change by helping the defeated nations to rebuild their war-torn cities, and (3) political change by ensuring that the postwar governments of Germany and Japan would be democratic.

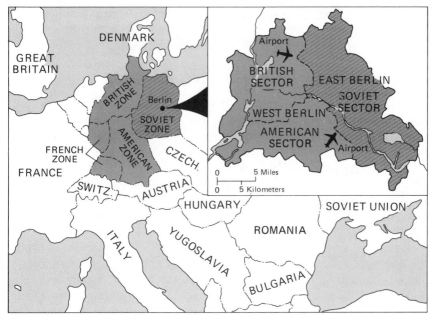

The division of Germany and Berlin, 1945

In Japan the United States took complete responsibility for seeing that these changes occurred. As you will see, U.S. efforts there were remarkably successful.

In Germany, however, the four wartime allies (the United States, Great Britain, France, and the Soviet Union) occupied four different sections of Germany. They also occupied different parts of Berlin, which was located in the Soviet section of Germany. It soon became clear that the Soviet approach to occupying and administering its territory in eastern Germany was very different from the American, British, and French approach in western Germany. The latter three managed to work out a common policy for disarming, rebuilding, and bringing democracy to the territory under their control. The Soviets, on the other hand, forced the East Germans to accept a Communist system that was harsh and undemocratic.

# B. CIVIL WAR IN CHINA

China was another U.S. ally in the war. Now that Japan was defeated, U.S. policymakers hoped that China would eventually become a strong and prosperous democracy. But this U.S. hope for a democratic China was soon threatened. In the late 1940s an army of Chinese Communists led by Mao Tse-tung fought against the government of China's wartime leader, Chiang Kai-shek. The Communist forces scored one victory after another. China was thus in serious danger of falling under the control of a Communist government. From the U.S. point of view, this was an alarming development.

## C. TURMOIL IN THE EMERGING NATIONS

A major result of World War II was the collapse of the colonial empires that had once belonged to Great Britain, France, the Netherlands, and other European powers. The peoples of Asia, Africa, and the Middle East were impatient to end colonial rule and to form independent nations of their own. In the postwar years they expected to achieve their goal of nationhood.

The American people generally sympathized with these movements for independence. At the same time it was clear that nationalist uprisings created problems for U.S. policymakers. In Southeast Asia, for example, the Vietnamese people fought for independence from the longtime colonial rule of France. The French fought a losing battle to keep control of its colony (known as Indochina). U.S. policymakers had mixed feelings about this struggle. On the one hand they recognized that the age of imperialism and colonialism was past. On the other hand they feared that, if the Vietnamese gained independence, their new nation might fall under Communist control.

## D. ORIGINS OF THE COLD WAR

By far the biggest U.S. worry of the postwar years concerned the ambitions of the Soviet Union. Leaders of the Western democracies believed that the Soviet Union was intent on expanding its power by supporting Communist revolutions and gaining control over other nations. How and why did U.S. fears originate?

**U.S.–Soviet Relations Before the Cold War**   The U.S.–Soviet conflict began as far back as 1917 when Communists came to power in Russia and established the Soviet Union as a new state. **Communism** was the name given to the Soviet system (and other systems like it). In theory Communism gave total power to the working class by giving the government total control of all means of production, including factories, farms, and mines. In practice, however, Communist leaders established a dictatorship over the people. The Soviet government declared its hostility to all nations that had a capitalist system of privately owned businesses. It asserted that every nation of the world would eventually become a Communist country like the Union of Soviet Socialist Republics (the USSR, or Soviet Union).

It is no wonder then that many Americans viewed the Soviet revolution of 1917 as a threat. President Woodrow Wilson refused to recognize the Soviet government as legitimate. In 1918 he sent U.S.

troops to northern Russia and eastern Siberia to keep the Germans from attacking northern seaports and capturing Allied war supplies. Later these troops helped to support a counterrevolution against the Communists. The three Republican presidents of the 1920s—Harding, Coolidge, and Hoover—also refused to deal with the Soviet government. Only in 1933 did the United States under President Franklin Roosevelt agree to send an ambassador to Moscow. In so doing the United States gave diplomatic recognition to the Communist regime.

In 1941 the United States and the Soviet Union joined to fight a common enemy, Germany, in World War II. Immediately after the war, however, Americans again began to fear Soviet ambitions when the Soviets gained control of Eastern Europe despite wartime agreements that promised free elections.

**Soviet Fears**  For its part the Soviet government also had reasons to fear U.S. power. In 1945 the United States was the only nation with atomic, or nuclear, weapons. It had dropped two atomic bombs on Japan. Also Soviet leaders distrusted the United States and other Western democracies because they were capitalist states.

**What Was the Cold War?**  You can see then that postwar hostility between the Soviet Union and United States was based on two opposing **ideologies** (belief systems). The two nations' rivalry in the postwar period was known as the **cold war**. The conflict was "cold" in the sense that Soviet and U.S. armies never fought each other. But the Soviet Union and the United States fought in many other ways, including:

- An arms race: Attempting to build more powerful nuclear weapons than those of the enemy
- Local and regional wars: Giving military aid either to rebel forces or government forces depending on which side in a civil war leaned toward communism
- Espionage: Spying on each other
- Propaganda: Creating and distributing messages that condemned the opposing nation and its way of life
- Space race: Attempting to impress world public opinion by being the first to make gains in space exploration
- Disputes in the United Nations: Using meetings of the UN General Assembly to condemn the actions of the rival power.

These cold war methods dominated world politics for about 44 years (from 1945 to 1989). This chapter describes only the first phase of the cold war, from 1945 to 1963.

**Cold War Leaders**  Pictured on the following pages are the leaders of the rival powers, or **superpowers**, in the cold war's first phase.

### U.S. Leaders of the Cold War

HARRY TRUMAN (1945 to 1953) Truman was the Democratic vice president when Franklin Roosevelt died. He was elected president in his own right in 1948. Truman and his secretary of state, George Marshall, took the first steps to halt Soviet expansion. Truman's policies served as a guide for later presidents.

DWIGHT D. EISENHOWER (1953 to 1961) The former army general in World War II served two terms as a Republican president. In fighting the cold war, Eisenhower relied on the advice of his secretary of state, John Foster Dulles, a strong opponent of Soviet expansion.

JOHN F. KENNEDY (1961 to 1963) Kennedy was the youngest president since Theodore Roosevelt. In his conduct of foreign policy, Kennedy experienced his greatest success and his greatest failure in two crises in Cuba.

# II. The Cold War in Europe

As soon as World War II ended, the Soviet Union used its troops of occupation in Eastern Europe to achieve political control of that region. Angry U.S. reaction marked the beginning of the cold war.

## A. SOVIET SATELLITES IN EASTERN EUROPE

At wartime conferences at Yalta and Potsdam (see Chapter 12), the Soviet leader Joseph Stalin had agreed that postwar governments of

## Soviet Leaders of the Cold War

JOSEPH STALIN (in power from 1924 to 1953) More than any other Soviet leader, Stalin ruled his nation with an iron hand as the party boss, or dictator, of the Communist party of the Soviet Union. He was more ruthless than many of the czars that had ruled Russia before the Communists came to power.

NIKITA KHRUSHCHEV (premier from 1958 to 1964) One of the highlights of Khrushchev's term as Soviet premier was his trip to New York City in 1959 to speak at the United Nations. Sometimes he would make hostile speeches against the United States. At other times, however, he would chat with U.S. leaders in a friendly spirit. He believed that communism would eventually "bury" the United States.

Eastern Europe should be elected freely and fairly. In 1945 and 1946 elections took place in Poland, Romania, Bulgaria, and Hungary. However, elections were far from free. Communist parties in each of these countries had the support of the occupying Soviet army. In each country Communists took control of the police, the newspapers, and the radio stations. Elections were rigged ("fixed") and Communist candidates elected. Only in Czechoslovakia did free elections take place—until 1948. In that year Communists forced the Czech leaders to leave office. Thus Czechoslovakia too fell to the country's Soviet-backed Communist party.

Soviet satellites in Eastern Europe

After coming to power, the Communist party of each Eastern European country took orders from the Communist party of the Soviet Union. In effect, as the map shows, seven Eastern European states were now Soviet **satellites**—countries whose policies were dictated by a foreign power, the Soviet Union. An eighth nation, Yugoslavia, was also under Communist rule but managed to remain free of Soviet control.

Counted among the seven satellites was the part of Germany assigned to Soviet control. Originally, at the end of the war, Americans expected Germany to be occupied briefly and then united under a democratically elected government. Instead, because of the conflict between the Soviet Union and the other occupying powers, Germany remained divided into two parts: a freely elected western part (West Germany) and a Communist-controlled Soviet satellite (East Germany).

## B. THE U.S. RESPONSE: CONTAINMENT

In the United States the last year of war, 1945, was a time for celebrating victory and looking forward to the return of peace. As in the post-World War I period, many Americans wanted to leave Europe to resolve its own postwar problems. However, President Truman and congressional leaders believed that the lack of U.S. involvement would leave Europe wide open to Soviet domination.

**Churchill's "Iron Curtain" Speech**   The American public began to see the need for involvement after the great British wartime leader Winston Churchill made a startling speech at Fulton, Missouri, in 1946. Churchill said that an **iron curtain** had descended across the continent of Europe. In other words, the Soviet control of Eastern Europe was so strong that there would be little contact between those nations and the democracies of Western Europe.

**The Concept of Containment**   What was the United States to do if the Soviet Union continued to support Communist uprisings in various countries of the world? A scholar and diplomat named George Kennan proposed an answer in an article that he wrote in 1947. Kennan argued that "the main element of any United States policy toward the Soviet Union must be that of a long-term, patient but firm and vigilant containment of Russian expansive tendencies. ..." The word **containment** was picked up by U.S. policymakers in Washington, including President Truman. It was a good label, or name, for U.S. policy toward the Soviet Union in the postwar world.

**The Truman Doctrine**   Truman used Kennan's idea of containment almost immediately. In 1947 the government of Greece was in serious danger of being overthrown by a force of Greek Communists. If Greece fell, then Turkey too could be in danger of being swept into the Soviet orbit. Truman decided to contain the Communist pressure. He asked Congress for $400 million in U.S. military aid for Greece and Turkey. In his statement to Congress, known as the **Truman Doctrine,** Truman said: "The free people of the world look to us for support in maintaining their freedoms. If we falter in our leadership we may endanger the peace of the world—and we shall surely endanger the welfare of our own Nation." Congress granted Truman's request in a **foreign aid** bill—the first of many foreign aid bills in the cold war. As hoped, U.S. aid to Greece and Turkey helped these countries deal sucessfully with the Communist threat.

**The Marshall Plan**   In 1947 the economies of the nations of Western Europe were still in desperate shape from the destructive effects of war. Communist parties in France and Italy made the most of people's discontent and won large numbers of supporters in both countries. To contain the rising tide of communism and Soviet influence, Truman's secretary of state George Marshall proposed an ambitious program of foreign aid. From 1948 to 1951, Congress approved $12 billion of economic assistance to Europe, a huge sum for that time. The **Marshall Plan,** as the aid program was called, helped to bring

## DOCUMENTS: THE TRUMAN DOCTRINE

On March 12, 1947, President Truman delivered a speech to Congress about the need for giving U.S. economic aid to Greece and Turkey. The part of the speech quoted below gives Truman's view of the state of the world in 1947.

To what extent is Truman's approach to world politics, as stated here, still valid in the 1990s?

The peoples of a number of countries of the world have recently had totalitarian regimes forced upon them against their will. The Government of the United States has made frequent protests against coercion and intimidation ... in Poland, Rumania and Bulgaria. I must also state that in a number of other countries there have been similar developments.

At the present moment in world history nearly every nation must choose between alternative ways of life. The choice is too often not a free one.

One way of life is based upon the will of the majority, and is distinguished by free institutions, representative government, free elections, guarantees of individual liberty, freedom of speech and religion, and freedom from political oppression.

The second way of life is based upon the will of the minority forcibly imposed upon the majority. It relies upon terror and oppression, a controlled press and radio, fixed elections, and the suppression of personal freedoms.

I believe that it must be the policy of the United States to support free peoples who are resisting attempted subjugation by armed minorities or by outside pressures.

I believe that we must assist free peoples to work out their own destinies in their own way.

I believe that our help should be primarily through economic and financial aid which is essential to economic stability and orderly political processes.

about European recovery. By 1951 Communist control of France and Italy was no longer a serious possibility, although the Communist party in both countries remained strong. (Interestingly, the United States had offered Marshall Plan aid to all nations in Europe, but it was refused by the Soviet Union and its satellites.)

The originator of the assistance plan, George Marshall, had been a leader in war as well as peace. As the armed forces' chief of staff during World War II, Marshall had been in charge of planning overall military strategy. In recognition of his postwar strategy for peace (the Marshall Plan), Marshall received the Nobel Peace Prize in 1953.

**The Berlin Airlift**    Truman's and Marshall's containment policy took a slightly different form in Berlin. Recall that the victors of World War II had divided both Germany and Berlin into zones of occupation. Berlin happened to be within the zone under Soviet control. In 1948 the Soviet Union announced that the British, French, and Americans could no longer use the land routes to Berlin that passed through the Soviet zone of occupation.

This meant that food and other vital supplies would be unable to reach the people living in West Berlin. Truman announced that the United States would not abandon West Berlin, as the Soviets had hoped. He ordered the U.S. Air Force to bring supplies to West Berlin by air. This operation, known as the **Berlin Airlift,** flew in supplies day after day for almost a year. Finally in 1949 the Soviets yielded to Western determination and ended their blockade of land routes to West Berlin.

**North Atlantic Treaty Organization (NATO)**    By 1949 U.S. policymakers recognized that the Soviet Union and its bloc (group) of Communist states in Eastern Europe threatened the security of Western Europe. For the first time in its history, the United States committed itself to a permanent military alliance in peacetime. In 1949 the president signed and the Senate approved a treaty with 11 nations (Great Britain, France, Italy, Belgium, the Netherlands, Denmark, Norway, Iceland, Portugal, Luxembourg, and Canada). The treaty created an alliance called the **North Atlantic Treaty Organization (NATO).**

In the treaty the allies agreed "that an armed attack against one or more of them in Europe or North America shall be considered an attack against all." The common defense of the NATO nations rested on a shield-and-sword concept. European and American ground troops would act as a "shield" against any Soviet attack. U.S. atomic weapons would act as a "sword." The purpose of the NATO alliance was to deter the Soviet Union from aggression and thus to avoid war.

**Two Powers with Nuclear Weapons**    The year of the NATO treaty, 1949, was also the year that the Soviet Union tested its first atomic bomb. Suddenly the United States was no longer the only nation to possess the most destructive weapon ever made. In 1952 the United States announced that it had developed a weapon thousands of times more destructive that the atomic bomb, or A-bomb. Its new weapon was the **hydrogen bomb, or H-bomb.** But only one year later, the Soviet Union announced that it too had developed and tested an H-bomb.

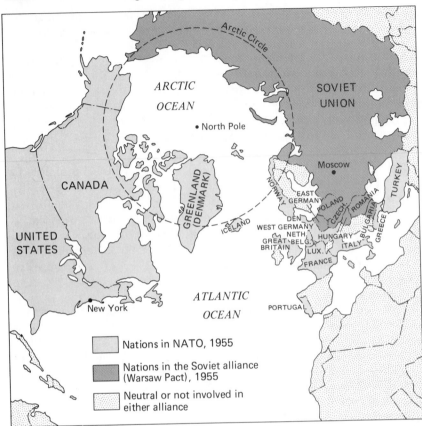

The global context: cold war alliances

The world now entered into a frightening time when its two most powerful nations competed with each other to produce more and more nuclear weapons. People of the 1950s soon recognized that much of the world might be destroyed if the cold war ever turned into a hot, nuclear war.

## C. CONTAINMENT UNDER NEW LEADERSHIP: EISENHOWER AND KENNEDY

When Truman left office in 1953, his Republican successor Dwight Eisenhower faced two problems. First, how could he stop Soviet aggression? Second, how could he avoid a nuclear showdown with the Soviet Union?

**Policy of "Massive Retaliation"**   Eisenhower's secretary of state, John Foster Dulles, used forceful language to impress the Soviet Union with U.S. determination to stop Soviet aggression in Europe.

Any aggressive move, he said, would be met by **massive retaliation.** Dulles did not mention nuclear weapons as such, but they were clearly implied.

**Uprisings in Hungary and Poland**    Fortunately, the United States did not have to act on its warning. Only once in the 1950s did the Soviet Union use troops in Europe. In 1956 anti-Soviet riots broke out in the Eastern European countries of Poland and Hungary. The Soviet Union agreed to slightly loosen its control of the Polish government. In Hungary, however, Soviet tanks rolled into the capital city of Budapest and quickly crushed the Hungarian uprising.

While he sympathized with the Hungarian "freedom fighters," President Eisenhower offered them no military assistance. Eisenhower recognized that the Soviet Union had established a "sphere of influence" in Eastern Europe. In response to NATO, the Soviets had arranged a military alliance of its own with its Eastern European satellites—an alliance known as the **Warsaw Pact.** To avoid war, Eisenhower was careful not to interfere in the Soviet "sphere of influence." At the same time the Soviet Union did not challenge the NATO alliance.

***Sputnik* and the Space Race**    In 1957 the cold war literally reached into outer space. In that year the Soviet Union launched ***Sputnik,*** a small metal sphere that orbited the earth. It came as a shock to the American people and their government that the first artificial satellite into space was Russian-made, not American-made. Both Eisenhower and his successor, Kennedy, wanted to show the world that U.S. space technology was superior to Soviet space technology. Under their leadership Congress committed vast resources to the "race for space." Between 1957 and 1963 the United States launched many satellites and began training human "astronauts" for earth-orbiting missions. At the same time the shock from the *Sputnik* setback caused the U.S. government to spend large sums on science education.

**The U-2 Incident**    U.S. prestige suffered another setback in 1960 when the Soviet Union shot down a U.S. spy plane, the U-2. During the **U-2 Incident** the Soviet leader, Nikita Khrushchev, angrily charged that the only purpose of the U-2 plane was to spy on their country from high altitudes. Eisenhower at first denied that this was true but later admitted that U-2 planes were commonly used for spying. The American pilot, Gary Powers, survived the crash of his plane and was later exchanged for a Soviet spy. As a result of the U-2 incident, Khrushchev canceled a summit conference with President Eisenhower, and cold war tensions increased.

**The Berlin Wall**    Almost as soon as John Kennedy moved into the White House in 1961, he was tested by Khrushchev. The test concerned the future status of the German city of Berlin. Recall that Berlin had been divided in 1945 into an eastern section under Soviet control and a western section supported by the British, French, and Americans. By 1961 West Germany had become far more prosperous than Soviet-controlled East Germany. It now appeared as if Germany might be permanently divided into two different nations. In 1955 West Germany had joined the NATO alliance, and East Germany had joined the Warsaw Pact. The German situation embarrassed the Soviet Union because East Germans were constantly leaving East Germany and East Berlin to enjoy the greater freedom and prosperity of West Germany.

In August 1961, the Soviets and their East German allies startled the world by erecting a wall of concrete blocks and barbed wire all along the border between East Berlin and West Berlin. The purpose of the **Berlin Wall** was to prevent any more East Berliners from moving into the western section of the city. But many East Berliners defied the barrier by trying to climb over the wall, tunnel under it, or even swim around it. Some succeeded, while others were shot by East German guards. The Berlin Wall served as a grim reminder of the iron curtain and of Soviet inability to meet people's economic and political needs.

Kennedy's response to the Berlin Wall was to travel to West Berlin to assure the people there that the United States would never give in to Soviet pressures. West Germans roared their approval when he told them: *"Ich bin ein Berliner"* (I am a Berliner). He meant by this that any threat against West Berlin would be viewed as a threat against the United States.

# D. AN ASSESSMENT OF THE CONTAINMENT POLICY IN EUROPE

Was the U.S. policy of containment an effective policy? Did it succeed in preventing the spread of Soviet power beyond Eastern Europe? The evidence shows that the policy *did* succeed. After the Communist takeover of Czechoslovakia in 1948, the Soviet Union made no further gains in Europe. Consider these facts:

- U.S. aid to Greece and Turkey under the Truman Doctrine helped block Communist takeovers of these countries.

- U.S. aid to the nations of Western Europe under the Marshall Plan helped to prevent Communist parties in France and Italy from gaining power.

- The forming of the NATO alliance convinced the Soviet Union that any attack on Western Europe would be extremely risky.

Not once did the Soviets challenge NATO by moving troops into NATO-protected territory.

- Despite the Soviet blockade of West Berlin in 1948 and the building of the Berlin Wall in 1961, West Berlin did not fall under Soviet control. In fact, in 1989 the East Germans took down the hated wall in Berlin and voted the Communist party out of office. In 1990 East Germany joined with West Germany in a united German nation.

## In Review

The following questions refer to section I: An Overview of the Postwar World and section II: The Cold War in Europe.

1. Define *cold war, containment, iron curtain, communism,* and *satellite nation.*
2. For each Soviet action listed below, state how the United States responded to the action.
   - Cutting off access by land to West Berlin, 1948
   - Sending troops into Hungary to put down a revolt, 1956
   - Launching the *Sputnik* satellite, 1957
   - Building the Berlin Wall, 1961
3. Explain why a president's foreign policy decisions in the 1950s and early 1960s involved unusually great risks.

# III. The Cold War in Asia

The cold war rivalry between the United States and the Soviet Union extended to all parts of the world, including Asia. On that continent the U.S.–Soviet rivalry was complicated by the politics of two powerful nations: Japan and China.

## A. THE RECONSTRUCTION OF JAPAN

After their nation was defeated in war in 1945, the Japanese people surprised the U.S. occupying army with their willingness to cooperate. General Douglas MacArthur was the supreme commander of the occupation. Acting on instructions from the U.S. government, MacArthur carried out the enormous task of transforming Japan from a military power into a nation without any military weapons.

Besides demilitarizing the country, MacArthur was also responsible for democratizing it. He supervised Japan's adoption of a new constitution (1947), which took away all political power from the Japanese emperor and guaranteed free elections and representative government. The constitution also banned the raising of an army and navy and declared that Japan would never again go to war.

The economic reconstruction, or rebuilding, of Japan required millions of dollars of U.S. aid. By 1955 only ten years after the war, Japan was again a prosperous nation closely allied with the Western nations that had defeated it. (West Germany too had taken only ten years to regain its former industrial strength.)

## B. COMMUNIST VICTORY IN CHINA

From the U.S. point of view, the occupation of Japan was a great success. Events in China however, were disappointing.

**The Opposing Forces**   China, the most populous nation in the world, had hundreds of millions of peasants who toiled in poverty. A discontented young peasant named Mao Tse-tung decided in the 1920s that the time had come for the Chinese working class (industrial workers and peasants) to take control of their government and adopt a Communist system. Through the 1920s and 1930s a rebel army under Mao's leadership fought with the government's army. The government leader was Chiang Kai-shek, head of a ruling party known as the Nationalists. Mao's Communists and Chiang's Nationalists stopped fighting their civil war during World War II in order to fight the Japanese. But as soon as Japan was defeated, the civil war resumed.

**U.S. Aid to Chiang**   President Truman and his advisers knew that the Chinese Communists received military aid from the Soviet Union. To contain and defeat Mao's forces, the U.S. Congress voted large amounts of economic aid and military supplies to support Chiang and the Nationalists. Unfortunately, however, Chiang made himself unpopular with the Chinese people by misusing government funds and failing to improve conditions of life for the common people. Chiang ignored U.S. advice to change his ways. At the same time Mao's army attracted peasant recruits by the millions. In 1949 Chiang and his Nationalist supporters fled to the island of Taiwan, off the Chinese coast.

**Problem of the "Two Chinas"**   There were now two Chinese governments—Mao's Communist government on the mainland and Chiang's Nationalist government on Taiwan. Each contended that it was the only legitimate government for the Chinese nation. Most Americans were shocked by the "loss of China" to communism. President Truman sided with Chiang, and so did his successors, Eisenhower and Kennedy. Through the 1950s and 1960s, the United States recognized only one Chinese government as legitimate— Chiang's Nationalist government. The United States refused to recognize Mao's Communist government.

Because Chiang's government had controlled China when the United Nations was formed in 1945, Nationalist China continued to be a UN member through the 1950s and 1960s. Communist China (the People's Republic of China) was excluded from UN membership. The United States and its NATO allies firmly opposed attempts by the Soviet Union to unseat the Nationalists.

During Eisenhower's presidency two small islands under Taiwan's control—Quemoy and Matsu—were bombarded by guns from the mainland. The United States stood ready to defend its ally, Chiang. But Mao stopped short of invading Quemoy and Matsu, and the crisis passed. By the end of the 1950s, an uneasy peace developed between the "two Chinas."

## C. WAR IN KOREA

Only five years after the end of World War II, the United States became involved in a war in Korea. One of the war's underlying causes was U.S. opposition to communism. The immediate cause was a sudden attack by a North Korean army against the territory of South Korea.

**A Divided Korea**   Korea, a proud nation with an ancient past, had lost its independence in 1910 when Japanese armies occupied the country. At the end of World War II, the Japanese were driven out of Korea by Soviet armies arriving from the north and American armies arriving from the south. Soviets and Americans agreed that the 38th parallel of latitude should be the temporary dividing line between their zones of occupation. After the cold war began, the 38th parallel seemed more like a permanent border between North Korea with its Soviet-backed Communist government and South Korea with its U.S.-supported government. The United Nations had helped to organize the South Korean government. Hoping that the United Nations could manage Korea's problems, U.S. troops left the country in 1949.

**The North Korean Attack and U.S. Response**   In June 1950 a North Korean army marched across the 38th parallel into South Korea. This was precisely the kind of aggressive act that the U.S. policy of containment was supposed to prevent. Truman did not hesitate. He ordered U.S. troops into South Korea and called upon the United Nations to undertake the defense of the South Korean government. Coincidentally, the Soviet Union had previously withdrawn its representative from the United Nations and thus, for the time being, had lost its veto power in the Security Council. Although many nations contributed troops to the UN-sponsored defense of South Korea, by far the largest number came from the United States and of course, South Korea.

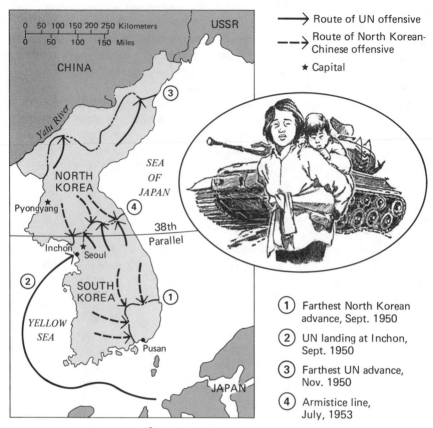

The Korean War, 1950 to 1953

Truman did not ask Congress to declare war. Instead, he used his power as commander in chief to conduct an undeclared war in Korea, which he called a **"police action."**

**General MacArthur's Strategy**  The commander of the UN forces was the brilliant U.S. general, Douglas MacArthur. At first MacArthur's forces suffered a series of defeats. But then a surprise attack behind enemy lines pushed the North Koreans backward toward the Chinese border. MacArthur's decision to pursue them caused China to come to the aid of North Korea. Overwhelmed by the Chinese assault, the UN forces and the South Koreans retreated below the 38th parallel.

**The Firing of General MacArthur**  During the heavy fighting MacArthur urged President Truman to permit him to bomb Chinese bases in Manchuria, a part of China, in order to stop the Chinese attack. Truman refused to give his permission. He feared that such action would probably result in a far larger and more dangerous war. MacArthur conveyed his thoughts to congressional leaders and continued to campaign for the bombing of Chinese territory. At this point in 1951 President Truman removed MacArthur as the commander of UN forces in Korea. Truman concluded that he could not allow MacArthur to challenge the president's authority as commander in chief.

The decision to remove MacArthur took courage because the general was popular with the American people. Returning to the United States, MacArthur received a hero's welcome in a huge ticker-tape parade in New York City. In a speech to Congress, he delivered a statement that became famous: "Old soldiers never die, they just fade away."

Despite MacArthur's popularity, most Americans supported President Truman's policy of avoiding a full-scale war with China.

**Stalemate and Truce**   The war in Korea dragged on through 1951 and 1952. Despite much loss of life, neither side could win decisive victories, and the war became stalemated near the 38th parallel. The Republican candidate for president—former general Dwight Eisenhower—promised to "go to Korea," if elected, to end the fighting. He carried out his promise in 1953. Soon afterward a truce established the 38th parallel as the line between the opposing forces.

**Assessing the Korean Conflict**   Truman's objective in Korea was to fight a limited war. His goal was *not* to defeat North Korea and take over its territory. Nor did he want to involve the Soviet Union and China in a full-scale Asian war. Truman's one goal was containment: saving one part of Korea from Communist control. This goal was achieved—but at the price of 54,000 Americans who lost their lives in the conflict.

# D. OTHER U.S. COMMITMENTS IN ASIA

In the 1950s the makers of U.S. foreign policy were committed to containing communism everywhere in the world. Toward this end, the United States signed several treaties of alliance with countries of Asia:

- In 1951 the United States signed a peace treaty with Japan agreeing to end U.S. occupation. At the same time Japan agreed to allow U.S. troops to stay in the country to provide military protection.

- In 1951 the United States signed a treaty with Australia and New Zealand, the ANZUS pact, promising military aid if either nation was attacked.

- In 1954 the United States formed an alliance in Southeast Asia similar to the NATO alliance in Europe. It was known as the

Southeast Asia Treaty Organization, or SEATO. Treaty members were Great Britain, France, the United States, Australia, New Zealand, Pakistan, Thailand, and the Philippines. (The Philippines had been granted its independence from U.S. control in 1946.)

U.S. alliances in both Asia and Europe were based on a single assumption, which was generally accepted at the time. The assumption was that the Soviet Union masterminded Communist movements in all countries of the world. Thus, Americans viewed communism as a single force. Only later, in the 1960s and 1970s, did U.S. policymakers begin to realize that Chinese Communists and North Korean Communists had national goals different from those of Soviet leaders in Moscow.

## In Review

The following questions are based on section III: The Cold War in Asia.

1. Evaluate President Truman's decision to remove General MacArthur from command in Korea. Do you agree or disagree with the decision? Why?
2. Describe one success and one failure of U.S. foreign policy in Asia between 1945 and 1955.
3. Compare U.S. foreign policy in Asia from 1945 to 1960 with U.S. foreign policy in Europe during the same period.

# IV. Containment in the Middle East and Latin America

The Soviet Union borders on Iran in the Middle East, while the United States borders on Mexico and has a special interest in Latin America. Both in the Middle East and in Latin America, the cold war struggle for supremacy led to several dangerous crises.

## A. STRUGGLE FOR POWER IN THE MIDDLE EAST

After World War II British and French colonies in the Middle East achieved independence. Taking their place among the independent nations of the world were Egypt and Jordan (formerly British colonies) and Lebanon and Syria (formerly French colonies). These and other Arab states in the region strongly opposed the creation of another new nation, Israel.

**The Creation of Israel**  Before World War II the territory of Palestine in the Middle East had been under British control. Jews and Arabs had been living side by side in Palestine for generations. When Germany's Nazi government began persecuting German Jews in the 1930s, Jewish emigration to Palestine increased significantly. In 1948 the General Assembly of the United Nations voted to divide Palestine into the Jewish state of Israel and a new Palestine state for Arabs. Both the United States and the Soviet Union quickly recognized the independence of these new nations. However, Arab nations of the Middle East refused to accept Israel's right to exist. An Arab-Israeli war—the first of several—ended in 1949 in Israel's victory. An African American diplomat in the United Nations, Ralph Bunche, arranged a cease-fire to end the war. For his efforts, Bunche won the Nobel Peace Prize in 1950, the first African American to be so honored.

**U.S. Policy**  The United States has consistently supported Israel in its struggles to defend itself from Arab hostility. At the same time U.S. presidents did not want to antagonize the Arab states for fear that they might fall under Soviet influence and control. It was never easy to walk this diplomatic tightrope between support for Israel, on the one hand, and support for the Arab allies of the United States, on the other.

**The Suez Crisis**  The dilemma became painfully evident in 1956 when the Egyptian leader, Gamal Abdel Nasser, decided to take over the Suez Canal that ran through his nation. During the **Suez Crisis** Nasser **nationalized** the canal, meaning that a property formerly belonging to either a colonial power or a private company was seized

PALESTINE, 1923

ISRAEL TODAY

The division of Palestine

by the government. Nasser was hostile to Israel, suspicious of the Western powers, and increasingly dependent on Soviet military and economic aid. Seeking to regain control of the canal, Great Britain, France, and Israel carried out a joint attack against Egypt. Furious with his allies for acting without U.S. approval, President Eisenhower condemned the attack. Eisenhower worried that the Soviet Union might enter the conflict on Egypt's side. As a result of U.S. pressure, the invading forces withdrew, and a UN force moved in to keep the peace. The Suez Canal remained under Egyptian control.

**The Eisenhower Doctrine**     Most Arab nations objected to U.S. support of Israel, even though they too received U.S. economic aid. Arab resentment against both Israel and the United States led to growing Soviet influence in the Middle East, especially in Syria. To prevent Soviet influence from spreading further, President Eisenhower in 1957 stated that the United States would send troops to any Middle Eastern nation that requested such help against communism. This policy, known as the **Eisenhower Doctrine,** was first applied in Lebanon. In 1958 the presence of U.S. troops in Lebanon helped that country's government deal successfully with a Communist threat.

## B. LATIN AMERICA

In the twentieth century U.S. relations with Latin American countries have been friendly—but also troubled. As you learned in Chapter 9, the people of Haiti and Nicaragua deeply resented U.S. Marines being sent into their countries to keep order and collect debts. This U.S. policy of intervention (from about 1900 to 1925) was changed to a Good Neighbor policy in the 1930s.

**The Good Neighbor Policy**     In the 1920s presidents Coolidge and Hoover tried to improve U.S. relations with Latin America. But the president who did the most to change U.S. policy toward this region was Franklin Roosevelt. In 1933 he announced his intention of following "the policy of the good neighbor." He meant by this that he would avoid intervening in the internal affairs of Latin American nations. To establish a **Good Neighbor policy**, Roosevelt did the following:

- He persuaded Congress to cancel the Platt Amendment, which had given the United States the right to intervene in Cuba.
- He withdrew U.S. troops from Haiti.
- He stated: "The definite policy of the United States from now on is one opposed to armed intervention."

**Latin American Allies in World War II**     During World War II most Latin American nations declared war against Germany and its allies (but only Mexico and Brazil sent troops overseas). After the war the United States recognized that its security was tied closely to the security of other countries of the Western Hemisphere. In Rio de Janeiro, Brazil, in 1947, the United States and almost all Latin American countries signed the Rio Treaty, pledging that an attack against any one nation in the region would be viewed as an attack against the other nations. Also in 1948 the **Organization of American States (OAS)** was established. The United States and Latin American members of OAS agreed to settle their disputes peacefully and cooperate in regional defense.

**A Communist Government in Cuba**   In 1959 the U.S. policy of containment suffered a setback. A young Cuban revolutionary named Fidel Castro overthrew the government of a military dictator, Fulgencio Batista. At first the United States thought the change in government might be beneficial, since Batista had ruthlessly suppressed Cuban liberties. But Castro promptly seized American-owned properties in Cuba and established a regime similar to the Communist regime of the Soviet Union. Suddenly U.S. policymakers realized that Cuba—a nation only 90 miles from U.S. shores—had fallen under Soviet influence.

**Disaster at the Bay of Pigs**   What could the United States do to remove Castro from power and thus remove a threat to U.S. security? Military advisers to President Eisenhower thought the best method would be to provide training and support to a band of Cuban exiles in Guatemala. These Cubans were enemies of Castro and wished to lead a revolt against him. When Kennedy became president in 1961, he supported the plan for assisting in an invasion of Cuba. But he rejected the idea of supporting the invasion with U.S. air power. Kennedy hoped that the Cuban exiles could succeed without such air support. The invasion was launched in April, 1961, off Cuba's southern coast, an area known as the **Bay of Pigs**. It was a complete failure. Castro's forces easily overcame the invading force of 1,500 men, most of whom were killed or captured. For the young president, John Kennedy, the poorly planned and executed invasion was a great embarrassment.

**The Cuban Missile Crisis**   In October, 1962, another crisis involving Cuba nearly led to war between the Soviet Union and the United States. Photographs of Cuba taken from U.S. spy planes showed the presence of Soviet missiles (nuclear weapons). The missiles, so close to the shores of the United States, posed a direct threat to U.S. security. Kennedy considered many options including an air strike against Cuba. He finally decided to send U.S. Navy ships into Cuban waters to intercept Soviet ships that might be carrying missiles. In a message to the Soviet leader Nikita Khrushchev, Kennedy demanded

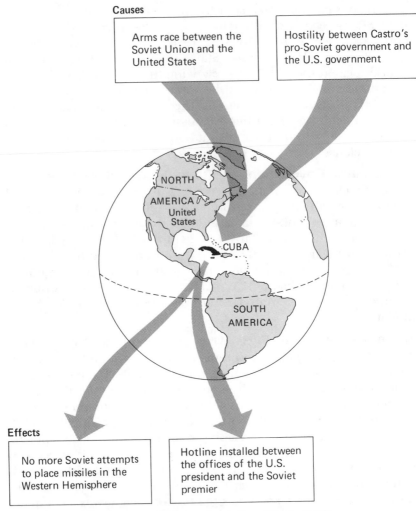

**Causes**

| Arms race between the Soviet Union and the United States | Hostility between Castro's pro-Soviet government and the U.S. government |

**Effects**

| No more Soviet attempts to place missiles in the Western Hemisphere | Hotline installed between the offices of the U.S. president and the Soviet premier |

Causes and effects: the Cuban Missile Crisis

that Soviet ships carrying missiles to Cuba turn around and that the missiles already in Cuba be removed. Kennedy announced his actions in a televised speech to the American people that caused great concern. People wondered what would happen if Soviet ships tried to break through the U.S. naval blockade. Would shots be fired, and if so, would this trigger an exchange of nuclear weapons between the superpowers?

Fortunately, Khrushchev backed down. He agreed to order the Soviet ships to turn around and later to remove the missiles from Cuba. In return Kennedy agreed that the United States would not again support an invasion of Cuba. Kennedy's handling of the **Cuban**

**Missile Crisis** was considered the greatest success of his presidency (just as the Bay of Pigs invasion was his greatest failure). After the crisis passed safely, there seemed less danger of a nuclear confrontation. Both the Soviet Union and the United States became more cautious in their dealings with each other. Neither wanted to provoke another crisis like the one that almost led to world disaster.

**Improved U.S.–Soviet Relations**   One sign of improved U.S.–Soviet relations after the crisis was the signing of a nuclear test-ban treaty in 1963. The two superpowers agreed to end the testing of nuclear weapons in the atmosphere, in outer space, and underwater. Also a direct telephone line—or "hot line"—was established between the office of the U.S. president and that of the Soviet premier to enable the two leaders to communicate in a time of crisis.

**The Alliance for Progress**   Kennedy wanted a plan of economic aid that would do for Latin America what the Marshall Plan had done for Europe. He hoped an ambitious program of aid would (1) promote economic growth in a region whose people suffered from poverty and (2) contain the threat of communism spreading from Cuba to other Latin American countries. Kennedy called his aid program for Latin America the **Alliance for Progress.** Under this program the United States offered to provide all Latin American nations, except Cuba, $20 billion in aid over a ten-year period.

The program did not work out as planned. Latin America lacked the democratic tradition of Western Europe. Aid dollars, instead of helping the poor, tended to be used for political purposes to support a country's ruling class. Eventually Congress allowed the program to die out.

# V. Effects of the Cold War: Global Reach and Presidential Power

The cold war reached into all aspects of American life. Foreign policy was the primary campaign issue in all presidential campaigns of the 1950s and 1960s. In Chapter 14 you will see how a a U.S. senator from Wisconsin named Joseph McCarthy carried fear of communism to an extreme. Basic American freedoms—freedom of speech and the press—suffered as a result.

This section examines only the effects of the cold war on (1) U.S. foreign policy toward the third world and (2) the powers of the president.

## U.S. Foreign Policy, 1945 to 1963

| The Situation Abroad | The U.S. Response |
|---|---|
| **A. EUROPE** | |
| Soviet expansion in Eastern Europe | Containment policy adopted, 1947 |
| Greece threatened by a Communist takeover | Truman Doctrine, 1947 |
| Desperate economic plight of war-torn Europe | Marshall Plan, 1947 |
| Soviet decision to cut off access to West Berlin | Berlin Airlift, 1948 to 1949 |
| Possibility of a Soviet military attack against Western Europe | North Atlantic Treaty Organization (NATO), 1949 |
| Hungarian uprising against Soviet control, 1956 | Words of support for the Hungarians but no military aid, as the United States recognized Soviet "sphere of influence" in Eastern Europe |
| Soviet launching of *Sputnik*, 1957 | U.S. commitment to an ambitious space program |
| Building of Berlin Wall, 1961 | Kennedy's speech pledging U.S. commitment to West Berlin |
| **B. ASIA** | |
| China under Communist control, as Nationalists flee to Taiwan, 1949 | U.S. refusal to recognize Communist government as legitimate |
| North Korean invasion of South Korea, 1950 | U.S. troops sent to fight in Korea (with backing of the United Nations) |
| Possibility of Communist expansion in Asia | Two alliances formed: ANZUS, 1951 and SEATO, 1954 |
| **C. OTHER REGIONS** | |
| Creation of Israel and Arab-Israeli War, 1948 to 1949 | U.S. economic and military aid to Israel as well as to some Arab nations |
| Israeli, British, and French attack on Egypt in the Suez Crisis, 1956 | U.S. demand that the attack be halted and the forces withdrawn |
| Threat of Communist takeovers in the Middle East | Eisenhower Doctrine, 1957, and U.S. troops to Lebanon, 1958 |
| Establishment of Communist dictatorship in Cuba, 1959 to 1960 | Training of Cuban exiles for an invasion that fails (Bay of Pigs, 1961) |
| Placement of Soviet missiles in Cuba | Naval blockade of Cuba and demand that missiles be removed (Cuban Missile Crisis, 1962) |
| Widespread poverty in third world countries | Point Four Program, 1949, and Peace Corps, 1961 |

## A. FOREIGN AID FOR THE THIRD WORLD

In the 1950s it became common to view the world as divided into three groups of nations. Anticommunist nations of the West were the first world. Communist nations allied with the Soviet Union were the second world. Newly independent and economically underdeveloped nations of Asia and Africa were the **third world**. Also included in the third world were older nations of Latin America whose economies were underdeveloped or not industrialized.

U.S. policymakers feared that poverty in the third world countries might lead to political unrest, which in turn might lead to Communist uprisings. U.S. foreign aid for the third world was intended to bring about economic growth and thereby contain the spread of communism.

**Truman's Point Four**   The first president to use economic aid to fight the cold war was Harry Truman. In his inaugural address of 1949, Truman listed several points as the basis for his foreign policy. Most important was his fourth point concerning world poverty. Truman said: "More than half the people of the world are living in conditions approaching misery. Their food is inadequate. They are victims of disease. Their economic life is primitive and stagnant. I believe that we should make available the benefits of our store of knowledge in order to help them realize aspirations for a better life." The foreign aid voted by Congress for third world countries in Asia, Africa, and Latin America was known as Truman's **Point Four Program**.

**Kennedy's Peace Corps**   In his inaugural address of 1961, John Kennedy inspired the nation with a call to patriotic service. "Ask not what your country can do for you," said Kennedy. "Ask what you can do for your country." Later Kennedy suggested a way for idealistic young Americans to serve their country. In a foreign aid program called the **Peace Corps**, volunteers would go abroad to assist the people of an African, Asian, or Latin American country. They would help others to help themselves by teaching the skills of reading and writing and modern methods of agriculture and health care. In addition to teaching needed skills, the Peace Corps also aimed to build good will for the United States through person-to-person contact with citizens of third world countries.

## B. THE GROWTH OF PRESIDENTIAL POWER

The Constitution gives the president greater power in foreign policy than in domestic policy. It gives the president the role of commander in chief of the armed forces. It also gives the president the power to make treaties (though treaties require the Senate's approval). During the cold war, as foreign policy grew in importance, the president's power also grew. Consider these examples:

- Truman made his decision to fight in Korea strictly on the basis of his power as commander in chief. Never did he ask Congress to participate in the decision to declare war.

- Congress relied upon President Eisenhower's leadership in responding to the Suez Crisis in 1956 and sending U.S. troops to Lebanon in 1958.

- In dealing with Cuba, President Kennedy and his team of advisers made the decisions concerning both the Bay of Pigs invasion and the Cuban Missile Crisis.

Recall that, after World War I, Woodrow Wilson became the first president to travel abroad to an international peace conference. During the cold war such travel was common for presidents. In 1955 President Eisenhower met Premier Khrushchev for a summit meeting at Geneva, Switzerland. In 1961 President Kennedy met Khrushchev at another summit meeting in Vienna, Austria. Though little was accomplished, the two conferences enhanced the president's power as "chief diplomat."

Finally, presidential power grew simply because of the existence of nuclear weapons. By 1960 missiles from both the Soviet Union and the United States could reach each other's territory in only a few minutes. If a sudden attack occurred in the nuclear age, the president did not have time to take the matter to Congress. A decision under such circumstance had to be made at once by the commander in chief—the president.

## GLOSSARY OF KEY TERMS: CHAPTER 13

**Alliance for Progress**   a program of economic aid to Latin American nations begun by President Kennedy.

**Bay of Pigs**   the site of an unsuccessful invasion of Cuba in 1961 for the purpose of overthrowing Fidel Castro's government.

**Berlin Airlift**   the U.S. policy of flying in food and other supplies to West Berlin after the Soviet Union had closed land routes to the city in 1948.

**Berlin Wall**   a long wall between East Berlin and West Berlin built by Soviet forces in 1961 to stop East Berliners from moving to the West.

**cold war**   a condition of rivalry and open hostility between the United States and the Soviet Union that continued for many years after World War II.

**communism**   an economic and political system based upon Karl Marx's theory that the working class should control society and that a working-class government should own and operate all the economic resources of the nation.

**containment**   a U.S. policy that attempted to prevent Soviet power and communism from expanding into non-Communist nations.

**Cuban Missile Crisis**   an international crisis of October and November, 1962, in which the United States blockaded Cuban ports, intercepted Soviet ships, and thus forced the removal of missiles already installed in Cuba.

**Eisenhower Doctrine**   a policy proposed by Eisenhower and approved by Congress in 1957 providing for U.S. troops being sent to a Middle Eastern country at the request of that country's government.

**foreign aid**   grants or loans of money from the U.S. government to other governments.

**Good Neighbor policy**   President Franklin Roosevelt's policy of respecting the political independence of all Latin American countries and not interfering in their internal affairs.

**hydrogen bomb (H-bomb)**   a nuclear weapon of the 1950s that was thousands of times more powerful than the atomic bombs dropped on Japan in 1945.

**ideology**   a system of ideas and beliefs.

**iron curtain**   Winston Churchill's term for the Soviet control of the countries of Eastern Europe.

**Marshall Plan**   the policy of giving U.S. economic aid to the nations of Europe to help them rebuild their war-torn economies.

**massive retaliation**   a cold war policy developed by Secretary of State John Foster Dulles in the 1950s suggesting U.S. readiness to use nuclear weapons if the Soviet Union attacked a free nation.

**nationalize**   to bring private property under the control of a nation's government.

**North Atlantic Treaty Organization (NATO)**   a military alliance of the nations of Western Europe, the United States, and Canada.

**Organization of American States (OAS)**   an international organization created in 1951 to promote the economic development of Latin America and cooperation between the United States and its Latin American neighbors.

**Peace Corps**   a foreign aid program begun by President Kennedy in which Americans volunteer to teach their knowledge and skills to people of third world countries.

**Point Four Program**   a foreign aid program begun by President Truman for extending U.S. economic and technical assistance to less developed nations.

**"police action"**   the use of military force in an undeclared war (a war not declared by Congress)—for example, the Korean War.

**satellites**   nations whose governments take orders from a more powerful nation.

**Sputnik**   a small sphere, or artificial satellite, launched into space by the Soviet Union in 1957 as the first such satellite in history.

**Suez Crisis**   a British, French, and Israeli attack against Egypt in 1956 for the purpose of regaining control of the Suez Canal from Egypt.

**superpowers**   the United States and the Soviet Union.

**third world**   nations of Africa, Asia, and Latin America that followed a policy of neutrality in the cold war.

**Truman Doctrine**   President Truman's policy (1947) of aiding the governments of Greece and Turkey in their attempt to defeat Communist rebels.

**U-2 incident**   the downing of a U.S. spy plane by the Soviet Union in 1960 and the Soviet accusations that followed.

**Warsaw Pact**   a military alliance between the Soviet Union and nations of Eastern Europe.

# TEST YOURSELF

## A. Multiple Choice: Facts, Main Ideas, Skills

*On a separate sheet of paper, write the number of the word or expression that, of those given, best completes the statement or answers the question.*

### Reviewing the facts

1. During the 1950s the term *cold war* referred to problems that existed between the United States and   (1) Great Britain   (2) Germany   (3) the Soviet Union   (4) Japan

2. The Truman Doctrine and the formation of the North Atlantic Treaty Organization (NATO) were attempts to   (1) balance the U.S. budget   (2) stop the spread of communism   (3) boost U.S. chances of winning the space race   (4) prevent European countries from interfering in Latin America

3. NATO is an alliance based on the principle of collective security. This means that   (1) the countries of Eastern Europe are members   (2) an attack on one member nation would be considered an attack on all member nations   (3) no member nation can make treaties with any other member nation   (4) only democracies are permitted to join the alliance

4. The purpose of the Marshall Plan was to provide Europe with   (1) defensive military weapons   (2) economic aid   (3) cultural exchange programs   (4) a political alliance

5. The Korean War can best be described as   (1) a U.S. effort to contain communism   (2) an attempt by Chinese Nationalists to regain control of the mainland   (3) a direct military conflict between Soviet and U.S. forces   (4) a military defeat for the United States

6. Korea was divided in 1945 as a result of   (1) popular elections   (2)

a civil war (3) a compromise political solution reflecting cold war realities (4) a dispute in the United Nations

7. President Truman's decision to replace Douglas MacArthur as the commanding general in Korea was made on the basis of (1) a vote of Congress (2) the president's responsibility as commander in chief (3) a ruling by the Supreme Court (4) a vote among the leading generals in the armed forces

8. The Alliance for Progress in Latin America was most similar in purpose to the (1) NATO alliance (2) Eisenhower Doctrine (3) Marshall Plan (4) Truman Doctrine

9. The Point Four Program and the Peace Corps were similar in that both represented (1) military aid to Western Europe (2) nonmilitary assistance (3) economic and financial aid to Greece and Turkey (4) attempts to develop peaceful relations with the Soviet Union

10. The "hot line" and the nuclear test-ban treaty were attempts to (1) reduce tensions between the United States and the Soviet Union (2) contain Soviet power (3) contain Chinese communism (4) create a new alliance between the United States and the Soviet Union

## Reviewing the main ideas

11. Which is a valid conclusion based on a study of the years immediately after World War II? (1) Defeated nations quickly resume militaristic foreign policies. (2) Challenging international problems arise as a result of war. (3) Participation in war leads the United States to pursue an actively expansionist foreign policy. (4) The existence of world organizations ensures peace.

12. U.S. foreign policy in the decade after World War II was intended to (1) support revolutionary groups by using U.S. troops to help them overthrow Communist governments (2) support the efforts of free peoples to resist communism (3) ensure U.S. neutrality in international affairs (4) allow Communist expansion in exchange for trade concessions

13. Following the end of World War II, U.S. foreign policy changed significantly in that the United States (1) assumed a more isolationist stance (2) began to rely on appeasement to reduce world tensions (3) perceived the containment of Communist expansion as a major goal (4) concentrated most heavily on events within the Western Hemisphere

14. In the period following World War II, the United States developed a policy of containment mainly in response to the (1) perceived threat of Soviet expansion (2) building of the Berlin Wall (3) needs of third world nations (4) spread of nuclear weapons

Base your answer to question 15 on the quotation below and on your knowledge of social studies.

"I believe that it must be the policy of the United States to support free peoples who are resisting attempted subjugation by armed minorities or by outside pressures. I believe that we must assist free peoples to work out their own destinies in their own way. I believe that our help should be primarily through economic and financial aid. . . ."

**15.** The recommendation made in this quotation resulted from the U.S. need to  (1) prepare for a third world war  (2) fight Nazi aggression  (3) oppose Communist expansion during the early post-World War II period  (4) justify the withdrawal of U.S. forces from Korea

**16.** Which trend in U.S. foreign policy of the 1940s and 1950s did the Truman Doctrine, Marshall Plan, and Eisenhower Doctrine best represent?  (1) continuous support of the United Nations  (2) increased commitment to NATO  (3) granting of economic, technical, and military assistance to nations threatened by communism  (4) effort to increase trade with Asian and European countries

**17.** The cold war of the 1950s and 1960s centered on  (1) worldwide economic growth  (2) imperialistic struggles between France and Great Britain  (3) Japan's need for markets and raw materials  (4) tensions between the United States and the Soviet Union

**18.** "Let every nation know, whether it wishes us well or ill, that we shall pay any price, bear any burden, meet any hardship, support any friend, oppose any foe to assure the survival and success of liberty." This statement by John F. Kennedy best supports a foreign policy of  (1) colonialism  (2) neutrality  (3) noninvolvement  (4) containment

"Let's get a lock for this thing"

## Developing critical thinking skills

*Base your answers to questions 19 and 20 on the cartoon on page 410 and on your knowledge of U.S. history and government. (Note: The two figures in the cartoon are John Kennedy and Nikita Khrushchev.)*

**19.** Which statement offers the best interpretation of the message of the cartoon?  (1) There is no way of containing the threat of nuclear war.  (2) The United States and the Soviet Union will always be at odds.  (3) The United States and the Soviet Union should make a joint effort to limit the risk of nuclear war.  (4) Kennedy and Khrushchev were not very effective leaders.

**20.** Which event in the cold war most likely led to the creation of this cartoon?  (1) the truce in Korea  (2) the Berlin Airlift  (3) the Cuban Missile Crisis  (4) the Suez Crisis

## B. Enduring Issues

*Select two of the enduring issues from column A. For each issue chosen, explain how the historical example in column B relates to the issue.*

| A. Enduring Issues | B. Historical Examples |
|---|---|
| 1. National power—limits and potential | The forming of military alliances with anticommunist nations in Europe, Asia, and Latin America |
| 2. Presidential power in wartime and foreign affairs | Kennedy's decision in the Cuban Missile Crisis |
| 3. Separation of powers and the capacity to govern | Truman's ordering of troops to Korea without a declaration of war |
| 4. Constitutional change and flexibility | Increased presidential power in the age of nuclear weapons |

## C. Essays

*Level 1*

Since the end of World War II, situations in world affairs have affected U.S. national security. Some of these situations are listed below.

- Soviet influence in Cuba
- Conflict in the Middle East
- Communist governments in China and North Korea
- Political changes in Eastern Europe

Choose *three* of the situations listed. For *each* one chosen, (1) identify one specific action or event related to the situation that has aroused U.S.

concern since 1945,  (2) explain why the action or event concerned the United States, and  (3) discuss how the United States responded to the action or event.

*Level 2*

Foreign-policy actions taken by U.S. presidents have important results.

**A.** Listed below are foreign-policy actions taken by three presidents:

| President | Action |
|---|---|
| Harry Truman | Provided economic aid to Western Europe |
| Harry Truman | Ordered U.S. troops to South Korea |
| Dwight Eisenhower | Refused to aid the Hungarians in their revolt against Soviet control |
| John Kennedy | Ordered a blockade of Cuba |

Choose *two* of the actions listed. For *each* one chosen, give one reason for the action and one result of the action.

**B.** Base your answer to part B on your answer to part A. Write an essay discussing the foreign-policy actions you chose. Include in your essay both a reason for each action and a result of each action.

# UNIT SIX

# A World in Uncertain Times, 1945 to 1974

*In the 30-year period* described in this unit, a new kind of society rapidly took shape. American society was now characterized by an advanced technology (televisions, computers, and satellites in space) and a new living standard (suburban homes, luxurious private cars, and more leisure time). In the 1950s and 1960s the U.S. economy and the way of life that it supported were the envy of the entire world.

At the same time, minorities in the U.S. population demanded increased political rights and equal economic opportunities. Beginning around 1955 the movement for civil rights for African Americans gained strength.

There were tragedies as well that cast a shadow over the era. Most disturbing of all was a war in Vietnam—a war that ended finally in U.S. defeat and much turmoil and bitterness.

| Chapter | Topics |
|---|---|
| 14. Domestic Issues in the 1940s and 1950s | ● How the fear of communism influenced U.S. politics<br>● Early victories in the African-American movement for civil rights |
| 15. Decade of Change: The 1960s | ● The climax of the civil rights movement<br>● The liberal politics of Presidents Kennedy and Johnson<br>● Achievements in space |
| 16. The Limits of Power: From Vietnam to Watergate | ● The Vietnam War and its impact on U.S. society<br>● The policies of Richard Nixon<br>● Scandal in the White House: the Watergate Affair |

# Chapter *14*

# Domestic Issues in the 1940s and 1950s

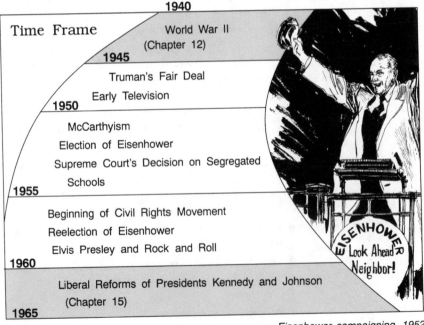

| Time Frame | |
|---|---|
| **1940** | |
| | World War II |
| | (Chapter 12) |
| **1945** | |
| | Truman's Fair Deal |
| | Early Television |
| **1950** | |
| | McCarthyism |
| | Election of Eisenhower |
| | Supreme Court's Decision on Segregated Schools |
| **1955** | |
| | Beginning of Civil Rights Movement |
| | Reelection of Eisenhower |
| | Elvis Presley and Rock and Roll |
| **1960** | |
| | Liberal Reforms of Presidents Kennedy and Johnson |
| | (Chapter 15) |
| **1965** | |

*Eisenhower campaigning, 1952*

## *Objectives*

- To describe the domestic policies of the postwar period.
- To analyze the impact of the cold war on domestic policy.
- To describe early victories in African-Americans' struggle for civil rights.
- To observe how protests against injustice have brought about significant changes in the law.
- To examine changes in American society in the 1950s.

By the end of 1945, after almost four years of war, the American nation was finally at peace. Americans had passed through many years of crisis—a worldwide depression in the 1930s followed by a world war in the 1940s. Now they looked forward to a time of peace and prosperity. But as they were soon to find out, these postwar years presented new troubles and challenges.

In the preceding chapter you read about the international challenges posed by the cold war with the Soviet Union. In this chapter you will examine the many national, or domestic, issues that confronted the American nation in the postwar period. The presidents who dealt with these issues were Harry S Truman (1945 to 1953) and Dwight D. Eisenhower (1953 to 1961).

# I. Postwar Problems

As a senator from Missouri in the 1930s, Harry Truman did not expect to be president. In the 1944 election, he had been the successful Democratic candidate for vice president when the president, Franklin Roosevelt, was reelected to a fourth term. Nobody—least of all Truman—was prepared for the shocking news of Roosevelt's death in April 1945 (less than four months after his inauguration). Truman, though unprepared, knew his constitutional duties and showed great courage in leading the nation through the last months of World War II.

## A. BRINGING THE TROOPS HOME

The first major task of peacetime was demobilizing the armed forces. Since the normal course of their lives had been interrupted by military service, millions of young Americans returning from the war needed help in adjusting to civilian life. As a form of compensation for their service, Congress had enacted the Servicemen's Readjustment Act—or GI Bill of Rights—in 1944. (Review Chapter 12.)

The GI Bill of Rights had a positive impact, not only on war veterans, but also on colleges, universities, and the U.S. housing industry. Under the law any veteran could apply for federal aid in paying for tuition, books, and other costs at a college or vocational school. Eight million veterans—about half of those who had served in the armed forces in World War II—took advantage of these educational benefits at a cost to the government of about $13.5 billion. Also under the law veterans could apply for federally guaranteed, low-interest loans for buying a home or investing in a farm or business. The GI Bill of Rights made it possible for millions of young families to own their own homes.

## B. RETURNING TO A PEACETIME ECONOMY

Just as troops were demobilized in 1945 and 1946, so too was the wartime economy. During the war the U.S. government had tried to prevent inflation (higher and higher prices for consumer goods) by regulating the prices businesses could charge for products. Such regulations are called **price controls.**

**Inflation**  When the war ended, most business owners wanted price controls to be removed. Reluctantly President Truman agreed to do so. The result was predictable—sudden jumps in the prices of everything in the marketplace. Consumers were in a buying mood for goods that had been in short supply during the war. Now automobiles, gasoline, and rubber products were available again, and the demand for them was enormous. Without price controls to keep a lid on, prices increased by 25 percent in just one year (mid-1945 to mid-1946).

**Strikes for Higher Wages**  Businesses showed greater interest in raising prices than in raising wages. Demanding higher pay, labor unions called one strike after another. They argued that consumer prices were rising while workers' incomes were declining. (One reason for the decline was that in peacetime there was less opportunity for overtime pay.) President Truman was normally a supporter of labor's objectives. But strikes in critical industries—steel, automobiles, coal, and railroads—threatened to cripple the economy. In 1946 Truman moved boldly to prevent economic disaster. In response to the coal strike, he ordered U.S. troops to operate the coal mines. In response to a railroad strike, he asked Congress for power to draft striking railroad workers into the army and have them work the mines as soldiers.

## C. CONFLICT WITH A REPUBLICAN CONGRESS

After the war the Republicans won control of Congress and often battled with the Democratic president.

**Taft-Hartley Act**   Over Truman's veto, Congress enacted a law intended to limit the power of labor unions. The **Taft-Hartley Act** of 1947 provided for the following:

- Union officials had to sign a loyalty oath declaring that they were not Communists and did not advocate the violent overthrow of the government.

- A labor union could no longer demand a **closed shop**—an arrangement in which the employer agrees to hire only dues-paying members of one union.

- A labor union could not conduct a **secondary boycott.** In a **boycott,** striking workers refuse to buy their employer's products. In a secondary boycott, strikers also refuse to buy products from firms that do business with their employer.

- An employer had the right to sue a union for breach of contract (failure to carry out the terms of a contract).

- The president could call for an 80-day "cooling-off" period to delay a strike that threatened the U.S. economy or national security.

The passage of the Taft-Hartley Act brought to an end the pro-labor legislation that had marked the New Deal years. For years afterward, labor unions lobbied to repeal (erase) the Taft-Hartley law, which they viewed as unfair.

**The Defeat of Truman's Domestic Programs**   Republicans and Democrats in Congress had generally cooperated during the war emergency. In other words the war years had been characterized by **bipartisanship** (two parties acting together for the national good). But during Truman's presidency, Republicans and Democrats were at odds on almost every domestic issue.

As a Democrat, Truman proposed reform laws similar to the New Deal programs of Franklin Roosevelt. He favored (1) a national health insurance program, (2) federal aid to education, (3) an expanded public housing program, and (4) greater Social Security benefits.

But the Republican majority in Congress rejected every one of Truman's proposals. The president launched his campaign for election in 1948 by telling voters that the Republicans had created a "do-nothing" Congress.

## D. THE ELECTION OF 1948

Republicans thought they had an excellent chance of winning the presidency, which had not been in Republican hands since Herbert Hoover's election back in 1928. Election polls showed that their candidate, Thomas E. Dewey of New York, was far ahead.

**A Divided Democratic Party** Opposition to Truman came not only from Republicans but also from within the ranks of his own party. In fact two groups in the Democratic party were so opposed to his policies that they both organized independent parties. A **liberal** group led by Henry Wallace thought Truman's foreign policy was too tough on the Soviets. A **conservative** group led by Strom Thurmond of South Carolina objected to Truman's support of civil rights bills for African Americans. The Southern conservatives who backed Thurmond for president were known as "Dixiecrats."

**Truman's Campaign** Throughout the campaign Truman fought an uphill battle. Opinion polls showed a Dewey victory to be almost certain. But Truman had a fighting, never-say-die spirit that impressed

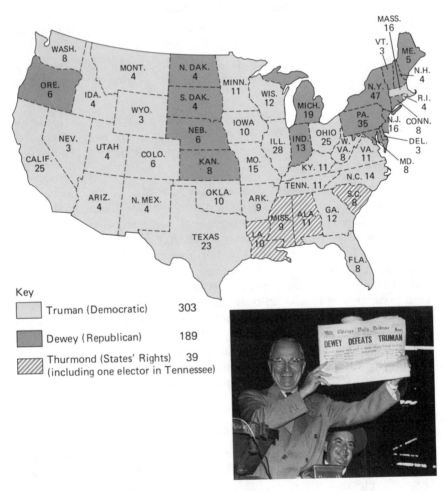

Key

☐ Truman (Democratic)  303

☐ Dewey (Republican)  189

▨ Thurmond (States' Rights)  39
(including one elector in Tennessee)

The election of 1948—and the surprised winner, Truman

many voters. During his "whistle-stop" campaign he traveled from one end of the country to the other and gave short speeches from the rear platform of his train. "Give 'em hell, Harry," people would say when the president hammered away at the "do-nothing" Congress.

The election was close, but Truman won it. His energetic campaign and the strong support of labor unions, farmers, and minorities had helped carry him to victory. The Republicans and newspaper writers were astonished. The morning after the election, a grinning president held up the front page of the *Chicago Tribune*. "DEWEY DEFEATS TRUMAN," read the headline. The newspaper had made the mistake of relying on election polls and early voting returns instead of the final vote.

## E. TRUMAN'S FAIR DEAL

In his inaugural address of 1949, Truman said he would try to achieve a "fair deal" for the American people. Truman's domestic program, known as the **Fair Deal,** added to the reform ideas of Franklin Roosevelt's New Deal. The Congress elected in 1948 passed some parts of the Fair Deal while rejecting other parts.

Congress approved the following measures:

- An increase in the minimum wage from 40 cents an hour to 75 cents an hour
- An extension of Social Security benefits to ten million people not covered under the original law
- Federal funds for the construction of low-income housing and slum clearance
- Increased federal funds for flood control, irrigation projects, and electric-power projects.

However, Congress also rejected these measures:

- A national health insurance plan
- Federal aid to education
- A law protecting the civil rights of African Americans (described later in this chapter, pages 433–434).

# II. The Cold War at Home

Communism was on the march in the postwar years. In just five years (1945 to 1950), Communists took over the governments of an entire region, Eastern Europe, and also won control of the world's most populous nation, China. In this time of Communist expansion, many Americans wondered whether their own country might be a target of Communist plots. They feared that Communist spies and Communist sympathizers might be anywhere, working as secret agents of the Soviet government.

Thus, the cold war abroad led to a cold war at home. During the presidencies of Truman and Eisenhower, the U.S. government took measures to determine whether civil service employees and others might be "disloyal" to the United States. Many of the actions taken by the government restricted freedom of speech.

This section illustrates the tension that may develop between a government's concern about national security, on the one hand, and a citizen's basic rights, on the other hand.

## A. LOYALTY CHECKS

In 1946 newspapers reported that several workers employed in Canada's government had been giving secrets about the American atomic bomb to the Soviet Union. To prevent this from happening in the United States, President Truman began a system of **loyalty checks** of federal employees. To determine whether an employee was likely to be loyal or disloyal, Truman ordered the Federal Bureau of Investigation (FBI) and the Civil Service Commission to find out about the employee's past associations. Had the person ever belonged to a Communist or subversive organization as defined by the U.S. government? (*Subversive* means "seeking to overthrow [the government].") The U.S. attorney general listed 90 organizations whose members *might* be disloyal or subversive. Many of these organizations, however, were never proved to advocate the overthrow of the U.S. government.

Between 1947 and 1951 some three million government workers were investigated. More than 200 of them lost their jobs as "security risks." In addition, 2,900 civil servants resigned for various reasons. Some resigned in protest, believing that the loyalty checks violated their constitutional rights. Others resigned to avoid being investigated.

## B. HOUSE UN-AMERICAN ACTIVITIES COMMITTEE

Also in the 1940s a special committee of the House of Representatives—the **House Un-American Activities Committee**—held a number of hearings on disloyalty. Testimony at these hearings received much attention in the press.

**The Watkins Case**  Called before the House committee, a labor organizer named John Watkins answered questions about his own dealings with Communist groups. But he refused to answer questions about the activities of other persons that he knew. He believed that such questions were not relevant to the committee's work. Watkins was convicted of violating a federal law that made it a crime to refuse to answer a congressional committee's questions. Watkins appealed to the Supreme Court.

In *Watkins v. United States* (1957) the Supreme Court decided that Watkins's conviction was not valid. The Court ruled that a witness at a congressional hearing may properly refuse to answer any committee question that does not relate to the committee's lawmaking task.

**The Hiss Case**   The most sensational case of suspected disloyalty in the 1940s involved a former member of the U.S. State Department, Alger Hiss. In 1945 Hiss had accompanied Franklin Roosevelt to the Yalta Conference. He had then resigned from the State Department to direct a private organization for world peace. Few people had heard of Alger Hiss until 1948. In that year an editor of *Time* magazine and a former Communist, Whittaker Chambers, appeared before the House Un-American Activities Committee. Chambers testified that Hiss had been a Communist spy in the 1930s and had provided Chambers with secret government documents. Hiss denied Chambers's accusations. Nevertheless, a federal court convicted Hiss of perjury (lying under oath) and sentenced him to five years in prison.

# C. TWO CASES INVOLVING ATOMIC WEAPONS

One of the greatest fears of government officials and the American public was that the Soviet Union might learn how to build an atomic bomb. Only the United States had this weapon during the first few postwar years.

**The Case of the Rosenbergs**   The Soviet Union tested its first atomic bomb in 1949. The next year, 1950, a married couple named Julius and Ethel Rosenberg were arrested and charged with passing secrets about the atomic bomb to the Soviet Union. At their trial they were found guilty of conspiracy to commit espionage (spying). The Rosenbergs maintained that they were innocent and appealed to both the Supreme Court and President Eisenhower. Despite worldwide appeals on their behalf, including those of Pope Pius XII and Albert Einstein, the Rosenbergs were executed in 1953.

**The Case of J. Robert Oppenheimer**   A brilliant physicist, Dr. J. Robert Oppenheimer, had been one of the scientists responsible for building the atomic bomb at Los Alamos, New Mexico, in 1945— shortly before the weapon was used in Japan. Oppenheimer later opposed the U.S. development of the hydrogen bomb. He feared that this weapon would lead to an uncontrolled arms race and ultimate destruction of the world. The U.S. government reacted negatively to Oppenheimer's public stand against the H-bomb. The government labeled him a security risk and in 1954 withdrew his security clearance.

In the Oppenheimer case, you see again how the government's fear of disloyalty can sometimes clash with a citizen's right to dissent.

## D. ANTICOMMUNIST LAWS

In addition to loyalty checks, congressional investigations, and spy trials, the cold war at home led to the passage of two anticommunist laws: the Smith Act (1940) and the Internal Security Act, or McCarran Act (1950).

**The Smith Act**   Congress had enacted this law even before U.S. entry into World War II. The law prohibited any group from advocating or teaching the violent overthrow of the U.S. government and also prohibited any person from belonging to such a group. In effect, since U.S. Communists advocated the overthrow of capitalist governments (although not necessarily by violence), the Smith Act made it illegal for U.S. citizens to join the Communist party.

**Supreme Court Cases Testing the Smith Act**   The First Amendment guarantees a citizen's right to freedom of speech and freedom of association. Did the Smith Act violate the First Amendment? The first important court case to test the law was *Dennis et al. v. United States* (1951). Eugene Dennis and ten others admitted to having been members of the Communist party in the 1940s. Dennis had made a number of speeches that, in the government's view, threatened the national security. He and his associates had been arrested and convicted under the Smith Act. They appealed to the Supreme Court, which decided that their First Amendments rights had *not* been violated. The Supreme Court noted that a speech may be prohibited if it presents a clear and present danger of overthrowing the government by force and violence. Dennis's speeches, in the Court's view, did present such a danger to the national security.

In a later case, *Yates v. United States* (1957), the Supreme Court shifted from its position on the Smith Act. For the law to be violated, said the Court, a speaker must encourage people to *do* something, not merely believe in something. Any idea could be advocated so long as the speaker did not urge people to commit dangerous acts.

**The McCarran Act**   Congress passed a second anticommunist law in 1950. The Internal Security Act, or **McCarran Act,** was aimed primarily at "Communist-front" organizations. Such groups did not identify themselves as Communists but were accused of either receiving support from Communists or including Communist members. The law required all Communist and Communist-front organizations to file membership lists and financial statements with the U.S. attorney general. It also prohibited (1) the employment in national defense plants of Communists or members of Communist-front organizations and (2) entry into the United States of Communists or former Communists.

# E. THE ACCUSATIONS OF SENATOR McCARTHY

Fear of Communist influences and subversion was especially intense during the years that the Korean War was being fought, 1950 to 1953. The person most responsible for arousing public fears was a senator from Wisconsin, Joseph McCarthy.

**McCarthy's Rise to Power**  In 1950 Senator McCarthy gave a speech in which he claimed that he held in his hand a list of known Communists who worked for the U.S. State Department. A Senate subcommittee found no evidence to support his accusations. Nevertheless, because McCarthy skillfully played upon the anticommunist fears and suspicions of the American public, he soon became an extremely powerful person. Other public officials began to fear McCarthy's accusations even more than communism.

McCarthy portrayed himself as a patriotic defender of American security. He conducted Senate committee hearings in which he accused many government officials of being "Communist sympathizers." McCarthy's committee investigated actors, writers, educators, and others and accused them of being either Communists or Communist sympathizers. Their constitutional rights were disregarded, and many lost their jobs because of false charges. They had trouble finding new employment because businesses would "blacklist" (refuse to hire) those who were under investigation.

**McCarthy's Fall from Power**  Early in 1954 McCarthy began to look for Communists in the army. The army counterattacked by accusing McCarthy of seeking special favors for one of his former Senate aides. McCarthy demanded that his committee investigate the army. These committee hearings, unlike earlier ones, were televised.

Between April and June, 1954, a huge TV audience of 20 million people watched the Army-McCarthy hearings. Television exposed McCarthy, as many people saw him in action for the first time. They did not like what they saw. He interrupted and bullied witnesses and made reckless use of unsubstantiated charges. These tactics offended the American sense of fair play. As public opinion turned against him, McCarthy soon lost both his supporters and his power. In December, 1954, the Senate voted to censure (officially criticize) McCarthy for improper conduct that damaged the reputation of the Senate.

The term **McCarthyism** has come to mean "the use of reckless and unfair accusations in the name of suppressing political disloyalty."

# DOCUMENTS: A SPEECH AGAINST McCARTHYISM

**Margaret Chase Smith**

Margaret Chase Smith was a Republican senator from Maine. She was the only woman to have served in both the U.S. House of Representatives (1940 to 1949) and the U.S. Senate (1949 to 1973). Senator Joseph McCarthy was also a Republican, but this did not stop Senator Smith from criticizing McCarthy's methods of investigating those he labeled as Communists. On June 1, 1950, Senator Smith invited members of the press into her Senate office and delivered the speech quoted below.

Why did Senator Smith think that Senator McCarthy was ignoring "some of the basic principles of Americanism"? Do you agree or disagree with her point of view?

**Joseph McCarthy**

I think that it is high time that we remembered that we have sworn to uphold and defend the Constitution. I think that it is high time that we remembered that the Constitution, as amended, speaks not only of the freedom of speech but also of trial by jury instead of trial by accusation.

Whether it be a criminal prosecution in court or a character prosecution in the Senate, there is little practical distinction [*difference*] when the life of a person has been ruined.

Those of us who shout the loudest about Americanism in making character assassinations are all too frequently those who, by our own words and acts, ignore some of the basic principles of Americanism:

the right to criticize;
the right to hold unpopular beliefs;
the right to protest;
the right of independent thought....

The American people are sick and tired of being afraid to speak their minds lest they be politically smeared as "Communists" or "Fascists" by their opponents. Freedom of speech is not what it used to be in America. It has been so abused by some that it is not exercised by others.

## In Review

The following questions refer to section I: Postwar Problems and section II: The Cold War at Home.

1. Identify three problems of the postwar period and state how President Truman dealt with them.
2. Compare Truman's Fair Deal to Franklin Roosevelt's New Deal. Explain why Truman had less success than Roosevelt in enacting his domestic program.
3. Discuss both specific and general reasons for anti-Communist fears in the postwar years.
4. Evaluate (a) the Smith Act and (b) the loyalty tests in terms of whether or not, in your view, they were allowed by the U.S. Constitution.

# III. Eisenhower's Domestic Policies, 1953 to 1961

A war hero, Dwight D. Eisenhower, was the Republican candidate for president in 1952. During World War II Eisenhower had been the supreme commander of Allied forces in Europe. In the postwar years he had been president of Columbia University and then a commander of NATO. Popularly known as "Ike," the Republican candidate easily defeated his Democratic opponent, Governor Adlai Stevenson of Illinois. In 1956 President Eisenhower won election to a second term, defeating Stevenson by an even greater margin.

When Eisenhower moved into the White House in 1953, he was the first Republican to be president in 20 years. As a Republican, would he make major changes in the domestic programs established by the Democratic presidents, Roosevelt and Truman? Or would he leave the programs of the New Deal and the Fair Deal largely intact? It soon became clear that the new president wished only to trim and modify the programs of his predecessors. He did not favor drastic change.

## A. DECREASING GOVERNMENT INVOLVEMENT IN THE ECONOMY

On domestic issues Eisenhower tended to be conservative. In other words he believed that private businesses should be allowed a large amount of freedom from government control. He also believed in restoring to the states some of the power exercised by the federal government.

**The Issue of Offshore Oil**  In the early 1950s oil wells off the coast of Texas, Louisiana, and California were producing large quantities of oil. The governments of these states claimed that it was within their power to regulate and tax the oil drilled a short distance from their coastlines. During his presidency Harry Truman had argued that **offshore oil** rights were under the authority of the federal government. But Eisenhower sided with the states. In 1953 he signed legislation allowing states to control the oil rights within their territorial waters.

**The Issue of the TVA**  Eisenhower also sided with private power companies and spoke critically about the U.S. government's own power projects run by the Tennessee Valley Authority (TVA). He said the TVA was an example of "creeping socialism." The president even favored the idea of the TVA giving up its function as a supplier of electric power. This proposal, however, was widely criticized and soon abandoned.

## B. RETAINING AND EXPANDING SOCIAL PROGRAMS

While favoring business interests, Eisenhower disagreed with those Republicans who wished to cut back the social programs begun by the Democrats. To show that the Republican party also cared about people's welfare, Eisenhower persuaded Congress to enact the following laws and programs.

- A law increasing the minimum wage from 75 cents an hour to one dollar an hour
- A law increasing Social Security benefits for retired persons and bringing many more workers under the protection of the Social Security system
- A law creating a new cabinet-level department of the executive branch—the Department of Health, Education, and Welfare. (To head the new department, Eisenhower chose a woman, Oveta Culp Hobby.)
- An ambitious program for building interstate highways, with 90 percent of the funds coming from the federal government and the remainder from the states. (Of course, the billions of federal dollars spent on new highways gave a tremendous boost to a number of important industries—the automobile industry, the tourist industry, the trucking industry, the housing industry, and others.)
- A program of government loans for students to attend college.

## C. SUPREME COURT APPOINTMENTS

One of President Eisenhower's most important decisions was his choice of a California governor, Earl Warren, to be the new chief justice of the U.S. Supreme Court. Under Warren's leadership (1953 to 1969) the Supreme Court made dozens of controversial decisions about the civil rights of African Americans and the rights of persons accused of committing crimes. In this chapter you will read about the Warren Court's landmark decision in the civil rights case of *Brown v. Board of Education of Topeka* (1954). (Chapter 15 treats the Warren Court's decisions on the rights of persons arrested for crimes.)

Eisenhower made three other appointments to the Supreme Court: John Harlan, Potter Stewart, and William Brennan. When he made his appointments, the president could not guess that Earl Warren and William Brennan would make bold decisions that tended to please liberals while displeasing conservatives.

Usually a president tries to nominate to the Supreme Court justices who share the president's own political views. But a justice, once chosen, may surprise the president who nominated him or her. Supreme Court justices can act independently because their appointments are for life and not subject to election politics.

When President Eisenhower left office, he was asked whether he had made any mistakes. He replied, "Yes, two, and they are both sitting on the Supreme Court." He was referring to Justices Warren and Brennan.

# IV. The Civil Rights Movement

When World War II ended, African Americans had lived for many decades under Jim Crow laws in the South that denied them equal rights. In Northern cities too, they had suffered from discrimination in housing and jobs. After World War II, however, discriminatory laws and customs began to break down. The civil rights movement, begun by W. E. B. DuBois and others early in the century, became a significant force for social change during the presidencies of Truman and Eisenhower.

## A. TRUMAN'S EFFORTS FOR CIVIL RIGHTS

More than any president before him, Truman recognized that a country claiming to be a democracy could not deny fundamental rights to a large group of its citizens. He did not like the long-time policy in the U.S. armed forces of segregating troops according to race. Therefore, one of his first acts as president was to issue an executive order ending racial segregation in the armed forces. At the same time Truman established a Fair Employment Board to ensure that African Americans were given an equal opportunity to hold civil service jobs in the U.S. government.

As an important part of his Fair Deal, Truman urged Congress to enact **civil rights laws** that would (1) abolish the poll tax and (2) punish those guilty of lynching African Americans. Congress failed to enact the civil rights laws proposed by the president. Even so, Truman's strong support for civil rights paved the way for the laws adopted later in the 1950s and 1960s. According to the historian Arthur Schlesinger, Jr., Truman's repeated efforts to make progress in civil rights represented his "boldest initiative in the domestic field."

# B. BREAKING DOWN THE BARRIERS OF SEGREGATION

Although a president could help their cause, African Americans were chiefly responsible for winning significant victories against discrimination in the late 1940s. World War II had given them an expectation of change. After all, they reasoned, many thousands of African Americans had fought in the war. They had played a significant role in liberating other peoples in Asia and Europe. If worldwide freedom and democracy were among the goals of the U.S. war effort, then it was surely time for equal rights and freedom from racial discrimination to be won at home.

**Breakthrough in Union Membership** Labor unions were among the first institutions in American life to do away with racial barriers. In 1935 only 190,000 African-American workers were union members. Ten years later, the number had increased to more than one million.

**Breakthrough in Higher Education** Another sign of change was the admission in 1948 of an African-American student, Edith Mae Irby, to a medical school at the University of Arkansas. Until this time many universities in the South had made it a policy to reject African Americans who applied for admission.

**Breakthrough in Sports** The most dramatic and widely publicized breakthrough in the 1940s was achieved by a talented and courageous baseball player, Jackie Robinson. When Robinson joined the Brooklyn Dodgers in 1947, he was the first African-American athlete to play for a major league baseball team. At first Robinson had to endure the jeers of whites in the crowd and the racial insults of many white ballplayers on his own team as well as opposing teams. He also had to stay in segregated motels and rooming houses when his Brooklyn team (now the Los Angeles Dodgers) played in other cities. But his talents as an athlete and his determination to keep calm, in spite of

## Baseball Greats, 1946 to 1955

The following baseball players were chosen the "most valuable player" (MVP) in their respective leagues. How many do you recognize?

| | National League | American League |
|---|---|---|
| 1946 | Stan Musial (St. Louis Cardinals) | Ted Williams (Boston Red Sox) |
| 1947 | Bob Elliott (Boston Braves) | Joe DiMaggio (New York Yankees) |
| 1948 | Stan Musial (St. Louis Cardinals) | Lou Boudreau (Cleveland Indians) |
| 1949 | **Jackie Robinson** (Brooklyn Dodgers) | Ted Williams (Boston Red Sox) |
| 1950 | Jim Konstanty (Philadelphia Phillies) | Phil Rizzuto (New York Yankees) |
| 1951 | Roy Campanella (Brooklyn Dodgers) | Yogi Berra (New York Yankees) |
| 1952 | Hank Sauer (Chicago Cubs) | Bobby Shantz (Philadelphia A's) |
| 1953 | Roy Campanella (Brooklyn Dodgers) | Al Rosen (Cleveland Indians) |
| 1954 | Willie Mays (New York Giants) | Yogi Berra (New York Yankees) |
| 1955 | Roy Campanella (Brooklyn Dodgers) | Yogi Berra (New York Yankees) |

**Jackie Robinson turning a double play**

all obstacles, won for him the admiration of millions. An outstanding ball player, Robinson in 1962 was elected to the Baseball Hall of Fame—the first of many African Americans to win the honor.

## C. LANDMARK CASE: *BROWN V. BOARD OF EDUCATION OF TOPEKA* (1954)

More than any event of the twentieth century, a Supreme Court decision of 1954 marked a turning point in the movement for civil rights for African Americans. The landmark case of *Brown v. Board of Education of Topeka* came before the Court shortly after Earl Warren had become its new chief justice.

**Background to the Case**  Until 1954, in earlier cases concerning racial segregation, the Supreme Court had determined that railroads, schools, hotels, and other facilities could be segregated under the Constitution *if* those facilities were "separate but equal." In other words segregation was allowed if the state made sure that separate facilites for the use of African Americans were roughly equal to the facilities set aside for whites. The "separate but equal" rule had originated in 1896 in the Supreme Court case of *Plessy v. Ferguson.* (Review Chapter 5.)

**Facts of the Case**  In the early 1950s the school system of Topeka, Kansas, was segregated by law. A young African American named Linda Brown lived closer to one of Topeka's all-white elementary schools than to the city's all-black elementary school. Her father attempted to enroll her in the white elementary school, but school officials turned him down. Aided by the National Association for the Advancement of Colored People (NAACP), Linda Brown's father brought suit against the Topeka Board of Education. A lower federal court rejected Brown's suit on the grounds that Topeka's schools were properly "separate but equal." Brown and the NAACP then appealed to the U.S. Supreme Court.

**The Decision**  The main lawyer representing Brown was an African American employed by the NAACP—Thurgood Marshall. Marshall and his associates used not only legal arguments but also psychological evidence from the studies of Kenneth Clark, an African-American psychologist. The studies demonstrated that African-American children tended to feel inferior as a direct result of living in a segregated society.

The Supreme Court's decision in the case reversed its previous position. It declared that segregated schools could *not* be equal, because of the psychological damage that they inflicted on minority children. Led by Warren and Brennan, all justices on the Supreme Court agreed that segregation on the basis of race deprived children

## DOCUMENTS: *BROWN V. BOARD OF EDUCATION OF TOPEKA* (1954)

Writing for a unanimous Court, Chief Justice Earl Warren gave several arguments for desegregating the nation's schools. One of his arguments is presented below. How would you state the argument in your own words?

Earl Warren

Today, education is perhaps the most important function of state and local governments. Compulsory school attendance laws and the great expenditures for education both demonstrate our recognition of the importance of education to our democratic society. It is required in the performance of our most basic public responsibilities, even service in the armed forces. It is the very foundation of good citizenship. Today it is a principal instrument in awakening the child to cultural values, in preparing him for later professional training, and in helping him to adjust normally to his environment. In these days, it is doubtful that any child may reasonably be expected to succeed in life if he is denied the opportunity of an education. Such an opportunity, where the state has undertaken to provide it, is a right which must be made available to all on equal terms.

We come then to the question presented: Does segregation of children in public schools solely on the basis of race, even though the physical facilities and other "tangible" factors may be equal, deprive the children of the minority group of equal educational opportunities? We believe that it does.

of equal educational opportunities. The Court concluded therefore that Topeka's school system and other systems like it violated the Fourteenth Amendment's guarantee of equal protection of the laws.

Shortly afterward the Supreme Court ruled that any segregated school system in the country would have to become racially desegregated with "all deliberate speed."

Thurgood Marshall, the lawyer who had helped achieve this breakthrough for civil rights, was appointed to the Supreme Court in 1967.

**Two Kinds of Segregation** In practical terms, what did the Supreme Court's decision mean for the nation's schools? Clearly state and local laws requiring segregation would now be considered unconstitutional. Laws of this kind were known as **de jure segregation.** But there was an even more common form of segregation known as **de facto segregation.** Instead of laws causing schools to be segregated, schools could be segregated in fact (de facto) by the custom of admitting only students living within the neighborhood. After the decision in the *Brown* case, the federal courts ruled in a series of cases that both forms of school segregation were unconstitutional.

## D. CRISIS IN LITTLE ROCK

Many Southern whites opposed the Supreme Court's ruling to desegregate their school systems. Some were determined to resist the ruling and prevent African-American students from entering schools that had previously been all-white. The first major challenge to the Court's decision occurred in Little Rock, Arkansas, in 1957. This city's board of education had drawn up a desegregation plan and ordered a formerly all-white high school to admit a few African-American students.

Arkansas's governor, Orval Faubus, posted units of the Arkansas National Guard around the Little Rock high school to stop African-American students from entering the building. Faubus explained that the state troops were there to maintain order. A federal court responded by reaffirming the students' right to enter the school and forbidding the governor to interfere. Faubus finally did remove the troops but only after a mob of whites had stopped the African-American students from entering the high school.

President Eisenhower was reluctant to become involved in the crisis. He recognized, however, that Governor Faubus's actions challenged the authority of the national government and the U.S. Supreme Court. He called the Arkansas National Guard into federal service and ordered it back to the high school, this time to protect the right of the African-American students to enter the building. In addition he sent hundreds of U.S. soldiers to Little Rock to keep order and to prevent any further trouble. Although Governor Faubus referred to these measures as an "occupation," most Americans supported the president's actions.

## E. PROTESTS IN THE SOUTH

Schools were only one institution that began to change in response to the civil rights movement. Other institutions—segregated buses, segregated lunch counters, and segregated movie theaters—also began to change.

**Bus Boycott in Montgomery** The civil rights movement gained momentum from an incident in Montgomery, Alabama, in 1955. As in many Southern cities, it was the rule in Montgomery for African Americans to sit in the rear section of a bus. Returning home from work one afternoon, an NAACP official named Rosa Parks refused to give up her seat in the front of the bus to a white person. She was arrested and charged with violating the segregation laws. Protesting Rosa Park's arrest, a 26-year-old Baptist minister, Martin Luther King, Jr., urged African Americans in Montgomery to boycott the city's buses by refusing to ride in them. The bus boycott lasted for more than a year and was extremely effective. It hurt both the bus system and business in general. Under the pressure of the boycott, the city of Montgomery gave in and agreed to desegregate its transportation system.

The reformers' victory in the heart of the South paved the way for boycotts and demonstrations in other cities. Another result of the bus boycott in Montgomery was the rise of a supremely gifted leader and speaker, Martin Luther King, Jr.

**King's Philosophy of Protest**   King believed in organizing public demonstrations that were nonviolent. He believed that groups of protesters who joined together to disobey unjust laws would eventually prevail. This approach, known as **civil disobedience,** had been taught by earlier reformers. In the 1840s the American writer Henry David Thoreau had advocated civil disobedience as a method for opposing slavery and the Mexican War. In the 1930s and 1940s India's great leader Mohandas Gandhi had demonstrated the power of civil disobedience in opposing British rule. Now in the 1950s and 1960s Martin Luther King, Jr., effectively applied the philosophy of nonviolence and civil disobedience to protesting the segregation laws of the South.

**Student Sit-ins**   A student group that believed in nonviolent protest called itself the Student Nonviolent Coordinating Committee (SNCC). Beginning in 1960 college students belonging to SNCC organized sit-in demonstrations in major cities of the South. They would walk into a restaurant that practiced segregation and sit at the counter waiting to be served. As expected, the restaurant would refuse to serve them, and they in turn would refuse to leave their seats. Many of the demonstrators were arrested. But combined with the powerful tactic of boycotting segregated businesses, the sit-ins led several cities including Dallas, Atlanta, and Nashville to do away with segregation.

# F.  CIVIL RIGHTS LEGISLATION

Ever since Reconstruction ended in the 1870s, African Americans in the South had difficulty exercising their constitutional right to vote in elections. State laws were especially designed to discriminate against them. Also many had reason to fear for their lives and property if they appeared at the local polling place and asked for a ballot. (Review Chapter 5, page 144.) To a majority of lawmakers in Congress, a federal law to protect the voting rights of Southern blacks seemed long overdue.

In 1957 Congress enacted a civil rights law that called upon the U.S. Justice Department to stop any illegal practices designed to prevent African Americans from voting. In 1960 another civil rights law called for the use of federal "referees" in situations where voting rights were being denied.

These two laws were weak and failed to provide real protection for African-American voters. Even so, they were the first civil rights laws passed since Reconstruction. They prepared the way for stronger laws that would follow in the 1960s (described in Chapter 15).

### In Review

The following questions refer to section III: Eisenhower's Domestic Policies, 1953 to 1961 and section IV: The Civil Rights Movement.

1. For each topic on the left, explain how it was affected by the event or presidential action to the right.
   (a) Truman's Fair Deal—the election of Dwight Eisenhower
   (b) Segregated schools—the appointment of Earl Warren to the Supreme Court
   (c) Civil rights for African Americans—the bus boycott in Montgomery
2. Define and evaluate the philosophy of Martin Luther King, Jr., as it has been used to protest unjust laws.

# V. Prosperity and Consumerism

In the depression decade of the 1930s, the American people had been chiefly concerned with economic security. U.S. entry into World War II in 1941 brought back prosperity, as factories strained to turn out increasing quantities of war goods. Many consumer goods were in short supply during the war. But when the war ended, Americans had plenty of money to spend—and they spent it on all the things that they had lived without during the Great Depression and war. Their purchases of new homes, appliances, cars, and televisions created a new society of middle-class consumers tending the lawns of their new suburban homes and spending hours watching their favorite TV shows. Their urge to acquire more and more possessions was known as **consumerism.**

## A. NEW CARS, NEW HOMES, NEW SUBURBS

In the postwar years millions of Americans bought new cars. Automobile sales spurred the growth of other industries that supplied the raw materials—such industries as steel, rubber, and glass. Spending on travel, tourism, restaurants, and motels increased, as people took to the open road in record numbers. Filling the tank with gas was no problem in the 1950s when gasoline was both plentiful and cheap (about 30 cents a gallon).

Record sales of new cars went hand in hand with record sales of new homes. **Suburbs** seemed to spring up overnight as more and more people moved out of city apartments into new suburban homes. Suburbanites used their automobiles to make the daily trip from their suburban residences to city office buildings and back again. Those who chose not to drive in the heavy traffic became railroad commuters instead.

Suburban homes of the 1950s were often built in large developments in which one home looked almost exactly like every other. The advantage of such homes was that they could be bought at relatively low prices. Middle-income families in the suburbs filled their homes with the latest electrical equipment—washing machines, dryers, dishwashers, and air conditioners.

## B. TELEVISION

Television was a new consumer item of the postwar years that profoundly influenced American society. Though developed by several inventors during the 1920s, television sets became common in American homes only in the early 1950s. By 1953 more than half the households in the United States had at least one television. Most TV images in the early 1950s were in black and white (even though color technology was available as early as 1951).

**Impact on the Entertainment Industry**   Television was partly like the radio, since its regularly scheduled programs were paid for by advertisers. It was also partly like the movies because it was a visual medium that showed old movies as part of its featured programming. Most of the early TV shows were broadcast "live" (as they happened). Much as filmmakers had to make the challenging transition from "silents" to "talkies," radio stars tried to adapt to the demands of being seen as well as heard. Through the medium of television, TV stars like Lucille Ball, Milton Berle, and Jackie Gleason became household names.

**Impact on Consumerism**   Every TV show had a commercial "sponsor"—a corporation whose purpose in paying for the show was to advertise its products to a huge audience. Because of their visual impact, TV ads were even more effective than radio ads in promoting the sale of automobiles, electrical appliances, and other consumer goods. Often a TV show included the name of its corporate sponsor—for example, "The Kraft Television Theater" and "The Palmolive Comedy Hour."

Scene from "I Love Lucy"—Lucille Ball, Desi Arnaz, Vivian Vance

**Impact on Popular Culture**  The most important effect of television was its influence on the tastes and habits of the American people. Watching TV for hours at a time became a daily habit of millions. Most people turned on the television for light entertainment in the form of sports, comedy shows, and adventure movies. Programs of a more serious and educational nature tended to be much less popular. People who watched many hours of TV a week had fewer leisure hours for more meaningful activities such as reading books or going on family outings. Critics of television in the 1950s and later decades believed that television had a generally negative effect on the values and habits of those who watched it most—young, school-age Americans. On the other hand, millions of Americans now had daily access, not only to a free form of entertainment, but also to some excellent cultural programs (plays, concerts, news commentary, and documentaries).

## C. THE EMERGENCE OF A TEENAGE CULTURE

Television was just one of the amusements of the youthful generation that grew up in the 1950s. More than any teenage group of the past, the youth of the 1950s had their own distinct culture. Late in the decade, it became a culture centered on the enjoyment of material pleasures and leisure activities.

**Values of the Young** During the early 1950s most young people had little interest in politics and generally accepted traditional values. They were known as the "quiet generation." At the same time, however, teenagers showed some signs of restlessness and rebellion. Many of them admired two new stars of the movies, James Dean and Marlon Brando, who portrayed moody and rebellious youths. A popular novel, J. D. Salinger's *The Catcher in the Rye* (1951), featured a teenage boy as its hero and raised searching questions about American society.

**Rock-and-Roll Music** A new kind of music helped to give the generation of the 1950s an identity different from that of their parents. Based on the "rhythm and blues" music of African-American musicians, **rock and roll** had a pulsing beat and fast tempo. The older generation called the new music nothing but noise, but teenagers of the late 1950s loved it. New recording stars such as Little Richard, Fats Domino, and the Platters burst upon the scene. Even more appealing to millions of young Americans were the rock-and-roll songs of their idol, Elvis Presley.

**The Baby Boom** One reason that teenagers attracted a lot of attention in the late 1950s was because there were so many of them. In the time of prosperity that followed World War II, married couples decided to have more children than in the prewar period. The result was a dramatic increase in the birth rate known as the **baby boom.** The greater number of children was one reason for increased sales of homes, cars, and appliances as well as children's toys and teen clothing. Cities and suburbs built new schools to make room for the growing youth population.

The *birth rate* is the number of births per 1,000 women aged 18 to 44.

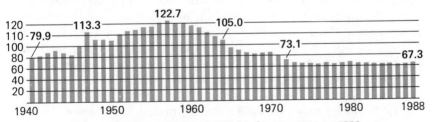

Baby boom—and baby bust: U.S. birth rate, 1940 to 1988

# VI. Immigration in the Postwar Years

While middle-class Americans moved from the cities into the suburbs, new immigrants from Latin America moved into the cities. By the 1950s the Hispanic (Spanish-speaking) part of the U.S. population had become a significant and growing minority.

## A. IMMIGRATION FROM LATIN AMERICA

Most of the newcomers from Latin America came from Mexico, Cuba, and Puerto Rico.

**Mexican Immigrants**   After World War II poverty in Mexico and economic opportunity in the United States caused many thousands of Mexicans to seek work in California, Texas, and other states of the Southwest. Hoping to escape unemployment at home, most Mexicans came to the United States as *braceros* (a Spanish word meaning "laborers") to harvest the fruit crops on Southwestern farms. Many entered the United States legally in compliance with the immigration laws. Others, however, crossed the border illegally.

**Puerto Rican Migration**   The Caribbean island of Puerto Rico became a U.S. territory as a result of the Spanish-American War of 1898. The U.S. Congress granted the Puerto Rican people full U.S. citizenship in 1917 and granted their island country special status as a commonwealth in 1952. Commonwealth status meant that Puerto Ricans could elect their own governor and did not have to pay federal taxes. On the other hand they could not participate in elections for Congress or the presidency. Immigration laws did not apply to Puerto Ricans who, as U.S. citizens, could enter or leave any part of the United States at will.

After World War II many Puerto Ricans migrated to New York and other cities of the Northeast in search of jobs.

**Cuban Immigrants**   Fidel Castro's revolution in Cuba in 1959 caused hundreds of thousands of Cubans to flee to the United States. Many settled in Miami and other Florida cities. Most of the Cuban immigrants were from middle-income and upper-income groups.

**Contributions of Hispanic Americans**   Like other immigrant groups, Hispanic Americans contributed their own rich culture to the American nation. Their distinctive styles of music gradually won the appreciation of a wide public. (The emergence of Hispanic leaders in the 1960s and 1970s is treated in Chapter 16.) In economic terms Puerto Rican workers stepped into jobs in the garment industry that had once been filled by Jewish and Italian immigrants. Mexicans in the 1950s and 1960s provided a hard-working labor force that was essential to harvesting the crops of the Southwest. Most Latin American immigrants received low wages. But their American-born children (like the children of other immigrant groups) had greater opportunity than their parents to go to college and pursue careers in high-income professions such as medicine, business, and law.

**Problems of Hispanic Americans**   Despite success and progress in many areas, Spanish-speaking ethnic groups in the United States have faced a number of obstacles in adapting to American life. The wages paid Mexican **migrant workers** were so low in the 1950s that all members of the family, including the children, had to work long hours. As a result, those who could not attend school were deprived of the advantage of an education. In Los Angeles and other large cities of the Southwest, gangs of "Anglo" (white) youths challenged the right of Mexican Americans to attend "Anglo" schools. This led to gang warfare, which became a serious urban problem.

Puerto Ricans also suffered from the hostility of the "Anglo" majority and the rivalry of other ethnic groups. Those who moved to New York City generally had little money and few skills. Too often they found only low-paying jobs and poor housing.

Adjusting to American schools was a serious problem for those immigrant children who were raised in a Spanish-speaking culture. Because they spoke Spanish at home, many Hispanic children struggled with lessons taught only in English. Thus, the percentage of Puerto Ricans who completed high school in New York City in the 1950s was much smaller than that of other groups.

## B. THE EFFECT OF IMMIGRATION LAWS ON OTHER GROUPS

Immigration laws in the 1950s kept out large numbers of people by assigning quotas to different countries.

**McCarran-Walter Act (1952)**  Congress passed this law over President Truman's veto. It provided for the following:

- The quota system was retained. The United States would admit more immigrants from Western Europe than from Eastern and Southern Europe.

- The U.S. attorney general could deport any aliens considered to be subversive.

- Asians could immigrate to the United States at the rate of 2,000 a year.

**Asian Immigrants**  Although 2,000 was a tiny quota for the world's most populous continent, it was more than the earlier quota for Asia. After the new law went into effect, Chinese neighborhoods grew slightly larger, and Korean immigrants began to arrive in small numbers.

**Survivors of the Holocaust**  President Truman favored an immigration policy that permitted Jewish refugees from Europe—survivors of the Holocaust—to enter the United States. The Displaced Persons Act of 1950 allowed as many as 341,000 refugees to be admitted as immigrants.

# In Review

The following questions refer to section V: Postwar Prosperity and Consumerism and section VI: Immigration in the Postwar Years.

1. Discuss the ways in which consumerism in the 1950s changed the nature of American society.
2. Explain the significance of television as a force for change in American society.
3. Compare the experience of Latin American immigrants in the 1950s with that of other groups of immigrants. (Review Chapter 7.)

## GLOSSARY OF KEY TERMS: CHAPTER 14

**baby boom**   a significant increase in the U.S. birth rate between 1946 and 1964.

**bipartisanship**   the support of a president's policies by both Republicans and Democrats.

**boycott**   a group's refusal to buy products from a certain business in order to compel the business to change its policies.

***Brown* v. *Board of Education of Topeka***   a Supreme Court case of 1954 in which racially segregated schools were declared unconstitutional.

**civil disobedience**   the strategy of purposely disobeying laws that are considered to be unjust.

**civil rights laws**   laws to enforce the right of African Americans, other minorities, and women to vote and to have equal access to public facilities.

**closed shop**   a company that agrees to hire only workers who belong to a single labor union.

**conservative**   a person who believes that the federal government's role in the economy should be kept to a minimum.

**consumerism**   the tendency of consumers to buy more and more products during a time of prosperity.

**de facto segregation**   racial segregation that results from two races living in different neighborhoods rather than from laws requiring segregation.

**de jure segregation**   laws that require African Americans to use facilities separate from those reserved for whites.

***Dennis et al.* v. *United States***   a Supreme Court case of 1951 declaring that a speaker may be penalized if his or her speech encourages people to revolt against the U.S. government.

**Fair Deal**   President Truman's domestic program.

**House Un-American Activities Committee**   a special committee of the

U.S. House of Representatives that investigated those whom the committee suspected of being Communists or disloyal Americans.

**liberal** a person who believes that the federal government should intervene in the economy and give assistance to people in need.

**loyalty checks** the policy begun by President Truman in which government employees were investigated to determine whether they had ever supported the Communist party or other radical group.

**McCarran Act** a federal law of 1950 requiring members of Communist and Communist-front organizations to register with the government; also known as the Internal Security Act.

**McCarran-Walter Act** a U.S. immigration law of 1952 that set national quotas for immigrants and provided for checking the loyalty of aliens.

**McCarthyism** the practice of recklessly accusing someone of supporting or belonging to the Communist party.

**migrant workers** farm workers who move, or migrate, from one place to another to harvest seasonal crops.

**offshore oil** oil located in seabeds close to the coastline.

**price controls** a policy in which government officials establish price levels for different products in order to avoid extreme inflation.

**rock and roll** popular music characterized by a heavily accented beat.

**secondary boycott** a labor union's refusal to buy merchandise from a firm that does business with another firm that is the primary target of the union's strike.

**suburbs** communities outside a major city but near enough to the city for residents to travel to and from city workplaces.

**Taft-Hartley Act** a federal law of 1947 whose purpose was to reduce the power of labor unions.

**"whistle-stop" campaign** the campaign technique in which a candidate delivers speeches from the rear platform of a train at different station stops.

***Yates v. United States*** a Supreme Court case of 1957 in which the Court ruled that statements of policy were protected under the First Amendment and that only statements leading to dangerous action could be prohibited.

## TEST YOURSELF

### A. Multiple Choice: Facts, Main Ideas, Skills

*On a separate sheet of paper, write the number of the word or expression that, of those given, best completes the statement or answers the question.*

### Reviewing the facts

1. The major purpose of the GI Bill of Rights was to (1) provide an employment service for returning veterans (2) aid returning war

veterans with funding for education (3) extend the tour of duty for soldiers scheduled to leave the service (4) assist soldiers with voter registration

2. A major goal of Truman's Fair Deal was (1) improving economic benefits for working people (2) extending trading privileges to Communist nations (3) ending the role of the Tennessee Valley Authority (TVA) in providing cheap electricity (4) shifting the funding of education from state and local governments to the federal government

3. Senator Joseph McCarthy built his power on the issue of (1) housing for senior citizens (2) the poor performance of U.S. students relative to Soviet students (3) the extent of Communist influence in government agencies and organizations (4) the military buildup in the Soviet Union

4. President Truman's most important contribution to the civil rights movement was (1) ending segregation in public education (2) ending discrimination in housing (3) desegregating the armed forces (4) desegregating major league baseball

5. The significance of the civil rights laws of 1957 and 1960 was that they (1) succeeded in ending discrimination in public facilities (2) were the first civil rights laws passed since Reconstruction (3) opened the doors to equal opportunity in employment (4) provided protection for women as well as racial minorities

6. In the case of *Brown v. Board of Education of Topeka* (1954), the Supreme Court ruled that segregated public schools (1) provided an appropriate education for all students (2) must be made equal to nonsegregated schools (3) must comply with federal standards (4) provided an unequal education

7. Martin Luther King, Jr., believed that improvements in racial attitudes would best be achieved through (1) eliminating the Thirteenth Amendment (2) establishing a separate nation for African Americans (3) using nonviolent methods of protest (4) supporting a policy of school segregation

8. The increased immigration from Mexico and migration from Puerto Rico in the post-World War II period was fueled primarily by (1) the desire for political freedom (2) a belief in bilingual education (3) the desire for increased economic opportunity (4) an appreciation for the popular culture of the United States

9. Both Henry David Thoreau and Martin Luther King, Jr., supported the idea of (1) social control (2) conformity (3) suspension of civil liberties (4) civil disobedience

## Reviewing the main ideas

10. The domestic policies of Truman and Eisenhower demonstrate that both presidents (1) accepted most of the social programs of the New Deal (2) favored private rather than public ownership of power plants (3) believed that offshore oil rights belong under state rather than

federal control (4) preferred a Supreme Court that makes bold decisions in civil rights cases

11. Since World War II the integration of U.S. public schools has been most significantly stimulated by (1) decisions of federal and state courts (2) passage of constitutional amendments (3) leadership of school boards in the South (4) actions of state legislatures

12. The Supreme Court decision in *Brown* v. *Board of Education of Topeka* is important in the civil rights movements because it established that (1) racial discrimination is legal (2) the "separate but equal" principle is constitutional (3) the use of poll taxes is illegal (4) segregating students by race is unconstitutional

13. A landmark Supreme Court case in 1954, a bus boycott in 1955, and sit-in demonstrations in 1960 were all concerned with (1) equal rights for women (2) discrimination against Latin American immigrants (3) the shift of the white middle class from central cities to the suburbs (4) the movement for civil rights for African Americans

14. In the early 1950s the American people were *most* divided over the issues of (1) nationalistic loyalty versus an individual's right to dissent (2) improving schools versus saving tax dollars (3) the need for nuclear power versus fear of radiation effects (4) the growth of big business versus its impact on the environment

15. Which was a major effect of the cold war on the United States in the 1950s? (1) Congress passed laws prohibiting U.S. contact with Communist countries. (2) The United States refused to enter military alliance with other nations. (3) Participation in so-called "radical" groups was viewed as un-American. (4) Americans were required to take loyalty oaths before registering to vote.

16. Critics of McCarthyism in the 1950s stressed the idea that (1) the government should always be on guard against Communist subversion (2) fears of subversion can lead to the erosion of constitutional liberties (3) loyalty oaths can prevent espionage (4) communism is likely to gain influence in times of prosperity

*Base your answers to questions 17 and 18 on the quotation below from a U.S. Supreme Court decision and on your knowledge of social studies.*

"We conclude that in the field of public education the doctrine of 'separate but equal' has no place. Separate educational facilities are inherently unequal."

17. The Supreme Court based its decision on the idea that segregated schools are likely to (1) cause members of a minority group to feel socially inferior to the majority (2) create unnecessary administrative problems in the nation's schools (3) place excessive burdens on school transportation systems (4) result in unfair tax increases to support dual school systems

18. This Supreme Court decision marked the beginning of the end of (1) racial violence (2) public education (3) legal racial discrimination (4) the civil rights movement

## Developing critical thinking skills

*Base your answers to questions 19 and 20 on the information below and on your knowledge of social studies.*

| Year | Event |
| --- | --- |
| 1954 | Supreme Court decision declaring the segregation of public schools to be illegal |
| 1955 | Supreme Court decision declaring the segregation of public transportation to be illegal |
| 1957 | Passage of a civil rights act providing federal protection for African Americans registering to vote |

**19.** From the above information, what can you correctly infer about civil rights in the 1950s? (1) All civil rights problems were solved after 1957. (2) Civil rights issues were less important in the 1960s than in the 1950s. (3) Congressional action on civil rights issues was more important than court action. (4) The U.S. government in the 1950s generally supported the idea of equal civil rights for African Americans.

**20.** Which document was most important to the Supreme Court's decisions of 1954 and 1955 listed above? (1) the Declaration of Independence (2) the U.S. Constitution (3) President Eisenhower's inaugural address (4) President Lincoln's Emancipation Proclamation

## B. Enduring Issues

*Select two of the enduring issues from column A. For each issue chosen, explain how the historical example in column B relates to the issue.*

| A. Enduring Issues | B. Historical Examples |
| --- | --- |
| 1. Federalism—the balance between nation and state | The conflict between President Eisenhower and Governor Faubus |
| 2. The judiciary—interpreter of the Constitution or shaper of policy | The Supreme Court's decision in *Brown* v. *Board of Education of Topeka* |
| 3. Civil liberties—balance between government and the individual | Loyalty tests under President Truman |
| 4. Rights of ethnic and racial groups under the Constitution | Civil rights movement in the 1950s |
| 5. Separation of powers and the capacity to govern | The McCarran-Walter Act passed by Congress over President Truman's veto |
| 6. Property rights and economic policy | The issue of offshore oil during Eisenhower's presidency |
| 7. Constitutional change and flexibility | The Supreme Court's reversal of its "separate but equal" decision in *Plessy* v. *Ferguson* (1896) |

## C. Essays

### Level 1

In different periods of U.S. history, a more democratic society has come about both by government action and by the individual actions of concerned citizens.

1. Describe *three* specific actions of the U.S. government in the 1950s that helped to bring about a more democratic society.
2. Describe *three* specific actions of concerned citizens in the 1940s and 1950s that helped to bring about a more democratic society.

### Level 2

After World War II, members of minority groups struggled to gain equal rights.

A. List *two* rights that were denied to African Americans in the 1940s. Then list *two* ways by which African Americans tried to gain their rights in the 1950s.
B. Base your answer to part B on your answer to part A. Write an essay explaining how and why African Americans struggled to gain their rights in the 1940s and 1950s.

# Chapter *15*

# Decade of Change:
# The 1960s

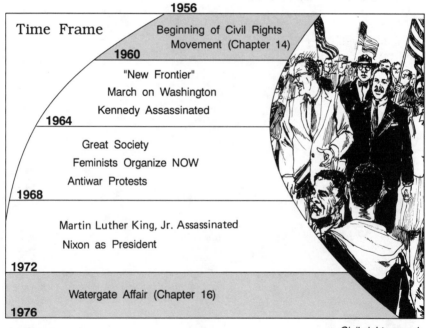

| Time Frame | |
|---|---|
| **1956** | |
| | Beginning of Civil Rights Movement (Chapter 14) |
| **1960** | |
| | "New Frontier" |
| | March on Washington |
| | Kennedy Assassinated |
| **1964** | |
| | Great Society |
| | Feminists Organize NOW |
| | Antiwar Protests |
| **1968** | |
| | Martin Luther King, Jr. Assassinated |
| | Nixon as President |
| **1972** | |
| | Watergate Affair (Chapter 16) |
| **1976** | |

*Civil rights march,
Alabama, 1965*

## Objectives

- To understand the changes that occurred in the 1960s in American society and politics.
- To compare the leadership of two presidents of the 1960s, Kennedy and Johnson.
- To note the achievements of African Americans in their movement for civil rights.
- To describe other movements for social justice by women, Native Americans, and persons with disabilities.
- To analyze landmark cases of the Supreme Court that redefined the rights of people accused of crimes.

The 1960s were years of great change and turmoil. In some respects, the changes were positive. U.S. society became more democratic in the 1960s, as minorities, the handicapped, and women made significant progress toward equality. Also the Supreme Court made decisions that expanded the protections of the Bill of Rights. Astonishing gains in science and technology enabled the United States to land a man on the moon in 1969.

In other respects, however, the 1960s was a tragic decade. Assassinations took the lives of a president (John Kennedy), a presidential candidate (Robert Kennedy), and three African-American leaders (Medgar Evers, Martin Luther King, Jr., and Malcolm X). Racial tensions caused riots to erupt in almost every major U.S. city. Drug use among American youths increased. Large numbers of college students took part in massive demonstrations protesting the war in Vietnam.

The Vietnam War and the protest against it will be treated in the next chapter. This chapter focuses chiefly on the positive aspects of change—the progress achieved by women and minorities in their movement for equal rights.

# I. The New Frontier and the Great Society

Politically, the 1960s were dominated by two Democratic presidents: John F. Kennedy (1961 to 1963) and Lyndon B. Johnson (1963 to 1969). Both Kennedy and Johnson stressed the need for social reforms. Kennedy called his reform program the **New Frontier,** while Johnson called his program the **Great Society.**

## A. THE POLICIES OF PRESIDENT KENNEDY

In many respects the brief presidency of John F. Kennedy was unique. Elected in 1960 at the age of 43, he was the youngest candidate to win the presidency and the first president born in the twentieth century. (Theodore Roosevelt was 42 when he took office in 1901, but he became president only as a result of President McKinley's assassination.) Kennedy was also the first Roman Catholic to be president.

**Candidate for President, 1960**   Kennedy came from a wealthy Irish-American family in Massachusetts that had long been active in politics. After fighting in World War II and winning a medal for bravery, Kennedy won election to the U.S. House of Representatives and then to the U.S. Senate. A well-financed campaign, an effective speaking style, and a likeable personality helped him to win the Democratic nomination for president in 1960. His Republican opponent, Richard Nixon, was better known by most voters, having served as vice president under President Eisenhower for eight years. But Kennedy caught up with Nixon in the opinion polls after debating him on television. Watching the first of four debates on their TV screens, most Americans thought Kennedy looked more self-assured and confident than his Republican rival. The Kennedy–Nixon debates showed the amazing power of television to sway voter opinion. If these debates had not occurred, Kennedy would probably have lost the election, since his margin of victory in the 1960 election was slight—303 electoral votes for Kennedy to 219 votes for Nixon.

**Inspiring Inaugural Address**   The youthful president inspired the American nation—especially the youth of America—with his forceful inaugural address of 1961. Speaking of the cold war with the Soviet Union, Kennedy said: "Let every nation know, whether it wishes us well or ill, that we shall pay any price, bear any burden, meet any hardship, support any friend, oppose any foe, to assure the survival and the success of liberty." His most memorable phrase appealed to the idealism of American youth: "Ask not what your country can do for you. Ask what you can do for your country."

**Foreign Policy**   In Chapter 13 you read about President Kennedy's efforts to apply the cold war policy of containment. His greatest successes in foreign policy were (1) his support of the people of West Berlin after the Soviets and East Germans erected the Berlin Wall, (2) his decision to use the U.S. Navy in forcing the Soviet Union to remove missiles from Cuba, and (3) his idea for a Peace Corps of American volunteers to aid nations of the third world. On the other hand, as you shall see in Chapter 16, Kennedy's efforts to contain communism in Vietnam were partly responsible for U.S. involvement in a costly and unsuccessful war.

**Domestic Policy: The New Frontier**   In the tradition of his Democratic predecessors, Roosevelt and Truman, President Kennedy gave a name to his reform program. His New Frontier included proposals for federal aid to education, greater Social Security benefits, assistance to Appalachia (a poverty-stricken region of the Southeast), protection of African-Americans' civil rights, and public health insurance for the elderly.

Even though both houses of Congress had Democratic majorities, Kennedy succeeded in winning passage of only a few of his New Frontier programs. Among those passed were:

- A bill granting federal funds for urban renewal (the rebuilding of rundown city neighborhoods)
- A bill increasing the minimum wage to $1.25 an hour
- A bill providing federal loans to aid impoverished families in the Appalachian Mountains and other "distressed areas."

Among the programs rejected were:

- A bill to provide federal grants of $2.3 billion to the states for school construction and teacher's salaries
- A bill to provide **Medicare,** or public health insurance, for elderly Americans through the Social Security system
- A new civil rights law to enable the federal government to take bolder action in cases of racial discrimination and segregation.

Even though Kennedy's most important programs were defeated by conservative Republicans and conservative Democrats, they were later adopted during the presidency of Lyndon Johnson.

**Assassination**   In late November, 1963, President Kennedy and his wife, Jacqueline Kennedy, traveled to Dallas, Texas. While riding in an open car through Dallas, the president was killed instantly by bullets fired from a high-rise building. The police arrested Lee Harvey Oswald for the crime. But another assassin killed Oswald before his case could come to trial. Thus, there is still a mystery surrounding the death of President Kennedy. Why did it happen? Did Oswald act alone, or were others involved in the crime?

The American nation went into a state of deep shock and mourning over the sudden death of its youthful leader. The assassination proved to be the first of a series of violent episodes (involvement in war, protests against war, racial unrest, more assassinations) that marked the decade of the 1960s.

## B. LYNDON JOHNSON AND THE GREAT SOCIETY

The next president was a more experienced politician than Kennedy. Until being elected vice president in 1960, Lyndon Johnson had served several terms in the U.S. Senate and had become a master of the lawmaking process. Johnson's personality and political style contrasted sharply with Kennedy's. He was a Southerner from Texas (not a New Englander from Massachusetts). He had grown up on a farm and lived close to poverty (unlike Kennedy's wealthy and urban background). As a Democrat, however, Johnson shared Kennedy's belief in liberal reforms. Using his boundless energy and shrewd political tactics, President Johnson managed to push through Congress more important legislation than any other president since Franklin D. Roosevelt.

**First Year of Reform, 1964**   Finishing the term begun by Kennedy, Johnson was quick to show his skills as a legislative leader. First, he persuaded Congress to enact the most important civil rights law in U.S. history (see page 457). Second, he announced an "unconditional" **War on Poverty.** Johnson said that a country as prosperous as the United States should be able to eliminate poverty. As the first step toward this goal, he persuaded Congress to pass the Economic Opportunity Act (1964), which authorized one billion dollars of federal money for antipoverty programs.

**Elected by a Landslide**   Johnson wanted to be elected president in his own right—and he was. In 1964 the Democrats chose him to be their presidential candidate. His Republican opponent, Senator Barry Goldwater from Arizona, wanted voters to understand that he was deeply committed to conservative ideas. Goldwater, however, was out of touch with the liberalism of the times. President Johnson won by a landslide, 486 electoral votes to only 52 for Goldwater.

**Johnson's Domestic Program**   Following his overwhelming electoral victory, Johnson proposed a far-reaching program of social and economic reform, which he called the Great Society. It was to affect nearly all areas of American life: health, education, housing, employment, immigration, and civil rights. Johnson's ideas for social legislation were not new. They had been proposed by other Democratic presidents, Truman and Kennedy. But Congress had rejected many of the earlier proposals of the Fair Deal and the New Frontier. Now in 1965 Johnson managed to persuade a Democratic Congress to enact all of the following laws:

- Elementary and Secondary Education Act. *Purpose:* To provide federal funds for schools with large numbers of children from low-income families. *Provisions:* Authorized the spending of $1.3 billion on educational programs such as **Head Start** (giving instruction to preschool children from disadvantaged backgrounds).

- Higher Education Act. *Purpose:* To enable qualified students from low-income families to attend college. *Provisions:* Authorized the granting of federal scholarships to capable but needy college students.

- Housing and Urban Development Act. *Purpose:* To assist low-income individuals and families to meet their needs for better and more affordable housing. *Provisions:* Authorized $2.9 billion in federal grants for building new low-rent apartment buildings in the nation's cities.

- Appalachian Development Act. *Purpose:* To help develop a rural and depressed region known as Appalachia (consisting of Eastern states from Pennsylvania to Alabama). *Provisions:* Authorized $1 billion in federal assistance for the region.

- Medicare Act. *Purpose:* To help senior citizens pay for the high costs of hospital care, doctor care, and other medical needs. *Provisions:* Established a public health insurance program known as Medicare, which became part of the Social Security system. Under the program, persons over 65 were insured for a large part of the costs of health care. Also, states received federal grants to pay the medical bills of needy persons. Such grants of outright aid were known as **Medicaid.**

- Immigration Act. *Purpose:* To change the system for admitting immigrants from one that favored Western Europeans to one that admitted greater numbers of people from Asia and Latin America. *Provisions:* Abolished the national quotas first established in the 1920s. (See page 555 for specific provisions of this law.)

**African Americans Appointed to High Positions**     More than any president since Lincoln, President Johnson attempted to assist African Americans and other minorities in their struggle to achieve both economic advancement and equal voting rights. The **Civil Rights Act of 1964** and the **Voting Rights Act of 1965** (discussed in section II of this chapter) probably would not have passed without the strong backing of the Great Society president. In addition Johnson made sure that African Americans were appointed to high-level positions in government. In 1966 he appointed Robert C. Weaver to be the secretary of a newly created cabinet department—the Department of Housing and Urban Development (HUD). Weaver was the first African American to serve in a president's cabinet. In 1967 a vacated seat on the Supreme Court gave Johnson the opportunity to appoint Thurgood Marshall as the first African American to serve on the nation's highest court.

**Foreign Policy: Deepening Involvement in Vietnam**     Unfortunately, President Johnson's hopes for creating a "great society" and eliminating poverty ran upon a major obstacle. The obstacle was largely of his own making, because he decided in 1965 to greatly increase U.S. involvement in a war in Southeast Asia—the Vietnam War. As you shall see in Chapter 16, it proved to be economically impossible to achieve ambitious domestic goals while also fighting a costly war abroad.

# II. The Civil Rights Movement Continues

When the 1960s began and John Kennedy moved into the White House, the civil rights movement was already a major force for change. Recall from Chapter 14 that Martin Luther King, Jr., had emerged as a civil rights leader during the 1950s. Also the Supreme Court had declared segregated schools to be unconstitutional. During the presidencies of Kennedy and Johnson, the civil rights movement continued to grow stronger and achieved some remarkable victories.

## A. DIFFERENT GROUPS IN THE MOVEMENT

A large number of organizations took part in the civil rights movement. Some were moderate in their goals and methods. They wanted nothing more than equal rights under the U.S. Constitution and a fair chance to participate in the political and economic system. Other groups were more radical, stressing "black pride" and "black power."

**Moderate Groups** Those organizations that stressed the goal of ending segregation were:

- The National Association for the Advancement of Colored People (NAACP). Organized in the early 1900s, the NAACP acted as the legal arm of the civil rights movement. It concentrated on winning victories for racial justice by arguing cases in court. The NAACP was chiefly responsible for winning the landmark case of *Brown v. Board of Education of Topeka* in 1954.

- The **Urban League.** Allied closely with the NAACP, this organization sought to end discrimination in employment and housing and to increase job opportunities for African Americans.

- The Student Nonviolent Coordinating Committee (SNCC). The students who joined this organization participated in sit-ins and other peaceful demonstrations against Jim Crow laws in the South.

- The **Southern Christian Leadership Conference (SCLC).** Martin Luther King, Jr., founded this organization in 1957 to coordinate the antisegregation efforts of African-American leaders in the South. Its nonviolent methods of protesting racial injustice included boycotts, sit-ins, and marches.

- The **Congress of Racial Equality (CORE).** Organized during World War II, activists in CORE carried out peaceful demonstrations against racial discrimination in both the North and the South. During the 1960s, under the leadership of James Farmer, CORE started a dramatic form of protest known as the **freedom ride.** Protesters against Jim Crow laws would ride in long-distance buses to make sure that bus terminals in the South were not segregated. Freedom riders included both white Americans and African Americans.

Jewish, Catholic, and Protestant members of CORE were willing to suffer attacks and beatings by angry mobs of racists without fighting back. This willingness to endure punishment for a good cause without resorting to violence is called passive resistance.

- Union alliances. Union leaders such as A. Philip Randolph and Bayard Rustin formed alliances between civil rights groups and labor unions. They persuaded their unions to support the political and legal goals of the civil rights groups. At the same time the civil rights groups gave support to the unions' struggle for economic progress.

**Radical Groups** In the mid-1960s new organizations arose that called for "black power." Nonviolence as a method for change was attacked by those dissatisfied with the pace of progress. Leaders among the radicals—Eldridge Cleaver, Stokely Carmichael, and Angela Davis—spoke of the need for a racial revolution. Said Cleaver in his book, *Soul on Ice:* "We shall have our manhood. We shall have it, or the earth will be leveled by our attempts to gain it."

Two groups committed to the cause of black power were the **Black Muslims** and the **Black Panthers.**

- *Black Muslims, or the Nation of Islam.* Black Muslims are African-American followers of Islam, one of the major religions of Africa as well as the Middle East. The founder of the Black Muslims was Elijah Muhammed. He advocated the separation of races, a separate African-American state within the United States, and pride in being black. One of the best known Black Muslims was Malcolm X, who broke from the main body of Muslims to form his own group in 1963. Malcolm X rejected passive resistance and urged his followers to fight back against those who violently abused them. "We don't teach you to turn the other cheek," he said. "We teach you to obey the law ... But at the same time, we teach you that anyone who puts his hands on you, you do your best to see that he doesn't put it on anybody else."

A famous convert to the Nation of Islam was the heavyweight champion of the world, Cassius Clay, who took the Islamic name of Muhammad Ali. In 1967, during the Vietnam War, Muhammad Ali refused induction into the armed forces, saying that he was a minister of Islam and a conscientious objector to war. He was convicted of draft evasion, and the boxing championship was taken from him. In 1970, however, his conviction was overturned. He then resumed his boxing career, once again winning the heavyweight championship.

- *Black Panthers.* Organized in 1966 the Black Panthers advocated the use of force to achieve "black power." Violence by whites, they said, should be answered with violence by blacks. For this purpose they formed a semi-military organization, wore a kind of uniform (leather jackets and black belts), and carried rifles. They also called for "better education, better medical care, and better housing" for African Americans. Their chief spokesman was their minister of information, Eldridge Cleaver.

# B. CIVIL RIGHTS UNDER THE NEW FRONTIER

President Kennedy was a Democrat with liberal views on racial issues. As such, he gave encouragement to African Americans' struggle to end segregation.

**Desegregating Interstate Buses**   When President Kennedy took office, he appointed his brother Robert Kennedy as U.S. attorney general. Both the president and the attorney general had to deal with a new tactic in the civil rights movement: freedom rides. By crossing state lines on interstate buses, the freedom riders demonstrated that segregation on buses was a matter that involved the interstate commerce clause of the U.S. Constitution. Therefore it was a federal matter, not a matter limited to local laws. Robert Kennedy urged the Interstate Commerce Commission (ICC) to **desegregate** the buses. The ICC did so when it ruled that segregation in interstate bus travel must end.

**Desegregating a University**   In 1962 a young African American, James Meredith, attempted to enroll as a student at the University of Mississippi. This university had previously admitted only white students. Mississippi's governor told Meredith that he could not enroll. But Meredith was determined to do so, despite a huge crowd of whites who threatened to attack him. To contain the crowd and protect Meredith's rights, President Kennedy ordered 400 federal marshals to the university campus. Thus protected, Meredith became the first African American to attend classes and finally to graduate from the University of Mississippi. Soon other Southern colleges and universities began admitting African-American students.

**Protest in Birmingham**   In the early 1960s several cities in the South decided to do away with their segregation laws. But the city of

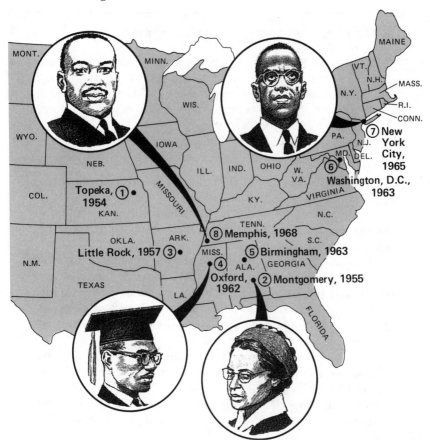

1. Schools desegregated by the Supreme Court's decision in *Brown* v. *Board of Education of Topeka*. 2. Bus boycott following the arrest of Rosa Parks 3. U.S. troops aid in desegration of Little Rock's high school 4. James Meredith enrolled as a student at the University of Mississippi 5. Peaceful demonstration violently broken up by Birmingham police 6. Huge demonstration for civil rights, the March on Washington 7. Assassination of Malcolm X 8. Assassination of Martin Luther King, Jr.

The struggle for civil rights: selected events

Birmingham, Alabama, was not one of them. Protesters led by Martin Luther King, Jr., went to Birmingham to participate in a peaceful march through the center of the city. The Birmingham police attacked the marchers with dogs, powerful jets of water from fire hoses, and electric cattle prods. Television cameras brought the confrontation to a national audience. Among the marchers arrested and jailed in Birmingham was their leader, Martin Luther King, Jr.

Writing from jail, King explained his reasons for breaking laws that he considered unjust. "One who breaks an unjust law must do so

## DOCUMENTS: "I HAVE A DREAM"

On August 28, 1963, Martin Luther King, Jr., stood on a speaker's platform near the Lincoln Memorial in Washington, D.C., and addressed a crowd of more than 200,000 people as well as a huge TV audience. In the most famous part of his speech, the civil rights leader spoke of his dream for a more democratic nation.

To what extent do you think the speaker's dream has become a reality?

I still have a dream. It is a dream deeply rooted in the American dream.

I have a dream that one day this nation will rise up and live out the true meaning of its creed. We hold these truths to be self-evident that all men are created equal.

I have a dream that one day out in the red hills of Georgia the sons of former slaves and the sons of former slaveowners will be able to sit down together at the table of brotherhood.

I have a dream that one day even the state of Mississippi, a state sweltering with the heat of oppression, will be transformed into an oasis of freedom and justice.

I have a dream that my four little children will one day live in a nation where they will not be judged by the color of their skin but by their character. . . .

This is our hope. This is the faith that I will go back to the South with. With this faith we will be able to hew out of the mountain of despair a stone of hope.

With this faith we will be able to transform the jangling discords of our nation into a beautiful symphony of brother-hood.

With this faith we will be able to work together, to pray together, to struggle together, to go to jail together, to climb up for freedom together, knowing that we will be free one day.

openly, lovingly, and with a willingness to accept the penalty. I submit that an individual who breaks a law that conscience tells him is unjust and who willingly accepts the penalty of imprisonment in order to arouse the conscience of the community over its injustice is in reality expressing the highest respect for law."

**March on Washington**   In the summer of 1963, Martin Luther King, Jr., and other civil rights leaders organized a huge demonstration in the nation's capital. This **March on Washington,** as it was called, was to alert Congress and the American people to the need for stronger civil rights laws. More than 200,000 people came to Washington, D.C., and heard Martin Luther King deliver a powerful and inspiring speech. (See Documents: "I Have a Dream.")

King's words reached out to the nation. It was now apparent that the civil rights movement had grown into a powerful force for change. The nation had come a long way since the 1920s when the most dramatic march in Washington had been conducted by the Ku Klux Klan.

## C. CIVIL RIGHTS UNDER THE GREAT SOCIETY

President Kennedy strongly supported both the March on Washington and a civil rights bill that Congress was then considering. Kennedy expected to lead the fight for the bill's passage. But less than three months after the march, he was assassinated. Lyndon Johnson as the new president pledged his determination to see that Kennedy's civil rights bill passed into law. In 1964 he kept his pledge by persuading Congress to adopt the most important civil rights law since Reconstruction.

A constitutional amendment of 1964 and a voting rights law of 1965 were additional triumphs of the civil rights movement in the Johnson years.

**Civil Rights Act of 1964** This law authorized the U.S. attorney general to bring suit if an individual's civil rights were violated. It also prohibited various forms of racial discrimination. **Discrimination** is the act of denying an individual equal opportunity because of some factor other than ability—a factor such as race, ethnicity, gender, or religion. These were the discriminatory practices banned by the **Civil Rights Act of 1964:**

- No discrimination in the services provided by such businesses as restaurants, hotels, motels, and gas stations
- No discrimination in the use of government- operated facilities such as public parks and pools
- No discrimination in federally supported programs (such as urban renewal and antipoverty programs)
- No discrimination either by employers of 100 or more workers or by labor unions of 100 or more members (a number later reduced to 25).

In effect, this far-reaching law meant that all Jim Crow laws and practices of the past were now abolished. Race could no longer be a reason to deny anyone equal rights or opportunities.

**Twenty-fourth Amendment**  Also in 1964 an amendment previously proposed by Congress was ratified by the necessary number of states. The Twenty-fourth Amendment banned the use of the poll tax in elections for president, vice president, and Congress. This amendment was especially important to African Americans in the South, many of whom were too poor to pay the poll tax required to vote. The amendment applied to federal elections only. Soon afterward, however, many states abolished the poll tax as a requirement for voting in state and local elections.

**Voting Rights Act of 1965**  Another major victory of the civil rights movement was the passage in 1965 of a law to give greater federal protection to African-American voters in the South. The **Voting Rights Act** prohibited the practice of using literacy tests to keep African Americans from voting. Furthermore, the new law authorized the U.S. government to identify places in the South where only a small percentage of African Americans had registered to vote. Federal registrars would then go to these places to assist African Americans in registering. Only one year after the law was passed, the number of Southern blacks registered to vote went from 870,000 to 1,289,000— an increase of about 50 percent.

## D. RACIAL TENSIONS AND TRAGEDY

The civil rights movement challenged long-established customs in the South. Activists in the movement could expect strong and even violent opposition from white defenders of segregation. In several tragic episodes the violence ended in the deaths of innocent people.

**Violent Episodes**  Two weeks after the March on Washington in 1963, a bomb exploded in a Baptist church in Birmingham, Alabama. Four African-American girls died in the explosion. Before the 1960s ended, more than 30 African-American churches would be bombed.

Among those who died in the fight for civil rights were three young activists who had traveled to Mississippi in 1964 to register African-American voters. James Chaney was a Southern black, while his two coworkers, Andrew Goodman and Michael Schwerner, were white, Jewish students from New York. The three were killed in a Mississippi town by unknown assailants. Although the Ku Klux Klan was thought to be responsible for the murders, the case was never solved.

In another violent episode in 1965, civil rights marchers in Selma, Alabama, were attacked and beaten by the police. To rally support for registering African-American voters in Alabama, Martin Luther King, Jr., organized a long-distance march from Selma to the state capital of Montgomery. The marchers were beaten by state troopers and harassed by hostile crowds. The marchers finally reached Montgomery only after President Johnson sent federal troops to protect them. One of the protesters, an Italian-American woman from the North named Viola Liuzzo, was killed shortly after the march had reached its goal.

**Riots in the North**  In cities of the North, most African Americans lived in crowded neighborhoods where poverty and unemployment were all too common. While aware that civil rights laws helped Southern blacks, African-Americans living in Northern cities saw no immediate benefits from these laws in improving the quality of their lives. Also, as they followed the news of churches being bombed and civil rights marchers being attacked and killed, many young African Americans became increasingly angry and distrustful of whites. The result was a violent outburst of discontent. The first riots took place in the Watts neighborhood of Los Angeles in 1965. Rioting lasted six days and resulted in the deaths of 28 people and damage to property totaling about $200 million.

Riots erupted again in the summer of 1966 and the summer of 1967. More than 167 cities were affected by these outbreaks. Among the worst hit were Detroit, Michigan, and Newark, New Jersey.

Investigating the causes of the rioting, a national commission called the **Kerner Commission** issued a controversial report. It noted that the United States was rapidly becoming two "separate but unequal" societies, one black and one white. It recommended that the government adopt major programs to relieve urban poverty and increase the job opportunities of African-American youths.

**Assassinations**  Racial tensions in the 1960s also led to the violent deaths of three African-American leaders. Medgar Evers, a leader of the NAACP in Mississippi, was killed in 1963, probably by white racists. Malcolm X was killed in 1965. Three Black Muslims were convicted for the slaying.

The most shocking assassination of all was the killing of Martin Luther King, Jr., in Memphis, Tennessee, in 1968. The civil rights leader had gone to Memphis to support the demands of sanitation workers for higher wages. While standing on the terrace of his motel room, he was shot by a Southern white, James Earl Ray. News of his death touched off riots in many cities. Throughout the nation Americans paid tribute to the man who had so courageously led the struggle for racial justice and democratic reform.

## In Review

The following questions refer to section I: The New Frontier and the Great Society and section II: The Civil Rights Movement Continues.

**Word Wheel**

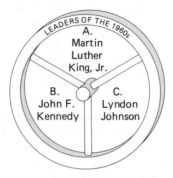

1. Explain why each person in the word wheel might be called a "liberal" leader.

2. Create a chart comparing the domestic policies of two presidents, Kennedy and Johnson.

3. Select *one* of the leaders in the word wheel, and discuss his contribution to making the United States a more democratic nation.

# III. The Movement for Women's Rights

African Americans were not the only group in the United States who suffered from discrimination. Their movement to win equal rights led women and other groups to organize reform movements of their own.

## A. ROLE OF WOMEN FROM 1920 TO 1960

Recall that an earlier movement for women's rights had focused on winning the right to vote. (Review Chapter 8.) When the women's suffrage amendment (the Nineteenth Amendment) was adopted in 1920, it seemed to many men that equal rights for women had been fully achieved. In fact women had a long way to go to attain equal rights in the workplace, not just equal rights in the voting booth.

In the 1920s urbanization and the automobile were partly responsible for allowing women greater social freedom. During the depression of the 1930s, women continued to enter the work force in large numbers to earn income desperately needed by their families. After U.S. entry into World War II in the 1940s, millions of women took jobs in factories and shipyards—jobs vacated by men called to service in the war. Women also volunteered for military service, joining the WACS (army) and the WAVES (navy).

When the war ended, many women left their jobs, as ex-servicemen returned to the work force in large numbers. During the 1950s most women living in middle-income homes believed that their most important role was to stay at home for the benefit and care of their families. Their husbands would provide the family's income while they looked after the house and children. This traditional view of a woman's role as mother and homemaker was challenged in the 1960s by women known as **feminists.**

## B. BEGINNINGS OF THE NEW MOVEMENT

We may date the beginning of the new movement for women's rights with the publication in 1963 of a book by Betty Friedan.

*The Feminine Mystique*   Betty Friedan was a college-educated woman who, as a suburban housewife in the 1950s, began to question the traditional assumptions concerning women's roles. The book that she wrote, *The Feminine Mystique,* criticized the common assumption that women are happiest at home rather than in the workplace. She argued that women, far from being the "weaker sex," were as capable as men in all respects and should have equal opportunity to pursue high-level jobs in business and the professions. Widely read and discussed, Friedan's book challenged women to redefine their role in society and to break away from a limited view of themselves.

**Discrimination in the Workplace**   If women's preferred role was in the workplace, then career opportunities for women should be equal to opportunities for men. But as Friedan and other feminists pointed out, male employers tended to favor male workers and discriminate against female workers. Median (average) income for men in the mid-1960s was $7,500 a year, compared to only $5,600 a year for women. Most women found it difficult to obtain high-level positions in finance and management. When applying to law and medical schools, male applicants were generally given preference over female applicants.

**The Founding of NOW**   In 1966 Friedan and other feminist leaders formed the **National Organization for Women (NOW).** Goals of the organization included equal pay for equal work, day-care centers for the children of working mothers, and the passage of antidiscrimination laws. Another goal was to increase the awareness of women and men about the various ways that men unfairly dominated their lives.

Many members of NOW had been active in the struggle to win civil rights for African Americans. Drawing upon this experience, they organized marches and demonstrations and thereby attracted national attention. NOW also supported female candidates for office and lobbied for changes in the laws. Able spokespersons for women's rights such as Gloria Steinem and Bella Abzug became nationally known. In the 1970s Abzug won election to Congress as a representative from a district in New York City.

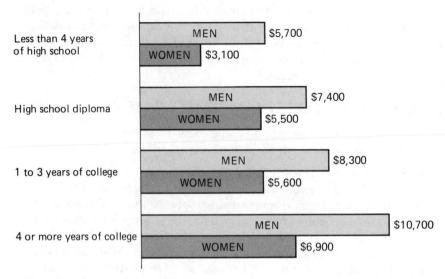

Source: U.S. Bureau of the Census

Median incomes of men and women workers by education, 1971

## C. ANTIDISCRIMINATION LAWS

Advocates of equal rights for women won a number of notable victories in Congress.

**Civil Rights Act (1964)**  The main purpose of this act was to protect the civil rights of African Americans. In addition one clause of the act made it illegal for employers to discriminate on the basis of a person's sex.

**Equal Employment Opportunity Act (1972)**  This act required that employers give equal pay for equal work. It also banned discriminatory practices in hiring, firing, promotions, and working conditions.

**Title IX (1972)**  Amendments to an education act included a provision known as **Title IX**. Its purpose was to promote equal treatment in schools for female staff and students. It stated that "no person in the United States shall, on the basis of sex, be excluded from participation in, be denied the benefits of, or be subjected to discrimination under any education program or activity receiving Federal financial assistance." An important consequence of this act was that schools and colleges greatly increased their sports programs for girls and young women. Previously, athletic programs in most schools had concentrated on supporting male teams in all sports, while restricting female athletics to only a few sports.

**Equal Rights Amendment**   In 1972 Congress proposed a contro-versial amendment to the Constitution. Called the **Equal Rights Amendment (ERA),** it stated: "Equality of rights under the law shall not be denied or abridged by the United States or any state on account of sex." For ten years, NOW and other feminist organizations campaigned for ERA to be ratified by the necessary number of states. By 1977 they had won ratification by 35 states, just three states short of their goal. But opposition to the ERA was also strong. Some women feared that the ERA might spell the end of their exemption from military service and might permit divorced men to neglect financial responsibilities to their former wives. Opponents of the ERA eventually prevailed. In 1982, the last year that the ERA could have been ratified according to Congress's deadline, supporters failed to persuade the required number of state legislatures to ratify the proposed amend-ment.

## D. SUPREME COURT DECISIONS

Even without an equal rights amendment, lawyers for NOW could argue that discrimination against women violated the equal protection clause of the Fourteenth Amendment. According to this clause no state may "deny to any person within its jurisdiction the equal protection of the laws." Feminist lawyers used this clause successfully to challenge government support of all-male schools, such as Stuy-vesant High School in New York City.

Of the many discrimination cases decided by the U.S. Supreme Court in the 1970s, two were especially important.

***Reed* v. *Reed* (1971)**   In this case a mother had been denied the right to be the administrator of her deceased son's estate solely because she was a woman. (In the past courts usually gave the legal responsibility for the handling of property to men.) The Supreme Court ruled that the mother's right to equal protection of the laws had been violated.

***Roe* v. *Wade* (1973)**   In this case a pregnant young woman living in Texas wanted to have an abortion but could not do so because of Texas's law prohibiting abortions. The Supreme Court decided that the Texas law was unconstitutional because it violated a woman's constitutional right to privacy. The Court ruled that a woman could choose whether or not to have an abortion during the first six months of pregnancy. During the last three months of pregnancy, however, a state may ban an abortion to protect the unborn child, or fetus, since at this stage the fetus may be considered a person.

The decision in ***Roe* v. *Wade*** sparked controversy for years after-ward. Supporters argued that the right to privacy applies to a woman's body. Opponents argued that even during the first six months of pregnancy, the fetus is a person who has a right to life equal to that of any person after birth.

# IV. The Rights of Minorities

Other groups in the United States also argued during the 1960s that their rights to equal protection under the Constitution were often violated. These groups—Mexican Americans, Native Americans, and persons with handicaps—organized marches and protest demonstrations to call attention to their cause.

## A. MEXICAN AMERICANS

Just as African Americans began to speak of "black power," Mexican Americans began to organize a movement for "brown power." A gifted and determined leader of the movement was a labor organizer named Cesar Chavez.

**Organizing the United Farm Workers**  Like thousands of other Mexican Americans in the Southwest, Chavez had worked long hours for low pay as a migrant farm laborer. He observed that employers often exploited migrant workers whose need for work at any wage was great. Migrant workers had no permanent residence and were therefore extremely difficult to organize into a labor union for group action. Despite the difficulties, Chavez succeeded in organizing a strong union of migrant workers called the United Farm Workers.

**La Causa**  For five years, 1965 to 1970, Chavez's union struggled for *La Causa*—the goal of winning both better pay and greater respect for migrant farm laborers from California's landowners who employed them in harvesting grapes. The union conducted a strike against the grape growers and also urged the American people not to buy California grapes. Like Martin Luther King, Jr., Chavez insisted that the movement be completely nonviolent. Eventually the strike and the boycott put enough pressure on California's grape growers to win major concessions for the union and the workers. In 1970 the largest grape growers in the state agreed to sign a contract with Chavez's union.

## B. NATIVE AMERICANS

Native Americans had longstanding grievances against the U.S. government, which had taken away their lands in the eighteenth and nineteenth centuries. Inspired by the civil rights movement, Native Americans from different reservations joined forces in an attempt to assert "red power."

**Grievances and Goals**  An organization called the National Congress of American Indians complained bitterly about the government agency that supervised Indian life on the reservations. The U.S. Bureau of Indian Affairs, or BIA, had failed for decades in raising the standard of living of Indians. A study made in 1960 found that Indians had a life expectancy of only 46 years, compared with 70 years for the U.S. population as a whole. More than any other ethnic minority, Indians suffered from high rates of malnutrition and unemployment.

Activists in the movement for Indian rights wanted the following:

- Less supervision by the BIA and greater freedom to manage reservation life as Native Americans saw fit. As one Native American put it, "We simply want to run our lives our own way."

- The return of fishing and hunting rights that Indians had once enjoyed, even if this meant changing state game laws for their benefit

- Greater economic assistance in combating problems of poverty

- The return of lands that had once belonged to the ancestors of the Indians and that U.S. treaties had guaranteed would not be taken from them.

**Protest at Wounded Knee**  Though united in their goals, Native Americans disagreed on how best to achieve them. Some favored peaceful protest, while others resorted to the use of armed force. In 1972 a radical group, the American Indian Movement (AIM), occupied the offices of the BIA in Washington, D.C., and demanded that the U.S. government honor treaties signed a century or more earlier. The next year, 1973, more than 200 members of AIM took up arms and gained control of the village of Wounded Knee on a Sioux reservation in South Dakota. Wounded Knee had been the site of the massacre of Indians by U.S. troops in 1890. For two months the invaders of Wounded Knee held the village and demanded that old treaty rights be granted. Even though they won no concessions, they may have prepared the way for the court victories later won by several Native American tribes.

**Victories in Court**  Through the 1970s Indians from Maine to California went to court to sue for lands promised to them by treaties in earlier centuries. One court granted the Narragansett Indians of Rhode Island the return of 1,800 acres. To settle their suit, the Penobscots of Maine won both thousands of acres and millions of dollars. The Sioux of South Dakota won another case, in which the court ruled that seven million acres of land had been taken from their people illegally.

## C. HANDICAPPED PERSONS

People with physical disabilities protested in the 1960s that federal and state laws treated them unfairly. These people also suffered from discrimination in the job market.

**Historical Background**  The movement for handicapped, or disabled, persons had its origins in reforms of the nineteenth century.

Reformers such as Dorothea Dix believed that the best way to treat handicapped persons was to place them in large and humane institutions. Education and training were also stressed. In Hartford, Connecticut, in 1817, Thomas Gallaudet began the first school for the hearing impaired. In 1865 President Lincoln signed a law establishing Gallaudet College, which continues to this day as a major institution of higher learning for students whose hearing is impaired.

In the early twentieth century, emphasis began to shift to a policy of "normalization." The new goal was to enable disabled persons to enter into the "mainstream" of society and lead a normal social life as much as possible. After World War I the training programs offered to wounded and disabled veterans were applied to all persons with disabilities. Both the Vocational Rehabilitation Act of 1920 and the Social Security Act of 1935 provided federal funds to help persons cope with various disabilities (loss of sight and hearing, for example.)

**Increased Public Awareness**  President Kennedy increased national awareness of the problems and abilities of handicapped persons. He created a President's Council on Mental Retardation and began a "Special Olympics" for those with physical disabilities. As the brother of a mentally retarded sister, President Kennedy had personal knowledge of the need for greater national action.

As wounded veterans of the Vietnam War returned home, there was increased public awareness of the needs of people with amputated or paralyzed limbs. The doors and stairs of courthouses, schools, and other public buildings made no allowance for the needs of people in wheelchairs. To protest these conditions, disabled persons organized demonstrations in front of buildings that had no access ramps and therefore, in effect, shut them out.

**Legislation of the 1970s**  Two acts of Congress went a long way toward protecting the rights of disabled persons.

A 1973 amendment to the Vocational Rehabilitation Act prohibited discrimination against the physically disabled in any federal program and in any state program supported by federal funds. Under this law the federal government issued a number of regulations to ensure that handicapped persons had full access to all buildings. It required for example, (1) ramp accesses in public buildings, (2) specially equipped buses for passengers in wheelchairs, (3) suitable bathroom facilities in public places, and (4) interpreting programs in signs for the hearing impaired on public television stations.

A second law of 1975, the **Education for All Handicapped Children Act,** provided strong support for children with learning disabilities. This law provided for testing to identify handicaps, a list of rights for handicapped children and their parents, and funds to assist states and local school districts in providing programs in special education. Many educators view this act as a "bill of rights" for handicapped children and their parents.

**Victories in Court**  Two court cases of the early 1970s were especially important in protecting the rights of children with mental handicaps.

- *P.A.R.C.* v. *Commonwealth of Pennsylvania* (1971) The question in this case was whether the state of Pennsylvania could prevent mentally retarded children in the state from participating in a free public education program. The U.S. district court ruled against the state's action. It argued that equal protection of the laws required a state to provide appropriate programs for the educational needs of mentally retarded children.

- *Mills* v. *Board of Education of District of Columbia* (1972) This U.S. Supreme Court case established the right of all children, including those with emotional and mental disabilities, to receive public schooling. It declared that no child between the ages of 7 and 16 could be excluded from regular classes unless the school district provided a program suited to the child's special needs.

## D. RIGHTS DEFINED BY THE WARREN COURT

During the 1960s the U.S. Supreme Court under Chief Justice Earl Warren made several controversial decisions concerning clauses of the Bill of Rights. Americans with conservative views accused the **Warren Court** of interfering with law enforcement and the police powers of the states. On the other hand, people with liberal views generally applauded the Court's decisions. They argued that fair police procedures are required by the Fourth, Fifth, and Sixth Amendments.

**Rights of Persons Accused of Crimes**  Could evidence obtained by the police without a search warrant be used in court? Could a trial be fair if the defendant had no lawyer to represent him or her? The Warren Court gave its answers to these and other questions in the landmark cases summarized below.

- *Mapp v. Ohio* (1961) This case involved the Fourth Amendment's protection against "unreasonable searches and seizures" of a suspected person's property. A court in Cleveland, Ohio, had convicted a woman named Dollree Mapp of a crime on the basis of evidence that the police had obtained without a search warrant. The Supreme Court ruled that the accused person's rights had been violated. It said that evidence wrongly obtained by the police could not be admitted as evidence in the suspect's trial.

- *Gideon v. Wainwright* (1963) This case involved the Sixth Amendment's guarantee that a citizen accused of a crime shall "have the assistance of counsel for his defense." Accused of breaking into a Florida poolroom, Gideon was too poor to pay for a lawyer at his trial. Florida provided lawyers for defendants in capital cases (those punishable by death) but not in minor criminal cases like Gideon's. The Supreme Court ruled that Gideon's rights to a fair trial had been violated. It said that a state must provide lawyers to indigent (poor) defendants in criminal cases whether or not the crime is a capital one.

- *Escobedo v. Illinois* (1964) This case also involved the Sixth Amendment's guarantee of an accused person's right to counsel (or his or her right to be defended by a lawyer). The police in Illinois arrested Danny Escobedo as a suspect in a murder. During questioning, the police refused to grant Escobedo's request to see a lawyer. Escobedo made statements to the police that were later used at his trial to convict him of murder. The Supreme Court ruled that Escobedo's right to counsel under the Sixth Amendment had been violated.

- *Miranda v. Arizona* (1966) One difference between this case and the *Escobedo* case was that the suspect Miranda did not ask to see a lawyer when questioned by the Arizona police. After two hours of questioning, Miranda signed a written confession of his crime (kidnapping and rape). Later, however, a lawyer representing Miranda appealed the case to the Supreme Court. The Court ruled that the police cannot question someone about a crime before informing that person of his or her constitutional rights. The Supreme Court's decision stated: "Prior to any questioning, the person must be warned that he has a right to remain silent, that any statement he does make may be used as evidence against him, and that he has a right to the presence of an attorney." These warnings are now known as "*Miranda* rights." The police now read the warnings to arrested suspects before questioning.

**Rights Concerning Religion**   Other controversial cases of the 1960s concerned the common practice in many schools of beginning class with a prayer or a reading from the Bible. The Supreme Court ruled that such practices were unconstitutional. They violated the First Amendment's clause prohibiting the government from "establishing" (or supporting) a religion.

- ***Engel v. Vitale*** (1962) In this case the parents of several pupils in New York schools objected to a prayer composed by a state agency, the New York State Board of Regents. The prayer was meant to be nondenominational (neither Christian nor Jewish nor Muslim). The board recommended that students recite the prayer on a voluntary basis in public school classrooms at the beginning of each day. The Supreme Court ruled against the use of the prayer, arguing that it violated the principle of the separation of church and state.

- ***Abington School District v. Schempp*** (1963) This case involved a Pennsylvania law requiring that at least ten Bible verses be read in public schools at the beginning of each day. The Schempps, a family in Abington, Pennsylvania, sued the school district for relief from this practice. They said that daily Bible readings went against their religious beliefs. The Supreme Court ruled in favor of the Schempps. It declared that reading from the Bible in a public school violated the First Amendment's guarantee against an establishment of religion.

## *In Review*

The following questions refer to section III: The Movement for Women's Rights and section IV: The Rights of Minorities.

1. Identify the goals of reformers in each of the following movements: (a) women's rights, (b) rights of Native Americans, and (c) rights of handicapped persons.
2. Describe the methods of Cesar Chavez, and compare them with the methods of Martin Luther King, Jr.
3. Select two U.S. Supreme Court cases of the 1960s and 1970s for analysis. For each case, (a) identify the constitutional issue involved, and (b) summarize the Supreme Court's decision.

# V. Progress in Space and Technology

While movements for equal rights were making headlines, equally important changes were taking place in science and technology. During the 1960s computers were changing people's habits of work, and explorations of outer space were changing people's views of the solar system.

## A. AUTOMATION IN THE FACTORY

In the 1950s and 1960s the U.S. economy surged ahead with spectacular gains in productivity. A chief reason for U.S. economic

growth in these decades was **automation**—a new method of manufacturing products. Automation is a process in which one set of
machines regulates other machines. This enables manufactured goods
to be assembled almost automatically, with a minimum need for
human labor. Not only does automation increase the speed of
production, but it also reduces the possibility of human error.

Though generally benefiting the U.S. economy, automation worried
factory workers and labor unions. Automation reduced the number
of factory jobs, especially those repetitive jobs that required little
education or skill. It became obvious that unskilled jobs would
decrease and that almost all careers of the future would depend on
having at least a high school education. Those lacking such an
education faced a bleak future of frequent unemployment and poverty-
level incomes.

## B. COMPUTERS IN THE OFFICE

The automation of American industries depended in part upon
the invention of an electronic device known as the computer. The
origins of this device go back to 1890. In that year an inventor named
Herman Hollerith created a tabulating machine (or counting machine)
to speed the process for taking the census. However, advanced
electronic computers did not appear until after World War II.

**First Generation: The Vacuum-Tube Computer**  To help the U.S.
armed forces make rapid calculations, an immense computer weigh-
ing 30 tons began operating in 1946. Known as ENIAC (Electronic
Numerical Integrator and Calculator), it consisted of 18,000 vacuum
tubes. As an electric current flowed through the tubes, the machine
performed thousands of mathematical calculations in only a few
seconds. Other computers designed by International Business Machines (IBM) in the 1950s also relied upon the bulky vacuum tube.
Technology advanced so rapidly, however, that this "first generation"
of electronic computers was replaced in the 1960s by a new and
more powerful type of computer.

**Second Generation: The Transistor Computer**  Instead of the
vacuum tube, the basic electronic building block of the "second
generation" computer was a transistor. Less then one-tenth the size
of the vacuum tube, the transistor could perform the same functions
with even greater speed and reliability.

**Third Generation: The "Chip" Computer**  Another breakthrough
in 1969 enabled more powerful computers to be made at lower cost.
Replacing the little metallic transistor was an even smaller and more
compact "chip"—a thin square of silicon with electronic circuits
printed on it. The trend in computer design was now clear. The goal

among computer engineers was to invent ways for computers to process more information at higher speeds for less cost. By 1970 it was clear to most observers that the Age of the Computer was at hand.

**Uses and Impact of the Computer**  By today's standards, even the first "chip" computers were heavy and expensive machines. Only government agencies and large corporations could afford to purchase them. Even so, the early computers of the 1950s and 1960s had a large variety of uses. They helped to automate factories. They kept track of business receipts and expenses. They stored vast amounts of data for agencies like the IRS. They helped scientists to solve complicated problems. For example, computers of the 1960s were essential to figuring out how to send three men from the earth to the moon and back.

## C. EXPLORING OUTER SPACE

President Kennedy announced in 1961 that he intended the United States to be the first nation to land a human being on the moon. The goal was in fact achieved before the 1960s ended.

**Space Race with the Soviet Union**  In Chapter 13 you read about *Sputnik*, the artificial satellite launched by the Soviet Union in 1957. Shocked that the Soviets had scored this triumph, President Eisenhower signed the Space Act of 1958, which created a new agency, the National Aeronautics and Space Administration (NASA). This agency aimed to compete with the Soviets in space. In 1961, however, the Soviet Union scored again in the space race by sending Yuri Gagarin into orbit as the first human to circle the earth in outer space.

**American Astronauts in Space**  Scientists at NASA worked furiously to compete with the Soviets. In 1961, less than a month after Gagarin's journey through space, a NASA rocket at Cape Canaveral, Florida, lifted an American astronaut, Alan Shepard, into space. Although he did not orbit the earth, Shepard returned safely in his space capsule. The U.S. manned space program had its first triumph.

After Shepard's flight, other breakthroughs soon followed. In February, 1962, an astronaut named John Glenn spent five hours in space orbiting the earth. His dramatic achievement matched that of the Soviets and thrilled millions of Americans who followed reports of Glenn's voyage on television. Glenn later became a U.S. senator from Ohio.

Not every rocket launching was a success. Practicing for a space launching in 1967, three astronauts (Virgil Grissom, Edward White, and Roger Chaffee) lost their lives when a fire broke out in their space

Astronaut Edwin E. Aldrin, Jr., on the moon

capsule. Subsequently, however, three other astronauts circled the moon and photographed it.

**Moon Landing**    In July, 1969, a spacecraft known as *Apollo 11* carried three astronauts from the earth to the moon. While Michael Collins remained behind in the spacecraft, Neil Armstrong and Edward Aldrin set off for the surface of the moon in a small capsule called a lunar module. Since the event was televised, millions of people around the world watched in amazement as Armstrong set foot on the gray lunar surface. President Kennedy's promise had been kept. The United States had landed a man on the moon before the end of the decade.

Although the moon landing took place many years ago, few people who viewed the event will forget Neil Armstrong's words as he stepped out of the spacecraft onto the moon. Said Armstrong, "That's one small step for a man, one giant leap for mankind." Nor should the world forget the plaque left on the moon at the end of the historic voyage. It read simply, "We came in peace."

## GLOSSARY OF KEY TERMS: CHAPTER 15

*Abington School District v. Schempp*    a U.S. Supreme Court case of 1963 that declared unconstitutional a Pennsylvania law requiring the reading of Bible passages in public schools.

**Apollo Project** a manned space mission in which two U.S. astronauts landed on the moon in July 1969.

**automation** a method of manufacturing in which special machines control the operations of other machines, thereby reducing the amount of human labor involved in the production process.

**Black Muslims** African-American followers of Islam.

**Black Panthers** a revolutionary group of African Americans who believed in violent methods for remedying racial injustice.

**Civil Rights Act of 1964** a federal law declaring discrimination on the basis of race and sex to be illegal.

**Congress of Racial Equality (CORE)** an organization of African-American activists who conducted freedom rides and other peaceful demonstrations for civil rights.

**desegregate** to end the practice of racial segregation in schools, restaurants, and other public places.

**discrimination** the practice of favoring one group in the population while blocking or restricting another group.

**Education for All Handicapped Children Act** an act of Congress of 1975 providing funds to states and local districts for teaching handicapped children and also listing these children's rights.

**Engel v. Vitale** a U.S. Supreme Court case of 1962 that declared unconstitutional the reciting of an official prayer in the public schools.

**Equal Employment Opportunity Act** an act of Congress of 1972 requiring that employers give equal pay for equal work.

**Equal Rights Amendment (ERA)** a constitutional amendment proposed by Congress in 1972 and advocated by those wishing to guarantee equal rights for women.

**Escobedo v. Illinois** a U.S. Supreme Court case of 1964 that declared that the police must grant an arrested person's request to have a lawyer present during interrogation.

**feminist** a person who is concerned about the economic and social inequality between men and women and supports efforts to achieve women's rights.

**freedom ride** a form of protest of the 1960s in which African Americans and white Americans joined together to desegregate buses and bus depots used in interstate commerce.

**Gideon v. Wainwright** a U.S. Supreme Court case of 1963 that declared that states must provide an attorney to a defendant in a criminal case if the defendant is too poor to pay for one.

**Great Society** President Johnson's program of social and economic reforms.

**Head Start** a federally funded program for disadvantaged preschool children.

**Kerner Commission**   a body of government officials who investigated the causes of urban riots in the 1960s and reported that U.S. society was rapidly dividing along racial lines.

**Mapp v. Ohio**   a U.S. Supreme Court case of 1961 that declared that evidence obtained in violation of the search and seizure provisions of the Fourth Amendment is inadmissible in court.

**March on Washington**   a 1963 demonstration for civil rights in Washington, D.C., led by Martin Luther King, Jr., and involving more than 200,000 people of all races and religions.

**Medicaid**   a government welfare program that provides funds for the medical care of the poor.

**Medicare**   a government insurance program under the Social Security system that pays for the medical care of elderly citizens.

**Miranda v. Arizona**   a U.S. Supreme Court case of 1966 that declared that police officers must inform an arrested person of his or her constitutional rights before they can question the suspect.

**National Organization for Women (NOW)**   an organization of women that attempts to end discrimination based on sex.

**New Frontier**   President Kennedy's program of social and economic reforms.

**Roe v. Wade**   a Supreme Court case of 1973 that declared that women's right to privacy was violated by state laws against abortion.

**Southern Christian Leadership Conference (SCLC)**   an organization of African-American leaders of the South, including Martin Luther King, Jr., that conducted demonstrations for civil rights.

**Title IX**   a provision of a federal law that prohibited discrimination on the basis of sex in any educational program receiving federal funds.

**Twenty-fourth Amendment**   a constitutional amendment abolishing the use of a poll tax in federal elections.

**Urban League**   an organization that seeks to end racial discrimination in employment and housing and to increase job opportunities for African Americans.

**Voting Rights Act of 1965**   a federal law to defend the right of African Americans of the South to register to vote.

**War on Poverty**   President Johnson's efforts to end poverty in the United States.

**Warren Court**   the Supreme Court during the years 1953 to 1969 when Earl Warren was the chief justice.

# TEST YOURSELF

## A. Multiple Choice: Facts, Main Ideas, Skills

*On a separate sheet of paper, write the number of the word or expression that, of those given, best completes the statement or answers the question.*

# Reviewing the facts

1. The "I Have a Dream" speech of Martin Luther King, Jr., in 1963 strongly appealed to African Americans because (1) the United States was deeply divided by the war in Vietnam (2) many in the audience had long been deprived of their civil rights (3) 18-year-old citizens insisted on the right to vote (4) the speech suggested the need for a violent revolution

2. The Civil Rights Act of 1964 was an attempt to abolish (1) the poll tax (2) discrimination based on race and sex (3) federal interference with states' rights (4) disloyalty by federal employees

3. Which is generally considered the most ambitious reform program since the New Deal? (1) Truman's Fair Deal (2) Eisenhower's domestic program (3) Kennedy's New Frontier (4) Johnson's Great Society

4. Opposition to reform in the 1960s is best illustrated by (1) the policies of John Kennedy (2) the goals of CORE and the NAACP (3) police action in Birmingham, Alabama, in 1963 (4) the organization of NOW

5. Supporters of the Warren Court's decisions in the 1960s believed that persons accused of crimes (1) were entitled to the full protection of the Bill of Rights (2) should be treated as if they were guilty (3) were treated properly by local and state police (4) were the concern of state and local authorities only, not the U.S. government

6. In what respect was the civil rights movement of African Americans similar to the movement of Native Americans? (1) Both concerned treaty rights. (2) Both concerned the unfair treatment of an ethnic minority. (3) Both were inspired by the women's movement of the nineteenth century. (4) Both movements were ignored by the white majority.

7. Which was *not* involved in explaining the successful landing of American astronauts on the moon in 1969? (1) U.S. rivalry with the Soviet Union (2) President Kennedy's policies (3) the civil rights movement (4) new computer technology

8. The U.S. Supreme Court has ruled that accused persons who cannot afford a lawyer must (1) be provided with a lawyer at government expense (2) plead guilty to the offense (3) act as their own defense (4) not stand trial until someone can be found to pay a lawyer

9. Which action has the U.S. Supreme Court found to be a violation of the principle of separation of church and state? (1) a minister giving a sermon on a political issue (2) a chaplain serving in the armed services (3) a coin bearing the motto "In God we trust" (4) the recitation of prayers in a public school

# Reviewing the main ideas

10. Which provision of the U.S. Constitution would a group most likely use as the basis for bringing legal action to end discriminatory

practices? (1) search and seizure clause of the Fourth Amendment (2) free speech clause of the First Amendment (3) reserved powers clause of the Tenth Amendment (4) equal protection clause of the Fourteenth Amendment

11. Which statement concerning African Americans' movement for civil rights in the 1960s is accurate? (1) It stimulated the growth of other reform movements. (2) Its leaders failed to use the U.S. Congress as a means of achieving its goals. (3) White support and participation was rejected from the very beginning of the movement. (4) The movement failed to achieve significant progress.

12. The major goal of the women's movement during the 1960s and 1970s was to (1) gain voting rights for women (2) provide equality of opportunity (3) obtain the right of women to join unions (4) pass laws limiting the right of men to seek divorces

13. Which is a major result of the women's movement in the United States? (1) Fewer women attend college. (2) Fewer women are employed outside the home. (3) There is increased legal pressure to provide equal opportunities for women. (4) The birth rate in the United States has increased.

14. Both the New Frontier and the Great Society shared the idea that (1) foreign trade should be cut to a minimum (2) the federal government should meet the economic and social needs of the less fortunate (3) taxes should be raised to stimulate consumer spending (4) key industries should be nationalized

15. Which statement is most accurate about government in the United States during the 1960s? (1) The two-party political system was replaced by a multiparty system. (2) There were no disagreements between branches of the federal government. (3) The judicial branch had less and less influence. (4) The federal government assumed powers formerly exercised by the states.

16. The U.S. Supreme Court is sometimes said to fulfill a legislative function because (1) its members are appointed by the president (2) its judgments may determine the effect of the law (3) its members serve only so long as Congress approves (4) it meets regularly with Congress to advise on the appropriateness of proposed laws

17. Which description best characterizes the decisions of the U.S. Supreme Court of the 1960s under Chief Justice Earl Warren? (1) activist, with a liberal approach to interpreting the Constitution (2) cautious, with a philosophy of strict construction (3) traditional, with an emphasis on states' rights (4) conservative, with a strong emphasis on "cracking down" on criminals

18. In the United States, informing suspects of their legal rights during an arrest procedure is required as a result of (1) customs adopted from English common law (2) state legislation (3) decisions of the U.S. Supreme Court (4) laws passed by Congress

## Developing critical thinking skills

*Base your answer to question 19 on the cartoon below and on your knowledge of social studies.*

"Founding Fathers! How come no Founding Mothers?"

**19.** Which is a valid generalization that can be drawn from the cartoon? (1) Women have not had an important role in U.S. history. (2) Women have become more appreciative of American art. (3) Women have become more conscious of their role in American society. (4) Women artists are demanding greater respect for their contributions to the field.

## B. Enduring Issues

*Select* two *of the enduring issues from column A. For each issue chosen, explain how the historical example in column B relates to the issue.*

| A. Enduring Issues | B. Historical Examples |
|---|---|
| 1. Federalism—the balance of power between the federal government and state governments | Antipoverty programs of the Great Society |
| 2. The judiciary—interpreter of the Constitution or shaper of policy? | U.S. Supreme Court cases: either *Gideon* v. *Wainwright* or *Engle* v. *Vitale* |
| 3. Civil liberties—balance between government and the individual | Decisions of the Warren Court in the 1960s |
| 4. Rights of the accused and protection of the community | U.S. Supreme Court cases: either *Mapp* v. *Ohio* or *Miranda* v. *Arizona* |

| A. Enduring Issues | B. Historical Examples |
|---|---|
| 5. Rights of women under the Constitution | U.S. Supreme Court cases: either *Reed* v. *Reed* or *Roe* v. *Wade* |
| 6. Rights of ethnic and racial minorities under the Constitution | Adoption of the Twenty-fourth Amendment |
| 7. Avenues of representation | Effect of the civil rights movement on laws enacted by the U.S. Congress |
| 8. Constitutional change and flexibility | U.S. Supreme Court's interpretation of the equal protection clause of the Fourteenth Amendment |

## C. Essays

### Level 1

The U.S. Supreme Court has acted as an interpreter of the U.S. Constitution on these topics:

> Rights of women
> Rights of accused persons
> Separation of church and state.

For *each* topic:

**1.** Identify a specific Supreme Court case that dealt with the topic.
**2.** State the specific issue involved in the case.
**3.** Discuss the Court's decision in the case.

### Level 2

Since its beginning as a nation, the United States has moved closer to equality for all of its people.

**A.** List *four* important events or changes that have led to greater equality for women, disabled citizens, and members of minority groups.

**B.** Base your answer to part B on your answer to part A. Write an essay discussing how the United States has moved toward greater equality for all Americans.

# Chapter *16*

# The Limits of Power: From Vietnam to Watergate

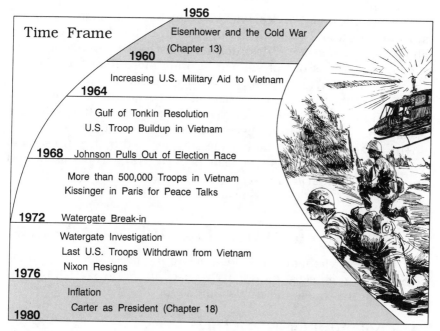

| Time Frame | 1956 | |
|---|---|---|
| | Eisenhower and the Cold War (Chapter 13) | |
| **1960** | | |
| | Increasing U.S. Military Aid to Vietnam | |
| **1964** | | |
| | Gulf of Tonkin Resolution U.S. Troop Buildup in Vietnam | |
| **1968** | Johnson Pulls Out of Election Race | |
| | More than 500,000 Troops in Vietnam Kissinger in Paris for Peace Talks | |
| **1972** | Watergate Break-in | |
| | Watergate Investigation Last U.S. Troops Withdrawn from Vietnam Nixon Resigns | |
| **1976** | | |
| **1980** | Inflation Carter as President (Chapter 18) | |

*U.S. troops in Vietnam*

*Objectives*

- To understand that the American political system is subject to a variety of public pressures.
- To realize that modern war technology is not always effective in dealing with nationalistic uprisings.
- To explore the consequences of U.S. involvement in Vietnam.
- To analyze and compare the policies of two presidents, Lyndon Johnson and Richard Nixon.
- To assess the impact of the Watergate Affair on the presidency.

No war in U.S. history was as controversial as the one fought in the Asian country of Vietnam between 1965 and 1973. It came as a shock to the American people that their country's armed forces—better equipped than any other military force in history—could not achieve victory in the jungles of a relatively small nation. Many people, particularly students in high school and college, questioned whether it was necessary for the United States to fight in Vietnam. Public protests against the war were one reason that Lyndon Johnson surprised the world in 1968 by announcing that he would not seek reelection.

The next president to deal with Vietnam, Richard Nixon, also faced student unrest and the growing discontent of the American people about the war's cost and destructiveness. Nixon adopted a policy of pulling U.S. troops out of Vietnam. During more than five years as president, he tried to deal with the changing realities of world politics. But he made the tragic mistake of failing to recognize the constitutional limits on his power. The result was a political crisis—the Watergate Affair—that caused him to resign from the presidency.

This chapter is about the hard lessons learned by two presidents and the American people between 1965 and 1974. They discovered in these years that there were limits to their nation's power—and also limits to a president's power.

# I. War in Vietnam: The Johnson Years

The war in Vietnam began long before the presidency of Lyndon Johnson in the 1960s. Its origins go back to World War II and the revolution that broke out in Vietnam as soon as that war ended.

## A. CIVIL WAR IN INDOCHINA

Vietnam is part of a region in Southeast Asia known as Indochina, which is located just south of China. The region fell under French control during the imperialist era of the late 1800s. It remained a French colony until World War II, when invading Japanese armies occupied it. After the Japanese left Indochina in 1945, a nationalist leader of the Vietnamese, Ho Chi Minh, proclaimed the independence of his people from colonial rule. But the French regained military control of the region. Ho Chi Minh led his followers to the northern part of Vietnam, where they began a guerrilla war against the French. In **guerrilla warfare**, small bands of soldiers conduct quick hit-and-run attacks against larger but less mobile forces. In such a war advanced technology has only limited effectiveness.

## B. THE BEGINNING OF U.S. INVOLVEMENT

The French had great trouble fighting the Vietnamese guerrillas. After the loss of a major battle at Dien Bien Phu in 1954, they decided to withdraw from Indochina. The region now consisted of three separate nations—Cambodia, Laos, and Vietnam. Each nation had problems adjusting to independence, as Communists competed with other groups to win political control.

**President Eisenhower and the "Domino Effect"**    Recall that in the early 1950s, the cold war had reached an intense stage. Chinese Communists under Mao Tse-tung had taken control of mainland China. Also, with UN backing, the United States had fought a war to prevent a Communist takeover of South Korea. Now that the French were leaving Vietnam, this Asian country looked as if it too might fall to Communist forces. If this happened, President Eisenhower feared what he called a **"domino effect."** He compared the countries of Southeast Asia to a lineup of falling dominoes. If Vietnam fell to communism, for example, other "dominoes" in the region (Cambodia, Laos, and Thailand) might also fall.

**The Division of Vietnam at Geneva**    In 1954 a conference took place at Geneva, Switzerland, to resolve the conflicts in Indochina. The United States took part in the conference as an "observer," not a full participant. French, Vietnamese, and other diplomats agreed to divide Vietnam at the 17th parallel of latitude into a Communist north and a noncommunist south. They further agreed that, within two years, elections would be held to unite the two halves of Vietnam under a single government.

The nationwide elections, however, never took place. Instead, a civil war broke out in the south between forces supporting Ho Chi Minh and forces backing South Vietnam's government led by Ngo Dinh Diem.

**U.S. Support of South Vietnam**    To prevent a Communist victory in the civil war, President Eisenhower decided to increase U.S. support

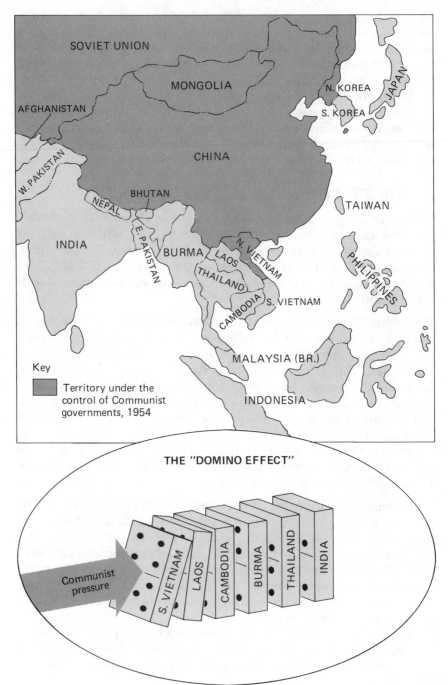

The global context: Asia in 1954

of South Vietnam's government. During his second term, Eisenhower sent U.S. military advisers to Vietnam to help train South Vietnamese soldiers loyal to Diem.

## C. DEEPER INVOLVEMENT UNDER PRESIDENT KENNEDY

When John Kennedy became president in 1961, he adopted Eisenhower's policy of supporting South Vietnam's government with military aid. He increased the number of U.S. military advisers from 2,000 in 1961 to 16,000 in 1963. He hoped that U.S. support would enable Diem's government to prevent a Communist takeover. He also hoped Diem would take steps to reduce poverty and make democratic reforms.

Instead, Diem, a Roman Catholic, acted ruthlessly to crush Buddhist opposition to his regime. He ordered his soldiers to arrest Buddhist priests and raid Buddhist temples. As oppression increased, so did opposition to Diem's rule. In 1963 Diem was assassinated by South Vietnamese military leaders.

## D. FULL-SCALE INVOLVEMENT UNDER PRESIDENT JOHNSON

Lyndon Johnson, who became president after Kennedy's assassination, promised "no wider war" in Vietnam. But he soon changed this policy when it became clear that the new leaders of South Vietnam were even less capable than Diem of winning the civil war against the Communists.

**Decision to Commit U.S. Troops**  In 1964 President Johnson concluded that South Vietnam's government was in danger of losing control of the country to the **Viet Cong** (the Communist guerrillas in South Vietnam). To counter the strong support given to the Viet Cong by the North Vietnamese government, Johnson decided that the use of U.S. troops was now necessary. He and many of his advisers wanted to prevent the Vietnam "domino" from falling to communism so as to save the rest of Southeast Asia from the same fate.

**The Gulf of Tonkin Resolution**  An incident occurred in August, 1964, that provided President Johnson with a specific reason for sending U.S. troops into combat. In the Gulf of Tonkin off the coast of North Vietnam, two U.S. ships had been attacked by North Vietnamese gunboats. President Johnson used this event to ask Congress for a resolution supporting increased military aid to South Vietnam. The resolution authorized the president "to take all necessary measures to repel any armed attack against the forces of the United States and to prevent further aggression."

Congress approved the **Tonkin Gulf Resolution** overwhelmingly, with only two senators voting against it. In effect the resolution turned over to the president the power to use the armed forces in Vietnam in any way he saw fit. For several years afterward Congress entrusted the president with the power to make war. Thus, like the earlier war in Korea, the Vietnam War was fought without a formal declaration of war by the U.S. Congress.

**Escalating the War Effort**   President Johnson waited until after the election of 1964 to begin a major military assault against North Vietnam. Early in 1965 U.S. planes began bombing enemy targets in the north. At the same time U.S. combat troops arrived in South Vietnam by the thousands. In little more than three years, the number of U.S. troops in Vietnam rose from 184,000 in 1965 to 536,100 in 1968. TV and newspaper reports referred to the steady buildup of American forces in Vietnam as a policy of **escalation**.

**Protests Against the War**   As more and more young Americans were drafted into military service and sent to fight in Vietnam, many people raised questions about Johnson's war policy. They began to doubt whether the United States was fighting for a worthwhile cause. They objected to fighting a war against an enemy on the other side of the world—an enemy that had little ability to threaten the United States. Many college students adopted various strategies for protesting the war policy. They gathered in groups and publicly set fire to their draft cards. They occupied buildings on college campuses and chanted defiant slogans such as "Hey, hey, LBJ, how many kids did you kill today?" In addition thousands escaped the draft law by moving to Canada.

The radical methods of the protesting students angered conservative groups who rallied to the flag and defended the U.S. war effort. By 1966 the nation was sharply divided between "doves" (those opposed to war) and "hawks" (those favoring even greater use of U.S. military power in Vietnam).

**Arguments for the War**   As U.S. involvement in the war escalated, Americans wanted to know: "Why are we in Vietnam?" In a 1965 speech at Johns Hopkins University, President Johnson gave these reasons:

- "We are there," said the president, "because we have a promise to keep." Ever since 1954 the United States had pledged to help South Vietnam.

- To end U.S. commitments to South Vietnam would cause other nations to doubt whether they could trust U.S. commitments to them.

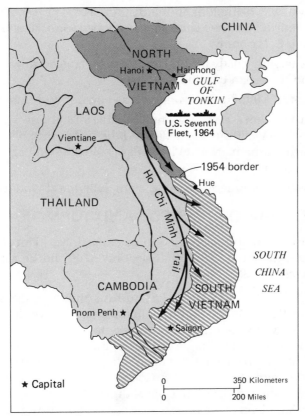

The war in Vietnam

- A Communist victory in South Vietnam would threaten neighboring countries in Southeast Asia and foster Communist aggression throughout the region.
- The Communist government of the People's Republic of China supported North Vietnam's war effort as part of "a wider pattern of aggressive purposes."

Underlying Johnson's arguments was an assumption that the two Communist powers, China and the Soviet Union, had plans to take control of much of Asia.

**Arguments Against the War**   Opponents of U.S. involvement in Vietnam argued as follows:

- The Communist nation of North Vietnam did not take orders from China or the Soviet Union. In fact, China and Vietnam had a long history of hostility and distrust toward one another.

- The war was being fought in a distant area that was not vital for U.S. security. Neither were Vietnam's economic resources vital to the U.S. economy.

- It was terribly costly for U.S. troops to be bogged down in a land war on the Asian continent.

- The South Vietnam government was corrupt and undemocratic.

- South Vietnam's army was not capable of fighting successfully against the Viet Cong guerrillas and the highly disciplined troops of North Vietnam. (North Vietnamese soldiers had begun fighting in South Vietnam in 1963.)

- Thousands of Americans were being killed and wounded.

# E. 1968: YEAR OF TRAGEDY AND TURMOIL

The war abroad and protest at home caused President Johnson to leave office rather than run for reelection. Why did he rapidly lose popularity after 1965?

**"Credibility Gap"**  The president and his military advisers stated many times that U.S. and South Vietnamese forces would eventually win the war. Many Americans, however, no longer accepted official reports about the war. They were more impressed by news reports on television, which showed that most villages in the South Vietnamese countryside were still under Viet Cong control. The commitment of more and more U.S. ground troops did not seem to make much difference. Members of the press spoke of a **"credibility gap"** between the government's view of the war and the public's view. Increasing numbers of people questioned the government's policy, and opposition to the war increased.

**Tet Offensive**  The "credibility gap" became much worse in January, 1968, when Communist forces launched an all-out attack against targeted cities in South Vietnam. TV news reports showed major Communist gains and the capital of Saigon in peril of being taken. Eventually, the attackers were pushed back, but the **Tet Offensive** dramatically demonstrated the strength of the Communist forces.

**Hippies and the Counterculture**  As 1968 began, a new movement among the nation's youth was in full swing. People in the movement were against the war and preached love and nonviolence. In addition, some students on college campuses adopted a style of life and dress that offended the older generation of their parents. Many people thought of radical students as wearing their hair long and taking drugs, even though only a minority did either of these things. Rebellious youths valued personal honesty and creativity as ideals and generally opposed marriage, patriotism, and business. Those

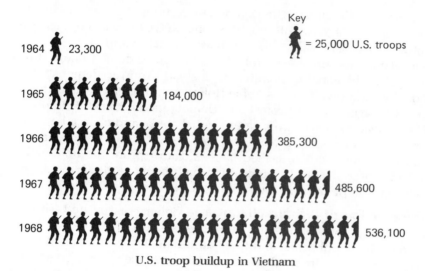

Key

1964 🪖 23,300

🪖 = 25,000 U.S. troops

1965 🪖🪖🪖🪖🪖🪖🪖 184,000

1966 🪖🪖🪖🪖🪖🪖🪖🪖🪖🪖🪖🪖🪖🪖🪖 385,300

1967 🪖🪖🪖🪖🪖🪖🪖🪖🪖🪖🪖🪖🪖🪖🪖🪖🪖🪖🪖 485,600

1968 🪖🪖🪖🪖🪖🪖🪖🪖🪖🪖🪖🪖🪖🪖🪖🪖🪖🪖🪖🪖🪖 536,100

U.S. troop buildup in Vietnam

adopting an extremely original lifestyle were known as **"hippies"** and "flower children." Their lifestyle was known as the **counterculture.**

**Johnson's Decision Not to Seek Reelection** The beginning of 1968 was also the beginning of campaigns for the presidency. Most Americans assumed that President Johnson would be nominated for reelection by the Democratic party. But young people rallied to the support of an antiwar candidate, Senator Eugene McCarthy of Minnesota. In an early primary in New Hampshire, McCarthy surprised the nation by winning more than 40 percent of the vote. Another challenger to Johnson's leadership, Robert Kennedy, announced his candidacy for the Democratic nomination. Following these events, President Johnson made a television address to the American people. He said that, in the interests of peace, he was ending the bombing of North Vietnam and opening up peace negotiations with the enemy. At the same time, to prevent politics from interfering with the success of his peace plan, Johnson announced that he would neither seek nor accept the nomination of his party for reelection.

**Assassinations** Even more startling events soon followed. In April, 1968, an assassin shot and killed Martin Luther King, Jr. Only two months later, while Robert Kennedy was campaigning in California, he was shot and killed by an Arab nationalist named Sirhan Sirhan. The nation now mourned the second Kennedy to be killed by an assassin. Many believed that Robert Kennedy, if he had lived and won the presidency, could have helped to unite the country and overcome the divisions between young and old, blacks and whites.

A World in Uncertain Times (1945 to 1974)

**Violence in Chicago**  The Democratic National Convention in 1968 took place in Chicago. Although Eugene McCarthy was popular with antiwar Democrats, he did not have enough support to win the nomination for president. Johnson's vice president, Hubert Humphrey, would win the nomination instead. Antiwar demonstrators led by well-known radicals Abbie Hoffman and Bobby Seale gathered in a Chicago park to protest the Democrats' choice of Humphrey. The Chicago police overreacted to verbal abuse and charged into the crowd of protesters. On television, people watched in dismay as the image on their screen flashed back and forth from the nomination of Humphrey inside the convention hall to the battle in the streets between the police and the protesters.

**The Election of Richard Nixon**  The violence associated with the Democratic convention and Humphrey's support of the war effort helped the Republicans and their candidate, Richard Nixon. A third-party candidate from Alabama, George Wallace, promised to take away thousands of votes in the South from both major candidates. Although Nixon was well ahead early in the campaign, Humphrey gained steadily in the opinion polls. On Election Day, Nixon emerged as the winner of one of the closest elections in U.S. history.

# II. War in Vietnam: The Nixon Years

When sworn into office in January, 1969, President Nixon was confronted with a double problem: how to deal with the war in Vietnam and how to deal with the antiwar movement at home.

## A. PURSUING BOTH PEACE AND WAR

President Johnson had carried out his 1968 promise to send U.S. diplomats to Paris to discuss peace terms with representatives from North Vietnam. The peace talks continued under President Nixon, but so did the war in Vietnam.

**New Proposal for Peace**  Nixon and his national security adviser, Henry Kissinger, proposed that both North Vietnam and the United States pull their troops out of South Vietnam at the same time. (Formerly, Johnson had proposed that the United States would withdraw troops only after the North Vietnamese did so.) The North Vietnamese in Paris rejected the U.S. proposal.

**Vietnamization and Heavy Bombing**  As his military strategy in Vietnam, Nixon announced that U.S. troops would gradually be withdrawn from Vietnam. At the same time South Vietnamese troops would receive intensive training to carry on the war by themselves. This strategy was called **Vietnamization**.

To avoid public debate and criticism, Nixon carried out another part of his strategy in secret. He ordered a series of bombing raids over Cambodia. His purpose in doing this was to cut off Cambodian roads and supply routes that the North Vietnamese relied upon for sending men and materials to the south. The U.S. military argued that the bombing of North Vietnam could not be effective unless U.S. planes also bombed the trails over which enemy troops and supplies traveled. So secret was the bombing of Cambodia that even Congress was at first unaware of it.

**More Protests**   Many Americans who had previously supported the U.S. war effort began to join the antiwar movement. On October 15, 1969, antiwar groups throughout the United States participated in a full day of peaceful protest. On November 15, 1969, more than 250,000 protesters gathered in Washington, D.C., and marched from the Washington Monument to the White House. Shortly afterward President Nixon appeared on television and appealed to the "silent majority" to support his efforts to end the war. In response to this appeal, many thousands of Americans sent telegrams of support to the White House.

Opposition continued, however, especially after the nation learned in 1970 of the bombing of Cambodia. News of the bombing touched off protests on college campuses across the country. At Kent State University in Ohio, four students were killed and several wounded when the National Guard opened fire to break up a peaceful demonstration.

**More Bombing**   In 1972, as more U.S. troops left Vietnam, Nixon ordered the continuous bombing of North Vietnam. Its capital, Hanoi, was bombed for the first time in the war. Also its harbor of Haiphong was mined to cut off shipments of oil and other supplies. At the same time, however, South Vietnamese forces lost ground to the Communists.

**The End of U.S. Involvement**   In Paris meanwhile, Henry Kissinger continued to negotiate with the North Vietnamese. Finally, in early 1973, he and President Nixon agreed to terms that had the approval of South Vietnam, North Vietnam, and the United States. According to this agreement:

- the last U.S. troops (down to less than 50,000 in 1972) would leave Vietnam;

- North Vietnamese forces in South Vietnam would be permitted to remain;

- South Vietnam's government would remain in place until elections could determine the South's future;

- the Vietcong would return all American prisoners of war and provide a full accounting for Americans missing in action (MIAs).

This agreement meant the end of U.S. involvement in Vietnam. However, the civil war in Vietnam continued for almost two more years.

**Victory of the North Vietnamese**　Without U.S. troop support, South Vietnam's government could not long survive. In 1975 a combined force of Vietcong and North Vietnamese swept into the South's capital of Saigon and thus won control of all of Vietnam. Also in 1975 Cambodia and Laos fell to Communist forces. The loss of South Vietnam, despite U.S. military power and financial aid, demonstrated both the limits on the presidency and the limits on national power.

# B. CONSEQUENCES OF THE VIETNAM WAR

The Vietnam War had a profound effect on U.S. public opinion, the U.S. economy, and U.S. foreign policy.

**Casualties and Costs**　About 58,000 Americans died in the Vietnam War, and 365,000 were wounded. A memorial in Washington, D.C., lists the names of the dead. The economic cost of the war to the United States came to a staggering sum: about $150 billion.

Economically, the indirect effects of the war continued long after the last soldier returned home. Government spending on the war was so great that it put a severe strain on the U.S. economy. Since the government was also spending vast sums for domestic programs (Johnson's Great Society), the government had to borrow billions of dollars. The national debt (the total sum owed by the government to purchasers of its bonds) jumped to a record figure. Also inflation became a serious problem both during and after the war.

**Impact on U.S. Foreign Policy**　Only a minority of Americans actively protested the war. Millions of others, however, doubted the wisdom of involving U.S. armed forces in a distant Asian war. The 1950s policy of containing communism everywhere in the world came under criticism. As you shall see, partly because of Vietnam, President Nixon tried to modify the U.S. approach to the cold war. Through the 1970s both the American people and Congress were reluctant to become involved in another foreign conflict.

**Congress and the War Powers Act**　Many members of Congress regretted the Tonkin Gulf Resolution, which had given total war-making power to President Johnson. To limit the president's power in the future, Congress passed the **War Powers Act** in 1973. These were the act's major provisions:

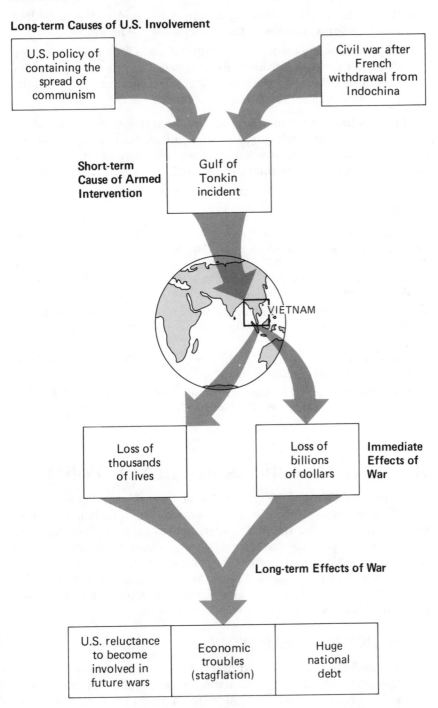

**Long-term Causes of U.S. Involvement**

U.S. policy of containing the spread of communism

Civil war after French withdrawal from Indochina

**Short-term Cause of Armed Intervention**

Gulf of Tonkin incident

VIETNAM

Loss of thousands of lives

Loss of billions of dollars

**Immediate Effects of War**

**Long-term Effects of War**

U.S. reluctance to become involved in future wars

Economic troubles (stagflation)

Huge national debt

Causes and effects of the Vietnam War

- Within 48 hours of sending troops into combat, the president must inform Congress of the reasons for the action.
- If U.S. troops are involved in fighting abroad for a period of more than 90 days, the president must obtain Congress's approval for continuing the use of troops. If Congress does not approve, the president must bring the troops home.

Congress has not yet applied the War Powers Act. President Nixon and his successors, including President Bush, have argued that the act's provisions are unconstitutional because they encroach on the president's power as commander in chief.

## In Review

The following questions refer to section I: War in Vietnam: The Johnson Years and section II: War in Vietnam: The Nixon Years.

1. Identify *guerrilla warfare, "domino effect," Tonkin Gulf Resolution, Vietnamization, Henry Kissinger,* and *War Powers Act.*
2. Explain (a) why President Johnson committed U.S. troops to the defense of Vietnam and (b) why President Nixon began withdrawing U.S. troops.
3. Evaluate whether or not U.S. policymakers made the right decision in the 1960s concerning Vietnam.
4. Describe the change in Amerian public opinion toward U.S. involvement in Vietnam between 1963 and 1973.

# III. New Directions in Foreign Policy

During the 1950s, as Eisenhower's vice president, Richard Nixon had often expressed hostility to the Soviet Union, China, and other Communist nations. However, after becoming president in 1969, Nixon adopted policies that were designed to lessen cold war tensions and also to scale back U.S. military commitments.

In making foreign policy, Nixon depended on the advice of his assistant for national security affairs, Henry Kissinger. In 1973 Nixon appointed Kissinger to be his secretary of state.

## A. POLICY OF REALPOLITIK

Nixon and Kissinger believed that U.S. foreign policies should have a single goal—supporting the national self-interest of the United States. Kissinger argued that all nations pursued their own self-interests. Therefore, he thought, the United States should do the same in order to devise realistic and successful policies. This approach to world politics, which focuses on realities rather than ideals, is known as **realpolitik.**

During his years as president (1969 to 1974), Nixon attempted to apply realpolitik and to reshape U.S. relations with the major Communist powers, the Soviet Union and China.

## B. PURSUING DÉTENTE WITH THE SOVIET UNION

Nixon's attempt to reduce, or relax, cold war tensions and to improve U.S.–Soviet relations was known as the policy of **détente,** which is a French word meaning "to relax."

**Disarmament Talks**   A principal goal of détente was to set limits on the production of nuclear weapons. During Nixon's first term as president, diplomats from the United States and the Soviet Union held a series of talks called the **Strategic Arms Limitations Talks (SALT).** They negotiated an important breakthrough in the arms race by setting fixed limits on both long-range nuclear missiles, or inter-

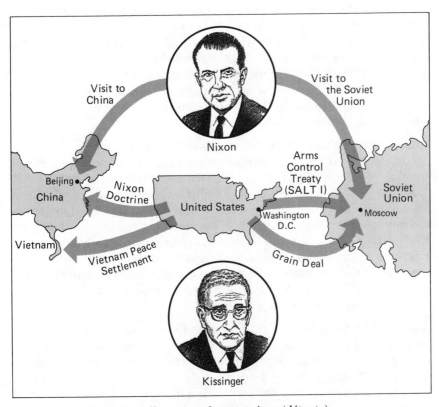

U.S. efforts to reduce tensions (détente)

continental ballistic missiles (ICBMs), and defensive missiles, or anti-ballistic missiles (ABMs).

**Nixon's Trip to the Soviet Union** In 1972 Nixon traveled to the Soviet Union where he met with Soviet Premier Leonid Brezhnev. The leaders of the two superpowers signed the SALT agreement. Also the president agreed to end a U.S. trade ban of 1949, which had prohibited the shipping of U.S. goods to the Soviet Union. To help the Russian people through a bad food shortage, Nixon offered (and Congress later approved) the sale to the Soviets of $750 million worth of U.S. wheat. The U.S.–Soviet "grain deal," as it was called, pleased not only the Soviet Union but American farmers as well.

**Seabed Agreement** The United Nations proposed another disarmament agreement in 1972. The 100 nations that signed this Seabed Agreement agreed never to place nuclear weapons on the ocean floor. Both the Soviet Union and the United States were among the signers.

## C. NORMALIZING RELATIONS WITH CHINA

The most dramatic change in U.S. policy during Nixon's presidency concerned the two governments that claimed to rule China. Recall from Chapter 13 that the United States had refused to recognize the Communist government of China established by Mao Tse-tung in 1949. The United States recognized instead the Chinese government on the island of Taiwan—a government established by Mao's anti-communist rival, Chiang Kai-shek. (Chiang's Nationalist party had ruled China through the 1930s and 1940s.)

**China's Rift with the Soviet Union** During the 1960s, however, Mao's Communist government in China began denouncing the Soviet Union. This surprised many Americans who had assumed that Communist nations were tightly bound together as allies and would follow identical policies. Previously, Americans had thought of all Communist countries as forming a **monolith,** a single and undivided force. Nixon perceived that China was growing extremely suspicious of its giant northern neighbor, the Soviet Union. Under these circumstances he and Kissinger believed that the time had come to establish normal relations with the People's Republic of China (the Chinese Communists' name for their nation).

**Nixon's Trip to China** In 1971 Kissinger traveled on a secret mission to Beijing, China's capital. His goal was to prepare the way for improved U.S. relations with the People's Republic. Following Kissinger's trip, President Nixon surprised the world by announcing that he would go to China to seek an understanding with its Communist leaders. The president's trip to China succeeded in bringing about a major shift in U.S. policy. In effect, the United States stopped taking the side of the anticommunist government on the island of Taiwan. Instead, it stressed the importance of fostering trade and good relations with mainland China.

After Nixon's trip China and the United States exchanged performing troupes and athletic teams. But they did not exchange ambassadors until 1979, when the United States formally recognized the People's Republic of China.

## D. OTHER POLICIES OF THE NIXON ADMINISTRATION

You have read about Nixon's policy of winding down U.S. involvement in Vietnam by withdrawing troops and negotiating an agreement with North Vietnam. To avoid U.S. involvement in other Asian wars, the president announced a policy known as the **Nixon Doctrine.**

**The Nixon Doctrine**  In the future, Nixon said, the nations of Asia would have to carry the main burden of their own defense. They would no longer be able to rely on the United States supplying massive amounts of military aid.

**Kissinger's Negotiations in the Middle East**  No sooner were U.S. troops out of Vietnam than a new crisis erupted in the Middle East. In October, 1973, Arab nations of the Middle East launched a surprise attack against Israel. Their immediate objective was to take from Israel the territories it had won during an Arab–Israeli war of 1967. Henry Kissinger traveled to the warring nations of the Middle East in an effort to arrange a cease-fire. At stake was not only the security of Israel but also the relations between the United States and the Soviet Union. The United States supported Israel in the conflict, while the Soviet Union supported the Arab nation of Syria. A cease-fire was finally arranged after Israeli troops had successfully crossed into Egyptian territory.

The end of the military crisis led immediately to the beginning of an economic crisis. Angered by U.S. support of Israel, several Arab nations announced an embargo on the shipment of oil to the United States and its Western allies. You will learn how the United States responded to this embargo in Chapter 19.

# IV. New Directions in Domestic Policy

Foreign affairs during the Nixon presidency had a direct effect on domestic affairs and the U.S. economy. In fact, as the 1970s began, Americans became aware that all nations of the world were **inter-**

**dependent**—tied together in a common system. Through trade and new technologies, decisions made in Tokyo and London affected the U.S. economy almost as much as decisions made in Washington, D.C. President Nixon tried to formulate policies that took account of the new global economy.

## A. A TROUBLED U.S. ECONOMY

Partly because of the billions of dollars spent on the war in Vietnam, the U.S. economy in the 1970s was in a troubled condition. It suffered from too much government money being spent for too many purposes (both a costly war and costly social programs). It also suffered from the high-quality and low-priced imports from Japan and Western Europe that in the 1970s began to compete strongly with U.S. products. Because of high government spending, consumer prices increased steadily—a condition called inflation. At the same time, a decline in the sale of U.S. products resulted in factory closings and unemployment. Stagnant economic growth and inflated prices produced a disturbing condition called **stagflation.**

**Wage and Price Controls**   In an effort to bring inflation under control, President Nixon placed wage and price controls on U.S. businesses. In August, 1971, he announced that for a period of 90 days no business could raise either its prices or its wages. After this period ended, however, inflation continued to be a serious problem.

**Effect of the Oil Crisis**   The Arab oil embargo of 1973 added to the woes of the American economy. Between 1973 and 1974 the price of a barrel of oil jumped from $3 to $11. The price increases affected not only the price of gasoline but also the price of almost all other manufactured products, since factory equipment cannot operate without oil. The U.S. automobile industry was badly hurt as American consumers bought fewer American cars and more of the smaller, fuel-efficient imports from Japan and Europe.

**Changed Policy Toward the U.S. Dollar**   During the years following World War II, the U.S. economy was very strong. People considered the dollar to be "as good as gold"—or as stable in value as gold. But when the U.S. economy weakened and lost its trade advantage, the *true* value of the dollar also declined. Therefore in 1971 Nixon decided to stop exchanging gold for U.S. dollars held by other nations. Now the dollar could move up or down against other currencies in a system of flexible exchange rates. In effect, the dollar traded at a cheaper rate enabling foreign consumers to purchase American products at cheaper prices. The purpose of the cheaper dollar was to increase U.S. exports. However, even though the new policy may have done some good, American manufacturers still felt the effects of foreign-made goods cutting into their sales in the United States.

Though Nixon tried to rescue the U.S. economy from stagflation, it remained in trouble throughout his presidency.

## B. COPING WITH A POLLUTED ENVIRONMENT

In the 1960s public attention was focused mainly on the civil rights movement and the war in Vietnam. At the same time Americans became aware that industrial wastes and exhaust fumes from millions of cars and trucks were causing terrible damage to the natural environment. The first presidents to take action on this problem were Kennedy, Johnson, and Nixon.

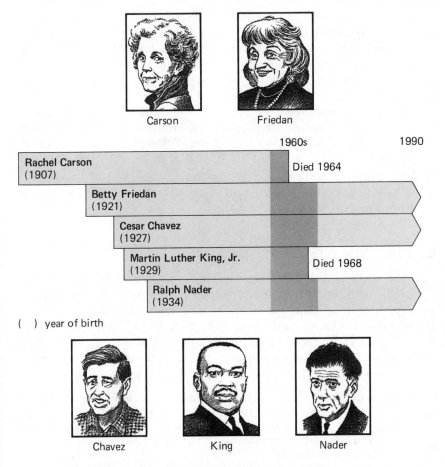

Parallel lives: reformers of the 1960s

**Increased Awareness in the 1960s**  Americans began to understand the dangers to their environment after the publication in 1962 of *Silent Spring*, an alarming book by Rachel Carson. Carson wrote: "Along with the possibility of the extinction of mankind by nuclear war, the central problem of our age has . . . become the contamination of man's total environment." The author pointed out how the pesticide DDT, a chemical spray widely used by farmers to kill insects, caused the deaths of enormous numbers of birds and fish. She also explained the damaging effects to the entire environment if wildlife vanished as a result of chemical pollution. In response to Carson's book, an environmental movement gained strength. Under presidents Kennedy and Johnson, Congress enacted several laws to control pollution and protect the nation's land, air, and water.

**Legislation in the 1970s**  In 1970 the Sierra Club and other environmental groups organized a nationwide demonstration called Earth Day. Hundreds of thousands of Americans who took part in the demonstration wanted to rouse the consciousness of the nation and pressure the government to enact tougher antipollution laws. President Nixon responded by persuading Congress to establish the **Environmental Protection Agency (EPA).** This agency, created in 1970, had the power to enforce 15 previously enacted federal programs for protecting the environment against various hazards. Under a Clean Air Act of 1970, the EPA could set federal standards for monitoring the quality of the air. Under a Clean Water Act of 1972, the new agency could assist states and local governments in funding projects for cleaning up polluted rivers and lakes. Also during Nixon's administration, the use of DDT was banned.

## C. PROTECTING THE CONSUMER

In the 1960s people began to fear, not only health hazards from a polluted environment, but also hazards from unsafe products such as cigarettes and defective cars. Once again, a best-selling book launched a new movement—the **consumer protection movement.** Ralph Nader's *Unsafe at Any Speed* (1965) attacked the U.S. automobile industry for failing to take important measures for the safety of drivers and passengers.

**New Laws of the 1960s**  Nader continued to be a leading advocate for American consumers. The movement that he helped to organize was responsible for the following laws enacted during Johnson's presidency.

- The Traffic Safety Act (1966) established safety standards in the design and equipment of new automobiles.

- The Truth-in-Lending Act (1968) required that consumers be given accurate information about the rate of interest they would pay when buying a product on credit.

**New Laws of the 1970s**  The consumer protection movement won other important victories during Nixon's presidency. An act of Congress of 1971 banned cigarette advertising on radio and television. Two other acts of 1972 created new agencies to protect people both at home and at work. The consumer agencies founded under Nixon were:

- The Consumer Products Safety Commission, which enforced safety standards for household objects such as ladders, power tools, and toys
- The Occupational Safety and Health Administration (OSHA), which provided for the inspection of factories to see that they met safety and health standards.

# D. NIXON'S CONSERVATISM

Some of President Nixon's policies were liberal (support for environmental and consumer protection). In general, however, he leaned toward conservatism. He judged many of the programs of the Great Society to be wasteful and unworkable. He therefore attempted to reduce the amount of federal money spent on aid to education, housing, job training, and welfare assistance. He persuaded Congress to eliminate altogether the Office of Economic Opportunity, which had administered many of Johnson's programs for aiding the poor.

**Appointment of a Conservative Chief Justice**  Nixon had a major opportunity to affect the future of the Supreme Court when Chief Justice Earl Warren announced his retirement in 1969. To fill the place of the liberal chief justice, Nixon selected a conservative judge, Warren Burger. Later in his presidency, three other vacancies arose on the nation's highest court. The Senate rejected two of Nixon's nominees to the Court. But those judges who finally did win Senate approval (Harry Blackmun, Lewis Powell, and William Rehnquist) were conservative in their views. As Nixon hoped, the decisions of the Burger Court in the 1970s tended to be far more conservative than those of the Warren Court in the 1960s.

**The "New Federalism"**  Conservatives also applauded a policy that Nixon called the "New Federalism." Arguing that the states understood the needs of their people better than the national government, Nixon proposed giving the states much greater freedom to decide how to use federal funds. In other words, he wanted the federal government to "share" its revenues with state and local governments. In 1971

Congress approved the idea of **revenue sharing** by passing a number of bills that permitted a state or community to use federal funds for whatever purpose it wished.

## In Review

The following questions refer to section III: New Directions in Foreign Policy and section IV: New Directions in Domestic Policy.

**Word Wheel**

1. For each labeled section of the wheel, describe a change in U.S. policy that occurred during Nixon's presidency.
2. Identify *détente, revenue sharing, SALT, realpolitik, Environmental Protection Agency*, and *stagflation*.
3. Summarize the methods used by President Nixon to improve the state of the U.S. economy.

# V. The Watergate Affair: End of the "Imperial Presidency"

The American people had not completely trusted the military policy and public statements of Lyndon Johnson. Their distrust grew even greater during Nixon's second term in office because of his involvement in a political crisis and scandal known as the **Watergate Affair.**

## A. CRISIS IN PRESIDENTIAL LEADERSHIP

**Break-in at the Watergate**   The crime that caused the crisis occurred early in the Republican party's campaign to elect Nixon to a second term. In 1972 the Democratic party had nominated a liberal senator from South Dakota, George McGovern, as its candidate for president. The Democrats' campaign was being run from an office in Washington, D.C.—a building called the Watergate. To get information about the Democrats' campaign, five men tried to break into the

Democrats' office late at night. A watchman on duty called the police, who arrested the burglars.

**Investigations**   In the November election, President Nixon won by a huge margin. But no sooner did he begin his second term than the Watergate crisis broke. In 1973 the newspapers and TV news were full of stories about the Watergate break-in of the previous summer. The news reports suggested that the crime might have been planned by members of the White House staff and perhaps by the president himself. The Federal Bureau of Investigation (FBI) began investigating the Watergate Affair. Also an unofficial investigation by two reporters for the *Washington Post* revealed that certain officials close to the president might have planned the break-in.

The most dramatic investigation was conducted by a Senate committee and televised to the nation. The witnesses who answered the committee's questions were members of the president's White House staff. Throughout 1973 Nixon stated again and again that he had no previous knowledge of the break-in and that he had not attempted to cover it up.

**White House Tapes and "Executive Privilege"**   In the course of its investigation, the Senate committee learned that the president had taped every conversation that took place in his White House office. The committee requested that the president turn over the tapes as evidence for its hearings. Nixon released some tapes and offered summaries and transcripts of others. But he refused to turn over certain tapes, arguing that it was his **"executive privilege"** to keep possession of them. Nixon argued that he would be violating the principle of separation of powers if he turned over the tapes to a Senate committee or even to a special prosecutor.

The case eventually went to the Supreme Court, which ruled that due process of law is more important than "executive privilege." The president then released the requested tapes. They revealed that, only a few days after the Watergate break-in, Nixon had participated in an effort to protect those responsible for the crime. His actions, if he were convicted of them, would be criminal, since to cover up a crime is itself a crime.

**A President Resigns**   In 1974 a committee of the House of Representatives voted to recommend that the president be impeached. Republican advisers urged Nixon to resign and thus prevent Congress from removing him by impeachment. He reluctantly agreed. On August 8, 1974, he announced on television that he would resign his office and turn over the presidency to the newly appointed vice president, Gerald Ford. It was the first time in U.S. history that a living president left office before the end of his term.

## DOCUMENTS: ARTICLES OF IMPEACHMENT

In the last week of July, 1974, the House Judiciary Committee voted to recommend the following articles of impeachment. Do you think the three reasons given by the committee are strong enough to justify the removal of a president from office?

*Article I:* On June 17th, 1972, ... agents of the Committee for the Reelection of the President:

Committed unlawful entry of the headquarters of the Democratic National Committee ... for the purpose of securing political intelligence. . . . Richard M. Nixon, using the powers of his high office, engaged personally and through his subordinates and agents in a course of conduct or plan designed to delay, impede, and obstruct the investigation of such unlawful entry; to cover up, conceal, and protect those responsible; and to conceal the existence and scope of other unlawful covert activities.

*Article II:* Richard M. Nixon ... has repeatedly engaged in conduct violating the constitutional rights of citizens, impairing the due and proper administration of justice in the conduct of lawful inquiries, or contravening the laws of government agencies of the executive branch and the purposes of these agencies.

*Article III:* Richard M. Nixon ... has failed without lawful cause or excuse to produce papers and things as directed by duly authorized subpoenas issued by the Committee on the Judiciary of the House of Representatives. . . .

In all this Richard M. Nixon has acted in a manner contrary to his trust as President and subversive of constitutional government, to the great prejudice of the cause of law and justice and to the manifest injury of the people of the United States.

Wherefore, Richard M. Nixon by such conduct warrants impeachment and trial and removal from office.

**Ford Takes Over**   Gerald Ford was in an unusual situation when he took the oath of office as the new president. The American people had not elected him to either the vice presidency or the presidency. In 1973 the elected vice president, Spiro Agnew, had resigned his office after he had fallen under suspicion of having taken bribes while serving as governor of Maryland. Nixon had then appointed Ford as

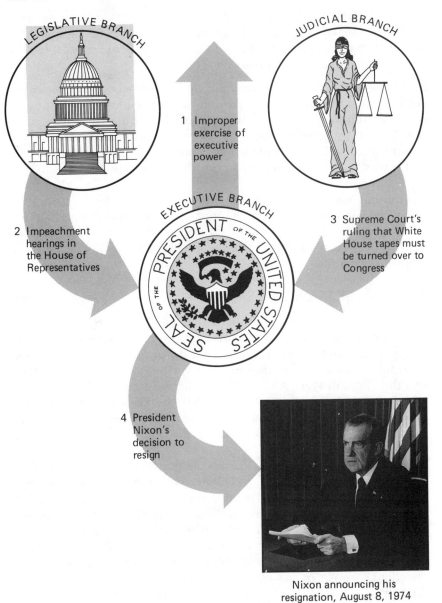

1 Improper exercise of executive power

2 Impeachment hearings in the House of Representatives

3 Supreme Court's ruling that White House tapes must be turned over to Congress

4 President Nixon's decision to resign

Nixon announcing his resignation, August 8, 1974

**Checks and balances in the Watergate Affair**

his vice president in accordance with a section of the Twenty-fifth Amendment. (The section reads: "Whenever there is a vacancy in the office of the Vice President, the President shall nominate a Vice

President who shall take the office upon confirmation by a majority of both houses of Congress.") The new president was an experienced politician, having served 25 years in the U.S. House of Representatives as a Republican from Michigan.

**Ford's Pardon of Nixon**   Only a month after becoming president, Ford announced that he was pardoning ex-president Nixon for any crime committed in the Watergate Affair. Critics of this action wondered if the pardon was legal, since no court had even charged Nixon with a crime. President Ford defended his action by saying that it was time for the nation to put the Watergate Affair aside and move forward.

Although Nixon was pardoned, other members of his White House staff were less fortunate. Among those convicted and imprisoned for covering up the Watergate Affair and committing perjury (lying under oath) were Nixon's former attorney general John Mitchell and key White House aides.

# B. AN ASSESSMENT

Until the Watergate Affair, there had been a steady increase in presidential power. Beginning with Franklin Roosevelt's strong presidency in the 1930s, the power exercised from the White House was enormous, especially in times of war (World War II, the Korean War, and the Vietnam War). A historian, Arthur Schlesinger, Jr., published a book in 1973 warning the nation that the growth in presidential power was beginning to get out of hand. He said presidents like Johnson and Nixon acted as if they could ignore both Congress and the American people.

The Watergate Affair and Nixon's resignation brought an end to the **"imperial presidency"** (as Schlesinger called the abuse of presidential power). Congress, the Supreme Court, and an independent press had fully asserted themselves in checking Nixon's power. Americans breathed a sigh of relief to see the constitutional system of checks and balances work as it had been intended to work. Congress had forced a president to leave office because of that president's abuse of his power. Nixon's fall was a lesson for later presidents, not to overstep the limits on power that are basic to our system of government.

## *In Review*

The following questions refer to section V: The Watergate Affair: End of the "Imperial Presidency."

**1.** Give a reason for each decision: (a) Vice President Agnew's decision to resign (b) President Nixon's decision to resign (c) President Ford's decision to pardon Nixon.

**2.** Define *"imperial presidency,"* and explain why Nixon's presidency was thought to be an example of this.

**3.** Explain how the system of checks and balances applied to the Watergate Affair.

# GLOSSARY OF KEY TERMS: CHAPTER 16

**consumer protection movement**   a movement advocating laws to protect consumers from dangerous products.

**counterculture**   the lifestyle and beliefs of those who rebelled in the 1960s against traditional American values.

**"credibility gap"**   the widespread public suspicion that President Johnson's statements about the Vietnam War were not trustworthy.

**détente**   the policy of attempting to reduce cold war tensions between the United States and the Soviet Union.

**"domino effect"**   the argument that the fall of Vietnam to communism would lead to Communist victories in other countries of Southeast Asia.

**doves**   those who opposed continuing military involvement in Vietnam.

**Environmental Protection Agency**   a federal agency for enforcing U.S. laws to protect the nation's land, air, and water from pollution.

**escalation**   to increase; in the context of this chapter, the regular increases in the number of U.S. troops engaged in the war in Vietnam.

**executive privilege**   a president's right, or alleged right, to withhold certain information from the legislative and judicial branches.

**flexible exchange rates**   the policy of permitting the U.S. dollar to rise and fall in value relative to other currencies.

**guerrilla warfare**   a form of warfare in which bands of soldiers launch surprise hit-and-run attacks against a stronger enemy.

**hawks**   those who favored a greater use of military power in Vietnam.

**hippies**   young people of the 1960s who protested the Vietnam war and adopted a style of dress and behavior that defied conventional tastes.

**"imperial presidency"**   the tendency of modern presidents, especially Johnson and Nixon, to ignore or bypass constitutional limits on their power.

**interdependent**   the condition of two or more things mutually depending upon each other.

**monolith**   a single undivided force or system.

**New Federalism**   President Nixon's policy of giving the states greater responsibility for controlling welfare programs.

**Nixon Doctrine**   President Nixon's policy of telling Asian countries that they would be responsible for their own defense in the future.

**realpolitik**  the idea that foreign policies should be based on national self-interest rather than on ideals.

**revenue sharing**  the policy of allowing state and local governments to decide how federal grants in aid shall be used.

**stagflation**  the economic condition of high unemployment combined with rising prices.

**Strategic Arms Limitation Talks (SALT)**  meetings of Soviet and U.S. diplomats that resulted in a 1972 agreement between the superpowers to limit the production of specific types of nuclear weapons.

**Tet Offensive**  a full-scale attack by Communist forces in 1968 against major cities of South Vietnam.

**Tonkin Gulf Resolution**  a resolution of Congress (August, 1964) giving President Johnson full authority to employ U.S. armed forces in Vietnam.

**Viet Cong**  the Communist revolutionaries who were native to South Vietnam and fought to overthrow its government.

**Vietnamization**  President Nixon's policy of reducing the number of U.S. troops in South Vietnam and also strengthening the South Vietnamese armed forces.

**War Powers Act**  an act of Congress of 1973 that placed strict limits on a president's power to engage in a foreign war without Congress's approval.

**Watergate Affair**  a political scandal of 1973 and 1974 leading finally to President Nixon's resignation.

# TEST YOURSELF

## A. Multiple Choice: Facts, Main Ideas, Skills

*On a separate sheet of paper, write the number of the word or expression that, of those given, best completes the statement or answers the question.*

### Reviewing the facts

1. Which is the most accurate definition of détente as it was applied to U.S.–Soviet relations? (1) a policy to improve peace prospects in the Middle East (2) a policy to reduce tensions and improve relations (3) a U.S. policy of protection for Soviet dissidents (4) a Soviet policy of threatening to use force in the cold war

2. During the administration of President Richard Nixon, U.S. policy toward China was characterized by (1) repeated attempts to introduce democratic principles into Chinese elections (2) increasing hostility and isolation (3) the signing of a mutual defense pact (4) a relaxation of strained relations

3. The decisions to divide Korea in 1945 and to divide Vietnam in 1954 were (1) made as a direct result of popular elections (2) reached by Korea and by Vietnam without the interference of other nations (3) worked out as compromise political solutions reflecting cold war realities (4) based on the principle of national self-determination

4. Which statement about U.S. involvement in the Vietnam War is accurate? (1) It came about only after a formal declaration of war. (2) It was based on the Open Door policy. (3) It was due exclusively to the actions of President Lyndon Johnson. (4) It reflected the U.S. commitment to a policy of containment.

5. U.S. participation in the undeclared war in Vietnam during the 1960s and 1970s raised a serious question about the (1) loyalty of U.S. military commanders (2) authority of the president to make war (3) intervention of the Supreme Court in matters of national security (4) ability of Congress to finance a war

6. U.S. actions in the Vietnam War demonstrated that (1) the "domino effect" is an effective military tactic (2) military policy in a democracy is affected by popular opinion (3) advanced technology ensures victory (4) limited use of tactical nuclear weapons can be successful

7. The War Powers Act of 1973 was passed mainly in response to concern that presidents Johnson and Nixon (1) had made treaties without informing the Senate (2) could involve the nation's armed forces in combat without congressional approval (3) had failed to control harmful antiwar protests (4) had refused to present military budgets to Congress

8. The resolution of the Watergate Affair was significant because it reinforced the idea that (1) the United States has a limited government based on laws (2) the chief executive can do no wrong (3) Congress is not effective in dealing with a constitutional crisis (4) the Supreme Court is reluctant to make decisions about matters involving the presidency

## Reviewing the main ideas

9. Why does presidential power often increase during wartime? (1) Many members of Congress leave Washington to serve in the armed forces. (2) The Constitution makes the president a dictator during wartime. (3) Quick action is often needed. (4) The Bill of Rights is suspended.

*Base your answer to question 10 on the headline below and on your knowledge of social studies.*

**NIXON MUST SURRENDER TAPES,
SUPREME COURT RULES, 8 TO 0;
HE PLEDGES FULL COMPLIANCE**

10. Which feature of the U.S. constitutional system is best illustrated by the headline? (1) checks and balances (2) "executive privilege" (3) power to grant pardons (4) federalism

11. In the 1960s and 1970s the United States and the Soviet Union built many nuclear weapons in order to (1) prevent each other from starting and winning a major war (2) follow the rules of the United Nations Security Council (3) win small-scale conflicts and wars (4) eliminate the need for allies

12. Recognition by both the United States and the Soviet Union of their mutual ability to destroy the world has encouraged both nations at times to (1) seek an alliance between them (2) pledge to use only conventional (nonnuclear) weapons in any future war (3) seek agreements to limit the number of nuclear weapons (4) place great emphasis on civil defense programs

## Developing critical thinking skills

*Base your answers to questions 13 and 14 on the cartoon below and on your knowledge of U.S. history and government.*

"Let's talk about not watering them."

13. The main idea of the cartoon is that preserving world peace depends largely upon the   (1) continuance of a balance of terror   (2) agreement of superpowers to stop the arms race   (3) adoption of isolationist policies by the nuclear powers   (4) formation of military alliances between the United States and the Soviet Union

14. The cartoon was most likely drawn to comment on   (1) the conflict in Vietnam   (2) the negotiation of a SALT agreement   (3) the grain deal between the United States and the Soviet Union   (4) the outbreak of a war in the Middle East

## B. Enduring Issues

Select two of the enduring issues from column A. For each issue chosen, explain how the historical example in column B relates to the issue.

| A. Enduring Issues | B. Historical Examples |
| --- | --- |
| 1. National power—limits and potential | Final outcome of the Vietnam War |
| 2. The judiciary—interpreter of the U.S. Constitution or shaper of policy | The U.S. Supreme Court's decision concerning Nixon's claim to executive privilege |
| 3. Presidential power in wartime and foreign affairs | Tonkin Gulf Resolution |
| 4. Separation of powers and the capacity to govern | Congress's investigation of the Watergate Affair |
| 5. Constitutional change and flexibility | The Twenty-fifth Amendment and the appointment of Gerald Ford as vice president |

## C. Essays

### Level 1

A president's actions either in domestic policy or foreign policy can sometimes lead to limits being placed on presidential power. Listed below are two presidents and problems that they faced during their administrations.

*Presidents—Problems in Domestic or Foreign Policy*

Lyndon Johnson—Vietnam War
Richard Nixon—Watergate Affair

For *each president:*

- Describe the action taken by the president and congressional reaction to it.
- Discuss how the president's actions in response to the problem resulted in limits being placed on presidential power.

*Level 2*

Presidents of the past have sometimes run into trouble by failing to recognize limits on their power.

**A.** Identify *two* presidents who did not recognize limits on their power. Also identify a problem that was caused by *each* president.

**B.** Base your answer to part B on your answer to part A. Write an essay discussing how two presidents failed to recognize limits on their power. Mention the problems that their actions caused.

# UNIT SEVEN

# Living in a Global Age

*You will remember* many of the years described in this unit. The era of your childhood, youth, and young adulthood was different from earlier eras in the following ways:

- The nations of the world recognized that they were closely linked in a global economy of trade and electronic communications.

- The U.S. role as leader of the world's economy was challenged. Japan and the nations of Western Europe came to dominate many industries in which the United States had once been supreme.

What other changes will occur in this era of computers and global change? By reading in this unit about events through the mid-1990s, you will better understand the changes and upheavals that are certain to make news before the beginning of the twenty-first century.

| Chapter | Topics |
|---------|--------|
| 17. Toward a Postindustrial World | • How the nature of the U.S. economy changed to an emphasis on services and information<br>• Evidence that nations were becoming ever more interdependent |
| 18. Domestic Issues, 1974 to the Present | • The conservative policies of presidents from Gerald Ford to George Bush<br>• Bill Clinton's "reinvention of government" and the Republican "Contract With America"<br>• Issues involving the rights of women and minorities<br>• Technological changes and their effects on U.S. society |
| 19. Foreign Policy, 1974 to the Present | • Conflicts in the Middle East<br>• U.S. policy changes: Asia, Africa, Latin America<br>• The end of the cold war; civil unrest and war in Eastern Europe |

# Chapter 17

# Toward a Postindustrial World

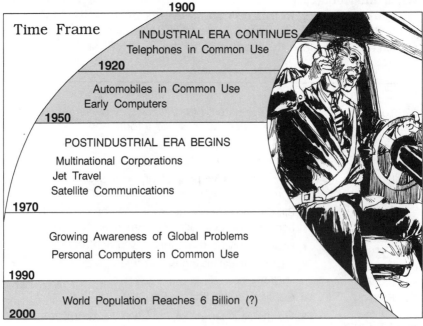

| Time Frame | 1900 |
|---|---|
| | INDUSTRIAL ERA CONTINUES<br>Telephones in Common Use |
| 1920 | |
| | Automobiles in Common Use<br>Early Computers |
| 1950 | |
| | POSTINDUSTRIAL ERA BEGINS<br>Multinational Corporations<br>Jet Travel<br>Satellite Communications |
| 1970 | |
| | Growing Awareness of Global Problems<br>Personal Computers in Common Use |
| 1990 | |
| | World Population Reaches 6 Billion (?) |
| 2000 | |

*Car phone in the
Information Age*

*Objectives*

- To understand the increasingly interdependent nature of the world.
- To explain how the United States is changing from an industrial to a postindustrial nation.
- To describe current changes in technology and their impact on both the United States and the world.

The industrial revolution that began about 1750 continued to change the world for about 200 years. Beginning in the 1950s there were signs in the United States and other industrialized countries that a new economic revolution was under way. People observed that the world was entering into a new postindustrial era. As this era continues to the end of this century and beyond, all nations of the world are likely to undergo rapid change.

Social scientists have proposed different names for this revolutionary age of new technology and new economic systems. Some call it the **"information age"** and others the **"postindustrial age."** The changes occurring in this age affect not only the United States but the entire world. This chapter briefly describes the forces that have transformed—and will continue to transform—our nation and the world during the last half of the twentieth century.

# I. The New Age: Emphasis on Information and Services

Daniel Bell, a social scientist at Harvard University, observed in the 1960s that the United States was fast becoming a "postindustrial society." He explained in his book *Coming of Post-Industrial Society* (1973) that most Americans had changed the way they earned their living. In the past they had worked at making products—either growing crops on a farm or manufacturing goods in a factory. But beginning in the 1950s there was an entirely new emphasis. Instead of making products, most workers in the United States produced services of one kind or another.

There were services of a traditional kind—for example, barbering, hairdressing, gardening, and waiting on tables. Even more common were services dealing with information. Teachers transmitted information to their students. Postal clerks transmitted information by mail. Office clerks stored information either in paper files or in computers. People in banks, business offices, medical laboratories, universities, libraries, and hundreds of other institutions did little

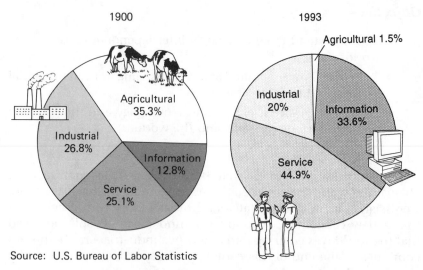

Source:  U.S. Bureau of Labor Statistics

Changes in the U.S. labor force, 1900 to 1993

else but record and interpret information. By 1993 only one out of five workers in the U.S. labor force produced goods in a factory or on a farm. Four out of five workers either dealt with information (creating it, transmitting it, or storing it) or performed some other service such as selling or transportation.

Bell observed that in the postindustrial society, "Information is power. Control over communication services is a source of power. Access to communication is a condition of freedom." In the past, almost all information took the form of words and numbers printed in books and documents. In the postindustrial age, however, more and more information was electronic in form. People in this new age learned to store information, or data, on computer discs and transmit it to other computers over the telephone lines. Bell and others predicted a time when practically every household would be part of a vast network of people communicating by computer. By 1990, only a small percentage of U.S. households used computers in this way. Even so, most businesses, universities, and government offices had adopted the new computer technology. As the twentieth century neared its end, it became obvious that an economy of services and information would depend more and more on a powerful new tool—the computer.

# II. Changes Within the United States

In addition to the computer, other technologies were also transforming the U.S. economy in the last decades of this century.

# A. NEW SOURCES OF ENERGY

The industrial age had relied for its energy on the burning of two fuels, coal and oil. Throughout the twentieth century, people in industrialized nations daily consumed huge quantities of these energy sources. Automobiles, trucks, and airplanes could not operate without oil. In fact, the entire industrial economy depended upon oil for fueling its factories, heating its buildings, and supplying the raw materials for making everything from tires to T-shirts.

However, the supply of oil was limited. Scientists predicted that the earth might use up its last gallon of oil sometime in the twenty-first century. In the 1970s nations around the world became aware that the days of burning oil at home and gasoline on the road might soon come to an end. In the postindustrial age what new forms of energy could be substituted for the oil supply that was running out?

**Nuclear Power** One answer to this question was to generate energy and heat by splitting the uranium atom. In the 1950s both the U.S. government and electric power companies had high hopes that **nuclear power plants** might be the energy source of the future. Such plants did not pollute the air with smoke. They produced electric power cheaply and efficiently.

The only question was whether nuclear plants could also supply energy safely. Because they were radioactive, the waste materials from nuclear plants presented a risk to the environment. The greatest risk of all was the possibility of an accident causing the nuclear core of a power plant to burn through the plant's protective walls. If such a "meltdown" occurred, the area near the plant could become radioactive for miles around. A disaster like this almost happened in 1979 at a nuclear power plant at Three Mile Island in Pennsylvania. An accident at this plant, although it did not lead to a "meltdown," made people aware of the dangers of nuclear power.

For years afterwards, groups of citizens successfully fought power companies' attempts to build more nuclear plants. They became even more determined after a disastrous accident occurred in the Soviet Union in 1986. A nuclear power plant near the Soviet city of **Chernobyl** caught fire and sent radioactive smoke streaming into the air. Winds carried the radiation across Europe. Millions of people around the world feared that radioactive dust blown from Chernobyl might contaminate their own land.

**Energy from the Sun and the Wind** Scientists recognized that an ideal substitute for oil would need to be both safe to the environment and practical to use. The light and heat from the sun offered one possibility. Nothing could be safer than trapping the sun's rays to heat a home or to provide power for a small automobile. Unfortunately, the devices created so far to harness **solar energy** have only limited uses. The same is true of modern windmills and other energy technologies for tapping the forces of nature (winds, tides, and underground heat).

## B. AN AGE OF PLASTICS AND LIGHT METALS

The postindustrial world is largely made of plastic. Consider these things that you may own—calculators, computers, compact discs, wristwatch bands, car seats, radios, cameras, and carpets. These and millions of other items are made entirely or in part from various plastics that did not exist before 1900. In fact, except for cellophane (invented in 1908), most plastics came into common use only in the 1940s and 1950s.

Another symbol of the new age is the throwaway aluminum can. Aluminum is the metal of the late 1900s (just as steel had been the chief metal of the late 1800s). Consumers have been wrapping their food in aluminum foil ever since its invention in 1947. They have been drinking from aluminum cans (instead of glass bottles) ever since the 1960s. Lightweight cars made from aluminum alloys came into use in the 1970s. The lighter cars made it easier to save gas.

Making products out of plastics and aluminum had negative side effects on the environment. Unlike natural materials, plastic wrappings and cups do not decompose when thrown away. Millions of tons of discarded plastics piled up over the years. By the 1980s finding ways to dispose of garbage had become a nearly insoluble problem.

The production of light metals like aluminum posed a different problem. The process for manufacturing aluminum consumed huge amounts of energy. In order to reduce these energy requirements and the many tons of waste, communities throughout the United States began requiring citizens to separate aluminum cans from the

Source: U.S. Environmental Protection Agency

The garbage crisis in the United States (figures are in millions of metric tons)

rest of their garbage so that the aluminum could be reused, or recycled.

## C. MULTINATIONAL CORPORATIONS

The light metal cars and plastic computers of the postindustrial world were not made in just one nation. The corporations that manufactured them had plants and selling outlets in many countries at once. Such globe-straddling firms were known as **multinational corporations (MNCs).** Leading examples of such firms were General Motors (GM)—automobiles—and International Business Machines (IBM)—computers.

U.S. firms would typically keep their office headquarters in U.S. cities but open manufacturing plants in countries of the third world. Wage rates outside the United States were usually far below American rates. It was therefore cheaper for manufacturing companies to make goods abroad. By the 1980s the largest U.S. corporations had turned themselves into multinational firms. By 1985, there were about 200 U.S. companies that operated in six or more countries.

What were the causes and consequences of U.S. companies globalizing their business?

**Causes**   One of the chief causes was technological. The telephone, the computer, the communications satellite, and the jet plane made it possible to manage businesses that circled the globe.

Jets began carrying business travelers across the Atlantic Ocean in the 1950s. By the 1970s international travel by air had become commonplace. From an airport outside New York City, a business executive could reach any major city in the world in 24 hours or less. Major cities were tied to other cities in a vast and complex network of international air routes.

Sending electronic messages around the world was of course even faster. Signals bouncing off satellites in outer space traveled at the speed of light. Data entered into a computer in Tokyo or Paris or New York could be relayed via satellite to any place on earth—and it would reach that place instantly! Thus banks and stock exchanges in all the major cities of the world are today part of a single financial system. Whether a bank is American, Japanese, British, German, or Swiss, its decision to lend money at a certain rate instantly affects all other banks.

**Consequences**   The trend of businesses becoming multinational has had both beneficial and harmful effects on the U.S. economy. On the positive side it has vastly increased world trade and opened up world markets for U.S. goods and services. On the negative side it has resulted in the closing of U.S. factories and the loss of manufacturing jobs for American workers.

## *In Review*

The following questions refer to section I: The New Age: Emphasis on Information and Services and section II: Changes Within the United States.

1. Explain what is meant by the term *information age*.

2. Identify *two* characteristics of a postindustrial society that distinguish it from an industrial society.

3. Define *multinational corporation*, and explain the ways in which it depends on modern technology.

## OBSERVERS OF AMERICAN LIFE: THREE VIEWS OF THE UNITED STATES IN A GLOBAL AGE

On July 4, 1976, the United States celebrated the bicentennial, or 200th-year anniversary, of its existence as a nation. The event attracted attention around the world. Writers from various countries commented on the impact of the United States in the past and its continued role in shaping the world's future. Comments by journalists from France, Nigeria, and India are given below.

On the whole, do the three writers view the United States as a positive or negative force in the world?

### *The View From France*

The U.S. is celebrating the 200th anniversary of its independence this year. How far has it come? And how far have we come? America, the most criticized country in the world, is also the most imitated, and nothing that goes on in America is wholly alien to Europe or the rest of the world, including China and the Soviet Union.

The Russians depend on American agriculture in order to feed themselves, and without American technology Siberia would remain barren. The European leftists who demonstrated against the Vietnam War were dressed in jeans and listened to Bob Dylan every night.

—From *L'Express*, Paris, France
May 17, 1976

### *The View From Nigeria*

Since July 4, 1776, the U.S. has grown to become the most powerful nation in the world, the richest, and most affluent.

# III. Changes in the World

The United States is already industrialized. It has passed through the industrial revolution and is moving into another economic stage—the postindustrial revolution. Many other countries, however, are still in the process of industrializing. Whether they are industrialized or not, all nations belong to the same global economy. What happens in one country indirectly affects what happens in other countries.

This section presents an overview of the total world picture. All Americans need to develop a worldview because, more than ever in U.S. history, our nation can neither escape nor ignore the problems of other nations.

She has become a colossus, feared by small and big nations alike. She's made many friends and a lot of enemies.

Though the U.S. has not been a major participant in the African scene, she has nonetheless demonstrated her desire to help in the building up of the continent. American technological, scientific, educational, and cultural aid is what Africans want from America. We want the cooperation of the U.S. in the development of our friendships.

What we Africans do not want, however, is American imperialism and domination, the American CIA, and the undermining of our national efforts. We strongly resent any attempt by America to dictate to us the terms of our friendship or who should be our friends.

—Babatunde Jose, Jr., in *Sunday Tide*,
Port Harcourt, Nigeria, July 3, 1976

*The View From India*
The U.S. has entered the third century of its existence as an independent nation full of doubts regarding its own future. And yet no other country is as vigorous, innovative, productive, and well placed to influence the course of events in coming years and decades. Indeed, it will not be much of an exaggeration to say that peace and stability in our era and the well-being of the rest of mankind are to no small extent dependent on the strength and prosperity of the U.S.

—Girilal Jain, in the *Times of India*,
Bombay and New Delhi, July 7, 1976

## A. DEVELOPED AND DEVELOPING NATIONS

Take the United States as an example of a developed (industrialized) nation and the African country of Zaire as an example of a **developing nation** (one that is industrializing). Compare them using the following data.

**A Comparison of Two Nations**
Statistics from the 1992 *World Almanac and Book of Facts*

|  | United States | Zaire |
|---|---|---|
| Population | 248.7 million | 35.3 million |
| Per capita income | $16,444 | $140 |
| Passenger cars in use | 141 million | 24 thousand |
| Television sets | 145 million | 16 thousand |
| Literacy | 99 percent | 55 percent |

A huge gap exists between the so-called **"have" nations** of the world (developed and industrialized) and the **"have-not" nations** (developing and industrializing).

**Economic Relationships**   Ever since World War II, the United States and other developed countries have given economic aid to less developed countries in the form of (1) loans, (2) outright grants, and (3) technical assistance (expert advice). In addition, MNCs have invested heavily in the poorer countries of Asia, Africa, and Latin America. They have opened up factories and mines and given employment to millions, though at wage rates far below U.S. standards. The United States and other developed countries have benefited from this relationship. The raw materials and labor that they can purchase cheaply in third world countries enable companies to sell goods for relatively low prices. The high standard of living enjoyed by the citizens of industrialized countries is largely due to this fact.

**Political Relationships**   The relationship between rich countries and poor ones is far from equal. Because of development loans that they have been unable to pay back, third world countries are heavily in debt to the industrialized nations of Europe, Canada, the United States, and Japan. The burden of debt grows heavier every year. More and more of a poor nation's governmental budget must be used to pay interest on its international debts. Thus, the gap between rich nations and poor nations continues to widen.

It so happens that most of the industrialized nations occupy the northern part of the globe. (Exceptions are Australia and New Zealand.)

At the same time, most of the third world countries lie to the south near the equator. Roughly speaking then, "have" nations tend to be in the north and "have-not" nations in the south.

The poorer nations resent the economic dominance of the richer nations. In the United Nations, they demand that the industrialized countries change their policies in order to provide the developing countries with relief from the crushing burden of debt.

# B. WORLD POPULATION GROWTH

The division between north and south, rich and poor, grows more serious every day as the world's population keeps increasing. Population growth in the United States and other industrialized countries has decreased in recent years. On the other hand, a high birth rate in Africa and other third world regions means that the population of the poorer part of the world is growing much faster than that of the richer part. By the year 2000, experts predict that China and the "have-not" nations of the south will have 80 percent of the world's population.

**Billions More People**   During the last decades of this century, the number of people in the world went from three billion in 1959 to four billion in 1974 to five billion in 1986. Currently the world population increases by about 90 million *every year*. At this rate there will be six billion people in the year 2000.

**The Green Revolution**   How could the world's food supply keep pace with its growing population? In the 1960s scientists hoped that they had found the answer in new agricultural technology. They had developed varieties of rice, corn, and wheat that would increase the crop yields on farms of the third world. The **Green Revolution,** as scientists called it, produced spectacular results. High-yielding wheat in India and high-yielding rice in Southeast Asia succeeded in greatly expanding the food supply. Unfortunately, methods for growing the improved grains also damaged the environment. The insects that attacked the new crops could be controlled only by the heavy use of pesticides.

**Pressure on the Land**   The Green Revolution did not work well in many parts of Africa where soil conditions were poor. In fact, attempts to produce more crops to feed more people only weakened the soil further and turned millions of acres into desert lands. This process of **desertification** had a disastrous effect on the economies of many African countries. In the 1980s and 1990s millions of Africans died from hunger and malnutrition.

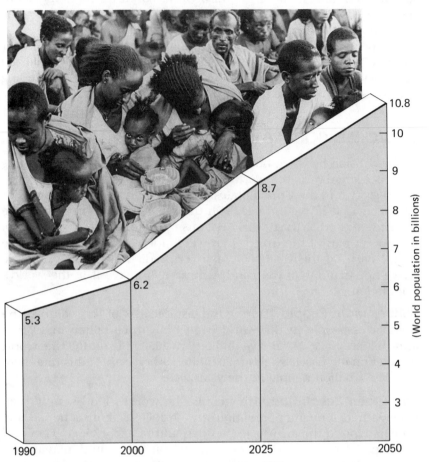

Source: U.S. Bureau of the Census, *World Population Profile: 1987*

Predicted growth of world population, 1990 to 2050

## C. THREATS TO THE GLOBAL ENVIRONMENT

Rich countries and poor countries of the world were alike in at least one respect. They all contributed to the problem of a deteriorating environment.

**Destruction of the Brazilian Rain Forest**   Environmentalists throughout the world warned that Brazil's vast rain forest was in danger of being destroyed. Day after day, year after year, industrial developers in Brazil opened up huge holes in the forest in order to dig for its underground deposits of gold, tin, bauxite (an aluminum ore), and other minerals. Poverty-stricken families also went into the forest and burned down trees to clear the land for farming. In the process, hundreds of species of tropical birds and animals became extinct. The burning of millions of trees released huge quantities of carbon dioxide into the atmosphere, enough to upset the world's climate.

**The Greenhouse Effect**   In the 1980s scientists warned that the burning of forests and exhaust fumes from automobiles might cause a condition similar to what happens in a greenhouse. As more and more carbon dioxide entered the earth's atmosphere, the sun's infrared rays would become trapped. The likely result would be the **greenhouse effect**—a gradual increase in the earth's average temperatures. Such a change in climate would melt the Antarctic ice caps, flooding coastal cities, and generally harm all forms of plant and animal life, including human life.

**Depletion of Ozone**   Another environmental worry of the 1980s concerned a layer of gas high above the earth's surface. The ozone layer blocks the sun's ultraviolet light, which is harmful to living

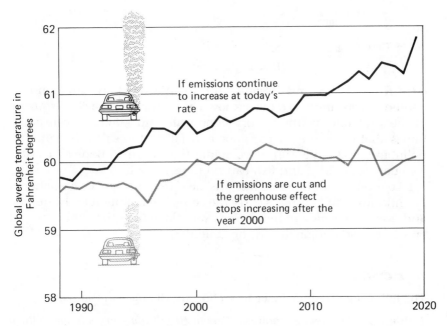

Source: Goddard Institute for Space Studies

Predictions of a warmer planet, 1990 to 2020

things. Such light can cause skin cancer. The ozone layer's protection against ultraviolet light may no longer exist if deodorant sprays, Styrofoam cups, and other consumer items continue to emit an ozone-destroying gas into the atmosphere. Canada, the United States, and the nations of Western Europe have agreed to try to prevent further damage to the ozone layer. They have pledged to ban all production of the damaging substances (chlorofluorocarbons) by the year 2000.

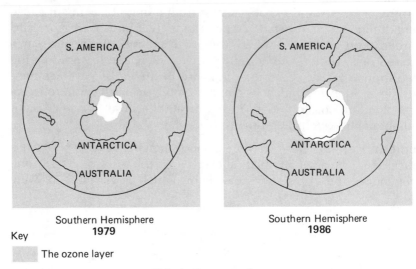

Key
■ The ozone layer

Hole in the ozone layer

**Acid Rain**   Lakes and streams around the world are threatend by another environmental danger known as **acid rain.** The chief sources of the problem are the factory chemicals and automobile exhaust fumes that enter the air as vapor and fall to the earth in rain. The pollutants make the rain more acidic than normal. Bodies of water also become acidic, and fish can no longer live in them.

Like other environmental hazards, acid rain recognizes no national boundaries. Wind currents carry the source of pollution for hundreds and even thousands of miles. For example, half of the acid rain that falls in Canada originates in the United States.

## In Review

The following questions refer to section III: Changes in the World.

**1.** Identify *developing country, Green Revolution, greenhouse effect, desertification, ozone layer,* and *acid rain.*

**2.** Explain why nations must cooperate if they are to solve their environmental problems. Give an example.

**3.** Compare and contrast the economy of one "have" nation with the economy of one "have-not" nation.

## GLOSSARY OF KEY TERMS: CHAPTER 17

**acid rain**   a type of rain that has become acidic due to pollution by industrial chemicals and exhaust fumes.

**Chernobyl disaster**   an accident to a nuclear power plant in the Soviet Union in 1986 that contaminated land, air, and water with radioactive material.

**desertification**   the process by which overuse of land for farming causes that land to become dry and lifeless as a desert.

**developing nation**   a nation that is not yet fully industrialized and whose people are mainly poor.

**greenhouse effect**   a predicted change in the world's climate caused by excessive amounts of carbon dioxide in the atmosphere; also known as global warming.

**Green Revolution**   an increase in the world's food supply brought about by new, high-yielding varieties of rice, wheat, and corn.

**"have" nations**   those nations that are fully industrialized or developed.

**"have-not" nations**   those nations that are only now becoming industrialized; also known as developing nations.

**"information age"**   the modern era, so named because a high percentage of workers now manage the flow of information in both electronic forms (computer data) and print forms (books, magazines, and newspapers).

**multinational corporations (MNCs)**   business firms that have offices, factories, or both in more than one country.

**nuclear power plant**   an electric power plant that derives its energy from the splitting of uranium atoms.

**ozone layer**   a layer of gas high above the earth that provides natural protection from the effects of ultraviolet light.

**postindustrial society**   a society that has passed through the industrial revolution and now specializes in processing information and providing services.

**solar energy**   the energy derived from the sun's heat and light.

# TEST YOURSELF

## A. Multiple Choice: Facts, Main Ideas, Skills

*On a separate sheet of paper, write the number of the word or expression that, of those given, best completes the statement or answers the question.*

## Reviewing the facts

1. One consequence of the formation of multinational corporations was (1) increased risk of a major war (2) a decline of manufacturing jobs in the United States (3) increased poverty of third world countries (4) further depletion of the ozone layer

2. The main reason that solar energy has not yet replaced oil and coal is that (1) oil will always be the cheaper fuel (2) the supply of oil and coal has steadily increased (3) current technologies for using solar energy have only limited uses (4) solar energy is likely to pose a threat to the environment

3. Which of these is the best example of production in the "information age"? (1) a textile mill that makes sweaters (2) a factory that makes bicycles (3) a dairy farm that produces cheese (4) a hospital laboratory that makes use of computers

4. A predicted change in the earth's climate due to increased quantities of carbon dioxide is known as (1) the greenhouse effect (2) the Green Revolution (3) desertification (4) ozone depletion

5. The region whose population will probably increase the most in the 1990s is (1) Europe (2) North America (3) Africa (4) Australia and New Zealand

6. The Green Revolution has been most important in increasing the world's (1) population (2) food supply (3) environmental problems (4) communications technology

7. Which of the following affects the environment of the United States? (1) damage to the Brazilian rain forest (2) acid rain from Canada (3) a hole in the ozone layer (4) all of the above

8. Which suggestion is most often cited by experts as a way to help solve the problem of the shortage of food in most developing nations? (1) Increase the number of farmers in third world nations. (2) Apply new agricultural technology. (3) Reduce the amount of fats consumed in the developed nations. (4) Attempt to change world weather and climate.

## Reviewing the main ideas

9. Which is an advantage of living in an age of computers? (1) Large amounts of information can be processed quickly. (2) Computerization helps to reduce unemployment. (3) The use of computers has created a more personalized society. (4) Workers have a greater sense of self-esteem.

10. Which is a global effect of the growth of technology? (1) Economic activity has become more dependent on domestic natural resources. (2) International cooperation has broken down. (3) High-speed communications link the economies of all countries. (4) Governments view nationalism as an obstacle to progress.

**11.** A negative effect of new technologies on U.S. industry is (1) a decline in the number of well-paid factory jobs (2) a decline in the number of service jobs (3) a high failure rate among multinational corporations (4) a consumer revolt against the use of new technologies

## Developing critical thinking skills

*Base your answers to questions 12 and 13 on the graph below and on your knowledge of social studies.*

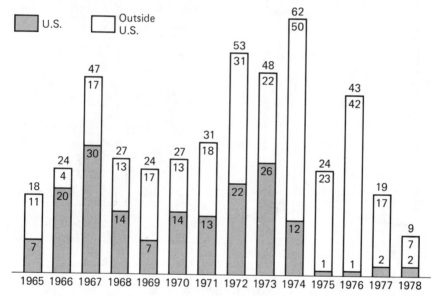

Source: Kidder, Peabody & Co.

Nuclear reactor orders (figures do not include reactors later canceled)

**12.** Which is a valid conclusion based on the data in the graph? (1) Nuclear reactors are an unsafe source of energy. (2) Orders for nuclear reactors reached their peak in the early 1970s. (3) Inflation is chiefly responsible for the variations in the numbers of nuclear reactors ordered. (4) Nations have become less dependent upon nuclear reactors as an energy source because of the popularity of solar converters.

**13.** Which development would be most likely to help reverse the trend that occurred since the early 1970s in nuclear reactor orders? (1) discovery of major new oil reserves in the Atlantic Ocean (2)

agreement of the United States and the Soviet Union on a nuclear arms limitation treaty  (3) expansion of solar energy applications (4) development of safer means of producing nuclear power and disposing of nuclear wastes

*Base your answers to questions 14 and 15 on the graphs below and on your knowledge of social studies.*

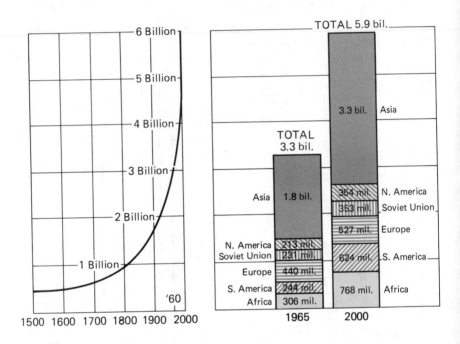

**Projected world population**

14. Which conclusion is best supported by the data in the graphs?  (1) In 1965 the populations of Asia and Africa were about equal.  (2) The world population was relatively stable until after World War II. (3) The population of North America is growing faster than the population of South America.  (4) The population of the world will have almost tripled between 1900 and 2000.

15. Which prediction is best supported by the data in the graphs?  (1) Population changes will reduce international tensions in the future. (2) The rate of world population growth will peak before 2000.  (3) Asian influence in world affairs is likely to increase.  (4) The influence of older people in world politics will increase by the year 2000.

## B. Enduring Issues

*For each issue in column A, explain how the historical example in column B relates to the issue.*

| A. Enduring Issues | B. Historical Examples |
|---|---|
| 1. National power—limits and potential | Increase in the number and influence of multinational corporations |
| 2. Federalism—the balance between nation and state | The issue of whether protecting the environment is chiefly a local or national matter |

## C. Essays

### Level 1

Since the 1950s economic changes have affected many areas of life including the following:

> Energy sources
> Technology
> Forms of business organization
> Forms of employment

Choose *two* of the areas of life given. For *each* one chosen:

**1.** Describe a specific change that has occurred since the 1950s.

**2.** Discuss one positive and one negative result of that change on American society.

### Level 2

Many important changes have occurred since 1950 that have affected people's lives.

**A.** List *four* changes since 1950 that have affected how Americans live.

**B.** Base your answer to part B on your answer to part A. Write an essay discussing *two* ways that people's lives have changed since 1950.

# Chapter *18*

# Domestic Issues, 1974 to the Present

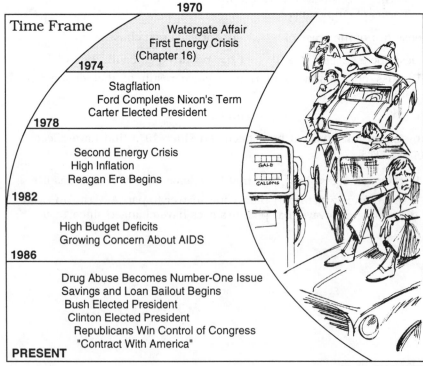

**Time Frame**

1970

Watergate Affair
First Energy Crisis
(Chapter 16)

1974

Stagflation
Ford Completes Nixon's Term
Carter Elected President

1978

Second Energy Crisis
High Inflation
Reagan Era Begins

1982

High Budget Deficits
Growing Concern About AIDS

1986

Drug Abuse Becomes Number-One Issue
Savings and Loan Bailout Begins
Bush Elected President
Clinton Elected President
Republicans Win Control of Congress
"Contract With America"

PRESENT

SALE

GALLONS

*Energy Crisis, 1979*

*Objectives*

- To understand that periods of upheaval in history are often followed by conservative reactions.
- To analyze the social and economic issues of the current period.
- To explain how domestic policies are influenced by global interdependence.
- To compare and contrast the domestic policies of recent administrations.

The 1960s had been a decade of liberal reform (civil rights, Great Society programs) as well as radical protest (the antiwar movement). The decades that followed—the 1970s and 1980s—were strikingly different. U.S. involvement in the Vietnam War ended in 1973. The Watergate scandal ended in Richard Nixon's resignation as president in 1974. Following these events, the American people largely abandoned the liberal hopes that had stirred them in the 1960s. The majority now expressed conservative tastes in their private lives and conservative choices in their public lives as citizens. (For definitions of "liberal" and "conservative," review the Glossary in Chapter 14.)

# I. The Trend Toward Conservatism

Five successive presidents—Nixon, Ford, Carter, Reagan, and Bush— followed policies that were far more conservative than those of Kennedy and Johnson. Only one of them, Jimmy Carter, was a Democrat. Even Carter was more conservative than any other Democratic president of the twentieth century. Only with the election of Bill Clinton in 1992 did presidential politics turn in a more liberal direction.

## A. FORD AND CARTER

In Chapter 16 you read about the swearing in of a new president, Gerald Ford, after the Watergate Affair caused Nixon to resign. In a televised speech to the nation, Ford promised to restore trust in the U.S. government. "Our national nightmare is over," he said. But memories of Watergate lingered for months and even years afterward. Ford's decision to pardon Richard Nixon, even before the courts acted to indict him, caused great controversy. (Review page 504.)

Like Nixon before him, President Ford followed policies that were moderately conservative. The chief domestic issue of his brief presidency (1974 to 1977) was how to bring inflation under control. His solution to this serious economic problem was to veto dozens of spending bills that, in his view, would put the U.S. government deeper into debt and cause consumer prices to rise even more.

**Appointment of a Vice President**   Another issue concerned the vice presidency. Now that Ford had moved into the presidency, who was to replace him in the vice presidency? He selected the former governor of New York, Nelson Rockefeller. A Senate committee conducted a long and probing investigation of Rockefeller before finally recommending that his nomination be approved. At last the United States had both a president and a vice president who could be trusted to carry out their constitutional duties.

**Election of 1976**   Honesty in government was an important issue in the presidential election of 1976. More than a dozen Democrats entered the race for their party's nomination. Each hoped to convince voters that, because of the Watergate Affair, Republican leadership in the White House was suspect. The candidate who eventually won the Democratic nomination was Jimmy Carter, a former governor of Georgia. Although only a few people had ever heard of Carter, they soon became familiar with his winning smile on TV debates and news shows. Carter's campaign stressed his honesty and lack of previous involvement in the politics of Washington, D.C. Millions of Democratic voters found Carter to be an attractive, likeable, and trustworthy candidate.

The Republican nominee, President Gerald Ford, started his campaign well behind Carter in the opinion polls. But after debating Carter on TV, the incumbent president closed the gap. The results of the election were close. Carter emerged with 297 electoral votes to Ford's 240 votes. For the first time since the election of Zachary Taylor in 1848, the United States was to have a president from the South.

**Carter's Style of Leadership**   Carter proved to be a hardworking, honest, and dedicated president. There was never much doubt about his good intentions and concern for human rights. There was some doubt, however, about his effectiveness as a leader. At times he would tell Congress and the American people that a certain law was urgently needed. But then he would not follow through on his proposals to make sure that the Democratic majority in Congress voted for them. He angered and frustrated lawmakers in his own party by sometimes changing his policies at the last minute. Public opinion polls during his four years in office (1977 to 1981) showed a decline in his popularity, especially after he failed to deal forcefully with an energy crisis in 1979 and failed to win the release of American hostages in Iran (see pages 565–566).

President Carter's most notable achievements were in foreign policy—persuading the Senate to ratify a treaty with Panama, arranging a peace treaty in the Middle East, and arranging an arms limitation treaty with the Soviet Union. These events are described in Chapter 19.

## B. EIGHT YEARS OF REAGAN CONSERVATISM

Carter was defeated for reelection in 1980 by a former movie star and two-term governor of California, Ronald Reagan. Since Reagan dominated U.S. politics in the 1980s, it is important to know who he was and what he stood for.

**A Brief Biography**   Born in 1911, Ronald Reagan grew up in Illinois where he acted in school plays both in high school and college. After graduating from college, he became a sports broadcaster on radio. Later he became an actor in Hollywood movies. He played romantic and heroic roles in such movies as *Knute Rockne—All American* (1940) and *King's Row* (1941). During the late 1940s he served as president of the Screen Actors Guild, a labor union. In the 1950s millions of Americans knew Reagan as an entertainer and TV host of a program called "The General Electric Theater." They knew nothing of Reagan's politics until the election of 1964 when he used his talents as a speaker to support Barry Goldwater, the conservative Republicans' candidate for president. Conservatives loved what Reagan said in his speeches. His career in politics was now launched.

Reagan was elected governor of California in 1966 and reelected in 1970. As a rising star in the Republican party, he almost won that party's nomination for president in 1976 but was narrowly defeated by President Gerald Ford. Reagan won the Republican nomination easily in 1980 and went on to defeat the Democrats' choice, President Carter, in a landslide victory.

**Conservative Principles of a Popular President**   Reagan proved to be an extremely popular president. As an experienced entertainer, he knew how to use the TV medium to project a pleasing personality to a mass audience. Unlike Jimmy Carter, Reagan took a firm stand on domestic issues. He believed in reducing taxes, reducing government spending on social programs, and increasing government spending on defense. As you will read, his policies had both a positive effect on business and a negative effect on the poor.

In the election of 1984, Reagan's popularity was demonstrated by an overwhelming victory over his Democratic challenger, Walter Mondale. In the electoral college, the president won the votes of 49 states. (The one state voting for Mondale was his own home state of Minnesota.)

## C. POLICIES OF GEORGE BUSH

Even when Reagan left office after serving two full terms, his conservative policies were carried into the 1990s by his successor, George Bush. As Reagan's vice president for eight years, Bush was closely identified with Reagan's basic philosophy. He had no trouble winning the Republican nomination for president in 1988 and not much trouble defeating the Democrats' candidate, Governor Michael Dukakis of Massachusetts.

Before becoming president, Bush had gained wide and varied experience as congressman from Texas, director of the Central Intelligence Agency (CIA), U.S. ambassador to the United Nations, and vice president. In his campaign he promised to fight against drugs, protect the environment, and improve education without raising taxes.

As president, Bush called for states to assume a larger role in domestic programs. For the most part, however, his first two years in office focused on foreign policy.

## D. POLICIES OF BILL CLINTON

The election of a Democrat, Bill Clinton, in 1992 marked a shift away from the conservative policies of Presidents Reagan and Bush. After his inauguration, Clinton moved quickly to fulfill his campaign promises to address many social and economic problems.

The new president provoked a storm of controversy by removing the long-standing ban against homosexuals serving in the armed forces. To make the military more comfortable with the change, Clinton said that gays could serve but only if they remained silent about their sexual preferences ("don't ask, don't tell").

Clinton appointed a number of women to top posts. In 1993, Janet Reno became the attorney general. Ruth Bader Ginsburg was Clinton's choice for appointment to the U.S. Supreme Court.

Working with Democratic majorities in both houses of Congress, Clinton succeeded in passing a number of important reform measures. Congress approved: (1) the president's plan for reducing the federal deficit, (2) a gun control bill (the Brady Bill) that imposed a waiting period on the sale of handguns, (3) a family leave bill that granted employees 12 weeks leave from work to care for newborn infants, and (4) a program called Americorps for enlisting young people in community service projects. The president's wife, Hillary Rodham Clinton, was chiefly responsible for drawing up the terms of a new system of national health insurance. (See page 564.)

## Recent Presidents

| President | Experience | Actions on Domestic Policy | Actions on Foreign Policy |
|---|---|---|---|
| Gerald Ford (1974 to 1977) Republican, Michigan | Minority leader of U.S. House of Representatives Vice President, 1973 to 1974 | Pardoning of Nixon Voluntary wage and price controls Attempts to cut spending | Détente with Soviet Union Granting asylum to Vietnam refugees |
| Jimmy Carter (1977 to 1981) Democrat, Georgia | Governor of Georgia | Decontrolling price of natural gas Voluntary wage-price guidelines | Emphasis on human rights Mediating Egypt-Israeli peace treaty Arranging to give control of Panama Canal to Panama Efforts to win release of hostages in Iran |
| Ronald Reagan (1981 to 1989) Republican, California | Governor of California | Tax cuts and tax reform Cutting government spending for social programs | Summit meetings with Soviet leader Military aid to "contras" of Nicaragua Troops sent to Lebanon and Grenada |
| George Bush (1989 to 1993) Republican, Texas | Member of U.S. House of Representatives Director of CIA Vice president, 1981 to 1989 | "War on drugs" Educational reform Higher taxes, lower Medicare payments | Invasion of Panama Organized Operation Desert Storm to oppose Iraq's invasion of Kuwait |
| Bill Clinton (1993 to —) Democrat, Arkansas | Governor of Arkansas | Supported health care reform Gun control law National service program (Americorps) Reduced federal spending, federal jobs, and budget deficit | Troops sent to ease civil war in Somalia NAFTA Agreement Restoration of democracy in Haiti Trade negotiations and agreements with China and Japan Participated in NATO effort to quell civil war in Bosnia |

# E. EFFORTS TO CHANGE THE CONSTITUTION

Some of the major issues of the 1980s and 1990s focused on three conservative goals: to restore prayer in public schools, to outlaw abortions, and to protect the American flag.

**The School Prayer Issue**   In the 1960s the U.S. Supreme Court had ruled that the reciting of prayers and reading from the Bible in public schools violated the First Amendment right to "separation of church and state." (In other words, government could not support a particular religion or religious practice.)

Conservative members of religious organizations strongly objected to the Supreme Court's decisions concerning prayer and Bible-reading. They argued that brief religious practices had once been part of the school day and should be allowed. In the 1980s a religious group known as the "moral majority" campaigned for an amendment to the U.S. Constitution that would permit public schools to require daily prayer. Although President Reagan supported the amendment, it was not adopted because of strong opposition by groups committed to the principle of "separation of church and state."

**The Abortion Issue**   The Supreme Court's decision in *Roe* v. *Wade* (1973) established a woman's right to have an abortion in the early months of pregnancy, if she chose to do so. Opponents of the Supreme Court's decision in this case wanted to overturn it by persuading the nation to adopt an anti-abortion amendment to the U.S. Constitution. Those who favored such an amendment organized a movement known as the "right to life" movement. Those who defended the Supreme Court's position in *Roe* v. *Wade* organized a "pro-choice" movement. They did not necessarily believe in abortions as such, but strongly believed that every woman should be permitted the choice of either having an abortion or not having one. An anti-abortion amendment was not adopted in the 1980s. However, the Supreme Court modified its position on abortion rights in the following cases:

- *Harris* v. *McRae* (1980) The Court ruled in this case that the federal government is not required to pay for the abortions of the poor through Medicaid. Nor must a state government pay for abortion costs.

- *H. L.* v. *Matheson* (1981) A Utah law required a physician to "notify if possible" the parents of a minor upon whom an abortion is to be performed. The Supreme Court ruled that Utah's law was allowed by the Constitution.

- *Webster* v. *Reproductive Health Services* (1989) The most controversial case of the 1980s concerned a Missouri law that placed restrictions on doctors performing abortions, even in the early months of pregnancy. In a 5 to 4 decision, the Supreme Court ruled that states may pass laws determining the circumstance under which abortions would be allowed.

- *Planned Parenthood* v. *Casey* (1992) In this case, five abortion clinics in Pennsylvania challenged the state's law requiring teenagers to obtain their parents' consent for an abortion. The Supreme Court upheld this law as constitutional. On the other hand, it said that its original ruling in *Roe* v. *Wade* was still valid. A state could limit but could not ban abortions.

**The Flag Issue**  If a person burned a U.S. flag in public, could that person be arrested and punished under a state law? This question was answered by the Supreme Court in 1989 in the case of *Texas* v. *Johnson*. The Court ruled that the First Amendment right to freedom of speech applied to a U.S. citizen who had burned the U.S. flag as an act of protest. Therefore Texas's law against desecrating (harming) the U.S. flag was declared unconstitutional.

# II. Government's Role in the Economy

Presidents Ford, Carter, Reagan, and Bush tried to redefine the role of the U.S. government in the economy. All four believed that the government had grown too large and needed to be trimmed back.

## A. POLICIES TO FIGHT INFLATION

In 1974, the year that Ford replaced Nixon as president, the U.S. inflation rate climbed to a frightening 11 percent. The problem was partly the result of government spending on the Vietnam War. It was also the result of high oil prices caused by an Arab **oil embargo** (see page 564). Both Ford and Carter attempted to bring inflation under control. But neither succeeded. The failure of these presidents to find a cure for inflation was one reason that neither was elected to a second term.

**Ford's Approach: Vetoes and Voluntarism**  Ford regarded inflation as the nation's number-one problem. To bring down the soaring prices, he vetoed 66 bills enacted by a Democratic Congress—bills that would have increased government spending on social programs. He also called upon Americans to participate voluntarily in an anti-inflation effort called W.I.N. (Whip Inflation Now). Ford argued that energy prices would go down if Americans tried to save on the use of electricity, oil, and gasoline in their daily lives.

Acting independently, the Federal Reserve Board tried to control inflation by raising interest rates on bank loans. The results of this

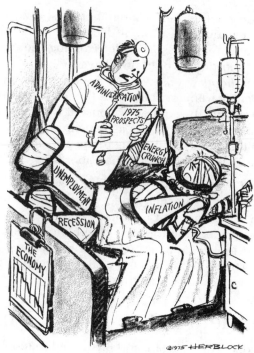

"Now for the bad news—"

policy were mixed. While the inflation rate came down to 6 percent, the unemployment rate shot up to 9 percent. For the unemployed a business recession was even harder to endure than high consumer prices.

**Carter's Approach: Voluntary Controls**   Inflation became even worse during Carter's presidency. In 1978 he urged businesses not to charge higher prices and asked labor unions not to demand higher wages. For the most part the president's call for voluntary restraint was ignored. After another huge increase in energy prices, the inflation rate hit a new high: 15 percent in the first half of 1980. Again the Federal Reserve Board tried to put the brakes on inflation by raising interest rates. Again the result was a business recession and loss of jobs.

The U.S. automobile industry was especially hurt by inflation, high energy prices, and competition from lower-priced and more fuel-efficient foreign cars. Several years of poor sales put the Chrysler Corporation on the verge of bankruptcy. To prevent this huge company from going under and to save the jobs of its thousands of workers, President Carter and leaders of Congress agreed to rescue, or "bail out," Chrysler with a government loan. In 1979 Congress voted $1.5 billion in federal funds to keep Chrysler afloat.

Critics of the **Chrysler bailout** said that it violated the U.S. tradition of allowing private businesses to succeed or fail on their own without being rescued by government whenever they ran into trouble.

**Reagan's Approach: Tax Cuts and Budget Cuts**  The next president to deal with inflation solved this problem only to create another— huge budget deficits. Reagan's approach to the economic muddle was based on a theory called **supply-side economics.** Conservatives who supported this theory believed that the economy would benefit if government spent less money and businesses spent more. The best way to arrange this, according to the supply-siders, was to cut federal taxes. Businesses would then be left with more money to invest, and consumers would be left with more money for buying goods and services. At the same time the government would make major cuts in welfare programs, which were considered wasteful by Reagan and other conservatives.

In 1981 Reagan persuaded Congress to enact the largest income tax cut in U.S. history. The Economic Recovery Tax Act (ERTA) provided for a 25-percent reduction in personal income taxes over a period of about three years. It also allowed generous tax credits for corporations.

At the same time the Federal Reserve decided to keep interest rates at a high·level. Its anti-inflation policy began to have an effect during Reagan's first two years in office. The inflation rate dropped to 6 percent in 1982 and less than 4 percent in 1983. Unfortunately, another cause of the lower inflation was a severe business recession. By late 1982 about 11 percent of the labor force had no jobs.

Prosperity returned in 1984 and continued for the remainder of the decade. Inflation ceased to be a serious problem. But another problem took its place: the problem of staggering budget deficits.

## B. COPING WITH BUDGET DEFICITS

Every year the executive branch of the U.S. government submits a budget to Congress. The **budget** is a document listing both what the government expects to spend for the year ahead and what it expects to receive in income. If the government spends more than it collects in taxes, it ends the year with a **deficit.** (The opposite result—more money received than money spent—is known as a **surplus.**)

Beginning with the depression years of the 1930s, the U.S. government almost always ended its spending year (or fiscal year) with a deficit. To make up the difference between expenses and income, it had to borrow millions and even billions of dollars each year. In other words the government went heavily into debt. The debt was kept at a reasonably manageable level through the early 1960s. After the Vietnam War, however, the national debt exceeded $500 billion and rapidly climbed to nearly $1 *trillion* when Ronald Reagan submitted his first budget to Congress in 1981.

**Effects of "Reaganomics"**   Critics of President Reagan's economic policy warned that **"Reaganomics"** (as they called the supply-side theory) would result in huge deficits. They were right. Reagan's tax cuts of 1981 meant lower government revenues. At the same time increased spending for defense meant higher government expenditures. The result: record deficits for eight years in a row and a national debt well above $2 trillion by the end of the 1980s.

Many economists were alarmed by these runaway budget deficits. They pointed out that, as deficits rose, so did the burden of paying interest on the national debt. By 1990 interest payments cost the government about $150 billion annually. Partly because of the debt burden, the government was less able to spend adequate sums for urgent national needs such as highway repair and health care.

**Bush's Policies: Tax Increases**   Although President Bush had promised not to raise taxes, he reached an agreement with the Democratically controlled House and Senate to raise taxes and cut federal spending. Taxes were then raised, but Congress did not reduce spending. As a result, the federal deficit continued to rise.

**Clinton's Policies: The "Reinvention of Government"**   President Clinton began his term of office by reducing both federal spending and federal employment. He and his vice president, Albert Gore, promised to examine every federal expenditure to determine if it were necessary and wise. They called this program the "reinvention of government." Thus, in 1995, Clinton claimed that he was the first president in the last 12 years to reduce the federal deficit. Nevertheless, the deficit was more than $4 trillion and still a matter of national concern.

**Republican Midterm Victories**   By 1994, there was increasing dissatisfaction with the Clinton administration. Some Americans believed he was too liberal on social issues. Others were disappointed with his leadership and his failed national health plan. As a result, Republicans won control of both the House and the Senate for the first time in 40 years. Senator Bob Dole from Kansas became the Senate majority leader, and Representative Newt Gingrich from Georgia became Speaker of the House.

In these congressional elections, the Republicans campaigned on a platform known as the "Contract With America." They pledged to pass within 100 days legislation on a balanced budget amendment, term limits for Congress, and welfare reform. They argued that the federal bureaucracy was wasteful and that the federal government's spending was out of control. They wanted a small central government, with many of its functions and powers transferred to the states.

For example, Republicans proposed that federal spending on welfare be replaced by block grants to the states, with few federal guidelines about how the states should use the money. By eliminating federal guidelines and reducing the federal bureaucracy, Republicans hoped to cut government spending. President Clinton opposed major portions of the Contract With America, since he feared it would hurt the poor and the middle classes.

**Bailout of Savings and Loan Associations**　Another heavy burden on the government and the economy was the failure of hundreds of **savings and loan associations (S & Ls).** The problem was caused by unwise, reckless, and perhaps illegal investment and loan decisions by S & L owners. Since the U.S. government insured the savings deposited in the bankrupt businesses, it was obligated to rescue each S & L by taking over its properties and paying the claims of thousands of insured depositors. In 1990 conservative estimates on how much the **savings and loan bailout** would cost ranged from $300 to $500 billion. The cost would be borne by taxpayers, most of whom were outraged.

**The Tax Issue**　For obvious reasons lowering taxes is always more popular with voters than raising them. Having already cut taxes in his first term, Reagan decided to reform the tax system during his second term. At his urging, Congress passed the **Tax Reform Act** in 1986. Previous tax laws had divided taxpayers into several brackets, according to their earned income. The higher the taxable income,

the higher the percentage of income paid in taxes. The new law created only two tax brackets. Lower-income people were taxed at 15 percent of taxable income, and upper-income people at 28 percent.

People with very high incomes benefited most from this reform law. Instead of being taxed at a 50-percent rate, as formerly, they paid just 28 percent. Thus a millionaire was in the same tax bracket as a person earning $30,000 a year. The new law closed some "loopholes" in the old tax code so that wealthy taxpayers could not deduct as much from their income to lower their taxes.

During his election campaign of 1988, George Bush was often asked whether he would ever raise taxes in order to reduce the budget deficit. "Read my lips," he would always say, "no new taxes." President Bush remained true to his campaign pledge until the summer of 1990, when he stated that new taxes might be necessary after all.

**Crisis Over Deficit Reduction**   In 1990 neither the president nor Congress could avoid raising taxes any longer. According to the 1985 **Gramm-Rudman-Hollings Act,** measures had to be taken to balance the federal budget by the early 1990s. If Congress failed to devise a plan for reducing deficits to zero, the law provided for automatic budget cuts in all departments of the executive branch.

In October, 1990, after months of debate, Congress and the president agreed upon a deficit-reduction plan. It provided large cuts in military spending and smaller cuts in a number of social programs. On the income side of the plan, the income tax rate for the wealthy was raised from 28 to 31 percent. Federal excise taxes on cigarettes, alcoholic beverages, and gasoline also went up.

Conservatives and liberals alike objected to the new tax law. Conservatives criticized President Bush for agreeing to new taxes, thereby violating his campaign pledge. Liberals attacked Bush's unwillingness to make the very wealthy bear more of the tax burden.

The problem of the federal deficit did not go away. How to deal with the problem was a major issue in the presidential election of 1992. One of Bill Clinton's first acts as president was to submit to Congress a comprehensive plan for reducing the deficit. Because his plan called for higher taxes, it was opposed by every Republican in Congress as well as many Democrats. But in August, 1993, the deficit reduction bill passed by one vote each in the Senate and House. The measure provided for (1) an increase in the top income tax rate (to 36 percent), (2) a slight increase in the federal tax on gasoline, and (3) a deficit reduction totaling $496 billion over five years.

## C. DEREGULATION OF BUSINESS

The twentieth century began with the Progressive Era and the founding of regulatory agencies to protect the consumers. In the late 1970s and 1980s, conservative presidents argued that regulation of business had gone too far. Carter and Reagan adopted policies to deregulate the economy. **Deregulation** meant removing many governmental rules that had limited and controlled business competition.

President Carter was responsible for deregulating four industries: oil, natural gas, airlines, and trucking. Oil and natural gas were both forms of energy whose prices to the American consumer were kept artificially low by government price controls. Carter decided to phase out such price controls in order to encourage U.S. companies to expand their search for new sources of oil and natural gas. In 1978 the president persuaded Congress to eliminate the Civil Aeronautics Board (CAB), which had regulated the airline industry for 40 years. The CAB had limited airline competition by assigning the routes they could use and the rates they could charge. The CAB scaled back its rule making and rate setting and in 1985 went out of existence. U.S. airlines were now free to compete for customers without restriction (except for observing federal safety standards).

President Reagan went even further than Carter in calling for deregulation. He ordered the dozens of regulatory agencies in the executive branch to cut back their rule making and allow businesses greater freedom. Reagan weakened a number of regulatory agencies by appointing opponents of regulation to head the agencies. The Reagan years saw a huge increase in business mergers, since little was done to enforce the antitrust laws. Also, President Reagan speeded up the deregulation of the oil industry (a policy begun by Carter).

## D. FARM POLICY AND THE DECLINE OF THE FAMILY FARM

The history of farm production in the United States is a great American success story. Between 1940 and 1970, farmers doubled the amount of wheat they could grow on a single acre. In the same period production of all crops per acre increased 66 percent.

At the same time, however, both the number of farms and the number of people engaged in farming steadily declined. In 1990 less than 3 percent of the American people earned their living as farmers (compared to 38 percent in 1900). The decline of the small family farm was closely linked to the mechanization of farms in the twentieth century. Expensive equipment made possible gains in productivity on large and medium farms. But small farms that could not afford such equipment found that they could not compete. By 1995, most farm acreage was controlled by large farm corporations.

**Farm Subsidies**   Ever since the Great Depression, the federal government had paid subsidies to farmers to help them survive years when crops brought low prices. (A **subsidy** is a grant of money from the government to a private enterprise.) Laws enacted by Congress in 1973 and 1977 established **target prices** for basic crops such as wheat, corn, and cotton. If the market price for a crop fell below its target price, the U.S. government would pay farmers the difference between the two prices. The government policy encouraged farmers to produce more crops. On the other hand, the government also paid farmers if they used less of their land for farming. By 1995 many in Congress began to oppose farm price supports as too expensive.

**Feast in the 1970s**   Farmers are always subject to sudden changes in the world demand for their crops. Theirs is a business of either feast (high demand, high prices) or famine (low demand, low prices). The 1970s was largely a boom time for American farmers. Prices for farm products were high partly because of increased exports to the Soviet Union and other nations. Encouraged by the federal government, farmers borrowed money to modernize farms and increase production. They made spectacular gains in productivity. In 1972 one American farmer produced enough to feed 53 people; by 1982 the same farmer could feed 78 people.

**Famine in the 1980s**   But feast turned to famine in the 1980s. Farmers became the victims of their own success. When world demand for their crops declined, they were left with millions of tons of unsold grain and received low prices for the rest. Contributing to the lower prices was an embargo on the sale of grain to the Soviet Union. (As explained in Chapter 19, the grain embargo was President Carter's response to the Soviet invasion of Afghanistan in 1979.) Farmers now faced high debts and declining income. Thousands of family farms went bankrupt. In the 1990s exports of grain again helped to increase farm income.

## E.  ECONOMIC CYCLES IN THE 1980s AND 1990s

A business boom in the 1980s was marked by heavy consumer spending, high interest rates, and a low savings rate. The general prosperity ended in 1991 as the economy slipped into recession. Layoffs in most industries pushed the unemployment rate up to seven percent. The federal government cautiously tried to effect a recovery. Hoping to increase consumer and business borrowing, the Federal Reserve Board reduced the discount rate (interest charged to member banks). In his 1992 State of the Union message, President Bush urged Congress to pass tax reductions to help both consumers and investors.

By 1994, during the Clinton administration, the recession's end was signaled by a significant decline in unemployment. This economic upturn occurred despite layoffs by major corporations and several interest rate hikes by the Federal Reserve Board to curb inflation. By 1995 the economy appeared to be healthy.

## F. THE ELECTION OF 1992

The economy remained sluggish as the 1992 presidential campaign began. As expected, the Republicans nominated President George Bush and Vice President Dan Quayle for re-election. In his campaign, Bush pointed to his achievements in foreign policy, citing, in particular, the victory in the Gulf War and the end of the cold war. He also blamed the Democratic majority in Congress for stalling his economic programs. The young governor of Arkansas, Bill Clinton, won the Democratic nomination for president. Clinton and his running mate, Senator Al Gore of Tennessee, blamed Bush for the nation's economic troubles. The Democratic team stressed the idea that it was "time for a change" in presidential leadership.

A Texas business leader and billionaire, H. Ross Perot, entered the race as an independent candidate for president. Perot used millions of dollars of his own money to finance a series of unusually long TV advertisements. He promised to cut the deficit to zero and revive U.S. competitiveness in the global economy. Perot excited significant interest among the electorate. But his following decreased after he dropped out of the race, only to reenter it again later.

The biggest election turnout in 30 years brought victory for Clinton and Gore. After 12 years of conservative leadership under Reagan and Bush, a moderate Democrat was again in the White House. President Clinton supported some liberal legislation, such as health care reform and gun control. However, he viewed himself as a fiscal conservative and cut federal spending, federal jobs, and the budget deficit.

## *In Review*

The following questions refer to section I: The Trend Toward Conservatism and section II: Government's Role in the Economy.

1. Identify *supply-side economics, budget deficit, savings and loan bailout, Gramm-Rudman-Hollings Act, deregulation,* and *target price.*

2. Give *four* examples of the trend toward conservatism in the 1970s and 1980s.

3. Compare President Carter's approach to economic problems to President Reagan's approach.

4. Identify the president who adopted *each* policy given below:

   a. supply-side economics
   b. W.I.N. (Whip Inflation Now)
   c. cutting tax rates for the wealthy
   d. "Read my lips. No new taxes."
   e. deregulation of the airlines
   f. a package of budget cuts and tax increases to reduce the federal deficit

# III. Promoting the General Welfare

The U.S. economy received more attention than any other domestic issue in the conservative era from 1974 to 1990. Americans were also aware that their entire society was undergoing change and stress in these years. Social problems existed that put a severe strain on every U.S. institution including schools, courts, prisons, welfare agencies, hospitals, and families.

## A. COPING WITH POVERTY

After World War II most Americans lived comfortably on incomes high enough to sustain an **affluent,** or prosperous, life-style. Even so, during the 1960s, there were still millions of Americans who lived in poverty. President Johnson declared a "war on poverty" in 1964 partly because of an eye-opening book about poverty written by Michael Harrington.

**The Other America** Harrington's book, *The Other America* (1962), depicted the lives of the poor in urban neighborhoods and rural communities. Harrington discussed the effect of poverty on the elderly, racial minorities, migrant farm workers, and the homeless. He urged the federal government to assume the responsibility of helping the poor overcome the forces that kept them from participating fully in the American economy.

**Results of the War on Poverty** As you have read, Johnson's Great Society was largely concerned with aiding those who lived in poverty. To a certain extent his programs of assistance succeeded. Between 1960 and 1969 the number of poor Americans as classified by the government dropped from 40 million to 24 million. However, in the 1970s the economic condition of stagflation (rising inflation coupled with unemployment) led to increases in poverty. In 1981 President Reagan argued that government programs to reduce poverty were not a solution but part of the problem. He believed that financial aid to all except the "truly needy" caused the poor to be permanently dependent on government funds. Many Americans, concerned about high taxes and budget deficits, supported the president's efforts to cut back on federal poverty programs.

**Increased Gap Between the Rich and the Poor** Michael Harrington had observed in the 1960s that the poor were largely "invisible" to people living in affluent neighborhoods. They were no longer invisible in the 1980s when increasing numbers of homeless people slept in bus terminals and makeshift shelters on the streets of major cities. Critics of Reagan blamed his cuts in welfare programs for the increasing numbers of homeless people. But some social scientists argued that the poor might represent a permanent "underclass" in American society and that no amount of government aid could effectively deal with the problem.

Americans who suffered most from poverty included children, divorced women with children to support, African Americans, Native Americans, Latinos, migrant farm workers, and unemployed factory and mine workers.

Increased poverty was one cause of two other trends: an increase in the crime rate and an increase in the school dropout rate. In the 1980s an inexpensive addictive drug, crack, worked its way into poor urban neighborhoods. Drug use, drug wars, and crime made life more difficult for millions living in U.S. cities.

At the other end of the income scale, the wealthiest fifth of the U.S. population commanded a greater and greater share of total national income. In the 1980s social scientists called attention to this fact and warned of the negative effect on American democracy if the income gap between rich and poor continued to widen.

## B. HEALTH CARE FOR THE ELDERLY

People aged 65 and older are classified as "elderly" or "senior citizens." Because of advances in medicine and health care, the numbers of elderly Americans increased steadily until in 1990 they represented 13 percent of the U.S. population (compared to only 5.5 percent in 1930).

**Victory for the Gray Panthers**  As the number of elderly increased, so did their political influence. They knew that their health problems and medical bills would increase during years of retirement—years when their incomes would be relatively low. Many relied for their support on the monthly Social Security checks mailed to them by the U.S. government. For millions of elderly Americans in the 1970s and 1980s, the most important political issue was the future of the Social Security system.

The elderly organized powerful pressure groups that lobbied Congress for greater Social Security benefits. The **Gray Panthers**, as they were called, wanted higher monthly checks to keep pace with inflation. They also sought wider coverage of Medicare, the government's insurance plan for paying retired persons' hospital and doctor bills. Senior citizens won a major legislative victory in 1975 when a law of Congress linked Social Security benefits to the cost of living. Under this law, if inflation caused the cost of living to increase, Social Security benefits would also rise automatically. The new provision was known as a **cost-of-living adjustment (COLA)**.

**Increased Social Security Taxes**  Though needed by senior citizens, the increased Social Security benefits were extremely expensive, especially in the inflationary years of the late 1970s. To prevent the Social Security system from going bankrupt, Congress passed two laws:

- a law of 1977 raising the Social Security tax. (Since the passage of the original Social Security Act in 1935, a Social Security tax has automatically been collected from  (a) workers' paychecks and  (b) employers. The taxes collected from both workers and employers go into a special fund that pays the benefits of retired workers.)

- the **Social Security Reform Act** of 1983. This law saved the Social Security system from financial collapse by (a) speeding up planned increases in Social Security taxes and (b) delaying for six months a scheduled increase in benefits.

Ever since the reform of 1983, money coming into the Social Security system has been enough to pay the benefits to which the elderly are entitled. However, social scientists predict that the system may again be in trouble early in the twenty-first century as the huge number of baby boomers (those born in the late 1940s and 1950s) retire from the work force.

Social Security is a help, but life is still difficult for many of the elderly, who are apt to suffer from loneliness and fear of crime. Nursing homes and programs such as "meals on wheels" have attempted to meet their needs. But the quality of nursing-home care is uneven. For many of the elderly, the term "golden years" is questionable.

## C. THE FAMILY IN CRISIS

In the last decades of the twentieth century, one change stood out as supremely important for the future of American society. It was a change in which *all* Americans of every age participated. In little more than a generation, between 1960 and 1990, the American family weakened and lost some of its ability to care for children's economic and emotional needs.

**Increased Divorce Rate**  When the twentieth century began, divorce had become far more common than in an earlier period. Even so, people in the 1950s still assumed that a marriage would probably continue until the death of one of the partners. In the following decades, however, a marriage was almost as likely to end in divorce as to continue into old age. In 1966 the divorce rate was twice as high as in 1950. Divorce became so common that two out of every five children born during the 1970s could expect to see their parents' marriage break up before these children turned 16. By the 1990s, half of all marriages ended in divorce.

The high divorce rate severely affected two groups: women and children. As single parents, divorced women suffered income loss and emotional strain. Some children suffered emotionally from seeing their parents separate. If they lived with their mother, which most did, they shared her economic plight, which increased when fathers withheld child support. At least 11 states began to revoke the driver's licenses of wage-earning scofflaw parents.

**Mothers in the Work Force**   The women's movement of the 1960s was one reason for increasing numbers of women pursuing careers in business and the professions. Another reason was the need for two incomes from two careers just to pay a married couple's bills. Married women sought employment outside the home in record numbers during the 1970s and 1980s. By 1990 60 percent of married women were in the labor force (compared to just 25 percent in 1950). Also in the labor force were thousands of single mothers.

In a previous generation young mothers customarily left their jobs and careers in order to provide full-time care for their children. Although millions of mothers observed this tradition, millions of others returned to work soon after giving birth. In fact, as the 1990s began, the number of mothers of preschool children working for wages was about equal to the number staying home.

Traditionally, men and women alike had assumed that child care was the mother's responsibility. Feminists questioned this assumption, asking why fathers should be relieved of the hundreds of tasks involved in the care of children and the home. Although some men tried to adopt new habits in the home, most left the burden of child care and other domestic chores to their wives. Thus, whether they were married or divorced, women with children at home and a job outside the home were badly overburdened. The day-care centers to which they brought their young children were seldom ideal or even adequate. Through the 1980s the women's movement focused on winning the support of lawmakers and businesses for providing satisfactory day-care and nursery-school centers.

**Redefining the Family**   What was a family anyway? The definition used to be simple. In 1960 more than 70 percent of U.S. households consisted of an income-earning father, a housekeeping mother, and one or more children. By 1988 less than 15 percent of U.S. households could be described in these terms. There were now millions of families with two working parents, other families with a single parent, and other families with no children. Increasingly rare was the household that included three generations: grandparents, parents, and children. Members of the older generation are today likely to live in retirement communities or nursing homes far from their children and grandchildren. The loosening of ties between generations appears to be a characteristic of the late-twentieth-century family.

## D. THE EFFECTS OF DRUG ABUSE

The use of illegal drugs has been a problem from the late 1940s to the present. On college campuses in the 1960s, increasing numbers of students smoked marijuana and adopted the slogan, "Tune in, turn on, and drop out." At the same time teenagers and even preteens began buying and selling illegal drugs as part of a widening network of organized crime. Drug abuse increased further in the 1980s with the sale of a low-priced drug, crack.

The effects of illegal drugs on U.S. society were devastating. City police departments and state and federal courts had to devote more and more of their resources to arresting and prosecuting "pushers" (sellers) of illegal drugs. But because of the demand for drugs among people of every social class, law enforcement officials found it nearly impossible to stop or even reduce the illegal sale of drugs in Washington, D.C., New York City, and other major cities. To control drug abuse, Congress created the Drug Enforcement Administration (DEA) in 1973. Fulfilling a campaign promise, President Bush in 1989 declared an all-out "war on drugs" involving the expenditure of more than $7 billion a year.

The statistics on drugs and drug-related problems were grim. More than half the students graduating from high school in 1985 had used marijuana at least once, and 17 percent had used cocaine. In New York City during the 1980s, the number of mothers using crack and other illegal drugs increased five times. These alarming figures started to decline in the early 1990s, perhaps in response to the government's "war on drugs." In 1991, less than 40 percent of high school seniors reported using marijuana and less than 10 percent had ever taken cocaine. Nevertheless, drug abuse in the 1990s was still a major problem.

Addiction to drugs was partly responsible for increases in violent crime (murder, rape, robbery, and assault) and property crime (burglary, larceny, and auto theft). In the 1980s, the rate of violent crime went up by nearly 30 percent. Law enforcement officials ascribed much of the increase to the widespread use of illegal drugs.

Drug abuse also contributed to the AIDS epidemic. Unknown before 1981, **AIDS (acquired immunodeficiency syndrome)** had caused the deaths of more than 200,000 people by the mid-1990s. The two most common ways for the AIDS virus to enter a person's body was through sexual contact and the practice of sharing needles to inject an illegal drug into the bloodstream.

## E. CONCERNS ABOUT EDUCATION

Throughout the twentieth century, Americans placed enormous stress on the benefits of public education. They expected that 12

A cartoonist's view of U.S. education

years of schooling would equip everyone in society with the ability to read with understanding and write with competence. Ever since the early 1970s, however, educators have issued alarming reports about low levels of student performance on standardized tests. For example, average scores on the Scholastic Aptitude Test (SAT) dropped lower and lower for 11 years in succession from 1970 to 1981. Since then slight gains in test scores have been almost insignificant. At the same time one out of every four students drop out of high school before graduation.

In 1983 a National Commission on Excellence in Education reported that the nation was "at risk" because of the millions of young Americans who left school without adequate skills and knowledge. Their lack of preparation put the U.S. work force at a disadvantage in competing with better-educated work forces of other industrialized countries.

Few agreed about how to improve schools and student performance. Conservatives urged a "back to basics" approach (more math, reading, and writing). Liberals proposed restructuring schools to make teachers, parents, and students part of the decision-making process. By 1990, however, government at all levels lacked funds for such ambitious programs. Nevertheless, in the mid-1990s, a reformist goal of achieving national standards in education set off debate among conservatives, moderates, and liberals.

## F. REAGAN'S "NEW FEDERALISM"

Another issue was whether it was primarily the job of the federal government or of the state governments to combat crime, reform schools, and provide for the general welfare. The Republican presidents of the 1970s and 1980s (Nixon, Ford, Reagan, and Bush) believed that the chief responsibility for social welfare lay with state and local authorities. Nixon used the term "New Federalism" to describe his idea for giving the states freedom to decide how to use federal grants. (Review Chapter 16.) Reagan adopted the same policy and urged the states to take more responsibility for solving social and economic problems.

Through the 1980s as the federal government trimmed its own budget and cut back social programs, the states did increase their spending on everything from police salaries to hospital beds. But they soon reached a limit on new programs, when citizens objected to paying higher taxes for improved public services. Candidates for election in 1990 added to the public outcry against taxes by promising not to raise taxes either at the federal level or the state level.

# IV. Adjusting to a Pluralistic Society

The civil rights movement of the 1960s and the women's movement of the early 1970s changed Americans' view of their society. Increasingly, minorities and women began to play a more prominent role in the nation's political and economic life.

## A. AFFIRMATIVE ACTION

Starting with the presidency of Lyndon Johnson, the U.S. government adopted a policy known as **affirmative action.** The purpose of the policy was to make sure that past discrimination against women and ethnic minorities did not continue into the future. To accomplish its purpose, the government encouraged businesses to increase the job opportunities of women and minorities. Government also encouraged colleges and universities to admit more students who were female or nonwhite. A college failing to adopt an affirmative action plan for recruitment would lose financial aid. A business failing to adopt such plans would lose its government contracts.

**Arguments For and Against the Policy** In the 1970s for the first time in the nation's history, women and members of ethnic minorities were given preference when applying for certain jobs and seeking admission to certain colleges. For the first time men of European ancestry felt that they were being discriminated against in the job market.

Supporters of affirmative action said there was no other way to compensate for all the past years of discrimination against women and minorities. On the other hand, opponents argued that affirmative action led to "reverse discrimination."

**Decisions of the U.S. Supreme Court**   Many cases involving affirmative action came to the U.S. Supreme Court for final decision. Two of the most important decisions are summarized here.

- *Regents of the University of California* v. *Bakke* (1978) Allan Bakke, a white man, had twice applied to the medical school of the University of California. Twice the university rejected Bakke's application even though his overall scores on standard entrance requirements were higher than those of many students who had been admitted. The university argued that it had set aside 16 out of 100 openings for minority students in order to fulfill its affirmative action goals. Bakke sued the university, arguing that its "quota system" violated the equal protection clause of the Fourteenth Amendment.

  Ruling in favor of Bakke, the Supreme Court declared that the university's approach to affirmative action was unconstitutional because it involved racial quotas. However, it said in the **Bakke case** that race could be one factor, but not the only factor, in deciding whom to admit to a university program.

- *Kaiser Aluminum and Chemical Corporation* v. *Weber* (1979) This case involved an affirmative action plan for correcting racial imbalance in the work force at the Kaiser Aluminum and Chemical Corporation. The workers at Kaiser had been almost exclusively white. To change this situation, both the steel workers union and the company agreed to develop a special training program in which half of the trainees would be African Americans. At a Kaiser plant in Louisiana, a white worker named Brian Weber was rejected for the training program even though he had greater seniority (years of service) than the African Americans who were selected. Weber brought suit, claiming that he had been discriminated against for reasons of race.

  The Supreme Court ruled against Weber. It argued that the affirmative action plan at Kaiser was a reasonable means for correcting racial imbalance. The court approved the plan because it was only temporary and did not result in white workers losing their jobs.

Not all decisions of the Supreme Court favored affirmative action. In a case involving the fire fighters of Memphis, Tennessee, the Court ruled that African-American workers hired to reduce racial imbalance could be first to be laid off if they had less seniority (years on the job) than white co-workers. And in 1995 the Court ruled against favoritism being shown to women and minority business people who bid on government contracts.

## B. WOMEN IN THE WORK FORCE

The women's movement continued to be a powerful force for change in the last decades of the twentieth century. Women entered occupations that had formerly been restricted to men. By 1985 professional women made up 17 percent of the nation's physicians, 18 percent of the lawyers and judges, 34 percent of the computer programmers, 35 percent of the economists, and 51 percent of the editors and reporters. Among the many women who achieved national recognition were: Sandra Day O'Connor, who in 1981 became the first woman appointed to the U.S. Supreme Court; Geraldine Ferraro, who in 1984 was the first female candidate of a major party to run for vice president; Jeane Kirkpatrick, who in the early 1980s was U.S. ambassador to the United Nations; and Janet Reno, who in 1993 became the first woman to serve as U.S. attorney general.

Women also gained stronger representation in Congress after the election of 1992. Barbara Boxer and Dianne Feinstein of California, Carol Moseley-Braun of Illinois, and Patty Murray of Washington won Senate seats. The number of women in the House increased from 28 to 47.

Also during the 1980s and early 1990s, women workers began to close the gap between themselves and men workers. In 1991 they

Reuters/Bettmann

President Clinton and Attorney General Janet Reno

earned 70 percent as much as men (up from 62.5 percent in 1979). On the other hand, despite laws against discrimination, this still left a 30-percent gap between the average wages of men and women holding comparable jobs. Full equality for women was often limited by custom- and tradition-based antifeminist attitudes.

## C. THE NEW IMMIGRANTS

In 1986 Americans celebrated the one-hundredth anniversary of a great national symbol—the Statue of Liberty. Ever since its completion, this statue had greeted the arrival in New York harbor of immigrants from Europe. In the 1980s (as in the 1880s) the U.S. population changed rapidly as a result of a new wave of immigration. The "new immigrants," as they were called, did *not* come from Europe. They came instead from Asia and Latin America. At the same time, immigrants from areas in turmoil (the Soviet Union, Eastern Europe, and Iran), as well as immigrants from India and Pakistan, added to the large number of new arrivals.

**Effects of the Immigration Act of 1965**  Between 1921 and 1965, U.S. immigration laws had favored nationalities from Western Europe and discriminated against people from other parts of the world. (Review Chapter 7.) This old quota system was ended in 1965 by a new immigration law that set the following criteria for determining who would be admitted as immigrants each year:

- No more than 20,000 from any one country
- No more than 120,000 from countries of the Western Hemisphere (Canada and Latin America)
- No more than 170,000 from countries of the Eastern Hemisphere (Asia, Africa, Europe, and Australia)
- Preference given to skilled workers and professionals and to those with family ties to U.S. citizens.

In addition, under a 1953 law, the president had the authority to admit refugees fleeing from political oppression. President Ford used this authority to admit hundreds of thousands of Vietnamese, Laotians, and Cambodians after their countries fell to communism.

The graphs on page 556 summarize the effects of the new immigration policy. Newcomers now came chiefly from (1) Asia (Taiwan, Korea, the Philippines, India, and Vietnam); (2) the Caribbean (Cuba, Haiti, and the Dominican Republic); and (3) Central America (Mexico and El Salvador).

**Illegal Immigrants**  In addition to the millions of "new immigrants" admitted legally, there were millions of others who crossed the U.S.–

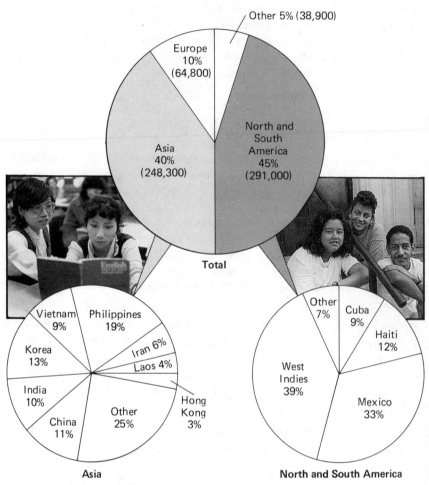

Other 5% (38,900)

Europe
10%
(64,800)

North and
South
America
45%
(291,000)

Asia
40%
(248,300)

Total

Vietnam
9%

Philippines
19%

Korea
13%

Iran 6%

Laos 4%

India
10%

Other
25%

Hong
Kong
3%

China
11%

**Asia**

Other
7%

Cuba
9%

Haiti
12%

West
Indies
39%

Mexico
33%

**North and South America**

Source: U.S. Immigration and Naturalization Service

**Legal immigration to the United States, 1989**

Mexican border illegally. Facing high unemployment and poverty in Mexico, they escaped detection as they waded across the shallow Rio Grande. U.S. employers were often glad to hire them for low wages. In the early 1990s, fences were installed along sections of the border between Texas and Mexico to help stop the illegal immigration.

U.S. labor unions feared that the illegal Mexican aliens would undercut American workers by taking jobs for less than the minimum wage. (One report, however, said that three-fifths of the immigrants arrested as illegal workers earned *more* than the minimum.)

There were other reasons for opposing illegal immigration: (1) illegal aliens did not pay taxes, and yet, because of their numbers, they placed a strain on city services and added to the cost of city government. (2) To permit illegal immigration to continue would be unfair to those other immigrants who had to wait patiently for years to gain lawful entry to the United States. These were two of the arguments used by members of Congress who wanted to control, and if possible, eliminate illegal immigration.

**Simpson-Mazzoli Act (1986)**    Enacted with President Reagan's approval, the Immigration Reform and Control Act, or the **Simpson-Mazzoli Act**, placed heavy fines on employers who knowingly hired illegal aliens. At the same time the law permitted illegal aliens who had entered the United States before 1982 to remain here as legal residents. Opponents of the law warned about its potentially damaging effects. They argued that employers would fear to hire, not just illegal aliens, but also the millions of Hispanic Americans who were legal residents, since certain proof of legality would be hard to obtain.

Whether wise or unwise, the immigration control act has not stopped the flow of illegal immigrants across the Mexican–U.S.border.

**Arguments for Encouraging Immigration**    Many social scientists have pointed out the economic benefits of increased immigration. They note that immigrants add to the economy by (1) purchasing goods and services and (2) paying taxes. In effect, immigrants may create jobs for native-born Americans rather than taking jobs away. Furthermore, if a decreased birthrate produces a future labor shortage, there will be a growing need for skilled workers from abroad.

# D. THE CHANGING CHARACTER OF THE AMERICAN PEOPLE

Like other immigrant groups before them, the "new immigrants" from Asia and Latin America struggled to adapt to the English-speaking culture that they found here. They also contributed aspects of their own culture (their foods, customs, music, family values, and respect for education) to the American way of life.

In the 1980s it became clear to many observers that the dominant group of the past—Americans of European ancestry—might some-day be in the minority. Already in 1990 one out of every four Americans was either a Hispanic American or nonwhite. An article in *Time* reported: "By 2056, when someone born today [1990] will be 66 years old, the 'average' U.S. resident ... will trace his or her descent to Africa, Asia, the Hispanic world, the Pacific Islands, Arabia—almost anywhere but white Europe."

**Hispanic Americans**    The fastest growing minority in the United States are the Hispanic Americans—those who either speak Spanish or have Spanish-speaking ancestors. Aside from sharing (or once sharing) a common language, they are a mixed group of people with origins from such regions as Mexico, Cuba, Puerto Rico, and South America. Just as German Americans have a different cultural background from Italian Americans, each Spanish-speaking group has its own unique tradition and identity.

Even so, Mexican Americans, Puerto Ricans, and other groups recognize that, as Spanish-speaking people, they form a strong and growing subculture in the U.S. population. They have common problems that can be solved through common action.

Economically, millions live in poverty (although growing numbers of Hispanic Americans are entering the middle class as business owners, public service employees, salespeople, and professionals). Since the early 1970s the unemployment rate among Hispanic Americans has been about 50 percent higher than among other groups of Americans. In the 1980s one out of every four Hispanic-American families lived in poverty (compared to one out of ten non-Hispanic-American families). Discrimination partly accounts for Hispanic Americans' difficulty in competing for middle-level and high-level jobs. Although affirmative action helped to remove this barrier in the 1970s, President Reagan's cuts in antipoverty programs represented a setback for the Latino poor in the 1980s.

By 1990 there were encouraging signs that Hispanic Americans, like earlier immigrant groups of a previous century, were entering into the mainstream of American life. Mexican restaurants that had once been popular only in the Southwest became extremely popular nationally during the 1980s. Celebrities in sports included such Hispanic Americans as José Canseco in baseball and Nancy Lopez in golf. In the 1980s Miami elected its first Cuban-born mayor, Xavier Suarez, and Florida elected a Hispanic-American governor, Bob Martinez. In 1988 President Reagan appointed Lauro Cavazos to lead the U.S. Department of Education. Cavazos thus became the first Hispanic-American member of the cabinet. In New York City, Ramon Cortines became the third Hispanic-American chancellor (chief executive officer) of the city's huge school system in 1993.

**Asian Americans**   Many Asian immigrants to the United States successfully adapted to the U.S. economic system. Korean families often pooled their money, worked long hours, and acquired the business know-how to succeed as owners of such businesses as groceries, fish stores, stationery stores, and dry cleaning establishments. Chinese immigrants from Taiwan, Hong Kong, and mainland China demonstrated a willingness to work hard for academic success in school and economic success in business. Recognizing that high grades in school were one key to success, many Asian-American students pushed themselves to attain top honors.

The U.S. economy benefited from the advanced training of Asian immigrants, who in the 1980s became the leading foreign source of U.S. engineers, doctors, and technical workers.

Even so both foreign-born Asians and native-born Asian Americans suffered from discrimination. Affirmative action and the setting of ethnic quotas tended to work *against* Asian applicants to U.S. colleges and universities. In 1990, for example, the U.S. Department of Education found that highly qualified Asian applicants to a university in Los Angeles (UCLA) were rejected for reasons of racial discrimination. In the business world racial discrimination has prevented many Asian-American managers from being promoted to top executive jobs.

In cities with large ethnic populations, many Asian Americans, especially recent arrivals, live in poverty and work at low-paying jobs—victimized by business owners, landlords, and gangs. In a city such as Las Vegas, Nevada, few visitors see how poor Asian-American workers live in tenements beyond the glittering hotels.

**Jesse Jackson and the "Rainbow Coalition"** In the 1980s a civil rights leader, the Reverend Jesse Jackson, recognized that ethnic minorities were a growing force in U.S. politics. After winning a strong following as a leader of African Americans, Jackson began to broaden his appeal and reach out to other minorities, women, and discontented farmers and workers. He referred to this multiracial and multicultural blend of peoples as the **"Rainbow Coalition."** In the election years 1984 and 1988, Jackson campaigned for the Democratic nomination for president. Though he fell short of winning a majority of delegate votes, he won national attention and came closer to being a presidential candidate than any other nonwhite American. In 1992 Jackson supported the election of Bill Clinton.

**Riots in Los Angeles** In Los Angeles, the nation's largest city, racial tensions erupted into rioting and looting in late April 1992. Touching off the violence was a jury's verdict in the much publicized case of Rodney King, an African American. Arrested for a traffic violation, King had been beaten repeatedly by four white police officers. When the jury acquitted the police officers of criminal acts, thousands of blacks rioted, broke into stores, and set fire to buildings in one section of Los Angeles. Before the National Guard could restore order, 52 people were killed. Hundreds of small businesses, many of them owned by Los Angeles' large Korean American community, were wiped out. The Rodney King riots, as they were called, were the most destructive riots in U.S. history. The incident showed that racial hatred was a continuing problem in American society.

## *In Review*

The following questions refer to section III: Promoting the General Welfare and section IV: Adjusting to a Pluralistic Society.

1. Identify *affirmative action, the Bakke case, Simpson-Mazzoli Immigration Act, Lauro Cavazos,* and *Jesse Jackson.*

2. Give *three* examples of the discrimination often encountered by Hispanic Americans and African Americans.

3. Select *three* social problems of the 1980s that you consider to be the most important. Summarize *each* problem and explain its significance.

4. Evaluate the policy of affirmative action, giving reasons why you *either* favor *or* oppose such a policy.

# V. Adjusting to Technological Change

Technological changes occurred so rapidly in the postindustrial age that nobody—not even scientists—could keep up with all that was happening. The following account gives only a small sampling of new technologies of the 1970s and 1980s and their effects on U.S. society.

## A. EXPLORATION IN SPACE

After American astronauts explored the moon's surface in 1969, other remarkable achievements in space quickly followed. Both the Soviet Union and the United States continued their ambitious programs to (1) explore space with manned and unmanned flights and (2) make practical use of ingeniously designed space satellites.

**Manned Flights**  In 1973 the United States launched into outer space a laboratory for gathering scientific data. The crew aboard the first **Skylab** performed medical experiments for 28 days. The second *Skylab* to rocket into space became the home and workstation for a three-man crew for nearly two months. At the same time the Soviets were also experimenting with their own space stations. In 1975 the Soviets and Americans carried out a cooperative space venture. Both their space crafts, the *Apollo* and the *Soyuz*, linked up, and their crews shook hands in space in a gesture of friendship.

In the early 1980s the U.S. space agency, the National Aeronautics and Space Administration (NASA), thrilled the American people by launching the first spacecraft capable of landing on a runway like an airplane rather than splashing down at sea. In April, 1981, the space shuttle *Columbia* flew in space for two days and returned safely to earth ready for another mission. Six other crews flew the *Columbia* safely, each time performing tasks that established new firsts in space.

A second space shuttle, however, came to a disastrous end. Ready for its tenth flight in January, 1986, the *Challenger* left its launching pad and then burst into a ball of flame. Killed instantly were six astronauts and a schoolteacher named Christa McAuliffe, who was

# OBSERVERS OF AMERICAN LIFE: THE "FIRST TEACHER IN SPACE"

*After being chosen to be the "first teacher in space," Christa McAuliffe of Concord, New Hampshire, granted interviews to dozens of writers and reporters. One of them was a New Hampshire writer named Joyce Maynard, who was curious about the daily routine of the woman destined to circle the earth. The following is Maynard's account of her interview with the teacher-astronaut.*

*How was a day in the life of Christa McAuliffe typical of American society in the 1980s? What does her daily routine say about the responsibilities of women in modern life?*

Christa McAuliffe

Well, she was meeting one reporter at eight and another one at eight forty-five. Someone else at nine-thirty. That's how it went, all day long, with breaks in between for her son Scott's Little League practice and picking up her daughter Caroline at day camp. But there was an hour at seven a.m., and she said I could come then.

She met me at the door with her hair still wet, in stocking feet, and I followed her through the rooms of her house as she talked, and as she looked for Scott's sleeping bag (he was going to a friend's house), took the chicken out of the freezer to defrost, and started the wash. There were lots of phone calls too: NASA one minute. The cleaners, to say her husband's shirts were ready the next.

There were piles of letters and newspaper clippings all over the house at that point; also helium balloons and flowers and signs saying things like "Reach for the Stars" and "Out of This World." I guess some people might've said the place was a mess, but you could tell something else too: This woman was organized. In her pocket she had a two-page list of things to do, and there was another one taped to the dashboard of her car. She had NASA's phone number attached to her refrigerator with alphabet magnets, right next to her kids' drawings. In the middle of a sentence, she'd suddenly reach for her pencil and jot something down. "Black high-top sneakers for Scott."

chosen by NASA to show that space travel might someday be available to average citizens. The **Challenger disaster** caused NASA to suspend its manned space program and concentrate on unmanned flights. In 1988 NASA resumed its manned space program by successfully launching a redesigned shuttle, *Discovery*. In 1990 it carried the Hubble Space Telescope—an instrument far more powerful than any earthbound telescope—into orbit.

A new first in space flights came in 1994, when a Russian astronaut flew aboard a U.S. spacecraft. Then, in 1995, a U.S. space shuttle rendezvoused with a Russian space station as a test run for future cooperative ventures in space.

**Unmanned Flights**   By 1986 two unmanned spacecraft, *Voyager 1* and *Voyager 2*, had already traveled millions of miles into outer space. Both had been launched in 1977 to send back scientific data about the planets Jupiter, Saturn, Uranus, and Neptune. *Voyager 1* made its closest approach to Jupiter in 1979. The amazing pictures that it sent to earth revealed that the planet had rings. Hurtling farther into space, *Voyager 1* came close to Saturn in 1980 and signaled back to earth that Saturn had more rings than had been previously imagined. Meanwhile, *Voyager 2* was on its way to Uranus (passing by it in 1986) and Neptune (1989).

**Satellites in Space**   By the 1970s satellites with sophisticated electronic gear had become a vital part of everyday life on earth. Shaped like a bug with two flat wings, the communications satellite *INTELSAT* helped relay telephone calls and TV programs around the earth. Distances between places no longer mattered in a satellite-linked communications system that turned the world into a "global village." To aid weather forecasting, a satellite called *GOES* relayed pictures of the earth's inner atmosphere every 30 minutes.

## B. THE COMPUTER REVOLUTION

Of all the new technologies, computers were the most revolutionary. In Chapter 15 you read about the rapid changes in computer design from bulky vacuum tubes to tiny silicon chips. The changes continued at a dizzying pace through the 1970s and 1980s.

**The Personal Computer**   Until 1977 most Americans thought of computers as expensive, complicated machines useful only in business. Two men just out of school disagreed. They believed the average consumer would buy a reasonably priced computer that was easy to use. Steven Jobs and Stephen Wozniak designed such a computer and called the second model Apple II. In its first year, 1977, it sold by the thousands. Thus the **personal computer** was born.

Through the 1980s major computer-makers such as IBM competed with Apple to produce better and faster personal computers for lower prices. Every year millions more Americans decided to enter the computer age by seeing what the latest, state-of-the-art model could do. By 1990 the personal computer was widely recognized as a powerful communications tool with nearly infinite uses—as a tool of instruction in the classroom, a high-powered typewriter, or word processor, a keeper of records, a calculator and problem solver, and a means for tapping into information files known as data bases. A vast computer network, the Internet, became a major attraction for personal computer users and speculative business entrepreneurs eager to exploit the new technology for profit.

**The Privacy Issue**    One problem with computerized files of information was that they might permit businesses and government agencies to invade a person's privacy. After all, for a small user's fee, almost anyone could look at a data base listing names of people who had, for example, once been arrested or failed to pay a debt. What was to stop strangers from gaining access to embarrassing or harmful information? Should there be laws regulating the use of computerized records? By the mid-1990s, citizens were gradually becoming aware of this potential threat to their basic rights to privacy.

## C. ADVANCES IN MEDICINE

In the field of medicine in the late twentieth century, there was both good news and bad news. The good news was that progress in medical knowledge enabled people to live longer. The bad news was that doctors and hospitals could keep extremely ill people alive by artificial means and perhaps prolong their suffering and the suffering of their families for months and even years.

**Increased Life Expectancy**    In 1900 there were no known cures for such common diseases as tuberculosis, influenza, pneumonia, and polio. Over the next 60 years breakthroughs in medical science brought these and other diseases under control. One of the most important discoveries was by a British scientist, Sir Alexander Fleming. In 1928 he discovered that some infections from open wounds could effectively be treated with penicillin, a bacteria-killing acid derived from a mold. The discovery of penicillin (an **antibiotic**) and other life-saving drugs accounted for major gains in life expectancy. In 1900 only 41 out of 100 Americans lived to age 65. By 1990 the number had risen to 79 out of 100. According to some population experts, the average baby born in the year 2010 will live to be 90.

**Ethical Dilemma**    If a person has no hope of recovery from severe injury or illness, should he or she be kept alive indefinitely through the use of life-sustaining equipment? This question has arisen only because of the advanced nature of modern medicine. Lawyers suggest that one solution to the dilemma might be a **living will**. A person wishing *not* to be kept alive by extraordinary means can say so in a living will, which states his or her wishes in the matter. Even so, somebody must interpret the will and decide whether or not it applies to a specific situation. Who should have the final word if the injured person cannot speak: a doctor, lawyer, judge, or family member?

**Clinton's health care plan**   Paying for the rising costs of modern medicine was another complex problem. When his presidency began in 1993, Bill Clinton assigned to his wife, Hillary Rodham Clinton, the job of heading a task force to propose a plan for reforming the U.S. health care system. The plan that the Clintons proposed to Congress had two main objectives: (1) to ensure that all Americans were covered by health insurance and (2) to prevent the total costs of medical care from consuming more and more of the national wealth. The president's plan proposed the following:

- Universal health insurance for all Americans (including the more than 37 million Americans who had no coverage in 1993)

- A choice of three kinds of health plans: low-cost care by a group of doctors (health maintenance organization, or HMO); higher-cost care by whatever doctor the patient chooses; or a middle-level plan combining some aspects of the other two.

Hillary Rodham Clinton speaking to the press about health care

- Businesses to pay for at least 80 percent of the cost of premiums for employees.

Various groups vigorously opposed the plan, and their views were widely reflected in Congress. By mid-1994 it was clear that legislative action on health care reform would be indefinitely delayed.

# VI. Oil Shortages and Global Awareness

From vehicles launched into space came back pictures of the earth as a small blue ball suspended in a black void. These pictures gave Americans a new view of the world as a single, undivided sphere. Many became aware for the first time of living in a global age and of the need for protecting the total planet. A series of global crises also contributed to global awareness. Each crisis concerned a world resource whose supply was daily declining. That resource was oil.

## A. THE FIRST ENERGY CRISIS

Americans first became aware of their dependence on foreign oil when an Arab-Israeli war broke out in 1973. As you read in Chapter 16, the Arabs used their control of oil fields in the Middle East to punish the United States for its support of Israel. Saudi Arabia, Iraq, Iran, and other nations placed an embargo on the sale of their oil to the United States and its allies.

The embargo made Americans realize that a significant percentage of the oil they used came from the Middle East, where the price of oil and its output were controlled by Arab members of the **Organization of Petroleum Exporting Countries (OPEC)**. (Japan and Western Europe depended almost totally on OPEC oil.) OPEC's 1973 embargo made worldwide oil prices soar. The oil shortage, or **energy crisis**, also led to long lines at gas stations. OPEC lifted its embargo in 1974 but continued to limit production and to keep oil prices high.

Presidents Nixon and Ford both urged Americans to conserve energy in their homes and on the road. When the crisis passed, however, the nation became even more dependent on foreign oil.

## B. THE SECOND ENERGY CRISIS

President Carter had to deal with an even worse energy crisis in 1979 when a revolution in Iran caused a major cutback in that country's production of oil. (See Chapter 19.) Oil prices climbed from about $11 a barrel to $40 a barrel. The shock to the world economy was severe. At U.S. gas stations motorists waited in long lines to refill their tanks and then had to pay more than a dollar a gallon for gas (compared to about 80 cents a gallon before the oil shortage). People became frustrated and angry having to start or end their workday in long gas lines.

The second oil crisis reminded Americans that they were at the mercy of OPEC and upheavals in the Middle East. President Carter had already persuaded Congress to set up a new cabinet department, the Department of Energy. Now he urged that the department expand its search for practical forms of energy other than oil. In 1980 Congress voted $20 billion in research funds to develop synthetic fuels.

## C. THE THIRD ENERGY CRISIS

Gradually, the price of oil declined from $40 a barrel in 1980 to $10 a barrel in 1986. Lower prices were the result of more fuel-efficient automobiles, oil discoveries outside the United States, and the increased flow of oil through a newly completed Alaska pipeline. Another Middle East crisis in 1990 caused the price of gasoline and heating oil to increase sharply. This time, oil-producing Iraq invaded its oil-producing neighbor Kuwait. To pressure Iraqi forces to withdraw, the United States and the United Nations voted to place an embargo on Iraqi oil. The resulting drop in oil supplies quickly led to higher prices at gas stations nationwide. Throughout the early 1990s, the price of oil stabilized at approximately $20 a barrel.

In Chapter 19, you will read further about the Iraqi invasion and U.S. response.

### In Review

The following questions refer to section V: Adjusting to Technological Change and section VI: Oil Shortages and Global Awareness.

1. Explain the significance of *each* event: (a) the discovery of penicillin; (b) the invention of the Apple II computer; (c) the *Challenger* disaster; (d) the energy crisis of 1979.

2. Discuss the effects that you think the computer will have on American democracy.

3. Identify *three* alternatives for dealing with U.S. dependence on foreign oil.

## GLOSSARY OF KEY TERMS: CHAPTER 18

**acquired immunodeficiency syndrome (AIDS)**   a new fatal disease of the 1980s that grew to the level of an epidemic late in the decade.

**affirmative action**   an employer's or university's policy of giving preference to women and members of ethnic minorities in order to correct past discrimination against these groups.

**affluent**   having a large supply of material possessions.

**Bakke case**   a landmark case of the U.S. Supreme Court in 1978 that placed limits on affirmative action programs in universities.

**budget**   a plan for spending money in a future year based upon the amount of income expected for that year.

***Challenger* disaster**   the mechanical failure of a U.S. space shuttle in 1986, resulting in the deaths of all seven crew members.

**Chrysler bailout**   the U.S. government's decision in 1979 to grant the Chrysler Corporation a loan of $1.5 billion to keep that company from going bankrupt.

**cost-of-living adjustment (COLA)**   a sum of money automatically added to a person's Social Security benefits whenever inflation causes the cost of living to rise.

**deficit**   the budgetary gap when expenditures are greater than revenues.

**deregulation**   the policy of reducing or eliminating governmental controls or rules concerning business practices.

**energy crisis**   an acute shortage of oil leading to an increase in oil prices.

**Gramm-Rudman-Hollings Act**   a law Congress passed in 1985 to reduce the federal deficit and bring about a balanced budget by 1991.

**Gray Panthers**   senior citizens organized as an interest group.

**"New Federalism"**   the policy of Presidents Richard Nixon and Ronald Reagan of returning to the states greater financial responsibility and cutting back federal involvement in social welfare programs.

**living will**   a document declaring a person's wishes about medical treatment and artificial life-support systems if that person should ever suffer extreme loss of physical and mental functions.

**oil embargo**   the action of Arab nations of the Middle East in 1973 in refusing to sell oil to the United States and its Western allies.

**Organization of Petroleum Exporting Countries (OPEC)**   an organization of oil-producing countries that regulates the production of oil in order to control its price.

**personal computer**   a small, relatively low-priced computer designed to perform record-keeping and other tasks in the average home.

**pluralistic society**   a society of many ethnic groups.

**racism**   the belief that a person's character and qualifications depend upon his or her racial inheritance or skin color.

**"Rainbow Coalition"**   the ethnic and racial minorities and the economically disadvantaged who supported Jesse Jackson as a candidate for president in 1988.

**"Reaganomics"**  President Reagan's economic policies, otherwise known as supply-side economics (see below).

**savings and loan association (S&L)**  a business that holds the savings of depositors and invests them chiefly in home mortgage loans.

**savings and loan bailout**  the federal government's costly effort to rescue troubled savings and loan associations by taking them over.

**Simpson-Mazzoli Act**  a 1986 law prohibiting the hiring of illegal immigrants; also called the Immigration Reform and Control Act.

**Skylab**  A U.S. space vehicle in which astronauts conduct scientific experiments.

**Social Security Reform Act**  a 1983 law increasing the Social Security taxes of workers in order to ensure adequate funds for making benefit payments to the elderly.

**subsidy**  government funds paid to support a private enterprise.

**supply-side economics**  the policy of reducing taxes in order to leave businesses with more money to invest in productive enterprises.

**surplus**  the budgetary balance when revenues exceed expenditures.

**target prices**  the prices for farm goods that the U.S. government considers normal and fair; if the market price of a particular farm product falls below the target price of that product, the government begins paying subsidies to farmers to make up the difference.

**Tax Reform Act**  a change in the tax laws passed by Congress in 1986 and representing President Reagan's policy of reducing taxes, especially for upper-income persons.

**yuppies (young urban professionals)**  a group of ambitious young men and women who aimed for material success and expressed the conservative values of U.S. society in the 1970s and 1980s.


# TEST YOURSELF

## A. Multiple Choice: Facts, Main Ideas, Skills

*On a separate sheet of paper, write the number of the word or expression that, of those given, best completes the statement or answers the question.*

### Reviewing the facts

1. Which trend indicates that U.S. families have adapted to changing social and economic conditions during the last 20 years?  (1) increase in the number of children who work in factories  (2) rise in the number of day-care facilities  (3) decrease in the number of women working outside the home  (4) decrease in average family income

2. Issues related to living wills and legal definitions of death have increased in recent years because  (1) population control has become

a critical necessity in the United States  (2) advancing medical technology has created new ethical problems  (3) demand for health care has outstripped society's ability to provide it  (4) an increasing number of people are dying without providing for the legal transfer of their estates

3. The United States has a deficit in its international trade balance. This means that  (1) imports are greater than exports  (2) too much money is being spent on public works  (3) the banking system is short of funds  (4) consumers owe too much of their incomes in taxes.

4. Which is the most basic cause of the U.S. government's budget deficit?  (1) The government prints too much money.  (2) The president spends too little money on social programs.  (3) Congress refuses to allow the president to spend money.  (4) The government spends more money than it receives.

5. President Ronald Reagan's federal budget proposals came under sharp criticism because they  (1) lowered interest rates and decreased inflation  (2) increased social welfare spending  (3) included very large deficits  (4) advocated raising the income tax

6. As a result of federal deficits in the 1980s, the national debt  (1) increased greatly  (2) declined on a per capita basis  (3) is owed almost wholly to foreigners  (4) must be secured by a gold reserve

7. Which statement about U.S. agriculture since 1970 is most valid?  (1) The number of farms has increased.  (2) Farmers have become more efficient producers.  (3) The average farm has continued to get smaller.  (4) The cost of farm machinery has gone down.

8. Increased life expectancy in the United States will most likely mean that  (1) more schools will be needed  (2) dealing with the problems of old age will become more important  (3) there will be less need for low-cost housing  (4) there will be more young workers available for employment

9. Since the late 1960s, most immigrants to the United States have come from  (1) Africa and Asia  (2) Europe and Asia  (3) Latin America and Asia  (4) Europe and Africa

10. Present-day U.S. immigration laws provide for  (1) a quota system for all countries outside Western Europe  (2) admission of only displaced persons and professionals  (3) transfers of unused quotas of Western European nations to Asian nations  (4) admission of immigrants on the basis of their skills and education

## Reviewing the main ideas

11. Which would be a logical outgrowth of the philosophy of the Progressive Era? (*Note:* If necessary, review Chapter 8.)  (1) the deregulation of key industries  (2) increased regulation of savings and loan associations  (3) an emphasis on supply-side economics  (4) the merging of large corporations

12. Which condition would be most likely to cause a society to adopt a policy of bilingualism? (1) high literacy rate (2) multiparty political system (3) high population density (4) patterns of cultural pluralism

13. "Changes in the role of women have had a significant impact on U.S. society in the 1970s and 1980s." Which statement could correctly be made to support this quotation? (1) Women have become dominant in big business. (2) Women hold most of the jobs in the federal government. (3) Most men and women would prefer not to marry. (4) Employment opportunities for women have altered the life-style of the family.

14. An important similarity between the economic programs of President Roosevelt in the 1930s and those of President Reagan in the 1980s is that both programs (1) attempted to reduce the government's role in the economy (2) were significantly different from the economic programs of the preceding administration (3) were developed in response to major foreign policy mistakes of the preceding administration (4) received the nearly unanimous support of economists.

15. What problem was faced by U.S. agriculture both in the 1930s and 1980s? (1) a lack of modern farm machinery (2) the poverty of most American consumers (3) low prices for farm products (4) a flood of cheap money and credit

## Developing critical thinking skills

*Base your answers to questions 16 and 17 on the graph below and on your knowledge of U.S. history and government.*

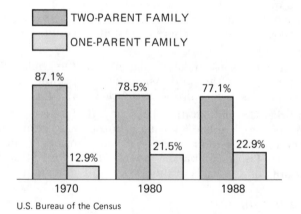

U.S. Bureau of the Census

**The family in transition: nuclear family vs. one-parent family**

16. According to the graph, from 1970 to 1984 the percentage of one-parent families (1) remained about the same (2) nearly doubled (3) decreased by one half (4) decreased and then increased

**17.** Which factor best accounts for the trend shown in the graph? (1) an increase in the divorce rate (2) an increase in inflation (3) a decrease in the birth rate (4) a decrease in the number of senior citizens

*Base your answer to question 18 on the cartoon below and on your knowledge of U.S. history and government.*

"I never tire of watching them"

**18.** The development in U.S. society that most concerns the cartoonist is that (1) computers are replacing individuals in the marketplace (2) the individual mind is becoming less important with the increasing use of computers (3) people's privacy is being threatened by the computerization of personal data (4) individuals are placing too much importance on the computer

## B. Enduring Issues

*On the next page, select two of the enduring issues from column A. For each issue chosen, explain how the historical example in column B relates to the issue.*

| A. Enduring Issues | B. Historical Examples |
|---|---|
| 1. Federalism—the balance between nation and state | President Reagan's "New Federalism" |
| 2. The judiciary—interpreter of the U.S. Constitution or shaper of policy | The U.S. Supreme Court decision declaring that flag burning could be considered an act of free speech |
| 3. Civil liberties—balance between the rights of the government and the rights of the individual | The government's practice of keeping computerized records of various aspects of a citizen's life |
| 4. Rights of ethnic and racial groups under the U.S. Constitution | Affirmative action as a government policy |
| 5. Avenues of representation | Jesse Jackson as a presidential candidate |

## C. Essays

### Level 1

Listed below are several problems facing the United States during the 1990s.

AIDS

Drug epidemic

Quality of education

Homelessness

Changing family

Choose *two* of these problems.

**1.** Describe the nature of *each* of the *two* problems.

**2.** Identify *two* alternatives for dealing with *each* problem.

### Level 2

Every year, the federal government must decide whether to spend more or less money on certain programs.

**A.** List *three* problems facing U.S. society on which the government spent money in the 1980s.

**B.** Base your answer to part B on your answer to part A. Write an essay on *one* problem. Discuss whether you think the U.S. government should spend more money or less money on that problem.

# Chapter *19*

# Foreign Policy, 1974 to the Present

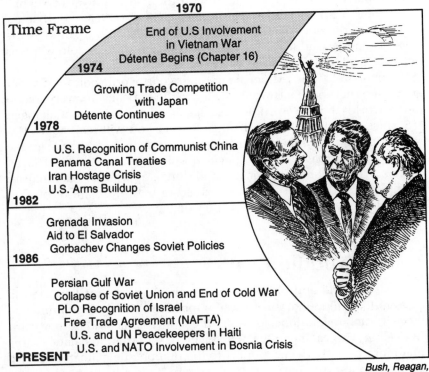

**Time Frame**

**1970**

End of U.S Involvement
in Vietnam War
Détente Begins (Chapter 16)

**1974**

Growing Trade Competition
with Japan
Détente Continues

**1978**

U.S. Recognition of Communist China
Panama Canal Treaties
Iran Hostage Crisis
U.S. Arms Buildup

**1982**

Grenada Invasion
Aid to El Salvador
Gorbachev Changes Soviet Policies

**1986**

Persian Gulf War
Collapse of Soviet Union and End of Cold War
PLO Recognition of Israel
Free Trade Agreement (NAFTA)
U.S. and UN Peacekeepers in Haiti
U.S. and NATO Involvement in Bosnia Crisis

**PRESENT**

*Bush, Reagan,
and Gorbachev, 1988*

573

## *Objectives*

- To examine changes in international politics in the Middle East, Asia, Africa, Latin America, and Eastern Europe.
- To analyze the forces and events leading to the end of the cold war.
- To identify and evaluate presidential responses to a hostage crisis in Iran, a civil war in Nicaragua, an invasion of Kuwait, and other challenges to U.S. foreign policy.

From the end of World War II (1945) to the end of the Vietnam War (1975), two situations were most important to the makers of U.S. foreign policy. First, the Soviet Union and the United States were cold-war rivals. Second, some crisis in this rivalry might lead to a world-destroying exchange of nuclear weapons.

After the Vietnam War, relations between the superpowers changed dramatically. During his first term in office, President Reagan increased cold-war tensions by calling the Soviet Union an "evil empire" and greatly increasing U.S. spending for new weapons. Reagan's second term in office, however, coincided with the rise to power of Mikhail Gorbachev, a Soviet leader committed to new policies. Gorbachev and Reagan developed a warmer U.S.–Soviet relationship. By 1991 the Soviet Union ceased to exist as a single nation, and the cold war was officially declared ended the following year.

Unfortunately, this extraordinary change in world politics did not guarantee that the 1990s would be a decade of peace. In every region of the world, there were violent struggles for power that challenged U.S. allies and U.S. interests. In this chapter you will read about U.S. responses to a number of crises, beginning with conflicts in the Middle East and a war against Iraq. You will see how a weakened Soviet economy, Gorbachev's policies, and long-suppressed nationalism brought an end to the cold war and led to both peaceful revolution and violent civil strife in Eastern Europe.

# I. The Middle East

Ever since the end of World War II, the Middle East has been in turmoil. The history of this region in modern times has been marked by civil wars, revolutions, assassinations, invasions, and border wars. In dealing with each conflict, U.S. policymakers tried to balance three main interests: (1) giving support to the democratic state of Israel, (2) giving support to Arab states to ensure a steady flow of Middle Eastern oil to the United States and its allies, and (3) preventing the former Soviet Union from increasing its influence in the region.

# A. CONTINUING ARAB-ISRAELI CONFLICT

From 1947 to 1973, Israel fought four wars with Arab neighbors. First, from 1948 to 1949, Arab states attacked Israel in a failed attempt to crush the independence of the new Jewish state. Second, in the Suez Crisis of 1956, Israel joined France and Great Britain in attacking Egypt. After the United States condemned the attack, Israel withdrew. Third, in 1967 Israel took only six days to defeat Jordan, Syria, and Egypt.

**Results of the 1967 War**   As a result of the 1967 Six-Day War, Israeli forces occupied the bordering territories of the Golan Heights (taken from Syria), the Sinai Peninsula and Gaza Strip (taken from Egypt), and the West Bank of the Jordan River (taken from Jordan). Israel refused to give back these territories that helped secure its borders against future attack. The embittered Arab nations hoped to regain the territories in yet another war.

**Yom Kippur War (1973)**   A fourth war broke out in October, 1973, when Arab nations, seeking to win back territories lost in 1967, launched a surprise attack against Israel on the Jewish holy day of Yom Kippur. After fierce fighting and initial Arab victories, Israel drove back the Arabs in a successful counterattack. The United States, fearful of Soviet intervention, used its influence to negotiate a cease-fire.

**Camp David Accords**   After the Yom Kippur War, Presidents Ford and Carter attempted to reduce tensions between Israel and its Arab neighbors. In 1978 President Carter persuaded Egypt's president Anwar Sadat and Israel's prime minister Menachem Begin to travel to the United States and informally discuss peace at Camp David, Maryland. Most world leaders doubted that peace would result from these talks and were therefore surprised when the Egyptian and Israeli leaders announced at Camp David that they had reached an agreement, or accord, on resolving problems dividing their countries. Later Egypt and Israel signed a treaty of peace based on the Camp David Accords. The treaty of 1979 provided for the following.

- Israel was to return the Sinai Peninsula to Egypt.
- Egypt formally recognized Israel as an independent nation.
- Israel and Egypt pledged to respect the border between them.

Many Egyptians as well as other Arabs bitterly condemned Sadat for making peace with Israel. Begin also faced severe criticism within his country for returning the Sinai Peninsula to Egypt. For their courage in agreeing to make peace with a former enemy, Anwar Sadat and Menachem Begin received the Nobel Peace Prize in 1978. Sadly, however, Sadat's peace policy cost him his life. In 1981 the Egyptian leader was assassinated by Muslim extremists.

**The Palestinian Problem** Complicating the Arab-Israeli conflict was the problem of Palestinian refugees and their demands for a nation of their own. After Israel's victories in the wars of 1948 and 1967, large numbers of Palestinians found temporary homes in refugee camps in neighboring Arab nations (Syria, Lebanon, and Jordan). The poverty of the refugee camps and nationalist feelings of the Palestinians gave rise to a political movement. Heading the movement was the **Palestine Liberation Organization (PLO).** Its goal was to eliminate Israel as a nation and turn it into a homeland for Palestinians. The PLO's leader was Yasir Arafat, and its main weapon was **terrorism**. (Rebels who lack an army sometimes resort to terrorism, which is the use of violence to spread fear and to disrupt the normal operations of government.) To the PLO, terrorism meant killing Israelis. Palestinian terrorists regularly attacked Israeli settlements, buses, beaches, and airplanes. They even carried their terrorism to countries outside the Middle East. In 1972 they murdered 11 Israeli athletes who had gone to Munich, West Germany, for the Olympic Games. In 1985 PLO terrorists hijacked an Italian cruise ship, the *Achille Lauro*, and killed an American passenger, an elderly Jewish tourist. In 1993 a massive bomb exploded in a garage below New York City's World Trade Center, killing six people and injuring more than 1,000. Those convicted in the bombing were Muslim fundamentalists with close ties to Islamic extremist groups in Egypt, where they were suspected of terrorism.

**The Intifadah** Among the territories taken by Israel in the 1967 war was the Gaza Strip (formerly part of Egypt) and the West Bank (formerly part of Jordan). More than a million Palestinians lived in these two captured territories. Beginning in 1987 Palestinian youths protested the presence of Israeli troops by throwing stones at them. Israeli forces occasionally responded to the stone throwing by firing at their assailants. Many young Palestinians were wounded, and some were killed. The **Intifadah**, as the Palestinians called their protest uprising, attracted international attention.

**Change in Israeli-Palestinian Relations** In a major diplomatic breakthrough in 1993, the Israeli prime minister Yitzhak Rabin and PLO leader Yasir Arafat shook hands in Washington, D.C., over an agreement granting Palestinians control over the Gaza Strip and the West Bank town of Jericho. In return, the PLO recognized Israel's right to exist and made a commitment to end terrorism. In 1994 negotiations officially ended the state of war between Jordan and Israel, and Israel and Syria held peace talks. Thus, a period of peaceful relations between Israel and its Arab neighbors seemed possible.

However, a new Palestinian movement, *Hamas*, used terrorism to undermine Israeli-PLO talks on expanding Palestinian self-rule. So killings and suicide attacks against Israelis increased.

## B. MARINES IN LEBANON

To the north of Israel is Lebanon, whose population is divided between Christians and different groups of Muslims. Lebanon's constitution provides for the sharing of power among various religious groups. By the 1970s, Lebanon's Muslims outnumbered Christians. Palestinians in Lebanon's refugee camps then began to protest the government's pro-Western policies. In 1975 a fierce civil war erupted between the Christians and the allied Palestinians and Muslims.

Syria intervened by supporting radical, pro-Communist Palestinians, while Israel sent troops into southern Lebanon to retaliate for PLO terrorist attacks on Israel. In 1982 Israel bombarded the capital, Beirut, and demanded and won a Palestinian withdrawal from the city. To keep the peace in Beirut and assist in the UN-supervised withdrawal, President Reagan ordered U.S. Marines to the embattled city as peacekeepers, but this effort ended in tragedy. In 1983 a terrorist bomb exploded at the marine barracks near Beirut, killing 241 Marines. In 1984 President Reagan removed the troops.

Following their departure, Syria assumed control over much of Lebanon, while Israel occupied a strip of southern Lebanon as a security zone to halt attacks against northern Israel. During the 1980s and 1990s, militant groups based in Lebanon launched rocket attacks and suicide raids against Israel, while Israeli forces retaliated with commando raids into southern Lebanon. The United States has urged both sides to resolve the conflict.

## C. HOSTAGE CRISIS IN IRAN

A low point in the history of U.S. foreign relations occurred during the Carter presidency. In 1979 Iranian revolutionaries, in violation of international law, broke into the U.S. Embassy in Iran's capital, Teheran. They captured 62 Americans, and held 52 as **hostages** (captives held until ransom is paid or demands are met) for over a year.

**Causes of the Crisis**  Many Iranians were angered by past U.S. policies toward their country. Since 1953 the United States had supported the regime of Iran's monarch, Shah Mohammad Reza Pahlavi. In return for U.S. military aid, the shah had let the United States use Iran as a base for spying on the Soviet Union. The shah had also employed a secret police to ruthlessly suppress dissent. Fundamentalist Muslims condemned the shah for modernizing Iran rather than following Muslim religious laws and customs strictly. A leader of these fundamentalists was the Ayatollah Khomeini. (*Ayatollah* is a Muslim title for an advanced religious scholar.)

In 1979 Khomeini led a successful revolution against the shah, who went into exile. President Carter allowed the ailing shah to enter the United States for medical treatment. This action angered the Iranian revolutionaries. Some of them seized Americans in the U.S. Embassy and demanded the return of the shah for trial. Carter refused and counterdemanded release of the hostages.

**Consequences of the Crisis**   The Iranians continued to hold the hostages through the early months of 1980. In April of that year, Carter decided to attempt a military rescue of the hostages. Unfortunately, the U.S. helicopters carrying U.S. troops broke down in the Iranian desert, and the rescue effort failed. Months passed without any change in the hostage situation, except for the death of the shah in Egypt in July. Running for re-election in 1980, President Carter suffered political damage by his inability to free the hostages. He lost the election partly because of the high rate of inflation and partly because of the frustrating situation in Iran.

On the day that Carter left office, January 20, 1981, Iran announced the release of the hostages, 444 days after their capture. The hostage crisis injured U.S. prestige. Coming only a few years after the loss of the Vietnam War, the crisis made many Americans wonder whether the nation was beginning to decline as a world power.

The ending of the hostage crisis did not improve U.S.-Iranian relations. Even into the 1990s, the United States continued an embargo on Iranian oil, a ban on the sale of U.S. business machinery and equipment to Iran, and a boycott of Iranian products sold by Iran. The United States also led an international embargo on the sale to Iran of materials used in developing nuclear weapons.

# D. WAR IN THE PERSIAN GULF

In the 1980s the four major producers of oil in the Middle East were Saudi Arabia (the largest), Kuwait, Iran, and Iraq. All four are located on the shores of the Persian Gulf. Between 1980 and 1988, Iran and Iraq fought a costly and brutal war. Iraq won small gains in territory.

**Iraq's Invasion of Kuwait**   Shortly after the Iran-Iraq War, Iraq's military dictator, Saddam Hussein, accused Kuwait of taking an unfair share of oil revenues. In August 1990, claiming that Kuwait was a part of Iraq, he invaded and occupied it. The invasion and occupation received wide news coverage around the world.

The Iraqi invasion alarmed President Bush and other world leaders for three reasons. First, it was an act of aggression by a strong nation against a weaker one. (Iraq in 1990 had the fourth largest military force in the world.) Second, the taking of Kuwait opened the way to an Iraqi conquest of the world's largest oil producer, Saudi Arabia. Third, Iraq's military power and aggressive actions would allow it to dominate the other countries of the Middle East.

To prevent further aggression, President Bush ordered 200,000 troops to Saudi Arabia, followed later by 300,000 more. "We have drawn a line in the sand," said the president, as he announced a defensive effort called Operation Desert Shield. U.S. troops were joined by forces from a UN-supported coalition of 28 nations, including Great Britain, France, Saudi Arabia, Syria, Turkey, and Egypt.

Members of the UN Security Council, including both the United States and the then Soviet Union, voted for a series of resolutions concerning Iraq's aggression. One UN resolution demanded Iraq's unconditional withdrawal from Kuwait. Other resolutions placed an international embargo on trade with Iraq and authorized UN members to use force if Iraqi troops did not leave Kuwait by January 15, 1991. As the January deadline neared, members of Congress debated whether or not to authorize the president to send U.S. troops into combat in the Persian Gulf. Both houses voted in favor of the war resolution.

**Operation Desert Storm**   After the deadline expired, thousands of planes from allied bases in Saudi Arabia took part in massive air strikes against military targets in Iraq and Kuwait. There was no effective resistance and little loss of life among U.S. and allied forces.

The major Iraqi response was to launch Scud (Soviet-made) missiles against targets in both Saudi Arabia and Israel. The missiles did some damage, even though most were intercepted and destroyed in the air by U.S. Patriot missiles. Recognizing that Saddam Hussein wanted to win Arab support by provoking an Israeli counterattack, Israel did not retaliate for the Scud attacks against its cities.

After more than a month of round-the-clock bombing attacks, U.S. and allied forces launched a massive ground attack against Iraqi positions in both Kuwait and southern Iraq. The demoralized Iraqis offered little resistance. Filing out of their underground bunkers, they surrendered by the tens of thousands as allied tanks swept across the desert toward Kuwait City and into Iraq itself. Saddam Hussein was now forced to concede defeat. In accordance with the UN resolution, all Iraqi forces not captured by the allies withdrew from Kuwait. On the evening of February 27—six weeks after the first air strike and only 100 hours after the ground war began—President Bush went on television to announce that the war had been won. He said, "Kuwait is liberated. Iraq's army is defeated. Our military objectives are met." Operation Desert Storm, as Bush called the U.S. war effort, had ended in a rapid and overwhelming victory.

**Effects of the War**   The Persian Gulf War liberated Kuwait and ruined Saddam Hussein's ambitions to control Mideast oil prices and supplies. The war also demonstrated military cooperation between the nations of Western Europe and the United States. Russia, faced with internal problems, supported U.S. resolutions in the UN.

The United States used its prestige as the war's chief victor to arrange peace talks between Israel and the Arab nations. After the war, however, Saddam Hussein remained in power as Iraq's dictator. UN inspection teams in Iraq suspected that Hussein might be seeking to acquire nuclear weapons. Another concern was that Hussein would order air attacks against Iraq's minority Kurdish population in the north. In order to prevent this and show humanitarian concern, the United States established a "no-fly" zone in northern Iraq.

# II. Asia

For almost 30 years after the end of World War II, U.S. foreign policymakers sought mainly to contain the advance of communism in Asia. Beginning in the 1970s, however, the United States became less concerned with Communist expansion and more concerned with economic competition from Japan, the nations of the Pacific Rim, and China. North Korea was being watched for another reason— fear of its growing nuclear capability.

## A. JAPAN AND THE PACIFIC RIM

Early in the 1970s Americans discovered that they were buying more and more goods from Japan. Japanese cars on U.S. highways were an increasingly familiar sight. Japanese motorcycles, cameras, TV sets, and radios were now standard equipment in millions of American homes. Although consumers benefited from these high-quality imports, U.S. manufacturers and labor unions worried about losing business and jobs to foreign competitors.

**Trade Imbalance**  Ever since World War I, the United States had been a creditor nation. In other words, the value of U.S.-made goods sold abroad (exports) was greater than the value of foreign-made goods sold in the United States (imports). In each year of the 1980s and 1990s, however, just the opposite occurred. The value of U.S. imports exceeded the value of exports by many billions of dollars ($115.5 billion in 1993). Instead of the world's largest creditor nation, the United States had become the world's largest debtor nation.

By far the widest gap between exports and imports was in U.S. trade with Japan. Thus, its **trade deficit** with Japan for 1993 was more than $59 billion.

**U.S. Trade Policy**  How could the U.S. government help American manufacturers sell more goods abroad, especially in Japan? From the 1970s through the 1990s, six presidents, from Nixon to Clinton, sought answers to this question. All were committed to cooperating with other nations in promoting world trade. Ever since 1947, most nations of the world, including the United States, had participated in a series of diplomatic conferences called the **General Agreement on Tariffs and Trade (GATT).** Each round of trade talks usually resulted in member nations of GATT lowering their tariffs.

Honoring U.S. commitments to GATT, Reagan, Bush, and Clinton favored keeping U.S. tariffs low. They feared that raising tariffs to protect U.S. manufacturing would result in tariff wars and hurt both the world and the U.S. economies. U.S. presidents, however, continued to pressure Japan's government to change its economic policies. They objected to Japan's practice of placing quotas on the number of foreign goods that it would allow Japanese businesses to buy.

In 1992 President Bush and U.S. business leaders traveled to Japan on a trade mission. Their prime objective was to urge the Japanese to increase U.S. imports. The Japanese agreed only to "targets" rather than specific increases. Incensed, some business leaders and government officials have called for a return to the traditional U.S. policy of raising U.S. tariffs and quotas on Japanese products. Others oppose such economic protectionism and stress the need for U.S. businesses to become more productive and competitive.

President Clinton continued to press Japan to import more American products, and his efforts achieved a minor success. In mid-1995 he threatened a 100-percent rise in import duties on certain popular, high-priced Japanese cars if Japan did not ease its foreign trade policies. U.S. and Japanese negotiators then met and worked out a compromise agreement by which Japan pledged to open its market for U.S. cars somewhat. Some observers thought that the agreement was more a compromise than an economic victory.

As Japan exported more to the United States than it imported, it accumulated a growing surplus of American dollars. This contributed to a decline in the value of the dollar and a corresponding rise in the value of the Japanese yen. In 1992 one dollar was equal to 160 yen; by 1995 one dollar equaled only 85 yen. One major result is that Japanese products have become more expensive for Americans, while American products have become cheaper for the Japanese.

**Countries of the Pacific Rim**   Japan is not the only Asian country whose businesses compete strongly with those of the United States. On the Asian coastline, or Pacific Rim, industry and trade grew rapidly in the 1980s and 1990s in South Korea, Taiwan, Thailand, and Malaysia, as well as the British colony of Hong Kong. The clothing, shoes, electric appliances, and steel produced in these areas sold well in foreign markets, including the United States. In 1993 the total value of U.S. imports from these other countries of the Pacific Rim almost equaled that of U.S. imports from Japan. Like Japan, South Korea and other Pacific Rim nations formerly had trade barriers against U.S. products. In 1994 President Clinton signed an agreement with the Pacific Rim countries to eliminate these trade barriers and move towards free trade over a period of several years.

## B. CHINA

As the world's most populous nation (about 1.2 billion people), China offers potentially the greatest market in the world for U.S. goods. Its violations of human rights, however, have posed a barrier to full-scale trade with the United States. Ever since President Nixon's trip to China in 1972, the United States has tried to establish normal relations with China's Communist government. The road to improved relations, however, has not been smooth.

**Eleven Years of Progress**   Between 1978 and 1989 the Communist leaders adopted a number of liberal and economic reforms. They permitted students to criticize government policies and suggest ideas for making the government more democratic. They encouraged people to organize their own small businesses. They opened their country to Western tourists and invited experts from the West to advise them on methods of improving their economy.

President Carter in 1979 formally recognized the Communist regime as the legitimate government of China. At the same time, the United States withdrew its recognition of the non-Communist government of Taiwan (also known as Nationalist China or the Republic of China). Diplomatic relations and military aid to Taiwan came to an end. However, the United States continued to carry on a far greater amount of trade with Taiwan than with the huge Chinese mainland.

**Massacre in Beijing**   The spring of 1989 saw a brutal end to the days of reform and openness in China. Hundreds of thousands of students had gathered in **Tiananmen Square,** a huge public square in the capital of Beijing, to demonstrate peacefully and urge the government to make democratic reforms in the Communist system. In reply, the government ordered troops to use their weapons. The square exploded with the sound of soldiers' rifle fire. In a few hours about 700 protesters were killed. A dazed onlooker told a U.S. reporter: "Tell the United Nations, tell the world what has happened in China. Tell them that the Chinese government is killing the Chinese people."

The United States joined other nations in protesting the massacre. For the most part, however, President Bush followed much the same policy toward China as before. He did not carry out economic sanctions (penalties) voted by Congress. The president wanted to avoid antagonizing the government of China, even though it had acted harshly. He argued that the United States could best help the Chinese people by keeping on good terms with China's government.

President Clinton continued this policy of keeping on good terms with China even while Chinese dissidents favoring democratic reforms were being arrested. The administration believed that increased trade with a prospering China would lead it to adopt a better human rights policy sooner than would economic sanctions.

## C. NORTH KOREA

One unresolved cold-war conflict was a divided North and South Korea. Communism had collapsed elsewhere, but the regime of dictator Kim Il-Sung and his son and successor Kim Jong-Il still ruled North Korea. In the early 1990s, there was growing concern that North Korea was developing nuclear weapons. While denying the charge, North Korea refused UN inspection of its nuclear power plants. Reacting to threats of UN economic sanctions, North Korea, in 1994, reached an agreement with the United States to freeze its nuclear program in exchange for two light-water reactors and economic and diplomatic concessions. (Light-water reactors make the production of nuclear weapons much more difficult.) Then, in 1995, President Clinton extended full diplomatic recognition to North Korea.

## *In Review*

The following questions refer to section I: The Middle East and section II: Asia.

1. Identify *Camp David Accords, PLO, terrorism, Intifadah, Yasir Arafat, Ayatollah Khomeini, Saddam Hussein, Persian Gulf War, GATT, trade deficit,* and *Tiananmen Square.*
2. Explain how each of the following posed a challenge to U.S. foreign policy: (a) PLO terrorism, (b) civil war in Lebanon, (c) revolution in Iran, (d) trade with Japan, (e) massacre in Beijing, and (f) Iraqi invasion of Kuwait.

# III. Africa

During the early years of the cold war (1947 to 1977), U.S. policymakers were mainly concerned about stopping Communist forces from gaining control of African governments. In later years, beginning with the presidency of Jimmy Carter, the focus shifted to a question of racial justice in South Africa. The question was: Should the United States continue to support an all-white regime that oppressed South Africa's black majority?

## A. AFRICA AND THE COLD WAR

Most African nations had achieved independence by the early 1960s. Unfortunately, many of the governments of the new African nations were unstable. Rival groups often fought each other in bitter and destructive civil wars. Often the Soviet Union would supply arms and training for one side in a civil war, while the United States supported the other side. Thus, for many years, the African nations were involved in a global struggle between the two superpowers. Some African governments were able to take advantage of the situation by accepting economic and military aid from both the Soviet Union and the United States.

Most African nations chose to remain neutral in the cold war. As nonaligned nations of the third world, they found that they shared a common outlook with nonaligned nations of Asia. In the General Assembly of the United Nations, the third-world countries of Africa and Asia made up a majority. President Carter recognized the growing power of the nonwhite (African and Asian) majority. He hoped to make a positive impression on third-world opinion when he appointed an African American, Andrew Young, to be the U.S. ambassador to the United Nations in 1977.

African civil wars and cold-war politics challenged the presidencies of both Carter and Reagan. In the 1980s, for example, the United States supplied arms to Somalia in its war against Soviet-backed Ethiopia. At the same time, south of the equator, a Communist government in Angola received military support from both the Soviet Union and Cuba. The United States supplied arms to a rebel group that fought unsuccessfully to overthrow Angola's government.

The United States supplied aid to African nations for humanitarian reasons as well. When hundreds of thousands of Ethiopians died in a terrible famine of 1984, many tons of U.S. food were sent to Ethiopia despite the Communist sympathies of that country's government.

## B. SOMALIA

During the last year of the Bush presidency, the United States provided humanitarian aid to Somalia, a nation suffering from famine and civil war. In addition to aid, U.S. troops joined a multinational UN force to help bring peace to the region. After significant multinational casualties, the United States withdrew its troops in 1994. By 1995 all UN forces had left Somalia.

## C. APARTHEID IN SOUTH AFRICA

U.S. policy toward South Africa had less to do with the cold war than with the issues of justice and basic human rights.

**Origins of Apartheid**   The Republic of South Africa was once a Dutch colony. The British took control of the colony after defeating the Dutch settlers in the Boer War (1899 to 1902). The Afrikaners, as people of Dutch descent called themselves, outnumbered the British and eventually, in 1948, won control of the government. Their republic broke all ties with Great Britain in 1961.

One of the first acts of the Afrikaner government in 1948 was to adopt a policy of strict racial separation. This policy of **apartheid** (an Afrikaner word meaning "apartness") separated the people of South Africa into four racial groups: whites, blacks, Asians, and "colored" persons (mixed ancestry). Apartheid applied to all aspects of life. Socially, blacks had to live apart from the other races. Politically, they could not vote. Economically, they could work only in the lowest paying occupations. Until only a few years ago, South African blacks had to carry identification passes and could enter white areas only for a limited time. South Africa's all-white government ordered many blacks to move to "tribal homelands" far from the coastal cities (even though blacks had never lived on the lands assigned to them).

**International Protests**  The huge majority of the world's nations consisted of people who were nonwhite. They viewed the racist policies of the South African government as an insulting carryover from the days when white Europeans ruled much of Afria and Asia. In the United Nations, countries of the third world voted for a long series of resolutions condemning apartheid and calling upon UN members to stop trading with South Africa.

**Change in U.S. Policy**  Until the 1980s the U.S. government did very little to oppose apartheid. Many U.S. businesses and even universities invested in South Africa's profitable gold, diamond, and uranium mines. However, the ruthless methods used by the South African government to enforce apartheid were widely reported on TV news shows and dramatized in the movies. At many U.S. colleges, students organized demonstrations against apartheid. A South African opponent of apartheid, Episcopal Archbishop Desmond Tutu, traveled to U.S. cities to urge that the United States stop trading with South Africa. In 1986 Congress passed (over President Reagan's veto) an act placing an embargo, or ban, on trade with South Africa.

Partly in response to the worldwide pressures being brought to bear on its economy, South Africa began to modify its policies. A new South African president, F. W. de Klerk, promised to integrate parks and beaches and to permit South African blacks to vote. In 1990, after spending 27 years in prison for opposing apartheid, the black leader Nelson Mandela was released. On a tour of the United States, Mandela urged Americans to continue the U.S. trade embargo until apartheid ended. However, in July, 1991, President Bush pointed to the progress South Africa had made in phasing out racist policies and persuaded Congress to lift the U.S. embargo.

**Transition to Majority Rule**  Mandela and de Klerk recognized the need for peaceful transition from white rule to a government elected by people of all races. In April, 1994, the first South African elections were held in which all races could vote. Mandela's party—the African National Congress (ANC)—won a majority of seats in the legislature, and Mandela became South Africa's first black president. This transition to multiracial democracy led to an end of all U.S. boycotts of South Africa and increased cooperation between the two nations.

# IV. Latin America

Ever since the beginning of the twentieth century, U.S. policy toward Latin America has followed two different paths. Presidents of the Progressive Era (Theodore Roosevelt, Woodrow Wilson, and William H. Taft) followed the path of intervention. Sending U.S. Marines into the Dominican Republic, Haiti, and Nicaragua caused much resentment not only in these countries but throughout Latin America. The United States reversed its interventionist policies in the 1930s. It then followed the path of the "good neighbor," as Franklin Roosevelt called his Latin American policy.

After World War II the United States tried to follow both the interventionist path and the "good neighbor" path at the same time. U.S. fears of Soviet influence and Communist revolutions caused President Kennedy to give aid to Latin American countries (the Alliance for Progress) and also to support an invasion of Cuba (the Bay of Pigs crisis). From then until the present day, U.S. policy has continued along both paths—economic assistance, on the one hand, and military intervention, on the other.

## A. CARTER'S EMPHASIS ON HUMAN RIGHTS

During his presidency (1977 to 1981), Jimmy Carter insisted that the United States could and should use its influence to stop oppressive governments from abusing the **human rights** of citizens. He knew that some violators (South Africa) were aligned with the West, while others (Cuba and Poland) were Communist countries. The United States, as a freedom-loving country, should require friend and foe alike to respect the basic rights of their citizens.

**Violations of Human Rights**   In Latin America (as in other regions of the world), human rights abuses were extensive. Military regimes in Argentina and Chile arrested many thousands of people and either imprisoned them without trial or killed them. The victims' only crime—or suspected crime—was joining political groups opposed to the regime. In Central America, El Salvador's friendly government and Nicaragua's hostile Communist government were both guilty of mistreating and killing citizens who opposed their policies.

**Carter's Policy**   At Carter's urging, Congress reduced or eliminated U.S. economic aid to countries like Argentina and Chile. Unwilling to reform, they accused Carter of meddling in their internal affairs.

Oppressed peoples were better helped by being admitted into the United States as refugees from tyranny. During Carter's presidency, Fidel Castro let thousands of Cubans go. Thousands of Haitians also left their island nation in a desperate effort to escape harsh laws and extreme poverty. Both groups sailed to Florida. Many Americans wanted to turn the "boat people" away since many were poor and unskilled, but Carter let them make the United States their new home.

## B. CHANGING RELATIONS WITH PANAMA

Ever since 1903 when Panama gained its independence, the United States has had a special relationship with that country. Panama's new government signed a treaty granting the United States the right to own and operate a canal through Panama and also to own a 10-mile-wide strip of land bordering the canal (the Panama Canal Zone). At first, the people of Panama welcomed U.S. efforts to build and protect the canal. Beginning in the 1960s, however, many Panamanians protested U.S. presence in their country. The time had come, they said, for the United States to give control of the canal to Panama.

**Panama Canal Treaties (1977)**   As a Democrat, President Carter favored the Good Neighbor policy of a Democratic predecessor, Franklin Roosevelt. He believed that U.S. troops in the Panama Canal Zone not only angered the Panamanian people but also offended other people of Latin America. Therefore, Carter negotiated two treaties with Panama. According to the first treaty, the United States promised to transfer ownership of the canal and canal zone to Panama by the year 2000. According to the second treaty, the United States and Panama agreed that the canal would always be neutral territory. If threatened by an outside power, the United States could use military force to defend it.

The **Panama Canal treaties** stirred much controversy in the United States. Many Americans were reluctant to have their country give up the canal. President Carter, however, managed to persuade two-thirds of the Senate to ratify both treaties. It was one of the major political victories of his presidency.

## C. MILITARY INTERVENTIONS BY REAGAN AND BUSH

As Republican presidents, Ronald Reagan and George Bush took a different view of politics in Latin America. They believed that the United States should readily intervene with military force if its interests were threatened. It was more important to act decisively in Latin America than to win Latin America's goodwill. This was in line with the traditional containment policy of opposing communism.

**The Grenada Invasion**   Grenada, an island nation in the Caribbean Sea, has a population of only 94,000. A few hundred American students were attending a medical school on the island when, in 1983, an uprising led to the overthrow of the democratic government by Communist forces. Shortly thereafter, believing that the medical school students were in danger, President Reagan ordered U.S. troops to invade the island. The invasion force quickly defeated the Cuba-backed Communist defenders and restored democratic rule to the island. Opinion polls showed that most Americans were pleased to see U.S. troops win this localized war.

**Aid to El Salvador**   Throughout the 1980s the Central American nation of El Salvador was torn apart by civil war. Both sides—the government's army and the rebel forces—were guilty of killing innocent people. President Reagan was convinced that the rebels, if successful, would establish a Communist government in El Salvador. To prevent this, he urged Congress to vote millions of dollars in military aid for El Salvador's government. Despite more than $600 million in U.S. aid, the civil war continued. Tens of thousands died in the bloody conflict. Finally, in late 1991, UN negotiators persuaded both sides to agree to a cease-fire and peace settlement.

**Aid to the Nicaraguan "Contras"**   Meanwhile in nearby Nicaragua, U.S. aid was helping a rebel group to fight Nicaragua's Communist government. That government, which came to power in 1979, was known as the **Sandinistas**. The anti-Communist, anti-Sandinista forces were known as the **"contras."** In 1982 and 1983 President Reagan urged Congress to supply the "contras" with financial and military aid. Congress did so. In 1984, however, Congress granted only financial aid for the "contras" and rejected the president's request for military aid. In 1986 Reagan once again persuaded Congress to approve $160 million in military aid for the "contras."

   The civil war in Nicaragua ended in 1990 when the Sandinista government permitted a free election to be held. The Sandinistas lost the election and peacefully turned over the government to the winning party and its moderately conservative leader. The United States provided aid to the new government. The "contras" disbanded, returning to civilian life.

**The Iran-"Contra" Affair**   President Reagan did not expect the civil war in Nicaragua to end peacefully. Since Congress had refused to vote military aid for the "contras" in 1984, he had urged supporters of his policies to make private donations to the rebel cause. At the

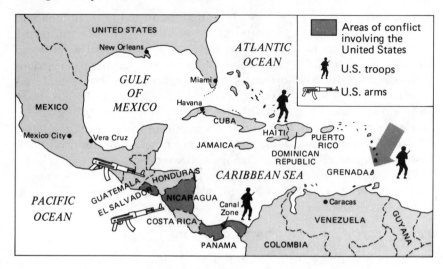

**U.S. interventions in Latin America in the 1980s and 1990s**

same time, in the Middle East, the president was having trouble freeing U.S. citizens who were being held hostage in Lebanon. What connection could there be between hostages in Lebanon and aid to the "contras" of Nicaragua?

In 1988 members of the press thought that they had found the missing connection. They discovered that U.S. officials had secretly arranged to sell weapons to Iran. This act alone violated a law of Congress banning the sale of U.S. weapons to that country. In addition, members of the press strongly suspected that the arms sale was made with the intention of winning the release of the American hostages in Lebanon. The press referred to this aspect of the affair as the "arms-for-hostages deal." Finally, money from the illegal sale of arms was secretly channeled to the "contras" of Nicaragua. This secret operation was carried out by a presidential aide and Marine lieutenant colonel, Oliver North. Investigating the **Iran-"Contra" Affair**, a congressional committee questioned Colonel North about his money-channeling operation. North testified that President Reagan knew nothing about his efforts to pass money from the Iranian arms sale to the "contras."

Although Colonel North's actions may not have been undertaken directly under orders by the president, some Americans compared the scandal to the Watergate Affair. Others believed that North had acted in the interests of his country.

**The Invasion of Panama** During his first year as president, George Bush decided to use U.S. troops to remove from power a Panamanian dictator named Manuel Noriega. Since coming to power in the late

1980s, Noriega had regularly violated the human rights of Panamanian citizens. He was also suspected of being involved in the smuggling of illegal drugs into the United States. Two U.S. grand juries indicted Noriega on drug trafficking charges. In December, 1989, President Bush decided to treat Noriega as an international outlaw. He ordered a surprise attack and invasion of Panama in order to (1) drive Noriega from power and (2) prevent the Panama Canal from falling under Noriega's control. The invading U.S. forces met little resistance. They captured Noriega and brought him to the United States for trial. Their task accomplished, most U.S. troops returned home.

The new government of Panama was friendly to the United States and received U.S. aid. Leaders of other Latin American countries, however, condemned the U.S. invasion as an act of aggression.

## D. CLINTON'S POLICIES IN LATIN AMERICA

The major problems confronted by President Clinton in Latin America occurred in Haiti, Cuba, and Mexico. There were attempts by many people from each country to enter the United States illegally. Their flight was caused by economic or political factors.

**Haiti**   In 1990 Father Jean-Bertrand Aristide was elected president of Haiti. Less than a year later, Aristide was ousted in a military coup and fled to the United States. In response to the illegal takeover, the United Nations imposed an oil and arms embargo on Haiti in 1993.

As political and economic conditions worsened in Haiti, the number of refugees trying to reach the United States soared. Some of them were returned to Haiti, others held in detention centers, and still others allowed to emigrate to welcoming countries.

In spite of the oil embargo, Haiti's military government continued to engage in violence and human rights violations. The military leaders refused to step down and return Aristide to office. As a result, in 1994 the UN authorized an invasion by a multinational force. With U.S. forces already on the way, the invasion was averted when the military leaders agreed to let Aristide resume office. As part of the agreement, thousands of U.S. troops were stationed in Haiti to restore order. Aristide returned and resumed office in October, 1994.

In 1995 U.S. forces were replaced by UN troops. However, a large number of U.S. troops remained as part of the international force.

**Cuba**   With the collapse of the Soviet Union in 1991 and the ongoing U.S. embargo on Cuban products, the Cuban economy was badly damaged. Fidel Castro resisted political and economic change, so thousands of Cubans left their homes and attempted to enter the United States illegally. As the exodus of "boat people" rose rapidly, the United States announced that Cuban refugees would be detained rather than being granted free entry, as in the past. As the exodus continued, the United States announced that it would now patrol the waters and intercept and turn back boats leaving Cuba. In 1994 a new U.S.–Cuba agreement ended the exodus and raised the yearly quota of Cubans allowed to enter the United States legally.

**Mexico**   Low wages and scarce jobs led many Mexicans to enter the United States illegally in search of a better life. There was also growing concern about the number of U.S. businesses moving production facilities to Mexico to take advantage of lower wages and weaker environmental rules there. In response, President Clinton completed negotiations begun by President Bush for the North American Free Trade Agreement (NAFTA) with Mexico and Canada. The agreement called for the three countries to gradually end tariffs on goods traded among them and thus create jobs and increase production. It was hoped that better economic conditions in Mexico would reduce illegal immigration to the United States.

In 1995 a crisis developed when the peso (the Mexican currency) steeply declined in value. With increased fear of inflation and unemployment in Mexico, President Clinton provided $20 billion to support the peso by guaranteeing the value of Mexican bonds.

## *In Review*

The following questions refer to section III: U.S. Policy in Africa and section IV: U.S. Policy in Latin America.

**1.** Identify *human rights, apartheid, Panama Canal treaties, Grenada, "contras," Iran-"Contra" Affair,* and *NAFTA*.

**2.** For *each* of the following countries, tell how it posed a challenge to U.S. foreign policy in the 1980s and 1990s. (*a*) South Africa, (*b*) Angola, (*c*) Haiti, (*d*) El Salvador, (*e*) Nicaragua, and (*f*) Panama.

# V. The Soviet Union and Eastern Europe

The most startling change in world affairs in recent years was the end of the cold war between the Soviet Union and the United States. During its final 15 years (1974 to 1989), the cold war went through three phases. First, Presidents Ford and Carter tried to improve U.S.–Soviet relations by continuing Nixon's policy of détente (the lessening of political tensions). Second, during Reagan's first term as president (1981 to 1985), relations between the superpowers once again became increasingly hostile. Third, after Mikhail Gorbachev came to power in the Soviet Union in 1985, he permitted the countries of Eastern

Europe to free themselves from Soviet control. In the Soviet Union as well as Eastern Europe, many aspects of communism were abandoned as unworkable. In effect, in 1989 and 1990, the Soviets more or less conceded that capitalism and Western-style democracies had their good points after all. They also began meeting with Presidents Reagan and Bush in a spirit of friendship and cooperation.

In greater detail, here is the history of the remarkable transition from cold-war hostilities to friendly relations.

## A. DÉTENTE AND DISARMAMENT

In Chapter 16 you read about President Nixon's efforts for détente with the Soviets. In 1972 he went to Moscow to meet with the Soviet leader, Leonid Brezhnev, and signed a treaty to limit the number of nuclear weapons in each country's arsenal.

**The SALT I Treaty (1972)** The first **Strategic Arms Limitation Talks Treaty (SALT I)** applied only to the future production of *defensive* nuclear missiles. Such missiles, which intercepted and destroyed attacking missiles, were known as antiballistic missiles, or ABMs. The United States and the Soviet Union agreed to set an upper limit on the number of ABMs that each would produce. Soviets and Americans alike hoped that this treaty would significantly reduce the risk of nuclear war. Now that defensive missiles were limited, there was less danger of one superpower's thinking that it could rely on its defense capabilities in order to defeat the other.

**Helsinki Accords** Another example of improved U.S.-Soviet relations in the mid-1970s was a diplomatic conference at Helsinki, the capital of Finland. Here the United States and the nations of Western Europe agreed to respect the Soviet sphere of influence in Eastern Europe. For their part, the Soviets and their Eastern European allies agreed to respect the human rights of their citizens, including the freedom to travel. In later years, however, the United States often accused the Soviet Union of violating the **Helsinki Accords** (1975) by deliberately preventing thousands of Soviet Jews from leaving the country.

**The SALT II Treaty (1979)** Meanwhile Soviet and American diplomats worked for years to devise a plan for limiting various *offensive*, or attacking, missiles. In 1979 President Carter and Soviet Premier Brezhnev signed a second strategic arms treaty, **SALT II.** It established a ceiling on the number of long-range offensive missiles that each superpower could produce. It also limited the number of cruise missiles (low-flying weapons) that could be launched from airplanes and submarines. Like the Washington Naval Conference of 1921 and the Kellogg-Briand Pact of 1928, the SALT agreements showed U.S. willingness to cooperate with other nations to reduce world tensions.

# B. RENEWAL OF THE COLD WAR

Many members of the U.S. Senate feared that the SALT II treaty left the Soviet Union with a military advantage. But the Senate never had a chance to vote either for or against SALT II. Early in 1980 President Carter withdrew the treaty from consideration after he received reports that Soviet troops had invaded Afghanistan.

**Soviet Invasion of Afghanistan** Afghanistan is a Muslim nation located on the Soviet Union's southern border. A rebellion broke out in Afghanistan in 1978 against the Soviet-backed Communist government. The Soviets invaded Afghanistan in December 1979 in an attempt to crush the rebellion. The movement of Soviet troops alarmed President Carter and his advisers, who feared that the Soviets might use Afghanistan as a base for seizing the oil fields in the Persian Gulf. To punish the Soviets for their aggression, Carter cut back the U.S. grain shipments to the Soviet Union. He also announced that U.S. athletes would not go to Moscow in 1980 to participate in the Summer Olympics there. In effect, because of the Soviet invasion of Afghanistan, the United States suspended its policy of détente.

**Arms Buildup under Reagan** Carter was especially disappointed in the Soviet Union because he had wanted détente to succeed. Ronald Reagan, on the other hand, had never believed that the Soviet Union could be trusted. In his 1980 campaign for the presidency, Reagan promised to increase military spending so that the United States could once again take the lead in the arms race. He kept his promise. In his first year in office, 1981, he asked Congress to approve huge increases in the defense budget for building new weapons systems. He wanted $1.5 trillion spent over a five-year period on new bombers, submarines, and missiles. While rejecting or trimming some of Reagan's program, Congress approved most of it.

The most ambitious and controversial of Reagan's proposals was to develop a "space shield"—the **Strategic Defense Initiative (SDI).** Critics of the idea thought it sounded like the popular movie *Star Wars*. The weapons, as conceived by defense experts, would orbit the earth and, from outer space, shoot down Soviet missiles before they could reach U.S. targets. Though skeptical about SDI's cost and practicality, Congress voted funds to explore the idea. Despite increased tensions, U.S.–Soviet relations generally improved. In 1993, the first defense budget of the Clinton administration cut off the SDI program after 10 years of development and an outlay of $30 billion.

# C. ECONOMIC DECLINE OF THE SOVIET UNION

While U.S. businesses prospered through most years of the 1980s, the Soviet economy was weakening. In fact, it was approaching a state of near collapse. More than any other factor, the weakness of the Soviet system for producing goods and services caused Soviet leaders to drop out of the arms race and abandon their cold war ambitions. Why did the Soviet economic system falter and fail? Three reasons are: lack of flexibility, lack of incentives, and too much emphasis on military goods.

**Lack of Flexibility** In a Communist system all important economic decisions are made by command, or direction, of the central government. Such a system is therefore called a **command economy**. The Soviet government in Moscow determined what products to produce,

CAUSE: Breakdown of the Soviet economy

EFFECTS

| End of Soviet control of Eastern Europe | | Reformed Soviet political system—glasnost |

| Arms control agreements with the United States | Reformed Soviet economic system—perestroika |

Cause and effects: Soviet economy and the cold war

what services to provide, and what prices to charge for goods and services. Usually, prices were unrelated to the cost of production. Nor did the price of a product, such as a TV set, reflect consumer demand. Government agencies might tell factories to produce too much of one product, too little of another. Rarely did they produce enough goods to satisfy consumer needs and wants.

**Lack of Incentives**   A second weakness in a command economy is that workers have little incentive to improve job performance. The government employs them and guarantees a certain wage, whether they work hard or not. The result is low productivity.

**Too Much Emphasis on Military Goods**   A nation has limited resources. If it uses them to produce guns, it cannot use them to produce butter. During the cold war, Soviet leaders spent much of their country's resources on producing military equipment and too little providing for people's basic needs for food, clothing, housing, and small luxuries—a new radio or a bar of soap. Consumers had to do without scarce products or wait in long lines at Soviet stores.

## D.  NEW POLICIES OF A NEW SOVIET LEADER

Leonid Brezhnev, the Soviet leader since 1964, died in 1982. He had presided over the slow decline of his country's economy. His first successor died after only 15 months in office; the second died after 13 months. In March, 1985, the Soviet Communist party selected as leader Mikhail Gorbachev. Relatively young and energetic, he recognized national problems and proposed sweeping reforms.

**Domestic Reforms**   Gorbachev wanted to reform and revitalize the Soviet system. First, he told the people to speak their minds openly about public issues and not to fear penalties. (In the past, critics of government policy were arrested and imprisoned.) Gorbachev's new policy was called **glasnost** (openness).

A second policy—for economic reform—was called **perestroika** (restructuring). Gorbachev encouraged local bureaucrats and factory managers to make their own decisions rather than take orders from the central government. He wanted more privately owned businesses that could decide how to produce goods and make profits. Perestroika was a move away from a command economy toward a mixture of private businesses and government welfare.

**Disarmament**   Gorbachev realized that the Soviet economy could not improve if a large percentage of the nation's resources went to its armed forces. He observed that, because of Reagan's arms buildup, the United States might soon be far ahead in the arms race. His country could no longer afford to strain its economic resources in an attempt to match U.S. armaments. Gorbachev was therefore eager to meet with U.S. leaders and reduce the costly and dangerous arms race. On three occasions he met with President Reagan to discuss arms control and other issues. At their third meeting in Washington, D.C. (December, 1987), the two leaders made a significant breakthrough by signing a treaty to reduce missiles in Europe. They were missiles of intermediate range that could travel hundreds of miles (compared with longer-range ICBMs that could cross oceans). The **Intermediate-range Nuclear Forces Treaty (INF Treaty)** went far beyond the SALT treaties. Instead of just limiting future production of weapons, the INF Treaty provided that all intermediate-range missiles in Europe be removed and dismantled. Gorbachev and Reagan established 1990 as the year when Europe would be completely free of intermediate-range nuclear weapons.

**Pulling out of Afghanistan**   The Soviet Union discovered that it had made a big mistake in invading Afghanistan. After years of fighting and much loss of life (more than 10,000 Soviets killed), Soviet troops had made virtually no gains in overcoming the tough rebel opposition. Afghanistan had turned into the "Russian Vietnam," as some called it. To relieve his country's failing economy, Gorbachev withdrew the last Soviet troops from Afghanistan in 1989.

**Collapse of the Iron Curtain**   Dramatic proof of the decline of communism occurred with amazing suddenness. For 42 years the nations of Eastern Europe had been under Communist rule. Whenever uprisings had occurred—in Hungary in 1956 and Czechoslovakia in 1968—Soviet tanks had moved in to crush them. In June, 1989, however, Poland held free elections, and the Communists lost. Since Gorbachev favored reform and openness, the Soviet Union accepted the result of the Polish election.

After that, one country after another in Eastern Europe followed Poland's example. The people of Hungary, Czechoslovakia, and Romania held mass demonstrations and demanded free elections and the end of Communist rule. In Romania, the long-time ruler, Nicolae Ceausescu, launched a bloody attack upon demonstrators, vowing to remain in power. Within days he was overthrown and executed. In most of Eastern Europe, the people voted to replace the Communist system with multiparty systems.

East Germany was the last country behind the "iron curtain" (under Communist and Soviet control). In 1989 Communist grip on power showed signs of weakening. In an effort to save itself, East Germany's government permitted East German citizens to travel freely to West Germany. In November, 1989, Germans on both sides of the Berlin Wall, a hated symbol of German division and the cold war, tore it down, and East Germans crossed directly into West Berlin. Soon, the West German government was accepted by East Germans as the government for all of Germany. The World War II allies—Great Britain,

France, the United States, and the Soviet Union—agreed to a reunited Germany, which became official in October, 1990. The government of the new Germany, meeting in Berlin, pledged never again to take military action against its European neighbors.

For the first time since the beginning of World War II, the nations of Eastern Europe were free from outside control. The "iron curtain" dividing Europe into two hostile camps had collapsed.

## E. END OF THE COLD WAR

George Bush began his presidency in 1989, the year that communism collapsed in Eastern Europe. Off the Mediterranean island of Malta, he and Gorbachev held their first summit. Most observers now believed that cold-war politics had passed into history. There were signs of a new world order. One was U.S. willingness to provide food and economic aid to the Soviet Union. Another was Soviet willingness to support U.S. policy against Iraq.

Besides the decline of communism and the dismantling of nuclear weapons systems in Europe, there was greater cooperation in the United Nations. During the cold war, the Security Council had usually been deadlocked by the rivalry between the superpowers. Now, the Security Council could pass important resolutions. In 1990, for example, it voted to condemn Iraq for its invasion of Kuwait. President Bush noted that the end of the cold war freed the United Nations to do its intended job—keeping the peace.

## F. COLLAPSE OF THE SOVIET UNION

In December, 1991, after months of turmoil, the Soviet Union ceased to exist. In its place were 15 independent republics, most of which joined a loose confederation called the Commonwealth of Independent States. How did this revolutionary change happen?

**Reasons for Collapse**  There were both economic and political reasons for the collapse of the former superpower:

1. *Economic failure.* Gorbachev had hoped that his reform policies of glasnost and perestroika would spur economic growth. Instead, the Soviet economy continued its rapid decline. Fewer goods reached the marketplace, and long lines formed for available goods. Critics called for an end to the old system.

2. *Yeltsin's rise to power.* Chief among those impatient with Gorbachev's policies was a radical reformer, Boris Yeltsin. In 1987 he broke with Gorbachev and resigned from the Communist party (then the only legal one). In 1990 Yeltsin and several other non-Communists were elected to the newly created Congress of People's Deputies. In 1991 Yeltsin was elected president of the Russian republic. His demands for reform and his openness made him a popular figure.

3. *The coup attempt that failed.* Increasingly, Gorbachev allied himself with conservatives in the Communist party. However, in August, 1991, these hard-liners tried to oust Gorbachev and seize control of the government. Their attempted coup (seizure of power) was quickly defeated when Moscow's citizens, led by Yeltsin, blocked the path of Soviet troops. The troops refused to attack the crowd. Those who plotted the coup were arrested. Yeltsin's decision to risk his life in fighting the coup leaders made him a national hero.

4. *Independence for the republics.* In 1991 all 15 republics in the Soviet Union demanded their independence. The first to succeed were the republics of Lithuania, Latvia, and Estonia, which had been taken over by the Soviet Union during World War II. Independence for the remaining republics became official on December 8, 1991, when the presidents of Russia, Ukraine, and Byelorussia (or Belarus) declared that the Soviet Union was "dead." They formed a new Commonwealth of Independent States, open to all republics. Shortly afterward, Gorbachev resigned as Soviet president.

**Effects on U.S. Foreign Policy** In a meeting at Camp David, Maryland, in February, 1992, President Bush and Boris Yeltsin, president of Russia, declared that the cold war had officially ended. The two leaders also agreed to make deep cuts in their arsenals of long-range nuclear weapons. Yeltsin assured the United States that nuclear missiles of the former Soviet Union would remain safely under central control. The United States joined other Western nations in pledging to give emergency aid to the struggling Russian economy. President Clinton continued to support Yeltsin, despite the following concerns:

- Russia's excessive use of force in subduing the Russian republic of Chechnya, which was attempting to become independent.
- Russia's opposition to the expansion of NATO, which would include countries in Eastern Europe.
- Russia's planned sale of nuclear reactors to Iran.

# G. BOSNIA

The major problem facing the Bush and Clinton administrations in Eastern Europe was the breakup of Yugoslavia and the ensuing civil war in Bosnia, one of its former republics. Bosnia consisted of three major ethno-religious groups—Bosnian Muslims, Serbian Orthodox Christians, and Croatian Roman Catholics. In 1991 Bosnia declared itself independent. The Serbs' opposition to this move led to a brutal civil war involving the three groups. Serbs killed thousands of Muslims and engaged in "ethnic cleansing" (expulsion of Muslims and non-Serbs from areas under Bosnian Serb control and from UN safe havens).

In 1994 Muslims and Croatian Christians in Bosnia agreed to create a Muslim-Croat confederation. Heavy Muslim-Serb fighting continued, with many civilian casualties. Bosnian Serbs controlled more than 70 percent of the country. They repeatedly rejected a U.S.-supported international peace plan that would give Serbs 49 percent of Bosnia and the Muslim-Croat confederation 51 percent. President Clinton called in vain for the arming of Bosnia's Muslims, military intervention by European allies, and NATO air strikes. He then decided to enforce the arms embargo against Bosnia that had been established by the major European powers. In addition, he supported an oil embargo against Serbia for supplying arms to Serbs in Bosnia.

In the United States, critics of the Bosnian crisis said that the nation had failed to live up to its role as world leader. Others warned that U.S. intervention would create a situation difficult to withdraw from.

## *In Review*

The following questions refer to section V: The Soviet Union and Eastern Europe.

1. Identify *SALT I, SALT II, Strategic Defense Initiative, INF Treaty, Mikhail Gorbachev, glasnost,* and *perestroika.*
2. Give *three* examples of how the policy of détente was carried out by U.S. presidents of the 1970s.
3. Explain why the policy of détente broke down after 1979.
4. Discuss the role of *each* of the following in bringing about an end to the cold war: (a) economics and (b) political leadership.

## GLOSSARY OF KEY TERMS: CHAPTER 19

**apartheid**   the policy of strict racial segregation enforced by the white minority government of South Africa against blacks and other racial groups.

**ayatollah**   the title of a Muslim scholar who has demonstrated advanced knowledge of Islamic law.

**command economy**   an economic system in which all major decisions concerning the economy are made by a central government.

**"contras"**   the rebel group that tried to overthrow the Sandinista (Communist) government of Nicaragua in the 1980s.

**General Agreement on Tariffs and Trade (GATT)**   an international organization whose member nations agree to keep tariffs low in order to promote world trade.

**glasnost**   Mikhail Gorbachev's policy of allowing greater freedom of speech and the press in the Soviet Union.

**Helsinki Accords**   an agreement signed by the United States, the Soviet Union, and other nations in 1975 declaring that they would respect the human rights of their citizens.

**hostages**   persons held in captivity either for ransom or, if politically motivated, for the purpose of putting pressure on a government to submit to the group's demands.

**human rights**   the right of the citizens of every nation to be treated fairly by their governments and to speak their political opinions freely and without fear of imprisonment, torture, or death.

**Intermediate-range Nuclear Forces Treaty (INF Treaty)**   a treaty of 1987 in which the United States and the Soviet Union agreed to remove and dismantle all intermediate-range nuclear missiles from Europe.

**Intifadah**   the uprising of Palestinian youths against continued Israeli control of territories occupied since the 1967 war.

**Iran-"Contra" Affair**   a political scandal involving the illegal sale of U.S. arms to Iran and the use of money from that sale to secretly aid the "contras" of Nicaragua.

**Panama Canal treaties**   two treaties of 1977 in which the United States agreed to turn over to Panama the ownership of both the Panama Canal and the Panama Canal Zone by the year 2000.

**Palestine Liberation Organization (PLO)**   an organization of Palestinian refugees who have employed terrorist methods in an effort to eliminate the State of Israel and establish a Palestinian nation.

**perestroika**   Mikhail Gorbachev's policy of trying to make the Soviet economy more productive by encouraging independent decision making by local industries as well as privately owned businesses.

**SALT I**   a strategic arms limitation treaty of 1972 in which the United States and the Soviet Union agreed to set an upper limit on the possession of defensive nuclear weapons.

**SALT II**   a strategic arms limitation treaty of 1979 in which the United States and Soviet Union agreed to set an upper limit on the possession of various types of offensive nuclear weapons; this treaty was never ratified by the U.S. Senate.

**Sandinistas**   the ruling group of Nicaragua that followed Communist policies in the 1980s and then lost power in free elections held in 1990.

**Strategic Defense Initiative (SDI)**   a defensive military system for using weapons in space to intercept and destroy an enemy's nuclear missiles.

**terrorism**   the use of violence against civilians and government officials as a means of bringing about political change.

**Tiananmen Square**   a public place in Beijing, China, where hundreds of Chinese demonstrators were killed by government forces in 1989.

**trade deficit**   the result of a nation's imports exceeding its exports in total value.

# TEST YOURSELF

## A. Multiple Choice: Facts, Main Ideas, Skills

*On a separate sheet of paper, write the number of the word or expression that, of those given, best completes the statement or answers the question.*

### Reviewing the facts

1. "Incidents such as the change of leadership in Iran in 1979 indicate that the United States had a serious foreign policy problem." This statement most likely refers to the idea that the United States (1) had supported pro-American leaders who failed to meet the needs of their people (2) had supported the pro-American leaders only verbally and not economically (3) had supported leaders who allowed too much pro-Communist activity (4) had failed to control the economies of these nations

2. The U.S. plan to turn over the Panama Canal to the Panamanians may be described as a victory of (1) free trade over protectionism (2) Panamanian nationalism over U.S. intervention (3) communism over capitalism (4) isolationism over nationalism

3. The use of U.S. military forces in Panama and Saudi Arabia in 1990 was legally justified by the (1) power of Congress to declare war (2) precedents established in the Nuremburg war crimes trials (3) provisions of the Monroe Doctrine (4) president's power as commander in chief

4. Apartheid is a policy of (1) mistreating Afrikaners (2) separating members of different races (3) favoring countries of the third world (4) improving U.S.–Soviet relations

5. Which event represented a major turning point in the cold war in the 1980s? (1) the election of Jimmy Carter as president (2) the outbreak of the Intifadah (3) the rise to power of Mikhail Gorbachev (4) the signing of the Panama Canal treaties

6. President Carter thought he could advance the cause of human rights by (1) threatening to use force against Cuba's dictatorship (2) intervening in the politics of Nicaragua (3) arranging summit meetings with the leaders of the Middle East (4) cutting off U.S. aid to dictatorial regimes

7. A major factor in bringing the cold war to an end was (1) the weakness of the Soviet economy (2) President Reagan's desire to reduce the defense budget (3) a revolution in Iran (4) terrorist acts of the PLO

8. Which of the following conflicts was *not* yet resolved by the year 1990? (1) the civil war in Nicaragua (2) the question of German reunification (3) the state of war between Egypt and Israel (4) Israel's conflict with Palestinians

## Reviewing the main ideas

**9.** Throughout the twentieth century the most important consideration in determining U.S. foreign policy has been (1) eliminating foreign investments in the United States (2) protecting the national self-interest (3) gaining new U.S. colonies overseas (4) keeping military expenses down

**10.** Which statement is the most valid conclusion based on a study of U.S. foreign policy? (1) The United States had no involvement in foreign affairs until the second half of the nineteenth century. (2) Historically, the president has exerted the most control in determining foreign policy. (3) The United States has consistently refused to intervene in the internal affairs of Central American countries. (4) The use of the armed forces to support U.S. foreign policy did not occur until 1917.

**11.** A major goal of U.S. foreign policy in the Middle East has been to bring about (1) a peaceful settlement of Arab–Israeli issues (2) an end to U.S. cooperation with Arab nations (3) ownership of oil resources by Western nations (4) permanent UN control of disputed territories

**12.** U.S. foreign policy toward nations in the Caribbean has generally been motivated by (1) social and humanitarian concerns (2) a desire to establish democratic governments in the area (3) economic and military defense concerns (4) a desire for noninvolvement

**13.** Which U.S. policy has been most frequently opposed by Latin American nations? (1) supporting the Organization of American States (2) sending military forces into Latin American nations (3) supporting international peace agencies (4) increasing imports from Latin American nations

**14.** An action most likely to reduce the U.S. trade deficit would be for the United States to increase its (1) foreign-aid programs (2) foreign investments and loans (3) exports (4) oil imports

**15.** "We live in a time when knowledge of world affairs is no longer simply nice to have or a luxury. It is essential to a nation's well-being." This quotation is based on a recognition of the crucial role in today's world of (1) terrorism (2) nativism (3) interdependence (4) assimilation

*Base your answers to questions 16 and 17 on the cartoon on page 603 and on your knowledge of U.S. history and government.*

**16.** This cartoon deals with U.S. foreign policy toward (1) Eastern Europe (2) the Far East (3) Latin America (4) Africa

**17.** The author of this cartoon suggests that the United States should (1) attempt to overthrow foreign governments (2) submit international disputes to the United Nations for binding arbitration (3) provide foreign nations with military aid (4) not interfere in the internal affairs of another nation

## B. Enduring Issues

*Select* two *of the enduring issues from column A. For* each *issue chosen, explain how the historical example in column B relates to the issue.*

| A. Enduring Issues | B. Historical Examples |
| --- | --- |
| 1. National power—limits and potential | The hostage crisis in Iran, 1979 to 1981 |
| 2. Presidential power in wartime and foreign affairs | President Bush's decision to order an air strike of Iraq |
| 3. Separation of powers and the capacity to govern | The SALT II Treaty was signed but not ratified. |

## C. Essays

### Level 1

Situations in world affairs have affected the interests of the United States. In the 1980s some of these international situations were:

    Expansion of Communist influence in Latin America
    Spread of international terrorism
    Tension in the Middle East
    Human rights violations in Africa

Choose *two* of the situations listed, and for *each* one chosen:

**1.** Identify *one* specific action or event related to the situation that has aroused U.S. concern.

**2.** Explain why the action or event has concerned the United States.

**3.** Discuss the response of the United States to the action or event.

*Level 2*

The actions of U.S. presidents in foreign policy have important results.

**A.** Listed below are four U.S. presidents and one foreign policy action taken by each.

| President | Action |
|-----------|--------|
| Richard Nixon | Opened relations with China |
| Jimmy Carter | Brought about a peace treaty between Egypt and Israel |
| Ronald Reagan | Signed the INF Treaty with the Soviet Union |
| George Bush | Sent U.S. troops into combat in Panama |

Choose *two* of these presidents. For *each* one, state briefly why the action was taken and state *one* result of the action.

**B.** Base your answer to part B on your answer to part A. Write an essay discussing the foreign policy action of *one* president you chose. In your essay state *one* reason for and *one* result of the president's action.

# APPENDIX

## How to Study for a Final Exam in U.S. History and Government

*The school year* is coming to an end, and your course in U.S. history is approaching its most challenging moment. In a short time you will face a final or standardized exam questioning you about presidents from George Washington to the current president, causes and consequences of wars from the American Revolution to Vietnam, and Supreme Court cases dealing with everything from slavery to abortion.

It's natural to panic and to think that you remember nothing if you can't, for example, instantly recall the policies of Zachary Taylor or the details of the Credit Mobilier scandal. Not to worry. Rarely do final exams in a high school course test for such detailed knowledge. Instead, educators who create tests covering a full year of study want to make sure that you have grasped the "big picture." Do you understand, for example, that the U.S. Constitution separates powers among three branches in order to protect citizens from possible abuses of power?

The test-taking tips that follow will help you to review history's main ideas and most significant facts. They will also provide strategies for answering multiple-choice and essay-type questions. After reviewing the highlights of the course and practicing test-taking strategies, you can go into the exam with confidence that you *do* know what happened between George Washington's time and your own. As a result you will be better prepared for your school or statewide examination.

# I. Developing a Test-Taking Strategy

In preparing for any test, it is important to assess (1) how much time remains between now and the test date and (2) the kind and amount of material that should be reviewed. Here is a formula for test-taking success:

**Long Period of Review (two weeks or more) + Organized Plan of Study = Strong Preparation and High Test Scores**

An opposite approach (overnight cramming and no organized plan of study) will almost certainly produce a negative result.

## A. HOW TO STUDY FOR THE FINAL EXAM

Instead of cramming your test preparation into one weekend, you'll have much greater success if you follow these guidelines:

- Separate the course of study into manageable units, limiting each night of study to no more than two chapters of material.

- Create a daily schedule for studying one unit at a time. Make sure this schedule allows you sufficient time to cover the full course before the exam date. (Consider, for example, the 14-day schedule suggested in section II below.)

- Before going to new material, allow about 15 minutes for reviewing what you had studied the night before.

- Study at times when you are alert rather than late at night when you may be tired and unable to concentrate.

- Study in a quiet place with few distractions. Avoid such diversions as talking on the phone or keeping one eye on a TV show and the other eye on your study notes.

## B. WHAT TO STUDY

When reviewing a text chapter or your class notes, always try to pick out the *main* idea, the *central* issue, the *key* term, and the *most important* historical person or event. Skip over small details because it is unlikely that these will appear on a final exam. Consider the difference between the items listed in columns A and B on the next page.

|              A              |              B              |
|-----------------------------|-----------------------------|
| Thomas Jefferson            | William Henry Harrison      |
| Andrew Jackson              | John Tyler                  |
| Franklin D. Roosevelt       | Chester A. Arthur           |
|                             |                             |
| federalist system          | bill of attainder           |
| due process of law          | writ of mandamus            |
| bill of rights              | Wilson-Gorman Tariff        |
|                             |                             |
| Monroe Doctrine             | Newlands Act                |
| "manifest destiny"          | Homestead Strike            |
| cold war                    | flappers                    |

The presidents, terms, and events in column A stand out as critically important to the history of the United States. Those in column B, although your textbook may mention them, are relatively minor. You can predict that questions *will* test your familiarity with most, if not all, of the items in column A.

How do you pick out from all the names and terms in a history text those that belong in the "most important" (most likely to be tested) column? To aid your study, the A-level names and terms are listed under each "aim" in the 14-day plan of study below.

# II. A 14-Day Plan for Reviewing U.S. History and Government

What follows is a method for linking your study to 14 learning objectives, or "aims." Allow one study session (about one to two hours) for reviewing the chapters and chapter sections relating to *each* aim question. There are 13 aims calling for review of historical content and one aim relating to basic skills (interpreting political cartoons, graphs, and maps). Therefore, the total study program could be completed in 14 days.

### Aim 1: How did the United States and its constitutional system come into being?

To achieve this aim, do the following:

- Review Chapter 1 of this text. Do not read the chapter word for word. Instead, scan its pages, noting the major headings and subheadings. If you can't remember anything about a heading, read a paragraph or two. Then continue scanning.

- Make sure that you know the meaning of the following key terms. First, try to define each term without looking it up. Then check your definition by turning to the Glossary at the end of Chapter 1.

| | | |
|---|---|---|
| democracy | Declaration of | federalism |
| limited government | Independence | Great Compromise |
| representative | Articles of | executive branch |
| government | Confederation | legislative branch |
| confederation | Bill of Rights | judicial branch |

- Review the multiple-choice questions for Chapter 1, especially those questions under Reviewing the Main Ideas.

- Study the diagram on page 16, and take notes on the sequence of great documents: Declaration of Independence—Articles of Confederation—Constitution—Bill of Rights.

### Aim 2: How does the U.S. Constitution divide power, and how can its rules be changed?

To accomplish this aim, do the following:

- Review Chapter 2, scanning its headings and subheadings.

- Make sure you know the following key terms. Try to define them first, and then look back at the Glossary at the end of Chapter 2.

| | |
|---|---|
| separation of powers | equal protection of the laws |
| checks and balances | due process of law |
| delegated powers | elastic clause |
| veto | electoral college |
| impeachment | lobbyist |
| unconstitutional | separation of church and state |
| ratification | |

- Review goals of the U.S. government given in the Preamble to the U.S. Constitution (pages 26–27).

- Review the main powers given to the president, Congress, and the Supreme Court.

- Identify some of the limits placed on the U.S. government, especially those in the Bill of Rights (Amendments 1 to 10).

- Identify amendments to the Constitution that have made our system of government more democratic.

- Be able to explain why the Supreme Court's power of judicial review has helped to make the Constitution a "living document."

- Understand the importance of Chief Justice John Marshall and two of the Marshall Court's decisions:

    *Marbury* v. *Madison*
    *McCulloch* v. *Maryland*

## Aim 3: How was the U.S. Constitution tested between 1789 and 1865?

To accomplish this aim, do the following:

- Review Chapters 3 and 4, scanning headings and subheadings.
- Make sure you understand the following terms. Try to define them first, and then look them up in the glossaries at the end of Chapters 3 and 4.

| | | |
|---|---|---|
| loose construction | Kansas–Nebraska Act | secession |
| strict construction | popular sovereignty | spoils system |
| neutrality | sectionalism | Compromise of |
| War of 1812 | nationalism | 1850 |
| Monroe Doctrine | Missouri | Gettysburg Address |
| abolitionist | Compromise | Emancipation |
| "manifest destiny" | nullification | Proclamation |

- Know the significance of one Supreme Court case: the Dred Scott case.
- Take *brief* notes on the accomplishments of the following American leaders. For each person, try to write no more than two to three phrases of identification.

| | | |
|---|---|---|
| George Washington | Abraham Lincoln | Harriet Tubman |
| Alexander Hamilton | Henry Clay | Harriet Beecher |
| Thomas Jefferson | John C. Calhoun | Stowe |
| James Madison | Elizabeth Cady | William Lloyd |
| Andrew Jackson | Stanton | Garrison |
| James K. Polk | Frederick Douglass | |

- For *each* president listed above (Washington to Lincoln), be able to give one decision or action that affected the American nation or the U.S. system of government—for example, Washington's decision to organize a cabinet and Jefferson's decision to purchase the Louisiana Territory.
- List the political issues and events that led to the Southern states' decision to secede from the Union in 1861.

## Aim 4: How were the civil liberties of African Americans gained during Reconstruction taken away in the years that followed?

To accomplish this aim, do the following:

- Review Chapter 5, scanning its headings and subheadings.

- Make sure you understand the following terms. Try to define them first, and then look them up in the Glossary at the end of Chapter 5.

| | | |
|---|---|---|
| Reconstruction | Freedmen's Bureau | Jim Crow laws |
| Radical Republicans | Ku Klux Klan | segregation |
| corruption | literacy test | separate but equal |
| disenfranchise | sharecropper | poll tax |

- Know what the Supreme Court decided in the case of *Plessy* v. *Ferguson* and why the case is important.

- Take brief notes (two to three phrases each) on the accomplishments of the following American leaders:

| | |
|---|---|
| Andrew Johnson | Booker T. Washington |
| Thaddeus Stevens | W.E.B. DuBois |

- Be familiar with the three post-Civil War amendments (the Thirteenth, Fourteenth, and Fifteenth Amendments).

- Compare the Reconstruction plan of Presidents Lincoln and Johnson with the Reconstruction plan of Congress.

- List the ways in which Southern states restricted the rights of African Americans after 1877.

## Aim 5: How did industrialization change U.S. society?

To accomplish this aim, do the following:

- Review Chapter 6, scanning its headings and subheadings.

- Make sure you understand the following terms. Try to define them first, and then look them up in the Glossary at the end of Chapter 6.

| | | |
|---|---|---|
| Industrial Revolution | monopoly | graduated income tax |
| corporation | Knights of Labor | primary election |
| capitalist system | American Federation of Labor | initiative |
| laissez-faire | Grangers | referendum |
| trust | Populist party | |

- Take brief notes (two or three phrases for each person) on the accomplishments of the following American leaders:

| | |
|---|---|
| Andrew Carnegie | Eugene V. Debs |
| John D. Rockefeller | William Jennings Bryan |
| Samuel Gompers | |

- Study the diagram on page 160, and take notes on the factors that encouraged industrial growth in the United States.

- Be able to explain the impact of industrialization on three groups: workers, farmers, and immigrants. (See Chapter 7 for the immigrant story.)

- Understand the impact of the Populist movement on U.S. politics and the political reforms of a later era.

## Aim 6: How did immigration and the settlement of the West change the United States?

To accomplish this aim, do the following:

- Review Chapter 7, scanning its headings and subheadings.

- Make sure you understand the following terms. Try to define them first, and then look them up in the Glossary at the end of Chapter 7.

| frontier | "new immigrants" | quota laws |
| homesteaders | assimilation | "melting pot" |
| reservation | nativism | cultural pluralism |
| Dawes Act | | |

- Be able to explain the impact of Western settlement on (1) U.S. society and (2) Native Americans.

- Be able to describe the changing pattern of immigration after 1880.

- Identify the factors that caused the United States to change from an open immigration policy to a quota system.

## Aim 7: What were the causes and effects of the United States becoming a world power after 1898?

To accomplish this aim, do the following:

- Review Chapter 9, scanning its headings and subheadings.

- Make sure you understand the following terms. Try to define them first, and then look them up in the Glossary at the end of Chapter 9.

| imperialism | intervention | Open Door policy |
| free trade | Roosevelt Corollary | "sphere of influence" |
| protectionism | dollar diplomacy | alliance |
| Platt Amendment | "watchful waiting" | |

- Take brief notes (two to three phrases per person) on the foreign policies of the following leaders:

William McKinley              Woodrow Wilson
Theodore Roosevelt           John Hay
William Howard Taft

- List the causes of the Spanish–American War. Make a separate list of the effects of that war on U.S. foreign policy.

- Give examples of U.S. involvement in Asian politics between 1900 and 1910.

- Give examples of U.S. involvement in Latin American politics between 1900 and 1920.

- Be able to explain U.S. imperialist policies in terms of the following: (a) economic self-interest and (b) national security.

## Aim 8: How was U.S. government changed by the reforms of the Progressive Era and the New Deal?

To accomplish this aim, do the following:

- Review Chapters 8 and 11, scanning the headings and subheadings.

- Make sure you understand the following terms:

| *From the early 1900s* | *From the 1930s* |
|---|---|
| Progressive Era | productivity |
| progressivism | Great Depression |
| suffragists | Great Crash |
| muckrakers | Bonus Army |
| conservation | New Deal |
| social justice movement | relief, recovery, and reform |
| "square deal" | Social Security system |
| New Freedom | Tennessee Valley Authority |
| Federal Reserve system | two-term tradition |
| "trustbusting" | "pack" the Court |
| NAACP | |

- Take brief notes (two to three phrases per person) on the reforms of the following:

Theodore Roosevelt    Franklin D. Roosevelt    Jane Addams
Woodrow Wilson        Susan B. Anthony         Eleanor Roosevelt

- Make three columns headed *T. Roosevelt*, *W. Wilson*, and *F. D. Roosevelt*, and list the major reform laws of these presidents. Limit each list by giving no more than five laws per president.

- Be able to explain the impact of the Great Depression on U.S. society and the need for increased governmental action.

- Give one action of President Franklin Roosevelt for achieving each of the three R's—relief, recovery, and reform.

- Study the diagram on page 327 showing the causes and effects of the Great Depression in 1929.

**Aim 9:  How did the United States become involved in two world wars?**

- Review Chapters 10 and 12, scanning the headings and sub-headings.

- Make sure you understand the following terms. Try to define them first, and then look them up in the Glossaries at the end of Chapters 10 and 12.

|          *From World War I*          |          *From World War II*          |
|---------------------------------------|----------------------------------------|
| dissenters                            | internationalists                      |
| "clear and present danger"            | aggression                             |
| Fourteen Points                       | Nazis                                  |
| self-determination                    | appeasement                            |
| League of Nations                     | cash-and-carry                         |
| Treaty of Versailles                  | Neutrality Acts                        |
| isolationism                          | "arsenal of democracy"                 |
| reparations                           | Atlantic Charter                       |
|                                       | United Nations                         |
|                                       | Yalta Conference                       |

- Know the significance of two Supreme Court cases involving civil liberties in wartime:

*Schenck* v. *United States*    *Korematsu* v. *United States*

- Summarize the changes in President Wilson's foreign policy toward Germany from 1914 to 1917. Then summarize President Franklin Roosevelt's foreign policy toward Germany and Japan between 1937 and 1941.

- Explain the role of isolationism in U.S. foreign policy *after* World War I (rejection of the League of Nations) and *before* World War II (the Neutrality Acts).

- Contrast U.S. involvement in foreign affairs after World War II to U.S. isolationism after World War I.

**Aim 10:  Have changes in U.S. society and domestic policy since World War II been for the better or the worse?**

- Review Chapters 14 and 15 and sections I and IV of Chapter 16.

- Make sure you understand the following terms. Try to define them first, and then look them up in the glossaries at the end of Chapters 14, 15, and 16.

| price controls | New Frontier | NOW |
|---|---|---|
| Fair Deal | War on Poverty | Equal Rights |
| McCarthyism | Civil Rights Act (1964) | Amendment (ERA) |
| civil disobedience | Great Society | stagflation |
| liberal | March on | Watergate Affair |
| conservative | Washington | "imperial |
| boycott | feminists | presidency" |
| migrant worker | discrimination | |

- Know the significance of each of the decisions in these Supreme Court cases:

    *Brown* v. *Board of Education*          *Engel* v. *Vitale*
      *of Topeka*                     *Abington School District* v.
    *Gideon* v. *Wainwright*              *Schempp*
    *Escobedo* v. *Illinois*              *Roe* v. *Wade*
    *Miranda* v. *Arizona*

- Compare the domestic policies of the following presidents: Truman, Eisenhower, Kennedy, L.B. Johnson, and Nixon.

- Take brief notes (two to three phrases per person) on the accomplishments of the following Americans:

| Jackie Robinson | James Meredith | Rachel Carson |
|---|---|---|
| Rosa Parks | Cesar Chavez | Ralph Nader |
| Martin Luther King, Jr. | Betty Friedan | |

- Evaluate the contributions of the following to redefining the rights of American citizens: (1) the civil rights movement, (2) the women's movement, (3) the Warren Court, and (4) the movement for the rights of people with disabilities.

- Be able to explain the influence on U.S. society of the following issues: (1) McCarthyism, (2) segregation, (3) Great Society programs, (4) rights of the accused, (5) U.S. involvement in the Vietnam War, and (6) the Watergate Affair.

## Aim 11: How did the United States respond to Soviet challenges between 1945 and 1975?

- Review Chapter 13 and sections I, II, and III of Chapter 16.

- Make sure you understand the following terms. Try to define them first, and then look them up in the glossaries at the end of Chapters 13 and 16.

|                |                 |                       |
|----------------|-----------------|-----------------------|
| ideology       | Truman Doctrine | Good Neighbor policy  |
| cold war       | Marshall Plan   | Cuban Missile Crisis  |
| communism      | NATO            | Tonkin Gulf Resolution|
| containment    | Berlin Wall     | War Powers Act        |
| "iron curtain" | space race      | détente               |

- Explain why the United States and the Soviet Union were cold war rivals.
- Give examples of crises and conflicts in the cold war to 1975. (See particularly the chart on page 404.)
- Explain the impact of the cold war on the powers of the U.S. presidency.
- Compare Lyndon Johnson's policies in Vietnam to Richard Nixon's Vietnam policies.

## Aim 12: In recent years, how have the nations of the world, including the United States, become interdependent?

To accomplish this aim, do the following:

- Review Chapter 17, scanning its headings and subheadings.
- Make sure you understand the following terms. Try to define them first, and then look them up in the Glossary at the end of Chapter 17.

|                          |                   |
|--------------------------|-------------------|
| postindustrial society   | greenhouse effect |
| information age          | developing nation |
| multinational corporation| third world       |

- Give examples of the changes that define the postindustrial society.
- Give examples of the ways in which the world has become interdependent.
- Study all the graphs in Chapter 17, and take notes on the trends that they illustrate.

## Aim 13: In our own times (1974 to the present), what changes have occurred in U.S. domestic and foreign policies?

To accomplish this aim, do the following:

- Review Chapters 18 and 19, scanning the major headings and subheadings.
- Make sure you understand the following terms. Try to define them first, and then look them up in the glossaries at the end of Chapters 18 and 19.

| supply-side economics | deregulation | "contras" |
| budget | national debt | SALT I and SALT II |
| deficit | trade deficit | INF Treaty |
| affirmative action | apartheid | terrorism |
| energy crisis | human rights | |

- Be able to discuss the changing status of women in U.S. society.
- Be able to discuss the status of ethnic minorities and the "new immigrants" in U.S. society.
- Give examples of conflicts in the Middle East, and know how the U.S. responded to each conflict.
- Evaluate U.S. interventions in Latin America in the 1980s.
- Study the chart on page 535 summarizing the domestic and foreign policies of Presidents Ford, Carter, Reagan, and Bush.
- Analyze the steps taken by the United States and the Soviet Union to avoid nuclear war (arms control agreement, détente, and summit conferences).

### Aim 14: How do political cartoons reflect some of the major issues of the twentieth century?

Reserve the last day of your test preparation for reviewing and practicing the skills of interpreting political cartoons, graphs, charts, and readings. You can anticipate that several multiple-choice questions in the final standardized exam will test one or more of these important skills.

To accomplish this aim, locate the political cartoons, graphs, and charts in Chapters 8 through 19 and examine them carefully. In the Test Yourself section of each chapter, complete the multiple-choice questions under Developing Critical Thinking Skills. Complete the questions in the Test Yourself sections that are based on specific readings.

# III. Tips for Answering Test Questions

Your final exam will probably include both multiple-choice questions and essay questions. Going into the exam, you should know certain techniques for dealing successfully with both kinds of questions.

## A. MULTIPLE-CHOICE QUESTIONS

Multiple-choice questions suggest four possible answers, only one of which is correct. How do you increase your chances of selecting the correct answer? Most important, of course, is how much you know about the subject. Even if you are well prepared, however, you can still make unnecessary mistakes by answering questions too hastily. For every question, *take enough time to consider all four choices before making your answer.* If you are not sure about your answer, put a mark next to the question. If there is time at the end of the exam, return to the marked questions and consider your choices a second time.

Also keep in mind the following tips for answering multiple-choice questions.

**1.** *The two-minute scan*   Take the first two minutes of exam time to scan, or look over, all the multiple-choice questions before answering any of them. If a question looks especially challenging, mark it in some way (perhaps with a TQ for "tough question"). You may wish to answer the easier questions first, then come back to the tougher ones.

**2.** *Spotting unlikely answers*   Even if you are not sure of the right answer to a question, you can improve your chances of making the right choice by eliminating choices that are unlikely to be right. Consider this question, for example:

> Which was a major result of the Civil War? (1) The power of the federal government was expanded. (2) States' rights were reinforced by constitutional amendments. (3) In the South, whites soon came to respect the equal rights of freed blacks. (4) Most freed blacks became landowning farmers.

Choice 2 is unlikely because the South had fought for states' rights, and the South lost the war. You know that choice 3 is most unlikely because of the well-known history of segregation in the South. Choice 4 is also unlikely, since most freed slaves became sharecroppers who did not own land. That leaves choice 1 as the answer most likely to be correct, which it is.

Some responses to multiple-choice questions make absolute statements that are unlikely to be true. Such choices contain words like "only" and "exclusively." For example:

> Which statement about U.S. involvement in the Vietnam War is accurate? (1) It came about only after a formal declaration of war. (2) It was based on the Open Door policy. (3) It was due exclusively to the actions of President Lyndon Johnson. (4) It reflected U.S. commitment to the policy of containment.

The words "only" in choice 1 and "exclusively" in choice 3 provide clues that these choices are unlikely to be correct. (The correct answer is choice 4.)

**3.** *Two names are easier than one*   The stem (beginning phrase) of a multiple-choice question may contain more than one name or term. This gives you an advantage because, if you know just one of the names or terms, you can confidently answer the question. For example:

> A major result of the Watergate and Iran-"Contra" Affairs is that they have (1) proven that politicians are loyal to political action groups (2) led to lower public confidence in public officials (3) shown that the media have no influence on public opinion (4) demonstrated that constitutional processes are not working

Suppose that you know only about the Watergate Affair, not the Iran-"Contra" Affair. You could still answer the question, knowing enough to select choice 2. You would make the same choice (and of course be equally correct) if you knew about the Iran-"Contra" Affair instead of Watergate.

**4.** *Key words*   You can expect that several multiple-choice questions will test for knowledge of key words or terms. For example:

> Which policy is an expression of economic nationalism? (1) foreign aid (2) protective tariff (3) free trade (4) laissez-faire

The key term in this question is "economic nationalism." You know that nationalism refers to a person's loyalty to his or her country. If you also know that a protective tariff is meant to protect a nation's businesses from foreign competition, you would then make the right choice (choice 2).

**5.** *Marking the standardized exam booklet*   When given to you at the beginning of the test, an exam booklet on a standardized test is your property. Unless you are specifically instructed not to do so, you may mark and make notes in the booklet. Cross out unlikely answers. Underline key words. Write notes to yourself in the margins. (If the examination is a schoolwide test, check first with the proctor before you mark the booklet.)

## B. ESSAY QUESTIONS

In most final or standardized exams (including those of New York State), one key to success in the essay sections is to consider the various choices of topics *before* you begin to write. A second and no less important test-taking principle is to make sure that you are fully carrying out the instructions in each question. If you take advantage of the following tips, you will very likely improve your essay-writing scores.

## Considering the Choices

**1.** *The five-minute scan*  Before writing anything, give yourself plenty of time—at least five minutes—to read all the essay questions. Circle or check those topics that you think you know fairly well. Recognize that you will have two kinds of choices to make: (1) You must choose between questions. (2) Within a question you may have a choice of topics relating to an overall issue or idea. For example, suppose you had two questions in a section of an exam dealing with U.S. government. These questions are presented below. The directions say that you must choose one of the two. What would be your choice?

*Answer one question from this part.* (15 points)

**1.** The United States has endured for 200 years in part because of its ability to adapt to changing times.

a. One way in which the Constitution can be changed is through the use of the formal amending process. Below is an excerpt from the Constitution as originally written.

SECTION 3. The Senate of the United States shall be composed of two Senators from each State, chosen by the Legislature thereof, for six Years; and each Senator shall have one Vote.

Discuss how this provision has been changed by amendment. Your discussion must include a clear description of the change and the reasons for the change. (5)

b. The Constitution has also been adapted to meet changing conditions through the use of the following methods:

● Judicial review
● Custom and usage
● Loose interpretation

Choose *two* of these methods. Discuss one way each method has been used to adapt the U.S. Constitution to meet changing conditions. In your response, describe the specific condition that required constitutional change, and describe the specific change that resulted. (5, 5)

**2.** At various periods in U.S. history, one of the three branches of the federal government has exercised particularly strong leadership.

*Branches/Periods*
Executive/1933–1945
Judicial/1800–1830
Legislative/1865–1877

a. Choose *two* of the branches listed above, and show how each branch exercised strong leadership during the time period indicated. Use specific historical examples to support your answer. (5, 5)

b. Some historians believe that since 1960 presidential power has grown at the expense of the other two branches. Discuss the extent to which this statement is valid. Refer to *two* specific examples since 1960 to support your position. (5)

*(From the New York State Regents Exams)*

**2.** *Analyzing your choices* When examining questions 1 and 2, you should select the question that will enable you to score the most points. Notice, first of all, that question 1(a) focuses on just one amendment. It calls for specific knowledge and offers no choices. The second part of the question, on the other hand, 1(b), is quite general and offers a choice of two out of three topics. Question 1 is a good choice for you if you know the change to which 1(a) refers (the change during the Progressive Era from state legislators electing U.S. senators to the voters electing them directly). Notice, also, that 1(a) is worth 5 points and 1(b) is worth 10 points. If you do not know 1(a) well, you will still have an opportunity to score up to 10 points on 1(b).

Would you do any better on question 2? The first part, 2(a), offers a choice of two out of three specific historical periods. You would have to know that 1933–1945 is the era of Franklin D. Roosevelt, that 1800–1830 is the era of Chief Justice John Marshall, and/or that 1865–1877 is the era of Reconstruction dominated by Congress. Know just two of these facts, and you have a good chance of scoring 10 points. The 5-point question that follows, 2(b), allows you to choose your own examples—only two required—for a long span of years, 1960 to the present. By picking the actions of any two presidents in modern times and linking those actions to the growth of presidential power, you have scored an additional 5 points.

Only you know which question is likely to yield the most points for you. But by thinking about your choices before writing, you can avoid an area of weakness and improve your chances of doing well.

**3.** *Jotting down ideas* Look again at the general question above, 2(b), that asks you to provide your own examples. How do you dig back into your memory to think of those examples? Just start writing something down on scrap paper or even right next to the question. First, write down the presidents since 1960 that you recall. Then select one you know well, such as Johnson. What did he do to demonstrate presidential power? Sending troops to Vietnam. *Or* initiating Great Society programs. Jot one idea down as a note to yourself:

*Sending troops to Vietnam*

Select another recent president—Reagan—and ask yourself again: What did this president do to demonstrate power? You might write:

*cutting back on domestic programs*

Examine your list of presidents since 1960 and see if you are aware of actions by other presidents that demonstrate presidential power. Then determine which two actions you know best.

### Following Directions

**4.** *From easy to hard*    Consider writing the required number of essay questions from the one you consider to be the easiest to the one that seems hardest. If you use this method, it is especially important that you identify each answer by numbering it clearly and completely.

**5.** *Doing all that is required*    If a question calls for *two* examples of something, give *two* examples (not one or three). Toward the end of the exam, check to see that the answers you have given match the directions.

**6.** *Putting the directions into your own words*    To make sure you know what is required by a question, put its directions into your own words. A question might read:

> Choose *three* of the developments listed. For *each* one chosen, describe the development that took place in the 1920s, and show how that development has had a continuing effect on U.S. society at any time since the 1920s.

You could tell yourself: "The question asks for three developments of the 1920s and their effects today. I'll start with the first development (automobile) and its effect today. Next, I'll describe the second development (radio) and its effect today. Finally, I'll describe the third development (woman's suffrage) and its effect today."

**7.** *Following the command words*    Be sure to observe the word of command that tells you how to handle a question. One question may direct you to "*identify*" topic X. Only a sentence or two is required to carry out this direction. Another question may direct you to "*describe*" topic Y. You can satisfy this direction by writing a paragraph that simply tells about the topic without offering any analysis or evaluation. A third question directs you to "*discuss*" topic Z. Here you must combine descriptive statements with statements of critical comment and argument—for example, whether you think Z had a positive or negative effect. A fourth question might ask you to "*show*" how X had an effect on Y. In this case you should cite a specific example that illustrates the given idea.

**8.** *Essays for a competency (level 2) exam*  The sample essay questions quoted above (pages 619–620) are from a challenging, higher-level type of exam. Here is an example of an essay question from a less demanding type of test:

> The United States is a nation of immigrants.
>
> **Part A**
> Identify *two* ethnic groups or nationalities who came to the United States in large numbers before 1900. State *two* reasons for immigrants coming to the United States.
> **Part B**
> Write an essay describing the reasons that the two immigrant groups identified in part A came to the United States.

Notice that this question is identical in form to the "level-2" essay questions at the end of every chapter of this book. In part A of the question, it is enough simply to make statements of fact. ("One reason that immigrants left their homelands was to escape conditions of poverty. A second reason was to escape harsh laws.") In part B of the question, you may use exactly the same facts as in part A—and other facts as well, if you wish. You could write one paragraph on reasons for immigrating and a second paragraph on problems of immigrants. In other words, in a level-2 essay, you should demonstrate the skill of (1) stating facts and (2) using those facts in a paragraph that develops an idea or topic.

**9.** *Checking your work*  If time remains after you have written your last essay, take every available minute to review your work—both your multiple-choice answers and your essays. Have you answered every question? Have you completely carried out every direction? Have you numbered your essays? Can you recall something now that you were unable to remember on your first try? In other words, take the time to fully review and improve your answers—and your final score.

# The Constitution of the United States of America

*Note:* Footnotes, headings, and explanations have been added to aid the reader. The explanations within the body of the text are enclosed in brackets [ ]. The parts of the Constitution that are no longer in effect are printed in *italic* type. Capitalization, spelling, and punctuation have been modernized.

## PREAMBLE

We the people of the United States, in order to form a more perfect Union, establish justice, insure domestic tranquility,[1] provide for the common defense, promote the general welfare, and secure the blessings of liberty to ourselves and our posterity [descendants], do ordain [issue] and establish this Constitution for the United States of America.

## ARTICLE I.  CONGRESS

**Section 1.  Legislative Power**  All legislative powers herein granted shall be vested in a Congress of the United States, which shall consist of a Senate and House of Representatives.

**Section 2.  House of Representatives**  [1] The House of Representatives shall be composed of members chosen every second year by the people of the several states, and the electors [voters] in each state shall have the qualifications requisite [required] for electors of the most numerous branch of the state legislature.

[2] No person shall be a representative who shall not have attained to [reached] the age of twenty-five years and been seven years a citizen of the United States, and who shall not, when elected, be an inhabitant of that state in which he shall be chosen.

---

[1]"Insure domestic tranquility" means *assure peace within the nation.*

[3] Representatives and direct taxes[1] shall be apportioned [divided] among the several states which may be included within this Union according to their respective numbers [population], *which shall be determined by adding to the whole number of free persons, including those bound to service for a term of years* [indentured servants], *and excluding Indians not taxed, three-fifths of all other persons.*[2] The actual enumeration [census] shall be made within three years after the first meeting of the Congress of the United States, and within every subsequent term of ten years, in such manner as they shall by law direct. The number of representatives shall not exceed one for every thirty thousand, but each state shall have at least one representative; *and until such enumeration shall be made, the State of New Hampshire shall be entitled to choose three, Massachusetts eight, Rhode Island and Providence Plantations one, Connecticut five, New York six, New Jersey four, Pennsylvania eight, Delaware one, Maryland six, Virginia ten, North Carolina five, South Carolina five, and Georgia three.*[3]

[4] When vacancies happen in the representation from any state, the executive authority [governor] thereof shall issue writs of election[4] to fill such vacancies.

[5] The House of Representatives shall choose their Speaker and other officers; and shall have the sole power of impeachment.[5]

**Section 3.   Senate**   [1] The Senate of the United States shall be composed of two senators from each state, *chosen by the legislature thereof,*[6] for six years; and each senator shall have one vote.

[2] *Immediately after they shall be assembled in consequence of the first election, they shall be divided as equally as may be into three classes. The seats of the senators of the first class shall be vacated at the expiration of the second year, of the second class at the expiration of the fourth year, and of the third class at the expiration of the sixth year,*[7] so that one-third may be chosen every second year; *and if vacancies happen by resignation, or otherwise, during the recess of the legislature of any state,*

---

[1] Modified by Amendment XVI, which granted Congress the power to levy a direct tax on individual incomes rather than on the basis of state populations.

[2] "Other persons" refers to slaves. Amendment XIII abolished slavery; Amendment XIV specifically eliminated the three-fifths formula.

[3] Temporary provision.

[4] "Issue writs of election" means *call a special election.*

[5] "Power of impeachment" means *right to charge federal officials with misconduct.*

[6] Replaced by Amendment XVII, which provided for popular election of senators.

[7] Temporary provision, designed to organize the first Senate in such a way that, thereafter, only one-third of its members would be subject to replacement at each successive election.

*the executive* [governor] *thereof may make temporary appointments until the next meeting of the legislature, which shall then fill such vacancies.*[1]

[3] No person shall be a senator who shall not have attained to the age of thirty years and been nine years a citizen of the United States, and who shall not, when elected, be an inhabitant of that state for which he shall be chosen.

[4] The vice president of the United States shall be president of the Senate, but shall have no vote, unless they be equally divided [tied].

[5] The Senate shall choose their other officers, and also a president pro tempore [temporary presiding officer], in the absence of the vice president, or when he shall exercise the office of president of the United States.

[6] The Senate shall have sole power to try all impeachments.[2] When sitting for that purpose, they shall be on oath or affirmation.[3] When the president of the United States is tried, the chief justice [of the United States] shall preside; and no person shall be convicted without the concurrence [agreement] of two-thirds of the members present.

[7] Judgment in cases of impeachment shall not extend further than to removal from office, and disqualification to hold and enjoy any office of honor, trust, or profit under the United States; but the party convicted shall nevertheless be liable and subject to indictment, trial, judgment, and punishment, according to law.

**Section 4.    Elections and Meetings of Congress**  [1] The times, places, and manner of holding elections for senators and representatives shall be prescribed [designated] in each state by the legislature thereof; but the Congress may at any time by law make or alter such regulations, except as to the places of choosing senators.

[2] The Congress shall assemble at least once in every year, *and such meeting shall be on the first Monday in December,*[4] unless they shall by law appoint a different day.

**Section 5.    Rules and Procedures of the Two Houses**  [1] Each house shall be the judge of the elections, returns, and qualifications of its own

---

[1]Modified by Amendment XVII, which permits a governor to select a temporary replacement to fill the vacancy until the next election.

[2]"To try all impeachments" means *to conduct the trials of officials impeached by the House of Representatives.* When trying such cases, the Senate serves as a court.

[3]If taking an oath violates a member's religious principles, that person may "affirm" rather than "swear."

[4]Amendment XX changed this date to January 3.

members,[1] and a majority of each shall constitute a quorum[2] to do business; but a smaller number may adjourn from day to day, and may be authorized to compel the attendance of absent members, in such manner, and under such penalties, as each house may provide.

[2] Each house may determine the rules of its proceedings, punish its members for disorderly behavior, and with the concurrence of two-thirds, expel a member.

[3] Each house shall keep a journal [record] of its proceedings, and from time to time publish the same, excepting such parts as may in their judgment require secrecy; and the yeas [affirmative votes] and nays [negative votes] of the members of either house on any question shall, at the desire of one-fifth of those present, be entered on the journal.

[4] Neither house, during the session of Congress, shall, without the consent of the other, adjourn for more than three days, nor to any other place than that in which the two houses shall be sitting.

**Section 6.  Members' Privileges and Restrictions** [1] The senators and representatives shall receive a compensation [salary] for their services, to be ascertained [fixed] by law and paid out of the treasury of the United States. They shall in all cases except treason, felony [serious crime], and breach of the peace [disorderly conduct], be privileged [immune] from arrest during their attendance at the session of their respective houses, and in going to and returning from the same; and for any speech or debate in either house, they shall not be questioned in any other place.[3]

[2] No senator or representative shall, during the time for which he was elected, be appointed to any civil office under the authority of the United States, which shall have been created, or the emoluments [salary] whereof shall have been increased, during such time; and no person holding any office under the United States shall be a member of either house during his continuance in office.

**Section 7.  Lawmaking Procedures** [1] All bills for raising revenue shall originate [be introduced] in the House of Representatives; but the Senate may propose or concur with [approve] amendments as on other bills.

[2] Every bill which shall have passed the House of Representatives and the Senate shall, before it becomes a law, be presented to the president of the United States; if he approve, he shall sign it, but if not, he shall return it, with his objections, to that house in which it shall have originated, who shall enter the objections at large on their journal, and proceed to reconsider it. If after such reconsideration two-thirds of

[1]This provision empowers either house, by a majority vote, to refuse to seat a newly elected member.

[2]A "quorum" is the *number of members that must be present in order to conduct business*.

[3]"They shall not be questioned in any other place" means that *they may not be sued for slander or libel*. Freedom from arrest during congressional sessions and freedom of speech within the halls of Congress—two privileges granted to members of Congress—are known as *congressional immunity*.

that house shall agree to pass the bill, it shall be sent, together with the objections, to the other house, by which it shall likewise be reconsidered, and, if approved by two-thirds of that house, it shall become a law. But in all such cases the votes of both houses shall be determined by yeas and nays, and the names of the persons voting for and against the bill shall be entered on the journal of each house respectively. If any bill shall not be returned by the president within ten days (Sundays excepted) after it shall have been presented to him, the same shall be a law, in like manner as if he had signed it, unless the Congress by their adjournment prevent its return, in which case it shall not be a law.[1]

[3] Every order, resolution, or vote to which the concurrence of the Senate and House of Representatives may be necessary (except on a question of adjournment) shall be presented to the president of the United States; and before the same shall take effect, shall be approved by him, or, being disapproved by him, shall be repassed by two-thirds of the Senate and House of Representatives, according to the rules and limitations prescribed in the case of a bill.

**Section 8. Powers of Congress** The Congress shall have power:

[1] To lay and collect taxes, duties, imposts, and excises,[2] to pay the debts and provide for the common defense and general welfare of the United States; but all duties, imposts, and excises shall be uniform [the same] throughout the United States;

[2] To borrow money on the credit of the United States;

[3] To regulate commerce with foreign nations, and among the several states, and with the Indian tribes;

[4] To establish a uniform rule of naturalization [admitting to citizenship], and uniform laws on the subject of bankruptcies throughout the United States;

[5] To coin money, regulate the value thereof, and of foreign coin, and fix [set] the standard of weights and measures;

[6] To provide for the punishment of counterfeiting[3] the securities and current coin of the United States;

[7] To establish post offices and post roads;

[8] To promote the progress of science and useful arts by securing for limited times to authors and inventors the exclusive right to their respective writings and discoveries;[4]

[9] To constitute tribunals [establish courts] inferior to [lower than] the Supreme Court;

[1]If Congress adjourns before the ten-day period is up, the president can kill a bill by ignoring it ("putting it in his pocket"). Therefore, this type of presidential rejection is called a *pocket veto*.

[2]"Duties, imposts, and excises" are forms of taxation. Duties and imposts are taxes on imports. Excises are taxes on goods produced or services performed within a country.

[3]Making an imitation with the intent of passing it as the genuine article.

[4]Copyright and patent laws, passed by Congress on the basis of this clause, protect the rights of authors and inventors.

[10] To define and punish piracies and felonies committed on the high seas[1] and offenses against the law of nations [international law];

[11] To declare war, grant letters of marque and reprisal,[2] and make rules concerning captures on land and water;

[12] To raise and support armies, but no appropriation of money to that use shall be for a longer term than two years;

[13] To provide and maintain a navy;

[14] To make rules for the government and regulation of the land and naval forces;

[15] To provide for calling forth the militia[3] to execute [carry out] the laws of the Union, suppress [put down] insurrections [rebellions], and repel [drive back] invasions;

[16] To provide for organizing, arming, and disciplining [training] the militia, and for governing such part of them as may be employed in the service of the United States, reserving to the states respectively the appointment of the officers, and the authority of training the militia according to the discipline [regulations] prescribed by Congress;

[17] To exercise exclusive legislation[4] in all cases whatsoever, over such district (not exceeding ten miles square) as may, by cession of particular states, and the acceptance of Congress, become the seat of government of the United States, and to exercise like authority over all places purchased by the consent of the legislature of the state in which the same shall be, for the erection of forts, magazines, arsenals, dockyards, and other needful buildings; and

[18] To make all laws which shall be necessary and proper for carrying into execution the foregoing powers and all other powers vested by this Constitution in the government of the United States, or in any department or officer thereof.[5]

**Section 9. Powers Denied to the Federal Government** [1] *The migration or importation of such persons as any of the states now existing shall think proper to admit shall not be prohibited by the Congress prior to the year 1808; but a tax or duty may be imposed on such importation, not exceeding ten dollars for each person.*[6]

[1]Open ocean; waters outside the territorial limits of a country.

[2]Letters of marque and reprisal are government licenses issued to private citizens in time of war authorizing them to fit out armed vessels (called *privateers*) for the purpose of capturing or destroying enemy ships.

[3]Citizen soldiers who are not in the regular armed forces but are subject to military duty in times of emergency; for example, the National Guard.

[4]"To exercise exclusive legislation ... over such district" means *to be solely responsible for making the laws for a designated area.*

[5]This is the so-called "elastic clause" of the Constitution, which allows Congress to carry out many actions not specifically listed.

[6]This temporary provision prohibited Congress from interfering with the importation of slaves ("such persons") before 1808.

[2] The privilege of the writ of habeas corpus[1] shall not be suspended, unless when in cases of rebellion or invasion the public safety may require it.

[3] No bill of attainder[2] or ex post facto law[3] shall be passed.

[4] No capitation [head] or other direct tax shall be laid, unless in proportion to the census or enumeration herein before directed to be taken.[4]

[5] No tax or duty shall be laid on articles exported from any state.

[6] No preference shall be given by any regulation of commerce or revenue to the ports of one state over those of another; nor shall vessels bound to, or from, one state be obliged to enter, clear, or pay duties in another.

[7] No money shall be drawn from the treasury, but in consequence of appropriations made by law; and a regular statement and account of the receipts and expenditures of all public money shall be published from time to time.

[8] No title of nobility shall be granted by the United States; and no person holding any office of profit or trust under them shall, without the consent of the Congress, accept of any present, emolument, office, or title, of any kind whatever, from any king, prince, or foreign state.

**Section 10.   Powers Denied to the States**  [1] No state shall enter into any treaty, alliance, or confederation; grant letters of marque and reprisal; coin money; emit bills of credit;[5] make anything but gold and silver coin a tender [legal money] in payment of debts; pass any bill of attainder, ex post facto law, or law impairing the obligation of contracts,[6] or grant any title of nobility.

[2] No state shall, without the consent of the Congress, lay any imposts or duties on imports or exports, except what may be absolutely necessary for executing its inspection laws; and the net produce [income] of all duties and imposts, laid by any state on imports or exports, shall be for the use of the treasury of the United States; and all such laws shall be subject to the revision and control of the Congress.

[3] No state shall, without the consent of Congress, lay any duty of

---

[1] A "writ of habeas corpus" is a court order obtained by a person taken into custody, demanding to know the reasons for imprisonment. If the court rules that the reasons are insufficient, the prisoner is released.

[2] A law that deprives a person of civil rights without a trial.

[3] A law that punishes a person for a past action that was not unlawful at the time it was committed.

[4] Modified by Amendment XVI.

[5] "Emit bills of credit" means *issue paper money.*

[6] "Impairing the obligation of contracts" means *weakening the obligations persons assume when they enter into legal agreements.*

tonnage,[1] keep troops[2] or ships of war in time of peace, enter into any agreement or compact with another state or with a foreign power, or engage in war unless actually invaded or in such imminent [threatening] danger as will not admit of delay.

## ARTICLE II.  THE PRESIDENCY

**Section 1.  Executive Power**  [1] The executive power shall be vested in a president of the United States of America. He shall hold his office during the term of four years,[3] and, together with the vice president, chosen for the same term, be elected as follows:

[2] Each state shall appoint, in such manner as the legislature thereof may direct, a number of electors, equal to the whole number of senators and representatives to which the state may be entitled in the Congress; but no senator or representative, or person holding an office of trust or profit under the United States, shall be appointed an elector.

[3] *The electors shall meet in their respective states, and vote by ballot for two persons, of whom one at least shall not be an inhabitant of the same state with themselves. And they shall make a list of all the persons voted for, and of the number of votes for each; which list they shall sign and certify, and transmit sealed to the seat of the government of the United States, directed to the president of the Senate. The president of the Senate shall, in the presence of the Senate and House of Representatives, open all the certificates, and the votes shall then be counted. The person having the greatest number of votes shall be the president, if such number be a majority of the whole number of electors appointed; and if there be more than one who have such majority, and have an equal number of votes, then the House of Representatives shall immediately choose by ballot one of them for president; and if no person have a majority, then from the five highest on the list the said House shall in like manner choose the president. But in choosing the president, the votes shall be taken by states, the representation from each state having one vote; a quorum for this purpose shall consist of a member or members from two-thirds of the states, and a majority of all the states shall be necessary to a choice. In every case, after the choice of the president, the person having the greatest number of votes of the electors shall be the vice president. But if there should remain two or more who have equal votes, the Senate shall choose from them by ballot the vice president.[4]*

[4] The Congress may determine the time of choosing the electors, and the day on which they shall give their votes; which day shall be the same throughout the United States.

---

[1] "Duty of tonnage" means a *tax based upon a vessel's cargo-carrying capacity.*

[2] Other than militia.

[3] Amendment XXII limits a president to two terms.

[4] Replaced by Amendment XII.

[5] No person except a natural-born citizen, *or a citizen of the United States at the time of the adoption of this Constitution*,[1] shall be eligible to the office of president; neither shall any person be eligible to that office who shall not have attained to the age of thirty-five years and been fourteen years a resident within the United States.

[6] In case of the removal of the president from office, or of his death, resignation, or inability to discharge the powers and duties of the said office, the same shall devolve on the vice president, and the Congress may by law provide for the case of removal, death, resignation, or inability, both of the president and vice president, declaring what officer shall then act as president, and such officer shall act accordingly, until the disability be removed, or a president shall be elected.[2]

[7] The president shall, at stated times, receive for his services a compensation, which shall neither be increased nor diminished [decreased] during the period for which he shall have been elected, and he shall not receive within that period any other emolument from the United States, or any of them.

[8] Before he enter on the execution of his office, he shall take the following oath or affirmation:

"I do solemnly swear (or affirm) that I will faithfully execute the office of President of the United States, and will, to the best of my ability, preserve, protect, and defend the Constitution of the United States."

**Section 2.  Powers of the President**  [1] The president shall be commander in chief of the army and navy [all the armed forces] of the United States, and of the militia of the several states, when called into the actual service of the United States; he may require the opinion in writing of the principal officer in each of the executive departments upon any subject relating to the duties of their respective offices; and he shall have power to grant reprieves[3] and pardons[4] for offenses against the United States except in cases of impeachment.

[2] He shall have power, by and with the advice and consent of the Senate, to make treaties, provided two-thirds of the senators present concur; and he shall nominate, and, by and with the advice and consent of the Senate, shall appoint ambassadors, other public ministers and consuls, judges of the Supreme Court, and all other officers of the United States whose appointments are not herein otherwise provided for and which shall be established by law; but the Congress may by law vest the appointment of such inferior officers as they think proper in the president alone, in the courts of law, or in the heads of departments.

[3] The president shall have power to fill up all vacancies that may

---

[1]Temporary provision.

[2]Modified by Amendments XX and XXV.

[3]A "reprieve" is a postponement of the execution of a sentence.

[4]A "pardon" is a release from penalty.

happen during the recess of the Senate, by granting commissions which shall expire at the end of their next session.

**Section 3.   Duties and Responsibilities of the President**  He shall, from time to time, give to the Congress information of the state of the Union, and recommend to their consideration such measures as he shall judge necessary and expedient [advisable]; he may, on extraordinary [special] occasions, convene both houses, or either of them, and in case of disagreement between them with respect to the time of adjournment, he may adjourn them to such time as he shall think proper; he shall receive ambassadors and other public ministers; he shall take care that the laws be faithfully executed, and shall commission [appoint] all the officers of the United States.

**Section 4.   Impeachment**  The president, vice president, and all civil officers[1] of the United States, shall be removed from office on impeachment for, and conviction of, treason, bribery, or other high crimes and misdemeanors [offenses].

# ARTICLE III.   THE SUPREME COURT AND OTHER COURTS

**Section 1.   Federal Courts**  The judicial power of the United States shall be vested in one Supreme Court, and in such inferior [lower] courts as the Congress may from time to time ordain and establish. The judges, both of the Supreme and inferior courts, shall hold their offices during good behavior, and shall, at stated times, receive for their services a compensation, which shall not be diminished during their continuance in office.

**Section 2.   Jurisdiction of Federal Courts**  [1] The judicial power shall extend to all cases in law and equity[2] arising under this Constitution, the laws of the United States, and treaties made, or which shall be made, under their authority; to all cases affecting ambassadors, other public ministers, and consuls; to all cases of admiralty and maritime jurisdiction;[3] to controversies [disputes] to which the United States shall be a party; to controversies between two or more states, between a state and citizens of another state,[4] between citizens of different states, between citizens

---

[1] "Civil officers" include executive and judicial officials, but not members of Congress or officers in the armed forces.

[2] "Cases in law" refers mainly to disputes that arise from the violation of, or the interpretation of, federal laws, treaties, or the Constitution. "Equity" is a branch of the law that deals more generally with the prevention of injustice.

[3] Legal disputes involving ships and shipping on the high seas, in territorial waters, and on the navigable waterways within the country.

[4] Modified by Amendment XI, which provides that a state may not be sued in the federal courts by a citizen of another state (or by a citizen of a foreign country). A state, however, retains the right to sue a citizen of another state (or a citizen of a foreign country) in the federal courts.

of the same state claiming lands under grants of different states, and between a state, or the citizens thereof, and foreign states, citizens, or subjects.[1]

[2] In all cases affecting ambassadors, other public ministers, and consuls, and those in which a state shall be a party, the Supreme Court shall have original jurisdiction.[2] In all the other cases before mentioned, the Supreme Court shall have appellate jurisdiction,[3] both as to law and fact, with such exceptions and under such regulations as the Congress shall make.

[3] The trial of all crimes, except in cases of impeachment, shall be by jury; and such trial shall be held in the state where the said crimes shall have been committed; but when not committed within any state, the trial shall be at such place or places as the Congress may by law have directed.

**Section 3.   Treason** [1] Treason against the United States shall consist only in levying [carrying on] war against them, or in adhering to [assisting] their enemies, giving them aid and comfort. No person shall be convicted of treason unless on the testimony of two witnesses to the same overt [open; public] act, or on confession in open court.

[2] The Congress shall have power to declare the punishment of treason, but no attainder of treason shall work corruption of blood or forfeiture except during the life of the person attainted.[4]

# ARTICLE IV.   INTERSTATE RELATIONS

**Section 1.   Official Acts and Records**   Full faith and credit shall be given in each state to the public acts, records, and judicial proceedings of every other state.[5] And the Congress may, by general laws, prescribe the manner in which such acts, records, and proceedings shall be proved, and the effect thereof.

**Section 2.   Mutual Obligations of States**   [1] The citizens of each state shall be entitled to all privileges and immunities of citizens in the several states.

[2] A person charged in any state with treason, felony, or other crime, who shall flee from justice and be found in another state, shall, on

---

[1]Modified by Amendment XI.

[2]"Original jurisdiction" means the authority of a court to hear cases that have not previously been tried by lower courts.

[3]"Appellate jurisdiction" means the authority of a court to review cases that have previously been tried by lower courts.

[4]Punishment imposed on someone for treason may not be extended to that person's children or heirs.

[5]The official acts of each state must be accepted by the other states. The "full faith and credit" clause applies to court judgments, contracts, marriages, corporation charters, etc.

demand of the executive authority of the state from which he fled, be delivered up, to be removed to the state having jurisdiction of the crime.[1]

[3] *No person held to service or labor in one state, under the laws thereof, escaping into another, shall, in consequence of any law or regulation therein, be discharged from such service or labor, but shall be delivered up on claim of the party to whom such service or labor may be due.*[2]

**Section 3.    New States and Territories**  [1] New states may be admitted by the Congress into this Union; but no new state shall be formed or erected within the jurisdiction of any other state; nor any state be formed by the junction [joining] of two or more states, or parts of states, without the consent of the legislatures of the states concerned as well as of the Congress.

[2] The Congress shall have power to dispose of and make all needful rules and regulations respecting the territory or other property belonging to the United States; and nothing in this Constitution shall be so construed [interpreted] as to prejudice [damage] any claims of the United States, or of any particular state.

**Section 4.    Federal Guarantees to the States**  The United States shall guarantee to every state in this Union a republican form of government, and shall protect each of them against invasion; and on application of the legislature, or of the executive (when the legislature cannot be convened), against domestic violence [riots].

# ARTICLE V.    AMENDING THE CONSTITUTION

The Congress, whenever two-thirds of both houses shall deem [think] it necessary, shall propose amendments to this Constitution, or, on the application of the legislatures of two-thirds of the several states, shall call a convention for proposing amendments, which, in either case, shall be valid, to all intents and purposes, as part of this Constitution when ratified by the legislatures of three-fourths of the several states, or by conventions in three-fourths thereof, as the one or the other mode [method] of ratification may be proposed by the Congress; provided *that no amendment which may be made prior to the year 1808 shall in any manner affect the first and fourth clauses in the ninth section of the first article; and*[3] that no state, without its consent, shall be deprived of its equal suffrage in the Senate.

# ARTICLE VI.    MISCELLANEOUS PROVISIONS

**Section 1.    Public Debts**  All debts contracted and engagements [agreements] entered into before the adoption of this Constitution shall be as

[1]The delivery by one state or government to another of fugitives from justice is called *extradition*.

[2]Since the phrase "person held to service or labor" refers to a slave, this clause was nullified by Amendment XIII.

[3]Temporary provision.

valid [binding] against the United States under this Constitution as under the Confederation.

**Section 2.  Federal Supremacy**  This Constitution, and the laws of the United States which shall be made in pursuance thereof, and all treaties made, or which shall be made, under the authority of the United States, shall be the supreme law of the land; and the judges in every state shall be bound thereby, anything in the constitution or laws of any state to the contrary notwithstanding.[1]

**Section 3.  Oaths of Office**  The senators and representatives before mentioned, and the members of the several state legislatures, and all executive and judicial officers, both of the United States and of the several states, shall be bound by oath or affirmation to support this Constitution; but no religious test shall ever be required as a qualification to any office or public trust under the United States.

## ARTICLE VII.  RATIFICATION

*The ratification of the conventions of nine states shall be sufficient for the establishment of this Constitution between the states so ratifying the same.*

Done in convention, by the unanimous consent of the states present, the 17th day of September, in the year of our Lord 1787, and of the independence of the United States of America the twelfth. In witness whereof we have hereunto subscribed our names.

*Signed by*     George Washington
[President and Deputy
from Virginia]
and 38 other delegates

---

[1]This "supremacy clause" means that federal laws always override state legislation in cases of conflict.

# Amendments to the Constitution

*Note:* The first ten amendments to the Constitution, adopted in 1791, make up the Bill of Rights. The year of adoption of later amendments (11 to 26) is given in parenthesis.

## AMENDMENT I.   FREEDOM OF RELIGION, SPEECH, PRESS, ASSEMBLY, AND PETITION

Congress shall make no law respecting an establishment of religion, or prohibiting the free exercise thereof;[1] or abridging [reducing] the freedom of speech or of the press; or the right of the people peaceably to assemble, and to petition the government for a redress [correction] of grievances.

## AMENDMENT II.   RIGHT TO BEAR ARMS

A well-regulated militia being necessary to the security of a free state, the right of the people to keep and bear arms shall not be infringed [weakened].

## AMENDMENT III.   QUARTERING OF TROOPS

No soldier shall, in time of peace, be quartered [assigned to live] in any house without the consent of the owner, nor in time of war, but in a manner to be prescribed by law.

## AMENDMENT IV.   SEARCHES AND SEIZURES

The right of the people to be secure [safe] in their persons, houses, papers, and effects [belongings] against unreasonable searches and seizures shall not be violated; and no [search] warrants shall issue but upon probable cause,[2] supported by oath or affirmation, and particularly describing the place to be searched, and the persons or things to be seized.

## AMENDMENT V.   RIGHTS OF THE ACCUSED; PROPERTY RIGHTS

No person shall be held to answer for a capital or otherwise infamous crime unless on a presentment or indictment of a grand jury,[3] except in cases arising in the land or naval forces, or in the militia, when in actual service in time of war or public danger; nor shall any person be subject

---

[1]"The free exercise thereof" refers to freedom of worship.

[2]"Probable cause" means *a reasonable ground of suspicion.*

[3]"A capital or otherwise infamous crime" refers to serious offenses punishable by death or by imprisonment. Before someone may be tried for such a crime, a grand jury must decide that sufficient evidence exists to bring that person to trial.

for the same offense to be twice put in jeopardy of life or limb;[1] nor shall be compelled in any criminal case to be a witness against himself; nor be deprived of life, liberty, or property without due process of law;[2] nor shall private property be taken for public use without just compensation.[3]

## AMENDMENT VI.   OTHER RIGHTS OF THE ACCUSED

In all criminal prosecutions [trials], the accused shall enjoy the right to a speedy and public trial by an impartial [fair] jury of the state and district wherein the crime shall have been committed, which district shall have been previously ascertained by law; and to be informed of the nature and cause of the accusation; to be confronted with the witnesses against him; to have compulsory process for obtaining witnesses in his favor;[4] and to have the assistance of counsel for his defense.

## AMENDMENT VII.   CIVIL SUITS

In suits at common law[5] where the value in controversy shall exceed twenty dollars, the right of trial by jury shall be preserved, and no fact tried by a jury shall be otherwise re-examined in any court of the United States, than according to the rules of the common law.

## AMENDMENT VIII.   BAILS, FINES, AND PUNISHMENTS

Excessive bail shall not be required, nor excessive fines imposed, nor cruel and unusual punishments inflicted.

## AMENDMENT IX.   RIGHTS NOT LISTED

The enumeration [listing] in the Constitution of certain rights shall not be construed to deny or disparage [weaken] others retained by the people.

## AMENDMENT X.   POWERS RESERVED TO THE STATES AND PEOPLE

The powers not delegated to the United States by the Constitution, nor prohibited by it to the states, are reserved to the states respectively, or to the people.

[1] A person may not be tried twice for the same offense (double jeopardy).

[2] "Due process of law" means *proper legal procedure*.

[3] The government has the power of *eminent domain*, or the right to take private property for public use. This provision requires the government to pay the owner a fair price for such property.

[4] The accused person has the right to request the court to issue an order, or subpoena, compelling a witness to appear in court.

[5] "Common law" is law based on custom and precedent (past decisions made in similar cases). Originating in England, it was brought to the English colonies by the early settlers and became the foundation of the American legal system.

# AMENDMENT XI.  SUITS AGAINST STATES (1798)

The judicial power of the United States shall not be construed to extend to any suit in law or equity, commenced or prosecuted against one of the United States by citizens of another state, or by citizens or subjects of any foreign state.

# AMENDMENT XII.  ELECTION OF PRESIDENT AND VICE PRESIDENT (1804)

[1] The electors shall meet in their respective states, and vote by ballot for president and vice president, one of whom at least shall not be an inhabitant of the same state with themselves; they shall name in their ballots the person voted for as president, and in distinct [separate] ballots the person voted for as vice president; and they shall make distinct lists of all persons voted for as president, and of all persons voted for as vice president, and of the number of votes for each, which lists they shall sign and certify, and transmit sealed to the seat of the government of the United States, directed to the president of the Senate.

[2] The president of the Senate shall, in the presence of the Senate and House of Representatives, open all the certificates, and the votes shall then be counted; the person having the greatest number of votes for president shall be the president, if such number be a majority of the whole number of electors appointed; and if no person have such majority, then from the persons having the highest numbers not exceeding three on the list of those voted for as president, the House of Representatives shall choose immediately, by ballot, the president. But in choosing the president, the votes shall be taken by states, the representation from each state having one vote; a quorum for this purpose shall consist of a member or members from two-thirds of the states, and a majority of all the states shall be necessary to a choice. And if the House of Representatives shall not choose a president whenever the right of choice shall devolve upon them, *before the fourth day of March next following*,[1] then the vice president shall act as president, as in the case of the death or other constitutional disability of the president.

[3] The person having the greatest number of votes as vice president shall be the vice president, if such number be a majority of the whole number of electors appointed; and if no person have a majority, then, from the two highest numbers on the list, the Senate shall choose the vice president; a quorum for the purpose shall consist of two-thirds of the whole number of senators, and a majority of the whole number shall be necessary to a choice. But no person constitutionally ineligible to the office of president shall be eligible to that of vice president of the United States.

[1]Changed to January 20 by Amendment XX.

# AMENDMENT XIII.  ABOLITION OF SLAVERY (1865)

**Section 1.  Slavery Forbidden**  Neither slavery nor involuntary servitude [compulsory service], except as a punishment for crime whereof the party shall have been duly convicted, shall exist within the United States, or any place subject to their jurisdiction.

**Section 2.  Enforcement Power**  Congress shall have power to enforce this article [amendment] by appropriate [suitable] legislation.

# AMENDMENT XIV.  CITIZENSHIP AND CIVIL RIGHTS (1868)

**Section 1.  Rights of Citizens**  All persons born or naturalized in the United States, and subject to the jurisdiction thereof, are citizens of the United States and of the state wherein they reside.[1] No state shall make or enforce any law which shall abridge the privileges or immunities of citizens of the United States; nor shall any state deprive any person of life, liberty, or property, without due process of law;[2] nor deny to any person within its jurisdiction the equal protection of the laws.[3]

**Section 2.  Apportionment of Representatives in Congress**  Representatives shall be apportioned among the several states according to their respective numbers, counting the whole number of persons in each state, excluding Indians not taxed.[4] But when the right to vote at any election for the choice of electors for president and vice president of the United States, representatives in Congress, the executive and judicial officers of a state, or the members of the legislature thereof, is denied to any of the *male* inhabitants of such state, being *twenty-one* years of age and citizens of the United States, or in any way abridged, except for participation in rebellion or other crime, the basis of representation therein shall be reduced in the proportion which the number of such *male* citizens shall bear to the whole number of *male* citizens *twenty-one* years of age in such state.[5]

**Section 3.  Persons Disqualified From Public Office**  No person shall be a senator or representative in Congress, or elector of president and

---

[1] This clause made the former slaves citizens.

[2] The primary purpose of this clause was to protect the civil rights of the former slaves. However, after the Supreme Court broadened the meaning of the word "person" to include "corporation," the clause began to be used to protect business interests as well.

[3] The "equal protection" clause has served as the legal basis for many civil rights cases.

[4] This clause nullifies the three-fifths formula of Article I, Section 2.

[5] Italicized words in this section were invalidated by Amendments XIX and XXVI.

vice president, or hold any office, civil or military, under the United States, or under any state, who, having previously taken an oath, as a member of Congress, or as an officer of the United States, or as a member of any state legislature, or as an executive or judicial officer of any state, to support the Constitution of the United States, shall have engaged in insurrection or rebellion against the same, or given aid or comfort to the enemies thereof. But Congress may, by a vote of two-thirds of each house, remove such disability.

**Section 4.   Valid Public Debt Defined**   The validity [legality] of the public debt of the United States, authorized by law, including debts incurred for payment of pensions and bounties [extra allowances] for services in suppressing insurrection or rebellion, shall not be questioned. But neither the United States nor any state shall assume or pay any debt or obligation incurred in aid of insurrection or rebellion against the United States, or any claim for the loss or emancipation [liberation] of any slave; but all such debts, obligations, and claims shall be held illegal and void.

**Section 5.   Enforcement Power**   The Congress shall have power to enforce, by appropriate legislation, the provisions of this article.

# AMENDMENT XV.   RIGHT OF SUFFRAGE (1870)

**Section 1.   African Americans Guaranteed the Vote**   The right of citizens of the United States to vote shall not be denied or abridged by the United States or by any state on account of race, color, or previous condition of servitude [slavery].

**Section 2.   Enforcement Power**   The Congress shall have power to enforce this article by appropriate legislation.

# AMENDMENT XVI.   INCOME TAXES (1913)

The Congress shall have power to lay and collect taxes on incomes, from whatever source derived, without apportionment among the several states, and without regard to any census or enumeration.

# AMENDMENT XVII.   POPULAR ELECTION OF SENATORS (1913)

[1] The Senate of the United States shall be composed of two senators from each state, elected by the people thereof, for six years; and each senator shall have one vote. The electors [voters] in each state shall have the qualifications requisite for electors of the most numerous branch of the state legislatures.[1]

---

[1]This amendment changed the method of electing senators as given in Article I, Section 3.

[2] When vacancies happen in the representation of any state in the Senate, the executive authority of such state shall issue writs of election to fill such vacancies: Provided, that the legislature of any state may empower [authorize] the executive thereof to make temporary appointments until the people fill the vacancies by election as the legislature may direct.

[3] *This amendment shall not be so construed as to affect the election or term of any senator chosen before it becomes valid as part of the Constitution.*[1]

# AMENDMENT XVIII.   PROHIBITION (1919)[2]

**Section 1.   Intoxicating Liquors Prohibited**   *After one year from the ratification of this article, the manufacture, sale, or transportation of intoxicating liquors within, the importation thereof into, or the exportation thereof from the United States and all territory subject to the jurisdiction thereof, for beverage purposes, is hereby prohibited.*

**Section 2.   Enforcement Power**   *The Congress and the several states shall have concurrent power to enforce this article by appropriate legislation.*

**Section 3.   Conditions of Ratification**   *This article shall be inoperative unless it shall have been ratified as an amendment to the Constitution by the legislatures of the several states, as provided in the Constitution, within seven years from the date of the submission hereof to the states by the Congress.*

# AMENDMENT XIX.   WOMEN'S SUFFRAGE (1920)

[1] The right of citizens of the United States to vote shall not be denied or abridged by the United States or by any state on account of sex.

[2] Congress shall have power to enforce this article by appropriate legislation.

# AMENDMENT XX.   PRESIDENTIAL AND CONGRESSIONAL TERMS[3] (1933)

**Section 1.   Terms of Office**   The terms of the president and vice president shall end at noon on the 20th day of January, and the terms of senators and representatives at noon on the 3d day of January, of the

[1]Temporary provision designed to protect those elected under the system previously in effect.

[2]This entire amendment was repealed in 1933 by Amendment XXI.

[3]This amendment is often called the "Lame Duck" Amendment because it shortened the period (from four months to two) between the elections in November and the time when defeated officeholders or officeholders who do not run again (known as "lame ducks") leave office.

years in which such terms would have ended if this article had not been ratified; and the terms of their successors[1] shall then begin.

**Section 2.   Convening Congress**   The Congress shall assemble at least once in every year, and such meeting shall begin at noon on the 3d day of January, unless they shall by law appoint a different day.[2]

**Section 3.   Presidential Succession**   If, at the time fixed for the beginning of the term of the president, the president-elect[3] shall have died, the vice president-elect shall become president. If a president shall not have been chosen before the time fixed for the beginning of his term, or if the president-elect shall have failed to qualify, then the vice president-elect shall act as president until a president shall have qualified; and the Congresss may by law provide for the case wherein neither a president-elect nor a vice president-elect shall have qualified, declaring who shall then act as president, or the manner in which one who is to act shall be selected, and such person shall act accordingly until a president or vice president shall have qualified.

**Section 4.   Selection of President and Vice President**   The Congress may by law provide for the case of the death of any of the persons from whom the House of Representatives may choose a president whenever the right of choice shall have devolved upon them, and for the case of the death of any of the persons from whom the Senate may choose a vice president whenever the right of choice shall have devolved upon them.

**Section 5.   Effective Date**   *Sections 1 and 2 shall take effect on the 15th day of October following the ratification of this article.[4]*

**Section 6.   Conditions of Ratification**   *This article shall be inoperative unless it shall have been ratified as an amendment to the Constitution by the legislatures of three-fourths of the several states within seven years from the date of its submission.[5]*

# AMENDMENT XXI.   REPEAL OF PROHIBITION (1933)

**Section 1.   Amendment XVIII Repealed**   The Eighteenth Article of amendment to the Constitution of the United States is hereby repealed.

**Section 2.   Shipment of Liquor Into "Dry" Areas**   The transportation or importation into any state, territory, or possession of the United States

[1]A "successor" is a person who is elected or appointed to replace another in a public office.

[2]This section changed the date given in Article I, Section 4.

[3]A "president-elect" is a person who has been elected to the presidency but has not yet assumed office.

[4]Temporary provision.

[5]Temporary provision.

for delivery or use therein of intoxicating liquors in violation of the laws thereof is hereby prohibited.[1]

**Section 3. Conditions of Ratification** *This article shall be inoperative unless it shall have been ratified as an amendment to the Constitution by conventions in the several states,[2] as provided in the Constitution, within seven years from the date of the submission hereof to the states by the Congress.[3]*

# AMENDMENT XXII. LIMITING PRESIDENTIAL TERMS (1951)

**Section 1. Limit Placed on Tenure** No person shall be elected to the office of the president more than twice, and no person who has held the office of president, or acted as president, for more than two years of a term to which some other person was elected president shall be elected to the office of the president more than once. *But this article shall not apply to any person holding the office of president when this article was proposed by the Congress, and shall not prevent any person who may be holding the office of president, or acting as president, during the term within which this article becomes operative from holding the office of president or acting as president during the remainder of such term.[4]*

**Section 2. Conditions of Ratification** *This article shall be inoperative unless it shall have been ratified as an amendment to the Constitution by the legislatures of three-fourths of the several states within seven years from the date of its submission to the states by the Congress.[5]*

# AMENDMENT XXIII. SUFFRAGE FOR WASHINGTON, D.C. (1961)

**Section 1. D.C. Presidential Electors** The district constituting [making up] the seat of government of the United States shall appoint in such manner as the Congress may direct:

A number of electors of president and vice president equal to the whole number of senators and representatives in Congress to which the district would be entitled if it were a state, but in no event more than

[1]This section allowed individual states to prohibit the use of intoxicating liquors if they wished to.

[2]This was the first amendment to be submitted by Congress for ratification by state conventions rather than state legislatures.

[3]Temporary provision.

[4]Temporary provision.

[5]Temporary provision.

the least populous state;[1] they shall be in addition to those appointed by the states, but they shall be considered, for the purposes of the election of president and vice president, to be electors appointed by a state; and they shall meet in the district and perform such duties as provided by the Twelfth Article of amendment.[2]

**Section 2.  Enforcement Power**  The Congress shall have power to enforce this article by appropriate legislation.

# AMENDMENT XXIV.  POLL TAXES (1964)

**Section 1.  Poll Tax Barred**  The right of citizens of the United States to vote in any primary or other election for president or vice president, for electors for president or vice president, or for senator or representative in Congress, shall not be denied or abridged by the United States or any state by reason of failure to pay any poll tax or other tax.

**Section 2.  Enforcement Power**  The Congress shall have the power to enforce this article by appropriate legislation.

# AMENDMENT XXV.  PRESIDENTIAL SUCCESSION AND DISABILITY (1967)

**Section 1.  Elevation of Vice President**  In case of the removal of the president from office or his death or resignation, the vice president shall become president.

**Section 2.  Vice Presidential Vacancy**  Whenever there is a vacancy in the office of the vice president, the president shall nominate a vice president who shall take the office upon confirmation by a majority vote of both houses of Congress.

**Section 3.  Temporary Disability**  Whenever the president transmits to the president pro tempore of the Senate and the Speaker of the House of Representatives his written declaration that he is unable to discharge the powers and duties of his office, and until he transmits to them a written declaration to the contrary, such powers and duties shall be discharged by the vice president as acting president.

**Section 4.  Other Provisions for Presidential Disability**  [1] Whenever the vice president and a majority of either the principal officers of the executive departments, or of such other body as Congress may by law provide, transmit to the president pro tempore of the Senate and the Speaker of the House of Representatives their written declaration that the president is unable to discharge the powers and duties of his office, the vice president shall immediately assume the powers and duties of the office as acting president.

[2] Thereafter, when the president transmits to the president pro

---

[1]At the present time, the District of Columbia is entitled to three electors.

[2]By providing for electors, this amendment gave residents of Washington, D.C., the right to vote for president and vice president.

tempore of the Senate and the Speaker of the House of Representatives his written declaration that no inability exists, he shall resume the powers and duties of his office unless the vice president and a majority of either the principal officers of the executive department, or of such other body as Congress may by law provide, transmit within four days to the president pro tempore of the Senate and the Speaker of the House of Representatives their written declaration that the president is unable to discharge the powers and duties of his office. Thereupon Congress shall decide the issue, assembling within 48 hours for that purpose if not in session. If the Congress, within 21 days after receipt of the latter written declaration, or, if Congress is not in session, within 21 days after Congress is required to assemble, determines by two-thirds vote of both houses that the president is unable to discharge the powers and duties of his office, the vice president shall continue to discharge the same as acting president; otherwise, the president shall resume the powers and duties of his office.

# AMENDMENT XXVI.   VOTE FOR 18-YEAR-OLDS (1971)

**Section 1.  Lowering the Voting Age**   The right of citizens of the United States, who are 18 years of age or older, to vote shall not be denied or abridged by the United States or by any state on account of age.

**Section 2.  Enforcement Power**   The Congress shall have power to enforce this article by appropriate legislation.

# AMENDMENT XXVII.   CONGRESSIONAL PAY RAISES (1992)

No law varying the compensation for the services of the Senators and Representatives shall take effect until an election of Representatives shall have intervened.

# INDEX

*Note:* Page numbers in *italics* indicate terms defined in the end-of-chapter glossaries. For example, a definition for **abolitionists** may be found in the glossary on page *98.*

# ACKNOWLEDGMENTS

**Cover** Photo B. Taylor/FPG.

**Photographs and Prints** page 8, Library of Congress; page 71, Chuck Asay, by permission of the *Colorado Springs Sun*; page 119, The Bettmann Archive; page 142, both Culver Pictures; page 188, Culver Pictures; page 253, Library of Congress; page 290, The Bettmann Archive; page 294, The Bettmann Archive; page 309, Reprinted by permission: Tribune Media Services; page 335, Franklin D. Roosevelt Library; page 346, Fred O. Seibell Collection (#2531), Manuscripts Division, Special Collections Department, University of Virginia Library; page 354, The Bettmann Archive.

Page 361, The Bettmann Archive; page 364, U.S. Coast Guard/Wide World Photos; page 368, UPI/Bettmann Newsphotos; page 377, from STRAIGHT HERBLOCK (Simon & Schuster, 1964); page 410, from STRAIGHT HERBLOCK (Simon & Schuster, 1964); page 418, UPI/Bettmann; page 429, UPI/Bettmann; page 436, The Bettmann Archive; page 472, National Aeronautics and Space Administration; page 477, Drawing by Dana Fradon, © 1972 The New Yorker Magazine, Inc.; page 503, UPI/Bettmann; page 508, Bissell, *The Tennessean*; page 522, UPI/Bettmann.

Page 538, from HERBLOCK ON ALL FRONTS (New American Library, 1980); pages 541, 544, and 551: Chuck Asay, by permission of the *Colorado Springs Gazette Telegraph*; page 556 (left), Laima Druskis/Photo Researchers, Inc.; page 556 (right), David M. Grossman/Photo Researchers, Inc.; page 565, from HERBLOCK ON ALL FRONTS (New American Library, 1980); page 571, Copyright 1978 by Herblock in the *Washington Post*; page 594, AP/Wide World Photos; page 603, Oliphant copyright 1989, Universal Press Syndicate, reprinted with permission.

**Print Material** Grateful acknowledgement is made to the following source for permission to use copyrighted material. *Pages 198–199*: "The Testimony of Standing Bear," by Thomas Henry Tibbles, in *Buckskin and Blanket Days*, copyright © 1957 by Vivien K. Barris: Doubleday & Co., Inc., reprinted in the 1985 Lakeside Classic edition (Chicago: The Lakeside Press), pages 253–254.